ENGLISH/LANGUAGE ARTS CURRICULUM RESOURCE HANDBOOK

A Practical Guide for
K-12 English/Language Arts Curriculum

CORWIN PRESS, INC.
A Sage Publications Company
Thousand Oaks, California

First Printing 1992

Library of Congress Cataloging-in-Publication Data

English/language arts curriculum resource handbook : a
    practical guide for K–12 English/language arts curriculum.
        p.   cm.
    Includes bibliographical references and index.
                    $19.95
    1. Language arts (Elementary)—United States—Handbooks,
manuals, etc. 2. Language arts (Secondary)—United States—
Handbooks, manuals, etc. 3. Curriculum planning—United
States. I. Kraus International Publications
LB1576.E497 1992
428'.0071'273—dc20   92-28559
ISBN: 978-0-8039-6369-6

CONTENTS

PART III: TEXTBOOKS, CLASSROOM MATERIALS, AND OTHER RESOURCES

PUBLISHER'S FOREWORD

T HE *English/Language Arts Curriculum Resource Handbook* is one of a new series of practical references for curriculum developers, education faculty, veteran teachers, and student teachers. The handbook is designed to provide basic information on the background of language arts curriculum, as well as current information on publications, standards, and special materials for K-12 English/language arts. Think of this handbook as the first place to look when you are revising or developing your language arts curriculum—or if you need basic resource information on English or language arts any time of the year.

This handbook does not seek to prescribe any particular form of curriculum, nor does it follow any set of standards or guidelines. Instead, the book provides a general grounding in the English/language arts curriculum, so that you can use this information and then proceed in the direction best suited for your budget, your school, and your district. What this handbook gives you is a sense of the numerous *options* that are available—it is up to you to use the information to develop the appropriate curriculum or program for your situation.

How To Use This Handbook

There are various ways to use this resource handbook. If you are revising or creating an English/language arts curriculum, you should read the Introduction (for an overall sense of the different philosophies of curriculum and how this will affect the program you develop), chapter 1 (for basic background on the trends and research in K-12 English/language arts), and chapter 2 (for a how-to guide to developing curriculum materials).

With this background, you can go through the other chapters for the specific information you need—ranging from topics to be covered at various grade levels (chapter 4) to state requirements (chapter 5) to publishers and producers (chapter 11).

If you know what type of information you need, then check the Table of Contents for the most appropriate chapter, or check the Index to see where this material is covered. For instance:

1. If you are looking for ideas on developing special writing projects or information on writing contests, turn to chapter 9.
2. If you are looking for a new textbook or supplementary materials (book, video, or software), turn to chapter 11.
3. If you need to contact state departments of education for language arts curriculum documents, check the list provided in chapter 6.

What's in the Handbook

The *Introduction* provides an overview of the ideologies and philosophies that have affected American curriculum through the years. This section will acquaint you with the various ideologies, so that you can determine whether your school is following one such philosophy (or a combination), and how this might influence the development of your curriculum. The Introduction is generic by design, since these ideologies pertain to all subject areas.

Chapter 1 provides an overview of *Trends and Issues in English/Language Arts Curriculum.* This chapter discusses the development of present-day curriculum and looks at the directions the curriculum is taking. The major research works are cited so that you can get more detailed information on particular topics.

Chapter 2 is a step-by-step description of *Curriculum Process and Design*. It is meant to be a practical guide to creating or revising English/language arts curriculum guides. This chapter is also somewhat generic, but includes examples specific to English/language arts.

Chapter 3, *Funding Curriculum Projects*, lists funding for programs that are studying or developing curriculum. Along with addresses and phone numbers, the names of contact persons are provided (wherever possible) to expedite your gathering of information.

Chapter 4 outlines *Topics in the English/Language Arts Curriculum, Grades K-12*. This is not meant to be a pattern to follow, but instead is a reflection of what most schools cover and what current research recommends.

Chapter 5, *State-Level Curriculum Guidelines: An Analysis*, describes the statewide frameworks and discusses the various emphases, philosophies, and coverage among the state materials.

Chapter 6, *State-Level Curriculum Guidelines: A Listing*, supplements the previous chapter by listing addresses of state departments of education and their publication titles.

Chapter 7 is a selection of *Curriculum Guides* for English/language arts.

Chapter 8 reprints an English/language arts curriculum guide, *Spelling Is a Tool*, to use as an example in creating your own curriculum materials.

Chapter 9 discusses *Ideas for Special Projects in Language Arts*. The chapter defines a special English project, the goals, and the methods used to create it. Also included is information on national writing contests.

Chapter 10 gives information on *Children's Trade Books* that can be used as supplementary texts in English/language arts classrooms. This chapter discusses the bibliographic tools to use in finding these trade books; it also cites the various published lists of children's books for English/language arts.

Chapter 11 is an annotated list of *Curriculum Material Producers* of textbooks, videos, software, and other materials for use in K-12 English/language arts.

Chapter 12, *Statewide Text Adoption*, lists the language arts textbooks adopted by each state.

Chapter 13 is an *Index to Reviews* of English/language arts textbooks and supplementary materials. Since these items are reviewed in a wide variety of publications, we have assembled the citations of appropriate reviews in index form (cited by title, author, publisher/distributor, subject, and grade level).

Chapter 14 provides a list of *Kraus Curriculum Development Library* (KCDL) subscribers; KCDL is a good source for models of curriculum guides in all K-12 subject areas.

Acknowledgements

The content of this handbook is based on numerous meetings and discussions with educators and curriculum specialists across the country. Our thanks go to the curriculum supervisors in schools across the United States; the faculty at education departments in the colleges and universities we visited; and curriculum librarians. Special thanks go to the members of the Curriculum Materials Committee (CMC) and the Problems of Access and Control of Education Materials (PACEM) committee of the Association of College and Research Libraries' Education and Behavioral Sciences Section (ACRL/EBSS). Our meetings with the committees during American Library Association Conferences continue to provide Kraus with valuable ideas for the handbooks and for future curriculum projects.

We also acknowledge with thanks the assistance of Anne Isner, Marjorie Miller Kaplan, Carrie Lesh, Paula Martin, Barbara Meyers, Jean Russo, and the indexers at AEIOU.

Your Feedback

We have a final request of our readers. At the back of this handbook is a user survey that asks your opinions about the book, its coverage, and its contents. Once you have used this book, please fill out the questionnaire—it should only take a minute or so—and mail it back to us. If the form has already been removed, please just send us a letter with your opinions. We want to keep improving this new series of handbooks, and we can do this only with your help! Please send questionnaires or other responses to:

Kraus International Publications
358 Saw Mill River Road
Millwood, NY 10546-1035
(914) 762-2200 / (800) 223-8323
Fax: (914) 762-1195

SERIES INTRODUCTION

P. Bruce Uhrmacher

Assistant Professor of Education
School of Education, University of Denver, Denver, Colorado

WHEN I travel by airplane and desire conversation, I inform the person sitting next to me that I'm in education. Everyone has an opinion about education. I hear stories about teachers (both good and bad), subject matter ("The problem with the new math is . . ."), and tests ("I should have gotten an A on that exam in seventh grade"). Many people want to tell me about the problems with education today ("Schools aren't what they used to be"). Few people are apathetic about schooling. When I do not wish to be disturbed in flight, however, I avoid admitting I'm in education. "So, what do you do?" someone trying to draw me out asks. I reply matter-of-factly, "I'm a curriculum theorist." Unless they persist, my retort usually signals the end of the dialogue. Unlike the job titles *farmer, stockbroker,* or even *computer analyst,* for many people *curriculum theorist* conjures few images.

What do curriculum theorists do? The answer to this question depends in part on the way curriculum theorists conceive of curriculum and theory. The term *curriculum* has over 150 definitions. With so many different ways of thinking about it, no wonder many curriculum theorists see their task differently. In this introduction, I point out that curriculum theorists have a useful function to serve, despite the fact that we can't agree on what to do. In short, like economists who analyze trends and make recommendations about the economy (and, incidentally, who also

agree on very little), curriculum theorists generate a constructive dialogue about curriculum decisions and practices. Although curricularists originally fought over the word *curriculum,* trying to achieve conceptual clarity in order to eliminate the various differences, in time educators recognized that the fight over the term was unproductive (Zais 1976, 93). However, the problem was not simply an academic disagreement. Instead, curricularists focused on different aspects of the educational enterprise. At stake in the definition of curriculum was a conceptual framework that included the nature of the role of the curricularist and the relationships among students, teachers, subject matter, and educational environments. Today, most curricularists place adjectives before the term to specify what type of curriculum they're discussing. Thus, one often reads about the intended, the operational, the hidden, the explicit, the implicit, the enacted, the delivered, the experienced, the received, and the null curriculum (see glossary at the end of this chapter). Distinctions also can be made with regard to curricularist, curriculum planner, curriculum worker, and curriculum specialist. I use the terms *curricularist* and *curriculum theorist* to refer to individuals, usually at the college level, who worry about issues regarding curriculum theory. I use the other terms to refer to people who actually take part in the planning or the implementation of curriculum in schools.

In order to trace the development that has

brought the field of curriculum to its present state, I will begin with a brief overview of the progression of curriculum development in the United States. First, I examine issues facing the Committee of Ten, a group of educators who convened in 1892 to draft a major document regarding what schools should teach. Next, I focus on the perennial question of who should decide what schools teach. Curriculum was not a field of study until the 1920s. How were curriculum decisions made before there were curriculum specialists? How did curriculum become a field of study? We learn that the profession began, in part, as a scientific endeavor; whether the field should still be seen as a scientific one is a question of debate. Finally, I provide a conceptual framework that examines six curriculum "ideologies" (Eisner 1992). By understanding these ideologies, educators will discern the assumptions underlying various conceptions of curriculum. Then they should be able to decide which ideology they wish to pursue and to recognize its educational implications.

What Should Schools Teach?

In the nineteenth century, curriculum usually meant "the course of study," and what many educators worried about was what schools should teach. Under the theoretical influence of "mental discipline" (derived from the ideas of faculty psychologists), many educators believed that certain subjects strengthened the brain, much like certain exercises strengthened body muscles. Greek, Latin, and mathematics were important because they were difficult subjects and thus, presumably, exercised the brain. By the 1890s, however, with the great influx of Italian, Irish, Jewish, and Russian immigrants, and with the steady increase of students attending secondary schools, a concern grew over the relevance and value of such subjects as Greek and Latin. Why should German or French be any less worthy than Greek or Latin? In addition, students and parents raised further questions regarding the merits of vocational education. They wanted curricula that met their more practical needs.

While parents pressed for their concerns, secondary school principals worried about preparing students for college, since colleges had different entrance requirements. In 1892 the National Education Association (NEA) appointed the Committee of Ten to remedy this problem. Headed by Charles W. Eliot, president of Harvard University, the committee debated and evaluated the extent to which a single curriculum could work for a large number of students who came from many different backgrounds with many different needs. In its final report, the committee suggested that colleges consider of equal value and accept students who attended not only the classical curriculum program, but also the Latin scientific, the modern language, and the English programs.

By eliminating the requirement of Greek for two of the programs and by reducing the number of required Latin courses, the committee broke with the traditional nineteenth-century curriculum to some degree. Yet, they were alert to the possibility that different kinds of curriculum programs taught in different ways could lead to a stratified society. Eliot had argued that the European system of classifying children into "future peasants, mechanics, trades-people, merchants, and professional people" was unacceptable in a democratic society (Tanner and Tanner 1975, 186). The committee believed all should have the opportunity for further studies under a "rational humanist" orientation to curriculum, a viewpoint that prizes the power of reason and the relevance and importance of learning about the best that Western culture has to offer.

The committee's report met with mixed reviews when it came out. One of its foremost opponents was G. Stanley Hall, a "developmentalist," who argued that the "natural order of development in the child was the most significant and scientifically defensible basis for determining what should be taught" (Kliebard 1986, 13). According to Hall, who had scientifically observed children's behavior at various stages of development, the committee did not take into account children's wide-ranging capabilities, and it promulgated a college-bound curriculum for everyone, even though many high school students would not go to college. Rather than approaching curriculum as the pursuit of a standard academic experience for all students, Hall and other developmentalists believed that knowledge of human development could contribute to creating a curriculum in harmony with the child's stage of interest and needs.

Thus far I have indicated two orientations to curriculum: the rational humanist and the developmentalist. We should understand, however, that at any given time a number of interest groups struggle for power over the curriculum. Historian Herbert Kliebard observes:

> We do not find a monolithic supremacy exercised by one interest group; rather we find different interest groups competing for dominance over the curriculum and, at different times, achieving some measure of control depending on local as well as general social conditions. Each of these interest groups, then, represents a force for a different selection of knowledge and values from the culture and hence a kind of lobby for a different curriculum. (Kliebard 1986, 8)

Who Should Decide What Schools Teach?

Thinking about curriculum dates back in Western culture to at least the ancient Greeks. Plato and Aristotle, as well as Cicero, Plutarch, and Rousseau, all thought about curriculum matters in that they debated the questions of what should be taught to whom, in what way, and for what purposes. But it wasn't until 1918 that curriculum work was placed in the professional domain with the publication of *The Curriculum* by Franklin Bobbitt, a professor at the University of Chicago. Although supervisors and administrators had written courses of study on a piecemeal basis, "Professor Bobbitt took the major step of dealing with the curriculum in all subjects and grades on a unified and comprehensive basis" (Gress 1978, 27). The term *curriculum theory* came into use in the 1920s, and the first department of curriculum was founded at Teachers College, Columbia University, in 1937. Of course, the question arises: If curricularists (a.k.a. curriculum specialists, curriculum theorists, and curriculum workers) were not making decisions about what should be taught in schools prior to the 1920s, then who was?

As we have seen, national commissions made some of the curricular decisions. The NEA appointed the Committee of Ten to address college–high school articulation in 1892 and the Committee of Fifteen to address elementary school curriculum in 1895. In the early 1900s the NEA appointed another committee to develop fundamental principles for the reorganization of secondary education. Thus, university professors, school superintendents, and teachers made some curricular decisions as they acted in the role of acknowledged authorities on national commissions.

Along with commissions, forces such as tradition have shaped the curriculum. One long-time student of curriculum, Philip Jackson, observes:

> One reason why certain subjects remain in the curriculum is simply that they have been there for such a long time. Indeed, some portions of the curriculum have been in place for so long that the question of how they got there or who decided to put them there in the first place has no answer, or at least not one that anyone except a historian would be able to give. As far as most people are concerned, they have just "always" been there, or so it seems. (Jackson 1992, 22)

Jackson also notes here that subjects such as the three R's are so "obviously useful that they need no further justification"—or, at least, so it seems.

Texts and published materials have also been factors in shaping the curriculum. Whether it was the old *McGuffey Readers* or the modern text-books found in almost any classroom in the United States, these books have influenced the curriculum by virtue of their content and their widespread use. According to some estimates, text materials dominate 75 percent of the time elementary and secondary students are in class-rooms and 90 percent of their time on homework (Apple 1986, 85). Textbook writers are de facto curriculum specialists.

National Commission committees, tradition, textbooks, instructional materials, and the influence from numerous philosophers (e.g., Herbart and Dewey) were focal in deciding what schools should teach. Of course, parents, state boards of education, and teachers had their own convictions as to what should be in the curriculum. However, as the United States moved toward urbanization (30 percent of 63 million lived in cities in 1890; over 50 percent of 106 million lived in cities in 1920 [Cremin 1977, 93]), new factors influenced schooling. In particular, the industrial and scientific revolutions commingled in the minds of some to produce new ways of thinking about work. Franklin Bobbitt applied these new ideas to education. Influenced by Frederick Winslow Taylor, the father of the scientific management movement, Bobbitt assumed that the kinds of accomplishments that had been made in business and industry could be made in education. What was needed was the application of scientific principles to curriculum.

Briefly, Bobbitt believed that "educational engineers" or "curriculum-discoverers," as he called them, could make curriculum by surveying the array of life's endeavors and by grouping this broad range of human experience into major fields. Bobbitt wrote:

> The curriculum-discoverer will first be an analyst of human nature and of human affairs.... His first task ... is to discover the total range of habits, skills, abilities, forms of thought ... etc., that its members need for the effective performance of their vocational labors; likewise the total range needed for their civic activities; their health activities; their recreations, their language; their parental, religious, and general social activities. The program of analysis will be no narrow one. It will be as wide as life itself. (Bobbitt 1918, 43)

Thus, according to Bobbitt, curriculum workers would articulate educational goals by examining the array of life's activities. Next, in the same way one can analyze the tasks involved in making a tangible object and eliminate waste in producing it, Bobbitt believed one could streamline education by task analysis, by forming objectives for each task, and by teaching skills as discrete units.

Bobbitt's push for the professionalization of curriculum did not replace other factors so much as it added a new dimension. By arguing that schools needed stated objectives and that curricularists should be chosen for the task since they were trained in the science of curriculum, Bobbitt opened up a new line of work. He and his students would be of direct help to practitioners because they would know how to proceed scientifically (analyze the range of human experience, divide it into activities, create objectives) in the making of curriculum, and this knowledge gave curricularists authority and power. The world was rapidly changing in communications, in agriculture, in industry, and most of all in medicine. Who could argue with the benefits of science?

If Franklin Bobbitt created the field of professional curriculum activities, Ralph Tyler defined it. In his short monograph, *Basic Principles of Curriculum and Instruction* (1949), Tyler offered a way of viewing educational institutions. He began his book by asking four fundamental questions that he believed must be answered in developing curriculum:

1. What educational purposes should the school seek to attain?
2. What educational experiences can be provided that are likely to attain those purposes?

3. How can these educational experiences be effectively organized?
4. How can we determine whether these purposes are being attained? (Tyler 1949, 1)

Tyler devoted one chapter to each question. Unlike some curricularists, Tyler did not say what purposes a school should seek to attain. He recognized that a school in rural Idaho has different needs from an urban one in Boston. Rather, Tyler suggested that schools themselves determine their own purposes from three sources: studies of the learners themselves, studies of contemporary life, and studies from subject matter specialists.

Tyler, like Bobbitt before him, wished to bring order to the complex field of education. Although there are differences between the two men, both believed there was work to be done by professional curricularists. Both men trained students in the field of curriculum, and both believed in the liberal ideals of rationality and progress. Curricularist Decker Walker summarizes the tradition that Bobbitt and Tyler started as follows:

> Since Bobbitt's day, planning by objectives (PBO) had developed into a family of widely used approaches to curriculum improvement. As a method of curriculum materials design, PBO focuses early attention on developing precise statements of the objectives to be sought. If the process is to be fully scientific, the selection of objectives must be rationally justifiable and not arbitrary. (Walker 1990, 469)

While Bobbitt and Tyler taught students how to become professional curricularists and encouraged them to conduct research, to write, and to attain university positions, differences of opinion on what curricularists should be doing soon mounted. At issue was not only the utility of scientific curriculum making, but also the specific endeavors many curricularists pursued.

A Framework for Thinking about Curriculum

Tyler produced a seminal work that provided curriculum workers with a way of thinking about curriculum. While some elaborated on his ideas (Taba 1962), others wondered whether indeed Tyler provided the best questions for curricularists to think about. During the 1970s, numerous educators began to seek other ways of thinking about curriculum work. William Pinar, for example, asked, "Are Tyler's questions . . . no longer pertinent or possible? Are they simply cul-de-sacs?" (Pinar 1975, 397). Reconceptualizing the term *curriculum* (race course) from the verb of the Latin root, *currere* (to run a race), Pinar goes on to argue:

> The questions of *currere* are not Tyler's; they are ones like these: Why do I identify with Mrs. Dalloway and not with Mrs. Brown? What psychic dark spots does the one light, and what is the nature of "dark spots," and "light spots"? Why do I read Lessing and not Murdoch? Why do I read such works at all? Why not biology or ecology? Why are some drawn to the study of literature, some to physics, and some to law? (402)

More will be said about Pinar's work later. My point here is that curriculum theorists do not necessarily agree on how one should approach thinking about curriculum. By trying to redefine curriculum entirely, Pinar drew attention to different aspects of the educational process.

Out of this continuing discussion among curricularists, various ideologies—beliefs about what schools should teach, for what ends, and for what reasons—have developed (Eisner 1992). In this section, I present six prominent curriculum ideologies that should prove useful in thinking about developing, adapting, or implementing curriculum. While these ideologies are important, they are not the only ones. Elliot Eisner writes of religious orthodoxy and progressivism and excludes multiculturalism and developmentalism. Some authors may include constructivism rather than developmentalism.

I remind the reader that few people actually wear the labels I describe. These conceptualizations are useful in helping one better articulate a set of assumptions and core values. They help us see the implications of a particular viewpoint. They also help us understand issues and concerns that may otherwise be neglected. Sometimes ideologies are specified in mission statements or some other kind of manifesto; at other times, ideologies are embedded in educational practice but are not made explicit. Rarely does a school adhere to one curriculum ideology—though some do. More often, because public schools are made up of people who have different ideas about what schools should teach, a given school is more likely to embrace an array of curricular ideas. While some readers may resonate strongly with a particular ideology because it expresses their inclinations, some readers may

appreciate particular ideas from various ideologies. In either case, it may be a good idea to examine the strengths and weaknesses of each one. Later in this chapter I argue that one does not need to be ideologically pure in order to do good curriculum work.

Rational Humanism

We have already seen, in the historical example of Charles Eliot and the Committee of Ten, an early exemplar of rational humanism. During Eliot's day, rational humanists embraced the theory of mental discipline, which provided a handy rationale for traditional studies. Why study Greek and Latin? Because these subjects exercised the mind in ways that other subjects did not. While mental discipline fell by the wayside, rational humanism did not. From the 1930s through the 1950s, Robert Maynard Hutchins and Mortimer Adler championed the rational humanistic tradition, in part by editing *The Great Books of the Western World*. Hutchins argued that the "great books" offer the best that human beings have thought and written. Thus, rather than reading textbooks on democracy, science, and math, one ought to read Jefferson, Newton, and Euclid.

Today, one may find the rational humanist ideology in some private schools and in those public schools that have adopted Adler's ideas as represented in the *Paideia Proposal* (Eisner 1992, 310). In short, the Paideia plan provides a common curriculum for all students. Except for the choosing of a foreign language, there are no electives. All students learn language, literature, fine arts, mathematics, natural science, history, geography, and social studies.

While Adler endorses lecturing and coaching as two important teaching methods, the aspect of teaching Adler found most engaging was maieutic or Socratic questioning and active participation. In essence, maieutic teaching consists of a seminar situation in which learners converse in a group. The teacher serves as a facilitator who moves the conversation along, asks leading questions, and helps students develop, examine, or refine their thinking as they espouse particular viewpoints. This process, according to Adler, "teaches participants how to analyze their own minds as well as the thought of others, which is to say it engages students in disciplined conversation about ideas and values" (Adler 1982, 30).

Another important educational feature of these seminars is that one discusses books and art but not textbooks. In a follow-up book to *The Paideia Proposal*, Adler (1984) provides a K–12 recommended reading list in which he recommends for kindergarten to fourth grade Aesop, William Blake, Shel Silverstein, Alice Walker, Jose Marie Sanchez-Silva, Langston Hughes, and Dr. Seuss, among other authors. I indicate these authors in particular because the charge that Adler's program embraces only the Western European heritage is not entirely accurate. While Adler would argue that some books are better than others, and that, in school, students should be reading the better ones, one can see that Adler includes authors who are not elitist and who are from culturally diverse backgrounds.

Developmentalism

Another approach to curriculum theory, which was discussed briefly in the historical section of this chapter, is developmentalism. Although a range of scholars falls under this heading, the basic point is that, rather than fitting the child to the curriculum, students would be better served if the curriculum were fitted to the child's stage of development. Why? One argument is that doing otherwise is inefficient or even detrimental to the child's development. It would be ridiculous to try to teach the Pythagorean theorem to a first grader, and it could be harmful (to use a fairly noncontroversial example) to teach a fourth grader to master throwing a curve ball. By understanding the range of abilities children have at various ages, one can provide a curriculum that meets the needs and interests of students. Of course, while the stage concept cannot pinpoint the development of a particular child at a given age, it serves as a general guide.

One might also pay attention to the idea of development when creating or adapting curriculum because of the issue of "readiness for learning." There are two ways of thinking about readiness. Some educators, in their interest to hurry development, believe that encouraging learners to perform approximations of desired behaviors can hasten academic skills. In this case, one tries to intervene in apparently natural development by manipulating the child's readiness at younger and younger ages. The research findings on whether one can greatly enhance one's learning processes are somewhat mixed, but, in my opinion, they favor the side that says "speed learning" is inefficient (Duckworth 1987, Good and Brophy 1986, Tietze 1987). I also think the more important question, as Piaget noted, is

"not how fast we can help intelligence grow, but how far we can help it grow" (Duckworth 1987, 38).

A different way of thinking about readiness for learning concerns not how to speed it up, but how to work with it effectively. Eleanor Duckworth, who studied with Piaget, believes the idea of readiness means placing children in developmentally appropriate problem situations where students are allowed to have their own "wonderful ideas." She believes that asking "the right question at the right time can move children to peaks in their thinking that result in significant steps forward and real intellectual excitement" (Duckworth 1987, 5). The challenges for teachers are to provide environmentally rich classrooms where students have the opportunity to "mess about" with things, and to try to understand children's thought processes. Students should have the opportunity to experiment with materials likely to afford intellectual growth, and teachers should learn how their students think. In this approach to curriculum, mistakes are not problems; they are opportunities for growth.

The developmental approach to curriculum teaches us to pay attention to the ways humans grow and learn. One basic idea underlying the various theories of human development in regard to curriculum is that the curriculum planner ought to understand children's abilities and capabilities because such knowledge enables one to provide worthwhile educational activities for students.

Reconceptualism

As noted earlier with Pinar's use of the term *currere*, during the 1970s numerous individuals criticized the technical aspects and linear progression of steps of the Tyler rationale. Loosely labelled as reconceptualists, some educators felt the following:

> What is missing from American schools . . . is a deep respect for personal purpose, lived experience, the life of imagination, and those forms of understanding that resist dissection and measurement. What is wrong with schools, among other things, is their industrialized format, their mechanistic attitudes toward students, their indifference to personal experience, and their emphasis on the instrumental and the out of reach. (Pinar 1975, 316)

Reconceptualists have focused on Dewey's observation that one learns through experience. Given this assertion, some important questions arise. For example, how can teachers, teacher educators, or educational researchers better understand the kinds of experiences individual students are having? To answer this question, reconceptualists employ ideas, concepts, and theories from psychoanalysis, philosophy, and literature.

Another question that arises when one reflects on understanding experience is, How can teachers provide worthwhile conditions for students to undergo educational experiences? Maxine Greene divides educational experiences into two types: "an education for having" and "an education for being." Education for having is utilitarian—for example, one may learn to read in order to get a job. Some students need this kind of experience. Education for being is soulful— one may learn to read for the sensual qualities it can provide. All students, she says, need the latter kind of experience. One problem is that the latter has often been neglected or, if not, often provided for the talented or gifted at the expense of others (Green, 1988a).

In their effort to reperceive education, reconceptualists such as Maxine Greene, Madeleine Grumet, and William Pinar do not usually offer specific educational ideas that are easily implemented. In part, this is because the kind of education with which they are concerned is not easy to quantify or measure. In general, reconceptualists do not believe their theories and ideas need quick utilization in schools in order to validate their worth. If in reading their writings you think more deeply about educational issues, then I think they would be satisfied.

Nevertheless, I can think of two practical challenges for education that stem from their writing. First, how could you write a rigorous and tough-minded lesson plan without using objectives? What would such a lesson plan look like? Second, if you wanted to teach students a concept such as citizenship, how would you do it? Rational humanists would have students read Thomas Jefferson or Martin Luther King, Jr. Reconceptualists, however, would wonder how teachers can place students in problematic situations (i.e., in the classroom or on the playground) where students would grapple with real issues concerning citizenship.

Critical Theory

The idea of critical theory originated at the Institute for Social Research in Frankfurt ("the Frankfurt school") in the 1920s. Today, scholars who continue to recognize the value and importance of Marxist critiques of society and culture draw from and build on ideas from critical theory. In education they reveal, among other things, that schooling comprises a value-laden enterprise where issues of power are always at play.

For instance, while many people perceive schools as neutral institutions, places that will help any hard-working student to get ahead in life, critical theorists suggest that, on the contrary, schools do not operate that way. Michael Apple points out, "Just as our dominant economic institutions are structured so that those who inherit or already have economic capital do better, so too does cultural capital act in the same way" (Apple 1986, 33). According to Apple, schools reflect the general inequities in the larger society. Rather than changing society through cultural transformation (teaching students to question or to be independent thinkers), schools actually maintain the status quo through cultural reproduction.

Unlike some curricularists who try to appear neutral in exercising judgments about curriculum matters, Apple's values are well known. He believes in John Rawls's insight that "for a society to be truly just, it must maximize the advantage of the least advantaged" (Apple 1979, 32). Apple encourages curricularists to take advocacy positions within and outside of education. While critical theory makes for a powerful theoretical tool, one question frequently asked of critical theorists is how this information can be used in the classroom. Teachers point out that they may not be able to change the school structure, the kinds of material they must cover, or the kinds of tests that must be given. Although admittedly application is difficult, one high school English educator in Boston who employs the ideas of critical theory is Ira Shor.

In an activity called "prereading," for example, Shor tells students the theme of a book they are about to read and has them generate hypothetical questions the book may answer. At first students are reluctant to respond, but after a while they do. Shor believes this kind of exercise has numerous functions. First, it provides a bridge for students to decelerate from the "rush of mass culture" into the slow medium of the printed word. Habituated to rock music and MTV, students need a slow-down time. Also, after creating a list of questions, students are curious how many will actually be addressed. Students may still reject the text, says Shor, but now it won't be a result of alienation. Perhaps most importantly, prereading demystifies the power of the written word. Rather than approaching the text as some kind of untouchable authority, "students' own thoughts and words on the reading topic are the starting points for the coordinated material. The text will be absorbed into the field of their language rather than they being ruled by it" (Shor 1987, 117).

Critical theory offers a radical way of thinking about schooling. Particularly concerned with students who are disenfranchised and who, without the critical theorists, would have no voice to speak for them, critical theory provides incisive analyses of educational problems.

Multiculturalism

In some ways, multiculturalists are in affinity with the critical theorists. Though critical theory traditionally is more concerned with class, most critical theorists have included race and gender in their analyses and discussions. Multiculturalism, however, deserves its own category as a curriculum ideology because it is rooted in the ethnic revival movements of the 1960s. Whether the purpose is to correct racist and bigoted views of the larger community, to raise children's self-esteem, to help children see themselves from other viewpoints, or to reach the child's psychological world, the multicultural ideology reminds educators that ethnicity must be dealt with by educators.

One major approach to multicultural education has been termed "multiethnic ideology" by James Banks (1988). According to Banks, Americans participate in several cultures—the mainstream along with various ethnic subcultures. Therefore, students ought to have cross-cultural competency. In addition to being able to participate in various cultures, Banks also suggests that when one learns about various cultures, one begins to see oneself from other viewpoints. The multiethnic ideology provides greater self-understanding.

When teaching from a multiethnic perspective, Banks advises that an issue not be taught from a dominant mainstream perspective with other points of view added on. This kind of teaching still suggests that one perspective is the "right one," though others also have their own points of view. Rather, one should approach the concept or theme from various viewpoints. In this case, the mainstream perspective becomes one of several ways of approaching the topic; it is not

superior or inferior to other ethnic perspectives. In addition to what takes place in the classroom, Banks also argues that a successful multiethnic school must have system-wide reform. School staff, school policy, the counseling program, assessment, and testing are all affected by the multiethnic ideology.

Cognitive Pluralism

According to Eisner, the idea of cognitive pluralism goes back at least to Aristotle; however, only in the last several decades has a conception of the plurality of knowledge and intelligence been advanced in the field of curriculum (Eisner 1992, 317). In short, cognitive pluralists expand our traditional notions of knowledge and intelligence. Whereas some scientists and educators believe that people possess a single intelligence (often called a "g factor") or that all knowledge can ultimately be written in propositional language, cognitive pluralists believe that people possess numerous intelligences and that knowledge exists in many forms of representation.

As a conception of knowledge, cognitive pluralists argue that symbol systems provide a way to encode visual, auditory, kinesthetic, olfactory, gustatory, and tactile experiences. If, for example, one wants to teach students about the Civil War, cognitive pluralists would want students not only to have knowledge about factual material (names, dates, and battles), but also to have knowledge about how people felt during the war. To know that slavery means by definition the owning of another person appears quite shallow to knowing how it feels to be powerless. Cognitive pluralists suggest students should be able to learn through a variety of forms of representation (e.g., narratives, poetry, film, pictures) and be able to express themselves through a variety of forms as well. The latter point about expression means that most tests, which rely on propositional language, are too limiting. Some students may better express themselves through painting or poetry.

One may also think about cognitive pluralism from the point of view of intelligence. As I mentioned, some scholars suggest that intelligence may be better thought of as multiple rather than singular. Howard Gardner, a leading advocate of this position (1983), argues that, according to his own research and to reviews of a wide array of studies, a theory of multiple intelligences is more viable than a theory about a "g factor." He defines intelligence as follows:

> To my mind, a human intellectual compe-
> tence must entail a set of skills of problem-
> solving—enabling the individual to resolve
> genuine problems or difficulties that he or
> she encounters and, when appropriate, to
> create an effective product—and must also
> entail the potential for finding or creating
> problems—thereby laying the groundwork for
> the acquisition of new knowledge. (Gardner
> 1983, 60–61)

Gardner argues that there are at least seven
distinct kinds of human intelligence: linguistic,
musical, logical–mathematical, spatial, bodily-
kinesthetic, interpersonal, and intrapersonal. If
schools aim to enhance cognitive development,
then they ought to teach students to be knowledgeable of, and to practice being fluent in,
numerous kinds of intelligences. To limit the
kinds of knowledge or intelligences students
experience indicates an institutional deficiency.

Applying Curriculum Ideologies

While some teachers or schools draw heavily on
one particular curriculum ideology (e.g., Ira
Shor's use of critical theory in his classroom or
Mortimer Adler's ideas in Paideia schools), more
often than not, a mixture of various ideologies
pervade educational settings. I don't believe this
is a problem. What Joseph Schwab said in the late
1960s about theory also applies to ideologies. He
argued that theories are partial and incomplete,
and that, as something rooted in one's mind
rather than in the state of affairs, theories cannot
provide a complete guide for classroom practice
(1970). In other words, a theory about child
development may tell you something about ten
year olds in general, but not about a particular
ten year old standing in front of you. Child
development cannot tell you, for example,
whether or how to reprimand a given child for
failing to do his homework. Schwab suggested
one become eclectic and deliberative when
working in the practical world. In simpler terms,
one should know about various theories and use
them when applicable. One does not need to be
ideologically pure. One should also reflect upon
one's decisions and talk about them with other
people. Through deliberation one makes new
decisions which lead to new actions which then
cycle around again to reflection, decision, and
action.

To understand this eclectic approach to using
curriculum ideologies, let's take as an example
the use of computers in the classroom. Imagine
you are about to be given several computers for
your class. How could knowledge of the various
curriculum ideologies inform your use of them?

Given this particular challenge, some ideologies will prove to be more useful than others. For
example, the rational humanists would probably
have little to contribute to this discussion because, with their interests in the cultivation of
reason and the seminar process of teaching,
computers are not central (though one of my
students noted, that, perhaps in time, rational
humanists will want to create a "great software"
program).

Some developmentalists would consider the
issue of when it would be most appropriate to
introduce computers to students. Waldorf educators, who base their developmental ideas on the
writings of philosopher Rudolf Steiner (1861–
1925), do not believe one should teach students
about computers at an early age. They would not
only take into account students' cognitive development (at what age could students understand
computers?), but they would also consider
students' social, physical, and emotional development. At what age are students really excited
about computers? When are their fingers large
enough to work the keyboard? What skills and
habits might children lose if they learned computers at too early an age? Is there an optimum age
at which one ought to learn computers? Waldorf
educators would ask these kinds of developmental questions.

Developmentalists following the ideas of
Eleanor Duckworth may also ask the above
questions, but whatever the age of the student
they are working with, these educators would try
to teach the computer to children through
engaging interactive activities. Rather than telling
students about the computer, teachers would set
up activities where students can interact with
them. In this orientation, teachers would continue to set up challenges for students to push
their thinking. Sustaining students' sense of
wonder and curiosity is equally important. In
addition to setting new challenges for students,
teachers would also monitor student growth by
trying to understand student thought processes.
In short, rather than fitting the child to the
curriculum, the curriculum is fitted to the child.

Reconceptualists' first impulse would be to
consider the educational, social, or cultural
meaning of computers before worrying about

their utility. Of course, one should remember that there isn't one party line for any given ideological perspective. Some reconceptualists may be optimistic about computers and some may not. Although I don't know William Pinar's or Madeleine Grumet's thoughts on computers, I imagine they would reflect on the way computers bring information to people. Pinar observes that place plays a role in the way one sees the world (Pinar 1991). The same machine with the same software can be placed in every school room, but even if students learn the same information, their relationship to this new knowledge will vary. Thus, to understand the impact of computers one needs to know a great deal about the people who will learn from and use them. Having students write autobiographies provides one way to attain this understanding. Students could write about or dramatize their encounters with technology. After such an understanding, teachers can tailor lessons to meet student needs.

Critical theorist Michael Apple has examined the issue of computers in schools. Though he points out that many teachers are delighted with the new technology, he worries about an uncritical acceptance of it. Many teachers, he notes, do not receive substantial information about computers before they are implemented. Consequently, they must rely on a few experts or pre-packaged sets of material. The effects of this situation are serious. With their reliance on purchased material combined with the lack of time to properly review and evaluate it, teachers lose control over the curriculum development process. They become implementers of someone else's plans and procedures and become deskilled and disempowered because of that (Apple 1986, 163).

Apple also worries about the kind of thinking students learn from computers. While students concentrate on manipulating machines, they are concerned with issues of "how" more than "why." Consequently, Apple argues, computers enhance technical but not substantive thinking. Crucial political and ethical understanding atrophies while students are engaged in computer proficiency. Apple does not suggest one avoid computers because of these problems. Rather, he wants teachers and students to engage in social, political, and ethical discussions while they use the new technology.

Multiculturalists would be concerned that all students have equal access to computers. Early research on computer implementation revealed

that many minority students did not have the opportunity to use computers, and when they did, their interaction with computers often consisted of computer-assisted instruction programs that exercised low-level skills (Anderson, Welch, Harris 1984). In addition to raising the issue that all students should have equal access to computers, multiculturalists would also investigate whether software programs were sending biased or racist viewpoints.

Finally, cognitive pluralists, such as Elliot Eisner, would probably focus on the kinds of knowledge made available by computers. If computers were used too narrowly so that students had the opportunity to interact only with words and numbers, Eisner would be concerned. He would point out, I believe, that students could be learning that "real" knowledge exists in two forms. If, however, computers enhance cognitive understanding by providing multiple forms of representation, then I think Eisner would approve of the use of this new technology in the classroom. For example, in the latest videodisc technology, when students look up the definition of a word, they find a written statement as well as a picture. How much more meaningful a picture of a castle is to a young child than the comment, "a fortified residence as of a noble in feudal times" (*Random House Dictionary* 1980, 142).

In addition to learning through a variety of sensory forms, Eisner would also want students to have the opportunity to express themselves in a variety of ways. Computers could be useful in allowing students to reveal their knowledge in visual and musical as well as narrative forms. Students should not be limited in the ways they can express what they know.

Each curriculum ideology offers a unique perspective by virtue of the kinds of values and theories embedded within it. By reflecting on some of the ideas from the various curriculum ideologies and applying them to an educational issue, I believe educators can have a more informed, constructive, and creative dialogue. Moreover, as I said earlier, I do not think one needs to remain ideologically pure. Teachers and curricularists would do well to borrow ideas from the various perspectives as long as they make sure they are not proposing contradictory ideas.

The chart on page 11 summarizes the major proponents, major writings, educational priorities, and philosophical beliefs of each curriculum ideology covered in this chapter. (Of course, this chart is not comprehensive. I encourage the

CURRICULUM IDEOLOGIES

Ideology	Major Proponent	Major Writings	Educational Priorities	Philosophical Beliefs	Teachers, Curriculum, or Schools Expressing Curriculum Ideology	Suggestions for Curriculum Development
Rational Humanism	R. M. Hutchins M. Adler	The Paideia Proposal (Adler 1982) Paideia Problems and Possibilities (Adler 1983) The Paideia Program (Adler 1984)	Teaching through Socratic method. The use of primary texts. No electives.	The best education for the best is the best education for all. Since time in school is short, expose students to the best of Western culture.	Paideia Schools. See Adler (1983) for a list of schools.	Teach students how to facilitate good seminars. Use secondary texts sparingly.
Developmentalism	E. Duckworth R. Steiner	Young Children Reinvent Arithmetic (Kamii 1985) "The Having of Wonderful Ideas" and Other Essays (Duckworth 1987) Rudolf Steiner Education and the Developing Child (Aeppli 1986)	Fit curriculum to child's needs and interests. Inquiry-oriented teaching.	Cognitive structures develop as naturally as walking. If the setting is right, students will raise questions to push their own thinking.	Pat Carini's Prospect School in Burlington, VT.	Allow teachers the opportunity to be surprised. Rather than writing a curriculum manual, prepare a curriculum guide.
Reconceptualism	W. Pinar M. Grumet	Bitter Milk (Grumet 1988) Curriculum Theorizing (Pinar 1975) Curriculum and Instruction (Giroux, Penna, Pinar 1981)	Use philosophy, psychology, and literature to understand the human experience. Provide an "education for having" and an "education for being."	One learns through experience. We can learn to understand experience through phenomenology, psychoanalysis, and literature.	See Oliver (1990) for a curriculum in accordance with reconceptualist thinking.	Write lesson plans without the use of objectives. Curriculum writers ought to reveal their individual subjectivities.
Critical Theory	M. Apple I. Shor P. Freire	Ideology and Curriculum (Apple 1979) Teachers and Texts (Apple 1986) Pedagogy of the Oppressed (Freire 1970) Freire for the Classroom (Shor 1987)	Equal opportunities for all students. Teaching should entail critical reflection.	A just society maximizes the advantage for the least advantages. Schools are part of the larger community and must be analyzed as such.	See Shor's edited text (1987) for a number of ideas on implementing critical theory.	Curriculum writers ought to examine their own working assumptions critically and ought to respect the integrity of teachers and students.
Multiculturalism	J. Banks E. King	Multiethnic Education (Banks 1988) Multicultural Education (Banks and Banks 1989)	Students should learn to participate in various cultures. Approach concept or theme from various viewpoints.	Students need to feel good about their ethnic identities. All people participate in various cultures and subcultures.	See King (1990) for a workbook of activities teaching ethnic and gender awareness.	Make sure that text and pictures represent a variety of cultures.
Cognitive Pluralism	E. Eisner H. Gardner	"Curriculum Ideologies" (Eisner 1992) The Educational Imagination (Eisner 1985) Frames of Mind (Gardner 1983)	Teach, and allow students to express themselves, through a variety of forms of representation. Allow students to develop numerous intelligences.	Our senses cue into and pick up different aspects of the world. Combined with our individual history and general schemata, our senses allow us to construct meaning.	The Key School in Indianapolis.	Curriculum lesson plans and units ought to be aesitetically pleasing in appearance. Curriculum ought to represent a variety of ways of knowing

reader to examine the recommended reading list for further works in each of these areas.) In the fifth column, "Teachers, Curriculum, or Schools Expressing Curriculum Ideology," I indicate places or texts where readers may learn more. One could visit a Paideia school, Carini's Prospect School, or the Key School in Indianapolis. One may read about reconceptualism, critical theory, and multiculturalism in the listed texts. Finally, in the sixth column, "Suggestions for Curriculum Development," I also include interesting points found in the literature but not necessarily contained in this chapter.

Recommended Reading

The following is a concise list of recommended reading in many of the areas discussed in this chapter. Full bibliographic citations are provided under *References.*

Some general **curriculum textbooks** that are invaluable are John D. McNeil's *Curriculum: A Comprehensive Introduction* (1990); William H. Schubert's *Curriculum: Perspective, Paradigm, and Possibility* (1986); Decker Walker's *Fundamentals of Curriculum* (1990); and Robert S. Zais's *Curriculum: Principles and Foundations* (1976). These books provide wonderful introductions to the field.

The recently published *Handbook of Research on Curriculum* (Jackson 1992) includes thirty-four articles by leading curricularists. This book is a must for anyone interested in research in curriculum.

For a discussion of **objectives** in education, Tyler (1949) is seminal. Also see Kapfer (1972) and Mager (1962). Bloom refines educational objectives into a taxonomy (1956). Eisner's (1985) critique of educational objectives and his notion of expressive outcomes will be welcomed by those who are skeptical of the objectives movement.

Good books on the **history of curriculum** include Kliebard (1986), Schubert (1980), and Tanner and Tanner (1975). Seguel (1966), who discusses the McMurry brothers, Dewey, Bobbitt, and Rugg, among others, is also very good.

Some excellent books on the **history of education** include the following: Lawrence Cremin's definitive book on progressive education, *The Transformation of the School: Progressivism in American Education, 1876–1957* (1961). David Tyack's *The One Best System* (1974) portrays the evolution of schools into their

modern formation; and Larry Cuban's *How Teachers Taught: Constancy and Change in American Classrooms, 1890–1980* (1984) examines what actually happened in classrooms during a century of reform efforts. Philip Jackson's "Conceptions of Curriculum and Curriculum Specialists" (1992) provides an excellent summary of the evolution of curriculum thought from Bobbitt and Tyler to Schwab.

For works in each of the ideologies I recommend the following:

To help one understand the **rational humanist** approach, there are Mortimer Adler's three books on the **Paideia school**: *The Paideia Proposal: An Educational Manifesto* (1982), *Paideia Problems and Possibilities* (1983), and *The Paideia Program: An Educational Syllabus* (1984). Seven critical reviews of the Paideia proposal comprise "The Paideia Proposal: A Symposium" (1983).

For works in **developmentalism** based on Piaget's ideas see Duckworth (1987, 1991) and Kamii (1985). Among Piaget's many works you may want to read *The Origins of Intelligence* (1966). If you are interested in Waldorf education see Robert McDermott's *The Essential Steiner* (1984) and P. Bruce Uhrmacher's "Waldorf Schools Marching Quietly Unheard" (1991). Willi Aeppli's *Rudolf Steiner Education and the Developing Child* (1986), Francis Edmunds's *Rudolf Steiner Education* (1982), and Marjorie Spock's *Teaching as a Lively Art* (1985) are also quite good.

A general overview of the developmental approach to curriculum can be found on pages 49–52 of Linda Darling-Hammond and Jon Snyder's "Curriculum Studies and the Traditions of Inquiry: The Scientific Tradition" (1922).

Two books are essential for examining **reconceptualist** writings: William Pinar's *Curriculum Theorizing: The Reconceptualists* (1975) and Henry Giroux, Anthony N. Penna, and William F. Pinar's *Curriculum and Instruction* (1981). Recent books in reconceptualism include William Pinar and William Reynolds's *Understanding Curriculum as Phenomenological and Deconstructed Text* (1992), and William Pinar and Joe L. Kincheloe's *Curriculum as Social Psychoanalysis: The Significance of Place* (1991).

Some excellent works in **critical theory** include Paulo Freire's *Pedagogy of the Oppressed* (1970) and *The Politics of Education* (1985). Apple's works are also excellent; see *Ideology and Curriculum* (1979) and *Teachers and Texts* (1986). For an overview of the Frankfurt School and the application of Jürgen Habermas's ideas, see Robert Young's *A Critical Theory of Education: Habermas and Our Children's Future* (1990).

For an application of critical theory to classrooms see the Ira Shor–edited book, *Freire for the Classroom* (1987) with an afterword by Paulo Freire.

In **multicultural education** I recommend James Banks's *Multiethnic Education: Theory and Practice* (1988) and Banks and Banks's *Multicultural Education: Issues and Perspectives* (1989). Also see Gibson (1984) for an account of five different approaches to multicultural education. Nicholas Appleton (1983), Saracho and Spodek (1983), and Simonson and Walker (1988) are also important. Edith King's *Teaching Ethnic and Gender Awareness: Methods and Materials for the Elementary School* (1990) provides useful ideas about multicultural education that could be used in the classroom. John Ogbu's work (1987) on comparing immigrant populations to involuntary minorities is also an important work with serious educational implications.

Important works in the field of **cognitive pluralism** include Elliot Eisner (1982, 1985, 1992) and Howard Gardner (1983, 1991). Some philosophical texts that influenced both of these men include Dewey (1934), Goodman (1978), and Langer (1976).

For $20.00, the Key School Option Program will send you an interdisciplinary theme-based curriculum report. For more information write Indianapolis Public Schools, 1401 East Tenth Street, Indianapolis, Indiana 46201.

Glossary of Some Common Usages of Curriculum

delivered curriculum: what teachers deliver in the classroom. This is opposed to Intended curriculum. Same as operational curriculum.

enacted curriculum: actual class offerings by a school, as opposed to courses listed in books or guides. *See* official curriculum.

experienced curriculum: what students actually learn. Same as received curriculum.

explicit curriculum: stated aims and goals of a classroom or school.

hidden curriculum: unintended, unwritten, tacit, or latent aspects of messages given to students by teachers, school structures, textbooks, and other school resources. For example, while students learn writing or math, they may also learn about punctuality, neatness, competition, and conformity. Concealed messages may be intended or unintended by the school or teacher.

implicit curriculum: similar to the hidden curriculum in the sense that something is implied rather than expressly stated. Whereas the hidden curriculum usually refers to something unfavorable, negative, or sinister, the implicit curriculum also takes into account unstated qualities that are positive.

intended curriculum: that which is planned by the teacher or school.

null curriculum: that which does not take place in the school or classroom. What is not offered cannot be learned. Curricular exclusion tells a great deal about a school's values.

official curriculum: courses listed in the school catalogue or course bulletin. Although these classes are listed, they may not be taught. *See* enacted curriculum.

operational curriculum: events that take place in the classroom. Same as delivered curriculum.

received curriculum: what students acquire as a result of classroom activity. Same as experienced curriculum.

References

Adler, Mortimer J. 1982. *The Paideia Proposal: An Educational Manifesto.* New York: Collier Books.

———. 1983. *Paideia Problems and Possibilities.* New York: Collier Books.

———. 1984. *The Paideia Program: An Educational Syllabus.* New York: Collier Books.

Aeppli, Willi. 1986. *Rudolf Steiner Education and the Developing Child.* Hudson, NY: Anthroposophic Press.

Anderson, Ronald E., Wayne W. Welch, and Linda J. Harris. 1984. "Inequities in Opportunities for Computer Literacy." *The Computing Teacher: The Journal of the International*

Council for Computers in Education 11(8): 10–12.

Apple, Michael W. 1979. *Ideology and Curriculum.* Boston: Routledge and Kegan Paul.

———. 1986. *Teachers and Texts: A Political Economy of Class and Gender Relations in Education.* New York: Routledge and Kegan Paul.

Appleton, Nicholas. 1983. *Cultural Pluralism in Education.* White Plains, NY: Longman.

Banks, James A. 1988. *Multiethnic Education: Theory and Practice.* 2d ed. Boston: Allyn and Bacon.

Banks, James A., and Cherry A. McGee Banks, eds. 1989. *Multicultural Education: Issues and Perspectives.* Boston: Allyn and Bacon.

Bloom, Benjamin S., ed. 1956. *Taxonomy of Educational Objectives: The Classification of Educational Goals, Handbook 1: Cognitive Domain.* New York: McKay.

Bobbitt, Franklin. 1918. *The Curriculum.* Boston: Houghton Mifflin.

Cremin, Lawrence A. 1961. *The Transformation of the School: Progressivism in American Education, 1876–1957.* New York: Vintage Books.

———. 1977. *Traditions of American Education.* New York: Basic Books.

Cuban, Larry. 1984. *How Teachers Taught: Constancy and Change in American Classrooms 1890–1980.* White Plains, NY: Longman.

Darling-Hammond, Linda, and Jon Snyder. 1992. "Curriculum Studies and the Traditions of Inquiry: The Scientific Tradition." In *Handbook of Research on Curriculum: A Project of the American Educational Research Association,* ed. Philip W. Jackson, 41–78. New York: Macmillan.

Dewey, John. 1934. *Art as Experience.* New York: Minton, Balch.

Duckworth, Eleanor. 1987. *"The Having of Wonderful Ideas" and Other Essays on Teaching and Learning.* New York: Teachers College Press.

———. 1991. "Twenty-four, Forty-two, and I Love You: Keeping It Complex. *Harvard Educational Review* 61(1): 1–24.

Edmunds, L. Francis. 1982. *Rudolf Steiner Education.* 2d ed. London: Rudolf Steiner Press.

Eisner, Elliot W. 1982. *Cognition and Curriculum: A Basis for Deciding What to Teach.* White Plains, NY: Longman.

———. 1985. *The Educational Imagination.* 2d ed. New York: Macmillan.

———. 1992. "Curriculum Ideologies." In *Handbook of Research on Curriculum: A Project of the American Educational Research Association,* ed. Philip W. Jackson, 302–26. New York: Macmillan.

Freire, Paulo. 1970. *Pedagogy of the Oppressed.* Trans. Myra Bergman Ramos. New York: Seabury Press.

———. 1985. *The Politics of Education.* Trans. Donaldo Macedo. South Hadley, MA: Bergin and Garvey.

Gardner, Howard. 1983. *Frames of Mind.* New York: Basic Books.

———. 1991. *The Unschooled Mind: How Children Think and How Schools Should Teach.* New York: Basic Books.

Gibson, Margaret Alison. 1984. "Approaches to Multicultural Education in the United States: Some Concepts and Assumptions." *Anthropology and Education Quarterly* 15: 94–119.

Giroux, Henry, Anthony N. Penna, and William F. Pinar. 1981. *Curriculum and Instruction: Alternatives in Education.* Berkeley: McCutchan.

Good, Thomas S., and Jere E. Brophy. 1986. *Educational Psychology.* 3d ed. White Plains, NY: Longman.

Goodman, Nelson. 1978. *Ways of Worldmaking.* Indianapolis: Hackett.

Greene, Maxine. 1988a. "Vocation and Care: Obsessions about Teacher Education." Panel discussion at the Annual Meeting of the American Educational Research Association, 5–9 April, New Orleans.

———. 1988b. *The Dialectic of Freedom.* New York: Teachers College Press.

Gress, James R. 1978. *Curriculum: An Introduction to the Field.* Berkeley: McCutchan.

Grumet, Madeleine R. 1988. *Bitter Milk: Women and Teaching.* Amherst: Univ. of Massachusetts Press.

Jackson, Philip W. 1992. "Conceptions of Curriculum and Curriculum Specialists." In *Handbook of Research on Curriculum: A Project of the American Educational Research Association,* ed. Philip W. Jackson, 3–40. New York: Macmillan.

Kamii, Constance Kazuko, with Georgia DeClark. 1985. *Young Children Reinvent Arithmetic: Implications of Piaget's Theory.* New York: Teachers College Press.

Kapfer, Miriam B. 1972. *Behavioral Objectives in Curriculum Development: Selected Readings and Bibliography.* Englewood Cliffs, NJ: Educational Technology.

King, Edith W. 1990. *Teaching Ethnic and Gender Awareness: Methods and Materials for the Elementary School.* Dubuque, IA: Kendall/Hunt.

Kliebard, Herbert M. 1986. *The Struggle for the American Curriculum, 1893–1958.* Boston: Routledge and Kegan Paul.

Langer, Susanne. 1976. *Problems of Art.* New York: Scribners.

McDermott, Robert A., ed. 1984. *The Essential Steiner.* San Francisco: Harper & Row.

McLaren, Peter. 1986. *Schooling as a Ritual Performance: Towards a Political Economy of Educational Symbols and Gestures.* London: Routledge and Kegan Paul.

McNeil, John D. 1990. *Curriculum: A Comprehensive Introduction.* 4th ed. Glenview, IL: Scott, Foresman/Little, Brown Higher Education.

Mager, Robert. 1962. *Preparing Instructional Objectives.* Palo Alto, CA: Fearon.

Ogbu, John. 1987. "Variability in Minority School Performance: A Problem in Search of an Explanation." *Anthropology and Education Quarterly* 18(4): 312–34.

Oliver, Donald W. 1990. "Grounded Knowing: A Postmodern Perspective on Teaching and Learning." *Educational Leadership* 48(1): 64-69.

"The Paideia Proposal: A Symposium." 1983. *Harvard Educational Review* 53 (4): 377–411.

Piaget, Jean. 1962. *Play, Dreams and Imitation in Childhood.* New York: Norton.

———. 1966. *Origins of Intelligence.* New York: Norton.

Pinar, William F., ed. 1975. *Curriculum Theorizing: The Reconceptualists.* Berkeley: McCutchan.

Pinar, William F., and Joe L. Kincheloe, eds. 1991. *Curriculum as Social Psychoanalysis: The Significance of Place.* Albany: State Univ. of New York Press.

Pinar, William F., and William M. Reynolds, eds. 1992. *Understanding Curriculum as Phenomenological and Deconstructed Text.* New York: Teachers College Press.

The Random House Dictionary. 1980. New York: Ballantine.

Saracho, Olivia N., and Bernard Spodek. 1983. *Understanding the Multicultural Experience in Early Childhood Education.* Washington, DC: National Association for the Education of Young Children.

Schubert, William H. 1980. *Curriculum Books: The First Eight Years.* Lanham, MD: Univ. Press of America.

———. 1986. *Curriculum: Perspective, Paradigm, and Possibility.* New York: Macmillan.

Schwab, Joseph J. 1970. *The Practical: A Language for Curriculum.* Washington, DC: National Education Association.

Seguel, M. L. 1966. *The Curriculum Field: Its Formative Years.* New York: Teachers College Press.

Shor, Ira, ed. 1987. *Freire for the Classroom: A Sourcebook for Liberatory Teaching.* Portsmouth, NH: Heinemann.

Simonson, Rick, and Scott Walker, eds. 1988. *The Graywolf Annual Five: Multi-Cultural Literacy.* St. Paul, MN: Graywolf Press.

Spock, Marjorie. 1985. *Teaching as a Lively Art.* Hudson, NY: Anthroposophic Press.

Taba, Hilda. 1962. *Curriculum Development: Theory and Practice.* New York: Harcourt Brace Jovanovich.

Tanner, Daniel, and Laurel N. Tanner. 1975. *Curriculum Development: Theory into Practice.* New York: Macmillan.

Tietze, Wolfgang. 1987. "A Structural Model for the Evaluation of Preschool Effects." *Early Childhood Research Quarterly* 2(2): 133–59.

Tyack, David B. 1974. *The One Best System: A History of American Urban Education.* Cambridge: Harvard Univ. Press.

Tyler, Ralph W. 1949. *Basic Principles of Curriculum and Instruction.* Chicago: Univ. of Chicago Press.

Uhrmacher, P. Bruce. 1991. "Waldorf Schools Marching Quietly Unheard." Ph.D. diss., Stanford University.

Walker, Decker. 1990. *Fundamentals of Curriculum.* New York: Harcourt Brace Jovanovich.

Young, Robert. 1990. *A Critical Theory of Education: Habermas and Our Children's Future.* New York: Teachers College Press.

Zais, Robert S. 1976. *Curriculum: Principles and Foundations.* New York: Thomas Y. Crowell.

1

TRENDS AND ISSUES IN ENGLISH/ LANGUAGE ARTS CURRICULUM

by Mary Erard
Human Relations Specialist
Fairfax County Public Schools, Fairfax, Virginia
and
Shirley T. McCoy
Minority Student Achievement Specialist
Fairfax County Public Schools, Fairfax, Virginia

T HE need for curriculum renewal or restructuring is as inevitable as change itself, and it can offer an opportunity to rethink practices and formulate a design for education that works for all children. In order to develop curriculum, planners must have a fuller, more replete view of what curricular planning involves. They must have a historical perspective, an understanding of our changing society, a grasp of the most recent research related to how children learn, and a clear vision of future goals for education.

English/language arts curriculum planners also need to know the latest trends in their subject area, together with some suggested strategies for implementing change. It is our hope that this chapter will provide English/language arts curriculum planners with the insights necessary to develop a curriculum that is productive and satisfying for both teachers and students.

Sources of the Curriculum

Historical Perspective

Schools mirror the dramatic changes that take place in society, and it is in the nation's schools more than any other place where evidence of this change is so dramatic and significant. While a historical perspective does not provide curriculum planners with a blueprint, it may serve to remind them of previous practices that have succeeded or failed. Even more importantly, a historical perspective builds a foundation from which we can appreciate and understand the forces that made our schools and the critics who wish to alter them (Pulliam 1968, 1).

Reform has been a major theme throughout the history of American education. From the time of the first European colonists, there have been debates over educational purposes, curriculum methods, and who should be taught.

The early immigrants in colonial times brought a simple notion of learning, grounded almost entirely in religious orientation. Elementary schools were to provide religious instruction as well as the rudiments of reading, writing, and arithmetic—for both boys and girls. Secondary schools were patterned after English grammar schools, with a very narrow classical curriculum suited to prepare boys for higher education. As the colonial period ended, commercialism, mercantilism, and a rising middle class created a need for the mandatory study of secular and utilitarian subjects (Lauderdale 1987, 10-11).

It was in the late eighteenth and early nineteenth centuries (national period), however, that a sense of urgency developed regarding the importance of schooling to the national welfare. It was Thomas Jefferson who most impressively addressed the issue of educational reform as a condition of national sovereignty.

With industrialization, urbanization, immigration, and westward migration came a web of religious, intellectual, political, and class conflicts that gave rise to one of the most important educational reform efforts in our history—the common school movement. Horace Mann, America's consummate advocate for social justice through education, unrelentingly crusaded for common schools "not in the traditional European sense of a school for common people but in a new sense of schools common to all people" (Cremin 1957, 8). Horace Mann believed that the seeds of excellence are implanted "equally in the mind of the ignorant peasant, and in the mind of the most profound philosopher" (Lauderdale 1987, 17). He set the tone for equity for both peasant and philosopher. Those committed to the improvement of schools today would do well to refresh their memories of the contributions of Horace Mann (Lauderdale 1987, 13-15).

By the mid-nineteenth century (Industrial Revolution), educational reform in America was defined by three issues: the role education could play in promoting democracy, the establishing of public order, and the accommodation of commercial interests. Two conflicting philosophies arose—those who wanted the western European tradition of classical education and those who advocated practical courses and vocational programs (Lauderdale 1987, 18-19).

Progressive education (twentieth century) represents a major effort to reform the schools. Progressive reform efforts began with attempts to broaden the school's role. John Dewey promoted the idea of a more open, democratic classroom environment. He believed that education is a social process. Attention was focused squarely upon the child and the importance of learner interest, as well as on learning relevant to life situations (Lauderdale 1987, 20-22). In contemporary times, a most important landmark in the history of American education took place in the 1954 *Brown* v. *Board of Education of Topeka, Kansas* case, which struck down the "separate but equal" doctrine established by *Plessy* v. *Ferguson.*

Another law that has had a far-reaching impact on education is Public Law 94-142, passed in 1975. This law requires schools to establish the least restrictive environment for handicapped students, which means mainstreaming students in a regular classroom whenever possible (Lauderdale 1987, 26-28).

Educational reform in America has had two major traditions—a concern for equity and a commitment to academic excellence. Historically, arguments on behalf of each have made them seem incompatible.

Two recent benchmarks in American education illustrate this conflict: the Elementary and Secondary Education Act of 1965 (ESEA) and *A Nation at Risk* (National Commission on Excellence in Education) in 1983. These two events symbolically represent the polarity of view on what should be the national priorities for education. With ESEA, President Lyndon B. Johnson clearly set his priority for serving the underprivileged. Under the banner of the Great Society, he established equality of educational opportunity as a national priority in place of academic excellence (Lauderdale 1987, 24-25).

Just two decades later, *A Nation at Risk* set in motion a spirited national dialogue on the failures of public education and a call for higher standards, accountability, and academic excellence (Lauderdale 1987, 24-25).

These concerns are being voiced at a time of dramatic increase in immigration. Suddenly we see very different cultural styles and worldviews brought together in one place, with the added dimension of language differences. These factors arising out of immigration will have their impact on the instructional program (Lauderdale 1987, 25).

Indeed, in less than two decades the dichotomous views of these two benchmark events in American education would make us believe that a concern for equity and a commitment to academic excellence are mutually exclusive (Lauderdale 1987, 23).

How does this historical perspective apply to the English/language arts curriculum? Perhaps the clearest connection can be found in James Miller's four sequential stages of English curriculum development. Miller's stages trace from the colonial period through the twentieth century and show how societal needs, beliefs, and values drove curriculum design (Inlow 1973, 93):

> 1. Authoritarian—a curriculum characterized by prescriptive grammar, extensive memory learning, heavy dependence on the classics, and an almost total disregard of learner interest and motivation.
> 2. Progressive—extensive learner permissiveness; emphasis on the here-and-now middle-class expectations of polite speech, thank-you notes, and "correct" business letters; and a resulting disregard of the in-depth literacy experiences.
> 3. Academic—the response of formal education to Sputnik 1; cognitively oriented; characterized by a "return" to the disciplines, a one-sided preoccupation with gifted learners, a "get tough" approach to all learners, and a gravitation toward homogeneously grouped classes.
> 4. Humanistic—the contemporary one, one whose goal is individual fulfillment; one in which honesty of feeling is legitimized; personal experience takes priority over product; direct instruction concedes to informal activity; and creative responses are regarded more highly than mechanically correct ones which lack feeling; a belief that the central purpose of any English curriculum needs to be the actualization of learners (Inlow 1973, 93).

What does this historical perspective teach language arts curriculum planners today? Perhaps the lesson is that the more things change, the more they stay the same. It is clear that many of the issues that confronted education in the past remain on the national agenda for education for the twenty-first century: How can schools achieve social justice? How can schools promote ethnic understanding? How can we make schools common to all people? How can we accommodate business interests? How can we make education a social process? How can we accommodate learner interests and make learning relevant to life situations? How can we meet the needs of the handicapped student in a mainstreamed situation? Who should be taught? What should be taught? How should it be taught? How can we provide equity with excellence?

Language arts curriculum planners must increasingly address themselves to the question, What is the basic function of a language arts curriculum, and can it meet societal needs?

Planners must preserve the best of the past but must not be limited by it. They must look at the language arts curriculum in a much broader sense, or they will be forced to repeat the failures of the past and the same issues will follow us into the twenty-first century.

Our purpose here has been to provide a historical perspective to the central theses of American education—equity and academic excellence. It is to alert language arts teachers that their challenge as curriculum planners is to create a language arts curriculum that incorporates a broad spectrum of social and cultural components so that all young people will have an equal opportunity to achieve academic excellence.

Societal Changes

America has experienced dramatic ethnographic, demographic, and status changes during the last few decades. The populations of today's schools represent a wide range of racial, religious, cultural, ethnic, and economic diversity. In 1982, the population of the United States was 245,000,000: 12 percent black, 6.4 percent Hispanic, 1.6 percent Asian, and 80 percent white. By the year 2030, the population will be 300,000,000: 15 percent black, 15 percent Hispanic, 10 percent Asian, and 60 percent white. If predictions hold, a majority of students under the age of 18 will be nonwhite, will come from varied experiential backgrounds, and will represent a diversity of interests, talents, languages (oral, native, written), and ability levels. These changes have created challenges for public schools.

Historically, school systems have attempted to accommodate change by adding on to the existing curriculum special focus classes, pull-out programs, and/or remedial courses. Most of these efforts failed to produce a significant change in students' academic achievement. If this process is to become more effective, curriculum writers must include student data as a critical element of curriculum planning. Language arts curriculum writers must give more attention to students who are now entering school with English as a second language, some of whom are illiterate in their native languages. They must have particular concern for those students who have deficient oral language backgrounds as well as those with limited exposure to prereading skills or the printed word.

In short, the challenge for language arts curriculum writers will be to create a curriculum that (1) provides developmentally appropriate learning experiences that will allow all students to master the basic skills and concepts; (2) builds background knowledge, to extend and expand students' knowledge base; (3) includes the development of thinking skills; and (4) provides meaningful experiences, to allow for the transfer of learning to real life. A functional language arts curriculum will be multicultural in content, allow for creative expression, encourage divergent thinking, and expose students to a variety of views through literature written by authors of different cultures. This curriculum should include space for student choice and sufficient blocks of time for students to engage in the practice of writing and reading.

Future Educational Goals

What implications for future educational goals are implied in these changes? First, curriculum planners within this framework must ask themselves the basic question, How shall curriculum be conceived? Curriculum must go beyond a sequence of course offerings; it must be viewed as the total learning environment, including content and delivery services, materials and textbooks, teaching practices and techniques, presentation models, instructional strategies, the teaching/learning environment, as well as learning outcomes. The curriculum must be well organized and flexible and respect the diversity of the student population.

Some characteristics of this nontraditional, futures-oriented curriculum follow. Such a curriculum will:
- facilitate continuous learning (throughout life)
- support gender equity
- develop understanding of the historical foundations for America's social, economic, and political institutions
- identify expected learning outcomes
- leave selection of teaching approaches that meet the needs of students up to teachers
- embody the psychology of empowerment (based on Glasser's Control Theory)
- foster student self directiveness rather than dependency
- acknowledge different learning styles, levels of maturity, goals, values and beliefs
- foster high expectations
- require frequent monitoring and feedback as a way of teaching independent learning
- employ outcome-based evaluation
- employ self-evaluation
- teach social skills and interpersonal skills
- emphasize higher level thinking processes
- integrate curriculum

- utilize alternative assessments
- make use of technology so that teachers can tailor instruction for individual students and allow for students to access information anywhere in the world (Erard and McCoy 1990, 6-7)

In short, this futures-oriented curriculum will have as its essence the transformation position, the aim of which is self-actualization. The National Standards Project, jointly developed by NCTE, IRA, and the Center for the Study of Reading at the University of Illinois at Urbana-Champaign, will also be dealing with the future needs of the English curriculum. The first results of this project will be ready in autumn 1993.

New Research-Based Theories Related to Learning

In order to meet these future goals, curriculum planners must have a grasp of the current research on how children learn. Three of the most significant areas of research are left/right brain theory, teaching/learning styles, and school climate.

Left/Right Brain Theory

Recent research indicates that the two halves of the cerebrum—the right hemisphere and the left hemisphere—while seemingly alike, serve different functions. The left hemisphere is analytical: it specializes in recognizing the parts that make up the whole; it is linear and sequential. The right hemisphere specializes in combining these parts to create a whole; it is engaged in synthesizing, seeking patterns, and recognizing the relationships between the parts. Williams's research sees the two hemispheres as complementary and believes that this complementary functioning gives the brain its power (Grady 1990, 16).

Tony Buzan (1974), in his book *Use Both Sides of Your Brain*, proposes that there are two upper brains that operate in different mental areas and require very different food to survive. According to Buzan, "The left side deals with logic, language, reasoning, numbers, linearity, and analyzes academic activities. The right side deals with rhythm, music, images and imagination, color, and patterns or map recognition" (14).

Researchers seemingly agree on the hemisphericity of the brain, and there appears to be little disagreement on the basic preferences or functions of each. Where the research does reveal a basic disagreement is in whether individuals are left-, right-, or whole-brain functioners. Most researchers support a complementary functioning theory, while conceding that some people may indeed have a decided preference for left- or right-brain activities.

The left/right brain theory offers enough evidence on the relationship between brain functioning and learning to warrant consideration by curriculum planners. Sperry (1985) noted that practices in the public schools tend to neglect right-brain functioning and concentrate more on gearing activities to the left-brain function (174). When this occurs, the learning environment is biased toward the student who learns in what has been termed the "traditonal modes." Other students may be shortchanged in a way that creates an inequitable learning environment. Curriculum design that reflects a balance of left- and right-brain instructional activities, strategies, and tools would appear to be more equitable.

Brain research has generated much interest in the styles of learners—thinking, learning, reading, and personality—and in determining how style impacts on teaching and learning.

Teaching/Learning Styles

During the past decade, educators have become increasingly aware that individual teachers/ learners approach academic tasks with different styles and that the varying styles can mean that some teachers/learners will be far more successful than others with particular tasks, situations, and people. A focus on learning styles is a significant step in promoting equity in schools. For instance, if the visual learner has less opportunity to learn than the auditory learner because of teaching behavior, not only has that learner been short-changed, but our society has been deprived of the optimum talents of that individual (Guild and Garger 1985, 5).

Learning style, as discussed here, is the way people concentrate on, internalize, and remember new and difficult knowledge and skills. It is composed of cognitive, motivational, and physi-ological elements that affect each person's ability to perceive, interact with, and respond to the learning environment (Dunn 1989, 22).

Once we acknowledge the differences in styles, how do we accommodate those differ-ences? In an individual teaching and learning situation, does the teacher adapt to the student or the student to the teacher?

Researchers on style have different opinions. Rita and Kenneth Dunn (1975) urge us to meet the needs of the individual learner as often and as

frequently as possible. Gregorc, on the other hand, encourages a direct accommodation of style some of the time and a conscious mismatch at other times, to help students stretch themselves. Charles Letteri, of the University of Vermont, believes that specific combinations of style characteristics are red flags for academic prob-lems. He argues that learners can and should be trained to develop success-oriented cognitive skills (Guild and Garger 1985, 88).

Bernice McCarthy describes four types of learners: idea people (Type 1); analyzers (Type 2); pragmatists (Type 3); and self-disclosers (Type 4). To accommodate these learners, McCarthy has come up with the 4MAT system, which moves through the learning cycle in sequence, teaching in all four modes. The sequence is a natural learning progression that starts with the teacher answering in sequence the questions that appeal to each major learning style: Why? (Type 1); What? (Type 2); How? (Type 3); If? (Type 4) (McCarthy 1988, 10).

The knowledge that diverse styles exist leads to the conclusion that teaching must be varied in content, delivery, structure, expectation, and assessment. It may not be as important to know the exact style of each student as it is for teachers and curriculum planners to act on the assumption that in any group of people a diversity of styles will be represented, thereby making it important to present students with a variety of options.

Expectations

School climate, accurately defined, encompasses all aspects of the school environment. Research-ers define it as "the norms, beliefs, and attitudes reflected in institutional patterns and behavioral practices that enhance or impede student achievement" (Lezotte et al. 1980, 8).

One area related to school climate that has received a great deal of attention over the past decade, and which is not included in this con-struct, is that of student/teacher expectations. According to Brophy and Good, the interaction between teacher and student profoundly impacts student achievement. An article by Good (1972) reports that they found several ways in which teachers' behaviors "co-vary with expectations":

1. Seating low-expectation students far from the teacher and/or putting them in a group together.
2. Paying less attention to "lows" in academic situations (smiling less often and not main-

taining eye contact).

3. Calling on "lows" less often to answer classroom questions or make public demonstrations.

4. Waiting less time for "lows" to answer questions.

5. Not staying with "lows" in failure situations (i.e., providing fewer clues, asking fewer follow-up questions).

6. Criticizing "lows" more frequently than "highs" for incorrect responses.

7. Praising "lows" less frequently than "highs" after successful responses.

8. Praising "lows" more frequently than "highs" for marginal or inadequate public responses.

9. Providing "lows" with less accurate and less detailed feedback than "highs." (26-27)

The effectiveness of any curriculum design is measured by the degree to which students learn what has been taught. Research indicates that students learn best in an environment that is characterized by motivating, encouraging, and nurturing messages relative to their abilities. Student/teacher expectations, therefore, have significant impact on the learning climate and, ultimately, on academic outcomes. One conclusion that can be reached from the research on expectations is that students are much more likely to achieve academic excellence in schools that foster high, nonnegotiable expectations for all students.

Theories Specific to Language Arts

In addition to the general research on learning, some theories specific to language arts have emerged. We will discuss these as they relate to each language arts component.

Reading

Current research about reading as a process includes the following:

1. Reading is the process of constructing meaning from written text. It is a complex skill that requires the coordination of a number of interrelated sources of information (Commission on Reading 1990, 3).

2. Reading is important in all disciplines.

3. Whether reading skills are best taught and learned in the context of actual reading is now being questioned. (See *Whole Language Instruction vs. Systematic Phonics Instruction*).

4. Whether students should use a basal reader or a variety of children's literature for beginning reading is also being debated. (See *Whole Language Instruction.*)

5. Reading skills are interrelated with writing, speaking, listening, and thinking skills.

6. Reading is an ongoing developmental process for all students (K-12).

7. The use of technology will have a significant impact on the teaching of reading. (See *Technology Integration.*)

8. Student-generated questions, rather than teacher-initiated ones, give students a way in which to monitor and control comprehension.

Writing

Current research about writing as a process and about students as individuals leads one to some basic assumptions:

1. Writing is important in all disciplines. It is the tool that helps students develop the knowledge and skills of a subject matter, and to gain awareness of how fragments of information relate to each other and how these fragments can be put together to make a cohesive whole.

2. Effective writing is refined thinking. Guided lessons in writing develop critical-thinking skills. It forces students to shape their experiences into meaning for themselves and others.

3. Writing skills are best taught and learned in the context of actual writing. Learning about writing will not take the place of learning to write.

4. Students should write for many different purposes and audiences.

5. Writing skills are interrelated with reading, speaking, and thinking skills; each skill stimulates and strengthens the others.

6. A positive relationship exists between increased reading and improved writing.

7. Writing is a process as well as a product (prewriting, composing, revising, and sharing).

8. Writing is an ongoing, developmental process.

9. Writing is not helped by grammar exercises, sentence diagramming, and other drill work.

10. The revision process is significant in improving student writing.

11. Evaluation should encourage rather than inhibit students to write.

12. Writing should be shared.

13. The use of technology will have a significant impact on the teaching of writing.

Spelling

A considerable body of research on the teaching of spelling has existed for the better part of this century, and its researchers are in more agreement here than in any other area of the curriculum. Unfortunately, however, it has been virtually ignored by most commercial spelling programs, which tend to take the form of workbooks or exercises that focus on spelling alone. To date, spelling research has revealed the following:

1. Spelling should be taught; it is not learned incidentally
2. The learning of rules is only marginally helpful
3. Spelling is a developmental process
4. There is a logic to the spelling patterns of early spellers and their errors change over time as they experiment with language
5. To master spelling, students need to perceive patterns that exist in words
6. Student's invented spellings indicate the tactics they use to determine the spelling of words
7. Words of highest frequency in student and adult writing should be the words studied
8. Learning the origin of a word and its relationship to others derived from the same root will often lead to correct spelling
9. Frequent opportunities to use spelling words in writing contribute greatly to the maintenance of spelling ability (Texas Education Agency 1991, 2-10)

In short, spelling makes sense only in the context of written work, where it serves the needs of both writers and readers. Spelling is the tool that assists writers in expressing themselves effectively.

Oral Language

Perhaps because virtually everyone can talk, parents and other adults have assumed in the past that oral language is a natural ability, and too few have seen the need for a structured program of oral experiences. Today, however, educators are focusing on the amount and kinds of oral language we use. Some work in this area has been done by writers who have examined the uses of oral language. Joan Tongh (1976) developed a category system that includes (1) self-maintaining language, (2) directing, (3) reporting, (4) logical reasoning, (5) predicting, (6) projecting, and (7) imagining. These category names include some functions that overlap those described by Halliday, who uses slightly different terminology: (1) instrumental, (2) regulatory, (3) interactional, (4) personal,

(5) heuristic, (6) imaginative, and (7) representational. These and other category systems help us to reconsider the kinds of instruction we provide.

As evidenced in much of the research on whole language, oral language development provides the foundation on which reading and writing are built. (See *Whole Language Instruction vs. Systematic Phonics Instruction.*) Teaching children to speak coherently for varied purposes will provide them with an invaluable tool as they grow up in today's world.

Our objectives for children might be grouped into four categories, to be introduced and developed at all levels: (1) acquiring verbal fluency, (2) extending the speaking vocabulary, (3) learning about the elements of speech, and (4) experiencing varied forms and styles of speaking. Under each of these categories, we can list specific topics or activities that will aid children in developing a command of spoken English.

1. Experiential background; frequency of opportunities to speak; self-esteem
2. Meanings of words; hearing words in context and language appropriate to specific situations; oral use of words; pronunciation
3. The science of the speech mechanism; discussing the voice and its effective use; interrelationships between speaking and listening; aspects of spoken language (dialectology, idiom)
4. Informal talking (discussion, conversation); formal speaking (oral report, debate)

Among the oral language activities that Tiedt (1983) cited for possible use across the curriculum are the following: guided discussion in small groups, creative drama, reader's theater, storytelling, reporting, debating, singing, ensemble speaking, pantomime, puppetry, audio/video taping (115-131). Tools for analyzing oral language could include taped samples.

Stewig (1988) describes a grid that Robert Ruddell developed which allows teachers to observe and quantify student language:

A sample of an oral presentation evaluation would consider such points as (1) Interest (enthusiasm of the speaker, audience response, expression of voice, gestures, attitude), (2) Voice (enunciation, clearness, pronunciation, volume, use of words, pace), (3) Organization (introduction, effect, organized points, knowledge of material, conclusion), and (4) Bearing (rising to speak, eye contact, posture, movement of body).

For specific types of speeches, the effectiveness can be tested by noting the results;

e.g., in telling a joke the effectiveness can be judged by audience response. When the student is assigned to explain how to do something, he/she will be successful if the listener can follow and produce what is described. (171-174)

Thinking

Children are perceived by some educational writers as "natural born philosophers who have the ability to learn logic and reasoning skills" (Johnson 1984, 214). Piaget's research on human development in adolescents would support this position. According to Day (1981), Piaget concluded that "all children beyond the age of 12 should be able to reason at a formal operations level." A student's ability to think can be improved by direct instruction (Stockton and Worsham 1986, 8). In support of these theories, several researchers believe that "Classrooms can create an atmosphere that encourages the · recognition, selection, and application of appropriate thinking skills" (Johnson 1984, 23); and that the K-12 curriculum offers the most supportive framework for the teaching of thinking. The development of thinking patterns and strategies is essential to all subject areas; therefore, thinking skills should not be taught as an add-on but should span the entire formal schooling experience (Beyer 1987, 7; Chuska 1986, 78).

Research on cognitive skill development indicates that if students are taught basic thinking skills and given practice in their use, their overall ability to solve problems will improve. Statistics show that students who receive focused instruction as a part of their English curriculum scored an average of 42 points higher on the verbal portion of the SAT than those in a control group who did not (Stockton and Worsham 1986, 8).

Researchers agree that thinking skills development should be a part of the curriculum; the questions are, *When, how much,* and *how* should it be done?

The curriculum models most discussed in the literature are infusion, inclusion, and separate courses. In the infusion method, thinking skills are taught through content or experiences not specifically designed to teach a particular thinking skill. Separate courses are designed specifically to teach thinking skills using either commercial or teacher-designed curriculum guides and materials. The inclusion method bases instruction on student needs, allows for teacher flexibility in the choice of skills to be taught, and uses the current curriculum objectives and course content (Stockton and Worsham 1986, 13-15). There are pros and cons to each. Some say the skills get lost in the infusion method; some say the separate course is too lockstep and requires expensive teacher training; and others say the inclusion method can get too unwieldy by allowing teachers to choose the skills to be taught. Curriculum planners should investigate each method thoroughly to determine which best fit into their school's process and plan.

The National Commission on Excellence in Education (1983) listed the following skills among its "Basics for Tomorrow": evaluation and analysis, critical thinking, problem solving, synthesis, application, and decision making (1-31). All of these are thinking processes. Students will need to be skillful thinkers now and, most assuredly, will be required to be skillful thinkers in the future. Skillful thinking does not develop on its own; it requires self-reflection, time to talk, and time to reflect (Beyer 1987, 235-36). A commonsense conclusion is that the mastery of higher-order curriculum objectives in any discipline area will require as a prerequisite the mastery of higher-order thinking skills.

Listening

Listening has been called "the forgotten skill." Very little attention has been directed toward listening skills in curriculum development. Yet, a diagram of the communication process would show that the average person spends 40 percent of the time listening; 9 percent, writing; 16 percent, reading; and 35 percent, talking (Burley-Allen 1982, 2-3).

Research findings indicate a strong correlation between reading and listening. Good listeners in kindergarten and first grade are more likely to become good readers by third grade. Good listeners in fifth grade are likely to do well on aptitude and achievement tests in high school. There is evidence that "listening is a moderate indicator of the level of comprehension a student will reach by grade three and the best predictor of the level of comprehension a student will achieve in high school" (Bennett 1986b, 15).

Listening is a teachable skill and, therefore, can be learned; however, little evidence can be found that it is formally taught in many of the nation's classrooms. An effective language arts curriculum plan should include many opportunities for students to learn and practice listening skills at all grade levels. Instruction can take the form of retelling stories, recalling segments of stories, repeating directions and instructions, or commenting on something someone else has said. Since most of the instruction in many schools is still delivered by lecture, the need for good listening skills is apparent.

Trends in Education with Implications for Language Arts Curriculum

New curriculum approaches and strategies have emanated from the research. Those most widely in use will be discussed in this section.

Interdisciplinary Curriculum

According to Heidi Jacobs (1989, 1991a, 1991b), common sense should provide the basis for curriculum integration. Learning is more effective when connections are made between the subjects studied and when knowledge is applicable to life.

Most of us can remember our teachers' saying, "It's time to put away your reading books and take out your social studies books." The thought of connecting the two never occurred. Using the reading of "The Cay" as a means of teaching social studies concepts relating to man's interaction with man and nature, or geography concepts of location and time, were not a conscious part of the curriculum. Everything had its own place and time. This isolation of content areas did little to heighten students' awareness of the interconnectedness of the concepts, skills, and knowledge of the various content areas. When these connections are not made, students learn information in a way that does not mirror real life and so appears to be of little value or utility.

We remember well the emphasis on the "teachable moment." This was an attempt to make connections between concepts of one field and those of another for students. However, the choice of making connections was left to the discretion of the teacher and was dependent upon his or her ability to seize the teachable moment. As a result, many of these moments are lost. A more formalized method for making connections between and among concepts learned in separate courses would be more efficient. When these connections are made, students will "have an understanding of what was, what is, and what may

be coming" (Palmer 1991, 57).

Future predictions of what students will need in order to be productive and competitive in the world of work have spawned specialization courses in such areas as substance abuse, sex education, thinking, cultural education, environmental education, global education, etc. These courses represent a "knee-jerk" approach to making learning more relevant for students, and create much of the fragmentation in the elementary school. At best, these add-on courses are producing minimal results. Clearly, a better approach is needed.

Some school districts have become totally interdisciplinary through a restructuring of the school curriculum. While this may be unrealistic or at least difficult for many school systems, there are curriculum integration models that are easier to implement.

The *concept model* focuses on the selection of a topic, theme, event, issue, or problem as an "organizing center." Students brainstorm ideas that relate to this center, and these ideas define the scope and sequence of the unit. Open-ended questions are developed from the brainstormed ideas. These questions are the basis for the activities which direct how the students will examine the center. They define the objectives, the outcome, and the evaluation process. The concept model is applicable to kindergarten through twelfth grade, when developmentally appropriate themes, activities, and outcomes are used (Jacobs 1989, 53-65).

Robin Fogarty (1991) describes three ways to integrate a curriculum: (1) within single disciplines, (2) across several disciplines, and (3) within and across learners. She identifies several views of each of these methods:

Integration within the single discipline. The single course is taught in isolation from others but connects skills and concepts within the subject field (i.e., archaeology and geology) and by connecting multiple skills within each subject area (i.e., social, thinking, and content-specific skills).

Integration across several disciplines. This model involves five views: sequenced, shared, webbed, threaded, and integrated. In the sequenced model, topics are taught separately but rearranged and sequenced to provide a broad framework for related topics. The shared model brings two disciplines together into a single focused image. The webbed model uses a theme to integrate subject matter and concepts (the concept model is a webbed model). The threaded model is a metacurricular approach; thinking skills, social skills, study skills, advance organizers, technology, and a multiple-intelligence approach are "threaded" throughout all content areas.

Integration within and across learners. This model is viewed as either immersed or networked. In the immersed model, the learner is totally involved in studies of subjects of personal interest. The network model implies what it says: "a connecting with, bouncing ideas off of, and learning from others with expertise in the field or related activities" (Fogarty 1991, 61-65).

A model currently being used by the Howard County, Maryland, public school system provides an interesting approach that involves teachers in the planning and implementation. This model is based on the philosophy that (1) it must keep the teacher's content area central, and (2) it must allow for the integration of logical, natural elements of associated contents. The model is called simply the "Planning Wheel." It allows the teachers to use a visual organizer to connect curriculum areas and to define activities, thereby teaching the basic theme or focus subject (Palmer 1991, 57-60).

Howard County planners offer suggestions of "promising practices" for curriculum planners to consider:

> In designing and developing a curriculum that lends itself to making connections planners should do the following: (1) Develop cross-curricular subobjectives within a given curriculum or grade; (2) Develop model lessons that include cross-curricular activities and assessments; (3) Develop enrichment or enhancement activities with a cross-curricular focus including suggestions for cross-curricular "contacts" following each objective; (4) Develop assessment activities that are cross-curricular in nature; and (5) Include sample planning wheels in all curriculum guides. (Palmer 1991, 57-60)

Whole Language Instruction vs. Systematic Phonics Instruction

Two approaches to reading instruction that have been hotly debated are whole language learning vs. systematic phonics instruction. Whole language proponents believe that children will develop their own phonetic principles as they read, write, speak, listen, and think. They oppose teaching phonics in any structured, systematic way. Proponents of phonics instruction believe that children learn best when lessons are struc-

tured and skills are taught directly, and that one cannot depend on haphazard instruction to teach something as critical as the alphabetic code.

Whole language enthusiasts operate from the theory that language, thought, and knowledge develop holistically and in support of each other; they view learning as child-centered and the teacher as a mediator who facilitates learners' transactions with the world (Goodman 1989); that teachers support learning rather than control it. Halliday (1984) concludes that we learn through language while we learn language. Every activity, experience, or unit is an opportunity for both holistic and cognitive development. Whole language emphasizes the importance of approaching reading, writing, speaking, listening, and thinking by building on the language and experiences of the child. The term whole language itself draws on two meanings of "whole": It is undivided, and it is integrated and unified (Goodman 1989, 209-221). Since whole language teachers view language arts as being holistic rather than a set of discrete skills, they use children's literature (trade books) for the heart of the curriculum. Teachers read to their students or tell them stories; they use poetry, songs, rhymes, riddles, plays, and other appropriate texts. Students tell and write their own stories and read stories of their own choosing. Writing in whole language classrooms involves generating ideas, revising, editing, and celebrating (publishing, presenting, and sharing pieces chosen by the author). In whole language classrooms, children learn to write with conviction and conventions by writing. They learn to make personal links to meaning through reading and writing, and they learn to work collaboratively. They have real reasons to read, write, listen, speak, and think (Watson 1989, 131-140).

Phonics proponents believe that there is a hierarchy of language acquisition (e.g., first listening, then speaking, then reading, finally writing) and a hierarchy of subskills within each language area, each to be mastered in a strict sequence. This hierarchical view of reading and writing places skills development at the core of the language arts program, with reading and writing to be done after students have demonstrated mastery of the skills (Walmsley and Walp 1990, 253). The role of the teacher in a phonics program is to instruct students so that they can master a series of specific skills: word recognition, phonetic analysis, structural analysis, contextual analysis, and comprehension (main idea, details, cause-effect relationship, sequencing, comparing/ contrasting, and levels of thinking [literal, inferential, critical, and creative]). The basal series is usually used to outline skills in a comprehensive and continuous sequence; workbooks are often used in conjunction with the basal text.

Having explored both points of view, it would appear that we need to embrace and retain the best of the new and old trends in education while, rejecting the excesses of each (MacGinitie 1991, 56). While there are indeed basic differences between the skill-development model (systematic phonics instruction) and the literature-based view (whole language), these approaches are not entirely incompatible. In a literature-based program, skills are not taught as ends in themselves; rather, the acquisition of skills becomes part of the understanding and enjoyment of stories. Students develop conventional reading skills as they learn to read, not the other way around. Teachers can integrate the full range of conventional reading skills in their reading instruction using trade books.

Most advocates of whole language agree with the claim that children must develop an understanding of phonics. However, instead of learning isolated letters and sounds and practicing them in workbooks, students learn them as they encounter them through rhyme and rhythm of books like *Chicken Little* and *Madeline* where sound-symbol relationship can be stressed. Most of the essential elements of phonics can be taught as students see the need to spell as part of the reading-writing connection. Structural analysis can be taught and stressed as children encounter roots, prefixes, and suffixes in stories (e.g., the function of "-ish" when Andrew turns "greenish" in *Freckle Juice*). As far as contextual analysis, students may need some initial help learning how to seek out clues to the meaning of unknown words, but this skill seems to develop as part of the normal process of reading meaningful segments of connected discourse. In the skill-development model, context clues are typically contrived through isolated sentences (Savage 1989, 1-4).

No matter what approach is taken, reading comprehension is an essential goal. All elements of interactive comprehension can be well illustrated and developed as students read and comprehend trade books.

To the proponents of direct instruction in phonics, we propose a more integrated and efficient form. To the proponents of whole language, we say that direct phonics instruction is,

in itself, an example of whole language learning. Using trade books and teaching reading skills do not have to be an either-or proposition; both can exist in harmony.

Multicultural Curriculum

Every day in many classrooms across the nation children sing of an America whose God will "crown thy good with brotherhood from sea to shining sea" and pledge allegiance to a flag that represents "one nation under God, indivisible, with liberty and justice for all." This America was not settled by accident. It was a deliberate action taken to provide for freedom of choice, where people could pursue life without threat, free of discrimination. As a result, this America was built upon the contributions of many—all of whom, with the exception of Native Americans, were foreigners to these shores. Out of this diversity emerged the American culture.

The population of America is changing dramatically. There is probably no other place that reflects this change as much as the nation's public schools. These population changes present public schools with the challenge of making the "American vision" a reality both for those who have been Americans for decades and for new immigrants. Singing the vision is one thing; making it a living reality is another. The curriculum planners have the challenge of endorsing, celebrating, embracing, and representing this diversity in a meaningful way through the instructional process of the school.

The language arts curriculum can be a prime vehicle for providing opportunities for students to explore multicultural perspectives and cultural understanding.

As in many other areas of curriculum revision, the question among educators is not *if*, but *what, how much, when,* and *how*? Clearly, past trends, such as international smorgasbords or celebrations, special days or months, or highlighting the contributions of a few superachievers, are not sufficient. While these activities have some merit, they fall short of meeting the goals of a multicultural curriculum in that they provide exposure with little in-depth learning. In the long run, they may be counterproductive and may trivialize and diminish the value of different cultural groups.

James Banks (1977) suggests instead that:
A conceptual approach will facilitate the implementation of a multiethnic curriculum which cuts across disciplinary boundaries. In

this approach the curriculum is organized around key concepts such as culture, socialization, power, and scarcity. Whenever possible these concepts should be viewed from the perspectives of disciplines such as the social sciences, art, music, literature, physical education, communication, the natural sciences, and mathematics. (29)

He offers this example:

Using the concept of culture—in literature students can read novels such as *Farewell to Manzanar, House Made of Dawn*, and *Bless Me Ultima*. They can determine what these novels reveal or do not reveal about the cultures of Japanese Americans, American Indians, and Mexican Americans. In drama students can produce a play based on the epic poem *I Am Joaquin* and discuss its treatment of Chicano history, contemporary life, and culture. They can examine the works of ethnic minority artists such as Jacob Lawrence, Charles White, and Roberto Lebron. The language arts can focus on the various ways in which symbols and communication styles differ between and within ethnic groups and how standard American English is influenced by the ethnic cultures within the United States. (29)

On the elementary level, a comparison study of several of 347 versions of the Cinderella story (e.g., *Mufaro's Beautiful Daughter* [African], *Cinderella* [European], and *Turkey Girl* [American Indian]) would provide students with the opportunity for cultural exploration on a developmentally appropriate level.

Curriculum planning committees will have a better chance of designing an effective curriculum approach if they themselves have a diverse composition that invites a broad range of insights and views. When committees lack this diversity, it is likely that the curriculum will reflect the narrow view of the homogeneous group.

Researchers seem to agree that multicultural education should begin early, while students are still receptive and open to different ideas and people.

Technology Integration

The technological changes that have moved society into the informational and biotechnical ages are having, and will continue to have, a profound impact on the traditional disciplines. Nowhere is this likely to be more evident than in English. Computers will be used for simulating problem-centered challenges, curriculum integration, knowledge acquisition, and individual programming of student-created programs. The job of the teacher will change from someone who creates process to someone who facilitates it. Goals and objectives will become broader and more inclusive. Both teachers and students will operate in a more open way with a much more democratic process. Evaluation will become a sharing of knowledge on something more substantial than a printed test. Problem solving will depend not so much on the omnipotence of the teacher as on the responsible participation of all (Kannel 1989, 22-23).

The types of activities that will be able to take place as we look at the integration of English and technology cannot but excite us. Computer-generated reading lists may be available from which students could select titles of interest (Wright 1988, 26-27). There may be greater use of live drama, because at least one wall of each classroom could have a high-resolution television screen. The hand-held television camera would permit classes to share field trips with each other. Other language arts technological possibilities include:

- Real world writing could replace the artificial and contrived
- Process writing, which is in effect in schools now, may include more time for students to think and talk in a workshop study environment
- The entire concept of revision can be vastly modified because of the student's facility with the word processor
- Students may be publishing a wide variety of works from meditations to poetry, essays, feature articles, folklore
- Special technology computer programs to aid instruction of the physically handicapped and learning disabled may be in place
- A thoroughly computerized World Library could be in place that could be accessed from school or home
- Technology of the future, as well as now, could help students master those things with which they have difficulty
- Holographic teleconferencing (being able to bring images of people from all over the world, such as famous authors and scientists) could be brought right into the classroom
- Students could interact face-to-face with students all over the world
- Media stations in classrooms could produce their own documentaries
- Students could show their knowledge on something larger than a printed test (Bruder 1990, 24-30)

In short, the future holds a new age for the teaching of English—one of technology with a heart. Students and teachers will be partners in learning—interacting with a real world, pursuing avenues of discovery, making full use of all available knowledge and talents—thus offering an opportunity for each student and teacher to develop his or her own full potential.

For this kind of education to occur, there must be a teacher who guides, a student who intends to learn, content to be learned, and the right climate in which guidance and learning occur—together with present and future technology (Frick 1991, 14-17). With such a scenario, the students would have many teachers communicating with them via technology; however, students would have one "executive" teacher (the classroom teacher) who could develop a personal relationship with, and design an individualized plan of instruction for, each student. The executive teacher might even have a cognitive map (made possible by an artificial intelligence program) of how students make decisions, how they think, their problem areas—across time or subject—to help build a stimulating learning environment for each student according to his or her needs and interests. Indeed, technology can and will empower both teachers and students.

Strategies for Implementing Current Trends

The Writing Process
A "paradigm shift" in the teaching of writing has occurred during the last decade. Substantive research on writing as a composing process has revealed that writing is a way of thinking, learning, and knowing. Traditionally, writing instruction has emphasized the final product. Now, the process of writing, as well as the product, receives attention. This new approach focuses on the process of writing through the following steps: prewriting, writing, thinking, and rewriting. The final step, postwriting, includes revising and final drafting. Teachers intervene in students' writing at each step. Although students write frequently, they are given sufficient time to complete the final product.

Other principles of this approach to writing include the following:
- Teachers invent strategies to help students generate thought, content, and purpose in writing
- Process writing considers audience, purpose,

and occasion
- Evaluation is based on how well the writing fulfills the author's intention and audience needs
- Writing is recognized as recursive and holistic rather than linear and compartmentalized

Process writing involves frequent writing practice, not always graded by the teacher, that is often shared and edited by peers and, in final form, is displayed to a wider audience through publication and other forms of schoolwide recognition. The writing process approach concludes that the isolated study of grammar and mechanics is not related to writing improvement; that instruction in grammar and mechanics is more logical when it is needed, as in the revision stage of writing (Pannwitt 1983, 1-2). For additional process writing strategies, curriculum developers may wish to consult Graves (1989), Hansen (1987), and Rhoades and Dudley-Marling (1988).

Teaching with Newspapers
The modern newspaper carries a vast array of news and information from around the world. It is packed with features and columns, opinions and think pieces, photographs, artwork, and stories of interest to all types of readers. It is one of the most readily available and highly motivating resources for teaching at all levels. It deals with what is happening in the world outside the classroom and provides information students can use in their daily lives. It has something to contribute to all areas of the curriculum.

In the elementary curriculum, newspapers are ideal for such activities as coloring, underlining, clipping, posting, and storytelling—all of which may contribute to the learning skills of reading, thinking, oral communication, and manual dexterity (Rhoades and Rhoades 1980, 11-15). In the secondary curriculum, newspapers are a rich resource. Using the newspaper puts students in touch with topics of adult conversation and raises issues about adult problems they will soon be facing.

Speaking and writing assignments based on news stories take on new importance, since they require understanding of and communicating about significant ideas. Newspapers provide relevant material for reading and writing on areas of interest to adolescents: appearance, making friends, dating, wearing the latest fashions, and being knowledgeable about the latest hit records, movies, and sports events. News stories, feature stories, editorials, and advertisements all provide models of different writing for different purposes (Rhoades and Rhoades 1980, 11-25).

Much of the impetus for using newspapers in the classroom has come from the Newspaper in Education programs, which offer such teaching aids as activity sheets, filmstrips, and sample lesson plans, as well as teacher workshops (Rhoades and Rhoades 1980, 11-25).

Film Study, Technology, and English

With the advent of the videocassette recorder, the future of film in the teaching of English is already upon us. No invention in cinematic history has so drastically changed the status of the film text. It is more accessible, familiar, and controllable on the one hand; and smaller, less compelling (both visually and psychologically), and more dismissable on the other. Students are now able to do some film "reading" at home, just as they now do literary reading. Brian Gallagher (1988) predicts the following in the near future:

1. The new video technology, because it permits and so encourages a concentration on the "micro-skills" of visual analysis, will bring the study of film and literature closer together.
2. Visual literacy and language literacy will increasingly reflect each other and so continue to provide a fruitful instructional way of moving from (interpreting to learning) practicing the act of writing.
3. The microcomputer will become an intermediary between visual and written texts and so help foster the connections between film and written language.
4. Laser disc technology will, to some extent, supplant videocassette technology in the classroom.
5. The new technology will imitate its predecessors' forms.
6. A new kind of hybrid text, written and graphic and perhaps even spoken, may come to replace, in part, the kind of traditional expository essay we now require of writing students. (58-61)

In the opinion of Charles Suhor, a writer on English curriculum, "The true power of the video disc should emerge through a yet undeveloped interactive program that combines print, image, and sound" (Gallagher 1988, 61).

Writing Across the Curriculum

Writing across the curriculum is a process that

emphasizes the teaching of writing in the content areas at the secondary level. In this process, the emphasis is on clarity, logic, and completeness of the ideas expressed rather than on the mechanics of writing. Students in this process learn to write for a varied audience. This approach assumes cooperation and collaboration between English and content area teachers: Content area teachers manage content and audience while English teachers manage the mechanics. Students are involved in a variety of writing activities, such as journals, applications, service requests, news articles, biographies, and historical pieces.

Reading Recovery

Reading recovery was developed by Marie Clay, a New Zealand educator. It is an intensive, one-on-one, short-term, early-intervention reading program designed to reduce reading failure among first-grade students.

In this model, the poorest readers in a class are targeted for reading recovery. In addition to their regular reading instruction, these children receive a daily, thirty-minute, one-on-one lesson with a reading-recovery-trained teacher. Each lesson includes reading "little" books, composing, and writing a story. Children develop strategies for hearing sounds and for monitoring and checking their own reading. They receive a new book every day which they are expected to read before the next class. The intervention ends when the child has developed strategies for independent reading. The program is intensive, limited to approximately twelve students per year per teacher, and requires extensive training from a reading recovery center.

The Publishing Center

Publishing centers are an outgrowth of the process approach to writing. The centers provide a way for students to showcase their individual and group writing products. Students select a piece of their writing that they wish to publish. The classroom teacher checks the work to make sure it is grammatically correct. The student then takes the book to the center where s/he consults with the "editor," a parent volunteer. The two collaborate on pagination, format, and illustrations. The story is typed by a parent volunteer, bound by the volunteer binder, and returned to the student. Books are shared in a number of ways, including library display, classroom display, and read-alouds. The publishing center is used extensively at all grade levels—elementary, middle, and secondary. It connects parents, students, and teachers in a cooperative, supportive liaison.

Authors-in-Residence

Authors-in-Residence is a program that brings authors of children's books into the school to discuss their works with children. The authors discuss origin of ideas, story development, writing style, research methods, layout, illustration, and marketing in large or individual classroom settings. Students sign up for a conference with the visiting author, who reads their writing drafts and makes suggestions for improving their work. Collections of the author's works are purchased and made available in the school and/or classroom library. Writing suggestions shared by the authors are used in regular English classes as students prepare their works for publication through the publishing center.

Poets Alive!

To motivate students to read and write poetry, poets are invited to the school to read and discuss their poetry with the children. This has been used most successfully at the middle school level. Students converse with the poet about ideas and styles of writing. During the year, students select poetry to dramatize for student and parent audiences. As they create a dramatic expression of the poem, they gain a greater understanding of the writer's message.

Summary

Language arts teachers as curriculum planners have to look beyond the traditional ways of planning and open their minds to a new way of looking at what curriculum planning really involves.

Our current language arts curricula are often outdated before they are put into practice, because they are planned in such limited ways. Expecting all children to learn the same material, in the same way, at the same pace, using the same process will no longer work. As our population continues to grow more diverse, it is essential that language arts curriculum planners look at the big picture. The following suggestions will broaden a

curriculum's perspective and will increase the probability that it will provide all children with an equal opportunity to achieve academic excellence in language arts. Teachers as curriculum planners should:

1. Identify their own belief system (a sense of values related to the purpose of curriculum). These beliefs must drive every decision made about language arts instruction for students.
2. Consider profiles of their students—who they are, what interests and competencies they possess, what they need in order to be successful learners, how they learn, what impacts on their learning, and what future competencies they will need—so that they can plan for appropriate learning experiences in language arts.
3. Analyze current language arts curricula and trends to determine whether they meet the identified needs, retaining, modifying, reconstructing, eliminating, or adding to them as needed.
4. Reexamine language arts course outcomes to determine what is developmentally appropriate or realistic. The outcomes must be clearly defined and understandable to all students and teachers so that there is no doubt or confusion about the desired outcomes. As the Cheshire Cat told Alice, "If you don't know where you are going, I suppose you will get someplace, but it may not be where you want to go."
5. Provide flexibility and choices in the curriculum development process so that teachers may exercise professional judgment in their diagnoses of and prescriptions for student learning in the language arts. They should not trade one outdated paradigm for another restricted paradigm that will ultimately prove to be just as ineffective in improving achievement. When flexibility and choice do not exist, students are still being required to learn in the same way, at the same pace, using the same process.
6. Provide a variety of opportunities within the language arts curriculum to develop and refine students' critical- and strategic-thinking skills through an integrated approach to content with a multicultural perspective.
7. Provide opportunities within the language arts curriculum for both independent and cooperative learning, for problem solving and creativity, for relevance, for looking at the

past and understanding the future, and for developing a foundation of effective learning tools that will allow students to expand, discover, and gain more knowledge. We can never teach students all they need to know, but we can teach them what questions to ask and how to find the answers.

In short, curriculum planners must reexamine old attitudes and approach curriculum planning with a new mind-set (similar to that of successful entrepreneurs)—one that reflects a knowledge of all the players, keeps the client close, and believes that people are the most valuable asset.

References

Banks, James. 1977. *Multicultural Education: Practices and Promises.* Bloomington, IN: Phi Delta Kappa.

Bennett, William J. 1986a. *First Lessons: A Report on Elementary Education in America.* Washington, DC: Department of Education.

———. 1986b. *What Works: Research about Teaching and Learning.* Washington, DC: Department of Education.

Beyer, Barry K. 1987. *Practical Strategies for the Teaching of Thinking.* Boston: Allyn & Bacon.

Brandt, Ron. 1982. "On School Improvement: A Conversation with Ronald Edmonds." *Educational Leadership* (Dec.): 13-15.

Brainard, Edward, Eugene Howard, and Bruce Howell. 1987. *Handbook for Conducting School Climate Improvement Projects.* Bloomington, IN: Phi Delta Kappa.

Bruder, Isabelle. 1990. "Education and Technology in the 1990's." *Electronic Learning* 9(4): 24-30.

Burley-Allen, Madelyn. 1982. *Listening: The Forgotten Skill.* New York: Wiley.

Buzan, Tony. 1974. *Use Both Sides of Your Brain.* New York: Dutton.

Caine, Geoffrey, and Nummela Caine. 1991. *Making Connections: Teaching and the Human Brain.* Alexandria, VA: Association for Supervision and Curriculum Development.

Carden, Guren. 1991. "Erasing Racism." *Parents and Kids* (Fall).

Cetron, Marvin. 1985. *Schools for the Future.* New York: McGraw-Hill.

Chuska, Kenneth R. 1986. *Teaching the Process of Thinking, K-12.* Bloomington, IN: Phi Delta Kappa.

Clarke, John H. 1990. *Patterns of Thinking.* Boston: Allyn & Bacon.

Cohen, Sheldon S. 1974. *A History of Colonial Education.* New York: Wiley.

Commission on Reading. 1990. *Becoming a Nation of Readers.* Washington, DC: The National Institute of Education, the National Academy of Education, and the Center for the Study of Reading.

Cooper, Harris M., and Thomas L. Good. 1983. *Pygmalion Grows Up: Studies in the Expectation Communication Process.* New York: Longman.

Cremin, Lawrence A. 1957. *The Republic and the Schools.* New York: Teachers College Press.

Day, M. D. 1981. "Thinking at Piaget's Stage of Formal Operations." *Educational Leadership* (Oct.): 44-47.

Dewey, John. 1938. *Experience and Education.* New York: Collier.

Dunn, Rita. 1989. "Learning Styles: Key to Improving Schools and Student Achievement." *NASSP Curriculum Report* 18(3): 1-4.

Erard, Mary T., and Shirley T. McCoy. 1990. *Curriculum and Instruction Handbook.* Alexandria, VA: National Association of Elementary School Principals.

Fogarty, Robin. 1991. "Ten Ways to Integrate Curriculum." *Educational Leadership* 49(2): 61-65.

Frick, Theodore W. 1991. *Restructuring Education Through Technology.* Bloomington, IN: Phi Delta Kappa.

Gallagher, Brian. 1988. "Film Study and the Teaching of English: Technology and the Future of Pedagogy." *English Journal* 77(7): 58-61.

Gold, Lillian. 1989. *The Elementary School Publishing Center.* Bloomington, IN: Phi Delta Kappa.

Good, Thomas L. 1972. "How Teacher Expectations Affect Results." *American Education* (Dec.): 25-30.

Goodman, Kenneth S. 1989. "Whole Language Research: Foundations and Development." *Elementary School Journal* 90(2): 207-21.

Grady, Michael. 1990. *Whole Brain Education.* Bloomington, IN: Phi Delta Kappa.

Graves, Donald. 1989. *Writing: Teachers and Children at Work.* Portsmouth, NH: Heinemann.

Guild, Pat Burke, and Stephen Garger. 1985. *Marching to Different Drummers.* Alexandria, VA: Association for Supervision and Curriculum Development.

Hansen, Jane. 1987. *When Writers Read.* Portsmouth, NH: Heinemann.

Hooper, David S. 1980. *Intercultural Education.* Bloomington, IN: Phi Delta Kappa.

Howard, Eugene, Edward Brainard, and Bruce Howell. 1983. *Handbook for Conducting School Climate Improvement Projects.* Bloomington, IN: Phi Delta Kappa.

Inlow, Gail M. 1973. *The Emergent in Curriculum.* New York: Wiley.

Jacobs, Heidi Hayes. 1989. *Interdisciplinary Curriculum: A Design for Implementation.* Alexandria, VA: Association for Supervision and Curriculum Development.

———. 1991a. "Planning for Curriculum Integration." *Educational Leadership* 49 (2): 27-28.

———. 1991b. "Curriculum Integration, Critical Thinking, and Common Sense." *Cogitare* (Winter): n.p.

Jalonga, Mary Renck. 1991. *Strategies for Developing Children's Listening Skills.* Bloomington, IN: Phi Delta Kappa.

Johnson, Tony W. 1984. *Philosophy for Children: An Approach to Critical Thinking.* Bloomington, IN: Phi Delta Kappa.

Kannel, Susan. 1989. "Program Planning for the Future." *Adult Learning* 1(1): 23-25, 29.

Lauderdale, William Burt. 1987. *Educational Reform: The Forgotten Half.* Bloomington, IN: Phi Delta Kappa.

Lezotte, Lawrence, et al. 1980. *School Learning Climate and Student Achievement.* Tallahassee, FL: Site Technical Assistance Center at Florida State Univ.

McCarthy, Bernice. 1988. "The 4MAT System: Teaching to Learning Styles with Right/Left Mode Techniques." *Human Intelligent Newsletter.*

MacGinitie, Walter H. 1991. "Reading Instruction Plus Ca Change," *Educational Leadership* 48(6): 55-58.

Morley, Franklin P. 1973. *A Modern Guide to Effective K-12 Curriculum Planning.* West Nyack, NY: Parker.

Myers, John W. 1984. *Writing to Learn across the Curriculum.* Bloomington, IN: Phi Delta Kappa.

National Commission on Excellence in Education. 1983. *A Nation at Risk: The Imperative for Educational Reform.* Washington, DC: Department of Education.

Palmer, Joan M. 1991. "Planning Wheels Turn Curriculum Around." *Educational Leadership* 49(2): 57-60.

Pannwitt, Barbara. 1983. "Teaching Writing Right Schoolwide." *NASSP Curriculum Report* 12(2): 1-12.

Peters, Thomas J., and Robert H. Waterman, Jr. 1982. *In Search of Excellence: Lessons from America's Best-Run Companies.* New York: Warner.

Pulliam, John D. 1968. *History of Education in America.* Columbus, OH: Merrill.

Ragan, William B., and Gene Shepherd. 1971. *Modern American Curriculum.* New York: Holt, Rinehart and Winston.

Rhoades, Lynn K., and Curt Dudley-Marling. 1988. *Readers and Writers with a Difference.* Portsmouth, NH: Heinemann.

Rhoades, Lynn, and George Rhoades. 1980. *Teaching with Newspapers: The Living Curriculum.* Bloomington, IN: Phi Delta Kappa.

Rutter, Michael. 1979. *Fifteen Thousand Hours.* Cambridge: Harvard University Press.

Savage, John F. 1989. *I'd Like to Teach Reading with Literature, But I'm Afraid My Pupils Will Miss out on Skills.* Littleton, MA: Sundance.

Sperry, Roger. 1985. "Consciousness, Personal Identity and the Divided Brain." In *The Dual Brain: Hemispheric Specialization in Humans,* ed. D. Frank Benson and Eran Zaidel. New York: Guilford Press.

Steeler, Arthur W. 1988. *Effective Schools Research.* Bloomington, IN: Phi Delta Kappa.

Stewig, John Warren. 1988. "Oral Language: A Place in the Curriculum?" *Clearing House* 62(4): 171-74.

Stockton, Anita J., and Antoinette Worsham. 1986. *A Model for Teaching Thinking Skills: The Inclusion Process.* Bloomington, IN: Phi Delta Kappa.

Texas Education Agency. 1991. *Spelling Instruction, A Proper Perspective.* Austin, TX.

Tiedt, Iris M. 1983. *The Language Arts Handbook.* Englewood Cliffs, NJ: Prentice-Hall.

Walmsley, Sean A., and Trudy P. Walp. 1990. "Integrating Literature and Composing into the Language Arts Curriculum, Philosophy, and Practice." *Elementary School Journal* 90(3).

Watson, Dorothy J. 1989. "Defining and Describing Whole Language." *Elementary School Journal* 90(2): 129-41.

Wright, Robert G. 1988. "Teaching English in the Year 2000". *Clearing House* 62(1).

■

2

CURRICULUM GUIDES: PROCESS AND DESIGN

by Jurg Jenzer
Director of Curriculum, Supervision, and Instruction
Lamoille North Supervisory Union, Hyde Park, Vermont

CURRICULUM designers face complex decisions in developing a quality English/language arts program. The stakes are high with judgments being made about what teachers should teach and what students should learn for years to come. Many factors are involved: district size, geographic location, funding capability, philosophy, state statutes, and demographic characteristics. Many are affected by these curricular decisions; therefore, many should participate in deciding on a course of action.

A district curriculum guide will often determine the development of language arts in the school and in the classroom. Since classroom teachers are the primary users of curriculum guides, their participation in development of the guide is essntial. For them, curriculum states and organizes instructional content between grade levels. A guidebook to school language arts does not, however, guarantee quality teaching unless teachers understand the usefulness and limitations of a language arts curriculum.

Textbooks still drive the curriculum in many districts. In many cases, language arts textbooks structure much of the teachers' knowledge regarding the curriculum. Textbooks offer a scope of language arts in terms of topics and the sequence in which they are to be taught and

learned. Unlike teachers, textbook authors have the time and logistical support to develop and test their programs before publication. As a result, for better or worse, teachers' dependency on textbooks has often been significant.

Textbooks have therefore been a powerful force on curriculum developed by states or by single school districts. It is not surprising to see textbook language and design reflected in the majority of locally developed language arts curricula.

Numerous critics have argued that the textbook has eroded the need to train teachers to design and evaluate curriculum (Apple 1979; Aronowitz and Giroux 1985; Giroux 1983). In contrast, designing curriculum at the district level challenges both the textbook industry and the dependency teachers may have on textbooks. A curriculum process, moreover, can be a rewarding experience for teachers. Alternatives to textbook-style scope and sequence programs in language arts are not only possible, but they can offer some interesting instructional alternatives.

Veteran teachers are already curriculum designers by practice. They tend to use textbooks eclectically, identifying strengths and weaknesses in each book. They pick and choose from all available resources. A formal, district-level curriculum fosters this development and is at odds with any single textbook series, unless the structure of the text is directly copied into the curriculum.

A curriculum development process with and for teachers provides insight into the decision making process that generates both textbooks and curriculum guides. It is the process, rather than the document, which provides an exciting opportunity: time to examine one's own assumptions and practices, an environment to discuss and test new assumptions and practices, and a reasonable incentive to get involved.

Curriculum is not so much a document as it is instruction. At its best, it teaches all those involved with its development and implementation. The actual curriculum in English, in reading, or in any other subject, is the one being taught. The taught curriculum may or may not resemble the planned curriculum (the adopted textbook or the curriculum guide). This point is crucial. The curriculum development process that is organized as a challenging learning opportunity will affect instruction far more than the document alone. A local curriculum process challenges the separation of planning and implementation, an issue all too often obscured by arguments for state or national curriculum initiatives. Unless teachers understand the process and decisions that generate a curriculum guide, implementation may be in jeopardy.

In general, the total process of curriculum guide design and implementation can be divided into numerous steps that curriculum designers and committees may need to deal with when developing or revising elementary or secondary language arts programs. These steps can be outlined as follows:

· Performing a needs assessment
· Defining the mission statement
· Choosing the participants
· Scheduling the project
· Forming a curriculum committee
· Budgeting
· Looking at standards
· Examining key topics in English/language arts
· Choosing curriculum features and design options
· Population analysis (target students)
· Field testing
· Public input
· Editing, ratification, production, and dissemination
· Adoption process
· Staff development and support

· Monitoring and supervision
· Evaluation and revision

Note that the steps described here are only *typical* of the process involved. The actual steps may differ in your district—there may be more steps or fewer ones, and some steps may occur in a different order. But you will most likely encounter many of these steps at some stage in the process, and this chapter is meant to acquaint you with these steps and many of the related decisions.

Before a curriculum can be written and implemented, curriculum designers plan and organize a process.[1] Just as importantly, these designers must set realistic expectations for the teachers who will ultimately be asked to turn these blueprints into meaningful experiences for children and young adults.

Performing a Needs Assessment

The needs assessment of the English/language arts program is an important part of curriculum planning, in that it provides a direction for the curriculum. The assessment defines the priorities of the curriculum (under local and state standards and in view of recommendations from national organizations), the goals of curriculum development in English, and the gaps that exist in the current curriculum.

In order to get a clearer picture of the school's needs in language arts, curriculum planners may wish to compare their current and planned curriculum program with those of other states and other districts (for further discussion on sources of curriculum materials, see below under *Examining Key Topics in English/Language Arts* and *Choosing Curriculum Features and Design Options*).

Defining the Mission Statement

The creation of the mission statement for the district or school is closely related to the needs assessment. While curriculum implementation may be the province of teachers and school administrators, the mission statement should be developed with members of the school board, teachers, parents, students, state education officials, the private sector, and others within the community. A widely shared understanding of the school district's mission statement in curricular and programmatic terms greatly enhances the odds for successful implementation. Formulating a new curriculum is expected to:

· Establish a relationship between district goals and instructional programs and methods
· Establish a relationship between local programs, state and national standards, laws, and policies
· Link curriculum and educational programs with important policy and budgetary decisions
· Inform communities about the schools' direction and programs
· Ensure a coordinated and planned educational program.

Choosing the Participants

Curriculum can affect a teacher's behavior and decision making in relation to the courses being taught. The teacher's understanding, acceptance, and implementation of a language arts curriculum are the most important and, oddly enough, the most commonly missed factors in the curriculum process.

All schools and school districts employ teachers of varying degrees of ability, from novice teachers to seasoned veterans. Their growth as professional educators will define their relationship with the curriculum.[2] Gaining insight into the quality and dynamics of the teaching staff for whom the curriculum is written is of critical importance. Some of the more important questions to be asked are:

· How many teachers will be charged with implementation? What are their experiences specifically with curriculum development? Have they worked with districtwide curricula before?
· What are the teachers' attitudes regarding the current curriculum? How well or to what extent are current curricula implemented?
· Can the school district support a curriculum process in which teachers have leverage over the curriculum?
· How many building administrators have experience specifically with curriculum development?

Interviewing prospective participants and reviewing appropriate records allow curriculum designers to actively recruit teachers best suited for the task ahead.

Scheduling the Project

When developing a reasonable timetable for a curriculum process, numerous factors must be faced. The following is a list of some of the more common concerns:

· Scope of the project (e.g., K-4, 5-8, 9-12, K-12)
· Mission of the project (complete revision, partial revision, etc.)
· Number of employees and students affected by the curriculum
· How the project fits into the participants' work schedules
· Staff development time that will be required to implement the new curriculum
· Available resources (also see below, under *Budgeting*)
· Deadlines (from the state, from local education agency, from federal agency mandates)
· Meeting times (see below)

Since teachers have relatively inflexible classroom schedules, a method must be chosen that will ensure their participation. Three of the more common methods used are *pull-out projects*, *after-school projects*, and *course projects*. Each method offers significant fiscal and procedural advantages.

Pulling teachers out of the classrooms for full-day work sessions allows them to concentrate on the project. Typically, this reduces the number of meetings necessary to complete the project. On the other hand, this method requires substitute teachers, with the resulting cost. Teachers who leave their classrooms for entire days must devote considerable effort to preparing substitutes. In addition, the frequency with which teachers are pulled from the classroom must be calculated to eliminate any potentially negative impact on students.

After-school projects avoid most of the negative implications of the pullout project. Some costs remain if contracts require compensation of personnel for extra duty. The most significant problem with this method, however, is that teachers are often tired after spending a day in the classroom; this minimizes their energy level and the quality of their work. This method also increases the number of meetings needed, because after school meeting time is limited.

Course projects are usually planned in collaboration with institutions of higher education. The strength of this method is its scheduling flexibility. Course projects can be organized as evening courses or as intensive two- or three-week work sessions during school vacations. Graduate credits issued by the cooperating college or university can be an attractive incentive for teachers who apply credits toward graduate degrees and/or salary schedules. One well-known problem with this method lies in potential conflicts between school district personnel and higher education faculty over controlling the project, the mission, and the curriculum itself.

Forming a Curriculum Committee

Curriculum designers, whether they be administrators, classroom teachers, or education professors, must be able to work effectively with adults. In addition, curriculum designers must have an excellent grasp of the subject, have classroom experience, and communicate effectively in order to be accepted and respected by teachers.

In forming a curriculum committee, curriculum designers encounter such questions as these:
· Who wants to participate? Who should be recruited?
· Which teachers can play leadership roles? Who will chair the committee?
· Should all affected schools and grade levels be represented?
· What are the advantages of small versus large committees?
· Should elementary committees work separately from middle level or secondary committees? How will they coordinate transitions between levels?
· What types of incentives are available to recruit quality committees?
· How committed are the school board and the administration to the committee's work?
· Are department heads, administrators, program specialists, guidance counselors, parents, students, board members, and business and community representatives on the committee?

The First Committee Meeting: Checklist
The importance of the first meeting cannot be overstated. Curriculum designers should carefully plan and orchestrate this meeting in order to develop team spirit and a sense of purpose within the committee itself.

Scheduling: If the first meeting is held during the school year, check with building principals

about events or meetings. If the meeting occurs after school, limit it to setting the agenda, getting to know one another, and starting a checklist of current topics and issues in language arts.

Committee Structure: Identify the committee's mission, meeting schedule, political conditions (level of administrative or school board support, etc.), and preliminary activities (needs assessment conducted, copies of obtained state statutes and regulations, important articles or resources, etc.).

Meeting Environment: If at all possible, meet outside the schools in a suitable room equipped with comfortable chairs, large tables, climate controls, chalkboard or overhead projector, and a steady supply of coffee and juice. In all-day meetings, do not skimp on lunch.

Budgeting

Resource Checklist
There are numerous factors to be considered when deciding about resources. The budget[3] and other logistical problems deserve careful consideration. Some of these factors are:

Logistics
· Secretarial assistance
· Access to computers
· Access to databases and other forms of information (e.g., ERIC, KCDL, libraries)
· A place for the committee to meet
· Possible collaboration with a local college or university
· Access to production facilities (e.g., graphics, desktop publishing, printing, copying, editing)

Budgetary Considerations
· Hiring substitutes
· Consultants
· Computers
· Secretarial
· Production (layout, paper, printing, copying, distribution, binders, graphics, etc.)
· Administrative
· Legal (reviews for compliance with state and federal laws)
· Other costs

Curriculum developers might want to explore the possibilities of outside funding to help support the extra costs involved in the project. Some national foundations provide grants for the development of particular curriculum; these organizations often have regional restrictions or will fund only certain types of curriculum. In addition, some corporations fund educational projects in their state or region. Chapter three provides a listing of foundations that offer grants for education projects; this list gives some idea of the types of funding available.

Looking at Standards

It is essential to consult existing standards—and to keep track of emerging ones—when designing or adopting curriculum guides. As arguments over national curriculum and testing systems fly back and forth, curriculum designers must be concerned first and foremost with understanding the present uncertainties over the direction of language arts (see chapter one for an overview of these trends). Undoubtedly, national standards will make a difference. However, major curriculum decisions remain to be made at the local level.

Every school district has standards that emerge from (*a*) community values, (*b*) the successes and failures of local reform and restructuring efforts in response to pressures from state and federal agencies, and (*c*) the curriculum in use. Curriculum designers must decide on standards with these factors in mind.

State and Local Standards

Copies of all statutes, regulations, and policies regulating a curriculum development or revision project should be made available to all parties participating in or affected by the curriculum process.

Under the United States Constitution, the state has the ultimate responsibility for education, and state education agencies define standards and conditions under which schools operate. This is where commonality ends, however, because the degree to which states regulate curriculum process and development varies widely. In some cases, the state sets standards for language arts and defines acceptable instructional resources for implementing that curriculum. In other cases, the curriculum process is largely controlled by local educational agencies (LEAs). Curriculum designers must ascertain the nature and scope of these standards as well as the degree of flexibility LEAs have in interpreting and implementing these standards (for details on particular states, please refer to chapter five).

When state regulations are generic, they allow for significant local variation. This opens the door for local emphases on issues such as literacy, reading, or written communication. Such emphases often find their way into curriculum guides and school board policies.

In addition to state regulations, there are other factors which may have resulted in de facto standards at the local level. For instance, the district may have adopted a particular way of teaching reading which unifies instruction in some way (i.e., a common textbook series). Just as significantly, when teachers "import" new ideas, materials, or methods into the school, they act as role models for other teachers. In fact, this is the most common way in which reading and other language arts can be transformed at the classroom level, and is an excellent indicator of what can be termed "local standards."

National Standards

The nation's concern over education has generated a demand for leadership and change. For example, the publication of mathematics standards and a core curriculum by the National Council for Teachers of Mathematics (1989, 1992) demonstrates the importance of a national consensus which supplies direction and focus to local curriculum efforts.

Starting in 1992, the National Council of Teachers of English (NCTE), the International Reading Association (IRA), and the Center for the Study of Reading at the University of Illinois at Urbana-Champaign began to develop a National Standards Project for K-12 English. NCTE started the project by collecting English frameworks from states, school districts, and county/regional agencies. The project schedule calls for the release of an overall framework by autumn 1993 (for comment); the development of standards, as well as examples of classroom practices, from summer 1993 to autumn 1994; and final development and dissemination from autumn 1994 to spring 1995. NCTE expects the profession to begin using the standards by summer 1995.

Until then, there is no equivalent to the NCTM standards in K-12 language arts, but there are numerous reports, documents, and model curricula which embody high standards and are considered exemplary. An excellent starting point for curriculum designers are two publications from the Wisconsin Department of Public Instruction: *A Guide to Curriculum Planning in English Language Arts* (1986a) and *A Guide to Curriculum Planning in Reading* (1986b); these books offer a great deal of practical insight into K-12 language arts curriculum development (see table 1 for a summary of concepts).

Table 1. Conceptual Standards in K-12 Language Arts	
Curriculum Development	Establish a curriculum process to ensure ownership of the program by staff. Decide controversies locally and reflect decisions in the program's philosophy. Formulate staff development programs to facilitate implementation.
Integrating the Language Arts	Strands in language arts (listening, reading, speaking, writing, and others) are closely interrelated; artificial separation for instructional purposes should be avoided.
Integrating the Language Arts with Other Subjects	The language arts are central to all other subject areas. Nevertheless, teaching language arts across the curriculum must be carefully planned.
The Spiral Curriculum	All language arts strands should be introduced at the earliest possible time, to build upon and to elaborate; this means focusing on concepts or skills in an increasingly sophisticated and challenging way.

Examining Key Topics in English/Language Arts

While the literature regarding elementary, middle, and high school language arts is rich and somewhat overwhelming, curriculum designers cannot afford to ignore it. The most critical decision to be made here deals with time. Should teachers be involved in reviewing and discussing this literature, or should the curriculum designer conduct a review and brief the other members of the curriculum committee? Committee participants should gain a critical perspective on current controversies in English language arts, as well as their own assumptions regarding what a language arts curriculum is and will be in the future.

An alternative approach is to review other school districts' curricula or current textbooks. On the one hand, this review yields a great deal of practical comparisons between districts as well as a sense of security (commonality) in the decision-making process. However, if the committee members are not fully knowledgeable about current trends and methods, this method could lead to the continued use of potentially obsolete curriculum design features and instructional topics.

Reviewing three types of information—the publishing sector (textbooks), the school sector (current curricula), and the academic sector (research)—will provide a balanced collection of data. The following examples are a selection of topics under discussion at the time of publication (for more detailed discussions of current controversies, see chapters 1 and 4):

· Selection of (appropriate) literature
· The structure of language
· Integrating media into the language arts
· Language and the cultural and situational context of learners
· Conventions of, and innovation in, language
· Formal vs. integrated grammar
· Formal vs. integrated spelling
· Formal vocabulary vs. integrated vocabulary programs
· Computers and young writers
· The role of parents in language development and proficiency
· District selection policies and practices (literature, textbooks, etc.)
· Assessment and evaluation in all language arts strands and areas
· Bilingual and bicultural learners
· Language instruction across the curriculum
· Translating writing goals into writing objectives and instructional strategies
· The value and purpose of big books and big print in primary classrooms
· Approaches to language arts: whole language, basal readers, phonics, process models, etc.
· Dictation: necessary or superfluous?
· Publishing the works of student writers: form, process, outcomes
· Spelling: should invented spelling be tolerated, encouraged, discouraged in primary grades?
· Whole language: what it is and what it isn't
· Selecting books for students: textbooks, readers, trade books, paperbacks, big books,

books on tape, books on video, etc.
· Writing and computers: what (hardware, software, keyboarding), when (age, grade, developmental level, etc.), why (benefit, support or dependency), and who (advanced learners, slow learners, handicapped learners, bilingual/bicultural learners, etc.)?
· Tracking students in language arts (advanced placement, curriculum preparation, general track, remedial track, etc.)
· Reading development (stages, process, remediation, SSR, etc.)
· Language arts environments (individualized vs. cooperative, reading corners, classroom libraries, media, message boards/boxes, etc.)
· Language arts pedagogy (individualized vs. cooperative, integrated vs. competency-based, multi-age vs. homogeneous classes, etc.)
· Appropriate techniques and resources for middle/junior high students
· Determining readability levels in language arts and other subject areas

Curriculum designers should develop their own checklists with the curriculum committee. These checklists will allow teachers to share questions linked directly to language arts instruction, topics and controversies which they are interested in, personal positions or philosophies, and an exploration of their colleagues' positions.

The next step could be the most difficult in the curriculum development and design procedures. The curriculum committee must now make choices regarding the organization of the guide, including the identification of strands or domains (i.e., reading, writing, spelling), the relationship between strands (i.e., should "handwriting" be separated from or integrated with writing?), and the specific topics to be covered at each grade level, grade cluster, or developmental level.

For a starting point, chapter 4 provides a detailed outline of language arts topics most often taught at each grade level, K–12. In addition, the Wisconsin guides (1986a, 1986b) can serve as models for the topics which you might be considering. These guides are organized in spiral fashion, featuring developmental levels of achievement rather than grade or age levels. As noted previously, the actual topics a school or district decides to cover will be based on its needs assessment, its curriculum mission, its state and local standards, and other factors that affect the school or district.

Choosing Curriculum Features and Design Options

When considering design and content of the curriculum, a developer must analyze the teachers as an audience, as well as what type of curriculum guide the teachers would find most attractive (besides being useful in the functional sense). This brings developers back to an earlier step (*Choosing the Participants*) and the expansion of the user analysis begun there. In general, the larger the audience (number of future users) for a language arts curriculum, the more difficult the search is for an appropriate design and content selection. The curriculum designer's own classroom experience and interaction with teachers will greatly facilitate the assessment of what teachers need and/or want.

Do some curriculum designs and content options work better than others? This depends upon the use of the guide and the audience. Here are some factors to consider:
· Which topics should be taught at certain grade levels in order to secure a high degree of achievement for most learners?
· How should these topics be described in the curriculum? Should they be described as "skills" students should master, or as discrete "content" areas teachers ought to cover?
· Should a curriculum be much like a textbook and describe all aspects of instructional work and implement state or local goals and objectives?
· Should a curriculum be brief and merely outline instructional scope and sequence in "blueprint fashion," thus leaving most curriculum decision making to teachers?
· Should curriculum guides contain one feature or multiple features or types of information?
· Does the actual curriculum content or design make any difference to teachers?
· Can curriculum guides be made attractive to teachers and thus shift the incentive for implementation from top-down mandates to the inherent benefits of the document itself?
· If teachers have greatly varied professional needs and practices, should the curriculum consist of multiple documents with varied content?

Different language arts curriculum guides offer choices of content features; some emphasize one feature above others, while other guides vary both the number and the combination of features.

One of the best ways to examine the different features of curriculum guides is to use actual guides as examples and models (see chapter 7 for information on recent language arts guides).

One good source for curriculum models is the Kraus Curriculum Development Library (KCDL). This annual program offers a large number of curriculum guides (commercial and noncommercial), all reproduced on microfiche. Of interest here is the subject area "English/Language Arts." Chapter 5 lists current KCDL customers, where the fiche collection can be viewed.

Another place for information on current guides is the Association for Supervision and Curriculum Development (ASCD). For many years ASCD has organized an exhibit of noncommercial curriculum materials for display at its annual conference. Most of these displays have included curriculum guides on reading, language arts, and related topics. In more recent years, ASCD has published a directory of the documents on display (the newer editions of this directory will be included in a CD-ROM package being planned by ASCD). Contact ASCD for information on the annual conference, and for the availability of directories for the noncommercial curriculum materials display.

In addition, the School of Education at the University of California, Sacramento, has begun to collect and catalogue the guides on display at the ASCD conferences. Once the cataloguing is completed, the guides themselves will be available on interlibrary loan.

The following list describes common curriculum features; examples for some are shown in full-page reproductions from published guides (figures 1 through 4):

A. Objectives/Instructional Strategies

Instructional objectives are written as specific topics that teachers must cover, described as specific knowledge areas (see figure 1).

B. Student Activities

Most often expressed in terms of student projects, games, or specific behaviors, this feature often "translates" instructional objectives into desired or proven methodologies that focus on engaging the student in the learning process as actively as possible (figure 2).

C. Skills/Competencies

This feature is by far the most common type of information in curriculum guides. The national agenda for accountability in education has clearly left its mark on guides published during the past decade. The focus on outcomes of instruction sets a baseline for testing or measurement of achievement, giving the teacher the result rather than the "what" or "how to." Many curriculum documents actually code skills in reference to standardized testing instruments.

D. Subject Information

This is perhaps the oldest feature found in curriculum guides. Its use dates back to the days when textbooks were the primary source for curriculum, and it focuses on the legitimacy and dominance of certain areas of knowledge over others. In some cases, excerpts from textbooks are copied directly into the guide.

E. Resources

This feature is prevalent in school district guides where the state adopts certain textbooks or instructional resources (figure 3).

F. Evaluation/Testing

Again, this feature is commonly found in curriculum guides, often in conjunction with *Skills/ Concepts,* which are then cross-referenced with specific testing instruments. A similar feature is the curriculum map, which places specific skills or objectives at specific age or grade levels to indicate mastery (see below).

G. Curriculum Maps

The chief purpose of curriculum maps is to give teachers information regarding where and how single units, chapters, or topics fit into the overall (i.e., K-12) program. Maps may also include cues regarding students' previous learning experiences which may be of consequence to the teacher's instructional style (e.g., introduce, reinforce, test, evaluate) (figure 4).

H. Document Size and Number of Features

Some school districts wish to increase both the number of features (e.g., to meet different types of needs) and the amount of detail. Other schools, however, deliberately minimize the number of content features (e.g., to provide emphasis or direction) as well as the size of the curriculum guides (e.g., to make the guides more manageable or to give teachers more opportunity to customize the curriculum).

There is little evidence, if any, suggesting that one format or a particular combination of

FIGURE 1. EXAMPLE OF INSTRUCTIONAL OBJECTIVES: SKILLS FOR A TENTH-GRADE ENGLISH COURSE

Grade 10

COURSE TITLE: English 020

TARGET GROUP: Students who have average ability and achievement in English

SKILL AREAS

COMPOSITION:

REVIEW   letter writing - all forms

DEVELOP   research skills, culminating in the production of a research paper

REFINE   a) ability to organize and write paragraphs
            b) writing essays, stressing logical order, coherence, unity, and transition
            c) writing reviews and reports
            d) creative writing
            e) proofreading and revising written work

GRAMMAR AND MECHANICS:

REVIEW   a) sentence structure
            b) parts of speech
            c) standards of usage
            d) mechanics

REFINE   a) use of all phrases - prepositional, appositive, verbal
            b) use of all types of dependent clauses - adjective, adverb, noun

LITERATURE

READING   Selected examples of the major genres for reading and analysis

            a) Short story
            b) Novel
            c) Drama
            d) Poetry
            e) Non-fiction

REVIEW   Literary elements and terms

ORAL COMMUNICATION:

INTRODUCE   group-discussion skills

REFINE   ability to prepare and deliver formal oral presentations

Source: Leominster Public Schools, *English Department Curriculum Descriptions, Grades 7-12* (Leominster, MA: 1986). Reproduced with permission.

FIGURE 2. EXAMPLE OF A STUDENT ACTIVITY: REWRITING A REPORT (CONTINUED ON NEXT PAGE).

```
                    STEP SEVEN

                    Rewrite


    Now cut your paper up!!!  Cut your paper into individual
paragraphs and look at each paragraph.  Not only do you need
to look at each paragraph, but at every sentence, every word.
Every word you use helps to build your paper.
```

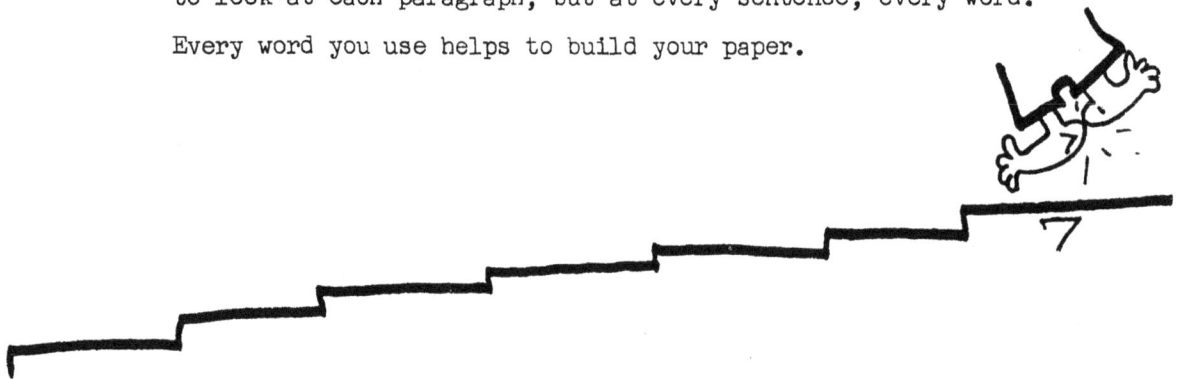

```
    After you are satisfied with each individual paragraph,
arrange the paragraphs in a logical order--introduction,
body, conclusion.  Re-read your paper.  If you are satisfied
with the order, tape your paper together.  If you aren't,
re-arrange them some more until you are satisfied.  NOW it
is time to neatly re-copy your final draft. (WHEW!)
```

17

Source: Volusia County Schools, *Rx for Report Writing*
(Daytona Beach, FL: 1982), pp. 17-18. Reproduced with permission.

FIGURE 2 (CONT'D)

When you have finished re-copying, you will have a whole new paper, and it's probably a lot better, too. Imagine how much you would have missed if you hadn't re-read and re-written it!

Writing is never really finished. There is always one more change to make. What you like about your writing today, you may not like tomorrow because every time you write, your writing level and your maturity increases.

18

FIGURE 3. EXAMPLE OF A RESOURCE LIST (KEYED TO STUDENT ACTIVITIES), FROM A READING CURRICULUM GUIDE.

READING

STRAND   2 - Vocabulary   GRADE   3

030202   The child will use context to select a missing word in a sentence and/or paragraph read silently by the student.

Suggested Activities	Instructional Resources, References and/or Materials	Evaluation
030202		
• Rebus Reading. In a rebus, pictures are substituted for nouns throughout a sentence or paragraph. Ask each child to create a rebus story to match a book that he/she has read. Have the student write or print the story on lined paper and paste in small pictures cut from magazines or catalogs. Some students might enjoy collecting a rebus reservoir by clipping pictures that look usable - objects, people, and animals- and placing them in a set of labeled envelopes for future rebus-writing sessions.	Criscuolo, Nicholas 125 Motivators for Reading, Pitman Learning, Inc. 1977	Teacher observation
• Each pair or group of students selects a word from the cards displayed and creates a clue to help others identify the word. (This creature wears its own house clam, shell. This creature builds its own house beaver, tunnel.) The others select the word.	Indrisano, Roselmina, Resource Activity Book, Ginn and Co. 1976 Cards for words that represent creatures and their habitats (worm, coyote, chipmunk, beaver; ground, field, forest, tunnel, river)	Teacher observation
• From a stack of word cards lying face down on a table, the first student draws three cards and begins a story, using all three words in appropriate context. The next student draws one word card from the pile and continues the story, using his/her word. The story develops as each student follows the same procedure. At any point in the story, a listener may challenge the story teller if he/she thinks that a word is being used out of context. The challenger must use the word appropriately in a sentence that adds to the story. The procedure then continues according to the original sequence.	Indrisano, Roselmina, Resource Activity Book, Ginn and Co., 1976 Cards prepared for words to be practiced	Student response

Source: Boone County Schools, *Elementary Reading Instruction Guide* (Florence, KY: 1986). Reproduced with permission.

FIGURE 4. EXAMPLE OF A CURRICULUM MAP.

LITERATURE–GRADE SEVEN THROUGH GRADE NINE

FICTION
The students should:

Grade Seven through Grade Nine (Short Story, Novel, Drama, Poetry)
    recognize what is involved in the setting.
    recognize plot as the basis for the structure of fiction.
    recognize the use of characterization as a major component of fiction.
    recognize and state the theme.
    recognize the differences between the short story and the novel.
    become aware of the characteristics of drama as well as various dramatic devices.
    recognize the various forms of poetry.

Grade Eight and Nine (Science Fiction–Optional)
    recognize point of view.
    identify literary devices used in fiction (foreshadowing, simile, metaphors, etc.).
    distinguish between major and minor characters.
    understand rhyme, rhythm, alliteration, personification, etc.
    identify the characteristics of science fiction as a type of fictional narrative. (Optional)

Grade Nine (Mythology)
    recognize the relationship between fiction and society.
    recognize that fiction provides a means of knowing and appreciating other groups and cultures.
    appreciate the origins, characteristics and characters associated with mythology.

NONFICTION
The students should:

Grade Seven through Grade Nine (Biography, Autobiography)
    identify the ways in which biography and autobiography differ from one another and other forms
        of prose.
    extend appreciation for human lives, values, and contributions through the reading of biography
        and autobiography.
    appreciate how accurate biography keeps notable individuals memorable and alive.

Grade Eight and Nine (Essay)
    recognize the characteristics and purpose of an essay.

Source: Bloomington Public Schools, *Language Arts: Curriculum Guide, K-12*
(Bloomington, MN: 1986), p. 29. Reproduced with permission.

features works better than another. Much is based on the characteristics of each school district, the mission of the curriculum project, administrative agendas to empower teachers or increase centralized control, and other decisive factors.

While these curriculum features are among the most common, there is no compelling reason to limit curriculum guides to these formats. In fact, educators and textbook publishers alike have challenged this tradition, including the assumption that a curriculum guide should be limited to one subject. For example, school districts are experimenting with integrated or interdisciplinary designs (Vars 1991). In the process they are challenging many fundamental assumptions about the nature of curriculum as well as about the nature of schooling.

A major element of interdisciplinary design relates to the structure of the school schedule itself. The artificial segregation of academic disciplines may have served to develop a specialized workforce, but it has not always produced versatile and broadly educated children and young adults. For most public school graduates, the world of work does not evolve around forty-five minutes of English followed by forty-five minutes of music. Their world presents problems that must be handled with knowledge and skills borrowed from mathematics, history, and other disciplines. The majority of designers using interdisciplinary models argue that the curriculum of the future ought to reflect those realities and provide similar learning situations.[4]

Most alternative designs result from locally developed experiments, often in conjunction with more traditional subject-based guides. Two possible designs, the thematic and interdisciplinary curriculums, are described below:

I. The Thematic Curriculum

An instructional unit or theme—chosen by teachers, administrators, students, parents, or combinations of these groups—serves as a focus for study and investigation for a given period of time. The theme is then examined from a variety of perspectives or traditional disciplines, such as writing, art, science, home economics, and physical education. For example, a unit on Steinbeck's *Grapes of Wrath* could revolve around a reading and analysis of the text but could also include discussions on the causes of the Great Depression (economics, modern history), the New Deal response to the Depression (politics), the WPA murals project (fine art), the crop

failures leading to the Dust Bowl (agriculture, environmental science), and how the Depression affected urban life (sociology). Connections could be made with the changing picture of migrant labor from the Depression to current times, how more recent recessions compare to the Great Depression, etc.

J. The Interdisciplinary Curriculum

This design model can focus on discrete skills that are considered essential for the students' future work or study, such as reading, collaborative skills, problem-solving techniques, test-taking skills, numeracy, research techniques, interpreting information, and others. Subject areas such as language arts, social studies, or physics serve as diverse contexts in which those skills are acquired and practiced.

Population Analysis (Target Students)

While teachers are the audience for whom curricula are written, the students are the true beneficiaries of high quality guides. The demographic characteristics of the student population represent a key factor in defining curriculum content (choosing features), scope, resource specifications, etc. For example, a curriculum developed in an affluent Los Angeles suburb may work very well there, but the same guide could fail completely when implemented in an inner-city Detroit school.

This consideration is particularly important for districts with diverse student populations and for schools in districts with diverse cultural and economic settings.

The characteristics of a given student population determine the teacher's ability to implement a curriculum. While a guide might be formatted to obtain performance expectations or to cover specific topics for *all* ninth graders or fifth graders, such *generic* design assumptions about student populations may simply ignore the realities that teachers must deal with on a daily basis. In fact, any given grade-level classroom will include students above and below grade level in reading ability. Some classes may have up to 25 percent of students on IEPs, requiring the teacher to make drastic adaptions to curriculum expectations. In this light, the blame for "failing to implement" may rest not with the teacher but with the designer. It also explains the surging interest in curriculum guides designed not for grade levels but for developmental levels.

Field Testing

There is no need to separate the drafting process from the field testing of a draft curriculum guide; indeed, it may be counterproductive. At its best, field testing involves a limited number of teachers who are either participants or who have been experimenting with changing a reading or language arts program (curriculum in use). Such tests should be conducted with the cooperation of the department chair and faculty.

There are many reasons to conduct field tests during the draft stage. First, it gives building-level teachers an early look at upcoming changes in the language arts program. If that new program, for example, heavily builds upon whole language concepts, the transition from a traditional phonics program to a whole language curriculum will require extensive staff development activities. Building ownership for a new program throughout the design process will greatly facilitate successful implementation.

The final stage of field testing should be conducted with a completed curriculum at a building or district level. A field test at the district level may require one or two years, to allow for a gradual transition. Teachers should be asked to provide feedback to the curriculum committee in order to provide practical information for final editing. This should include, if possible, one-on-one interviews with each teacher who participated in the field test, preferably conducted by curriculum committee participants. Some of the more important questions that can be posed are:

· Have you found the curriculum useful? How?
· Do you have any reservations or concerns you would like to share?
· Are suggested activities useful for implementation?
· What do you need to implement this curriculum?
· Is there anything else you would like the curriuclum committee to know?

Public Input

Schools—and the curriculum development process—can benefit a great deal from collaborating with parents, community-based organizations and agencies, the private sector, and institutions of higher education. The question for the curriculum designer is: How can this be organized and what do we do with the information?

There are a number of critical factors to consider in organizing public input:

1. Should public input be sought at the beginning of the curriculum process, in order to avoid the impression that such input amounts to mere formality after educators have made all the decisions?
2. Should public input be sought after field testing in order to give the curriculum an opportunity to prove itself?
3. Should public input be conducted through an open forum (public meetings, curriculum or parent nights at the school, press releases, etc.), or should such input be targeted by inviting feedback from specific individuals, constituencies, or organizations that are most likely to understand the issues and needs related to the teaching of language arts?

Public input, particularly when conducted in an open forum, can yield contradictory opinions and requests. It is critical for the implementation process, however, to combine public input with feedback received from future users. Regardless of the nature of public feedback, or whether or not such input translates into actual changes in the language arts curriculum, experienced curriculum designers (or school districts) must respond to those who have answered the invitation to participate.

Editing, Ratification, Production, and Dissemination

Editing

Editing a curriculum guide has two major purposes. First, it should minimize jargon and technical language without eliminating the technical detail that teachers need for clarity. Whenever possible, a school district should hire an outside curriculum specialist or auditor when editing new guides or curricula in use (English 1988).

Second, the curriculum committee edits the drafted curriculum guide in order to fix weaknesses or missing parts identified in the interviews with future users (discussed above, under *Field Testing*) and the public (see above, under *Public Input*).

Ratification

Curriculum guide designers need to discuss ratification procedures with the administration in order to comply with state statutes, regulations, and local school board policies. Such procedures often involve local school board action. If that is the case, it is important to plan this event carefully.

School boards and communities should be informed about curriculum changes on an ongoing basis rather than being confronted with finalized documents. School boards may choose to review the document themselves before granting final approval. When a board is ready to vote on the matter, the curriculum designer (or responsible administrator) should make a formal presentation. This gives the district as a whole an opportunity to celebrate its achievement, to congratulate all participants for their efforts (including recognition ceremonies), and to confirm the importance of curriculum and instruction matters publicly (Carr and Harris in press). This event should include participants and citizens and be publicized in the local media.

Production

Curriculum designers should consider ways to ensure a high-quality appearance of the guide, to accompany—and emphasize—the high-quality content. A well-designed and well-printed document reveals care for and commitment to the curriculum on the part of the district—and it may facilitate implementation.

Three-ring binders of various sizes offer significant advantages: (*a*) the name of the district, titles, and graphic designs can be silk-screened on binders at reasonable prices; (*b*) binders allow users to add new sections of the curriculum during revisions, remove outdated sections, or add their own instructional plans to it; (*c*) binders tend to have a longer life than cardboard covers or spiral-bound documents.

Curriculum production involves numerous decisions leading to printing and publication:
- Should the language arts curriculum guide be published in its entirety (K-12) in order to demonstrate a comprehensive approach to language arts?
- Should the English curriculum be published in sections or as separate documents (e.g., K-3, 4-6, 7-8, 9-12) to accommodate varying user needs, and/or to save paper?
- Should the curriculum be prepared by a layout specialist in order to prepare an attrac-

tive document (typeface, graphics, etc.)?
- Does the district have desktop publishing capacity, and can the district develop its own layout?
- Should the document be bound in book fashion (may prolong cohesion), be bound with plastic spirals (may save production costs), or be placed in three-ring binders?
- Who should be given authorship for the final document? (Note: It is recommended that the school district retain all rights; the district can issue letters or certificates to participating committee members to affirm their contribution.)

Production efforts should be entirely planned and coordinated by the curriculum designer or administrative staff. Production may involve the contracted services of a printing company (unless administrative staff can handle the job). The process for purchasing binders (or an alternative) may follow a similar route.

Dissemination

The dissemination of the new guide should be timed carefully. Summer breaks or vacations offer teachers an opportunity to read the documents and incorporate curriculum objectives into plans for upcoming quarters or semesters. An additional concern regarding dissemination addresses district plans for staff development or inservice training. It can be helpful to disseminate new curricula during staff development time; this provides time for reading and discussion among teachers or for carefully targeted workshops which address the new curriculum.

Adoption Process

By far the most challenging phase of the curriculum process is the adoption of the curriculum guide at the building level, along with the assurance that teachers plan instruction with the guide in hand. In this phase, curriculum is translated into instruction. The complexity of the curriculum, the degree to which assumptions about language arts are spelled out or hidden, the volume of the curriculum, and the teacher's disposition toward the curriculum guide are all factors that affect adoption.

In facing a mandatory curriculum, teachers must first decide whether or not they will work with that curriculum. This is a decision which can be mandated but not necessarily implemented. Because curriculum adoption at the classroom level is, at least in part, a personal decision, curriculum designers must take several factors into consideration which influence that decision:

· The degree to which teachers "own" the curriculum
· Level of experience working with district curriculum
· The degree to which the teacher depends on the textbook
· The administration's willingness and ability to support teachers
· Availability of necessary resources/materials
· Level of support from community, school board, state officials, etc.
· Availability and quality of staff development opportunities

Staff Development and Support

Staff development can be an effective implementation strategy, a fact that is voiced by many writers (Fullen 1990; Joyce and Showers 1988; Goodlad 1990; Holmes Group 1990; Loucks-Horsely et al. 1987; Schon 1987). From this standpoint, the teachers charged with implementing the curriculum may require specific training. Curriculum designers often see multiple training needs. To assess those needs as accurately as possible, administrators need to examine several factors:

1. Who are the users of the new curriculum? This information will determine the scale of training which will have to be provided to the district (e.g., how many classroom teachers per grade level, how many specialists, etc.).
2. Which local, state, or national goals and standards are being adopted? This information must be included in order to train and inform staff about adopted standards or goals effectively.
3. Has a timetable been adopted? This information defines the curriculum implementation timetable. Ideally, staff development targeted to facilitate curriculum implementation should be planned over several years and linked with a clear message to teachers that adoption is a longitudinal learning process.
4. What types of resources are needed/available? Available resources, such as trainers and staff development consultants, must be identified and included in the district's staff

development budget.
5. Who has served on the curriculum committee? Educators who have participated in the curriculum design process can be used as discussion leaders or to model implementation in their own classrooms.
6. What are current topics in K-12 English and language arts? Current topics, controversies, or problems in K-12 language arts should have been identified in the review of the literature; this information can be helpful in defining topics for staff development workshops. In addition, authors and researchers may be available to serve as trainers or lecturers.
7. Which design format has been adopted? If the chosen format differs significantly from that previously used in district curricula, some staff development may be required to instruct teachers in using the new materials.
8. What are the results from the field test? Teachers will often reveal staff development needs and topics when interviewed anonymously during the pilot testing process.

Monitoring and Supervision

Those supervisors who observe teachers will play a key role in supporting the implementation process; they provide opportunities for teachers to share and discuss problems and uncertainties with regard to their implementation efforts. In order for supervisors to be effective in this role, they must consider the following guidelines:

· Prove to teachers that supervision aims to support the teacher's many tasks. In order to do this, it may be necessary to separate the supervisor's two roles, and to emphasize the *supervision* role over the *evaluation* role.
· Be familiar with the curriculum and the teacher's professional development; focus on issues, students, lesson plans, and instructional techniques in reference to, and appropriate for, his/her classroom.
· Provide feedback to the curriculum designer or committee which has an impact on staff development plans or curriculum revision.

Evaluation and Revision

Evaluation
After all the dust has settled, all the decisions have been made, and, at long last, a new language

arts guide has been adopted for implementation, all participants surely deserve a rest. As far as the curriculum designer is concerned, however, the greatest challenge still lies ahead.

Curriculum documents—for language arts, for reading, and for most other subject areas—which are more than four or five years old require a thorough evaluation. Changes in language arts teaching, new research information, new standards, and better instructional methods appear quickly, making curricular adjustments necessary on an ongoing basis. This explains the necessity for school districts to have a curriculum process, rather than merely a document. Curriculum designers should communicate this issue to all educators, to parents, and to policymakers.

Traditionally, achievement scores are held to be indicators of the quality of a curriculum. Achievement scores, however, are only one source of curriculum evaluation data, and they are useful only insofar as the tested curriculum matches both the planned and the taught curriculum (English 1980).

Again, curriculum designers face some critical decisions:

1. What is the purpose of evaluating the curriculum? Is it a tool to evaluate teachers, students, or schools?
2. Who will participate in evaluating the curriculum? Should the same curriculum committee be used, or would a different perspective, and therefore a fresh committee, serve better?

The curriculum evaluation committee should be empowered to investigate the strengths and weaknesses of an implemented curriculum in pursuit of the truth.

Curriculum designers should clarify the evaluation process in advance, including the following:
- Who the evaluation committee *participants* will be
- To what degree curriculum process *goals* have been achieved
- Whether the overall *mission* of the curriculum project has been reached
- Whether curriculum *content* is appropriate in light of district characteristics and mission objectives
- Whether *instruction* is based on the curriculum
- Whether the *assessment* process measured the taught curriculum against the planned curriculum

Table 2 provides a sampling of the goals and

questions that could be addressed during evaluation of a language arts curriculum.

The evaluation will yield a *needs assessment* to clarify what types of resources, time demands, training and workshops, and supervision strategies must be in place in order for successful implementation (to continue). In addition, a *revision plan* should be issued for the curriculum guide itself, giving specifics for additions or deletions.

Revision

Planning for the next generation of language arts or reading programs begins now. The first step consists of educating the school board, the staff, and the community that implementation will yield a variety of positive experiences as well as numerous problems. Information of this sort must be collected and organized with an eye to future revisions of the curriculum. Any curriculum has room for improvement and must be dynamic enough to incorporate future changes in teaching the language arts.

Curriculum designers should therefore present a *curriculum development process,* if not at the outset, then certainly at the time of adoption and implementation. This will clarify the ground rules for all concerned. A development process at the district level should incorporate all curriculum areas. However, in order to remain manageable, the district should avoid revising all curricula during the same year. Revising a reading or language arts curriculum guide can be as complex as designing it in the first place. Numerous decisions must be made, and numerous sources of information should be considered, such as:
- Is a revision necessary in view of available information, or should the revision cycle be changed (to revise sooner or later than planned)?
- Should a committee be established to carry out the revision?
- Have conditions changed since the language arts curriculum was first implemented or most recently revised (new standards, new testing systems, new staffing patterns, significant changes in enrollment, budget crises, etc.)?

Curriculum designers often battle the assumption that completed curriculum guides finalize the curriculum process—in reality, a curriculum guide marks the *beginning* of a curriculum. A curriculum guide that looks the same five years after it was

Table 2. Sample Evaluation of K-5 Language Arts Curriculum		
Rationale	**Participants**	**Goals**
The evaluation will identify strengths and weaknesses in the K-5 language arts program.	Curriculum committee members; supervisory personnel; consultant; building prinicpals	Quality of document (design, format, volume, type of information); effectiveness of staff development; effectiveness of supervision; quality of achievement
Mission	**Revision**	**Content**
To what degree has the curriculum been implemented? Have adopted standards and goals been achieved? Have reading scores been raised? Have teachers adopted the curriculum?	Schedule meeeting with 4th-grade teachers; revise 4th-grade program; redesign 4-6 staff development program; incorporate NCTE guidelines for 3rd grade	Is the information in the document accurate, verifiable, measurable, "teachable," developmentally appropriate?
Needs Assessment	**Assessment**	**Instruction**
The 4th grade teachers must be involved in redesigning the commposition strand. The 4th grade curriculum is too demanding, geared to advanced students. Staff development efforts for 4-6 teachers ineffective. Grade 3 goals do not meet intent of NCTE guidelines.	Does the testing program cover this curriculum? Have teachers changed their assessment tools and strategies effectively to accommodate the curriculum? Have achievement scores changed with the implementation of this curriculum?	Do teachers have sufficient time to teach the curriculum? Have teachers changed instructional methods? Have teachers used the curriculum in planning instruction? Are instructional resources (textbooks, manipulatives, software, etc.) available?

written will most likely be outdated. Teachers tend to leave them on the shelf, and for good reason.

Each school or district must have a process in place for curriculum development and revision. The schools and districts that have an ongoing curriculum revision process can best react to new standards and methods in teaching reading, language arts, and all other K-12 subjects—and these are the schools that can best serve their students and prepare them for the world beyond graduation.

Notes

1. Other practical guidebooks are available to supplement this one. See Carr and Harris 1992; Frey et al. 1989; Tchudi 1991; Wisconsin Department of Public Instruction 1986a, 1986b.

2. Among the numerous outstanding resources which discuss the issue of teachers as adult learners in detail are Thies-Sprinthall 1986; Sprinthall 1983; McNergney 1981; Oja and Ham 1987.

3. Budget models based on curricular or programmatic priorities are discussed in Wood 1986.

4. For a comprehensive review of interdisciplinary curriculum models and procedures, see Palmer 1991; Jacobs 1989; Miller, Cassie, and Drake 1990; Drake 1991; Pappas 1990.

References

Anderson, S. A., et al. 1987. *Curriculum Process.* Yale, MI: Yale Public Schools.

Apple, M. W. 1979. *Ideology and Curriculum.* Boston: Routledge and Kegan Paul.

Argyris, C. 1982. *Reading, Learning, and Action: Individual and Organizational.* San Francisco: Jossey-Bass.

Aronowitz, S., and H. A. Giroux. 1985. *Education under Siege.* South Hadley, MA: Bergin & Garvey.

Brozo, W. G., and M. L. Simpson. 1990. *Readers, Teachers, Learners: Expanding Literacy in Secondary Schools.* New York: Macmillan.

Caine, R. N., and G. Caine. 1991. *Making Connections—Teaching and the Human Brain.* Alexandria, VA: Association for Supervision and Curriculum Development.

Campbell, M. et al. 1989. "Board Members Needn't Be Experts to Play a Vital Role in Curriculum." *American School Board Journal* 176 (April): 30-32.

Carr, J. F., and D. E. Harris. 1992. *Getting It Together: A Process Workbook for Curriculum Development, Implementation, and Assessment.* Boston: Allyn & Bacon.

Connelly, F.M., and D. J. Clandinin. 1988. *Teachers as Curriculum Planners: Narratives of Experience.* New York: Teachers College Press.

Doll, R. C. 1989. *Curriculum Improvement: Decision Making and Process.* 7th ed. Boston: Allyn & Bacon.

Drake, S. M. 1991. "How Our Team Dissolved the Boundaries." *Educational Leadership* 49 (2): 20-22.

English, F. W. 1988. *Curriculum Auditing.* Lancaster, PA: Technomic.

———. 1980. "Improving Curriculum Management in the Schools." Occasional Paper 30. Washington, DC: Council for Basic Education.

Frey, K., et al. 1989. "Do Curriculum Development Models Really Influence the Curriculum?" *Journal of Curriculum Studies* 21 (Nov.-Dec.): 553-59.

Fullen, M. G. 1990. "Staff Development, Innovation, and Institutional Development." *Association for Supervision and Curriculum Development Yearbook,* 3-25. Alexandria, VA.

Giroux, H. A. 1983. *Theory and Resistance in Education.* South Hadley, MA: Bergin & Garvey.

Glatthorn, A. A. 1987. *Curriculum Leadership.* Glenview, IL: Scott, Foresman.

Glickman, C. 1990. *Supervision of Instruction: A Developmental Approach.* 2d ed. Boston: Allyn & Bacon.

Goodlad, J. I. 1990. *Teachers for Our Nation's Schools.* San Francisco: Jossey-Bass.

Harris, D. E., and J. Jenzer. 1990. "The Search for Quality Curriculum Design: Four Models for School Districts." Paper presented to National Association for Supervision and Curriculum Development Conference, San Antonio, TX.

Harste, J. 1989. *New Policy Guidelines For Reading: Connecting Research and Practice.* Urbana, IL: National Council of Teachers of English.

Holmes Group. 1990. *Tomorrow's Schools: Principles for the Design of Professional Development Schools.* East Lansing, MI.

Irvin, J. L. 1990. *Reading and the Middle School Student.* Boston: Allyn & Bacon.

Jacobs, H. H. 1989. *Interdisciplinary Curriculum-Design and Implementation.* Alexandria, VA: Association for Supervision and Curriculum Development.

Joyce, B., and B. Showers. 1988. *Student Achievement through Staff Development.* White Plains, NY: Longman.

Kanpol, B., and E. Weisz. 1990. "The Effective Principal and the Curriculum—A Focus on Leadership." *NASSP Bulletin* 74 (April): 15-18.

Loucks-Horsely, S., et al. 1987. *Continuing to Learn: A Guidebook for Teacher Development.* Andover, MA: Regional Laboratory for Educational Improvement of the Northeast and the Islands.

McNeil, J. D. 1985. *Curriculum—A Comprehensive Introduction.* 3d ed. Boston: Little, Brown.

McNergney, R., and C. Carrier. 1981. *Teacher Development.* New York: Macmillan.

Miller, J., B. Cassie, and S. M. Drake. 1990. *Holistic Learning: A Teacher's Guide to Integrated Studies.* Toronto: Ontario Institute for Studies in Education.

Montana State Office of the Superintendent of Public Instruction. 1990. *The Curriculum Process Guide: Developing Curriculum in the 1990's.* Helena, MT.

National Council of Teachers of Mathematics. 1989. *Curriculum and Evaluation Standards for School Mathematics.* Reston, VA: NCTM.

National Council of Teachers of Mathematics. 1992. "A Core Curriculum: Making Mathematics Count for Everyone." In *Curriculum and Evaluation Standards for School Mathematics.* Addenda series. Grades 9–12. Reston, VA: NCTM.

Oja, S. N., and M. Ham. 1987. *A Collaborative Approach to Leadership in Supervision.* Project funded by U.S. Department of Education (OERI). ED no. 400-85-1056. Washington, DC.

Palmer, J. M. 1991. "Planning Wheels Turn Curriculum Around." *Educational Leadership* 49(2): 57-60.

Pappas, C. C., B. Z. Kiefer, and L. S. Levstik. 1990. *An Integrated Language Perspective in the Elementary School.* White Plains, NY: Longman.

Schon, D. 1987. *Educating the Reflective Practitioner.* New York: Basic Books.

Singer, H., and D. Duncan. 1989. *Reading and Learning from Text.* 2d ed. Hillsdale, NJ: Lawrence Erlbaum.

Sprinthall, N. A., and Thies-Sprinthall, L. 1983. "The Teacher as an Adult Learner: A Cognitive Developmental View." *Eighty-second Yearbook of the National Society for the Study of Education,* 13-35. Chicago.

Tchudi, S. 1991. *English Language Arts.* Alexandria, VA: Association for Supervision and Curriculum Development.

Thies-Sprinthall, L. 1986. "A Collaborative Approach to Mentor Training: A Working Model." *Journal of Teacher Education* 19 (Nov.-Dec.): 13-20.

United States Department of Education. 1983. *A Nation At Risk: The Imperative for Educational Reform.* Washington, DC.

Vars, G. F. 1991. "Integrated Curriculum in Historical Perspective." *Educational Leadership* 49(2): 14-15.

Weaver, C. 1990. *Understanding Language: From Principles to Practice.* Portsmouth, NH: Heinemann.

Wisconsin Department of Public Instruction. 1986. *A Guide to Curriculum Planning in English Language Arts.* Madison, WI.

———. 1986. *A Guide to Curriculum Planning in Reading.* Madison, WI.

Wood, R. C., ed. 1986. *Principles of School Business Management.* Reston, VA: Association of School Business Officials International.

Wulf, K. M., and B. Schave. 1984. *Curriculum Design.* Glenview, IL: Scott, Foresman.

Young, H. J. 1990. "Curriculum Implementation: An Organizational Perspective." *Journal of Curriculum and Supervision* 5(2): 132-49.

3

FUNDING CURRICULUM PROJECTS

THE greatest challenge curriculum developers often face is locating money to finance their projects. They hear that money is available for such projects, but are at a loss as to how it can be accessed. Frequently, it requires as much creativity to locate financing as it does to generate the curriculum. This chapter includes information on three types of funding that are available for education projects:

1. Federal programs that provide money for special school projects
2. Foundations and organizations that have recently endowed education projects
3. Foundations and organizations that proclaim education, including special projects, as a mission.

When seeking a potential funding source for a project, first review any information that is available about the organization. Specifically, look at the following areas:

· Purpose: Is a mission of the foundation to provide money for education?
· Limitations: Are there specific geographic requirements?Are there some areas that are disqualified?
· Supported areas: Does the organization provide funding for special projects?
· Grants: After reviewing the education projects that have been funded, does it appear that the organizations and projects are similar to yours?

Your search will be even more useful if you also keep these questions in mind:

· Has the foundation funded projects in your subject area?
· Does your location meet the geographic requirements of the organization?
· Is the amount of money you are requesting within the grant's range?
· Are there foundation policies that prohibit grants for the type of support you are requesting?
· Will the organization institute grants to cover the full cost of a project?Does it require that costs of a project be shared with other foundations or funding sources?
· What types of educational groups have been supported?Are they similar to yours?
· Are there specific application deadlines and procedures, or are proposals accepted continuously?

This information can be found in the annual report of the foundation or in *Source Book Profiles.* Many of the larger public libraries maintain current foundation directories. If yours does not, there are Foundation Center Libraries located at:

79 Fifth Avenue
New York, NY 10003-3050
(212) 620-4230

312 Sutter Street
San Francisco, CA 94180
(415) 397-0902

1001 Connecticut Avenue, NW
Suite 938
Washington, DC 20036
(202) 331-1400

1442 Hanna Building
1442 Euclid Avenue
Cleveland, OH 44115
(216) 861-1934

Identifying appropriate foundations is the first step in your quest for money. The next step is initiating contact with the foundation, either by telephone or letter. It is a good idea to direct your inquiry to the person in charge of giving; otherwise, you take a chance of your letter going astray. A phone call to the foundation will provide you with this information.

Federal Programs that Fund Special School Projects

Jacob B. Javits Gifted and Talented Students
Research Applications Division
Programs for the Improvement of Practice
Department of Education
555 New Jersey Avenue, NW
Washington, DC 20202-5643
(202) 219-2187
Provides grants for establishing and operating model projects to identify and educate gifted and talented students.

Technology Education Demonstration
Division of National Programs
Office of Vocational and Adult Education
Department of Education
400 Maryland Avenue, SW
Washington, DC 20202-7242
(202) 732-2428
Funding to establish model demonstration programs for technology education in secondary schools, vocational education centers, and community colleges.

The Secretary's Fund for Innovation in Education
Department of Education
FIRST
Office of Educational Research and Improvement
Washington, DC 20208-5524
(202) 219-1496
Funding for educational programs and projects that identify innovative educational approaches.

Foundations and Organizations that Have Recently Funded Education Projects

The Blandin Foundation
100 Pokegama Avenue, North
Grand Rapids, MN 55744
(218) 326-0523
Contact: Paul M. Olson, President
Funding limited to Minnesota, with an emphasis on rural areas.
   · $125,500 to Grand Rapids Independent School District 318, Rapids Quest Program, to continue imaginative enrichment programs for Grand Rapids students.
   · $25,000 to Independent School District #317, Deer River, to produce Ojibwe K-12 curriculum.
   · $50,000 to Mahnomen School District 432 for their Ojibwe curriculum.

Du Pont Community Initiatives Fund
Du Pont External Affairs
Wilmington, DE 19898
Matching-grant program for projects to encourage company sites to develop or adopt programs in their communities that will improve the quality of public education and increase public understanding of environmental matters.

W. Alton Jones Foundation, Inc.
232 East High Street
Charlottesville, VA 22901
(804) 295-2134
Contact: John Peterson Myers, Director
   · $70,000 to Episcopal School of New York for general school development and teacher professional development.

The Nellie Mae Fund for Education
50 Braintree Hill Park, Suite 300
Braintree, MA 02184
(617) 849-1325
Funding generally limited to the six New England states.
   · $10,000 to Volunteers in Providence Schools, Rhode Island, for after-school study centers in eleven sites throughout Providence
   · $12,000 to Winthrop School Department, Maine, to develop "Modeling for Success" project (positive role models for at-risk middle school students).

The Medtronic Foundation
7000 Central Avenue, NE
Minneapolis, MN 55432
(612) 574-3029
Contact: Jan Schwarz, Manager
Giving primarily in areas of company operations.
· $12,500 to Minneapolis Public Schools,
Minnesota, to work with the community on
general curriculum development.

The Reader's Digest Foundation
Pleasantville, NY 10570
(914) 241-5370
One hundred minigrants of up to $500 each to
fund innovative-teaching programs in
Westchester and Putnam counties, NY.

Z. Smith Reynolds Foundation, Inc.
101 Reynolds Village
Winston-Salem, NC 27106-5197
(919) 725-7541
Fax (919) 725-6067
Contact: Thomas W. Lambeth,
Executive Director
Funding limited to North Carolina. Will provide
funding for special K-12 projects.
· $10,000 to Children's Grammar School,
Asheville, North Carolina, for language arts
curriculum outline for pre-school and el-
ementary grades.

The Spencer Foundation
900 North Michigan Avenue, Suite 2800
Chicago, IL 60611
(312) 337-7000
Grants for various research projects related to
cultural variations, high-school teaching, mathematics, school choice, etc.

Steelcase Foundation
P.O. Box 1967
Grand Rapids, MI 49507
(616) 246-4695
Funding limited to areas of company operations.
· $20,000 to Forest Hills Education Founda-
tion, Grand Rapids, MI, for development of
a science curriculum for special education
students.

The Tandy Corporation
1800 One Tandy Center
Fort Worth, TX 76102
· Tandy Educational Grants to eleven schools
and colleges/universities for "Using micro-

computers for classroom management to
increase student/teacher productivity."

The Zellerbach Family Fund
120 Montgomery Street, Suite 2125
San Francisco, CA 94104
(415) 421-2629
Giving primarily in the San Francisco Bay area.
· $32,885 to Children's Own Stories, San
Francisco, to develop curriculum, training,
and dissemination of programs to encourage
reading readiness in children.

Foundations and Organizations that Provide Funds for Education, Including Special Projects, as a Mission

Aetna Foundation, Inc.
151 Farmington Avenue
Hartford, CT 06156-3180
(203) 273-6382
Contact: Diana Kinosh, Management Information Supervisor

The Ahmanson Foundation
9215 Wilshire Boulevard
Beverly Hills, CA 90210
(213) 278-0770
Contact: Lee E. Walcott, Vice President
& Managing Director
Giving primarily in southern California.

Alcoa Foundation
1501 Alcoa Building
Pittsburgh, PA 15219-1850
(412) 553-2348
Contact: F. Worth Hobbs, President
Giving primarily in areas of company operations.

The Allstate Foundation
Allstate Plaza North
Northbrook, IL 60062
(708) 402-5502
Contacts: Alan Benedeck, Executive Director;
Allen Goldhamer, Manager; Dawn Bougart,
Administrative Assistant

American Express Minnesota Foundation
c/o IDS Financial Services
IDS Tower Ten
Minneapolis, MN 55440
(612) 372-2643
Contacts: Sue Gethin, Manager of Public Affairs,
    IDS; Marie Tobin, Community Relations
    Specialist
Giving primarily in Minnesota.

American National Bank & Trust Co. of Chicago
    Foundation
33 North La Salle Street
Chicago, IL 60690
(312) 661-6115
Contact: Joan M. Klaus, Director
Giving limited to six-county Chicago metropolitan area.

Anderson Foundation
c/o Anderson Corp.
Bayport, MN 55003
(612) 439-5150
Contact: Lisa Carlstrom, Assistant Secretary

The Annenberg Foundation
Street Davids Center
150 Radnor-Chester Road, Suite A-200
St. Davids, PA 19087
Contact: Donald Mullen, Treasurer

AON Foundation
123 North Wacker Drive
Chicago, IL 60606
(312) 701-3000
Contact: Wallace J. Buya, VP
No support for secondary educational institutions
or vocational schools.

Atherton Family Foundation
c/o Hawaiian Trust Co., Ltd.
P.O. Box 3170
(808) 537-6333
Honolulu, HI 96802
Fax: (808) 521-6286
Contact: Charlie Medeiros
Funding limited to Hawaii.

Ball Brothers Foundation
222 South Mulberry Street
Muncie, IN 47308
(317) 741-5500
Fax(317) 741-5518
Contact: Douglas A. Bakker, Executive Director

Funding limited to Indiana.

Baltimore Gas & Electric Foundation, Inc.
Box 1475
Baltimore, MD 21203
(301) 234-5312
Contact: Gary R. Fuhronan
Giving primarily in Maryland, with emphasis in
Baltimore.

Bell Atlantic Charitable Foundation
1310 North Courthouse Road, 10th Floor
Arlington, VA 22201
(703) 974-5440
Contact: Ruth P. Caine, Director
Giving primarily in areas of company operations.

Benwood Foundation, Inc.
1600 American National Bank Building
736 Market Street
Chattanooga, TN 37402
(615) 267-4311
Contact: Jean R. McDaniel, Executive Director
Giving primarily in the Chattanooga area.

Robert M. Beren Foundation, Inc.
970 Fourth Financial Center
Wichita, KS 67202
Giving primarily for Jewish organizations.

The Frank Stanley Beveridge Foundation, Inc.
1515 Ringling Boulevard, Suite 340
P.O. Box 4097
Sarasota, FL 34230-4097
(813) 955-7575; (800) 356-9779
Contact: Philip Coswell, President
Giving primarily to Hampden county, Massachu-
setts, to organizations that are not tax-supported.

F.R. Bigelow Foundation
1120 Norwest Center
St. Paul, MN 55101
(612) 224-5463
Contact: Paul A. Verret, Secretary/Treasurer
Support includes secondary education in the
greater St. Paul metropolitan area.

Borden Foundation, Inc.
180 East Broad Street, 34th Floor
Columbus, OH 43215
(614) 225-4340
Contact: Judy Barker, President
Emphasis on programs to benefit disadvantaged
children in areas of company operations.

The Boston Globe Foundation II, Inc.
135 Morrissey Boulevard
Boston, MA 02107
(617) 929-3194
Contact: Suzanne Watkin, Executive Director
Giving primarily in the greater Boston area.

The JS Bridwell Foundation
500 City National Building
Wichita Falls, TX 76303
(817) 322-4436
Support includes secondary education in Texas.

The Buchanan Family Foundation
222 East Wisconsin Avenue
Lake Forest, IL 60045
Contact: Huntington Eldridge, Jr., Treasurer
Giving primarily in Chicago, IL.

The Buhl Foundation
Four Gateway Center, Room 1522
Pittsburgh, PA 15222
(412) 566-2711
Contact: Dr. Doreen E. Boyce,
    Executive Director
Giving primarily in southwestern Pennsylvania,
particularly the Pittsburgh area.

Edyth Bush Charitable Foundation, Inc.
199 East Welbourne Avenue
P.O. Box 1967
Winter Park, FL 32790-1967
(407) 647-4322
Contact: H. Clifford Lee, President
Giving has specific geographic and facility
limitations.

California Community Foundation
606 South Olive Street, Suite 2400
Los Angeles, CA 90014
(213) 413-4042
Contact: Jack Shakley, President
Orange County:
13252 Garden Grove Boulevard, Suite 195
Garden Grove, CA 92643
(714) 750-7794
Giving limited to Los Angeles, Orange, Riverside, San Bernadino, and Ventura counties, CA.

The Cargill Foundation
P.O. Box 9300
Minneapolis, MN 55440
(612) 475-6122

Contact: Audrey Tulberg, Program &
    Administrative Director
Giving primarily in the seven-county Minneapolis-St. Paul, metropolitan area.

H.A. & Mary K. Chapman Charitable Trust
One Warren Place, Suite 1816
6100 South Yale
Tulsa, OK 74136
(918) 496-7882
Contacts: Ralph L. Abercrombie, Trustee;
    Donne Pitman, Trustee
Giving primarily in Tulsa.

Liz Claiborne Foundation
119 West 40th Street, 4th Floor
New York, NY 10018
(212) 536-6424
Funding limited to Hudson County, NJ, and the
metropolitan New York area.

The Coca-Cola Foundation, Inc.
P.O. Drawer 1734
Atlanta, GA 30301
(404) 676-2568

The Columbus Foundation
1234 East Broad Street
Columbus, OH 43205
(614) 251-4000
Contact: James I. Luck, President
Giving limited to central Ohio.

Cowles Media Foundation
329 Portland Avenue
Minneapolis, MN 55415
(612) 375-7051
Contact: Janet L. Schwichtenberg
Funding limited to the Minneapolis area.

Dade Community Foundation
200 South Biscayne Boulevard-Suite 4770
Miami, FL 33131-2343
(305) 371-2711
Contact: Ruth Shack, President
Funding limited to Dade County, Florida.

Dewitt Families Conduit Foundation
8300 96th Avenue
Zelland, MI 49464
Giving for Christian organizations.

Dodge Jones Foundation
P.O. Box 176
Abilene, TX 79604
(915) 673-6429
Contact: Lawrence E. Gill, Vice President,
    Grants Administration
Giving primarily in Abilene.

Carrie Estelle Doheny Foundation
911 Wiltshire Boulevard, Suite 1750
Los Angeles, CA 90017
(213) 488-1122
Contact: Robert A. Smith III, President
Giving primarily in the Los Angeles area for non-tax-supported organizations.

The Educational Foundation of America
23161 Ventura Boulevard, Suite 201
Woodland Hills, CA 91364
(818) 999-0921

The Charles Engelhard Foundation
P.O. Box 427
Far Hills, NJ 07931
(201) 766-7224
Contact: Elaine Catterall, Secretary

The William Stamps Farish Fund
1100 Louisiana, Suite 1250
Houston, TX 77002
(713) 757-7313
Contact: W. S. Farish, President
Giving primarily in Texas.

Joseph & Bessie Feinberg Foundation
5245 W. Lawrence Avenue
Chicago, IL 60630
(312) 777-8600
Contact: June Blossom
Giving primarily in Illinois, to Jewish organizations.

The 1525 Foundation
1525 National City Bank Building
Cleveland, OH 44114
(216) 696-4200
Contact: Bernadette Walsh, Assistant Secretary
Funding primarily in Ohio, with emphasis on Cuyahoga County.

The Edward E. Ford Foundation
297 Wickenden Street
Providence, RI 02903
(401) 751-2966

Contact: Philip V. Havens, Executive Director
Funding to independent secondary schools.

George F. & Sybil H. Fuller Foundation
105 Madison Street
Worcester, MA 01610
(508) 756-5111
Contact: Russell E. Fuller, Chairman
Giving primarily in Massachusetts, with emphasis in Worcester.

The B. C. Gamble & P. W. Skogmo Foundation
500 Foshay Tower
Minneapolis, MN 55402
(612) 339-7343
Contact: Patricia A. Cummings, Manager of
    Supporting Organizations
Giving primarily for disadvantaged youth, handicapped, and secondary educational institutions in the Minneapolis-St. Paul, metropolitan area.

The Gold Family Foundation
159 Conant Street
Hillside, NJ 07205
(908) 353-6269
Contact: Meyer Gold, Manager
Support primarily for Jewish organizations.

The George Gund Foundation
1845 Guildhall Building
45 Prospect Avenue West
(216) 241-3114
Cleveland, OH 44115
Fax: (216) 241-6560
Contact: David Bergholz, Executive Director
Giving primarily in northeastern Ohio.

The Haggar Foundation
6113 Lemmon Avenue
Dallas, TX 75209
(214) 956-0241
Contact: Rosemary Haggar Vaughan,
    Executive Director
Limited to areas of company operations in Dallas and south Texas.

Gladys & Roland Harriman Foundation
63 Wall Street, 23rd Floor
New York, NY 10005
(212) 493-8182
Contact: William F. Hibberd, Secretary

Hasbro Children's Foundation
32 West 23rd Street
New York, NY 10010
(212) 645-2400
Contact: Eve Weiss, Executive Director
Funding for children with special needs, under
the age of 12.

The Humana Foundation, Inc.
The Humana Building
500 West Main Street
P.O. Box 1438
Louisville, KY 40201
(502) 580-3920
Contact: Jay L. Foley, Contribution Manager
Giving primarily in Kentucky.

International Paper Company Foundation
Two Manhattanville Road
Purchase, NY 10577
(914) 397-1581
Contact: Sandra Wilson, Vice President
Giving primarily in communities where there are
company plants and mills.

The Martha Holden Jennings Foundation
710 Halle Building
1228 Euclid Avenue
Cleveland, OH 44115
(216) 589-5700
Contact: Dr. Richard A. Boyd, Executive Director
Funding limited to Ohio.

International Reading Association
800 Barksdale Road
P.O. Box 8139
Newark, DE 19714-8139
(302) 731-1600
(800) 336-READ
A small grants division funds reading programs
and projects.

Walter S. Johnson Foundation
525 Middlefield Road, Suite 110
Menlo Park, CA 94025
(415) 326-0485
Contact: Kimberly Ford, Program Director
Giving primarily in Alameda, Contra Costa, San
Francisco, San Mateo and Santa Clara counties in
California and in Washoe, Nevada; no support to
private schools.

Donald P. & Byrd M. Kelly Foundation
701 Harger Road, No. 150
Oak Brook, IL 60521
Contact: Laura K. McGrath, Treas.
Giving primarily in Illinois, with emphasis on
Chicago.

Carl B. & Florence E. King Foundation
5956 Sherry Lane, Suite 620
Dallas, TX 75225
Contact: Carl Yeckel, Vice President
Giving primarily in the Dallas area.

Thomas & Dorothy Leavey Foundation
4680 Wiltshire Boulevard
Los Angeles, CA 90010
(213) 930-4252
Contact: J. Thomas McCarthy, Trustee
Funding primarily in southern California to
Catholic organizations.

Levi Strauss Foundation
1155 Battery Street
San Francisco, CA 94111
(415) 544-2194
Contacts: Bay Area: Judy Belk, Director of
   Contributions; Mid-South Region: Myra Chow,
   Director of Contributions; Western Region:
   Mario Griffin, Director of Contributions; Rio
   Grande: Elvira Chavaria, Director of Contributions; Eastern Region: Mary Ellen
   McLoughlin, Director of Contributions
Generally limited to areas of company operations.

Lyndhurst Foundation
Suite 701, Tallan Building
100 West Martin Luther King Boulevard
Chattanooga, TN 37402-2561
(615) 756-0767
Contact: Jack E. Murrah, President
Limited to southeastern United States, especially
Chattanooga.

McDonnell Douglas Foundation
c/o McDonnell Douglas Corp.
P.O. Box 516, Mail Code 1001440
Street Louis, MO 63166
(314) 232-8464
Contact: Walter E. Diggs, Jr., President
Giving primarily in Arizona, California, Florida,
Missouri, Oklahoma, and Texas.

Meadows Foundation, Inc.
Wilson Historic Block
2922 Swiss Avenue
Dallas, TX 75204-5928
(214) 826-9431
Contact: Dr. Sally R. Lancaster, Executive
    Vice President
Funding limited to Texas.

Metropolitan Atlanta Community Foundation,
Inc.
The Hurt Building, Suite 449
Atlanta, GA 30303
(404) 688-5525
Contact: Alicia Philipp, Executive Director
Giving limited to the metropolitan area of
Atlanta, GA, and surrounding regions.

The Milken Family Foundation
c/o Foundation of the Milken Families
15250 Ventura Boulevard, 2nd floor
Sherman Oaks, CA 91403
Contact: Dr. Jules Lesner, Executive Director
Giving limited to the Los Angeles area.

National Council of Teachers of English
Grants Office
1111 Kenyon Road
Urbana, IL 61801
(217) 328-3870
Funding for language arts programs and projects.
Reading Research Education.

The New Hampshire Charitable Fund
One South Street
P.O. Box 1335
Concord, NH 03302-1335
(603) 225-6641
Contact: Deborah Cowan, Associate Director
Giving limited to New Hampshire.

The New Haven Foundation
70 Audubon Street
New Haven, CT 06510
(203) 777-2386
Contact: Helmer N. Ekstrom, Director
Giving primarily in the greater New Haven, CT,
and lower Naugatuck River Valley areas.

Dellora A. & Lester J. Norris Foundation
P.O. Box 1081
Street Charles, IL 60174
(312) 377-4111

Contact: Eugene Butler, Treasurer
Funding includes secondary education.

The Northern Trust Company Charitable Trust
c/o The Northern Trust Co., Corporate Affairs
Div.
50 South LaSalle Street
Chicago, IL 60675
(312) 444-3538
Contact: Marjorie W. Lundy, Vice President
Funding limited to the metropolitan Chicago
area.

The Principal Financial Group Foundation, Inc.
711 High Street
Des Moines, IA 50392-0150
(515) 247-5209
Contact: Debra J. Jensen, Secretary
Giving primarily in Iowa, with emphasis on the
Des Moines area.

Sid W. Richardson Foundation
309 Main Street
Forth Worth, TX 76102
(817) 336-0497
Contact: Valleau Wilkie, Jr., Executive Vice
    President
Funding limited to Texas.

R.J.R. Nabisco Foundation
1455 Pennsylvania Avenue, N.W., Suite 525
Washington, DC 20004
(202) 626-7200
Contact: Jaynie M. Grant, Executive Director

The Winthrop Rockefeller Foundation
308 East Eighth Street
Little Rock, AR 72202
(501) 376-6854
Contact: Mahlon Martin, President
Funding primarily in Arkansas, or for projects
that will benefit Arkansas.

The San Francisco Foundation
685 Market Street, Suite 910
San Francisco, CA 94105-9716
(415) 495-3100
Contact: Robert M. Fisher, Director
Giving limited to the San Francisco Bay area,
California counties of Alameda, Contra Costa,
Marin, San Francisco, and San Mateo.

Community Foundation of Santa Clara County
960 West Hedding, Suite 220
San Jose, CA 95126-1215
(408) 241-2666
Contact: Winnie Chu, Program Officer
Giving limited to Santa Clara County, California.

John & Dorothy Shea Foundation
655 Brea Canyon Road
Walnut, CA 91789
Giving primarily in California.

Harold Simmons Foundation
Three Lincoln Center
5430 LBJ Freeway, Suite 1700
Dallas, TX 75240-2697
(214) 233-1700
Contact: Lisa K. Simmons, President
Given limited to the Dallas area.

Sonart Family Foundation
15 Benders Drive
Greenwich, CT 06831
(203) 531-1474
Contact: Raymond Sonart, President

The Sosland Foundation
4800 Main Street, Suite 100
(816) 765-1000
Kansas City, MO 64112
Fax (816) 756-0494
Contact: Debbie Sosland-Edelman, Ph.D
Funding limited to Kansas City, Missouri, and
Kansas areas.

Community Foundation for Southeastern
Michigan
333 West Fort Street, Suite 2010
Detroit, MI 48226
(313) 961-6675
Contact: C. David Campbell, Vice President,
    Programs
Giving limited to southeastern Michigan.

Springs Foundation, Inc.
P.O. Drawer 460
Lancaster, SC 29720
(803) 286-2196
Contact: Charles A. Bundy, President
Giving limited to Lancaster County and/or the
townships of Ft. Mill and Chester, SC.

Strauss Foundation
c/o Fidelity Bank, N.A.
Broad & Walnut Sreets
Philadelphia, PA 19109
(215) 985-7717
Contact: Richard Irvin, Jr.
Giving primarily in Pennsylvania.

Stuart Foundations
425 Market Street, Suite 2835
San Francisco, CA 94105
(415) 495-1144
Contact: Theodore E. Lobman, President
Funding primarily in California; applications
from Washington will be considered.

T.L.L. Tempee Foundation
109 Tempee Boulevard
Lufkin, TX 75901
(409) 639-5197
Contact: M.F. Buddy Zeagler, Assistant Executive   Director & Controller
Giving primarily in counties in Texas constituting
the East Texas Pine Timber Belt.

Travelers Companies Foundation
One Tower Square
Hartford, CT 06183-1060
(203) 277-4079
(203) 277-4070
Funding for school programs limited to Hartford.

Turrell Fund
111 Northfield Avenue
West Orange, NJ 07052
(201) 325-5108
Contact: E. Belvin Williams, Executive Director
Giving limited to New Jersey, particularly the
northern urban areas centered in Essex County.
Also giving in Vermont.

U.S. West Foundation
7800 East Orchard Road, Suite 300
Englewood, CO 80111
(303) 793-6661
Contact: Larry J. Nash, Director Administration
Limited to states served by US WEST calling
areas. Address applications to local US WEST
Public Relations Office or Community Relations
Team.

Philip L. Van Every Foundation
c/o Lance, Inc.
P.O. Box 32368
Charlotte, NC 28232
(704) 554-1421
Giving primarily in North Carolina and South
Carolina.

Joseph B. Whitehead Foundation
1400 Peachtree Ctr. Tower
230 Peachtree Street, NW
Atlanta, GA 30303
(404) 522-6755
Contact: Charles H. McTier, President
Giving limited to metropolitan Atlanta, GA.

Winn-Dixie Stores Foundation
5050 Edgewood Court
Jacksonville, FL 32205
(904) 783-5000
Contact: Jack P. Jones, President
Giving limited to areas of company operation.

The Zellerbach Family Fund
120 Montgomery Street, Suite 2125
San Francisco, CA 94104
(415) 421-2629
Contact: Edward A. Nathan, Executive Director
Giving primarily in the San Francisco Bay area.

This chapter includes a sampling of foundations
that can be contacted for funding your curriculum
project. By no means are these all the resources
that can be tapped. Remember, think creatively!
Are there any community service organizations
such as the Jaycees, Lion's Club, or Rotary
International that can be contacted? Is there a
local community fund that supports education
projects? Ask friends and neighbors about the
organizations they support. Ask if you can use
their name as a reference--and be sure to get the
names of the people to contact. Make initial
contacts and don't be discouraged by rejections.
The money is there for you. All you need to do is
be persistent!

References

Directory of Research Grants. 1992. Phoenix: Oryx
Press.
Information on a wide variety of funding
organizations; index includes terms for
elementary education, secondary education,
science education, teacher education, etc.
The Foundation Grants Index. 1992. New York:
Foundation Center.
Provides funding patterns and other information about the most influential foundations in
the U.S.
1991 Catalogue of Federal Domestic Assistance.
1991. Washington, DC: Government Printing
Office.
Source Book Profiles. 1992. New York: Foundation Center.
Information on the one thousand largest U.S.
foundations.

4

TOPICS IN THE ENGLISH/LANGUAGE ARTS CURRICULUM, GRADES K-12

by Irene D. Thomas
Lecturer, English and Education
Sonoma State University, Rohnert Park, California

ATTEMPTING to write a list of suggested topics to be taught in the English language arts today feels a bit like straddling separating landmasses during an earthquake. The curriculum, as most teachers know well, has undergone some considerable rumbling and has split into major divisions. The literature-based curriculum and the communication-based model are just two. Rarely has there been as much disagreement about the structure and content of a curriculum as there has been about the English language arts in the last few decades. If this sounds like a disclaimer, then it probably is: the topics that curriculum designers might consider essential will depend on their personal view of what the language arts base should be. In an attempt to reflect the diversity of our discipline, I am sure I have nonetheless left out topics that some readers will consider de rigueur and have included topics that to others are trivial. Still, there are some important trends we can point to (see chapter 5).

Then, too, a partial disclaimer must be made about the very essence of this chapter's purpose. Admittedly, when I began the project, I had my doubts as to the value of identifying grade level topics at a time when the trend is away from such specification. I wondered if creating a list of

topics wasn't just another encouragement toward "teaching toward the test" through drill and practice—a dangerous and often fruitless way to pursue literacy, as so many teachers have discovered. As an alternative, many teachers agree that the enlightened movement today is toward "whole language," and thus the integration of the language arts and the relegation of skills to the category of subskills. Subskills (spelling, punctuation, grammatical labeling, and so on) are so named because they are to be acquired in the larger context of writing and reading instruction, not as ends in themselves—the formerly hallowed objective of most drill and practice activities.

Nonetheless, with its limitations fully in mind, I came to see this making of a scope-and-sequence outline as creating a product of some value to those who design, implement, or evaluate curriculum. First of all, since I have attempted to reflect a cross-section of diverse regions of the country, with varying population and demographics, the users of this handbook may benefit from a more pluralistic view than their own state affords. Secondly, while attempting to accurately reflect the realities, I have also tried to pick and choose from what I judged to be the best practices found in my searches. And finally, I came to see the value of using a document like this to help teachers in one of their most difficult roles: student evaluation. In the mix of activities and skills that follow, teachers may find guidelines— not prescriptions—they might use in creating diagnostic tools and meaningful evaluative instruments for a student's performance at any given level.

That is not to suggest that this outline is as specific as everyone would wish. I have intentionally alternated between general topics and specific suggestions because that mix reflects the way state and local curriculum guidelines tend to be written today. Some guidelines, for example, are left open and general enough to allow teachers to apply the materials they have at their disposal. However, when I have offered a very specific piece of literature or teaching procedure as an example, it is because I judged it to be an exceptionally rich idea and worthy of special mention. At the risk of producing a possibly confusing model, I nonetheless decided to include sometimes inconsistent levels of specificity.

Similarly, please remember that this writer, like most educators today, subscribes to the Brunerian concept of the spiral curriculum (Bruner, 1960) which holds that any concept can be taught at any time in a child's development. The process that follows from the Brunerian theory allows students to focus on any one concept or skill in an increasingly sophisticated and challenging way throughout their education. It also means that few concepts or skills are too advanced to be introduced at the lower levels in appropriate contexts. For that reason, I suggest that early childhood specialists look ahead to the later levels as well, for ideas that may be genuinely applicable to early childhood even though not specified under K-3.

Keeping the spiral curriculum in mind may also help the teacher/curriculum specialist using this outline to select strands and make specific suggestions for implementing them beyond the admittedly sketchy suggestions offered here. For example, under "Literature," there is a strand for "relating self to literature" which appears beginning with kindergarten and continues through grade 12. How a teacher might effect this strand in the classroom is beyond the scope of this chapter, this being primarily a matrix rather than a teaching document.

A Note on Organization

While most state and district curriculum guides I examined are organized around loosely struc-

tured guidelines (goals rather than prescriptions), some states still include a more traditional scope and sequence. (Again, see chapter 5 for specific comparisons.) In order to reflect both of these realities, I have chosen to organize by grade level and subdivide by guideline objectives for each of the four language arts. Where relevant, I include subskills under the heading "Reading and Language Skills" in order to reflect the fact that these particular skills are often specified for that grade level. By specifying these skills, I do not suggest that they be taught in isolation, as ends in themselves. As mentioned earlier, I support the movement toward context-based skills instruction as a principle of the whole language and "language experience" approaches. The scope for each of the areas discussed below is adapted from the California State Department of Education's *English Language Arts Framework* (1987).

Scope for Grades K-3

For students in K-3, the understanding of meaning is the most important reason for learning language and may well be the primary focus of all language activities. Using the "language experience" model, students use common words from the environment and from their own dictated stories in order to read more easily because they already understand the meaning.

It is here that instruction in phonics can help students understand the relationships between letters and sounds so as to unlock meaning. And it is here that the writing process in all its stages can be introduced in the context of whole language.

Because of the wide variation in readiness, early language arts programs must provide for flexibility in pacing and content. For example, students at the emerging literacy stage benefit from a program that is rich in listening activities and language experience activities. All children at this level benefit from daily reading aloud by the teacher and by volunteers, as well as by having the opportunity to dictate their ideas to others, which then provide the wordstock for their very first reading and writing attempts. Teachers need to be especially alert for opportunities to reinforce children's language growth: opportunities to speak and be heard, to share their experiences, to help assess their accomplishments. All major movements today stress that while instruction in phonics should be direct in K-3, the conventions of spelling, handwriting, grammar, and punctuation should be taught only when needed to aid the written communication process.

Kindergarten (pre-primary)

I. Literature
  A. Comprehension and Response
  Listen to nursery rhymes, folktales, poetry, and stories
  Look at story pictures, films; discuss: who is it about? What happens? What is seen?
  Relate self to story, picture, or film: What would I do ...?
  Browse through library; notice how alphabetical order is used
  Explore ABC books
  Attend children's theater
  Attend story hour
  Illustrate story/poem: draw, pantomime, create collage
  Compare different illustrations
  Use language experience to "read" their own responses
  B. Understanding Self
  Relate literature to own life and surrounding world: "I feel like ..."; "I have seen ..."
  If I were [character] what would I do?
  C. Growth in Language
  Retell story, preserving sequence
  Repeat poetic language
  Begin to recognize words from language experience charts
  Learn new words: color words, high-frequency words
  Classify objects belonging in the same category
  Sequence events in a story
  Predict outcome of a story or event
II. Reading and Language Skills
(often taught directly at this level, ideally in context of language experience)
  Recognize letter names, upper and lower-case
  Recognize color words and high frequency sight words
  Identify words or pictures beginning with consonant sounds
  Recognize and use rhyming words
  Recognize different ways to spell one sound
  Use language experience model for building sentences and phonic activities

III. Speaking
  A. Purposes
  Memorize core works of poetry and nursery rhymes
  Focus on feeling, ritualizing, imagining
  Retell a story
  B. Audience
  Choral reading, programs for parents
  Choose topics of interest to self and others
  Talk to, but not for, others
  C. Language Skills
  Show normal vocabulary and grammatical development
  D. Evaluation/Feedback
  Begin to show acceptance of feedback, rather than purely personal reactions.
IV. Listening
  A. Attend and Discriminate
  Listen for story main idea
  Listen for sequencing
  B. Assign Meanings—Language Skills
  C. Respond
  Learn sounds and rhythms of language by listening and chanting familiar rhymes and stories
V. Writing
(the transition from speaking to writing)
  Participate in writing stories through:
  A. Prewriting
  Brainstorming, discussion, artwork, role playing
  B. Writing
  Make a picture and tell others about it
  Dictate class and individual stories, autobiographical incidents, and observations
  Dictate descriptive phrases or captions for artworks, science displays, maps, etc.
  Dictate vocabulary to be recorded on cards which can be arranged into sentences that have meaning for student
  Through language experience method, write and reads what it says
  C. Writing to Publish
  Make individual book, contribute to class story
  Display work
  Publish in class or school newsletter
  Begin writing for an audience and a purpose: a note or invitation to parents, a class book of biographies, a recommendation to a visitor of a place to see in your town

VI. Writing across the Curriculum
   Social Studies
   In kindergarten children first begin to understand that school is a place for learning and working. Most children are eager. Most will be working in groups for the first time. They will need to learn about sharing, taking turns, respecting the rights of others, taking care of themselves. Children can also discover how other people have learned and worked together by hearing stories of times past and through other literature.

   Examples
   Discuss stories, fairy tales, and nursery rhymes that incorporate conflict and raise value issues in terms of characters' behaviors and the consequences of those behaviors.

   Explore the school and its neighborhood—write and read about it through language experience method.

   Compare themselves with children of past eras, considering how their lives would have been different in other times and places; illustrate, write, and read a few sentences about this comparison.

   Science
   Students will identify the five senses and notice words in literature (read to them) that appeal to senses. They might label pictures of sensory experiences with the appropriate sense(s).

   Students will be exposed to classification of like objects, and subdivisions within classes, and be exposed to (perhaps recognize and write) the words that describe these: animal attributes; classroom objects; parts of the body; seasons; senses; objects in the nighttime and daytime sky.

   Critical Thinking
   Teacher may read aloud selections that deal with a character's attempts to be something s/he is not; e.g. *Harry the Dirty Dog* by Gene Zion. Students discuss how and why a character might finally decide to be him/herself. Students dictate or write their thoughts about similar characters from other stories or about real people they know.

   For more ideas on critical thinking at all grade levels, please see table 1, a chart utilizing Bloom's taxonomy.

   Example of an integrated language arts

lesson: students listen to a fable read aloud by the teacher. Students discuss several of Aesop's fables as they are encouraged to discover what fables have in common. In pairs, or in small groups, children choose a moral, animal characters, and a surprise ending, and write a fable of their own, which may then be made into an illustrated book.

Grades 1-3 (Primary)
   Continuing the language-rich environment of the kindergarten classroom, teachers of grades 1-3 help students to use language effectively and appreciate the language expression of others. Teachers provide diverse opportunities for stimulating all forms of communication, make available all sorts of materials, and integrate the language arts within daily lessons. For example, discussion helps to clarify ideas and issues; listening encourages appreciation for good writing; reading helps to prepare for writing; and writing uncovers critical questions that need discussion as well as gaps in critical thinking.

I. Literature
   A. Comprehension and Response
      Read literary "core" works together in class
      Select independent reading from class library
      Listen to stories and poems read aloud by teacher
      Begin reading predictable books, *Brown Bear,* etc., for reinforced vocabulary
      Become acquainted with classics of children's literature
      Talk about a literary work: who, what, when, and where?
      Predict outcome
      Identify main idea
      Discuss characters, choose a favorite, impersonate
      Dramatize story, poem: reader's theater, puppetry, choral reading
      Write about story, poem; discuss and perform in a group
      Summarize story in different ways: illustration, retelling
      Write a new ending for a story
      Grades 2 and 3: add legends, non-fiction, fantasy, stories that have different versions in different cultures
      Distinguish between fact and fiction
      Identify cause and effect

Name examples and traits of various genres read

B. Understand Self, Cultural Heritage, and Others

Relate self to literature: "What would I do if . . . ?" "When I was . . . "

Relate work to family, friends, school, and community: "I remember. . . . ; I have seen. . . ."

Read fable or fairy tale with strong value issue; e.g., "The City Mouse and the Country Mouse."

Discuss how different ways of thinking and living have advantages and disadvantages.

Students can write a "moral" to another fable.

C. Growth in Language

Predict, with teacher's help, which words students would expect to find in a story about a specific subject. Look for these during and after reading. Record these in a word-book.

Select words that are new in a story. Define these with context clues; record them in a personal word-book to be used again in writing.

Retell story in sequence

Identify characters and setting

Notice unusual uses of language

Learn new words

Continue language experience to acquire spelling and reading improvement

II. Reading and Language Skills

(often taught directly at this level, ideally in context of language experience)

Alphabetization

Use of alphabet in library and alphabet books

Color words, number words, sight vocabulary from reading

Introduction to synonyms and antonyms

Different ways to spell one sound

Continued use of language experience model for building sentences: students create word cards as a means to acquiring written vocabulary and performing phonic activities

Although controversial in principle, these following subskills are sometimes identified in school-district curriculum guidelines for this level. Advocates of "whole language" instruction, however, do not necessarily specify these skills but rather assume they will be acquired by students naturally as they participate in a rich language environment.

Language subskills

Correct singular and plural regular nouns

Correct forms of regular verbs

Common irregular verbs

Irregular plurals

Subject/verb agreement

Production of basic sentence patterns and variations

Reading skills sometimes identified (in sequence of expectations):

Phonic analysis of initial and final consonants

Long and short vowels

Recognize CVC and CVCe patterns, vowel digraphs

Compound words, inflectional endings

Root words, affixes (-ly, -er, -est, -ness)

Hear syllables and stressed syllable

Alphabetize by initial, then by second letter

Consult dictionary for pronunciation, meaning

III. Speaking

A. Purposes

Memorize core works of children's poetry and nursery rhymes

Gain experience speaking for self and interacting with a group

Read orally

Show and tell

Tell of personal experiences and feelings

Retell stories

Contribute ideas and information in group setting

Recognize persuasion as a purpose and identify reasons that persuade a peer or adult

Give a short sequence of directions

B. Audience

Choral reading, programs for parents

Establish relationship with listeners; begin to adapt to age, etc., of audience

Respond to thoughts expressed by others

Use visual aids effectively

C. Language Skills

Use appropriate words to describe

Pronounce clearly

Take turns, establish eye contact

D. Evaluation/Feedback

Ask appropriate questions

Become aware of importance of listeners' response

Learn how to accept and give constructive criticism

IV. Listening
  A. Attend and Discriminate
     Information, directions, main idea
  B. Assign Meanings—Language Skills
  C. Respond
     Sounds and rhythms of language by listening
        and chanting familiar rhymes and stories
     Listen for rhyme, alliteration, onomato-
        poeia
V. Writing
     A popular guideline: students become
  aware that writing is a means of clarifying
  thinking and that it is a process which embodies several stages, including prewriting, drafting, receiving responses, revising, editing, and
  postwriting activities.
     A guideline growing in popularity: students
  learn the conventions of the English language
  (usage, spelling, punctuation, and capitalization) through all the language arts and through
  direct instruction when necessary.

Purposes of Writing
     A number of state curriculum guides
  identify specific genres to be addressed at each
  grade level. Some teachers prefer to think in
  terms of the "domains of writing": sensory/
  descriptive, imaginative/narrative, practical/
  informative, analytic/expository. Others stay
  with the traditional and more directive terms:
  functions or purposes. For this grade level, we
  may see the following configuration of purposes, adapted from New York State's curriculum guide:
To express self:
  • Sequence of sentences recounting feelings
    or reactions to an experience (first oral
    then written)
  • Autobiographical sketch of one event
    (maintaining first-person point of view)
  • Friendly letter
  • Poem (using a poetic form and rhythmic
    language; possibly using a model or
    completing a prompt poem)
To narrate:
  • Personal narrative: who, what, when, why,
    how
  • Fictional story, beginning with a prompt
    or story starter, or writing a new ending
    to another story
  • Journal entry
To explain:
  • Word/phrase caption or label
  • Sentence: first dictated, then written with

punctuation
  • Sequence of sentences giving directions
  • Sequence of sentences explaining "how
    to"
  • Letter of invitation

To describe:
  • Words, phrases, captions (in response to a
    visiting pet, students produce words for
    what they see, hear, smell, touch
  • Sentence about a person, animal, or
    object (begin with completing sentence
    frame)
  • Several sentences about the above subject

The Processes
A. Prewriting
   Dictate dialogue to develop into a story,
     puppet show, readers' theater
   Dictate/write notes about a class experience,
     trip, interview
   Tap personal experiences for ideas
   Use brainstorming and story frames
   Recognize what it means to stay on the
     topic
B. Drafting
   Recognize that function of first draft is to
     capture ideas
   Recognize that writer aims for an audience
     and purpose
   Write brief descriptions and stories
   Narrate in chronological order
   Write simple chants, complete poems with a
     format model
   Classify differences and similarities of
     objects and events
   Arrange ideas and information for clarity
C. Revising
   Begin to see written work as a product
   Add additional information in subsequent
     drafts
   May discover what he or she means in the
     process of revising
   Write two or more alternative openings and
     choose which is best
   Develop tolerance for "messing up" a draft
     (here word processing is an advantage
     when available)
   Recognize some advantages to rearrange-
     ment for clarity, purpose, etc.
   Participate in peer response to writing by
     asking questions of each other; "read
     around groups"

IV. Editing
   The integrated approach: as the need arises,
   teacher provides direct instruction in punctuation of simple sentences, providing models that
   are posted and using students' own sentences
   whenever possible. Teachers can, for example,
   create sentence strips using students' sentences, with punctuation omitted. Students
   insert punctuation using punctuation cards or
   markers, and explain to each other why
   punctuation was needed there.

   Students come to realize that conventions of
      writing are used mostly to provide clarity
   Students may be allowed to use invented
      spellings through first grade
   Subsequently they learn to use a systematic
      method for spelling independently and
      look to spelling patterns for help
   Begin to recognize complete sentences and
      end-sentence punctuation
   Edit their work for sentence completeness
      after peer and teacher input
   Edit their work for capitalization in the
      context of complete sentences
   Join related sentences into paragraphs
   Rewrite using legible manuscript letters

Example of an integrated lesson for this grade level:
   Teacher presents two pieces of literature on
   the same theme, one through storytelling and
   one through reading aloud. Talk about the
   theme and how each work handles it. Students
   write/dictate a story of their own about the
   theme and receive feedback through the read-
   around method. The teacher leads a discussion
   to determine what students liked about each
   story. Students edit and revise for sentence
   completeness and punctuation, posting their
   work or collecting it in a class anthology.
VI. Writing across the Curriculum
   Science
      Teachers give directions for a science
   experiment such as growing lima beans.
   Students take notes, then write their observations of the process, perhaps keeping a journal
   of the plant's progress.
      During a lesson on shadows, students go
   outside to look at shadows and teacher uses a
   flashlight to show how shadows are formed.
   This is followed by reading stories and poems
   about shadows, such as: "My Shadow," by
   Robert Louis Stevenson; *Mi Amiga la
   Sombrera*, by Alma Flor Ada; "Shadow," by
   Marcia Brown.

Students discuss how shadows make them
feel. The unit can culminate in making shadow
puppets and writing poems/stories/memories
about shadows in their lives.

Social Studies
   After reading or hearing literature or
nonfiction about a place with vivid characteristics, such as the zoo, students write or dictate
dialogue to develop into a story about that
place. The story can then be performed as
puppet show or readers' theater.
VII. Critical Thinking
   Please see the taxonomy chart on page 76 for a
   critical-thinking matrix which can be adapted
   to any grade/age level. Teachers of grades K-3
   may find the chart useful by adapting the "cue
   words" to their students' vocabularies, and by
   constructing grade level activities/assignments
   around appropriate children's literature.

Scope for Grades 3-6

At about age ten, students become interested in
the world beyond their immediate environment.
It is here that background information brought in
by students or the teacher becomes especially
important for the language arts. Continue to
integrate the language arts into other curricula.
Fill classrooms with books and allow visits to the
library. Aim for a teaching plan that produces
eager readers who can communicate their
reactions to what they read. Continue to read
literature aloud, making choices that will stretch
students' vocabulary comprehension and acquisition. Sharing ideas in small groups and speaking
more formally to the whole group help to build
self-confidence and model good listening skills.
Students should write daily—even if only a brief
journal entry—and should revise and edit regularly. The conventions, for the most part, should
be taught in the context of purposeful reading
and writing tasks, always with the goal of communicating meaningfully as the major purpose.

   Author's note: the exception among conventions may be spelling skills. Students at this level
can benefit from regularly encountering the
principles of language change, systematic groupings, regularities and exceptions, as well as
principles and patterns, which may aid them in
the editing process.

I. Literature
   A. Comprehension and Response
      Read, silently and aloud, classics and award-winning books (core works) and free selection
      Decide which current candidates for book prizes deserve to win; vote on books
      Read fictionalized biographies, historical fiction
      Use film and other audiovisual media
      Attend theater
      Discuss why an author would write a certain work in a certain way
      Recognize difference between first and third point of view
      Relate one work to another
      Differentiate fact and opinion, cause and effect, motives and results of action
      Identify an implied main idea
      Compare different media versions of a story
      Give interpretive reading
      Prepare related speech
      Create sequel, new ending, illustration
      Impersonate character; improvise talk between two characters
      Select books for independent reading from a collection put together by teacher/ librarian on similar subjects or by same author
      Grades 5 and 6: recognize simile and metaphor as comparisons
      Recognize personification as a literary device.
   B. Understanding Self, Cultural Heritage and Others
      Relate self, family, community, school, and news of the day to literary work
      Read stories or biographies of immigrants; extend crosscultural awareness, e.g., interview students or family members who came from elsewhere. Report to class in groups through writing, video, audio
      Read with focus on characters, showing understanding through mock trials, story theater, reader's theater, impersonating character, writing new stories, episodes, or endings for them
      Respond to affective literature in writing; for example, teacher reads a story about someone who changes, e.g., "The Girl Who Loved the Wind," by Jan Yolen. Students write about how they accept change in their lives, giving examples of

what makes people change.
   C. Growth in Language
      Begin to recognize figurative language and employ unusual uses of language
      Locate words that are unfamiliar; explain contextual clues; hunt in other texts for similar words, new words, and contexts
      Begin structural analysis of base words, compound words, suffixes, syllables, stress pattern changes
      Identify literary devises such as alliteration, humor, exaggeration, puns
      Experiment with various poetic and story forms
      Identify and give examples of synonyms, homophones, and antonyms for specific words in story
      Predict, with teacher's help, words they would expect to find in a story about a specific subject. After reading, review which words they encountered and add them to their word-books
      Select new words encountered in a story. Define with context clues, and write these in personal word-book or file. Students might consult these periodically and reuse them in new writing
   D. Integrating with other subjects
      Science lesson on shadows: followed by reading stories about shadows
      Experience before reading; e.g., "Strega Nona" by Tomie de Paola—first experience pasta in the uncooked form, then cooked
      Use dictionary and encyclopedia to locate information about social studies and science topics
      Use graphic sources: tables, lists, charts, graphs, maps, globes, time-lines, scale drawings, transportation schedules. Compare information from medium to medium
      Introduce American dialects and link them to immigration patterns across the continent and in the home state

II. Reading and Language Skills
   Although controversial in principle, these following subskills are sometimes identified in school district curriculum guidelines. Advocates of whole language instruction, however, may not specify such skills but rather assume they will be acquired by students naturally as they participate in a rich language environment.

This writer believes that sentence combining, spelling principles, and topics in language history are worthy of classroom time at this level, especially in meaningful context.

Language Subskills Sometimes Identified
    Write correct possessive and pronoun forms
    Produce a variety of sentence patterns
    Coordinate and subordinate sentence elements appropriate to meaning
    Work toward more fluent sentences, avoiding choppy or run-on sentences.
    Introduction of sentence combining as a method for practicing all of the above skills
    Work on agreement between pronouns and antecedents

Reading Skills Sometimes Identified
    Understand more complex words in context, using context to unlock meaning
    Use more complex structural analysis— words with several prefixes, introduction to Greek and Latin prefixes/suffixes
    Use dictionary for definitions, determining levels of usage, word origins, and histories

Grades 5 and 6:
    Predict probable outcomes
    Draw logical conclusions
    Make generalizations
    Recall specific facts and details that support main idea
    Arrange events in sequential order when not overtly stated
    Arrange events according to degree of importance
    Recognize various persuasive devices

Spelling Skills Sometimes Identified
    Students at these levels are able to grasp the abstractions of categorizing and are therefore apt to benefit from occasional spelling instruction based on sound-to-spelling correspondences, their regularities and exceptions. Students should be able to group words according to spelling and tentatively formulate rules or mnemonic devices by induction. For example, c/k/ck ch/tch ou/ow oi/oy.
    Similarly, because their sense of historical time is now better developed, students will be interested in the historical origins of many mysteries of English spelling. For example, the principle that pronunciation changes but

spelling doesn't explains: igh, ign, kn, almost all the silent letters in English, and the borrowed spellings such as "ch" for /k/, qu, etc.

Handwriting Activities
    Students write letters to authors of books they like, trying to make a good impression through handwriting.

III. Speaking
  A. Purposes
    The five functions of speaking are often identified as: expressing feeling, ritualizing, imagining, informing, controlling. Students should have opportunities at this level to:
    Experience all five functions and expand their repertory
    Make organized oral presentations
    Give directions on "how to..."
    Interpret literature
    Adapt content and formality to purpose and audience
  B. Audience
    Use techniques to gain attention and develop interest of audience
    Keep to the subject
    Recognize need for background information (especially for persuasion)
  C. Experiences
    Role playing, asking relevant questions, telling stories with a moral
    Explaining spatial, temporal, causal relationships
    Creating ads for products
    Making introductions
    Develop interviewing skills: students can interview family members or other adults about their work, etc., first developing a questionnaire, and finally reporting to class
    Participate in committees and other group problem-solving activities
  D. Feedback and Evaluation
    Speaker and listeners together evaluate selection of criteria
    Speaker begins to give and receive tactful, constructive criticism
IV. Listening
  A. Attend and Discriminate
    Sense emotional language-hidden content
    Sense content of message
    Sense judgmental tone
    Determine a speaker's motive

Recognize patterns, transitions
Distinguishes fact from opinion
Follow logical organization of an oral
   presentation
B. Assign Meanings—Language skills
Listen for accuracy and memory: the game
   "gossip" (passing a "message" along
   through a group); play "secretary"
   dictating notes to one another for writing
   ideas, brainstorming, etc.
C. Respond
Ask appropriate questions from a speaker
Search memory for details to relate to new
   data
Refine note-taking skills
Study oral literature that survived through
   listening and memory; e.g., "tall tales"
   and how they reflect American values
Listen to tall tales read aloud and identify
   the exaggerations
Students might write their own tall tales in
   groups, and use storytelling to present
   the tales to the class.

V. Writing
    A popular guideline: students become
aware that writing is a way to clarify thinking,
and that it is a process which embodies several
stages, including prewriting, drafting, receiving
responses, revising, editing, and postwriting
activities.
    A guideline growing in popularity: students
learn the conventions of the English language
(usage, spelling, punctuation and capitalization) through all the language arts and through
direct instruction when necessary.

Purposes for writing
    A number of state curriculum guides
identify specific genres to be addressed at each
grade level. Some teachers prefer to think in
terms of the Domains of Writing as defined in
writing project terms: sensory/descriptive;
imaginative/narrative; practical/informative;
analytical/expository. Others stay with the
traditional and more directive terms "functions" or "purposes." For this grade level, we
may see the following configuration of purposes, adapted from New York State's curriculum guide:

To express self:
Paragraph(s) expressing personal feelings or
   reactions to an experience of event
Autobiographical sketch with a focus and a

conclusion
Journal entry: primarily a source of topics
   for fuller writings
Friendly letter: such as congratulations, get
   well, sharing an event
Poem: couplet, haiku, cinquain, free verse

To narrate:
Narrate actual experience, chronologically
   and consistently
Brief story: sequence, create, title, maintain
   consistent point of view
Animal fable
Invented folktale
Skit: dialogue
Feature article based on interview

To explain:
Give directions to get from place to place
How to, with procedural markers
Business letter of request
Report: notetaking, organizing, objective
   diction and tone
News article and headline
Biographical sketch based on an interview:
   maintain third person
Book report

To describe:
Paragraph(s) describing a real or imaginary
   person or place advertisement for a lost
   pet or object

To persuade:
Advertisement, commercial: connotative
   value of words, description, organization
Contest entry: adhering to requirements
Letter to persuade someone to adopt an
   opinion, accompanied or followed by a
   speech

The processes
A. Prewriting
Students begin to consider audience and
   purpose in writing
Students show some ability to plan and use
   outside resources
Teacher provides for wide variety of thinking and planning activities: brainstorming, quickwrites
Teacher helps child focus on audience and
   purpose
Teacher gives children experience with a
   variety of forms

B. Drafting

Students become capable of focusing on one topic

Students show more syntactic skill

Students may show willingness to improve text

Teacher models the writing process, going through drafts

Teacher models questioning strategies and tentativeness

Teacher encourages student interaction during composing

C. Revising

Students are more able to see writing as a product to be worked on

Students may tend to be overly concerned with mechanics or easily frustrated

Students may need help with logic and sequence

Teacher helps students to read critically

Teacher helps students to focus on the global issues first: content, organization, purpose

Teacher does not require revision of every assignment

Teacher encourages the "seeds" of peer response

Teacher models questioning and envisioning audience/purpose

D. Editing

Students may have better grasp of conventions

Students may be capable of referring to a handbook for help as well as some self-correction

Teacher uses patterns of error as a base of skills instruction:

• Doesn't require corrections in all areas simultaneously

• Gives focus to sentence completeness and end-punctuation

• Using overhead projector, engages students in editing sample paragraphs, and explaining insertion of punctuation

• Introduces sentence combining using students' sentences

• Tries "dictation" from student textbook as a "warm up" to editing. Students self-correct against original text

• Encourages students to help each other in response groups

• Gives students a rationale for editing

• Gives opportunities for class publications

Example of scenario typical of grades five and beyond: After brainstorming and writing a first draft, students respond in groups to each other's writing and, with teacher's help, use relevant handbooks to help each other edit.

VI. Writing across the Curriculum

Social Studies

Students write letters to England from a pilgrim's perspective. They brainstorm about the conditions, attitudes, feelings, and physical challenges facing the pilgrims. Then they write a letter to a loved one left behind, describing their life in the New World.

Students read books about life during the Revolutionary War period, then discuss and write about life during this period. To make the conflict come alive, students can be either British or Yankees and develop debates, mock trials, etc.

Since the study of your state is usually introduced in the intermediate grades, this is a propitious place in the curriculum to integrate language skills and practice with history, geography, demographics, and current events. The literature students encounter can come from the legends and folk stories of your state. If there is cultural and ethnic diversity in your state, this is a good time to introduce immigration patterns and the richness of experience available to residents as a result of diversity.

Writing/Social Studies

Students might listen to family histories of long-time residents who are invited to visit the classroom; they might take notes, read pioneer stories, interview older family members and neighbors, and write brief biographies of long-time residents to share with the class. One of many writing assignments could be a comparison of your state with another in terms of natural resources, settlement history, and industrial profile—all of which call for an introduction to the encyclopedia as a reference work.

Science

Along with their study and exploration of weather, students read stories dealing with weather (*The First Snow*, by Helen Coutant). Students can read nonfiction books about weather along with newspaper weather reports, TV weather reports, articles about weather disasters. Sixth graders can analyze effects of weather on economy, and research such topics as how to create weather on stage or sound effects on radio.

VII. Notes on Critical Thinking Skills

Critical thinking, as both a learning tool and as part of the composing process, has been much discussed in the last decade. Some teachers have utilized Bloom's taxonomy as a way of approaching the tasks we should ask students to perform in building their critical acuity (higher-order thinking skills). Wherever possible, it has been suggested, we need to ask students to use more than one thinking mode, and our writing assignments should reflect the application of more than one mode. (The activities described under *Writing across the Curriculum* are especially rich in overlapping thinking modes.)

In *Thinking/Writing*, a new book by Carol Booth Olson and her colleagues from the UC Irvine Writing Project, the author puts forth Bloom's taxonomy with a new slant—the integration of thinking and writing within the process writing model. The authors contend:

> We perceive all thinking, whether it be at the knowledge level or evaluation level, to be critical. Generative writing requires that teachers tap into all levels of the taxonomy.... However, these acts of cognition do not necessarily occur one at a time or progress in a certain order. At any stage, the writer may simultaneously tap two or more thinking levels. . . . We also contend that all thinking levels pose their own difficulty; knowledge is not always a simpler behavior than comprehension. (Olson, date 13)

And to illustrate this expansion of the taxonomy of critical thinking into writing tasks, the authors provide us with a Bloom-based chart, a simplified form of which appears below (table 1). Teachers of all grade levels may want to refer to this chart since its curricular implications cross all grade-level boundaries. Consider this the spiral curriculum at its best!

Scope for Grades 6-8

Many special needs must be addressed in the middle school grades. Students begin to think more abstractly and develop a broader base of knowledge, yet they are pulled in many direc-

tions. They demand independence, but still need stability and caring adults. Finding the balance is a challenge to teachers. More than ever, students need to find and experience real-world applications to keep them motivated, such as small group discussions, drama and speech groups, leadership campaigns—lots of opportunities for structured, purposeful communication. They should begin to acquire the research and questioning skills necessary for success in other subject areas. Most important perhaps is that between the ages of ten and fifteen, students enter a critical period for developing the pleasure-reading habit. Any way we can foster that habit can help to produce life-long learners rather than turned-off adolescents.

To expand their reading, a school library and staff are essential. Similarly, lots of writing for different purposes, informal and formal, should be encouraged. This is the ideal time to employ revising strategies, peer response and evaluation, and, if possible, to introduce the joys of word processing for all the stages of the writing process. A revising table or corner can be set up, stocked with dictionaries, thesauri, etc., where students who are editing can work in pairs to improve their writing for organization and correctness.

I. Literature

A. Comprehension and Response

Read literary works silently and aloud

Use film and other media representing literature

Attend theater

Read classics and high quality young adult books

Discuss motives of characters, results of human actions

Discuss why an author would write a work in this form

Compare written and visual version of selections

Write responses: imaginative, essay

Change form: story to play, poem to essay

Dramatize some parts of a work

Integrate with listening: teacher reads a short story aloud and chooses a particular word or sentence which has significant meaning as the theme. Students select a similar sentence in another work. They do a quick-write to explain their rationale, and in small groups they read papers aloud and compare according to a rubric.

Table 1. Taxonomy of Critical Thinking as Applied to Writing Tasks		
Thinking Level	**Cue Words**	**Sample Directions**
Knowledge (Recall: remembering previously learned material)	Observe, repeat, recall, recount, label/name, sort, cluster, outline, list, record, match, define, memorize	Recall names and relationships of characters in a drama. Cluster the characteristics of the author's style. Define denotation and connotation.
Comprehension (Translate: grasping the meaning)	Recognize, express, locate, explain, identify, review, restate, cite, paraphrase, document/ support, tell, describe, summarize, report, precis/abstract	Explain how words and actions affect our perceptions of a play's characters. Restate the story of [character] in your own words, incorporating all parts contributed by the class.
Application (Generalize: using the material in new and concrete situations)	Select, use, dramatize, illustrate, manipulate, sequence, imagine, show, organize, imitate, demonstrate, frame	Imitate a story by writing about a similar event in your own life. Apply the definition of a word as it is used in a story to another situation.
Analysis (Breakdown/discover: breaking down material so that it is more easily understood)	Examine, classify, outline, map, question, analyze, compare, research, interpret, refute, conclude, infer	Analyze which letter from a group of friends would be the most persuasive. Examine Thanksgiving from the points of view of a child, a parent, and a turkey.
Synthesis (Compose: putting material together to form a new whole)	Propose, plan, compose, formulate, design, construct, emulate, imagine, create, invent	Imagine you've discovered a new animal; write an encyclopedia entry for it. Speculate about a person based only on a photograph. Compose an alternate ending for a story.
Evaluation (Judge: judging the value of material for a given purpose)	Compare, rank, judge, decide, rate, evaluate, predict, criticize, argue, justify, convince, persuade, assess, value	Persuade a specific audience through letter. Assess a character's actions in terms of his values. Assess the overall learning experience of doing a writing assignment.

B. Understanding Self, Cultural Heritage and Others

Relate self to literary work

Relate one work to another

Discover and distinguish: fact and opinion, cause and effect, motive and result, fantasy and reality

Relate literary works to self, family and friends, school, community, news of the day, historic figures, and events

Read stories about a major event such as death, and relate them to similar events in their own lives

Read stories or poems set in the kind of environment students live in: rural, urban, town. Show slides, films, oral histories. Students write descriptive phrases, metaphors, similes that become the basis of original poems about their

environment.
C. Growth in Language
Recognize story elements: plot, character-
ization, setting, theme
Learn types and structure of a variety of
literary works
Relate content to literary form
Recognize and respond to literary features
and conventions
Expand vocabulary: teacher gives students
key vocabulary before they read aloud a
chapter of a novel. From context, students infer meaning and discuss inferences. Finally, someone reads aloud
dictionary definition.
D. Integration with other Subjects
Read *The Diary of a Young Girl* by Anne
Frank in the context of study of World War II.
Use the work also as a basis for extracting a
key statement and having students write about
that statement in terms of their own lives.

Read Helen Keller's biography or that of
another handicapped person. Students then
experiment with sensory deprivation and write
in journals about their feelings and responses.
Decide in small groups if their attitudes about
handicaps changed. Invite a special education
teacher to visit and speak about braille and
American Sign Language. An ideal time to
learn some finger spelling and learn about how
English syntax differs from ASL syntax.

Read novels dealing with a topic involving
two groups of people at odds; e.g., settlers and
Native Americans (*Edge of Two Worlds*, by
Weyman Jones; *Sign of the Beaver*, by Elizabeth
Speare). Groups take sides and write entries in
reading logs. This can serve as basis for
research, reflection, writing, oral report about
values and beliefs of both sides.
II. Additional Language Skills
Although controversial in principle, these
following subskills are sometimes identified in
school district curriculum guidelines. Even
advocates of "whole language" instruction, who
tend not to specify such skills, agree that at this
level a rich language environment includes
some attention to editing and correctness. This
writer believes that sentence combining,
spelling principles, and topics in language
history are worthy of classroom time, especially
in context.

Language Subskills Sometimes Identified
Produce correct subject/verb agreement

with personal pronouns, indefinite
pronouns, and compound subjects
Produce, coordinate, and subordinate
sentence elements appropriate to
meaning
Teacher provides models of various kinds of
sentences and does sentence combining
to reveal sentence "layering" in English,
which at the same time models skillful
subordination, variety, economy of
expression
Teacher helps students make effective use
of grammar and usage handbooks as
references in the revising/editing process.
Teacher provides spelling and punctuation
checklists during editing process.
Students consult lists of corrected examples
of specific writing skills, against which to
edit their own work.
Introduction to word processing (if this
hasn't happened earlier): learning to
type, use command keys, revising tools.
Suggested protocol for first guided
experiences:
1. Compose a first draft in response to a
prompt based on literature read by the
entire class
2. Meet in groups and respond to each
other's work, according to a rubric, with
teacher serving as a consultant
3. Return to word processor to revise and
edit
4. Submit final draft for evaluation

Reading Skills Sometimes Identified
Use prefixes, suffixes, and roots to unlock
words. Teacher may integrate with study
of Greek and Roman mythology and the
ancient world
Develop more sophistication in making
inferences about main idea, supporting
ideas
Recognize persuasive tone and various
persuasive devices
Use parts of a book: index, glossary, foot-
notes, appendices
Use graphic sources for information: tables,
lists, charts, graphs, maps, globes, time-
lines, scale drawings
Compare information on graphic sources
Use periodicals, card catalogs, and basic
reference works to locate information in
content areas
Look for and determine meaning of new

words through roots and affixes

In content areas (literature, social studies, science), students in groups predict the questions they expect to be answered in the next chapter. They discuss possible answers, and which predictions are most likely. Verify after reading, and locate exact information or inferential cues.

In content areas, arrange events in sequential order, according to time, degree of importance, cause and effect

Draw logical conclusions, make generalizations

Evaluate and make judgments about material read

III. Speaking

(The five functions of speaking are often identified as: expressing feeling, ritualizing, imagining, informing, controlling (persuading)

A. Purposes

Expand repertory of all functions: give a set of reasons to persuade; explain a process; make puns; tell riddles, anecdotes

Focus on appreciation of the skills, and ability to select and use each function appropriately

B. Audience

Adapt content and formality to fit audience

Show appreciation for supporting material

Become aware of feedback during the speech

Become aware of need to qualify, clarify, extend ideas

Begin to use emotional appeals appropriate to audience relationship

C. Experiences

Read literary selections aloud

Interpret news events

Participate in group discussion and choral reading

Recreate famous speeches

Speak to a variety of audiences (peers, parents, younger students)

Use appropriate language: figures of speech, nonverbal effects

D. Evaluation/Feedback

Speaker and listeners examine success of factors used: pleasing voice? Usage and style appropriate? Organization for objective?

IV. Listening

A. Attend and Discriminate

Perceive artistic uses of language, sounds

Attend to content of performance

Determine a speaker's motive, bias and point of view

Detect use of propaganda and over-generalization

Recognize theme

Discriminate between major ideas and supporting details

B. Assign Meanings—Language skills

Seek meaning at metaphoric level

Recognize stylistic devices

Distinguish literal/figurative/topical/universal/trivial/artistic

C. Respond

Provide feedback to elicit a specific gratifying response

Draw up and visualize past experiences as a base for comparison

V. Writing

A popular guideline: students become aware that writing is a means of clarifying thinking and that it is a process which embodies several stages, including prewriting, drafting, receiving responses, revising, editing, and postwriting activities.

A guideline growing in popularity: students learn the conventions of the English language (usage, spelling, punctuation, and capitalization) through all the language arts and through direct instruction when necessary.

Purposes for writing

A number of state curriculum guides identify specific genres to be addressed at each grade level. Some teachers prefer to think in terms of the Domains of Writing as defined in writing project terms: sensory/descriptive; imaginative/narrative; practical/ informative; analytical/expository; others stay with the traditional and more directive terms functions or purposes. For this grade level (often specified as grades 7-9) we may see the following configuration of purposes, adapted from New York's curriculum guide:

To Express Self

Journal entries: demonstrating introspective thinking, developing a voice, experimenting with language

Friendly letter: informal diction and tone in correct form and conventions

Personal response to literature: react to one selection, providing examples and sup-

porting details, and drawing conclusions
Poem: haiku, quatrain, ballad, free verse

To Narrate

Narrative of actual experience: maintain consistent point of view; include description and dialogue

Short story: use specific, vivid language, suggest a theme, create characters and setting

Skit: produce as a speaking/listening activity; build to a humorous, abrupt, or surprise ending

Feature article about a person or event: using "hook"; sustaining human interest focus through organization

Autobiographical sketch: use appropriate organization, unified theme, and closure

Myth: invent explanation of the origins of life, natural phenomenon; create superhuman characters

To Explain

Essay on a process: begin with demonstration, oral explanation

Business letter ordering merchandise

Research report: gather and organize information; maintain objective diction and tone

Accident report: use of precise language

News article: who, what, when, where, how, why; maintain third-person point of view; write headline

Biographical report: gather information from a variety of sources; include adequate and interesting details, begin with a lead that captures the essence of the person and ends with an idea that stirs the curiosity to know more

Deductive essay: select a general statement, proved support, demonstrate logical thinking

Character study: based on a character from a work of literature

Revise one of the above for a different audience/reader

To Describe

Describe a real or imaginary person

Feature article describing a place

Classified ad to sell an article

Revise one of the above for a different audience/reader

To Persuade

Book review: to interest a prospective reader

Ad about a new product: use propaganda techniques, such as bandwagon, testimonial, connotative language

Letter to editor in opposition to an issue: identify issue, state opinion, support, in acceptable business letter form

Editorial in favor of an issue: provide supporting reasons, examples, details

The Processes

A. Prewriting

Use materials for stimulating writing ideas: pictures, film and video, stories heard or read aloud, literature, classroom simulations of moral dilemmas and improvisational drama, role play of literary characters or imagined situations.

Students begin to consider audience and purpose in writing

Students help to generate questions about a topic they want to explore: what they already know, what they don't know, unanswered questions, where they might go for information

Teacher plans for movement from expressive to informative and persuasive writing

Teacher provides sources for gathering information

Students begin to show some ability to plan and to use outside resources

Teacher encourages students to reach out beyond the school to the community

Students begin to synthesize information from a variety of sources

Teacher helps motivate a purpose in writing: opinion surveys, field trips, debates on issues from literature read, "selling" a book to a peer, advertising a book

Teacher provides opportunities for students to interact and discuss their ideas and plans for writing; peers can ask questions to indicate what an audience wants to know from the writer

Teacher may use computer activity files as writing prompts to help students get started

Teacher and students make use of invention techniques, such as brainstorming, clustering, freewriting, first as a whole class experience, then as an individual or group pursuit

B. Drafting

Teacher models drafting and shares own drafts

Teacher models the questioning process when drafting

Teacher encourages tentativeness, freedom from constraints of mechanical correctness and neatness

Teacher encourages student interaction during the drafting process: read around groups or response groups/pairs

Students begin to show clear and logical thinking in developing a central idea

Students begin to show movement from loosely constructed ideas to more focused theme

Students begin to anticipate counter-arguments to an argument

C. Revising

Students develop tolerance for work-in-progress, seeing revision as more than recopying

Students begin to read more critically for selves and peers and learns to accept constructive criticism as part of the revising process

Teacher includes peer-response group as an occasional resource

Teacher focuses on global issues of content and organization first, style and usage second

Students participate in developing a rubric for issues of content and organization; they consider the purpose and audience

Teacher does not ask students to revise every piece of writing

D. Editing

Students begin to accept the necessity and appropriateness of editing some of their written work

Students are introduced to the use of references for usage, style, spelling, word meaning

Students work with peers and with checklists they have helped to generate

Students should have internalized some writing conventions and show growing mastery of spelling

Students may be encouraged to edit for: formal and informal language; word specificity, sentence completeness; tense consistency, clarity, and sentence effectiveness

Teacher focuses attention on one or two skills per writing assignment, so as not to overwhelm the student

Students should begin to recognize cliches and triteness and get help in replacing them with fresh language

Teacher may provide practice exercises in proofreading for: punctuation, spelling, capitalization, and sentence improvement. Ideally, these grow out of student drafts rather than from isolated examples.

Teacher may want to remind students about sentence-combining; show example sentences from student writing that could be improved by this principle

Teacher provides opportunity for class publication

VI. Writing across the Curriculum

Social Studies

After studying historical and contemporary figures who are seen as great leaders or heroes, students brainstorm about which features deserve those appellations. Then, using their notes, they write an essay, "Prescription for Greatness," using examples from people studied to illustrate their points. Response groups can critique.

Students read fictional stories about life in pioneer days of their state. They discuss and write about the insights they gained and compare with information gained in social studies. Did the author correctly represent the main characters?

Students read accounts of personal experiences during a specific historical event and compare the writer's experiences with more objective reportage from that era, such as from history texts, newspapers, and newsreels. Two excellent examples of personal accounts are *The Diary of a Young Girl* by Anne Frank, and *Farewell to Manzanar* by Jeanne Houston. In the comparing process, students focus on objective vs. subjective accounts and the value of each to understanding both human behavior and the relationship between external and internal events.

Students take a story with a historical setting and turn it into a script to be produced live or on video. Or, they select a time in the history of their state, write a script in groups depicting a typical day in that time. Watch for authenticity in language, lifestyles, occupations. Allow time for performing the script.

After introducing a new unit, the teacher may divide the class into groups of five to research a topic related to that unit. Students collaborate to develop questions they will need to explore and how to find the answers. The school librarian may serve as a helpful guide in the exploration stage.

Science

Students write a story about how it feels for a specific food item to go through the digestive process (not for the faint-hearted). Include each organ in the digestive system and use as many descriptive words as possible: crunch, gnash, tumble, contract.

Students keep a learning log, recording in their own words what they have learned or what confused them. Teachers might allow students to use these logs occasionally during exams.

Students try to explain a new term or concept more clearly than their textbook did, and then examine together the principles of clear writing.

Students assume the role of a scientist writing a letter to a newspaper in defense of his or her theory.

Math

To clarify a math problem and practice expository writing, students write a step-by-step explanation of the solution.

Students create a real-life situation that requires math; for example, they role-play, then write dialog for, a financial counselor explaining how to save in order to buy a sailboat.

Students write a story using math symbols in place of some of the words (math rhebus)

Translate formulae into word problems.

Media

Students explore the question of which medium delivers the best message according to the demands of the topic and the needs of the researcher. For example, which is best if you want to learn to dive, to draw cartoons, to recognize bird songs, to find batting averages? Possible answers: transparency, print, audio, filmstrip, video, magazine, slide, newspaper. Students might compare messages in different media and choose one to "teach" a skill they feel able to convey.

Students may profitably be introduced to the computer as a means of storing and retrieving information. Students enter short book reviews into a simple database. Students consult the database when choosing a book for pleasure reading, book reviewing, or searching for topical information.

VII. Notes on Critical Thinking Skills

Critical thinking, both as a learning tool and as part of the composing process, has been much discussed in the last decade. Some teachers have utilized Bloom's taxonomy as a way of approaching the tasks we should ask students to perform in building their critical acuity. Wherever possible, it has been suggested, we need to ask students to use more than one thinking mode, and we need to design their writing assignments with thinking skills in mind.

The activities described under *Writing across the Curriculum* (on the previous page) are especially rich in overlapping thinking modes. In addition, see table 1 for suggestions of thinking/writing tasks adaptable to this grade level.

Scope for Grades 9-12

At the high school level, students continue to read and study in depth a core of important literary works in all the major genres and media, and to extend their personal reading and writing, supported by a library system. Opportunities for lively oral activities should be encouraged, such as reading aloud, dramatizing, role-playing, simulations, debates, and panel presentations.

Here, reading and writing across the curriculum requires the cooperation of teachers in all the disciplines, but it is the English teacher who may need to lead the movement to include in all classes such activities as: vocabulary building, strategies for reading, note taking, essay exam writing, study skills, and research techniques. Other teachers—perhaps through all-school workshops—should learn to employ the principles of process-writing in their classes. At the very least, they should give students enough time to plan and revise their writing for each class.

In summary, students should be provided a challenging curriculum with (1) a significant body of important literary works at the core;

(2) teaching strategies that address the needs of all students and integrate all the elements of language arts instruction; and (3) support in the home and across all the school disciplines. With these elements in place, schools will graduate young people whose literacy enables them to respect themselves and others, succeed in the work place, and contribute to improving the human condition. (California State Department of Education 1988, 32)

Because of the inherent differences between high schools and the lower levels, and the vast differences among high schools even within one district, the outline of topics for this level will be arranged somewhat differently. We will focus on literature and writing only to the extent that one can identify discrete skills and activities. Even specialists generally agree that the integration of all the language arts and skills continues to be essential in curriculum design at these levels. For that reason, many teachers consider the process of identifying discrete skills a highly arbitrary pursuit. In a literature-based program, for example, the skills taught will have grown out of the literature read, combined with those skills needed to write effectively about literature.

The following topics and expectancies were drawn from a four-state sampling of district course descriptions and state curricular guides, as well as from the author's own experiences in visiting school districts.

I. Literature
  A. Comprehension and Response
    Read a wide variety of literary works
    Read several works that represent a particular theme
    Use media and attend theater
    Pursue interests in books
    Extend interests through books
    Read from both classic core works and popular works
    Analyze author's purpose, characterizations, and plot development
    Emphasize writing responses in the form of imaginative, persuasive, informative writing
    Create a play or film (in a group)
    Critique the print and visual forms of literature (plays, films, TV treatments)
  B. Understanding Self, Cultural Heritage, and Others
    Discover, discriminate, and evaluate fact and opinion, cause and effect, motive

and result, fantasy and reality
    Relate one work to another and to oneself
    Develop perspectives for viewing works of literature: individual, community, national, world, historical
    Recognize cultural attitudes and customs in literary selections
    Focus on American and English literature
  C. Growth in Language
    Become familiar with major genres of literature, in prose and poetry
    Learn about themes common in various types and periods
    Study major literary movements, styles, and significant writers
    Recognize literary devices: figurative language, symbolism, imagery, satire, parody, irony, tone, mood
    Recognize point of view in literary selections
    Distinguish between language used denotatively and connotatively
    Begin to employ criteria for evaluating a literary work

II. Language Topics that May Require Direct Instruction at this Level
(Many teachers at this level agree that skills such as these should, whenever possible be taught in context; for example, vocabulary study should be based on contextual clues from literature being read and from topics being pursued in writing assignments.)
    Use affixes to change words from one part of speech to another
    Produce well-formed sentences that convey coordinate and subordinate ideas appropriately.
    Choose appropriate words to convey intended meaning
    Analyze word parts to unlock meaning of new words
    Use context to determine meaning
    Recognize meanings and uses of colloquialism, slang, idiom, jargon
    Vary word and sentence choices for purpose and audience
    Demonstrate facility with word analogies and other forms of advanced vocabulary development
    Describe the history and major features of American dialects
    Recognize sociological functions of language
    Describe the major features of the origins and development of the English language

Analyze grammatical structure of sentences
    (parsing and diagramming)
    Note: Although it is lessening, there is still
controversy about the overt teaching of formal
grammar (analyzing grammatical structure).
Since the Writing Project movement has
gained momentum and acceptance, many
teachers have accepted its recommendations to
teach good usage, form, and correctness
through modelling and generative activities
(such as sentence-combining) rather than
through analysis and drill, which many claim do
not transfer to student writing. A similar
movement has also gained wide acceptance in
foreign language teaching, as well as in ESL,
and is favored by many applied linguists.
Concurrently, there is some interest in offering
a course in grammar analysis as a senior high
school elective, in which grammar is studied as
an end in itself, not necessarily as a prelude to
writing.
III. Reading Skills Which May Require Direct
Instruction (most of these skills, alternatively, can
be viewed as subsumed under I. part C, above)
    Recognize relevant details
    Identify stated or implied main idea
    Distinguish between fact and non-fact
    Draw conclusions and make inferences
    Predict outcomes and future actions
    Vary rate of reading according to purpose
    Identify main idea AND supporting details
    Use format and organization of a book—
        footnotes, appendices, cross references
    Use reference materials such as atlas, encyclo-
        pedia, almanac, bibliography
    Interpret complex maps, charts, tables, and
        complex dictionaries
    Determine an author's point of view, purpose,
        qualifications
    Recognize the devices of propaganda
    Take appropriate notes while both reading or
        listening
IV. Writing
    Purposes for writing
    A number of state curriculum guides
identify specific genres to be addressed at each
grade level. Some teachers prefer to think in
terms of the Domains of Writing as defined in
writing project terms. Others stay with the
traditional and more directive terms functions
or purposes. For this grade level (grades 9-12)
we may see the following configuration of
purposes described as classroom products,
adapted from New York's curriculum guide:

To Express Self
    Journal entries: explore basis for the feeling
        or value, experiment with voice and
        language
    Personal response to literature: use ex-
        amples, reasons, details to show how they
        support or contradict a personal attitude
    Poem: use sensory detail; use figurative
        language such as metaphor, simile,
        hyperbole, personification, oxymoron,
        pun

To Narrate
    Short story with an ironic or surprise ending
    Script: skit, scene, play
    Script adapted from literature
    Humorous newspaper column: analyze
        humorists' columns and use as models

To Explain
    Series of articles/essays on one topic, from
        different viewpoints
    Business letter of complaint
    Research paper
    Formal essay
    Character study based on literature
    Precis
    Letter of application
    Resume

To Describe
    Compare and contrast the same place at
        different times/seasons
    Describe a familiar place from an unusual
        perspective
    Write a poem appealing to a single sense
        (begin with clustering)

To Persuade
    Editorial (from several points of view)
    Literary analysis (begin with group effort
        and modeling)
    Argumentative essay (emphasis on logic,
        facts, and refutation)
    Critical review of an event or performance
        (ending with a recommendation)
    Formal speech: careful consideration of the
        audience; persuasive rhetoric

The Processes
A. Prewriting
    Students receive ample practice in a variety
        of generating strategies
    Students do free-writing on a nearly daily

basis

Students keep a journal as a source of topics

Teacher encourages content areas as source of writing

Literature is used as basis of response writing

Imagination is used as a source

B. Drafting

Teacher writes with students and shares drafts

Teacher observes, follows, and solves problems with students

Teacher models questioning, conferences with student

Teacher and students view writing as process of discovery

Students write multiple-paragraph compositions incorporating information from sources other than self

Students make rhetorical choices based on audience, purpose, form

Students write compositions with documentation (research or term paper)

Students write descriptive, narrative, expository paragraphs of increasing length and complexity

Students write literary discourse of a variety of types

Students write a variety of forms of informative and persuasive discourse

C. Revising

Students are better able to focus on content first, language second

Students become aware of frequent gap between text and intended meaning

Teacher steers students in the direction of global issues

Teacher helps with global issues, reordering lines of reasoning

Teacher organizes peer groups and models critical reading among peers; "read-around groups"

Students see and compare early drafts of an essay with polished one; in groups they discuss and take notes on what made the improvements

Teacher provides response sheets or check lists for students to complete when revising early drafts

Students evaluate content, organization, topic development, transition, clarity of language, diction, audience

D. Editing

Teacher provides publication, giving authen-

tic reason for editing process

Teacher focuses on only one or two skill areas at once

Uses variety of editing activities, using drafts as basis of skill instruction

Students proofread for punctuation, spelling, syntax, usage

Students refine sentences and paragraphs for unity and fluency

VI. Writing across the Curriculum

Social Studies

Students conduct a mock presidential or senatorial campaign. In groups of four or five, they create a candidate, write a biography of him/her, create a campaign strategy, editorials, commercials (ideally these can be videotaped), speeches. The culmination can be a live convention wherein a candidate is nominated (or a president elected).

Students write about a historical event from the point of view of two or three people who experienced it.

Students answer study questions that require them to discuss cause and effect, comparison and contrast, drawing conclusions and forming opinions.

Students explore social studies concepts they don't understand by conducting research and writing about their findings, using documentation.

Science

Students write questions and answers for possible use on an exam.

Students see films or videos on controversial topics such as organ transplants or other medical procedures relating to organs they are studying. They write brief reactions to what they see. Then they discuss matters of bioethics and write their emotional response, followed by their rational responses.

Business Education

English teachers and business teachers collaborate.

Students write and mail a variety of letters that will elicit responses.

Students plan a business of their choice and write promotional material to advertise.

Students type assignments for their other classes as partial course objectives.

Students write business letters and memos,

fill out purchase orders, application letters, and other letters designated by language arts curriculum.

Foreign Language

Have students keep lists of English words that were borrowed from or influenced by the foreign language.

Coordinate writing assignments with English department; students could, for example, write in English the plans and itinerary for a trip to the land of the target language.

Coordinate literary assignments when possible, so some students may read a foreign literary work (or a portion thereof) both in translation and in the original. Literary time-lines can introduce the principles of compara-tive literature, as well as setting an historical context for both literatures.

Language history can be reinforced by relating the target language to English and the Indo-European family tree.

Music, Drama, and Art

Students prepare notices and press releases for upcoming events in the art community

Students keep logs of what they achieve each week in their art form

Teachers arrange for guest artists to visit; students write their impressions, and write synopses of the experience.

Students attempt to describe in words their responses to a non-verbal art form.

Students regularly write critiques, develop rubrics for critiques, and share critiques of peer work.

Students research and write about the lives and careers of famous musicians, dramatists, painters, sculptors.

Health and Physical Education

Students keep personal records of their own progress and obstacles, problems and goals in a log or daily diary.

Students "write to learn" about a sport that is new to them.

VII. Thematic Units

Many English departments across the country organize their curricula around thematic units. Around a core group of classic and contemporary literature, teachers may integrate writing, speaking, and media activi-ties, as well as interdisciplinary links with other subject areas. Here are some of the most popular themes encountered:

> Search for Justice and Dignity
> New Americans and the Immigration Experience
> Experiences with War and Peace
> Individuals and the Need for Acceptance
> Passages and Transformations
> The Individual and Society
> Journey to Personal Fulfillment
> A Time for Courage
> The Meaning of Heroism
> Fantasy and the Unexplained
> Threats to the Environment
> Men and Women
> What is Important?

In the *English Teacher's Handbook,* by Stephen and Susan Tchudi, you will find the following classics gathered under the theme "Love and Romance" (153): *Jane Eyre, The Return of the Native, Tess of the d'Urbervilles, Wuthering Heights, Anna Karenina, Madame Bovary, Romeo and Juliet, Cyrano de Bergerac, Ethan Frome*

VIII. Typical Course Requirements (Objectives)

School districts vary widely in their curricu-lar guidelines for teachers of the Language Arts and English. The degree of specificity ranges from precise behaviors/goals toward which presumably every teacher should strive, to simple descriptions of outcomes and instruc-tional levels. Even the metalanguage differs from district to district: goals, objectives, expectancies, behaviors, products, focus, program outcomes. By way of example, consider the curricular course guides below. The first is an excerpt from a course objectives guide for a high school in Northern California. (The full document for this course runs to eighty-three items.) The second is from a list of "focus topics" and "program outcomes" from a Long Island, New York, school district.

Academic Expectations

Grade 9: Middle-Level Literature

1. Understands the cause/effect relationship between the protagonist/antagonist and the plot of a literary work.

2. Identifies the form of conflict in a literary work: person against person; person against society; person against nature;

person against himself or herself.
. . . .
9. Analyzes the ways in which setting influences the plot development of *To Kill a Mockingbird*.
10. Explains how a mockingbird is a symbol for Boo Radly and Tom Robinson in that work.
. . . .

Composition
47. Writes an effective introduction with a thesis statement.
51. Writes an effective essay on the theme, "A Time for Courage"

Vocabulary
64. Integrates new vocabulary from literary works into writing
66. Defines jargon and slang

Grammar
73. maintains verb agreement
74. distinguishes between whose and who's in sentences
76. punctuates introductory phrases

Speaking/Listening
77. Delivers a 3-5 minute prepared expository speech
78. Writes a critique of another student's expository speech
83. Delivers a 3-5 minute persuasive speech

Table 2. K-12 Language Arts Curriculum, Secondary Level

E = exposure   I = direct instruction
R = reinforcement   AI = advanced instruction

Program Outcomes	12	11	10	9
Reading: Students will read and interpret print media				
identify advertising techniques	AI	AI	R	I
translate information in visual aids	AI	AI	AI	AI
interpret political cartoons	AI	AI	AI	R
distinguish parts of a newspaper and magazine	R	R	R	AI
Writing				
write a letter of introduction	AI	I	-	-
write a letter of application	AI	I	-	-
write a personal letter	AI	AI	AI	AI
write a business letter	AI	AI	AI	AI
write an autobiographical essay	-	-	-	R
Listening/speaking				
communicate clearly, grammatically, and coherently in a group and interview setting	AI	AI	AI	AI

IX. Notes on Critical Thinking Skills

Critical thinking, as both a learning tool and as part of the composing process, has been much discussed in the last decade. Some teachers have utilized Bloom's taxonomy as a way of approaching the tasks we should ask students to perform in building their critical acuity. Wherever possible, it has been suggested, we need to ask students to use more than one thinking mode.

The activities described under Writing Across the Curriculum are especially rich in overlapping thinking modes. In addition, see table 1 for suggestions of thinking/writing tasks that are also appropriate to any grade level.

Recommended Readings

California State Department of Education. 1988. *English Language Arts Model Curriculum Guide K-8*. Sacramento.

———. 1987a. *English Language Arts Framework*. Sacramento.

———. 1987b. *Practical Ideas for Teaching Writing as a Process*. Sacramento.

———. 1986. *Handbook for Planning an Effective Writing Program K-12*. Sacramento.

———. 1985. *Model Curriculum Standards 9-12*. Sacramento.

Olson, Carol Booth, ed. 1992. *Thinking/Writing Fostering Critical Thinking through Writing*. New York: HarperCollins.

Tchudi, Stephen, and Susan Tchudi. 1992. *The English Teacher's Handbook*. Boston: Little, Brown.

Texas Education Agency. n.d. *English Language Arts Framework K-12*.

The University of the State of New York, State Education Department. 1991. *English Language Arts Syllabus K-12*. Albany.

Wisconsin Department of Public Instruction. 1991. *A Guide to Curriculum Planning in the English Language Arts*.

5

STATE-LEVEL CURRICULUM GUIDELINES: AN ANALYSIS

by Roger Farr
Associate Director, ERIC Clearinghouse on Reading and
Communication Skills; Professor of Education
Indiana University, Bloomington, Indiana
and

Beth Greene
Associate Scientist, Center for Reading and Language Studies
Indiana University, Bloomington, Indiana

L IKE every other area of the curriculum, English and language arts include a large number of identifiable subareas. Any guide written to describe the English/language arts curriculum must deal with all of these areas. More often than not, a curriculum guide reflects what leaders in the field think should be part of the curriculum. In order to adequately develop or build a curriculum guide, authors usually examine a number of sources, including similar or related guides. The curriculum guide then grows from this base. The opening secion of this chapter is designed to help interested individuals, groups of teachers, or school committees to write their own curriculum guide. In the section that follows, the English/language arts curriculum guides of thirty-eight states are discussed. In some cases, the state has a single guide for this curriculum area. There are also states with separate guides for the elementary and secondary grades. In still other cases, a separate guide is provided for the reading

curriculum. Other options exist as well. These can be seen below in the descriptive section and related discussion of the guides.

How to Use This Chapter

It is our hope that the information presented in this chapter will enable teachers, language arts coordinators, and curriculum committees to find models for their own English/language arts guides. Many states have mandates for the content of the English/language arts curriculum, and this information is contained in the guides. The guides range from the detailed--specifying numerous skills and instructional activities--to the highly philosophical--articulating a theory and view of language arts, but leaving the implementation of the curriculum to the local school district.

This chapter begins with a brief review of previous summaries of state curriculum guides and an overview of current trends in language arts. We then proceed to a description of the state guides, including some basic information about what tends to generate state curricula, what can be learned by examining the guides, an overview of the thirty-eight state guides that have been examined, a discussion of the stated and apparent philosophies that help structure them, and an analysis of their impact on curriculum development and language arts instruction.

The analysis then proceeds to describe skill-focused guides and to compare them to guides that are process-oriented. We discuss how these two approaches reflect current theory and knowledge of the language arts. A more detailed analysis of several state guides exemplifies some of these descriptions. Before drawing conclusions about the guides and the curricula they depict, we examine how the guides handle some of the key issues in language arts curriculum today.

Trends in Language Arts

What Topics and Issues are "Hot"?
For many years, the National Council of Teachers of English (NCTE) has published *Recommended English Language Arts Curriculum Guides, K-12* and has updated the set annually. Compiled by the NCTE Committee to Evaluate Curriculum Guides and Competency Requirements, the guides cited in these reviews represent "carefully planned and well-written curricula" (NCTE 1987, 1). For the most part, the committee highlights county, city, and town guides and includes relatively few state guides. Many of these guides are specific to limited grades or segments of the curriculum. Only a few are comprehensive. The most recent edition, *Commended English Language Arts Curriculum Guides, K-12,* 1990, covers the three-year period 1986-1989 and includes information and commentary for nineteen guides for 1988-1989.

Other summaries produced annually by NCTE are *Trends and Issues in English Instruction: Reports on Informal Annual Discussions of the Commissions of the National Council of Teachers of English.* Earlier reports have various titles but all are summaries compiled by the six NCTE commissions at their annual meetings. The 1991 edition (Piazza and Suhor) cites concerns about a widespread increase in legislative actions about teaching language arts, narrow conceptions

of literacy, practices in teaching literature, misuse of the term *whole language,* the use of computers in teaching language arts, changing aspects of evaluation and assessment in language arts, language arts textbooks, and the politics of literacy, teaching, and assessment. Several of these topics have persisted from year to year and remain as topics of great concern within the field.

In a recently published monograph, Tchudi (1991) addresses similar issues, but in a more theoretically motivated framework. His *Planning and Assessing the Curriculum in English Language Arts* presents a historical overview of English teaching and provides background on the "new English," followed by examples of successful curriculum development. He then offers guidelines for future curriculum developers. The monograph concludes with the NCTE specifications for the new English and criteria for evaluating curricula.

In their efforts to serve teachers and curriculum developers, the Association for Supervision and Curriculum Development (ASCD) produced a *Curriculum Handbook* for language arts to be used for staff development programs (ASCD 1991). The authors address a specific set of contemporary issues in the language arts and discuss how these issues affect teaching and learning.

Some Key Issues in the Field
There are always issues that persist within a discipline, issues that make us question what we do and why we are doing it. Language arts is not an exception. In the next few paragraphs, we address several of these issues: integration within language arts, integration across content areas, the role of literature, holism or wholism, skills, and assessment and evaluation.

Integration within Language Arts
The use of the term *integrated language arts* is widespread, but what does this mean in 1992? Typically, this term has meant avoiding the breakdown of language arts into separately considered subareas: reading, writing, speaking, and listening--yet including each subarea. No one disputes that these subareas constitute the language arts; the issue is the compartmentalization that often occurs, leading to the artificial separation of these areas in instructional practice. Furthermore, using this set of four subareas omits several others recently cited, *e.g.,* literature,

thinking, and media (see Piazza and Suhor 1990, 1991). Often the teaching of language arts is defined as teaching language; this definition is seen as a way to integrate the subareas.

Other uses of the term *integration* concern the integration of the language arts with content areas across the curriculum, a topic addressed in the next section, and students' integration of new information with what they already know. The latter concept is described by a variety of phrases including the traditional, *building background,* and the contemporary, *into the text.*

Integration across Content Areas

One aspect of language arts that addresses a broad spectrum of the curriculum is the place of language arts in other content areas, such as mathematics, science, and social studies. Students use language every day in content-area classrooms, but little instruction is focused on the integration of language skills across content areas. The notions of interdisciplinary studies, inquiry, integrated content, and core curriculum offer the prospect of having integration across content areas.

Curriculum developers advocate that curriculum planning should transcend the traditional curricular boundaries. Thematic studies or topical units provide a means to achieve this kind of integration. Writing across-the-curriculum is a major concern at all educational levels. The writing process and the reading-writing link also offer means to combine language arts and the content areas. Interestingly, the major textbooks on teaching gifted and talented students include detailed program descriptions of thematic or topical units (Gallagher 1985; VanTassel-Baska 1988). Perhaps all students could be taught this way.

The Role of Literature

There is no question that literature holds a central place in language arts. Teaching literature has always been a major component of the secondary curriculum in English. Literature plays an important role in the elementary grades as well. Literature-based reading instruction is well established as a general emphasis and as a method, and a number of guides include it in the elementary curriculum.

Across grades K-12, literature stands on its own as a major component of English and language arts. Literature serves well as instructional and recreational reading material. It

functions as a stimulus for writing. It also links to other areas of language arts such as drama, choral reading, and reader's theater. Another important role for literature is in other content areas as part of thematic teaching or topical units of study.

Holism or Wholism

Several issues revolve around the concept of the whole. There is concern for using intact, whole pieces of literature. There is also the whole language movement, a plea to deal with language as a whole. There is also another view that suggests putting the language arts into a communications framework as a way to maintain the whole. Others refer to language as learned in a holistic, meaning-centered environment or to the need to focus on the whole child (or student).

The Place of Skills

There is no question that there are many skills to be learned in the language arts, but the concern in this area is how these skills come to be learned. In the philosophy sections, as well as in the more specific sections of many of the guides, there is reference to learning language skills in the context of reading and writing activities, not through direct instruction--still another, and a very essential kind of integration.

Closely related to the place of skills is the use of the term *strategies.* Teaching students strategies as a means to pursue a goal or to solve problems is meritorious. However, the current tendency to use the word *strategies* merely as a synonym for the word *skills* does not offer anything to the field and may actually obscure the underlying issues.

Assessment and Evaluation

In language arts there is a move away from reliance on multiple-choice and standardized tests as a way to evaluate students. The use of performance and other alternative assessments in language arts already includes writing assessments for which students write in response to a supplied prompt, sometimes as first drafts but also with the opportunity (or the requirement) to review, revise, and rewrite. These responses are sometimes evaluated to rate both reading comprehension and writing, using carefully developed rubrics that can be field-tested to equalize evaluations across raters. Several states and numerous schools and teachers have developed writing assessments of this type.

The use of portfolios for assessment in language arts is another alternative that integrates reading and writing and that is becoming a viable evaluation alternative to traditional formal and informal tests.

Standardized reading assessment procedures are undergoing substantial change as well. Using long passages rather than short ones, having many questions rather than just a few, and including open-ended questions that require a constructed response are several recent alternative assessment practices in use.

This movement away from traditional testing—both criterion- and norm-referenced--has promising implications for the development of language arts curriculum.

Concerns and Theories

In the United States there is no single language arts curriculum taught nationwide. While this survey suggests that there are at least thirty-eight states with one or more language arts curricula, even these claim to be but directive guidelines for the formation of the curriculum at district and local school levels. However, in recent years, a kind of general agreement about what language development involves has evolved.

A theory of what reading and the other language behaviors are has emerged in recent years. This theory describes a *process* that relies on an individual's background and interests and that is initiated by some purpose. Invariably, too, language behavior is some kind of reciprocal activity between a sender or senders and a receiver or receivers. While educators, researchers, and theorists in the numerous fields related to language have come to accept this new understanding, there is no one language arts curriculum endorsed nationwide for teaching or developing student abilities to use language processes.

While this theory has been emerging, criticism of the teaching of reading and the other language behaviors has led to demands for more school accountability, and various testing programs have been installed by states to try to assure that children are taught the language behaviors they need in order to function as successful and content citizens. These tests have tended to assess language skills--particularly numerous skills associated with reading and language production—that have been labeled and taught for some time. Yet what is taught and tested varies considerably from state to state.

In some states, however, the minimum-competency testing program put in place seems an attempt to establish a state curriculum that all teachers and schools will follow in order to be accountable. In the past, language arts textbooks and standardized tests labeled and targeted numerous language sub-behaviors. As textbooks and tests interacted with accountability thrusts, the list of sub-behavior skills grew quite large; and other critics contended that attending to them instructionally turned language away from purposeful communication. In some schools, teachers prepared their students for the competency tests using a host of skill-drill exercises with very limited context and appeal to students.

Most language arts texts now respond to process-depicting theory and help to develop a young reader, for example, with texts that serve a genuine reader purpose. Many have responded in recent years to demands for literature-based programs, structuring activities that engage many reading sub-behaviors and the other language modes in intricate and complex ways--as opposed to providing drills designed to practice skills.

Yet there remains a demand for skill-focused materials in some states in the U.S., and textbooks have not altogether abandoned attention to the traditional skills. As these skills appear within texts generally built to reflect new theory and thrusts, the materials take on a kind of eclectic look. The question persists as to whether meaning is best constructed in a "bottom-up" fashion that builds from basic skills to more sophisticated ones, or whether learning occurs more readily during a "top-down" experience that concentrates on the student's interests, background, and purpose for using language.

Whether it is important or not for a student to analyze literary elements such as plot and character development in order to enjoy and profit from reading a story, a grasp of literary terms has remained the goal of traditional objectives for teaching literature or reading. Whether it is important for a young reader to recognize parts of speech and a sentence in order to read, comprehend, enjoy, and learn from a text is an issue that has not eliminated the study of usage and grammar from most language arts instruction. How important is it for a young writer to know thirty rules for capitalization, as opposed to developing a habit of thinking about audiences and of how ideas can be best organized to appeal to a particular audience? These questions represent issues that do not yet appear to be resolved by state language arts curricula.

So potentially varied are the language arts curricula of the different states, that no matter how traditional many educational objectives have become, no set of them constitutes a curriculum with national endorsement.

An Examination of the State Curricula

An analysis of what is prescribed for language arts instruction across the United States would need to examine an adequate sample of local curricula. Because of the high potential for differences, that task would require examining a great many curriculum guides--enlarging the NCTE analyses manifold. It would be a tremendous task, if not a life's work.

Meanwhile, the best way to learn how the states may be impacting on language arts curriculum development, is, of course, to examine the curriculum guides of the states that have them. Guides depicting part or all of a language arts curriculum have been received from thirty-eight states. It is only fair to note that several of these states, such as Michigan and Indiana, specify that their guides are drafts of curriculum development in progress. Others note that curriculum is always in a state of development, and they invite ongoing reactions from the teachers using the guides and from others interested in education. Several present their guides in a loose-leaf format to facilitate updating.

While every effort was made to collect all existing state curriculum guides in language arts, it is possible that some states with curriculum guides did not respond to our survey. It seems reasonable to assume, however, that this collection represents the large majority of state curriculum guides that actually exist--a sample that almost certainly includes at least 90 percent of the available pool.

Examination Approaches
Two general approaches to examining the state guides for the language arts have been used. One has been to read them, inductively accruing observations that appear valid for many. Specific guides that support our general observations have been described at some length. At the same time,

unique aspects or features found in a single state guide were sometimes of enough interest to be noted and described. The other approach to analyzing the state guides has been to look at them in response to predetermined issues inspired by language theory and instructional trends.

Certain state guides are highlighted as specific points are made. This does not mean that only the highlighted state reflects the point. These noted guides are examples, and other states may also share the attribute under discussion.

An Overview
One analysis of the guides from the thirty-eight states is presented in table one as an overview and reference. When different guides from the same state are written for different grade levels or for different aspects of language development, they are listed separately on the chart. As this and other analyses discussed subsequently suggest, there are sometimes significant differences between two or more curricula prepared within the same state.

Table 1 shows that only four states are using curriculum developed before 1985. A majority of the guides begin with statements about the philosophies on which their development was based. We used these statements and other evidence in the text to infer a *philosophy/focus* label for each curriculum. Many states, for example, claim to integrate the modes, language behaviors, or key aspects of the language arts in their curricula. A program labeled *Integrated Language Arts* is more apt to reflect current understanding of language.

Numerous other state guides receive the *Communication* label because they stress the basic concept and consideration that binds the various behaviors associated with the language arts. On the surface, a claim to follow a communication philosophy would suggest that the objectives of a curriculum are highly process- and performance-oriented. Among the guides that discuss a state's philosophy, only Michigan does not label itself in one of these two ways. That curriculum, which is presented as a draft in the process of development, is labeled *Outcome Model*--an appropriate label for a program that begins with the intention of focusing on both process and product.

The last column in the table indicates whether the guide includes instructional examples and whether they are general or specific.

Table 1 / 93

Table 1
State Curriculum Guides
General Characteristics

State	Title of Guide	Latest Update	Grd. Levels	Philosophy/Focus Label	Philosophy Statement	Instructional Activities Included
Alabama*	Alabama Course of Study - Language Arts	1987	K-12	Integrated Language Arts	Yes	General Examples
Alaska	Alaska Elementary Curriculum Guide - Kindergarten	1985	K	Integrated Language Arts	Yes	General Examples
Alaska	Language Arts Alaska Curriculum Guide	1989	1-12	Integrated Language Arts	Yes	General Examples
Arizona*	Language Arts Essential Skills	1989	K-12	Integrated Language Arts	Yes	General Examples
Arkansas*	Language Arts 1-8		1-8	Not Determined	No	No
Arkansas*	Language Arts 9-12		9-12	Not Determined	No	No
Arkansas*	Reading Grades 1-8		1-8	Not Determined	No	No
California*	English Language Arts Framework	1987	K-12	Integrated Language Arts	Yes	General Examples
Connecticut	A Guide to Curriculum Development in Language Arts	1981	K-12	Not Determined	No	No
Delaware	Kindergarten Content Standards	1986	K	Not Determined	No	No
Delaware	English Language Arts Content Standards	1986	1-12	Not Determined	No	No
Delaware	Reading Content Standards	1986	1-12	Not Determined	No	No
Florida*	Curriculum Frameworks 6-8	1990	6-8	Not Determined	No	No
Florida*	Curriculum Frameworks 9-12	1990	9-12	Not Determined	No	No
Georgia*	QCC English Language Arts		K-12	Not Determined	No	No
Georgia*	Reading Education Curriculum Guide - Primary		K-4	Integrated Language Arts	Yes	Specific Examples
Georgia*	Reading Education Curriculum Guide - Middle Grades (5-8)		5-8	Integrated Language Arts	Yes	Specific Examples
Georgia*	Reading Education Curriculum Guide- Secondary Grades (9-12)	1991	9-12	Integrated Language Arts	Yes	Specific Examples
Hawaii*	Language Arts Program Guide	1988	K-12	Communication	Yes	General Examples
Idaho*	Integrated Language Arts Course of Study	1992	K-8	Integrated Language Arts	Yes	No
Idaho*	Secondary English Language Arts Course of Study	1991	9-12	Integrated Language Arts	Yes	No
Illinois	State Goals for Learning and Sample Learning Objectives	1986	3-12	Integrated Language Arts	Yes	No
Indiana*	English/Language Arts Proficiency Guide (Draft)	1991	K-12	Not Determined	Yes	No

State	Title of Guide	Latest Update	Grade Levels	Philosophy/Focus Label	Philosophy Statement	Instructional Activities Included
Iowa	A Guide to Curriculum Development in Language Arts	1986	K-14	Communication	Yes	Specific Examples
Louisiana*	Language Arts Curriculum Guide	1986	K-12	Communication	Yes	Specific Examples
Maryland	English Language Arts - A Maryland Curriculum Framework		K-12	Integrated Language Arts	Yes	No
Michigan	Model Core Curriculum Outcomes	1991	K-12	Outcome Model	Yes	No
Minnesota	Model Learner Outcomes for Language Arts	1988	K-12 (Assumed)	Communication	Yes	General Examples
Mississippi*	Mississippi Curriculum Structure-English Language Arts	1990	K-12	Communication	Yes	No
Missouri	Core Competencies and Key Skills for Missouri Schools	1990	2-10	Not Determined	No	Specific Examples
Montana	Montana School Accreditation Standards and Procedures Manual	1989	K-12 (Assumed)	Communication	Yes	No
Nevada*	Elementary Course of Study	1984	K-8	Communication	Yes	No
Nevada*	Nevada Secondary Course of Study	1987	9-12	Communication	Yes	No
New Hampshire	Minimum Standards for New Hampshire Public Elementary School Approval	1987	K-8	Not Determined	No	No
New Hampshire	Standards/Guidelines for Middle/Junior High School	1978	5-8	Communication	Yes	No
New Hampshire	Standards for Approval of New Hampshire Public High Schools	1984	9-12	Not Determined	No	No
New Mexico*	An Elementary Competency Guide for Grades 1-8	1990	1-8	Integrated Language Arts	Yes	General Examples
New Mexico*	Graduation Requirements		9-12		No	No
New York	English/Language Arts Syllabus K-12	1991	K-12	Integrated Language Arts	Yes	General Examples
North Carolina*	Standard Course of Study - Introduction to Competency Based Curriculum	1985	K-12	Integrated Language Arts	Yes	No
North Carolina*	Teacher Handbook - Communication Skills K-12	1985	K-12	Integrated Language Arts	Yes	No
North Dakota	Language Arts Curriculum Guide K-12	1986	K-12	Not Determined	Yes	General Examples
Oklahoma*	Learner Outcomes Oklahoma State Competencies		1-2, 6-12	Integrated Language Arts	Yes	No
Oregon*	English Language Arts Common Curriculum Goals	1986	3-11	Integrated Language Arts	Yes	No

Table 1 / 95

State	Title of Guide	Latest Update	Grade Levels	Philosophy/Focus Label	Philosophy Statement	Instructional Activities Included
Pennsylvania	The Pennsylvania Framework for Reading, Writing and Talking Across the Curriculum	1990	K-12	Integrated Language Arts	Yes	Specific Examples
S. Dakota	Language Arts Curriculum Guide K-12	1982	K-12	Integrated Language Arts	No	No
S. Dakota	A South Dakota Curriculum Guide for Reading	1978	1-12	Communication	Yes	No
Tennessee*	Tennessee K-8 Curriculum Frameworks	1991	K-8	Integrated Language Arts	No	No
Tennessee*	Curriculum Framework for Secondary Language Arts Program 9-12		9-12	Communication	Yes	No
Texas*	English/Language Arts Framework K-12		K-12	Communication	Yes	No
Utah*	Language Arts Core Curriculum	1991	K-12	Integrated Language Arts	Yes	No
Vermont	Framework for the Development of an English/Language Arts Scope and Sequence	1986	K-12	Not Determined	No	No
Virginia*	Standards of Learning Objectives-- Language Arts	1988	K-12	Not Determined	No	No
West Virginia*	English/Language Arts Program of Study	1989	K-12	Integrated Language Arts	No	No
West Virginia*	Reading Program of Study	1989	K-12	Integrated Language Arts	No	No
Wisconsin	A Guide to Curriculum Planning in English Language Arts	1990	K-12	Communication	Yes	Specific Examples

*Indicates a textbook adoption state

Philosophies Claimed

Table 2 expands on table one with significant quotes from the introductions and other philosophy statements of guides that include them. These are particularly interesting because they should represent the rationale for the emphases in the various curricula. California's quote, for example, clarifies the eloquent simplicity of the rationale that led to what is perhaps the most directly stated literature-based program in the country. The philosophies of Georgia and Illinois, on the other hand, clearly indicate their intention to balance goals that reflect current understanding of language acquisition with traditional concerns that have long guided language arts instruction.

As the analysis developed, it became apparent that one needs to be cautious in accepting philosophical contentions in the guides at face value and without examining the actual proposed curriculum objectives. There are very significant differences, for example, among the states that profess to follow an integrated language arts philosophy and among those that contend that their guiding philosophy focuses on communication.

The analysis suggests that a more meaningful division might place the states into three categories: (1) those that follow a philosophy that relies heavily on skill orientation, (2) those that follow a philosophy that sees language behavior as one or more processes, and (3) those that make a claim to view language behaviors as process but reflect in their declaration of objectives an equal response to skills traditionally taught over the years. Since it is not always reliably possible to relate this categorization to the philosophies claimed by the states, table two must be used only as an interesting indication of what the states claim to be their guiding philosophies.

Organization of Objectives

Goals (objectives, outcomes, or whatever other tag a particular guide gives them) usually are presented under some classification scheme that either reflects the nature of the objectives or a view of what subareas are included in the language arts.

Both skills-oriented and process-oriented curricula may use the four language behaviors or modes--listening, speaking, reading, and writing--as the major categories of language arts. Variations of these--such as oral communications for a combination of listening and speaking--appear in some guides; and major language arts considerations are often added. For example, a state may add literature, study skills, viewing or media, thinking, and other aspects that the designers of the curriculum have decided are of equal importance to the basic language modes or behaviors. Table 3 presents those that are often mentioned.

The categories in a scheme resulting from such additions are parallel only in terms of their importance. For example, reading is a key language process or function; while thinking is also a function or process, it tends to be a key emphasis identified by the state--inherent in reading and all the other language modes or behaviors. Literature is clearly a textual, content emphasis that engages the other aspects identified. In some states, more particular objectives get promoted to equal status with the four basic language behaviors. In others, subcategories at one grade level are promoted to a major aspect at others.

Because of this tendency to freely select major categories to house language arts objectives, we frequently use the term *key aspects* to refer to these categories. Occasionally this same concept is expressed by the term *strands*, as in table three. Particular categorization schemes do not seem closely related to whether curriculum is skill-oriented or process-oriented, although theory-driven curricula tend to have fewer categories and to stress their interaction.

Physical Appearance

The first obvious factor in examining the guides is that they are physically quite different. Some, like Wisconsin's and California's, are professionally created, while others are obviously manufactured in-house. Some are only a few pages, while others are so long that one wonders how the state ensures that teachers actually read and subsequently use them to any significant degree.

The length of a guide often has a great deal to do with both its intent and whether it is based on a philosophy that is skill-focused or process-oriented. Generally, the skill-focused curricula are much longer than those that express objectives in terms of language processes. There are, of course, exceptions. New Hampshire's three brief guides, prepared for different grade spans, include a very standard but short list of skill-oriented goals.

Louisiana's, North Carolina's, and Wisconsin's are examples of very long guides. The Louisiana curriculum contains objectives that build "bottom-up," and it is skill-focused throughout. North Carolina's is composed of many traditionally articulated objectives. Wisconsin's guide, which is book-length, does not prescribe either objectives or content, although its discussion of language development would tend to recommend instruction that involves the student in meaningful language use.

Intent

The general intent of the guides is evident in their length and contents. There are four general types:

· Some guides are quite long and thorough, intending to depict the potential content of instruction across most grade levels rather thoroughly. Almost without exception, the objectives of these guides are highly skill-focused.

· Some guides mean to frame the objectives of the instruction--usually as skills--in a concise presentation. They do this in a general way, leaving the teacher and texts to itemize all the skills that might be listed under any objective such as "Use a variety of word-recognition techniques to identify words."

· Some guides avoid detailing the objectives of the curriculum, contending that that is the responsibility of the district or local educators and implying that the objectives might well vary from site to site. These guides tend to discuss theory, philosophy, and instructional methodologies at varying lengths as a source and inspiration for those who must do the job at the local level. One of these guides is book-length. Others average about 100 pages. They aim to assist planners but not to prescribe exact objectives. Others list some particular objectives in terms of what our knowledge of language acquisition suggests and in terms of what state testing programs will hold students responsible for learning.

· Some guides appear eager to perform a kind of task that seems obligatory at the state level. Such guides set only the broadest of guidelines and are, in effect, a kind of statement that the state is aware of its obligation to endorse the structure of what districts, schools, and/or teachers thoughtfully decide to teach.

Most of the guides have introductions, some of which include discussions of the philosophy that helped inspire the curriculum. Most guides assert that they are not intended to mandate what happens in the language arts classroom. An example of one that does give mandated standards is Mon-

tana, but it describes the mandates so briefly that they could be used only as a starting point for guidance. Even states that appear to have tried to list every skill that could be culled from various sources protest that teachers are not required to teach from the list. Interestingly, no guide with extensive skill lists invites teachers to *select* from the list. In several states with lengthy lists of skills as objectives, teachers are encouraged to *add* skills if they like--*not* to select; it is difficult to think of skills they might conceive that are not on the lists.

Even when inviting teacher modification, some states have obviously intended to be as all-inclusive as possible in presenting the language behaviors they want taught at particular grades or grade ranges. Other states openly refer to "mastery" of objective skills at particular grade levels. Most states, on the other hand, intend the guide to be just that--a guide and not a mandate of any kind.

The most popular term across the guides is *framework*. At least ten states either use the term in the title of the guide or in their introductions. The connotation of the term is well-described in Alaska's guide as a common frame of reference--a model, not a mandate. The Tennessee guide explains that the intent of its *Curriculum Frameworks* is to set broad objectives that ensure integration of language behaviors and to avoid dictating instructional methodologies. Other terms that indicate that the guides are intended as a beginning for forming more explicit local curricula are *guidelines, sample,* and *foundation.* Some states avoid the term *model*, but Connecticut and Michigan use it in discussing how their guides hope to model options for building local curricula.

Yet in a few of these states, the intention is that the curriculum be more mandatory than the term *framework* would suggest. The title of Arizona's guide refers to *Essential Skills.* Florida presents "guidelines for specific course content," and Virginia describes "standards of learning objectives," suggesting that the guides' recommendations are to be carefully followed. Nevada presents "standards to insure a quality education and to build on." These standards, its guide explains, are based on "common goals for the child of average abilities." New Hampshire presents "minimum standards and guidelines."

Texas refers to its guide charting *Essential Elements* of a language arts curriculum as a "reference" providing a "framework for determining what students should know at each grade level." Utah, which uses the term *core curriculum* rather than *framework*, gives its skills an elaborate coding system, suggesting that they are too important to ignore. New York's guide is intended as a "syllabus" to help teachers plan day-to-day instruction.

Most states whose curricula are tied to accountability-testing programs and that note the skills covered by the tests contend that districts, schools, and/or teachers are free to structure their own classroom emphases. Yet it seems that teachers would ignore or supplant the tested objectives at their own peril.

Guides that Assist Curriculum Development
The unmistakable intent of several state curriculum guides is to promote and assist the process of developing local curricula at the district and school--or even teacher--level. These guides may offer instructional ideas that tilt toward process emphases in classroom activities, but they offer little or no specification of goals or outcomes.

Wisconsin's textbook-like coverage of the aspects and issues of language education is an example of a state's response to curriculum planning that attempts to assist in the development of local curricula. It is a large book discussing what we have come to know about language behavior in terms of the impact that information might have on the classroom. At the same time, however, it explains non-process-oriented emphases and encourages teachers to discuss and select the philosophy that will guide their local curriculum development.

The Wisconsin book's attractive design and appealing writing style should attract teachers. If they read it and discuss its content, it can have considerable impact on curriculum development, as well as on teaching practices. The guide is packed with good illustrative teaching suggestions, and has a repeated feature that relates issues and concerns to parent involvement. It provides help in evaluating existing curricula, indicates different possible scopes and sequences for instruction matching varied philosophies, and has numerous examples of aids that can serve curriculum development--many of them presented as charts that can be duplicated and put to work by curriculum committees. The guide's references are selective, excellent, and current.

Yet this unusually valuable book may work better in teacher preparation and review than as

a guide to curriculum development. The book does not emphasize curriculum development as a sequenced process of recommended steps that can be followed. It does not extensively discuss who might participate in curriculum at the local level--what different kinds of persons have to offer, for example--and how such a task force might best be put together. It has a useful checklist on evaluating current curriculum, but it does not supply a detailed description of how this early phase of curriculum might best be carried out.

The book appears not to dictate particular development procedures any more than it dictates content or curriculum objectives. Yet one wishes for ample treatment of potential problems that might arise in curriculum development and some advice about how they might be handled. Left to articulate the philosophy that will guide the development of a curriculum, for example, how does someone who is directing and facilitating the process deal with a head-on clash between traditionalists, who want literature to serve a very traditional analysis of the aspects of fiction, and those who want to promote student-selected reading that grows out of individual interests and needs? Is a compromise possible? In what ways might it be achieved? Would it be desirable? How does one deal with a group of participants who want to overstress very particular values development in the language arts classroom? These are but a few examples of numerous issues that may surface as large numbers of persons participate in curriculum development.

Connecticut's guide is not nearly so thorough or engaging a treatment of the aspects and issues of language arts education as is Wisconsin's. Yet the Connecticut document is a much more helpful "how-to" guide on the process of developing language arts curriculum. Like the Wisconsin guide, it does not specify content or objectives. There is a general volume on curriculum development in all areas and a volume specifically for language arts. Considerations for writing local guides are discussed in some depth and within a process sequence in which they would arise. The guides tell how to coordinate committees working on curriculum development, how to evaluate existing and developing curricula, and how to coordinate curricula for different subjects.

It tells how to plan, assess needs, allocate resources, select a format and write the guide, plan evaluation, and implement and pilot the resulting curriculum. It explains several perspectives from which one could structure a philosophy on which to build a curriculum. These include a skill focus, a curriculum built on specific content, one with behavioral objectives, one built around themes, one addressing interesting problems and issues, and one designed to reflect what is known about concept acquisition.

Other options the guide discusses include organizational instructional patterns (individual/group size), whether student acquisition of terminology is important, whether instruction emphasis will be inductive or deductive, whether the curriculum will be mandated, to what extent metacognition will be stressed, and how text-bound instruction will be. A chapter on evaluating and implementing the curriculum includes a checklist and other sample graphic aids useful in that process.

Other states' guides discuss the curriculum development process, but in far less detail than the guides discussed above. Minnesota's contains details for the particular kind of performance-based curriculum that is to be written--including some mandated outcomes and lesson plans that demonstrate how language behaviors can be integrated. Yet it treats this material within an organization that is designed to advise those planning curricula.

Georgia's guide at the elementary and the high school level is basically a set of very short essays on issues of concern in curriculum development. Although quite brief, some are written by easily recognized scholars. This collection is quite traditional in focus, but like Wisconsin's, Georgia's guide is meant as a generator of ideas at the local level.

New York's guide has a short chapter on planning at the local level. Hawaii's chapter on implementation is a very general review of what is involved in curriculum development. Iowa's guide has a set of appendices to serve those who face the task. The Texas guide gives information essential to planning, such as recommended time allotments for covering specific objectives. The Alaska document discusses the process that was used in revising the guide itself, and some review reactions to earlier drafts are included.

Several states' guides have philosophy/issue focuses that suggest that their major intent is to serve curriculum development. These include North Dakota, with a philosophical emphasis; Montana, where theory-conscious goals suggest that the guide is to be used as a stepping-stone to curriculum development; and the Idaho guide for the high-school grades, which presents brief discussions intended to inspire discussions by those in curriculum development.

Guides that Include Instructional Advice
Some of the language arts curriculum guides prepared by the states offer teaching assistance, ranging from brief ideas that exemplify objectives to relatively complete courses and lessons that are intended to be models of what teachers can create.

The Arkansas guide backs its many skills with brief teaching ideas presented as "extensions" of its skills lists. The Louisiana guide contains the most extensive collection of teaching ideas and supplies the kind of detail for presenting them that one would find in a teacher's manual accompanying a textbook. Some of these are exercises that could be presented on the chalkboard. Many could be copied from the guide and used like workbook seat exercises. North Dakota and Idaho also have numerous teaching suggestions.

Iowa's guide offers many teaching suggestions to match the "functions" of language that organize its goals: imagining, feeling, controlling, informing, and ritualizing. Washington presents teaching ideas as "instructional implications" in its journalism curriculum. Utah's objectives often imply classroom activities. In a right-hand column, the Alaska guide gives "sample learning activities" that include exemplary specific reading selections. Both the Wisconsin and Connecticut guides include numerous short teaching ideas to help illustrate their discussions.

Florida's guides for grades 6-8 and 9-12 offer thirty-five specific courses across twelve subject/content areas. Some are designed for particular student populations. Each is several pages long.

Organization and Presentation of Information
The various ways in which the guides present skills and objectives should be of interest to those who are planning a language arts curriculum. A key term in the consideration of the organization and emphases in a curriculum is *strand*. While not all the guides use this term, it is useful to cover language-related behaviors, content emphases, and trend-supported concerns and issues. These are frequently presented as key factors in a state's curriculum. Thus, a language mode such as speaking may be put on equal footing with literature and a technology-centered strand on viewing skills.

As one reads references to and descriptions of parts of curricula in particular states, it may be helpful to skim across the strands for that state in table three to see which language behaviors and other factors are treated in the curriculum as key aspects of the language arts. By skimming the Arkansas entry, for example, one can quickly determine that the curriculum for that state combines a focus on skills such as word attack with key traditional focuses such as vocabulary and research skills. Or a quick skim down the *Study Skills* column will identify those states that have made such skills a major factor in designing their curricula.

Generally, the guides are organized in one of three ways. Those like the California guide, which discuss issues and aspects of language development, may present their objectives in running text, using a typical textual page divided by various levels of subheads to indicate goals and subobjectives. In the California guide, general objectives of the literature-based program are a part of the description of goals under two levels of subheads. The Michigan guide uses this simple presentation to present goals that represent both process and product. It discusses areas of general concern and related goals. Under that come related subgoals and then learning strategies that are related to the subgoals.

A second method of organization uses some kind of outline form in which numbers, letters, and other codes designate goals and objectives indented under them. A subordinate level of breakdown may subdivide objectives into more specific skills or illuminate them with examples, teaching suggestions, or evidence of how the teacher may know that the student has demonstrated acquisition of the skill or objective.

The most common type of presentation is in columns, with the more general description of the goal, objective, or skill to the left and the more explicit information to the right. Sometimes these columns appear in combination with subheads of one or two levels. The columnar approach is an easy one for the reader to use.

Emphases

Skill-Focused vs. Process-Oriented

The state language arts curriculum guides analyzed fall rather obviously into three groups: those that stress skills, those that emphasize process, and those that attempt to do both.

Skill-Focused State Curricula

The state guides that imply that the extensive skill lists they present are to play a major role in structuring local language arts curricula statewide usually do not contain much advice to curriculum planners or extensive discussion of their guiding philosophy. In effect, such guides tend to present the curriculum that local districts and schools should use as a checklist of the skills to be taught. Some of these guides are more "bottom-up" than others.

The Arkansas guides are obvious examples of a total skill focus. The state has separate guides for reading and language arts, and each offers a list of many numbered skills. There is no introductory discussion of the philosophy that directs this focus. "Basic" and "developmental" skills are listed under more general skill categories that vary a bit across the grades. While the "developmental" breakdown tends to apply the preceding basic skill in a relatively limited context, these curricula are made up almost entirely of isolated skills and seem to reflect little influence from the language-process theories of recent years.

Louisiana's guide stresses the interrelatedness of language behaviors as processes in its introduction; yet its list of objectives is as extensively skill-focused as that of Arkansas. Growing out of these breakdowns are "extensions," exercises, or applications that look much like pages from workbooks.

The Texas curriculum's emphasis on skills has been influential. In the minds of many educators, the state's extensive testing and intensive teaching of its *Essential Elements* has led many publishers to increase the skills they focus on in the language arts. Yet a long and difficult introductory overview of the Texas curriculum sounds philosophically in tune with current theory and understanding, contending that "Each skill is a part of an integrated whole." The four key aspects of language are described as *purposes and forms, arts, organization,* and *convention.* Each of these aspects contains objectives that cover either language mechanics or classification schemes of traditional terms such as *description, narrative, classification, evaluation.*

Mississippi's guide suggests that the state is perhaps the most skill-focused state of all. The guide lists over 400 language skills on a continuum, grade by grade. The skills are classified as "basic" (tested by state minimum-competency exams), "functional literacy" (covered on a functional literacy test), and "core," a less than clear category. This classification scheme does not suggest performance objectives or the integration of language behaviors. The objectives for composition seem to be related to the mechanics of language, with special emphasis on spelling and handwriting. Apparently, however, gifted students in Mississippi experience an alternative "accelerated English" curriculum, which promotes literature and a more process-conscious approach to developing writing.

Other states whose curricula feature an intensive skill focus, despite some claims to the contrary, include Missouri, where some higher-level reading comprehension objectives appear to have been eliminated in revision; Alabama, which begins with performance objectives at the lowest levels but quickly becomes very bottom-up and skill-focused, while including a few purpose-oriented skills; New Hampshire, North Dakota, and West Virginia, with very short, perfunctory, but traditional skill lists; North Carolina, where only the addition of *viewing* as a language behavior breaks a highly traditional mold of bottom-up skills that take hold after a highly process-oriented focus in the lowest grades; and Nevada, with a very traditional list like those once associated with language arts and reading textbook series.

The preceding list does not include all the states with a balance of skill-focused objectives across language behaviors. States such as Vermont, Florida, and Delaware have uneven focuses across grades and/or language behaviors; overall, however, they rely on traditional skills as objectives at most levels. Florida's objectives are presented within general course descriptions.

Skill-Focused Reading Objectives

Within the curricula for a surprising number of states, there is a distinct difference between the recommended approach for developing reading proficiency and the approaches recommended for developing other language behaviors. The frequent tendency is to present reading in a "bottom-up" or traditionally framed set of goals, even when instruction in speaking, and particularly in writing, are very process-oriented.

In such states, reading frequently begins with a host of word-recognition strategies, and leading the list are grapheme/phoneme correlations listed letter by letter. Unlike California, where the curriculum direction specifies teaching phonics in the lower grades within meaningful contexts, the guides for states with extensive bottom-up skill lists do not specify the context for this instruction.

The reason for this strong skill-focus in reading can only be surmised; one possibility is

that reading became the focus of criticism of the schools beginning in the 1950s, and thus it was reading curriculum that tended to respond to accountability concerns. School boards felt compelled to demonstrate that reading was being developed with the kind of skills that many of the critics insisted were both essential and neglected. Perhaps this is the reason why reading has remained more focused on numerous skills, while writing has developed with attention to the behavior as a language *process*. Whatever the reason or reasons for these differences, they can be detected in numerous states, including New Mexico and the following examples:

The Texas (K-8) curriculum has objectives for listening, speaking, and writing that begin with a clear emphasis on process and application of the behavior; yet its reading objectives faithfully reflect the stated intention to begin with very basic, simple skills and to build on those with more sophisticated skills. Alaska's (9-12) curriculum follows an uneven attempt in the elementary grades to structure a curriculum that develops language as a process and features reading objectives that are very traditional.

In Michigan, a state that succeeds for the most part in presenting performance, process-oriented goals, reading goals are nonetheless traditional. The Nevada (1-8) curriculum tends to integrate the other language behaviors and thinking into its objectives; yet reading is treated as a bottom-up list of very traditional skills.

A more detailed look at a part of Utah's language arts curriculum makes the point about the differences between reading and writing objectives in many guides quite dramatically. Compare the objectives (which are somewhat condensed below) for reading with those for writing at grade three:

Reading
· Know sound/symbol relationships
· Use structural analysis on compound words, contractions, possessives, singular and plural forms of words
· Identify affixes and read multisyllable words
· Read sight words required by the program
· Know antonyms, synonyms, homonyms, and multiple-meaning words for the level
· Identify pronoun referents in context
· Comprehend word and sentence meanings
· Discriminate between statement and question
· Read and follow directions
· Alphabetize up to the second letter

Writing
  · Generate ideas for writing
  · Write personal experiences, stories, poetry, friendly letters, etc.
  · Recognize complete sentences
  · Share and respond to own and others' written work
  · Use capital letters, punctuation, nouns, verbs

While this set of writing objectives does not include revision, it clearly implies process and suggests that mechanics are employed and considered as a part of it. The isolated nature of the reading objectives is curiously underlined by the need of the objective related to pronoun referents to note that this skill would have to be exercised in context. Nothing in the goals relates the context to the kind of student needs, interests, and purposes implied by the first goal for writing.

Skill-Oriented Study Skills

A majority of the state guides include the development of study skills within the language arts, and almost without exception study skills are treated as a very traditional list of library and source-material uses. Only in North Dakota, where the category *information gathering* includes eight sequenced steps as concepts that cross the language arts processes, do study skills get treatment atypical of that which has prevailed in U.S. classrooms for many years. The North Dakota emphasis promotes the option of letting study skills initiate many learning opportunities by supplying the ideas for language arts activities.

Teaching Language Conventions

The guides approach grammar in several ways. Some states that promote a process approach to language arts instruction have no problem combining the teaching of grammar and mechanics with focuses more closely related to contexts meaningful to students. The Connecticut guide has a chapter discussing ways to teach writing mechanics. In Michigan's process orientation, one of five major writing goals is concerned with mechanics. In Idaho and Maryland, language conventions are one of four major goals. Maryland's linguistics approach to such language concerns nonetheless includes a goal that has the student "understand that grammar provides a systematic description of how sentences are formed."

A few guides discuss grammar, writing mechanics, and other language conventions as topical considerations to be avoided in and of themselves. These curricula are influenced by holistic philosophies that see language as a process or processes to be performed in ways that integrate aspects often considered separately in more traditional teaching. Such states tend to replace a focus on grammar and mechanics with linguistic examinations of language--how it reveals culture, how it developed, and how certain conventions of language came about. Idaho strives to "develop increasing awareness of origins and use of conventions."

North Carolina considers grammar along with semantics, the history of language, and the understanding of dialects. The Montana guide states, "People label objects and ideas with words and . . . words and their meanings change over time and through usage." Wisconsin's volume promotes teaching students "how standard usage is shaped by historical, geographical, social, cultural, and economic forces."

As does Tennessee, most states with this philosophy incorporate questions of usage into instruction of how language functions as a process. Spelling and preferred usage, for example, are taught and practiced during the revision step of writing or in reacting to reading and writing. The California guide, for example, says that as a student writes, he should understand how the mechanics of the language can empower it. One way to make this point is to encourage student interaction to each other's writing as a kind of critical thinking, language appreciation, process editing, and metacognition-building activity. A curriculum with a process focus is highly unlikely to advise teaching subject-verb agreement, for example, without a genuine context, usually written by the student.

Other states, of course, approach writing or the separate consideration of usage and grammar in a bottom-up fashion. Mississippi, for example, has thirty-five objectives for mastering capitalization, and it lists scores of other objectives for punctuation and other mechanical/grammatical features of the language. Like some of the states where process is a more obvious focus, Texas makes language conventions one of the four major aspects of its curriculum. In Vermont, spelling gets top billing among the language objectives up through grade 6.

Process-Oriented Writing Instruction

Writing is often taught with more of a process

focus than is reading. While states such as Arkansas, with a notable skill focus, build the skills from the bottom up in both writing and reading, there are numerous examples of states where a process orientation in writing stands beside a bottom-up skill focus in reading.

Many state curricula treat writing as a process that begins with a writer's purpose growing out of his or her background. Texas begins with process goals for writing and then deals with the mechanics. New Mexico builds reading ability with bottom-up acquisition of skills, but develops listening, speaking, and writing as processes. Often some analysis of audience helps dictate the organization and thrust of the written product. The performance approach continues as the student becomes editor of his or her own writing (and sometimes of a peer's work), attending to the mechanics--the specific skill focus--as a part of the natural process.

The process approach is certainly evident in Idaho's secondary guide and in those from New York, Hawaii, Wisconsin, Virginia, Michigan, and Alaska. Hawaii's attention to the consideration of purpose, audience, and occasion when writing effectively incorporates thinking and stresses a purpose for writing that is basically overlooked in most other states' curricula: *Writing is a highly effective way to learn.* The Hawaii curriculum values writing as a tool for sharing experiences and meaning, for making decisions, for restructuring values, and for achieving self-discovery.

Wisconsin's guide, too, calls writing a "catalyst to thinking" and Michigan's has a set of goals for using writing to learn. Virginia's curriculum, which is not nearly so process-oriented overall, stresses the importance of using writing to learn and encourages the development of written student responses to peer writing. While at some grades this guide is structured on very traditionally classified approaches to critical thinking, a few grades employ student writing for problem solving.

Michigan mentions, but does not elaborate, on the use of student publications in structuring writing instruction as process, and Alaska's guide emphasizes revision and peer editing. No state guide, however, goes into explicit detail about how to produce student publications or details how each can underline the importance of understanding the writing process. In most guides that use the term *publication* in this way, the students are asked to pretend that what they write has its ultimate impact in print actually circulated to other readers.

Theoretical Understanding

The guides that promote the writing emphases discussed above are direct reflections of what current theory and research have suggested about language and language development. California's guide is a treatise that pointedly rejects a skill-drill focus and mandates a literature-based curriculum. Wisconsin's describes all types of curriculum emphases in order to promote discussion, yet there is something persuasive about the book's presentation of language as a communication process based on an awareness of purpose and audience. The same is true of the Connecticut guide. Hawaii's 100-page discussion of what is now known about language has clear implications for curriculum. Maryland's reading goals stress background, purposes, sources of information, and student attitudes and behaviors in developing reading as a personal activity.

The commitment to language-process instruction is less pronounced in other guides. Despite its discussion of language process, the Idaho guide places considerable emphasis on language conventions. Illinois makes no apologies for including skill emphases that will be tested. New York's curriculum at the lowest grades could be a model for process/performance-based curricula, but it changes dramatically after those initial grades. The same is true of North Carolina's curriculum up through grade 5. A heavy skill-focus sets in after that, and it looks far more like traditional curricula that have not intended to reflect current theory. With Michigan's present draft of its curriculum, reading and listening do not reflect the performance emphasis on process and product.

Alaska is the one of the states that try to cover all of the bases--reflecting what scholars would now argue defines language development, but also incorporating all that has traditionally been associated with language instructional goals. This can also be said of Virginia, Illinois, and Michigan, among others. Alaska's guide gives a kind of reasonable synthesis of some of the new understanding about language, while making use of all the skill tags that had developed in reading textbooks before recent editions. In a nutshell, Alaska's sensible perspective is well represented by its inclusion of both handwriting and keyboarding skills.

Both the Illinois and Texas guides articulately combine both process and skill focuses with an air of authority. However, the extent to which the influential Texas curriculum actually reflects current process theory is a matter of some debate. Communication cannot be meaningful, the Texas skill list of *Essential Elements* makes clear, without a firm and foundational control of language conventions.

Curricular Integration of Language Behaviors

While nearly every guide with any kind of introduction or rationale calls for, or at least mentions, the integration of language behaviors--listening, speaking, reading, and writing--not all of the curricula that claim to integrate the behaviors would ensure that this happens. One example of good intentions that may not produce the desired result is the New Mexico guide, which presents goals for the behaviors separately while arguing that they should be integrated in practice.

The Utah guide for grades K-6 claims to integrate the language behaviors with thinking and numerous drama activities as a total process of learning and applying what is learned, yet the implementation of this intention across the entire curriculum is spotty. At grade 5, for example, the goals for the literature strand become traditional after having been closely tied to reader purposes in grade 4. Reading goals are quite traditional, while writing goals in both grades are varied, purpose-oriented, and of high potential interest to students.

New York's guide calls for using all the behaviors to accomplish instructional tasks, yet its discussion tends to separate them while relating them to each other as a process of language implementation. The "receptives," reading and listening, are designated as creating understanding, while the "expressives," writing and speaking, are described as using the understanding facilitated by the receptives to solve problems.

In the Wisconsin volume, language behaviors are seen as the "arts" in language arts; the behaviors are to be integrated with other subjects, communication media, thinking, concepts, experiences, and a focus on purpose and audience.

Several other states structure their curricula in such a way as to promote, and even ensure, integration. North Dakota's process-oriented categories for goals, which begin with information gathering and include revision and reviewing, are applied to all the language behaviors, and that approach encourages integration.

Alaska promotes integration of the language behaviors, as well as subject content integration, by housing goals within the physical, social, emotional, cognitive, and creative development of the child. Some of the general topics under which Michigan groups objectives force a kind of integration of the behaviors: Michigan's objectives are classified as a cultural set, a language arts set, a technology set, and a career/employability set.

California's insistence on the use of texts that promote truly meaningful contexts for the student, ties reading to the other modes, especially writing, in a very genuine way. In effect, Wisconsin and Connecticut help promote the integration of language behaviors by using ample instructional suggestions throughout their guides. This approach may have the surest impact on teachers who use the guides.

Integrating Thinking into Language Use

Language theory suggests that thinking is the inherent link in language processes. Inspired both by the traditional emphasis on teaching critical thinking as a part of the language arts and by critical concerns that U.S. schools are not training thinkers, most curricula have installed thinking goals related to language processing and/or have retained and reemphasized instruction on the traditional thinking skills, such as comparison/contrast, classification, summarizing, etc.

Despite highly traditional objectives throughout the curriculum it describes, the North Dakota guide articulates the relationship between language and thinking as effectively as any. It would develop the students' abilities:

· to make increasingly more and finer distinctions among the elements of their experience
· to see increasingly more suitable connections among objects, forces, processes, people, and events.

Arkansas (grades 1-8), Vermont, Alaska, and Nevada (K-6) all stress the traditional objectives long associated with thinking. North Carolina places a pronounced emphasis on thinking in language processing and uses Bloom's taxonomy.

Hawaii is one of several states that include a more process-oriented incorporation of thinking into their curriculum objectives. In Hawaii, thinking is implicitly involved in the establishment of purpose for using language, in considering the audience or author perspectives, and in analyzing the situation in which language is to be used. Montana stresses thinking skills as problem solving. Like Wisconsin, Michigan, and Virginia, North Dakota ties language use directly to learning.

Literature-Based Curricula

The California *English Language Arts Framework* articulates the philosophy that guides the state's curriculum, citing literature as "the core of the curriculum"--affecting strategies for teaching listening, speaking, reading, and writing. That impact is clearly process- and performance-oriented. The overriding goal of the curriculum is to promote students' development by encouraging wide and thoughtful reading, reflected in writing and speaking done in a variety of useful formats that serve the reasonable purposes of language users. The objective is to integrate the language behaviors, as students are encouraged to relate important writings from many disciplines to their lives.

In comparing "effective features" with the "ineffective features" of English-language arts programs and in discussing instructional strategies, the California guide makes it clear that, in its philosophy, a literature-based program is almost diametrically opposed to a bottom-up skills focus. The guide, however, resists going beyond general recommendations for instruction, a few classroom examples that support them, and numerous brief examples of how students' performance and progress within the curriculum might be assessed.

While California's central focus on literature is unique, the resurgence of literature as a major focus of the language arts is not. Literature is one of four major goals in Idaho's secondary curriculum, for example. The four modes of language, plus a strand labeled "viewing" are integrated within themes, such as contemporary issues, American studies, and multicultural perspectives.

Many states, such as Alaska, whose guide includes exemplary specific reading selections within some sample learning activities, now profess to emphasize literature. In some of these, literature is identified as a key aspect of language arts along with the oral communication modes, writing, and sometimes reading--considered distinct from literature. Vermont is another example of a state that identifies literature as a key aspect of the language arts. As in several other states, the Vermont goals for literature are very "top-down" and reader-oriented at the lowest grade levels but are traditional after that. This is truer of literature than of other key aspects such as writing, media, and reasoning, where application of the instruction to the students' lives is stressed at one or more grade levels.

Yet in most of these curricula, attention to literature is much like that in others that do not claim a new emphasis on literature. Most states focus on traditional goals that have often been associated with "literature appreciation." This is the case, for example, in New York, where the guide articulately promotes process-oriented, theory-conscious instruction, yet treats reading quite traditionally.

Many states cover an emphasis on literature, almost exclusively with objectives that will enable students to identify genres and to analyze fiction according to literary elements such as plot, setting, and character development. While some of these states may mention the potential of literature to enlighten a student's understanding of life, they almost invariably return to traditional academic focuses when articulating particular goals. Seldom is literature used explicitly to promote value assessment, decision making, or an increased understanding of human behavior. Even in Hawaii, where thinking and language, including reading, are wedded for a purpose-dictated communication focus, literature tends to be treated as the recognition of genres.

Numerous state language arts curricula now state the importance of using literature to build awareness and appreciation of different cultures. Montana, which like California has a literature-based curriculum, mandates that a school's language arts program represent many cultures.

Other Issues

Other Emphases

If the state language arts curriculum guides can be identified as reflecting current theoretical understanding of language behavior, they might be expected to reflect issues of major concern in language arts instruction today. This is the case for some issues, but the lack of impact of other issues is somewhat surprising.

The Response to Technological Development

Two concerns regarding the technological developments affecting language use have had some impact on language arts curricula. One, of course, is computers; the other is often labeled in the guides as media or viewing.

While some states call only for basic familiarization with computers and with keyboarding, Alaska has specified new objectives under the headings *media study, computers, word processing,* and *new communication technologies.*

Nevada is one of the few other states to specify word processing as an objective, but it need not be mastered until the senior year in high school. No state details the potential for teaching the writing process by stressing word processing and its facilitation of the revision process. Nevada uses the term *computer literacy;* however, no guide exploits the computer as a communication tool by including objectives that will encourage exposing students to this now well-established technology.

The media get attention in some guides because they have created the need for critical viewing. States such as North Carolina, Tennessee, and Idaho (at the secondary level) have labeled viewing as a major category of language arts objectives, which tend to resemble critical thinking objectives more practically applied. New Mexico links media competencies with library use, and Vermont incorporates study skills and technology with performance goals and critical responses reserved for higher grade levels. In a general statement, Michigan recognizes the impact of technologies on language use; however, this general statement awaits specific objectives in a subsequent version of its guide. Michigan stresses the importance of learning the applications of technology, acquiring the skills to make the most of technology, understanding its limitations and power, learning to select the correct technology, using it to solve problems, and adapting technology to particular situations.

Accountability Testing

Numerous states with curriculum guides are among those that have some kind of minimum competency or accountability testing. Yet few states are as direct about acknowledging the link between testing and curriculum as Texas, which has carefully coordinated its language arts curriculum with the highly structured *Essential Elements*—skills that are covered by its testing program.

Mississippi denotes those skills that are tested as "basic" on its exhaustive list of objectives. The guide indicates at what levels such skills may be introduced, as a local option, but the grade by which they must be mastered is not optional. Students are tested on specific skills at specific grades by the state's *Basic Skills Assessment Program* (BSAP). Skills noted as "functional" are tested on the state's *Functional Literacy Test.* The guide cautions that "to promote maximum

performance on the BSAP and the Functional Literacy Test, teachers must be aware of the curriculum in all subjects and at all grade levels."

The Louisiana guide clearly indicates that it is part of the state's competency legislation. While the Illinois curriculum's goals are not nearly so numerous or explicit as those of Mississippi and Louisiana, the curriculum is geared directly to match state testing. That is why curriculum exists only for grades 3, 6, 8, 10, and 12--the grades tested statewide.

While other states may not be so direct about the relationships between their curricula and their testing, it is clear that many others are written to be compatible with, reflect, and endorse testing programs.

Textbook Adoption and Skill Orientation

A study of the link between state textbook adoption policies and language arts curricula might prove illuminating. While it might be hypothesized that states with textbook adoption policies would be more apt to have state curriculum guides and to articulate more traditional curricula, a cursory look at the guides does not necessarily support that assumption. (Generally, the adoption states are in the West and across the South of the nation to the East Coast.)

Few have considered what impact the emphases in language arts textbooks have on setting state goals, but it has been suggested that state textbook adoption policies have a significant impact on textbooks. It is important, of course, for publishers to have their books approved by states with adoption policies. Thus, it is highly conceivable that publishers pay attention to the goals in state curricula. Supposedly, populous states such as Texas have had an impact on reading textbooks, for example, which to be adopted in Texas must make a point of reflecting the state's *Essential Elements.*

Yet the guide from California, also a populous adoption state, describes a curricular thrust in language arts that provides no list of skills at all! If the Texas curriculum has influenced the development of language arts materials, so has California's; that probability makes it difficult, indeed, to make generalizations linking state textbook adoption policies with particular types of curricula.

Other Issues

Some important issues in language arts curriculum have had only limited impact on the state guides and only in a few states:

Metacognition: Alaska, Hawaii, and Michigan—which has a whole set of goals that develop students' awareness of how they are processing language—discuss metacognition. Alaska would have its students apply, analyze, and synthesize what they learn about the many uses of language. The Arkansas guide for grades 9-12 briefly discusses intrapersonal communication as a goal.

Language across the curriculum: Alaska is one of a very few states that pay much attention to the role of language in learning across the curriculum. Its guide argues that across-content instruction creates the opportunity for "holistic learning." Language, it notes, is the core of all curricula. Montana also calls for a cross-content instruction as does California, thus broadening the term *literature* in its literature-based program.

Performance assessment: The criticism of standardized assessment in the language arts continues, but there is only limited curricular response and in only a few states. Georgia's guide, which consists of a series of short essays on key issues in the language arts written by national authorities, includes one essay on assessment. It deals, for the most part, with the use of published tests.

Like California, some states specifically describe alternative forms of assessment that teachers can use in the classroom. Iowa does this in an appendix. North Carolina's explicit "measures" for its numerous objectives suggest a tireless and ongoing process of observation and assessment by teachers. Alaska puts emphasis on a variety of performance assessments, and Arizona recommends assessing reading with writing, a method now being developed at state and local levels as well as by several commercial publishers.

New York calls for informal, holistic assessment that matches the process-orientation it claims is its guiding philosophy:

> Procedures used for testing, appraising, and judging students' success in the English language area curriculum must necessarily be in harmony with the philosophy underlying that curriculum. Thus, in an integrated curriculum with an emphasis on meaning, evaluation should focus on how successful students are at discovering and creating meaning for themselves.

Parent involvement: Although several guides mention parents and suggest a few ways to involve them in the language development of their children, Wisconsin goes considerably further and treats the involvement of parents in a substantive way. Each chapter in the Wisconsin guide has a subsection for parents.

Curriculum adaptation for special audiences: Several states mention the importance of including materials for special audiences. These include states with large student populations for whom English is a second language: Alaska, Hawaii, California, and Texas. Wyoming is another state that mandates such adaptation.

The use of courses in lieu of graded objectives serves Florida well in this regard. Its guides include numerous optional courses for students for whom English is a second language. These courses tend to be more skill-focused than those they would replace.

Conclusions

Recommended Development

This analysis of the thirty-eight state language arts curriculum guides has revealed a host of considerations that could help guide those who are developing such a curriculum. The ideas that arise as one looks at the guides are too numerous to review here. These specific observations, however, can be summarized in several important general conclusions that states developing and revising language arts curricula should consider.

Clearly Articulated Philosophy

This study suggests that the most potentially effective state curricula grew out of a clearly articulated and well-understood philosophy. California's guide is the clearest example of an uncompromising adoption of a guiding philosophy. The guide proceeds to discuss how the literature-based, process-oriented philosophy should affect instructional goals and methods and assure the integration of key aspects of the language arts. If the presentation has a shortcoming, it is that these discussions are short. Teachers may want and need more examples—more extension of how a philosophy that is a clear mandate and policy can be implemented in their classrooms.

A state need not necessarily adopt a philosophy that so emphatically endorses a particular instructional approach, but its curriculum developers should openly clarify and describe any unique adaptation or mix of philosophies and demonstrate how the result has impacted on their curriculum. Many states, however, do not adequately articulate the beliefs about language and language development that have guided their efforts. Some of the guides present no such introductory discussion at all.

Another observation based on this study is that some states' articulation of the philosophy they followed (see table 2) does not stand up when one examines the resulting curriculum. Other states discuss key aspects of the language arts that add up to a kind of overriding philosophy, but those beliefs do not appear to have had a substantive effect on the formulation of the curriculum goals and objectives. Nearly every guide with such commentary professes a belief in integration of the major aspects of language arts, yet many of these states' curricula do not support that claim.

In still other states, the guiding philosophy's impact on the curriculum is spotty. Skill-focused objectives are stated for one language mode at a particular grade, and process-oriented goals are outlined for another mode at that same grade. At the next grade level, the emphases may be just the opposite. A high-school curriculum may appear to effectively integrate the language modes with literature, thinking, and critical analyses of self and society; yet these emphases may follow eight years of a strictly bottom-up curriculum that specifies little about content, purposes, or applications of the behaviors learned. If a state is going to endorse both direct instruction of language skills and instruction that develops the language arts through student performance, vacillating between the two does not appear the most effective way to establish the balance.

It is not enough for a state language arts curriculum guide merely to imply or even state that the rationale for its contents is a match for the content and focuses of the state assessment program. That content—in the tests and then in the curriculum—should come from a philosophy that can be openly and clearly stated. North Carolina, for example, demonstrates that a heavily skill-structured curriculum can be rationalized with a honest presentation of the beliefs that motivated it. The North Carolina guide openly contends that attention to language skills and direct instruction of them are essential.

The Texas guide's articulation of the state's philosophy may appear to be more process oriented than the curriculum itself. Yet a close analysis suggests that the philosophical statement puts a different spin on some of the terms that are more commonly associated with process-

oriented philosophies; at the same time, the many skills representing the Texas *Essential Elements* are built in a kind of developmental sequence that educators in the state truly believe is a valid representation of language process and the process of developing language abilities. One might disagree, and some might feel uneasy with the Texas use of process-oriented terminology, but the philosophy is laid open and carefully articulated, allowing those and other reactions to it.

States whose philosophy includes the conviction that curricula should be developed as nearly as possible for particular types of students need to present all philosophical facets of this issue that may guide local curriculum developers. Several states, such as Wisconsin and Connecticut, appear to have done a reasonable job of this.

Assisting Local Curriculum Development

Too many state guides imply or state that they are to be used as frameworks to build local curricula without indicating adequately how they are to be used. If such a guide presents hundreds of language skills across the grades and does not advise that the local developers are to select from the list, the guide appears to be unrealistic. If all of the skills listed for a grade are to be incorporated in a local curriculum, there is little left for the local developers to do, even if they are invited to add still more skills.

Guides that present a highly thought-provoking review of key language arts issues do a good job of stimulating the minds of local developers, but once the thought processes of those who will develop a curriculum have been set in motion, local educators would surely come to value the guide with respect directly equivalent to the amount of good advice it provided for getting the job done. The more audience-oriented a guide is in providing this help, the more it will consider the problems, decisions, and needs of the task force, committees, or individuals doing the job. Detailing the options for who might play what roles would surely be one chapter useful to a local school district beginning the development of a curriculum. If some of the guide's advice ended up seeming mundanely practical and even obvious to some people, it would be very useful to others and could only facilitate the curriculum-development process. Only the Connecticut guide comes close to doing a satisfying job in this regard.

Using a Consistent, Facilitating Presentation

Once the aspects, goals, objectives, and other features of a curriculum are determined, they should be presented in a format and organization that facilitates their grasp and application by teachers and others interested in education. The prose should be as explicit, logically organized, and clear as possible; and the structure or format selected should be consistent or at least complementary across grade levels. It ought to:

· make the information easier to understand; the relationships of the details of the curriculum more obvious; the key aspects, goals, and objectives parallel, distinct, reasonable, and achievable

· help the user understand distinctions such as: objectives that are mandatory and those that are optional; any objectives that the guide feels are best achieved sequentially; what student behavior, performance, or outcome is being recommended.

Imagine, for a moment, being a teacher just hired to teach in a state new to you. You pick up the state language arts curriculum guide and find—with or without an introductory rationale—a very long list of skills under the grade level you are to teach. You notice that they are arranged in skill categories and tend to run from the easiest to the more difficult. "What," you may ask yourself, "am I to do with this list?" Should you expect to teach them all, or do you select? If you may select, on what basis should you do so? If you attempt to teach them all, do you teach them one at a time in the order they are listed?

Or suppose your state's guide is, for the most part, an essay on the controlling philosophy, which recommends always treating the language arts as a process that serves a genuine student need--often communicating with a particular audience. The discussion introduces a very general list of goals, applicable across all the grades. These goals include "broadening understanding of diverse cultures," "developing self-awareness of how language is being used," and "encouraging the application of literature to the individual student's life, understanding, and values structure."

"Fine," you might say. "I agree!" But beyond the assurance that you are working in a state where your philosophy is valued, the guide leaves you on your own to elaborate on goals with objectives and to decide how you will achieve them. Did you have a right to expect a bit more direction from your state curriculum guide?

Providing Instructional Direction

Another thing that a curriculum *guide* should do is give the teacher some indication of how the objectives might best be achieved. As several of the guides demonstrate, this can be done without dictating exact methodologies. Since a curriculum is developed to affect instruction and learning, isn't the inclusion of exemplary teaching approaches something that might be expected, along with goals and objectives? Besides directing implementation of the curriculum, the inclusion of instructional ideas and models clearly indicates what impact the guiding philosophy and the curriculum itself will have in the classroom--a vital consideration to any educational professional applying the curriculum.

Recommending that guides supply instructional guidance does not mean that the state guide should attempt to become a basic source of instructional materials. However, teachers should be given some clear ideas of how to go about implementing various aspects of the curriculum. If a state language arts curriculum guide is to do its job—helping to structure effective instruction or promoting the development of local guides that do—teachers will need to be able to understand and use the guide. It is in each state's interest to make such implementation as easy as possible.

References

Association for Supervision and Curriculum Development. 1991. *ASCD Curriculum Handbook.* Alexandria, VA.

Gallagher, J.J. 1985. *Teaching the Gifted Child.* Boston: Allyn & Bacon.

NCTE Commission to Evaluate Curriculum Guides and Competency Requirements. 1990. *Commended English Language Arts Curriculum Guides, K-12.* Urbana, IL: National Council of Teachers of English. (ERIC Document Reproduction Service No. ED 322 522.)

NCTE Committee to Evaluate Curriculum Guides and Competency Requirements. 1987. *Recommended English Language Arts Curriculum Guides, K-12.* Urbana, IL: National Council of Teachers of English. (ERIC Document Reproduction Service No. ED 286 204.)

Piazza, S., and C. Suhor. 1990. *Trends and Issues in English Instruction, 1990: Six Summaries.* Urbana, IL: National Council of Teachers of English. (ERIC Document Reproduction Service No. ED 315 793.)

Piazza, S., and C. Suhor. 1991. *Trends and Issues in English Instruction, 1991.* Urbana, IL: National Council of Teachers of English. (ERIC Document Reproduction Service No. ED 335 699.)

Tchudi, S. 1991. *Planning and Assessing the Curriculum in English Language Arts.* Alexan-dria, VA: Association for Supervision and Curriculum Development.

VanTassel-Baska, J. 1988. *Comprehensive Curriculum for Gifted Learners.* Boston: Allyn & Bacon.

■

Table 2
Summary of the Philosophy for Each Curriculum Guide

State, (Grades), Philosophy/Focus Label	Philosophy
Alabama (K-12) Integrated Language Arts	"The study of language arts is the basic foundation of learning..." "Language study is, by necessity, a recursive process; that is, recurring learning activities appear at the various grade levels." "The language arts are interrelated..."p. 1
Alaska (K) Integrated Language Arts	"The purpose of education, and particularly kindergarten education, is to foster the development of the whole child, and to develop competency in all areas of life." "This integrated curriculum model is based on six premises, as stated by JoAnne Hendrick in her book, TOTAL LEARNING FOR THE WHOLE CHILD..." p.iv
Alaska (1-12) Integrated Language Arts	"Language arts is the heart and soul of every school's curriculum. This guide reflects a process approach to LA...stressing the inter-relationships between the language arts and connections with other disciplines." Also emphasized: culture, parental involvement, meaning, literature, and skills
Arizona (K-12) Integrated Language Arts	Their philosophy seems to be based on a list of 10 "widely held concepts about language arts instruction" p. 10-11 Examples listed below: 1) "Language and thinking are closely connected. Teachers can help students learn to think through learning to use language." 2) "Writing is one of the most powerful ways of teaching students to think because..." 3) "Language arts involves whole acts..." 4) "Language arts skills are not sequential." 5) "Students do not need to master one aspect of lang arts to be able to go on to the next." 6) "Evaluation in lang arts is not the same as evaluation in other content areas. 7) All of the strands reinforce each other 8) All strands are equally important
Arkansas (Lang Arts 1-12) Not Determined	
Arkansas (Reading 1-8) Not Determined	
California (K-12) Integrated Language Arts	"The main features of an English-language arts curriculum that reinforces that goals of our reform movement include: 1) a systematic literature program with a meaning centered approach based on intensive reading, writing, speaking and listening, 2) a clearly communicated sense of common values and common goals that respect diversity, 3) an emphasis on delight in the beauty and heritage of our language. Revitalizing English-language arts instruction through a literature-based curriculum is a critical part of our overall educational reform movement." p. v
Connecticut (K-12) Integrated Language Arts	
Delaware (K) Not Determined	
Delaware (Lang Arts 1-12) Not Determined	

Table 2 / 111

State, (Grades). Philosophy/Focus Label	Philosophy
Delaware (Reading 1-12) Not Determined	
Florida (6-8) Not Determined	
Florida (9-12) Not Determined	
Georgia (Lang Arts K-12) Not Determined	
Georgia (K-4) Integrated Language Arts	"Reading is the multisensory process for constructing meaning from written text. To accomplish this, the child must use a variety of complex and varied skills." "The major priority of the reading program should be to help the children to integrate information in the text with what they already know." p.iv
Georgia (5-8) Integrated Language Arts	"Reading is the multisensory process for constructing meaning from written text. To accomplish this, the child must use a variety of complex and varied skills." "The major priority of the reading program should be to help the children to integrate information in the text with what they already know." p.iv
Georgia (9-12) Integrated Language Arts	"Reading is the multisensory process for constructing meaning from written text. To accomplish this, the child must use a variety of complex and varied skills." "The major priority of the reading program should be to help the children to integrate information in the text with what they already know." p.iv
Hawaii (K-12) Communication	There is an appendix (p.102-3) that has samples of 3 philosophies from different public schools. I'm not sure this guide declares a philosophy, but instead gives instructions for a school to develop their own.
Idaho (K-8) Integrated Language Arts	"English language arts is the integrated and sequential study of literature, composition, and language through ...[strands]" "Ability in one of the language arts influences ability in the others; instruction in one affects learning in the others; exposure in one encourages growth in the others." p.1
Idaho (9-12) Integrated Language Arts	"English language arts is the integrated and sequential study of literature, composition, and language through ...[strands]" "Ability in one of the language arts influences ability in the others; instruction in one affects learning in the others; exposure in one encourages growth in the others." p.iii
Illinois (3-12) Integrated Language Arts	"The emphasis in language arts is on skills, not content areas." p.1 "The skills and knowledge of the LA are essential for student success in virtually all areas of the curriculum. They are also central requirements to the development of clear expression and critical thinking. The language arts include the study of literature and the development of skills in reading, writing, speaking and listening." p.3
Indiana (K-12) Not Determined	"The goal of the English/language arts curriculum is to develop proficient language users- readers, writers, speakers, listeners, thinkers-who can use language to think and learn independently, grow personally, participate in a democratic society.

State, (Grades). Philosophy/Focus Label	Philosophy
Iowa (K-14) Communication	"Language is a process of social interaction." "Language learning develops as the young child explores his or her immediate environment and interacts with the persons in it." "Language arts as a school program begins with the existing language capacities of individual students and involves interactive processes of composing and comprehending." "Educational equity is an important part of the language arts program." p.5
Louisiana (K-12) Communication	4 philosophical principles: 1. "Reading, writing, speaking & listening are inseparable components of the lang communication process. Listening & reading involve comprehension processes, speaking & writing involve production processes. Interrelationship of these components is presented graphically in the communication model..." p.xiii ... 2. "Because the language arts are interrelated, reading and writing communication can not be taught as a set of isolated skills, but instead must be taught in the context of actual reading and writing processes."... 3. "These 4 language arts strands are processes rather than content..." 4. "All varieties of language have value and are useful in different situations and with different audiences." ...
Maryland (K-12) Integrated Language Arts	"Through the English language arts, human beings use language to communicate, to create, and to comprehend experience. An English language arts integrates reading, writing, speaking, listening, language and literature." "The English language arts curriculum has two purposes: 1) to enable students to gain conscious control of their thought and language, and 2)to help students enjoy language as art and entertainment. Both these aspects, cognitive and affective, have content and process that are taught within the context of a balanced, integrated program.
Michigan (K-12) Outcome Model	"The outcomes defined in the draft Model Core Curriculum address both the content and process of learning." p.ii "The core outcomes, if successfully integrated and realized through a comprehensive curriculum, should prepare individuals to be functional, competent, productive participants in society who are able to apply knowledge in diverse and changing situations." p.ii "The outcomes defined within the draft Model Core Curriculum transcend traditional curricular boundaries by addressing real life skills and integrating problem solving, critical thinking, and decision making skills into all the curricular areas." p.iii
Minnesota (K-12) Communication	"Language is a tool by which we can satisfy our need to understand the world and through which we can understand how it acts upon us." They suggest that students should be encouraged to do the above through the use of the strands (speaking, etc.). Also emphasize that even when integrating all the strands, they must still "address the uniqueness of each". -Believe language arts has its base in oral language -Believe reading should be comprehension-centered -Believe in using cultural literature -Believe writing is important for personal growth -Believe that curriculum should be responsive to needs of students
Mississippi (K-12) Communication	"The English/Language Arts program offered by Mississippi schools includes the development of oral language skills, the writing process, and literature appreciation. The goal of the language arts curriculum is to help students develop effective and appropriate communication skills through the use of integrated listening, speaking, reading and writing activities. Realization of this goal will be reflected in students' competent use of receptive...and expressive language skills..." p. LA-1
Missouri (2-10) Not Determined	

Table 2 / 113

State, (Grades). Philosophy/Focus Label	Philosophy
Montana (K-12) Communication	"Language is at the core of successful schooling and living.... Thus, effective communication arts programs have a very high priority in the curricula of Montana schools. The education program in Communication Arts encompasses the study of languages and literatures, the development of reading, writing, listening, and speaking skills, effective media use, and the nurturing of creative, logical, and critical thinking." p.17
Nevada (K-8) Communication	"Language arts teach communication, the ability to receive, interpret and express experiences and ideas that are basic to all learning. The language arts program will provide these necessary skills." "Above all the language arts program fosters a love for language. The program is based on the creation and expression of ideas and the use of logical thinking skills. The development of effective communication is the process that allows students to use their thinking skills as they move from experience to expression. Language arts skills are interrelated and students experiences are expressed through a variety of activities for different audiences."
Nevada (9-12) Communication	"It [English] helps students acquire self-sufficiency and work independently in all disciplines." "It [English] offers students experiences... that aid their personal growth and academic enhancement. The study of English challenges the analytical and creative capabilities of students, expands the capacities of the human intellect, and preserves the tradition of free thought through active participation in a democratic society."
New Hampshire (K-8) Not Determined	
New Hampshire (5-8) Communication	"Language arts provide for the development of verbal, aural, visual and non-verbal skills of communication and thus are important for the middle school student." "Language arts provides opportunities for students to dramatize their thoughts and feelings and to express themselves fully and creatively through use of a variety of media and the theater arts." p.39
New Hampshire (9-12) Not Determined	
New Mexico (1-8) Integrated Language Arts	"Effective instruction will carefully integrate [strands] (and the studying competencies), rather than separate them; this approach will foster better language facility in our students and help them to develop higher order critical thinking skills. Additionally, effective instruction will provide all students, including who are limited-English-proficient, with meaningful contexts for using language for meaningful purposes."
New Mexico (9-12) Not Determined	

State, (Grades). Philosophy/Focus Label	Philosophy
New York (K-12) Integrated Language Arts	"An integrated curriculum in the English language arts is one in which: - reading, writing, listening, and speaking are taught with in a "literate environment" in context that are meaningful to the students - reading, writing, listening, and speaking are considered language processes that interact in various ways to allow communication to occur-language study happens naturally as part of helping students become clear, precise, effective communicators-formal evaluation of subskill mastery is de-emphasized in favor of methods that allow for observation of students actively engaged in the communication process." p.2
North Carolina (K-12) Integrated Language Arts	"The full integration of the processes of listening, speaking, reading, writing and viewing leads to improved thinking and problem solving. Learning experiences should be designed to enable students to apply those integrated processes in meaningful real-life situations. Language is learned through use." p.109
North Carolina Teacher Handbook Communication Skills (K-12) Integrated Language Arts	"The primary purposes of the [guide] and the competency-based curriculum are 1) to help students become responsible, productive citizens and 2) to help students achieve a sense of personal fulfillment."
North Dakota (K-12) Not Determined	"...to enable students to enhance and enjoy the social, cultural, business, and political life around them." "...students must be allowed to be active learners." "The chief goal of learning in the language arts is the intellectual development of students." "Students learn best when they can be challenged in an environment of support." pp. vi-viii
Oklahoma (1-2, 6-12) Integrated Language Arts	Language Arts Philosophy:"Language is a primary medium for thinking and communicating thought." "The mission of the language arts program is to enable students to be fluent, effective communicators and lifelong learners who have an understanding of themselves and the world around them." "Current research indicated that it is essential for students to learn language in a holistic, meaning-centered environment which integrates all of the language acts." p.3 Reading Philosophy:"The major goal in the instruction of reading is for students to become able to read various kinds of text to accomplish various purposes, so that as adults they will be able to participate fully in...their communities and nation." p.13
Oregon (3-11) Integrated Language Arts	"...language is central to learning, the basic of basics. It is through the experience, appreciation and use of language that the vital purposes of creative expression, rational thinking, effective communication, learning how to learn and understanding the human condition are made possible. Therefore, this curriculum takes an integrated approach to the language arts, where students use language skills and knowledge in interrelated and increasingly complex ways."
Pennsylvania (K-12) Integrated Language Arts	"Learning is meaning-centered, social, language-based, and human. (p. 11) These perspectives are not really separate or discrete,...the making of meaning is primary (p. 13);...learning occurs in a social context (p. 15);...all content areas involve the use of language (p. 17);...all learners use language to make meaning in unique ways (p. 20):...an integrative model of language across the curriculum" (p. 139).
S. Dakota (Lang Arts K-12) Integrated Language Arts	

Table 2 / 115

State, (Grades). Philosophy/Focus Label	Philosophy
S. Dakota (Reading 1-12) Communication	"Reading involves perceiving, understanding, interpreting and using printed symbols. Reading is one of the communicative arts. It is not possible to separate reading from auding, speaking, writing and thinking skills." "The reading program must provide balance between the development of word recognition skills and development of comprehension skills..." "Continuous evaluation is essential..."
Tennessee (K-8) Integrated Language Arts	
Tennessee (9-12) Communication	"We are engulfed by communication in all our daily affairs. Listening, thinking, speaking, writing, and reading function together to provide students with the necessary communication skills needed to become exemplary citizens." p.1
Texas (K-12) Communication	"The philosophy...centers around the belief that students, to be successful in and out of the classroom, must be competent users of language." "English language arts education, therefore, must help all students...to communicate more effectively and appropriately in ways that benefit the students and others." p.1
Utah (K-12) Integrated Language Arts	"The purpose of the language arts core is to help students attain language skills that generate and communicate thinking." "1) Thinking, reading, writing, speaking and listening, all interrelated processes, are the core of the curriculum. They are the most basic of all skills. These activities represent an integrated whole... 2) Language skills cannot be productively taught in isolation... 3) Language skills stretch across all mastery levels and subject areas 4) In general, the developmental sequence of language skills is: Fluency - Detail - Abstractions" p.i-ii
Vermont (K-12) Not Determined	
Virginia (K-12) Not Determined	
West Virginia (K-12) Integrated Language Arts	
West Virginia Reading (K-12) Integrated Language Arts	
Wisconsin (K-12) Communication	"...the task force believes that developing students' use of the language is the first curriculum priority of a language arts program. A functional, communication-based approach is the perspective that focuses most clearly on the approach." p.3 "Moffett's view of language as central to the process of communicating and learning has implications both within the language arts curriculum and beyond it in the schoolwide curriculum. Such a view will result in the integration of language arts in a number of ways." p.7

Table 3
Curriculum Strands Included in State Curriculum Guides

	Reading	Writing (Composition)	Listening	Speaking	Viewing	Literature	Study Skills (Learning Skills)	Thinking (Reasoning)	Media (Print/Visual)	Language: Concepts, Processes, Study	Vocabulary	Grammar (Lang. Struct./Usage)	Handwriting	Spelling	Reading/Writing	Listening/Speaking	Career Awareness	Word Attack/Recognition Skills	Comprehension	Research Skills	Expressive	Receptive
Alabama (K-12)	Yes	Yes	Yes	Yes																		
Alaska (K)															Yes	Yes						
Alaska (1-12)	Yes	Yes	Yes	Yes			Yes			Yes												
Arizona (K-12)	Yes	Yes	Yes	Yes						Yes												
Arkansas (Lang. 1-8)		Yes				Yes	Yes					Yes		Yes						Yes		
Arkansas (Lang. 9-12)		Yes				Yes						Yes		Yes						Yes		
Arkansas (Rdg. 1-8)	Yes		Yes	Yes		Yes	Yes				Yes							Yes	Yes	Yes		
California (K-12)	Yes	Yes	Yes	Yes	Yes																	
Connecticut (K-12)	Yes	Yes		Yes	Yes	Yes		Yes				Yes										
Delaware (K)	Yes		Yes	Yes	Yes																	
Delaware (1-12)		Yes	Yes	Yes		Yes	Yes															
Delaware (Rdg. 1-12)						Yes					Yes								Yes	Yes		
Florida (6-8)	Yes	Yes				Yes	Yes	Yes			Yes				Yes	Yes			Yes	Yes		
Florida (9-12)	Yes	Yes		Yes		Yes	Yes	Yes			Yes	Yes								Yes		
Georgia (Lang. K-12)	Yes	Yes	Yes	Yes		Yes	Yes					Yes								Yes		
Georgia (Rdg. K-4)	Yes	Yes					Yes												Yes			
Georgia (Rdg. 5-8)	Yes	Yes		Yes		Yes	Yes				Yes								Yes			
Georgia (Rdg. 9-12)	Yes	Yes				Yes	Yes	Yes														
Hawaii (K-12)	Yes	Yes		Yes		Yes				Yes												
Idaho (K-8)	Yes	Yes	Yes	Yes	Yes																	

Table 3 / 117

	Reading	Writing (Composition)	Listening	Speaking	Viewing	Literature	Study Skills (Learning Skills)	Thinking (Reasoning)	Media (Print/Visual)	Language: Concepts, Processes, Study	Vocabulary	Grammar (Lang. Struct./Usage)	Handwriting	Spelling	Reading/Writing	Listening/Speaking	Career Awareness	Word Attack/Recognition Skills	Comprehension	Research Skills	Expressive	Receptive
Idaho (9-12)	Yes	Yes	Yes	Yes	Yes			Yes														
Illinois (3-12)	Yes	Yes	Yes	Yes		Yes																
Indiana (K-12)	Yes	Yes	Yes	Yes				Yes														
Iowa (K-14)	Yes	Yes	Yes	Yes	Yes																	
Louisiana (K-12)		Yes					Yes				Yes	Yes		Yes				Yes	Yes			
Maryland (K-12)	Yes	Yes	Yes	Yes		Yes						Yes										
Michigan (K-12)	Yes	Yes	Yes	Yes		Yes																
Minnesota (K-12)	Yes	Yes	Yes	Yes																		
Mississippi (K-12)		Yes				Yes							Yes	Yes								
Missouri (2-10)	Yes	Yes														Yes						
Montana (K-12)	Yes	Yes	Yes	Yes		Yes		Yes	Yes	Yes												
Nevada (K-8)	Yes	Yes	Yes	Yes			Yes	Yes									Yes		Yes			
Nevada (9-12)	Yes	Yes	Yes	Yes		Yes		Yes												Yes		
New Hamp. (K-8)	Yes	Yes	Yes	Yes																		
New Hamp. (5-8)	Yes	Yes	Yes	Yes																		
New Hamp. (9-12)	Yes	Yes	Yes	Yes	Yes																	
New Mexico (1-8)	Yes	Yes	Yes	Yes			Yes															
New Mexico (Grad. Req.)	Yes	Yes	Yes	Yes			Yes															
New York (K-12)	Yes	Yes														Yes						
N. Carolina (Guide K-12)	Yes	Yes	Yes	Yes	Yes		Yes					Yes	Yes						Yes			
N. Carolina (Handbook)	Yes		Yes	Yes	Yes	Yes	Yes					Yes	Yes						Yes			

	Reading	Writing (Composition)	Listening	Speaking	Viewing	Literature	Study Skills (Learning Skills)	Thinking (Reasoning)	Media (Print/Visual)	Language: Concepts, Processes, Study	Vocabulary	Grammar (Lang. Struct./Usage)	Handwriting	Spelling	Reading/Writing	Listening/Speaking	Career Awareness	Word Attack/Recognition Skills	Comprehension	Research Skills	Expressive	Receptive
N. Dakota (K-12)	Yes	Yes	Yes	Yes																		
Oklahoma (1-2, 6-12)	Yes									Yes												
Oregon (3-11)																					Yes	Yes
Pennsylvania (K-12)	Yes	Yes	Yes	Yes				Yes		Yes				Yes	Yes	Yes						
S. Dakota (Lang. K-12)	Yes	Yes	Yes	Yes																	Yes	Yes
S. Dakota (Rdg. K-12)	Yes		Yes	Yes		Yes	Yes											Yes	Yes			
Tennessee (K-8)										Yes												
Tennessee (9-12)																					Yes	Yes
Texas (K-12)	Yes	Yes	Yes	Yes	Yes							Yes				Yes						
Utah (K-12)	Yes	Yes	Yes	Yes				Yes														
Vermont (K-12)	Yes	Yes				Yes		Yes	Yes			Yes		Yes		Yes						
Virginia (K-12)		Yes	Yes							Yes					Yes				Yes			
W. Virginia (Lang. K-12)	Yes	Yes	Yes	Yes				Yes														
W. Virginia (Rdg. K-12)	Yes																					
Wisconsin (K-12)	Yes	Yes	Yes	Yes		Yes		Yes				Yes										

6

STATE-LEVEL CURRICULUM GUIDELINES: A LISTING

THIS chapter provides bibliographic information on the state curriculum documents discussed in chapter 5. The publications are organized by state; for each state, we have provided the full address for that state's department of education, including the office to contact regarding curriculum publications (if such an office has been specified by the state department). The phone number shown is the best number to use for ordering the publications or for getting further information on the publications. We have also provided the addresses and phone numbers for states whose departments of education do not publish statewide curriculum frameworks. These states may produce curriculum materials on specific topics in English/language arts and in other disciplines, but they are not statewide guides as described in chapter 5.

For each publication, the listing provides the full title, document number and/or ISBN (if available), number of pages, year of publication (or reprinting), and price. Pricing is given on those publications for which Kraus had information; note that the prices shown are taken from the department's order form. Shipping and handling are often extra, and some states offer discounts for purchases of multiple copies. If a document is listed in ERIC, its ED number is shown as well.

Alabama

State Department of Education
Gordon Persons Office Building
50 North Ripley Street
Montgomery, AL 36130-3901

Division of Student Instructional Services
Coordinator, Curriculum Development/Courses
of Study
(205) 242-8059

Alabama Course of Study: Humanities
Bulletin 1983, no. 16, 57p., 1983. $3.00. ED 245
982.

Alabama Course of Study: Language Arts
Bulletin 1987, no. 57, 308p., 1987. $3.00. ED 325
827.

Language Arts, Curriculum Guide, Grades 4-6
Bulletin 1989, no. 41, 729p., 1989. ED 325 828.

Language Arts, Curriculum Guide, Grades 7-8
Bulletin 1990, no. 21, 731p., 1990. ED 325 829.

Alaska

State Department of Education
Goldbelt Building
P.O. Box F
Juneau, AK 99811

Division of Education Program Support
Administrator, Office of Basic Education
(907) 465-2841, Fax (907) 463-5279

Language Arts: Alaska Model Curriculum Guide
Second ed., 164p., 1989.

Arizona

State Department of Education
1535 West Jefferson
Phoenix, AZ 85007

Education Services
Instructional Technology
(602) 542-2147

Arizona Literature Essential Skills
47p., 1990. ED 321 296.

Essential Skills: Language Arts
DDD871, 50p., 1989. $2.12.

Arkansas

Department of Education
Four State Capitol Mall
Room 304 A
Little Rock, AR 72201-1071

Instructional Services
Coordinator, Curriculum and Assessment
(501) 682-4558

Language Arts, Grades 1-8
56p., 1987.

Language Arts, Grades 9-12. Arkansas Public School Course Content Guide
45p., 1987. ED 294 186.

Reading, Grades 1-8
35p., 1987.

California

State Department of Education
P.O. Box 944272
721 Capitol Mall
Sacramento, CA 95814

California Department of Education
Bureau of Publications
(916) 445-1260

English Language Arts Framework for California Public Schools, Kindergarten through Grade Twelve
ISBN 0-8011-0041-0, 62p., 1987. $3.75. ED 288 195.

Handbook for Planning an Effective Literature Program
ISBN 0-8011-0320-7, 64p., 1988. $3.50

Colorado

State Department of Education
201 East Colfax Avenue
Denver, CO 80203-1705

The Colorado State Department of Education does not produce statewide frameworks for K-12 English/language arts.

Connecticut

State Department of Education
P.O. Box 2219
165 Capitol Avenue
State Office Building
Hartford, CT 06106-1630

Program and Support Services
Division of Curriculum and Professional Development
(203) 566-8113

A Guide to Curriculum Development in Language Arts
122p., 1981. ED 262 423.

A Guide to Curriculum Development: Purpose, Practices and Procedures
72p., 1981.

Delaware

State Department of Public Information
P.O. Box 1402
Townsend Building, #279
Dover, DE 19903

Instructional Services Branch
State Director, Instruction Division
(302) 739-4647

Content Standards for Delaware Public Schools
233p., 1986. Includes content standards for
English/language arts.

State Content Standards for English Language Arts.
Volume I: Instructional Activities for Effective
Teaching, Grades 1-3
140p., 1989. ED 321 280.

State Content Standards for English Language Arts.
Volume II: Instructional Activities for Effective
Teaching, Grades 4-6
174p., 1989. ED 321 281.

State Content Standards for English Language Arts.
Volume III: Instructional Activities for Effective
Teaching, Grades 7-8
192p., 1989. ED 321 282.

State Content Standards for English Language Arts.
Volume IV: Instructional Activities for Effective
Teaching, Grades 9-12
270p., 1989. ED 321 283.

Florida

State Department of Education
Capitol Building, Room PL 116
Tallahassee, FL 32301

Curriculum Support Services
Bureau of Elementary and Secondary Education
(904) 488-6547

Curriculum Frameworks for Grades 6-8 Basic
Programs. Volume III: Language Arts/Intensive
English-ESOL
104p., 1990.

Curriculum Frameworks for Grades 9-12 Basic and
Adult Secondary Programs. Volume III: Language

Arts/Intensive English-ESOL
170p., 1990.

Georgia

State Department of Education
2066 Twin Towers East
205 Butler Street
Atlanta, GA 30334

Office of Instructional Programs
Director, General Instruction Division
(404) 656-2412

The Georgia State Department of Education
issues its statewide frameworks on diskette only.

Georgia's Quality Core Curriculum (K-12)
25-diskette set (AppleWorks version) $100.00, 17-
diskette set (IBM-WordStar version) $68.00,
1989. Includes section on English and language
arts.

Reading Education (Curriculum Guide, Elementary
Grades K-4)
175p., 3-diskette set (AppleWorks version)
$12.00, 2-diskette set (IBM-WordStar version)
$8.00, 1991.

Reading Education (Curriculum Guide, Middle
Grades 5-8)
70p., 3-diskette set (AppleWorks version) $12.00,
2-diskette set (IBM-WordStar version) $8.00,
1990, rev. 1991.

Reading Education (Curriculum Guide, Secondary
Grades 9-12)
114p., 2-diskette set (AppleWorks version) $8.00,
1 diskette (IBM-WordStar version) $4.00, 1991.

Hawaii

Department of Education
1390 Miller Street, #307
Honolulu, HI 96813

Office of Instructional Services
Director, General Education Branch
(808) 396-2502

Language Arts Program Guide
RS 88-4889, 110p., 1988.

The Hawaii Department of Education is revising its statewide frameworks; the new publications are scheduled to be available in 1993.

Idaho

State Department of Education
Len B. Jordan Office Building
650 West State Street
Boise, ID 83720

Chief, Bureau of Instruction/School Effectiveness
(208) 334-2165

Secondary English Language Arts: Course of Study
34p., 1991.

Illinois

State Board of Education
100 North First Street
Springfield, IL 62777

School Improvement Services, Curriculum Improvement
(217) 782-2826, Fax (217) 524-6125

State Goals for Learning and Sample Learning Objectives. Language Arts: Grades 3, 6, 8, 10, 12
4M 7-474B-26 no. 238, 63p., 1986. ED 277 001.

Indiana

State Department of Education
Room 229, State House
100 North Capitol Street
Indianapolis, IN 46024-2798

Center for School Improvement and Performance
Manager, Office of Program Development
(317) 232-9157

English/Language Arts Proficiency Guide
15p., 1991 (draft).

Iowa

State Department of Education
Grimes State Office Building
East 14th and Grand Streets
Des Moines, IA 50319-0146

Division of Instructional Services
Bureau Chief, Instruction and Curriculum
(515) 281-8141

A Guide to Curriculum Development in Language Arts. Curriculum Coordinating Committee Report
123p., 1986. ED 276 052.

Kansas

State Department of Education
120 East Tenth Street
Topeka, KS 66612

The Kansas State Department of Education does not produce statewide frameworks.

Kentucky

State Department of Education
1725 Capitol Plaza Tower
500 Mero Street
Frankfort, KY 40601

Office of Learning Programs Development
Division of Curriculum Development
(502) 564-2106

A List of Valued Outcomes for Kentucky's Six Learning Goals. Council on School Performance Standards
6p., n.d.

The Kentucky State Department of Education does not produce other statewide frameworks.

Louisiana

State Department of Education
P.O. Box 94064
626 North 4th Street
12th Floor
Baton Rouge, LA 70804-9064

Office of Academic Programs
Elementary Education (504) 342-3366
Secondary Education (504) 342-3404

*English Language Arts Curriculum Guide, Grades
K-6*
Bulletin 1588, 256 pp., rev. 1986. $6.25. ED 287
166.

*English Language Arts Curriculum Guide, Grades
7-12*
Bulletin 1795, 240 pp., rev. 1986. $6.25. ED 287
167.

Maine

State Department of Education
State House Station no. 23
Augusta, ME 04333

Bureau of Instruction
Director, Division of Curriculum
(207) 289-5928

The Maine State Department of Education does
not produce statewide frameworks.

Maryland

State Department of Education
200 West Baltimore Street
Baltimore, MD 21201

Bureau of Educational Development
Division of Instruction, Branch Chief, Arts and
Sciences
(410) 333-2307

Better English Language Arts
125 pp., n.d.

*English Language Arts. A Maryland Curricular
Framework*
30 pp., n.d.

Massachusetts

State Department of Education
Quincy Center Plaza
1385 Hancock Street
Quincy, MA 02169

School Programs Division
(617) 770-7540

The Massachusetts State Department of Education does not produce statewide frameworks.

Michigan

State Board of Education
P.O. Box 30008
608 West Allegan Street
Lansing, MI 48909

Instructional Specialists Program
(517) 373-7248

Model Core Curriculum Outcomes
73p., 1991 (working document). Contains educational outcomes for K-12 subjects, including
outcomes for language arts and for cultural and
aesthetic awareness.

Minnesota

State Department of Education
712 Capitol Square Building
550 Cedar Street
St. Paul, MN 55101

Minnesota Curriculum Services Center
(612) 483-4442

*Model Learner Outcomes for Language Arts
Education*
E721, 97 p., 1988. $8.00. ED 332 201.

Mississippi

State Department of Education
P.O. Box 771
550 High Street, Room 501
Jackson, MS 39205-0771

Bureau of Instructional Services
(601) 359-3778

Mississippi Curriculum Structure: English/Language Arts 59p., 1986 (sixth printing 1990).

Missouri

Department of Elementary and Secondary
Education
P.O. Box 480
205 Jefferson Street, 6th Floor
Jefferson City, MO 65102

Center for Educational Assessment, University of Missouri--Columbia
(314) 882-4694

Core Competencies and Key Skills for Missouri Schools. Grade 2: Reading/Language Arts
55p., 1991. $10.00, all subjects.

Core Competencies and Key Skills for Missouri Schools. Grade 3: Reading/Language Arts.
55p., 1991. $10.00, all subjects.

Core Competencies and Key Skills for Missouri Schools. Grade 4: Reading/Language Arts
60p., 1991. $10.00, all subjects.

Core Competencies and Key Skills for Missouri Schools. Grade 5: Reading/Language Arts
60p., 1991. $10.00, all subjects.

Core Competencies and Key Skills for Missouri Schools. Grade 6: Reading/Language Arts
60p., 1991. $10.00, all subjects.

Core Competencies and Key Skills for Missouri Schools. Reading/Language Arts, Grades 7 through 10
254p., 1990. $10.00

Montana

Office of Public Instruction
106 State Capitol
Helena, MT 59620

Department of Accreditation and Curriculum Services
Curriculum Assistance and Instructional Alternatives
(406) 444-5541

Montana School Accreditation: Standards and Procedures Manual
34p., 1989.

Nebraska

State Department of Education
301 Centennial Mall, South
P.O. Box 94987
Lincoln, NE 68509

The Nebraska State Department of Education does not produce statewide frameworks.

Nevada

State Department of Education
Capitol Complex
400 West King Street
Carson City, NV 89710

Instructional Services Division
Director, Basic Education Branch
(702) 687-3136

Elementary Course of Study
65p., 1984. Includes scope and sequence for reading and language arts. ED 278 511.

Nevada Secondary Course of Study. Volume 1: Academic Subjects
0-5282, 72p., n.d. Includes information on required courses in arts/humanities and English, plus information on elective courses in communicative arts.

New Hampshire

State Department of Education
101 Pleasant Street
State Office Park South
Concord, NH 03301

Division of Instructional Services
General Instructional Services Administrator
(603) 271-2632

Minimum Standards for New Hampshire Public Elementary School Approval, Kindergarten-Grade 8: Working Together
36p., 1987. Includes elementary school curriculum, K-8.

Standards and Guidelines for Middle/Junior High Schools
101p., 1978. Includes information on language arts including reading.

Standards for Approval of New Hampshire Public High Schools, Grades 9-12
53p., 1984.

New Jersey

Department of Education
225 West State Street, CN 500
Trenton, NJ 08625-0500

Division of General Academic Education
(609) 984-1971

New Jersey High School Graduation Requirements
1p., 1988.

The New Jersey Department of Education does not produce statewide frameworks.

New Mexico

State Department of Education
Education Building
300 Don Gaspar
Santa Fe, NM 87501-2786

Learning Services Division, Instructional Materials
(505) 827-6504

An Elementary Competency Guide for Grades 1-8
88p., 1987, rev. ed. 1990. Includes "Competencies by Subject Area" for language arts.

Graduation Requirements
SBE Regulation no. 90-2, section A.4.3, 12p., 1990. High school graduation requirements.

New York

State Education Department
111 Education Building
Washington Avenue
Albany, NY 12234

The University of the State of New York
The State Education Department
Publications Sales Desk
(518) 474-3806

English Language Arts Syllabus K-12. A Publication for Curriculum Developers
91-7138, 91-367, 93p., 1988, repr. 1991. $1.50. ED 299 578.

Handbook on Requirements for Elementary and Secondary Schools. Education Law, Rules of the Board of Regents, and Regulations of the Commissioner of Education
140p., second ed. 1989.

Improving Reading/Study Skills in Mathematics K-6
88-8417, 038900, 31p., repr. 1989.

North Carolina

Department of Public Instruction
Education Building
116 West Edenton Street
Raleigh, NC 27603-1712

Publications Sales Desk
(919) 733-4258

North Carolina Standard Course of Study and Introduction to the Competency-Based Curriculum
530p., 1985. $7.50. ED 264 640.

Teacher Handbook: Communication Skills, Grades K-12. North Carolina Competency-Based Curriculum
710p., 1985. $12.00.

North Dakota

State Department of Public Instruction
State Capitol Building, 11th Floor
600 Boulevard Avenue East
Bismarck, ND 58505-0440

Office of Instruction Supplies
(701) 224-2272

Language Arts Curriculum Guide, K-12
251p., 1986. $4.25.

Ohio

State Department of Education
65 South Front Street, Room 808
Columbus, OH 43266-0308

Division of Curriculum Instruction and Professional Development
(614) 466-2761

At present, the Ohio State Department of Education does not produce statewide frameworks for K-12 language arts.

Oklahoma

Department of Education
Hodge Education Building
2500 North Lincoln Boulevard
Oklahoma City, OK 73105-4599

School Improvement Division
Instructional Programs
(405) 521-3361

Learner Outcomes. Oklahoma State Competencies, Grade 1
87p., 1992. Includes learner outcomes for language arts, reading, information skills, and drama.

Learner Outcomes. Oklahoma State Competencies, Grade 2
87p., 1992. Includes learner outcomes for language arts, reading, information skills, and drama.

Learner Outcomes. Oklahoma State Competencies, Grades 6-12
265p., 1992. Includes learner outcomes for language arts, reading, information skills, and drama.

Oregon

State Department of Education
700 Pringle Parkway, SE
Salem, OR 97310

Publications Sales Clerk
(503) 378-3589

English Language Arts: Common Curriculum Goals-1986
25p., 1986. $2.00.

Pennsylvania

Department of Education
333 Market Street, 10th Floor
Harrisburg, PA 17126-0333

Office of Elementary/Secondary Education
Bureau of Curriculum Academic Services
(717) 787-8913

Chapter 5 Curriculum Regulations of the Pennsylvania State Board of Education. Guidelines for Interpretation and Implementation
32p., 1990.

The Pennsylvania Department of Education does not produce statewide frameworks.

Rhode Island

Department of Education
22 Hayes Street
Providence, RI 02908

Division of School and Teacher Accreditation
(401) 277-2617

The Rhode Island Department of Education does not produce statewide frameworks for K-12 English/language arts.

South Carolina

State Department of Education
1006 Rutledge Building
1429 Senate Street
Columbia, SC 29201

The South Carolina State Department of Education is revising its statewide frameworks; the revised publications will be issued in 1993.

South Dakota

Department of Education and Cultural Affairs
435 South Chapelle
Pierre, SD 57501

Division of Elementary and Secondary Education
Office of Curriculum and Instruction
(605) 773-3261/4670

A South Dakota Curriculum Guide for Reading. Guidelines, Abilities, Skills, Competencies, Resources: Primary-Twelve
140p., 1978. $1.50.

A South Dakota Curriculum Guide for Language Arts, Kindergarten-Twelve
40p., 1977. $3.50.

Tennessee

State Department of Education
100 Cordell Hull Building
Nashville, TN 37219

Curriculum and Instruction
(615) 741-0878

Tennessee K-8 Curriculum Frameworks
10p., 1991. Includes frameworks for language arts.

Texas

Texas Education Agency
William B. Travis Building
1701 North Congress Avenue
Austin, TX 78701-1494

Publications Distribution Office
(512) 463-9744

English Language Arts Framework, Kindergarten-Grade 12
CU837001, 126p., 1988. $3.00. ED 294 174.

Utah

State Office of Education
250 East 500 South
Salt Lake City, UT 84111

Division of Instructional Services
Coordinator, Curriculum
(801) 538-7774

Elementary Core Curriculum Standards: Levels K-6. Language Arts
30p., 1992.

Secondary Core Curriculum Standards: Levels 7-12. Language Arts (Drama)
151p. 1991.

Vermont

State Department of Education
120 State Street
Montpelier, VT 05602-2703

Basic Education
Curriculum and Instruction Unit
(802) 828-3111

Framework for the Development of a English/ Language Arts Scope and Sequence
17 in. x 22 in. folded sheet, 1986.

Virginia

Department of Education
P.O. Box 6-Q, James Monroe Building
Fourteenth and Franklin Streets
Richmond, VA 23216-2060

Instruction and Personnel
Administrative Director of General Education
(804) 225-2730

Standards of Learning Objectives for Virginia
Public Schools: Language Arts
27p., rev. ed. 1988.

Washington

Superintendent of Public Instruction
Old Capitol Building
Washington and Legion
Olympia, WA 98504

Curriculum/Student Services and Technology
Service
Curriculum Support
(206) 753-6727, Fax (206) 586-0247

English Language Arts: K-12 Curriculum Guide-
lines
143p., 1985. ED 294 211.

Journalism Curriculum Guidelines for Washington
Schools--K-12
IPS-613-90, 88p., 1990.

West Virginia

State Department of Education
1900 Kanawha Boulevard, East
Building G, Room B-358
Charleston, WV 25305

Division of Instructional and Student Services
(304) 348-2702

Reading Program of Study (Learning Outcomes)
24p., 1989.

English Language Arts Program of Study (Learning
Outcomes)
21p., 1989.

Wisconsin

State Department of Public Instruction
General Executive Facility 3
125 South Webster Street
P.O. Box 7841
Madison, WI 53707-7841

Publication Sales
(608) 266-2188

A Guide to Curriculum Planning in English/
Language Arts
Bulletin no. 6360, 274p., 1986, rev. ed. 1990.
$30.00

A Guide to Curriculum Planning in Reading
Bulletin no. 6305, 189p., 1986, repr. 1991. $24.00.
ED 271 726.

Classroom Activities in Listening and Speaking
Bulletin no. 1337, 275p., 1991. $30.00

Wyoming

State Department of Education
2300 Capitol Avenue, 2nd Floor
Hathaway Building
Cheyenne, WY 82002

Division of Certification, Accreditation and
Program Services
Accreditation/Special Services Unit
(307) 777-6808

School Accreditation
6p., n.d.

■

7

CURRICULUM GUIDES: A SELECTION

by Carl B. Smith

Director, ERIC Clearinghouse on Reading and Communication Skills
Indiana University, Bloomington, Indiana

THIS chapter provides a sampling of recent curriculum guides in English and language arts. Most of the entries in this listing resulted from numerous searches of the ERIC database (see below). The guides included here range from general language arts frameworks to documents that deal with specialized applications of language arts instruction. In some cases, articles and collections of papers are cited if they contain lesson plans or curriculum guidelines, or if they discuss particular curriculum strategies for language arts.

The bibliography starts with general materials, often guidelines and frameworks from state departments of education and city school systems. After this general section, the topic sections are as follows: Decoding and Phonics; Early Childhood and Language Arts; Integrated Language Arts; Listening/Speaking; Reading; Spelling; Vocabulary; Whole Language; Writing/Composition; and Specialized Topics for Language Arts. The chapter ends with a section on Lists/Resources, with descriptions of books that list language arts curriculum materials or literature appropriate for K–12 teaching.

One of the most useful information resources for language arts curriculum guides is *Commended English Language Arts Curriculum Guides,*

K–12, published by the National Council of Teachers of English (NCTE). The most recent edition (1990) includes guides recommended in 1987, 1988, and 1989. Full descriptions of the 1990 and 1987 editions are provided in the Lists/Resources section.

Most of the items in this bibliography show an ED number (for a publication or document) or an EJ number (for a journal article); this indicates that these documents can be found in the database of the Educational Resources Information Center (ERIC). ERIC is an information system sponsored by the U.S. Department of Education's Office of Educational Research and Improvement. The ERIC Documentation Reproduction Service (EDRS) can provide paper or microfiche copies of these ERIC documents. For pricing information, write to EDRS, 7420 Fullerton Road, Suite 110, Springfield, VA 22153-2852; or call 703-440-1400 or 800-443-3742. Use the ED numbers in this bibliography to identify and order documents from EDRS. Overnight delivery and fax services are provided by EDRS for customers who need to obtain ERIC documents quickly. For entries that are in the ERIC database, the annotations provided here are adapted from *Resources in Education,* a monthly publication of the U.S. Department of Education.

General Guides for English/Language Arts

Alabama State Department of Education. 1987. *Language Arts. Alabama Course of Study.* Bulletin 1987, No. 57. Montgomery. 295p. ED 325 827.

This course of study guide outlines the language arts skills and concepts to be taught at each grade level (K–12) in Alabama schools. Following an introduction, a listing of selected characteristics of an effective language arts program, and a short list of language arts goals for grades K–12, the guide deals with elementary and secondary programs in language arts (grade by grade), listing goals, objectives, and skills to be taught for listening, speaking, reading, and writing. Appendixes contain information on advanced placement courses in English; language arts for the exceptional student and for the gifted and talented; career education in the language arts program; instruction in ethics, moral values, and citizenship in the language arts; evaluating writing; time requirements for subject areas; and student habits, homework, and responsibilities. A glossary of terms, the Dolch word list, Wilson's essential vocabulary, a basic competency education spelling list, and a list of resources are also included.

Alabama State Department of Education. 1989. *Language Arts Curriculum Guide, Grades 4–6.* Bulletin 1989, No. 41. Montgomery. 729p. ED 325 828. EDRS price - MF04/PC30 plus postage.

Designed to help classroom teachers implement the "Alabama Course of Study: Language Arts," this curriculum guide is divided into three major sections. The first section is a table of contents that lists desired student outcomes under each of the major strands mandated by the course of study (listening, speaking, reading, and writing) and directs the user to classroom activities that address the specific outcome. The second and largest section of the guide consists of classroom activities, divided among the four strands. Each strand is subdivided into skills areas. The activities are preceded by student outcome statements and notes for the teacher. The third section summarizes the relationship of student outcomes to the original sources from which the outcomes were taken (the Alabama Course of Study, the Stanford Achievement Tests and the Alabama Basic Competency Tests). The guide is intended

to be used as a supplement to textbooks and locally developed curriculum materials. (Also *Language Arts Curriculum Guide, Grades 7–8.* Bulletin 1990, No. 21. 1990. 731p.)

Alberta Department of Education. 1987. *Junior High Language Arts Curriculum Guide.* Edmonton, Alberta, Canada. 159p. ED 286 198.

Based on the philosophy, goals, and objectives of Alberta, Canada's 1978 curriculum, this revised curriculum guide stresses the importance of students' active involvement in using language. The guide emphasizes the writing process, increases the prominence of personal response to literature, and aligns terminology and grammar with the reading and writing processes. The first chapter describes the rationale, philosophy, goals, and general objectives of the language arts program for grades 1–12, and then describes required and elective contents of the junior high program. Chapter 2 discusses the rationale behind the integration of the five language strands—speaking, listening, viewing, writing, and reading—and outlines the process of each. Chapter 3 focuses on teaching methodology. Chapter 4 discusses student evaluation. The final chapter reviews various learning resources, including books and computer courseware. Appendixes include charts for planning, evaluating, and analyzing class activities and student assignments.

Arkansas State Department of Education. 1987. *Language Arts.* Little Rock. 46p. ED 294 186.

The language arts course content guides presented in this manual cover English, oral communications, and journalism in grades 9–12. Within each subject area and at each grade level, skills are identified at three instructional levels: basic, developmental, and extension. The basic skills are skills that all students should master; developmental skills should be introduced and taught, but not mastered by all students; extension skills, for learners who have mastered the required basic and recommended developmental skills, stress higher-order thinking, processing, and problem-solving skills. The English curriculum consists of capitalization, punctuation, writing numbers (grade 9), syllabication (grade 9), usage, elements of the sentence, semantics, spelling, reference skills, literature, and composition. The oral communications curriculum includes intrapersonal and interpersonal communication, listening and critical thinking, nonverbal communication, group discussion, public speaking, parliamentary procedure, oral interpretation, and debate. Journalism subject areas include an introduction to journalism, history of journalism, terminology, news writing, feature writing, editorials, publication production, ethics, advertising, and careers in journalism.

Burbank Unified School District. 1987. Junior High School English 1 and 2, Grade 9. Burbank, CA. 474p. ED 296 373.
Designed for ninth-grade English teachers, this curriculum guide contains (1) a course description; (2) educational goals; (3) teaching perspective; (4) a set of general principles; (5) a list of questions that teachers ask, along with answers; (6) an overview; and (7) directions for writing as a process, higher-level thinking skills, how to measure more than recall, speaking and listening, and conventions of the English language. Also included in the guide are core works lesson plans and instructional materials for *Shane, A Christmas Carol, The Outsiders, The Pigman, Romeo and Juliet, Animal Farm, The Good Earth, Hiroshima, A Midsummer Night's Dream,* and *The Yearling.* A general appendix includes (1) reading activities; (2) writing activities; (3) a thirteen-page list for independent reading; (4) book report activities; and (5) study skills activities.

California State Department of Education, 1987. *English–Language Arts Model Curriculum Guide, Kindergarten through Grade Eight.* Sacramento. 41p. ED 288 193. Publications Sales, California State Department of Education, P.O. Box 271, Sacramento, CA 95802-0271, $2.25, plus sales tax for California residents.
As the language arts component of the California State "Model Curriculum Guides" series, this document sets guidelines for the elementary and middle school English/language arts curriculum. The guide suggests a learning sequence—core, integrated, and across the curriculum—and delineates concepts, skills, and activities appropriate for learners in grades K–3, 3–6, and 6–8. In keeping with the philosophy of a process approach, the content and model lessons of the guide are structured to help teachers lead discussions, frame questions, and design activities that contain multiple levels of learning. Twenty-two guidelines are presented, each followed by representative activities and suggested texts for the three grade groups. General guidelines

emphasize the study of significant literary works, basing instruction on students' experiences, and developing an interrelated program that is integrated across the curriculum. The guide concludes with a summary of the twenty-two guidelines.

California State Department of Education. 1987. *English–Language Arts Framework for California Public Schools, Kindergarten through Grade Twelve.* Sacramento. 62p. ED 288 195. Publications Sales, California State Department of Education, P.O. Box 271, Sacramento, CA 95802-0271. $3.00, plus sales tax for California residents.
This document presents a philosophical and practical framework for a literature-based English/language arts curriculum that will encourage students to read widely and in depth, write frequently in many formats, study important writings from many disciplines, and relate these studies meaningfully to their own lives. Chapter 1 describes the curriculum goals of preparing students to become informed citizens, effective workers, and fulfilled individuals. Chapter 2 provides the rationale for basing instruction in literature, using particular literary works, motivating reading through a variety of literatures, teaching composition through process writing, and using oral language activities. Chapter 3 discusses teaching methods and materials, including modeling, questioning, direct teaching, media and computer-assisted instruction, and multimodal approaches. Chapter 4 presents examples of integrated arts programs and lessons for grades K–3, 3–6, 6–9, and 9–12. Chapter 5 describes over twenty alternative methods of student and program assessment. Chapter 6 identifies the roles of teachers, community, staff, and administration in revising the curriculum. Appendixes include: (1) textbook and instructional materials standards; and (2) a bibliography and recommended readings.

Davis, Susan J., and Jerry L. Johns. 1990. *Language Arts for Gifted Middle School Students.* Teaching Resources in the ERIC Database (TRIED) Series. ERIC Clearinghouse on Reading and Communication Skills, Bloomington, IN; Indiana University, Center for Reading and Language Studies. 84p. ED 319 046. ERIC Clearinghouse on Reading and Communication Skills, Indiana University, Smith Research Center, Suite 150, 2805 East

10th Street, Bloomington, IN 47408-2698.
$9.95, plus $2.00 postage and handling.
Designed to tap the rich collection of instructional techniques in the ERIC database, this compilation of lesson plans focuses on language arts activities for gifted middle school students. The forty lesson plans in this book cover history, literature, mass media, reading, theater arts, thinking skills, and writing. The book includes an activities chart that indicates the focus and types of activities (such as communication skills, collaborative learning, vocabulary development, etc.) found in the various lessons. A forty-one–item annotated bibliography contains references to research and additional resources.

Delaware State Department of Public Instruction. 1989. *State Content Standards for English Language Arts.* Volume I: *Instructional Activities for Effective Teaching, Grades 1–3.* Dover. 140p. ED 316 881.
This book of instructional activities for grades 1–3 contains "Delaware's State Content Standards for English Language Arts," which were developed in 1985. (The complete series covers grades 1–12.) The standards were designed to guide instruction by detailing program objectives for teaching and expectations for student learning. The guide is divided into sections that contain instructional activities on listening, speaking, writing, literature, and study skills. Each section presents general objectives, specific objectives, and suggested procedures. Also Volume II: *Instructional Activities for Effective Teaching, Grades 4–6.* 1989, 174p., ED 321 281; Volume III: *Instructional Activities for Effective Teaching, Grades 7–8.* 1989, 192p., ED 321 282; Volume IV: *Instructional Activities for Effective Teaching, Grades 9–12.* 1989, 270p., ED 321 283.

DelFattore, Joan, ed. 1987. *Instructional Strategies for English/Language Arts: Ideas for Effective Teaching.* Dover, DE: Delaware State Department of Public Instruction. 150p. ED 303 833.
This guide contains sixty-five model lesson plans developed by Delaware public school English/language arts teachers for grades 1–12. Each entry lists content standards, the type(s) of activities involved in the lesson (for example, class discussion, oral reports, student writing), a description of the activity, and relevant elements of effective instruction. Appendix A lists the English/language arts standards; appendix B contains material from the manual for Delaware's

1986–1987 teacher effectiveness workshops; and appendix C provides an annotated bibliography of research reports.

Duncan, Verne A. 1987. *English Language Arts Comprehensive Curriculum Goals: A Model for Local Curriculum Development.* Salem, OR: Oregon State Department of Education. 176p. ED 290 168.
Designed as a model to demonstrate one way in which English/language arts common curriculum goals can be extended throughout grades K–12, this document is the integrated work of English/language arts educators and curriculum specialists. After outlining the steps necessary to adapt the model to fit local needs, the document provides a time line and guidelines for a three-year implementation period for grades K–12. The following portion advances two statements of purpose: (1) students will use listening, reading, and literature skills to understand and appreciate human experiences to share cultural commonalities and differences; and (2) students will use writing and speaking skills in a variety of modes of communication and self-expression. Specific learning outcomes are provided for each goal. Instead of providing instructional strategies, the document shows a sequential development of outcomes. The guide concludes with a glossary of terms and a list of information sources.

Fort Worth Independent School District. 1989. *Middle School English Language Arts: English Language Arts 6, Honors English Language Arts 6, Honors English Language Arts/Reading 6.* Fort Worth, TX. 81p. ED 315 786.
This grade 6 language arts curriculum guide attempts to promote greater student achievement through alignment of the written, the taught, and the tested curriculum, and to promote broader and higher levels of thinking through objectives, activities, and strategies that integrate content and cognition. (The full series covers grades 6–8.) The guide has four major sections. The first section, Middle School English Language Arts, presents acknowledgments, rationale and purpose, philosophy, goals and objectives, basic assumptions, points to consider, and prerequisites/entry criteria for honors courses. The guide's second section, English Language Arts 6, includes objectives, recommended course sequence, scope and sequence, and activities. The guide's third and fourth sections, Honors English Language Arts 6 and Honors English Language Arts/

Reading 6, list objectives for these areas. An addendum contains a twenty-five–item bibliography; an outline of essential elements in English/language arts; a forty-eight–page section on resources, strategies, and planning; and a teacher response form. Also *Middle School English Language Arts: English Language Arts 7, Honors English Language Arts 7, Honors English Language Arts/Reading 7*, 1989, 92p., ED 315 787; *Middle School English Language Arts: English Language Arts 8, Honors English Language Arts 8, Honors English Language Arts/Reading 8, English I*, 1989, 118p., ED 315 788.

Glatthorn, Allan A. 1988. "What Schools Should Teach in the English Language Arts." *Educational Leadership* 46(1): 44–50. EJ 376 245.
In this article, the author makes specific recommendations for the content of the English "mastery curriculum," grades 5–12. These include guidelines for the six strands of the English curriculum: literature, language, composition, speaking and listening, critical thinking, and vocabulary development.

Hawaii State Department of Education. 1988. *Language Arts Program Guide.* Honolulu: Hawaii State Department of Education, Office of Instructional Services. 238p. ED 303 791. EDRS price - MF01/PC10 plus postage.
This program guide, which provides a framework and philosophy of language arts, is intended primarily for teachers of language arts in grades K–12. The content of the guide is derived from effective classroom practices and research on language learning, and focuses on developing programs that will help students become competent communicators and contributing members of society. The guide is divided into seven sections: (1) Overview; (2) Framework; (3) Goals and Objectives; (4) Language across the Curriculum; (5) Issues in Language Arts; (6) Implementation; and (7) Resources. One hundred twenty-six references and two appendixes are included.

Indianapolis Public Schools. 1988. *I.S.T.E.P. Summer Remediation Curriculum: Reading, Language and Mathematics.* Indianapolis, IN. 80p. ED 300 784.
This curriculum and teaching guide outlines the ISTEP (Indiana Statewide Testing for Educational Progress) 1988 Summer Remediation Program in reading, language, and mathematics provided for students in grades 1, 2, 3, and 6 who

did not pass the minimum state standards for promotion to the next grade level based on the results of the ISTEP test. In addition to the major sections that cover the reading, language, and mathematics curricula, the guide includes the following minor sections: (1) a foreword; (2) ISTEP achievement standards; (3) program logistics and schedule; (4) waiver provisions for both remediation and retention waivers; (5) ISTEP extended-learning progress reports for grades 1, 2, 3, and 6; and (6) guidelines for curriculum development for the ISTEP extended-learning program.

Kaufmann, Felice A., ed. 1989. *Substitute Teachers' Lesson Plans: Classroom-Tested Activities from the National Council of Teachers of English.* Urbana, IL: National Council of Teachers of English. 54p. ED 310 418. National Council of Teachers of English, 1111 Kenyon Road, Urbana, IL 61801. Stock no. 48778-3020. $4.50 member; $5.95 nonmember.
This guide contains materials from "NOTES Plus," the National Council of Teachers of English's (NCTE's) journal for the exchange of ideas by teachers and other English professionals. The suggestions presented here are meant for use by substitute teachers. The activities are divided into five categories: (1) Thinking and Writing with Precision, (2) Imaginative Problem Solving, (3) Description and Detail, (4) Poetry, and (5) Word Play.

Lipton, Arlene, et al., eds. 1989. *Computers in the English Literature Classroom.* Brooklyn, NY: New York City Board of Education, Division of Computer Information Services. 236p. ED 314 756. Curriculum/Sales Unit, Division of Computer Information Services, Room 310, Gravesend Neck Road and East 22nd Street, Brooklyn, NY 11229.
This manual provides a resource for English literature teachers who wish to take advantage of available computer software materials to expand and strengthen classroom instruction. The manual presents selected lesson plans that facilitate the integration of computer-based instruction with regular teaching methods. These plans not only indicate the features of the software, but also represent a sharing of ideas on their application by teachers who have had successful experiences with computers in the literature classroom. The lessons in the manual (structured around the elements of the short

story, the novel, plays, and tales, myths, and fables) are intended to be a reference and guide. Appendixes contain information about software duplication guidelines, copying public domain disks for MS-DOS and Apple computers, and lists of software and literary works used in this manual.

Lytle, Susan, and Morton Botel. 1988. *PCRP II: Reading, Writing and Talking across the Curriculum.* Harrisburg: Pennsylvania State Department of Education. 183p. ED 313 658.
This book discusses PCRP II, an integrative framework for language and literacy. Chapter 1 offers an introduction and summary. Chapter 2 presents four perspectives for looking at the curriculum: learning as meaning-centered, social, language-based, and human. Chapter 3 defines each of five critical experiences (reading, writing, extending reading and writing, investigating language, and learning to learn), elaborates its specific research and theory bases, and suggests classroom activities applicable across the grades, across the curriculum, and for different grade levels and content areas. Chapter 4 addresses the integration of the five critical experiences in daily, weekly, and long-range instruction and curriculum planning, and deals with ways to use the PCRP II framework as a heuristic for critical reflection on current practice and for designing units and planned courses of study. Chapter 5 proposes six principles for designing evaluation procedures for an integrative model of curriculum. Chapter 6 discusses the rationale for PCRP II and for the statewide plan for implementing the framework, and provides a set of specific but adaptable suggestions for how this book may be used to effect change at district, school, and classroom levels. Twenty notes are included and an eleven-page bibliography is attached. An appendix contains the report of the Pennsylvania Department of Education conference on PCRP II.

Manitoba Department of Education. 1988. *English Language Arts Overview K–12.* Winnipeg, Manitoba, Canada. 141p. ED 319 061.
This guide reflects new understandings about language and literature—the close association between language and learning, language and thinking, and language and personal growth. The guide recommends that students be encouraged to use their personal, unstructured language to grapple with new ideas and come to terms with new experiences before they attempt to cope with

the more structured means of expressing what they have learned. The guide also supports integration of the language arts at all levels. The guide considers the importance of literature in the elementary school; the emphasis of studying literature at other levels is on experiencing a wider range of materials rather than analyzing a limited number of works. Sections of the curriculum guide include: (1) Rationale; (2) Major Emphases; (3) Language Needs; (4) Learning Goals K–12; (5) Correlation of Student Objectives and Goals; (6) Language Development; (7) Integrating the Language Arts; (8) Balance; (9) Time Allotments; (10) Evaluation; (11) Meeting Individual and Group Needs; (12) Meeting Special Needs; and (13) Goals and Objectives. Seventeen references and summaries of seven suggested readings are included.

New York State Education Department. 1988. *English Language Arts Syllabus K–12. A Publication for Curriculum Developers.* Albany. 101p. ED 299 578.
This syllabus outlines general criteria for an effective integrated curriculum in English/language arts, suggests the instructional objectives that need to be addressed, and provides direction for the evaluation of student progress and program effectiveness. A fifty-seven–item bibliography and six appendixes containing guidelines for keyboarding instruction, information regarding students with handicapping conditions, and other materials are included in the syllabus.

Paul, Richard, et al. 1990. *Critical Thinking Handbook: K–3rd Grades. A Guide for Remodelling Lesson Plans in Language Arts, Social Studies & Science.* Rohnert Park, CA: Sonoma State University, Center for Critical Thinking and Moral Critique. 420p. ED 325 803. Center for Critical Thinking and Moral Critique, Sonoma State University, Rohnert Park, CA 94928. $18.00; 10–19 copies, $16.00 each; 20–49 copies, $14.00 each; 50+ copies, $9.00 each.
The purpose of this handbook is to demonstrate that it is possible and practical to integrate instruction for critical thinking into the teaching of all subjects. The handbook discusses the concept of critical thinking and the principles that underlie it, and shows how critical thinking can be taught in language arts, social studies, and science. The book's first section contains nine chapters that: (1) provide an introduction to critical thinking and lesson remodelling; (2) discuss

making critical thinking intuitive by using drama, examples, and images; (3) delve into what education for critical thinking requires of teachers; (4) explain the thirty-five remodelling strategies, with suggestions on how to teach for them; (5) present sixty-nine remodelled lessons for language arts, social studies, science, and math; and (6) focus on remodelling lessons into thematic units. The handbook's second section, which contains seven chapters, compares didactic and critical views on education, outlines the curriculum changes required by a shift toward education for critical thought, provides practical ideas for facilitating staff development, presents short writings by teachers, and considers the problem of defining critical thinking. The seventh chapter is an analytic glossary of key words and phrases relevant to critical thinking and education. A list of recommended readings and critical thinking resources is appended. Also *Critical Thinking Handbook: 4th–6th Grades,* 1990, 442p., ED 325 804; *Critical Thinking Handbook: High School,* A Guide for Redesigning Instruction. 1989, 424p., ED 325 805.

Tennessee State Department of Education. [1987]. *Language Arts Curriculum Framework: 9–12.* Nashville. 70p. ED 296 356. EDRS Price - MF01/PC03 plus postage.
Developed by a statewide committee of language arts educators in accordance with the "Rules, Regulations, and Minimum Standards" of the Tennessee State Board of Education, this curriculum framework contains goals and terminal objectives for language arts courses in grades 9–12. The framework covers the disciplines of standard English, English as a second language (ESL), speech, drama, and journalism. Each section contains a brief description of the curriculum strands, followed by a list of objectives for the skill areas at each grade level. Standard English skill areas consist of reading (comprehension, word identification, reference and study, and literature); writing (handwriting, grammar/mechanics, spelling, and composition); and thinking and expression (thinking and organization, listening and viewing, and oral communication). ESL skill areas are listening and speaking (sound discrimination, linguistic structures, communication, and comprehension strands); reading (comprehension, word identification, reference and study skills, literature, and thinking); writing (handwriting, grammar/mechanics, spelling, and composition); and culture (cross-cultural issues). Strands for the speech skill area are thinking, writing, listening, and speaking; drama strands are writing, performance, reading, and critical viewing and listening. Journalism skill areas consist of communication (thinking and organizing, interviewing and broadcasting, composition, and mechanics) and production (layout and makeup, business management, organization, and career implications).

Tennessee State Department of Education. 1987. *English I. Language Arts Curriculum Guide.* Nashville. 176p. ED 296 358.
As part of the language arts curriculum framework developed in accordance with the "Rules, Regulations, and Minimum Standards" of the Tennessee State Board of Education, this English curriculum guide contains the goals, concepts, and terminal objectives for ninth-grade English courses. (The full series covers grades 9–12.) Following an introduction, a description of the framework categories, curriculum guide categories, and English strands, and a note on guide usage, the guide is divided into the following strands: (1) comprehension; (2) word identification; (3) reference and study; (4) literature; (5) handwriting; (6) grammar/mechanics; (7) spelling; (8) composition; (9) thinking and organization; (10) listening and viewing; and (11) oral communication. Each page of the guide addresses a strand objective, and consists of instructional objectives, associated content statements (including academic competencies), and skills and activities that may be used to enhance the understanding of the terminal objective. In addition, space for curriculum cross-references (indicating where the objective appears in the curriculum guide of another discipline) and a resource column, contingent on materials available to the teacher, are provided. Also English II (for grade 10), 1987, 156p., ED 296 359; English III (for grade 11), 1987, 166p., ED 296 360; and English IV (for grade 12), 1987, 146p., ED 296 361.

Tennessee State Department of Education. 1987. *Basic Skills First, K. Language Arts Curriculum Guide.* Nashville. 106p. ED 296 362.
This comprehensive language arts curriculum guide for kindergarten combines the Basic Skills First Reading Guide and the Language Arts Guide. The objectives in the guide are categorized according to the strands (divisions of skill areas) for grades 1–12 to show how the kindergarten curriculum prepares students for academic

learning in the later grades. The guide is divided into the following language arts strands: (1) handwriting; (2) spelling; (3) composition; (4) thinking and organizational skills; (5) listening skills; and (6) oral communication skills. Each page of the guide addresses a strand objective, and consists of instructional objectives, associated content statements, and skills and activities that may be used to enhance the understanding of the terminal objective. In addition, space for curriculum cross-references (indicating where the objective appears in the curriculum guide of another discipline) and a resource column, contingent on materials available to the teacher, are provided.

Tennessee State Department of Education. 1987. *Language Arts Curriculum Guide, 1.* Nashville. 115p. ED 296 363.
As part of the language arts curriculum framework developed in accordance with the "Rules, Regulations, and Minimum Standards" of the Tennessee State Board of Education, this English curriculum guide contains the goals, concepts, and terminal objectives for first-grade language arts. (The full series covers grades 1–8.) Following a brief introduction and description of the curriculum framework, each guide is divided into the following language arts strands: (1) handwriting; (2) grammar/mechanics; (3) spelling; (4) composition; (5) thinking and organizing skills; (6) listening skills; and (7) oral communication skills. Each page of the guide addresses a strand objective, and consists of instructional objectives, associated content statements, and skills and activities that may be used to enhance the understanding of the terminal objective. In addition, space for curriculum cross-references (indicating where the objective appears in the curriculum guide of another discipline) and a resource column, contingent on materials available to the teacher, are provided. (Also *Language Arts Curriculum Guide, 2,* 1987, 128p., ED 296 364; *Language Arts Curriculum Guide, 3,* 1987, 177p., ED 296 365; *Language Arts Curriculum Guide, 4,* 1987, 153p., ED 296 366; *Language Arts Curriculum Guide, 5,* 1987, 163p., ED 296 367; *Language Arts Curriculum Guide, 6,* 1987, 161p., ED 296 368; *Language Arts Curriculum Guide, 7,* 1987, 138p., ED 296 369; *Language Arts Curriculum Guide, 8.* 1987, 122p., ED 296 370.

Texas Education Agency. [1988]. *English Language Arts Framework: Kindergarten–Grade 12.* Austin: Texas Education Agency. 130p. ED 294 174.
This guide provides general guidelines for local school districts in Texas to follow in designing English/language arts programs to meet the needs of their students and the expectations of their communities. The guide reflects Texas State Board of Education rules and legal mandates and presents suggestions for implementing these rules. The first section provides an overview of the content of the English/language arts curriculum. Subject and course descriptions are provided together with scope and sequence illustrations of the English/language arts essential elements at all levels. In addition, the section details the required and suggested time allocations for the English/language arts essential elements as well as high school graduation requirements. The second section provides sample English/language arts lesson plans for grades 2, 4, 5, 7, 9, and 10. The third section provides general information about students and teachers, focusing on grading and staff development. The final section expands on language arts instruction for special populations, such as handicapped, gifted, and migrant students.

University of Illinois. 1990. *Language Arts CCA Basic Skills Curriculum. Instructor's Guide.* Urbana: University of Illinois, Computer-Based Education Research Laboratory. 100p. ED 319 051. University of Illinois, Computer-Based Education Research Laboratory, 103 South Mathews Avenue, Urbana, IL 61801. $4.50; $25.00 for a set of four (Reading, Language Arts, Spelling, and Math).
Designed and programmed by the staff of the Courseware and Curriculum Applications (CCA) Group (a unit of the Computer-Based Education Research Laboratory at the University of Illinois at Urbana–Champaign), this instructor's guide describes a computer-based language arts curriculum intended to move adult and adolescent students performing at the fourth-grade level to the eighth-grade level. The guide offers a curriculum that emphasizes usage; grammatical terminology is minimized. The guide outlines a curriculum composed of eight units of instructional materials, with lessons designed to teach basic punctuation, parts of speech, vocabulary, synonyms/antonyms, subject–verb agreement, and proofreading skills. Each unit consists of a pretest, computer instruction, and a posttest. An appendix lists files.

Wresch, William, ed. 1991. *The English Classroom in the Computer Age: Thirty Lesson Plans.* Urbana, IL: National Council of Teachers of English. 154p. ED 331 087. National Council of Teachers of English, 1111 Kenyon Road, Urbana, IL 61801. Stock no. 13761-0015. $12.95 members; $16.50 nonmembers.
Written by middle school, high school, and college writing teachers, these thirty lesson plans represent a mix of computer-based units for teaching writing. The lessons cover many types of writing, from journalism to literary essays, fiction, and poetry; and many aspects of the writing process, from brainstorming for ideas to prewriting warm-ups, electronic library research, revision, and desktop publishing. While most of the lessons in the book are adaptations of lessons used for years without computers, a small number are new activities. The lessons follow a format designed to help readers quickly determine which activities are most appropriate for them, and are divided into categories for students with little, moderate, or substantial computer experience. A directory of software and a list of contributors are included.

Yeager, Jim. 1989. "Three Ways to Incorporate Drama through Storytelling in Your Secondary English Class." *Drama/Theatre Teacher* 2(1): 20–22. EJ 429 689.
This article offers three variations of an activity designed to help teachers turn students on to performance within two weeks. A sample ten-day lesson plan on incorporating drama through storytelling is included.

Decoding and Phonics

Albert, Elaine Acker. 1990. *How the Alphabet Works: A Handbook for Teaching Someone to Read (Based on the 15th-Century Hornbook).* 66p. ED 324 661.
Written to be used as a manual for a tutor and not as a workbook or primer, this expanded version of a phonics book is designed to help parents teach their children to read and for those who wish to help older children and adults to read. Sections include: (1) Introduction; (2) What Went Wrong? (an essay); (3) HOW to Teach Someone to Read by Beginning with Basic Phonics (the main body of the manual); and (4) Special Problems. A chronology, a twenty-four–

item bibliography and a page depicting a "hornbook for the twentieth century" with brief instructions are attached.

Albert, Elaine Acker. [1991]. *Phonic Primer for "How the Alphabet Works" (Based on the 15th-Century Hornbook) Systematic Basic Phonics.* 59p. ED 335 639.
This primer supplies systematic basic phonics material for learning how to read, to be used by children. The primer includes instructions for the teacher, but it assumes that the user has read either the book, *How the Alphabet Works,* or the matching pamphlet, "Systematic Basic Phonics," which is included in the back of the primer.

Colvin, Ruth J., and Jane H. Root. 1987. *TUTOR. Techniques Used in the Teaching of Reading. A Handbook for Teaching Basic Reading to Adults and Teenagers.* 6th ed. Syracuse, NY: Literacy Volunteers of America, Inc. 111p. ED 292 949. Literacy Volunteers of America, Inc., 5795 Widewaters Parkway, Syracuse, NY 13214. $9.50.
This guide is intended to assist teachers and volunteer tutors who are teaching adults and teenagers to read. The nature and extent of the adult illiteracy problem and the process of learning to read are discussed in the first chapter. The characteristics that are desirable in basic reading tutors and those that are encountered in adult learners are described in the next two chapters; assessment and goal setting are examined next, and the fifth chapter deals with the following instructional approaches and techniques: language experience stories, sight words and context clues, phonics (consonants), and word patterns. Comprehension and thinking skills are the subject of the sixth chapter. Chapter 7 is devoted to instructional materials and learning activities, and Chapter 8 covers goal analysis and lesson planning. Materials that should be brought to a lesson, methods of identifying appropriate material, ways of incorporating handwriting into lessons, steps in developing lesson plans, and appropriate behavior for tutors are discussed in the next chapter. A series of sample beginning- and intermediate-level lesson plans is also included. Appendixes include guidelines for evaluating tutor competency (complete with illustrative case studies); a list of the 300 most frequently used words; basic and survival word lists for adults; useful words for filling out forms; signs in capitals; a glossary; suggested key words;

vocabulary building/syllabication guidelines; word patterns; guidelines for evaluating adult basic education reading material; a checklist of students' word attack skills; and lesson plan forms.

Spiegel, Dixie Lee. 1990. "Decoding and Comprehension Games and Manipulatives (Instructional Resources)." *Reading Teacher* 44(3): 258–61. EJ 416 395.
This article presents six key questions to ask about any instructional resource and suggests a few specific questions to ask when selecting decoding and comprehension games and manipulatives. Seven instructional games and manipulatives appropriate for classroom use are included.

Woodward, Helen. [1987]. *Reading Problems: More Phonics?* PEN 63. Rozelle, Australia: Primary English Teaching Association. 8p. ED 284 187.
Intended to discourage classroom reading teachers from relying on phonics instruction as a remedy for students' inadequate reading performance, this pamphlet presents reasons why phonics drills should not be taught at all, and offers a set of practical phonic awareness activities to help poor readers overcome reading difficulties. The pamphlet presents seven exercises that illustrate how meaning is made during the reading process and how sounding out letters interferes with the meaning-making process. It provides strategies that will enable children to use the more natural syntactic and semantic cueing systems that will allow the graphophonic cueing system to fall into place. References are attached.

Early Childhood and Language Arts

Adams, Velma A., and Donald G. Goranson, Jr., eds. 1988. *A Guide to Program Development for Kindergarten: Part I and Part II.* Hartford: Connecticut State Department of Education. 301p. ED 301 356.
Connecticut's two-part curriculum guide offers both a philosophical foundation and a practical direction for kindergarten program development. Part I discusses historical perspectives; the effect of growth and development in planning for young children; the interactionist theoretical model for program development; components of a high-quality kindergarten program; elements of social

and emotional development; organization of the kindergarten, including the extended-day kindergarten; approaches to building a home–school–community partnership; strategies for developing a continuum of experiences from preschool through the primary grades; and effective planning and evaluation. Part II details program content in the arts (creative dramatics, creative movement, music, and visual arts); foreign languages; language arts; mathematics; physical education (including health and safety); social studies; and science.

Spodek, Bernard, ed. 1991. *Educationally Appropriate Kindergarten Practices. NEA Early Childhood Education Series.* Washington, DC: National Education Association. 113p. ED 338 436. National Education Association Professional Library, P.O. Box 509, West Haven, CT 06516. Stock No. 3050-0-00. $11.95.
The basis for educationally worthwhile activities in kindergarten is examined in a series of papers that also provide examples of how kindergarten programs can be organized. Long-term projects or units are seen as useful vehicles of instruction, and organizing teaching around topics or themes is shown to help teachers present complex ideas. Theoretical discussions are combined with examples of practical application.

Integrated Language Arts

California State Department of Education. 1988. *Handbook for Planning an Effective Literature Program.* Sacramento, CA. 62p. Publication Sales, California State Department of Education, P.O. Box 271, Sacramento, CA 95802-0271. $3.00, plus sales tax for California residents.
This handbook is intended to give practical advice to teachers and parents, for developing and improving a literature program in school. Includes a discussion on the value of teaching literature, and provides a profile of an effective literature program, with teaching suggestions for using literature from kindergarten through high school. Also provides a checklist for assessing a school's literature program.

Green, Reginald Leon. 1989. "Cincinnati's Bold New Venture: A Unified K–12 Reading/Communication Arts Program." *Reading*

Improvement 26(3): 247–53. EJ 403 661.
This article describes the Cincinnati Public School
System's unified reading/communication arts
program, which uses new basal texts, support
materials, and a customized instructional system
for each grade level, and integrates listening,
speaking, reading, writing, and thinking skills.
Intervention strategies, customized materials,
instructional assessment, and expected outcomes
are also discussed.

Leigh, Cindy, et al. 1990. *Primary Guide for
Instructional Planning.* Jackson: Mississippi
University, Early Childhood Leadership
Institute. 1464p. ED 328 366.
Mississippi's guide for instructional planning for
the primary grades consists of six units and
appended materials. Research principles incorporated into the guide include: (1) a project approach that encourages the study of specific
topics; (2) an integrated language program based
on children's literature; (3) mathematics instruction using manipulatives, a variety of representational forms, and calculators, with a strong
emphasis on problem solving; (4) collaborative
student groups for projects and activities; and (5)
learning centers to enhance instruction in basic
skills. The six unit themes, and their suggested
time-lines, are: Living and Learning Together
(August–September); Our Town (October–
November); Then and Now (November–Decem-
ber); Investigations (January–February); Fantasy
and Fact (March); and The Big Backyard (April–
May). Each unit follows the same format, consist-
ing of title, topic web, general goals that guide
planning, methods of evaluation, specific unit
goals, a project section, and an activity section.
Required and recommended books are cited at
the end of each unit. Appendixes include teacher
resource materials; an informal test; a social skills
checklist; a reading interview note sheet; a subject
area checklist; and a developmental checklist.

Ridout, Susan Ramp, et al. [1990]. *An Integrated
Language Arts Practicum.* 50p. ED 315 766.
This document is a collection of materials used in
a pre–student-teaching practicum in language
arts, in which each pre-student teacher works
with two or three children in the fourth or fifth
grade for six reading and writing lessons using the
computer. The document also includes forms and
questionnaires used in collecting data on the
practicum from both pre-student teachers and
grade school students, and explanatory papers

sent to participating elementary school teachers.

Seminole County Board of Public Instruction.
1988. *Justice: Family Law. Curriculum Guide.
Grades Kindergarten–Three.* Sanford, FL:
Seminole County Board of Public Instruction,
Department of Curriculum Services. 71p. ED
327 460.
This curriculum guide suggests reading and social
studies activities to satisfy the Florida state
requirement on law education. Kindergarten and
first-grade lessons emphasize family situations
and learning personal manners. Second-grade
lessons help students identify rules and examine
consequences of personal actions. They also cover
trial procedures and include directions for
conducting a mock trial. Third-grade lessons
focus on gaining awareness of the elderly and the
need to recognize cultural differences. A list of
community resources for family law is included.

Shoemaker, Betty Jean Eklund. 1989. "Integrative Education: A Curriculum for the Twenty-
First Century." Eugene: Oregon School Study
Council. 57p. ED 311 602. *OSSC Bulletin,* 33(2)
October 1989. Publication Sales, Oregon
School Study Council, University of Oregon,
1787 Agate Street, Eugene, OR 97403. $6.00
prepaid; $2.00 postage and handling on billed
orders; quantity discounts. EDRS price -
MF01/PC03 plus postage.
Chapter 1 of this document discusses the various
meanings of integration and some approaches
taken to achieve integration. Chapter 2 addresses
why there is a call for integration at all levels of
schooling. Chapter 3 briefly describes nine
integrative models. Chapter 4 describes the first
draft of the elementary "Education 2000 Integrated Curriculum" in Eugene Public Schools.
Chapter 5 contrasts integrated and traditional
subject-centered curricula. Arguments in support
of integrative education are summarized.

Winget, Patricia L., ed. 1987. *Integrating the Core
Curriculum through Cooperative Learning.
Lesson Plans for Teachers.* Sacramento: Califor-
nia State Department of Education, Division
of Special Education. 222p. ED 300 975.
Resources in Special Education, 650 University
Avenue, Room 201, Sacramento, CA 05825.
$22.50.
Cooperative learning strategies are used to
facilitate the integration of multicultural students
and students of different ability levels into regular

education classrooms in California. This handbook is a sampling of innovative lesson plans that use cooperative learning activities to incorporate the core curriculum. Three papers introduce the cooperative learning process and give guidelines for its implementation. Twenty-seven lesson plans are presented; each outlines grade level (K–12), necessary materials, and procedures for setting, conducting, monitoring and processing, and evaluating the lesson. In the language arts/reading area, lesson plans include: Show and Tell, We'd Rather, The Goop, Brothers Grimm Fairy Tales, Jobs, Jobs, Jobs, Facts in Fives, Identifying Denial, Writing Complete Simple Sentences, and Garden Plot. A miscellaneous category includes Santa Claus, Roses Are Red, Family Squares Game, and an overview of cooperative learning for parents and teachers. Four excerpts from published works, one concerning competition and the others concerning aspects of cooperative and group learning, conclude the handbook. A list of contributors, an index by grade level, and a list of additional resource materials are appended.

Listening/Speaking

New York State Education Department. 1989. *Listening and Speaking in the English Language Arts Curriculum K–12.* 1989 Field Test Edition. Albany: New York State Education Department, Bureau of Curriculum Development. 182p. ED 335 726.

One of three manuals developed to supplement the English Language Arts Syllabus K–12 for the State of New York, this draft manual discusses listening and speaking in the English/language arts curriculum K–12. Designed to help teachers plan day-to-day instruction, the manual explains the rationale for listening and speaking instruction, defines expected learning outcomes, and suggests strategies for teaching listening and speaking from within a process perspective. The manual provides information on the components of an integrated English language arts curriculum, suggests general criteria for an effective curriculum, outlines the communication process and the roles of listeners and speakers in that process, explores the classroom as a communication environment, and discusses the integration of listening and speaking instruction with instruction in the other language arts and in the content areas. The manual also provides a chart of expec-

tations for K-12 student listeners and speakers, suggests methods of evaluating listening and speaking skills, and provides sample activities that show how identified listening and speaking objectives and focus skills can be integrated into the students' total learning program. A bibliography contains eight briefly annotated items. Appendix A contains samples of listening and speaking evaluation instruments. Appendix B provides information regarding instruction of students with handicapping conditions. A questionnaire for field review of the manual is attached.

Oklahoma State Board of Vocational and Technical Education. 1988. *Effective Communication. Successful Living Skills.* Stillwater. 313p. ED 303 571. Curriculum and Instructional Materials Center, Oklahoma Department of Vocational and Technical Education, 1500 West Seventh Avenue, Stillwater, OK 74074-4364. Order no. BS1008. $20.00.

One of a series of modules designed to help teach students to become more self-sufficient in their personal and professional lives, this module contains teacher and student materials that are planned to help students become more relaxed, prepared, and confident when using written and verbal communications. Six units cover the following topics: (1) understanding communications; (2) improving communication; (3) using words correctly; (4) giving oral presentations; (5) planning written communication; and (6) writing letters and reports. Each instructional unit follows a standard format that includes some or all of these eight basic components: performance objectives, suggested activities for the instructor, information sheets, assignment sheets, job sheets, transparency masters, tests, and answers to tests and assignment sheets. All of the unit components focus on measurable and observable learning outcomes, and are designed for use for more than one lesson or class period.

Speech Communication Association. 1991. *Guidelines for Developing Oral Communication Curricula in Kindergarten through Twelfth Grade.* Annandale, VA. 57p. ED 337 828. Speech Communication Association, 5105 Backlick Road, Building E, Annandale, VA 22003.

This booklet contains guidelines for developing oral communication curricula in grades K–12. The booklet discusses the following topics: enhancing the role of oral communication in elementary and secondary education; the objective, overview, and criteria of oral communication curriculum (offering thirteen guidelines—one for each grade, K–12—for the development of a comprehensive, developmental, elementary and secondary oral communication curriculum); oral communication competencies and content areas for grades K–12; resources and syllabi; and conclusions.

Tennessee State Department of Education. 1987. *Language Arts Curriculum Guide: Speech.* Nashville. 113p. ED 296 427.
Designed to provide direction and guidance for secondary classroom teachers in planning classroom instruction in speech, this guide is organized into four strands: thinking, writing, listening, and speaking. Each page, in chart form and headed by a terminal objective, shows instructional objectives, associated content statements, skills, and activities that may be used to enhance the understanding of the terminal objectives, and academic competencies. A page for suggestions is attached.

Wisconsin Department of Public Instruction. 1991. *Classroom Activities in Listening and Speaking.* Madison, WI. 275p. Publication Sales, Wisconsin Department of Public Instruction, 125 South Webster Street, P.O. Box 7841, Madison, WI 53707-7841. $30.00.
A collection of learning activities for integrating language arts into the curriculum, pre-kindergarten through grade twelve. The pre-K section provides activities to be used by teachers or parents, both in school or non-school settings. The middle level sequence has listening and speaking activities that can be integrated into middle-school English courses, or used to develop a separate course on listening and speaking. The high school section is designed to be used as a curriculum for a required course on listening and speaking. Uses the Comprehensive Listening and Speaking Sequence (CLASS) as a framework for the activities.

Reading

Alano, Becky, and Mary Morgan, eds. 1989. *Teaching the Novel.* Bloomington, IN: ERIC Clearinghouse on Reading and Communication Skills. 97p. ED 308 549. ERIC Clearing-

house on Reading and Communication Skills, 2805 East 10th Street, Smith Research Center, Suite 150, Bloomington, IN 47405. $12.95, plus $1.50 postage and handling. Teaching Resources in the ERIC Database (TRIED) Series.
This book of forty-one lesson plans, compiled from resources in the ERIC database, focuses on strategies for teaching the novel at the junior high and high school levels. Each lesson includes a brief description, objectives, and procedures. The book includes strategies for teaching specific novels, general strategies, a user's guide, an activities chart, and an annotated bibliography of related resources in the ERIC database.

Alaska State Department of Education. 1989. *Common Ground 1989: Suggested Literature for Alaskan Schools, Grades K–8.* Juneau. 130p. ED 314 757.
Intended to assist Alaskan school districts in their selection and promotion of reading and literature, this guide to literature for use in grades K–8 has five purposes: (1) to encourage reading and the use of literature throughout Alaskan schools; (2) to promote the inclusion of native Alaskan and minority literature, in addition to the traditional Eastern and Western classics; (3) to help curriculum planners and committees to select books and obtain ideas for thematic units using literature; (4) to stimulate local educators to evaluate the use of literature in their schools and consider ways to use it as core material and as recreational reading; and (5) to accompany the state's Model Curriculum Guide in Language Arts, K–12, and to promote the reading of literature as an activity expected of all Alaskan students. Also *Common Ground 1989: Suggested Literature for Alaskan Schools, Grades 7–12.* 1989, 153p., ED 309 447.

Bainter, Dolores, et al. 1988. "Using Literature To Teach in All Curriculum Areas K–3." Petaluma, CA: Old Adobe Union School District. (Paper presented at the Annual Northern California Kindergarten Conference, San Francisco, CA, January 23, 1988.) 69p. ED 294 694.
This paper presents ideas for learning activities that use books and stories to teach language arts, art, cooking, movement, health, music, and math to kindergarten and primary school students. Activities are organized around such topics as quilts, apples, teeth, hands, feelings, heroes,

letters, and bookbinding, and birthdays, Mother's Day, Father's Day, Ground Hog Day, and April Fools' Day. Each unit provides a statement of intent and a list of books and readings, as well as suggested learning activities. Materials designed to be duplicated and handed out to students are included.

Bass Nelson, Erlene. 1991. *Enriching and Increasing Kindergarteners' Knowledge, Ability to Recite, Write, and Appreciate Poetry Integrated across a Standardized Curriculum.* Ed.D. practicum, Nova University. 261p. ED 337 784.
Through the integration of poetry across the curriculum, this practicum was designed to improve thirty kindergarteners' understanding, and enjoyment of, and ability to compose poetry in order to enhance their cognition and reading skills. Surveys were administered to parents and children, pretests and posttests were administered to pupils, daily poetry experiences were organized, opportunities for display of children's work were provided, and a poetry production was presented to the school by the children. The results strongly demonstrated that using poetry daily can increase children's poetry skills and curriculum cognition; use of phonology, alliteration, and rhyme can facilitate early reading ability; and both teachers and parents can gain more competence and self-esteem by using poetry. Fifteen tables of data are included. Sixteen assessment instruments, forms, and checklists; a list of supplies, equipment, and materials; a poetry supplement to a standardized curriculum; and an essay entitled "Origin and History of Rhyme and Poetry" are attached.

Fuchs, Lucy. 1987. *Teaching Reading in the Secondary School. Fastback 251.* Bloomington, IN: Phi Delta Kappa Educational Foundation. 34p. ED 281 165. Phi Delta Kappa, Eighth and Union, Box 789, Bloomington, IN 47402. $0.90.
This publication was sponsored by the St. Leo Florida Chapter of Phi Delta Kappa. Intended for use by secondary school teachers in all subject areas, this booklet provides practical information, classroom activities, and strategies for the instructor who wants to incorporate reading instruction into a particular content area. Following an introductory chapter that emphasizes the need for reading skills, the booklet offers specific chapters on: (1) vocabulary development; (2) reading in the content areas; (3) incorporating

reading into lesson planning; (4) using questions to develop critical reading; (5) reading and study skills, such as outlining, note taking, and study methods; (6) guiding teenage reading choices; and (7) other reading activities, including reading newspapers (especially the sports pages), junk mail, and television-related material. The booklet also contains a bibliography.

Hancock, Maxine. 1987. *Reading 10: Senior High School Curriculum Guide, 1987.* Edmonton, Alberta, Canada: Alberta Department of Education. 68p. ED 284 188.
Based on recent reading research, this secondary school developmental reading curriculum guide presents a reading program to help students acquire strategies to begin independent reading of a variety of print materials and for a range of purposes. The introductory section of the guide presents a rationale, philosophy, statement of content, and list of resources. The next section provides a detailed description of the Reading 10 program, including recommended teaching/ learning activities and strategies. The last section suggests methods of teaching and evaluation that are appropriate to the philosophy of the Reading 10 program. A select bibliography concludes the guide.

Kansas State Department of Education. 1988. *Reading Treasures. Phase I and Phase II.* Topeka. 172p. ED 310 366.
Based on the premise that a school reading program must focus on the learner and the text, this guidebook is divided into two phases. Phase I, "Guidelines for Developing and Strengthening K–12 Programs," includes sections on The Reading Committee, Review of Research, Needs Assessment for Evaluating Reading Programs, Philosophy of Reading, K–12 Reading Curriculum Guidelines, and Implementation. Phase I also includes appendixes providing a K–12 reading curriculum guide and a list of instructional resources; a glossary of reading terms; and a bibliography. Phase II, "Reaching for Treasures: Instructional Strategies for Implementing Reading Treasures," contains two sections: Instructional Strategies for Reading Instruction in the Elementary School (describing strategies for each of seven goals) and Instructional Strategies for Reading Instruction in the Content Areas (describing strategies for before, during, and after reading). Twenty references are attached.

Katz, Kim, and Claudia Katz. 1991. *Reading Strategies for the Primary Grades. Teaching Resources in the ERIC Database (TRIED) Series.* Bloomington, IN: ERIC Clearinghouse on Reading and Communication Skills. 115p. ED 331 016. ERIC Clearinghouse on Reading and Communication Skills, Indiana University, 2805 East 10th Street, Suite 150, Bloomington, IN 47408-2698. $12.95.

Designed to tap the rich collection of instructional techniques in the ERIC database, this compilation of lesson plans focuses on reading strategies for the primary grades. The forty lesson plans in this book offer practical suggestions for the teacher on how to: (1) get started with beginning reading; (2) facilitate comprehension through vocabulary development; (3) read different kinds of text; (4) enhance reading by writing and writing by reading; and (5) promote reading by promoting the use of books. The book includes an activities chart that indicates the focus and types of activities (such as collaborative learning, use of literature, playing games, etc.) found in the various lessons. A thirty-seven–item annotated bibliography contains references to additional lessons and to other resources for teaching language-learning strategies in the ERIC database.

Lehman, Barbara A., and Patricia R. Crook. 1989. "Content Reading, Tradebooks and Students: Learning about the Constitution through Nonfiction." *Reading Improvement* 26(1): 50–57. EJ 394 872.

This article provides five lesson plans on the United States Constitution, in which students read multiple tradebooks in order to synthesize information from several sources in preparation for written or oral reports. A thirteen-item annotated bibliography of tradebooks about the Constitution is also included.

New York State Education Department. 1988. *Reading and Literature in the English Language Arts Curriculum, K–12* (draft). Albany: New York State Education Department, Bureau of Curriculum Development. 168p. ED 298 434.

As a supplement to the English Language Arts Syllabus K–12, this curriculum guide draft for reading and literature focuses on instruction that reflects reading as an active, meaning-centered process. The guide includes: (1) a description of an integrated program in the English/language arts; (2) the characteristics of an effective pro-

gram; (3) a description of the reading process; (4) recommendations for nurturing the reading process; (5) an overview of essential reading readiness experiences; and (6) expected instructional outcomes for grades K–12. Also included is a discussion of the role of literature in a comprehensive reading program and a chart describing the content of a balanced literature program. The role of word identification is addressed, and several informal approaches to assessing and monitoring student achievement in reading are presented.

"Practical Teaching Ideas (In the Classroom)." *Reading Teacher* 42(1): 90–96. October 1988. EJ 377 465.

This article describes ten practical ideas for classroom teaching at the elementary level, including "roulette" writing, story map raps, and theme cubes.

Taunton Public Schools. 1987. *Reading K–12.* Taunton, MA. 96p. ED 285 128. Prepared by the K–12 Reading Curriculum Committee.

This curriculum guide offers suggestions for reading improvement for grades K–12. Following an introduction and statement of philosophy, a section on the theoretical and research basis of the program outlines recommendations from the National Academy of Education's Commission on Education and Public Policy's *Becoming a Nation of Readers* (Robert Glaser), emphasizing parental involvement, phonics instruction, comprehension instruction, and continuing professional development for teachers. Sections four and five examine frequency of instruction and the scope and sequence of reading skills in grades K–8. Sections six through nine focus on word recognition and vocabulary development skills, reading comprehension, study skills, and recreational reading. Section ten outlines learning objectives for each grade level (K–8), while section eleven describes the reading program for the Taunton high schools, including information on a reading laboratory, individualized reading, and test-taking techniques.

Spelling

Green, Max. 1988. "Spelling within One School's Whole Language Framework." *Australian Journal of Reading* 11(1): 11–21. EJ 373 312.

This article explains how an elementary school's spelling program evaluation led to the formulation of a spelling policy reflecting the school's whole language approach to learning.

University of Illinois. 1990. *Spelling CCA Basic Skills Curriculum. Instructor's Guide.* Urbana, IL. 28p. ED 319 010. University of Illinois, Computer-Based Education Research Laboratory, 103 South Mathews Avenue, Urbana, IL 61801. $3.00; $25.00 for a set of four (reading, language arts, spelling, and math).
Designed and programmed by the staff of the Courseware and Curriculum Applications (CCA) Group (a unit of the Computer-Based Education Research Laboratory at the University of Illinois at Urbana–Champaign), this instructor's guide describes a computer-based spelling curriculum designed to help adult and adolescent students learn basic rules of spelling and to master some of the more commonly misspelled words. The first unit has four lessons on common spelling rules: final *e*, doubling, adding prefixes and suffixes, and changing *y* to *i*. The second through fifth units provide drill on commonly misspelled words that do not necessarily follow regular spelling rules. Each unit of the guide contains a pretest and computer instruction. An appendix lists the files used in this guide.

Woodburn, Mary Stuart. 1987. "Take the Drudgery Out of Spelling with this Individualized Program." *Learning* 15(5): 70–71. EJ 346 366.
A weekly plan is presented for teachers as an alternative to the more traditional spelling list and instructional techniques. Each student has an individualized spelling list of frequently misspelled words and content area vocabulary. Activities are designed to increase student confidence in spelling.

Vocabulary

DeSerres, Barbara. 1990. "Putting Vocabulary in Context (In the Classroom)." *Reading Teacher* 43(8): 612–13. EJ 408 419. Special Issue: Whole Literacy: Possibilities and Challenges.
This article describes a method for increasing vocabulary recognition of Chapter 1 elementary students by using mastery words from basal programs, sight word cards, and modified cloze stories.

Hadaway, Nancy L., and Viola Florez. 1988. "Five Strategies for Teaching Vocabulary as a Process." *Reading Horizons* 28(3): 165–71. EJ 368 565.
This article recommends five process-oriented strategies for teaching vocabulary: (1) teach words in context; (2) move from the known to the unknown; (3) group and categorize items; (4) relate content to students' interests; and (5) provide for constant review.

Moore, David W., et al. 1989. *Prereading Activities for Content Area Reading and Learning.* 2nd ed. Reading Aids Series. Newark, DE: International Reading Association. 82p. ED 300 786. International Reading Association, 800 Barksdale Road, P.O. Box 8139, Newark, DE 19714-8139. Book no. 233. $5.25 member; $7.75 nonmember.
Intended to be a practical guide to prereading activities, this book shifts the focus of instruction to student-centered applications. Chapters of the book cover such topics as: (1) preparing students to read in the content areas; (2) asking and answering questions prior to reading; (3) forecasting passages; (4) understanding vocabulary; (5) graphically representing information; and (6) writing before reading. Each chapter contains a statement of purpose and a list of teaching strategies, as well as a list of references.

Nagy, William E. 1988. *Teaching Vocabulary To Improve Reading Comprehension.* Urbana, IL: ERIC Clearinghouse on Reading and Communication Skills, and the National Council of Teachers of English; Newark, DE: International Reading Association. 52p. ED 298 471. National Council of Teachers of English, 1111 Kenyon Road, Urbana, IL 61801. Stock no. 52384-015. $4.95 member; $7.50 nonmember (ISBN-0-8141-5238-4). International Reading Association, P.O. Box 8139, 800 Barksdale Road, Newark, DE 19714-8139. No. 151. $4.95 member; $7.50 nonmember (ISBN-0-87207-151-0).
Based on the best available research, this publication describes the most effective methods of vocabulary instruction for the improvement of reading comprehension. Examples of useful approaches to vocabulary instruction aimed at students past the initial stages of reading are presented for use or adaptation by classroom teachers. The publication's main emphasis is on the use of prereading activities, but the primary

purpose is to provide the teacher with a knowledge of how and why vocabulary-related activities can be chosen and adapted to maximize their effectiveness. Sections of the publication discuss: (1) reasons for failure of vocabulary instruction; (2) partial word knowledge; (3) problems of traditional vocabulary instruction; (4) efficiency of vocabulary instruction; and (5) the trade-off between effective instruction and incidental learning. Fifty-five references are appended.

Oregon State Department of Education. 1989. *Vocabulary. English Language Arts Concept Paper Number 7.* Salem. 9p. ED 311 417.
Stressing that building vocabulary is a continuously developing skill, acquired over a lifetime and in a variety of ways, this concept paper suggests instructional strategies that lead to word knowledge. Following a research summary and a section on implications for instruction, the paper focuses on a variety of instructional strategies. A section on developing independent skills offers a step-by-step vocabulary overview guide as a model for students to use on their own to learn word meanings. A twenty-three–item bibliography is attached.

Sanacore, Joseph. 1988. *Linking Vocabulary and Comprehension Through Independent Reading.* 15p. ED 300 798.
Independent reading can serve as a practical context for linking vocabulary and comprehension; it complements other instructional approaches while it expands word knowledge in a naturalistic setting. While teachers should act as reading models during students' silent reading, they are cautioned about overdoing it and displacing independent reading. At times, teachers may vary their modeling by demonstrating to students ways in which context plays a role in grasping the meaning of words. What is needed is a balance of encouraging wide and varied reading and of modeling at appropriate times in clear, demonstrative, and motivational ways. Fifteen references, a model, and a brief outline of the paper are attached.

Whole Language

Clemmons, Joan, et al. 1991. "Engaging the Learner in Whole Literacy: An Immersion Approach." (Workshop presented at the

Annual Meeting of the International Reading Association, Las Vegas, NV, May 6–10, 1991.) 74p. ED 336 730.
This collection of administrative, planning, and teaching materials focuses on an immersion approach to engaging learners in whole literacy. The collection's six sections and authors are: (1) "Role of the Administrator" (Mary Dill); (2) "Role of the Reading Teacher" (Carleen Payne); (3)" Batteries and Bulbs" (DonnaLynn Estes); (4): "Bears" (Lois Laase); (5)" American Colonization and Revolution" (Joan Clemmons); and (6) "Portfolios" (DonnaLynn Estes, et al.). The third, fourth, and fifth sections are interdisciplinary teaching units on the topics noted, containing planning webs, unit descriptions and objectives, learning activities, and suggested books. An appendix contains work sheets, diagrams, and charts for learning activities.

Cromwell-Hoffman, Carole, and Linda Sasser. 1989. "A Literature-Based Cooperative Lesson for ESL." (Paper presented at the Annual Meeting of the California Association for Bilingual Education, Anaheim, CA, February 17, 1989.) 49p. ED 317 047.
In this cooperative lesson for students of English as a Second Language (ESL), students from different cultural and language backgrounds write folk tales from their native cultures and compile them into a book. The composition of each four-member team is based on student variables, such as ethnicity, personality, academic ability, language functioning, gender, and preference. Interdependence is facilitated by assigning roles to team members. Procedures for the six-day exercise are outlined and the following elements are delineated: materials, preparations, introduction and focus, input and evaluation, application(s) and evaluation, refocus when appropriate, and closure. Extension activities are also suggested. Five sample folk tales and sample work sheets for the unit are appended.

Ferguson, Phyllis. 1988. "Whole Language: A Global Approach to Learning." *Instructor* 97(9): 24–27. EJ 374 371.
The whole language approach to learning is used to develop reading, writing, and language skills in primary grades and science and social studies skills in intermediate grades. The program is described and its techniques of immersion, theme building, brainstorming, implementation, and flexible grouping are discussed.

Hudson, Jean. 1988. "Real Books for Real Readers for Real Purposes." *Reading* 22(2): 78–83. EJ 376 102.
This article attempts to justify the place of real books in the beginning reading curriculum, and suggests teaching strategies for developing a multi-cue approach to reading.

Schwartz, Susan, and Mindy Pollishuke. 1991. *Creating the Child-Centered Classroom.* Katonah, NY: Richard C. Owen. 100p. ED 329 893. Richard C. Owen Publishers, Inc., P.O. Box 585, Katonah, NY 10536. $19.95.
This book outlines the theory behind the child-centered classroom, which involves an understanding of whole language and active learning. The practical classroom strategies that are suggested for different curriculum areas are intended to provide a base from which to begin to modify and to adapt to fit teachers' and students' individual needs and strengths. The eight chapter titles include: (1) Whole Language and Active Learning: A Philosophical Model; (2) The Physical Set-Up of the Classroom; (3) Timetabling; (4) Classroom Atmosphere; (5) Whole Language; (6) An Integrated Child-Centred Curriculum; (7) Learning Centres; and (8) Record Keeping, Student Evaluation and Parental Involvement. Blackline masters are provided for student, teacher, and parent use. A list of favorite children's books is appended.

Whyte, Sarah. 1988. *Whole Language Using Big Books.* 73p. ED 298 479.
Designed as thematic units around Wright Company Big Books, the lessons in this guide demonstrate ways that Big Books can be used in a whole language first grade program. Each lesson indicates skill focus, needed materials, procedures, and additional thoughts or suggestions about the lesson. The following information is included in the appendix: a list of themes and Wright Books used; a thematic listing of poems/songs and their authors; a list of nursery rhymes for use in whole language activities; a thematic listing of tradebooks and their authors; possible Big Book material; a whole language and writing bibliography; and a teacher resource bibliography.

Writing/Composition

Collins, Cathy. 1991. "Reading Instruction That Increases Thinking Abilities." *Journal of Reading* 34(7): 510–16. EJ 424 211. Themed Issue: Thinking and Learning across the Curriculum.
This article analyzes the effects of eight reading and writing lessons designed to increase adolescent thinking ability. The lessons were found to increase the thinking abilities and scholastic achievement of middle school students, and to improve their self-esteem and communication skills.

Kneeshaw, Stephen. 1988. "Comparative History in the Classroom: A Lesson Plan." *OAH Magazine of History* 3(3–4): 43. EJ 391 313.
This article offers ideas for using comparative history in the classroom, including suggestions for using guided design, role playing, and sequenced writing exercises. The 1920s and 1970s are used for comparison, focusing on Teapot Dome and Watergate.

Mueller, Lyn Zalusky, et al. 1987. *Teaching and Testing Our Basic Skills Objectives (T & T). Writing: Grades 1–3.* Columbia: South Carolina State Department of Education, Office of Research. 103p. ED 288 196.
To stimulate students' growth in writing, this guide offers suggestions, lists, charts, and activities for classroom use in the primary grades. Following a preface and philosophy, the first section discusses young writers and the writing process, with subsections on stages of the writing process, conferencing, and Basic Skills Assessment Program (BSAP) objectives. The second section offers suggestions for helping young writers, including setting up a writing environment; involving teachers, parents, and administrators; writing across the curriculum; and tracking and assessing progress. The final section answers questions about implementing such a program, writing readiness, selecting good children's books, and integrating reading and writing. Four pages of resources are included. Appendixes include a list of professional organizations, ideas for publishing student writing, sample parent letters, ERIC Digests on spelling, and BSAP scoring criteria. Also *Writing: Grades 4–12*, ED 253 886.

Petroshius, Sandra. 1991. "Civic Writing Approaches in Language Arts." *Civic Perspective* 4(1): 1–4. EJ 428 380.

This article presents examples of classroom writing activities that can be incorporated into language arts textbooks for grades 2, 5, and 8 to encourage civic thinking on issues such as nationhood, leadership, cultural differences, taxation, and war.

Piper, Judy. 1991. "Classroom Writing Activities to Support the Curriculum." *Writing Notebook: Creative Word Processing in the Classroom* 8(3): 33. EJ 422 630.

This article provides three teaching strategies that integrate technology into the curriculum: inductive teaching, cooperative learning, and mnemonics.

Specialized Topics for Language Arts

Florida State Department of Education. 1987. *English Skills IV: Course No. 1001390: Parallel Alternative Strategies for Students.* Tallahassee, FL: Bureau of Education for Exceptional Students. 386p. ED 294 247.

One of a series of Parallel Alternative Strategies for Students (PASS) packages developed to provide Florida teachers with modified approaches for presenting content courses to mainstreamed exceptional students, this guide was designed as a supplementary text and workbook for a high school English course. The guide is divided into eight units of study: (1) Vocabulary; (2) Written Composition; (3) The Writing Process; (4) Reference Skills; (5) Literature; (6) Speaking Skills; (7) Media; and (8) Development of the English Language. Each unit contains a teacher's guide with the objectives listed at the beginning of the unit, as well as a section which lists various approaches and activities for presenting the content to students. The student materials in each unit include study sheets and learning activities, which may be reproduced for the students' use. Answer keys are located in the appendix. This PASS has been correlated to the intended outcomes adopted by the State Board of Education for the English Skills IV course and the state-suggested student performance standards. The correlation chart is found in the appendix.

Hanson, Cynthia, ed. 1990. *Thinking through Technologies; Integrating Technology Series.* St. Paul: Minnesota State Department of Education, Instructional Design Section. 57p. ED 337 133. Minnesota Curriculum Services Center, Capitol View, 70 Co. Road. B-2 W, Little Canada, MN 55117.

The lesson plans presented in this guide are intended to provide secondary teachers with examples of ways that students can use thinking and technology skills to solve problems and address issues they will be facing in their futures. The lessons are based on the Williams Model for Cognitive–Affective Interaction and are designed to fit into existing courses in language arts, science, and social studies. Each lesson lists the curriculum area, grade level, objectives, and activity, and briefly introduces the concepts involved. The appendixes contain a description of the Williams Model for Cognitive–Affective Interaction and a discussion of databases and their uses.

Harnett County School District. [1989]. *Harnett County Schools Academically Gifted Curriculum K–8.* Lilington, NC. 33p. ED 327 989.

The Harnett County curriculum for academically gifted students in grades K–8 uses a consulting model to extend and enrich the academic curriculum according to students' individual needs. The curriculum guide is designed to be flexible while providing for a standard course of study throughout the school system, and aims to enhance and enrich but not replace the North Carolina Competency Based Curriculum. The curriculum covers language arts (reading, spelling, creative writing, grammar, and research skills), mathematics, field trips, computer skills, science, and social studies. Each content area is divided into learning activities for students in grades K–3 and 4–8. Suggested resources are listed throughout the guide. In addition, a list of fifteen recommended readings for parents, teachers, and counselors is included, along with a list of eleven readings recommended for gifted students.

Morris, Vivian Gunn, and Kathleen Conroy. 1987. *Writing in Consumer and Homemaking Education Programs: A Guide for Reinforcing Basic Skills.* Vocational Home Economics Education. Glassboro, NJ: Glassboro State College. 170p. ED 288 073.

This guide is intended to assist home economics teachers in designing lessons and activities that will reinforce writing skills in consumer and homemaking education programs. Included in the guide are fifty-nine mini-lessons on the following areas: child development; family relationships; foods and nutrition; consumer education; housing, home furnishings, and equipment; and clothing and textiles. Each activity contains some or all of the following: content area, level of difficulty, home economics content objective, writing objective, learning activity, and source. An appendix contains the answers to all the activities. Also included is a matrix that details (1) the number(s) of the learning activities in which a particular writing skill is reinforced, and (2) whether a given writing skill is required to pass the New Jersey High School Proficiency Test.

Podany, Zita. 1989. *Ideas for Integrating the Microcomputer with Instruction.* Portland, OR: Northwest Regional Educational Laboratory. 43p. ED 319 360.
This report focuses on the integration of computers in elementary and middle school instruction: (1) desktop publishing for grades 4 and 5; (2) interpretive writing for any grade level; (3) student-authored word problems for grades 6, 7, and 8; (4) long-distance telecommunications for grades 3 and up; (5) teaching students how to learn for grades 4 and 5; (6) nutrition for grades 6, 7, and 8; and (7) mapping the Western Hemisphere for grades 5 and 6. Included for each lesson are a narrative description and a lesson plan that outlines target audience, hardware, software, instructional purpose, objectives, pre-activities, computer activities, follow-up activities, time requirements, schedule, management suggestions, instructional materials, and teacher preparation. A directory of producers of software mentioned in the report is attached.

Sorenson, Sharon. 1991. *Working with Special Students in English/Language Arts. Teaching Resources in the ERIC Database (TRIED) Series.* Bloomington, IN: ERIC Clearinghouse on Reading and Communication Skills. 81p. ED 326 902. ERIC Clearinghouse on Reading and Communication Skills, Indiana University, 2805 East 10th Street, Suite 150, Bloomington, IN 47408-2698. $9.95, plus postage and handling. Published by EDINFO Press.
This collection of thirty-four lessons offers practical suggestions for addressing the needs of special students (primarily those with learning disabilities or limited English proficiency) in the

English/language arts classroom at both the elementary and secondary levels. The collection includes an activities chart that indicates the focus and types of activities, including: classroom organization, community involvement, computer-assisted instruction, collaborative learning, graphic organizers, reading skills, student evaluation, and writing instruction. A twenty-one-item annotated bibliography of resources in the ERIC database is attached.

South Carolina State Department of Education. 1987. *Reinforcing Basic Skills through Vocational Education.* Columbia: South Carolina State Department of Education, Office of Vocational Education. 94p. ED 287 976.
This guide presents a statewide strategy to ensure that all South Carolina vocational educators are properly prepared to provide relevant basic skills reinforcement instruction as part of all vocational courses. The first section answers the following questions: (1) Why should basic skills be reinforced in vocational education? (2) What are basic skills? (3) How are basic skills currently reinforced in vocational education? and (4) What is South Carolina's strategy for increased implementation? The second section provides sample lesson plans that show how the state-adopted basic skills objectives could be taught in vocational courses. Each lesson plan emphasizes one basic skill in one vocational course and contains an objective, suggested measurement strategy, competency, performance objective, basic skill, basic skill objective, instructional activities, required instructional materials, evaluation, assignment sheets with answer keys, and student self-check with answers. The final section of the guide is an annotated list of resources.

Valencia Community College. [1991]. *Infusing Alcohol and Drug Prevention with Existing Classroom Study Units: Language Arts.* Orlando, FL. 133p. ED 337 121.
This report is part of a collection of programs, policies, and curricula developed by members of the Network of Colleges and Universities Committed to the Elimination of Drug and Alcohol Education, Office of Educational Research and Improvement in response to the 1989 Drug Free Schools and Communities Act. This curriculum module, one of seven in the Infusion Project, offers lessons on drug use prevention that can be integrated into an existing seventh-grade middle school language arts curriculum. The module,

based on a type of interactive learning called infusion learning, contains eighteen lessons that provide objectives, resource materials, student activities, suggestions for additional classroom or out-of-class activities, and teacher tips. Many lessons come with reproducible worksheets. The lesson topics are listening skills, vocabulary, writing, grammar, and library skills. Also included for teachers is "Just the Facts," a set of information units on alcohol, amphetamines, barbiturates, children of alcoholics, cocaine, designer drugs, driving under the influence, eating disorders, inhalants, lysergic acid diethylamide (LSD), marijuana, opiates, phencyclidine (PCP), steroids, tobacco, and nutrition,. There is also a general brochure booklet that introduces the program.

Lists/Resources

American Newspaper Publishers Association
   Foundation. 1986. *NIE Publications. More than 100 Teacher Guides and Curriculum Materials to Aid the Classroom Use of Newspapers.* 6th ed. Washington, DC. 64p. ED 308 541.
This bibliography lists 124 publications designed to answer the question of how to use the newspaper in the school curriculum. The bibliography is one facet of a continuing effort to assist hundreds of newspapers and school systems sponsoring Newspaper in Education programs. Most of the materials in the bibliography are published by newspapers, in close collaboration with curriculum developers in local school systems; many of the lesson plans and activities have been successfully teacher-tested in the classroom.

California State Department of Education. 1988.
   Recommended Readings in Literature: Kindergarten through Grade Eight (Annotated Edition). Sacramento: California State Department of Education. 128p. $4.50.
This book lists more than 1,000 titles of children's classics, modern literature, and storybooks, including books in languages other than English. The annotations for each book cited provide a description of content, and an indication of grade level and culture (as appropriate). An addendum (1990) lists more than 260 additional titles.

California State Department of Education. 1990.
   Recommended Literature, Grades Nine through Twelve. Sacramento. 115p. ED 316 869. Bureau

of Publications, Sales Unit, California State Department of Education, P.O. Box 271, Sacramento, CA 95802-0271. $4.50 each, plus sales tax for California residents.
Intended as a guide for local-level policymakers, curriculum planners, teachers, and librarians, this guide lists over 1200 books that exemplify good literature for high school students. The book is divided into two sections: (1) core and extended materials (books to be taught in the classroom and books to be assigned to supplement classwork); and (2) recreational and motivational literature (to guide students when selecting individual, leisure-time reading materials). Titles are listed within these sections by traditional categories: biographies; drama; folklore, mythology, and epics; nonfiction, essays, and speeches; novels; poetry; short stories; and books in languages other than English. Books are listed alphabetically by author, and a matrix is used to give information that will assist selectors when searching for a title. Title and author indexes and an appendix on storytelling are included.

California State Department of Education. 1991.
   Literature for History–Social Science: Kindergarten through Grade Eight. Sacramento. 128p. $5.25.
This publication was produced to provide a connection between literature and history, so that curriculum planners can include reading as part of social studies and history lessons. This publication lists over 1,000 works of literature that can be used in history or social studies classes. The chapters are arranged by grade level (K–6); within each chapter are a number of subject sections. A short annotation is given for each book cited. Included are works of literature and historical fiction, as well as biographies, fables, myths, and legends.

National Council of Teachers of English. 1987.
   Recommended English Language Arts Curriculum Guides, K–12. Urbana, IL: ERIC Clearinghouse on Reading and Communication Skills, and the National Council of Teachers of English. 34p. ED 286 204. National Council of Teachers of English, 1111 Kenyon Road, Urbana, IL 61801. Stock no. 39515-222. $2.25 member; $3.00 nonmember.
This guide is intended to help teachers and administrators develop exemplary English/ language arts curricula. The first part of the

booklet presents an annotated list of recommended curriculum guides representing a variety of curriculum frameworks and content units. Annotations for curriculum guides recommended in 1985, 1986, and 1987 are included. Information on grade level, content aims and objectives, and how to obtain the guide is provided. The second part of the booklet contains revised criteria for planning and evaluating English/language arts curriculum guides. These criteria are organized under the headings of philosophy, objectives, language, composition, reading, literature, media, organization, policies and procedures, and design.

National Council of Teachers of English. 1990. *Commended English Language Arts Curriculum Guides, K–12*. Urbana, IL. 46p. ED 322 522. Prepared by the NCTE Commission to Evaluate Curriculum Guides and Competency Requirements.
This guide, growing out of the annual evaluation by the National Council of Teachers of English (NCTE) of English Language Arts curriculum

documents (K–12), presents exemplary curriculum documents from the years 1986–1989. The guide presents documents that were commended by the NCTE reviewers and that demonstrate substantive, procedural, or presentational features that can serve as illustrative examples for other schools or school districts. Entries in the guide include a description of the curriculum document, a commentary about its applicability, and information about its availability (cost, a contact person or office, and the appropriate address). Following an introduction, the guide is divided into four main sections: (1) curriculum guides commended in 1988–1989; (2) curriculum guides commended in 1987; (3) curriculum guides commended in 1986; and (4) criteria for planning and evaluating English language arts curriculum guides. Information about the ERIC Document Reproduction Service concludes the guide.

■

8

CURRICULUM GUIDE REPRINT

Curriculum developers can often find ideas and models through the study of curriculum guides from state departments of education and school districts. In this chapter, we have reprinted the following material:

Spelling Is a Tool: Teacher's Guide 1990-91. Wichita Public Schools. Reproduced with permission.

This chapter reproduces this entire eighty-five-page teacher's guide. As the table of contents indicates, the guide progresses from an introduction covering basic questions such as "What is spelling?" through organization and strategies, to evaluation and testing. It concludes with five appendixes which contain samples of letters to students' parents, homework activities, lessons, charts of rules and guidelines, and spelling lists.

For a complete guide, please contact the Director, Elementary Education, Wichita Public Schools, Educational Services, 217 North Water, Wichita, KS 67202.

SPELLING

IS A

TOOL

Teacher's Guide
1990-91

USD 259
Wichita Public Schools
Curriculum Services Division
Elementary Language Arts

ACKNOWLEDGEMENTS

Spelling Guide Committee

Judith White
Mary Ann Lowry
Susan Graves
Janice Fanter
Connie Quintanilla
Trina Waddill
Berneice Garcia
Marilyn Tilton
Mary Ellen Isaac
Marti Garlett
Mychael Willon

Administration

Dr. Stuart Berger, Superintendent of Schools
Mr. Ron Naso, Associate Superintendent of Educational Services
Dr. Anna Chandler, Division Director of Curriculum Services Division
Judith White, Coordinator of Elementary Language Arts

1990-91

TABLE OF CONTENTS

INTRODUCTION

WHAT IS SPELLING?

Spelling is the art of forming words in the standard way society expects. Knowing how to spell words frees us to write what we want to write, whenever and wherever we want to write.

WHAT IS SPELLING?

- one tool of communication

- part of the writing process

- a developmental process

- a process dependent on learning style

WHAT IS A GOOD SPELLER?

- a child who freely explores language and is willing to risk

- a child who is usually a good talker and reader

- a child who has 'caught' spelling by the age of seven or eight (Hudson and O'Toole, 1983)

- a child who has good small muscle control and writes legibly and fluently

- a child who wants to spell correctly for publishing

- a child who has several spelling strategies

- a child who has developed a spelling conscience

2

WHAT IS MORE EFFECTIVE?

There is considerable agreement among spelling authorities concerning teacher behaviors which contribute to more and less effective spelling programs (Oregon Department of Education, May 1987). According to the research, more effective spelling programs result when **teachers provide opportunities for students**:

to write, listen, read, and speak EVERY DAY.

to see that learning to spell is a developmental process.

to develop a variety of spelling strategies.

to develop visual awareness of
- letter sequences and patterns,
- words within words,
- word structures.

to actively manipulate words using preferred learning styles (visual, auditory, and tactile).

to stretch spelling growth while safely risking learning to spell.

to be rewarded for coming close as well as for being right in spelling.

WHAT IS LESS EFFECTIVE?

According to the research, less effective spelling programs result when teachers

❑ teach spelling only as a separate, isolated, fragmented process;

❑ teach only a limited number of spelling strategies;

❑ teach spelling using only one learning mode (visual for example);

❑ have students write spelling words several times;

❑ use a spelling program that has too many lists and rules.

3

SPELLING AS PART OF THE LANGUAGE ARTS PROGRAM

Good spelling is a matter of good manners. As a courtesy, we expect others to spell correctly in their writing to us, and we owe others the same courtesy. Moreover, correct spelling makes things easier to read. Confusions and misinterpretations are less likely when written communications are spelled correctly. In the world of work, correct spelling is valued and demanded.

SPELLING AND SPEAKING

To understand how we learn to spell, it is helpful to look at how we learn to speak. As small children, we are surrounded by a variety of sources of speech and by others who expect us to successfully learn to speak. We are provided with a risk-free environment which allows trial and error. When we approximate speech ("dink"), we are rewarded for our try ("Good! **Dr**-ink, you want a drink.") We are rewarded for being close as well as for being right.

We are encouraged to speak often every day. We are encouraged to hear sounds within words (**dr**-ink), and to hear standard sentence structure (you want some milk). We naturally manipulate sounds using our dominant learning styles. This supportive environment helps us develop several speaking strategies to communicate. We all need many opportunities to try to learn to speak, to fail, and to try again. And so, virtually all of us learn to speak. This pattern of learning or developmental process of a risk-free environment which allows trial and error and rewards approximation, occurs over and over in our lives. The same developmental process helps children learn to spell.

4

SPELLING AND READING

While reading, writing, and spelling have many commonalities, *good readers are not always good spellers.* The process of reading requires decoding. The process of spelling requires encoding.

𝟀 Reading does not require muscle ability; spelling does.

𝟀 Reading is not an exact process; spelling is.

𝟀 The reading environment contains many clues to aid memory; the spelling environment does not.

𝟀 Reading does not require attention to every letter or pattern in words, spelling does.

SPELLING AND WRITING

Just as decoding is one tool used to read, spelling is one tool used to write. In order to communicate clearly in writing, we must use many skills together. We must know how to spell; capitalize; punctuate; use appropriate format, grammar, and syntax; and use legible handwriting skills (or skills in word processing).

THE TOOLS OF WRITING ARE NOT THE WRITING

The tools we use to write (spelling, grammar, handwriting, punctuation, usage, mechanics) are essential to effective writing. *These tools do not, by themselves, communicate. The message is the critical element.* Spelling is a tool for making the message clear. Teachers, students, and parents must be careful not to confuse the tools with writing.

5

SPELLING IS FOR WRITING

The first and most important task in speaking is to communicate a meaningful message. The first and most important task in writing is to communicate a meaningful message. We do not learn to speak in an environment which provides no purpose for speaking. Just so, we will not learn to write or spell correctly in an environment which provides no purpose for writing or spelling. As teachers concerned about spelling, we must provide a learning environment filled with reasons for writing and spelling correctly. This kind of environment stretches skills.

SPELLING WITHIN THE WRITING PROCESS

> We must help students successfully experience the process of learning to communicate meaning through writing and to learn about spelling within that process.

There are several models of the steps of writing process. During the 1990-91 school year, elementary teachers will be using several resources to teach language arts. While these resources do not all use the same terms, the writing process and the place of spelling within that process can be summarized in the following way:

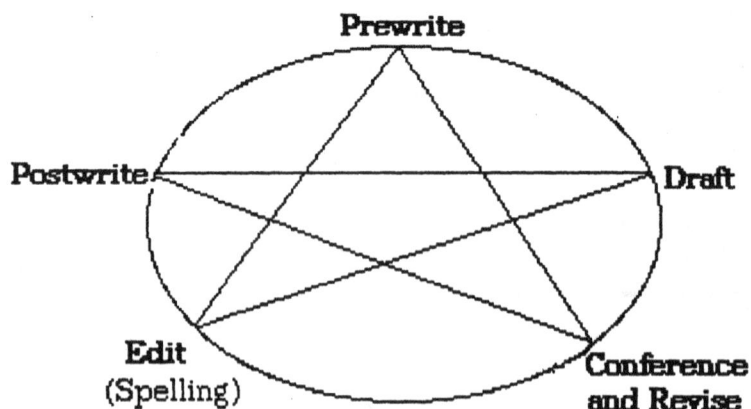

6

LANGUAGE ARTS RESOURCES

Descriptions of the steps of the writing process from each resource provided to each elementary teacher are included below. The appropriate place of spelling correctly in the different resources is highlighted. Teachers are encouraged to examine and study the sections concerning spelling in each resource more thoroughly.

Teaching Writing: Balancing Process and Product (Tompkins)

Prewrite-rehearse, choose audience/purpose, select form

Draft-basic content

Revise-share, discuss, and change

Edit-proofread own and others **(spelling)**

Share-with appropriate audience

Heath Reading Teachers' Guides

Prewrite-generate ideas, expand topic, discover known/unknown, determine approach/who/why/how to start

Write/Draft

Revise-meaning, word selection, organization

Edit-grammar/usage/**spelling**

Postwrite/Publish

If You're Trying to Teach Kids How to Write, You've Gotta Have This Book (Frank)

Motivate

Collect

Rough Draft

Re-read

Share

Edit **(spelling)**

Mechanics check **(spelling)**

Final Copy

Present

The Write Source

Prewrite-select subject

Plan-prepare to write

Write

Revise/edit **(spelling)**

7

THE DEVELOPMENT OF THE SPELLING/WRITING PROCESS

Both the writing process and the process of learning to spell correctly can be traced as children develop. Gail Heald-Taylor (1987) developed a Natural Writing Behavior Inventory to describe possible stages of development. While many children demonstrate behavior at each stage, others skip around within stages, and still others skip some stages completely.

	Date	Comments

Scribble Behavior
  The child:
• Scribbles with no intended message.
• Scribbles using vertical and horizontal movements.
• Scribbles to communicate ("reads" scribble).
• **Scribbles from left to right across the page.**
• **Consistently scribbles horizontally.**
• Uses a line of scribble to represent a thought (sentence).
• **Uses a scribble to represent each word,
   leaving spaces between scribbles.**
• **Makes the scribble match the length of word.**
• "Reads" the scribble story by rote, maintaining a consistent oral text.		

Consonant Spelling
  The child:
• **Uses random letters in writing (no intended communication).**
• **Uses letters and scribbles to communicate (no sound-symbol
   correspondence).**
• **Uses letters to communicate (no sound-symbol correspondence)**
• **Uses letters and sound-symbol correspondence
   (initial consonant spelling).**
• **Uses letter name spelling.**
• **Uses initial consonant spelling and scribble.**
• **Uses initial and final consonant spelling.**
• **Uses combinations of scribble and consonant spelling.**		

Invented Spellings
  The child:
• **Uses invented spellings
   with initial and final consonants and vowels.**
• **Uses known words in stories.**
• **Begins to make transition from invented spelling
   to standard spelling.**
• Begins to use punctuation at end of lines (not necessarily at end of a sentence).
• Writes stories up to three sentences long on one topic.
• Develops an awareness of capital letters for the word *I* and children's names.		

8

	Date	Comments
Early Transitional Behaviors The child: • **Uses more invented spellings than standard spellings.** • **Uses many vowels in invented spellings.** • Writes stories consisting of five or more sentences on one topic. • Sequences two or more events in stories. • Uses punctuation at end of lines. • Occasionally uses punctuation at end of sentences. • Uses capital letters for the word *I* and names.		
Later Transitional Spelling The child: • **Begins to make transition from invented spellings to standard spellings.** • **Uses equal number of invented spellings as standard spellings.** • Writes stories longer than five sentences on one topic. • Uses punctuation at end of sentences with consistency.		
Stabilization of Standard Spelling The child: • **Uses more correct spellings than invented spellings.** • Writes stories longer than five sentences. • Writes stories longer than five sentences, and the sentences are on one topic. • Can sequence three or more events. • Begins to use capital letters at beginning of sentences.		
Growth in Mechanics The child: • **Uses more correct spellings than invented spellings.** • Uses capital letters at beginning of sentences consistently. • Uses punctuation in addition to the period (? ! "). • Uses periods consistently. • Uses quotations in stories, but doesn't make marks accurately. • Begins to use quotation marks with some accuracy.		
Imaginative and Fantasy Stage The child: • Begins to use imagination in story writing. • Begins to use quotation marks appropriately. • Develops an awareness of a variety of purposes for writing (lists, letters, research, etc.).		
Writes for a Variety of Purposes The child: • Writes interesting stories. • Consistently uses punctuation accurately. • Consistently uses capitals accurately. • Writes for a variety of purposes (poetry, research, invitations, etc.).		

9

THE PURPOSE OF SPELLING INSTRUCTION

The purpose of spelling instruction is to help children communicate in writing. Learning to correctly spell a list of weekly spelling words is only one part of learning to spell. We all know that the ability to spell words correctly on a weekly spelling test does not necessarily transfer to the ability to spell words correctly in our writing. Filling in blanks in a spelling workbook correctly does not always help us spell words correctly in our writing. Playing a spelling game or winning a contest does not guarantee we will spell words correctly in our writing.

The purpose of spelling study is not correct performance on a spelling test, or in a workbook, or during a contest. **Competence in communicating a message through writing is the purpose**. While isolated or focused spelling skill instruction has a place in our school spelling programs, **it must not displace opportunities to communicate messages through writing** and to learn to spell correctly in that process.

WHEN TO BEGIN FORMAL SPELLING INSTRUCTION

According to Donoghue (1990), students cannot successfully be introduced to more formal spelling lessons until reaching the phonetic and transitional spelling stages (labeled consonant spelling and transitional stages in the chart on pages 8 and 9). Exposure to extensive writing experiences and to systematic reading instruction appears to be the key to the transition.

INVENTED SPELLING

In the classroom, an effective spelling program begins with invented spelling described in the Natural Writing Behavior Inventory. Invented spelling is the name used for children's misspellings before

10

they know the structure of the English language adults use to spell. Inventive spellers learn to write as they learned to talk.

Invented spelling does not interfere with learning to spell correctly. Like early attempts to talk or draw, early attempts to spell do not produce habits to be overcome. No one worries when first attempts to speak include "dink". No one worries when a child's first drawing of a person is a head on top of two stick legs. AND, no one should worry when a child writes "sno" for "snow". As children write using invented spelling, they practice and drill themselves at a pace and level of difficulty appropriate to their skills. No teacher has the time to motivate, diagnose, and assign the appropriate individualized spelling materials that can match the work children do when they write.

AUTHENTIC REASONS FOR SPELLING

When children have authentic reasons* to communicate in writing, they have real reasons to learn to spell correctly. Some examples of authentic reasons include

✐ making lists for others to read and use,

✐ writing news stories,

✐ writing about important events in their lives,

✐ writing stories for younger children,

✐ writing letters,

✐ writing directions or instructions,

✐ writing notes, and

✐ labeling.

* The adopted teachers' resource materials mentioned in the preface include many more examples of authentic writing opportunities. In particular see Tompkins and Frank.

11

GOALS OF THE SPELLING PROGRAM

STUDENTS

- Independently attempt to spell any word as they draft.

- Learn to use many spelling strategies and resources through the writing process.

- Develop a spelling conscience or the sense of words spelled correctly and words spelled incorrectly.

- Learn common letter groups and spelling patterns, spelling generalizations, and words most commonly used in writing.

TEACHERS

- Provide a risk-free environment in which to learn to spell.

- Teach spelling primarily through the writing process.

- Stretch spelling growth through the writing process.

- Teach standard spelling using many real models and authentic, ongoing, integrated activities.

12

MORE ABOUT THE GOALS

STUDENTS •**Independently attempt to spell any word as they draft.**

Good spelling is not a sign of high intelligence and absolutely no one is a perfect speller all of the time. The single most important goal and purpose of spelling instruction is for students to learn skills and strategies they will use as they write. In order for students to feel free to write, they must focus on expressing meaning not on spelling until the appropriate time in the writing process. This results in invented spelling or in the students spelling words in nonstandard ways. Teachers will need to use a phrase such as "give it a try," "try it yourself," or, "have a go" and use the phrase consistently with students during the drafting stage of writing. Also, teachers will need to have students circle words they are not sure how to spell to help delay any focus on correct spelling.

TEACHERS •**Provide a risk-free environment in which to learn to spell.**

Spelling skills can most effectively be learned in a risk-free environment which values trial and error as an integral part of learning to spell. Fear of misspelling a word should **never** keep students from expressing themselves during the first three steps (prewriting, drafting, revising) of the writing process. Teachers will need to be very persistent in expecting students to attempt to use invented spelling to independently spell any word during the first three steps of the writing process; because, some students will try very hard to focus on spelling or mechanics during this stage. Establishing a risk-free environment with some students will take time.

13

STUDENTS •**Learn to use many spelling strategies and resources through the writing process.**

During drafting, students will learn to try many spelling **strategies** including invented spelling. As they edit for spelling, they individualize their study of standard spellings of the English language. As part of editing, students will learn to use many **resources** including dictionaries, textbook glossaries, machines, individual lists and logs, and/or class lists or charts, their own knowledge and that of other students, and more.

TEACHERS •**Teach spelling primarily through the writing process.**

When teachers provide many opportunities to write and publish, students become interested in spelling correctly and will work hard during the editing process on spelling and other editing skills. Isolation of spelling skills without frequent (daily) opportunities clearly connected to writing and publishing is usually a waste of everyone's time. Every "real" writer (published author) has an editor.

STUDENTS •**Develop a sense of words spelled correctly and words spelled incorrectly.**

While students will attempt to spell any word they write, they will also develop a sense of correct and incorrect spelling to use during the editing and proofreading process. Teaching students to circle words they are not sure how to spell in their drafts is one technique which helps students learn to proofread. Proofreading skills are very important and are assessed in the district's norm-referenced testing program, the *Iowa Test of Basic Skills.*

TEACHERS •**Stretch spelling growth through the writing process.**

During the revising and editing stages of writing and during writing conferences, teachers will find many "teachable" moments to stretch spelling growth. These moments are best left as brief opportunities and not turned into lengthy lectures. When needed, mini-lessons can be based on student and teacher evaluation of spelling skill needs based on students' writings.

14

STUDENTS •Learn common letter groups and spelling patterns, spelling generalizations, and words most commonly used in writing.

Students will be held accountable for making progress toward knowledge and use of the more dependable of the patterns of the English language. This guide provides resource materials.

TEACHERS •Teach standard spelling using many real models and authentic, ongoing integrated activities.

As a result of many opportunities to read a variety of literature and to engage in authentic writing process activities, students become motivated to learn to spell correctly. Teachers need to provide not only opportunities for authentic writing process activities, but also knowledge about the spelling structure of standard English as students write. This manual, other adopted language arts teacher support materials, and materials from other curriculum areas will provide teachers with real models and authentic, ongoing, integrated spelling and writing activities.

15

ORGANIZING YOUR SPELLING PROGRAM

Like teachers everywhere, each teacher in Wichita is unique. We have many teaching styles, beliefs, and methods. The authors strongly believe Wichita teachers are educated and capable decision makers. As you organize the spelling program for your classroom, you need information and resources.

In the Wichita Public Schools, educators are effectively teaching many students how to spell. We are not teaching **all** students how to spell. Based on the goals of our spelling program and on research, there are three essential elements of designing an effective spelling program for **all** students:

THREE ESSENTIAL ELEMENTS

Write and read everyday.

Diagnose needs.

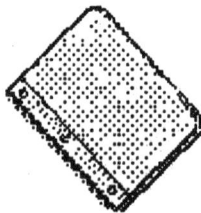

Stretch growth.

16

Extensive experience with writing and with reading provides the foundation for spelling growth as well as the basis for diagnosing the need for formal spelling instruction. Learning to spell is more an active, developmental process than it is a memorization process.

Since students cannot benefit from formal spelling instruction until they developmentally move into the appropriate spelling stage. Diagnosis is critical to an effective spelling program. Based on diagnosis, instruction can be very effective in helping all students learn to spell accurately.

Commercial spelling programs cannot guarantee all students will learn to spell accurately. Stetson and Boutin (1980) estimate students are probably able to spell 68% of the words in the spelling book for their grade level **before** the beginning of the year.

When teachers rely on a textbook-oriented, formal instructional approach to spelling, they tend to address whatever is next in the text regardless of students' needs for instruction. The purpose of textbook companies is primarily to sell texts and preferably to sell workbooks which are needed at least yearly. To improve spelling instruction, teachers must use available information from research. Many researchers believe their findings are not reaching the classroom due to reliance on both tradition and on commercial materials.

17

APPLYING THE ELEMENTS TO A PLAN

There is considerable agreement among spelling authorities concerning teacher behaviors which contribute to more and less effective spelling programs (see page 2) in terms of meeting individual student needs. Three sample plans are presented for the consideration of teachers. All three of the plans contain the essential elements of an effective spelling program.

Most Effective <——— <——— <——— <——— <——— <——— <——— <——— **Least Effective**

PLAN A	PLAN B	PLAN C
WRITE AND READ EVERYDAY	WRITE AND READ EVERYDAY	WRITE AND READ EVERYDAY
1. Students write and read extensively.	1. Students write and read extensively.	1. Students write and read extensively.
DIAGNOSE NEEDS	DIAGNOSE NEEDS	DIAGNOSE NEEDS
2. Teacher and students diagnose spelling needs and knowledge.	2. Based on identified student need, the teacher selects part of a word study list.	2. Based on identified student need, the teacher selects a word study list.
STRETCH GROWTH	3. Based on self-diagnosis, students add to the list.	STRETCH GROWTH
3. Students edit using many resources including those they make and keep for references and study: spelling dictionaries, spelling logs, word collections and more.	STRETCH GROWTH	3. A pretest-study-test-reteach-retest format is used.
4. A pretest-study-test-reteach-retest format is used.	4. Students are taught spelling strategies and the teacher provides ongoing, authentic activities to stretch spelling skills using WTA&A mini-lessons (see appendix).
4. Students are taught spelling strategies and the teacher provides ongoing, authentic activities to stretch spelling skills using WTA&A mini-lessons (see appendix).	5. Students are taught spelling strategies and the teacher provides ongoing, authentic activities to stretch spelling skills using WTA&A mini-lessons (see appendix).	

18

MORE ABOUT THE PLANS

Once students can developmentally benefit from formal spelling instruction (when they have reached the transitional stage), **no more than fifteen well-planned minutes per day** should be spent on direct instruction to stretch growth. Teachers are invited to devise PLAN AB, PLAN BC, and so forth using any combination plans. Any of the three plans or a mixture of plans can be used for any part of the school year. Students' spelling needs vary both individually and from classroom to classroom at different times during the school year. Our Heath Reading adoption supports the teacher as decision maker. Each teacher, in consultation with the building principal and with parents, is by far the best decision maker for the students.

Teachers are **strongly** encouraged to communicate their classroom plan to the parents of their students (see Appendix A for sample letters). Many parents may think that studying a weekly list is the most effective way to learn to spell. Those parents who are particularly insistent about a weekly spelling list for their child should be accommodated. The *Report to Parents* (report card) places spelling skills firmly in the context of writing. When parents realize that the results of weekly spelling test "grades" do not determine progress either on the report card or in terms of real spelling development, they will probably becomes less interested in spelling lists.

PLAN A

WRITE AND READ EVERYDAY

Students write and read everyday. Within editing, spelling is emphasized. Extensive reading provides the spelling models students need.

19

DIAGNOSE NEEDS

Spelling growth depends on continuous diagnosis and evaluation. During the writing process, students are involved in diagnosing their needs in spelling. Involving students in diagnosis, and in designing their own methods of stretching growth is important and frees the teacher for other tasks. As students use their resources and strategies during writing, natural "study" occurs.

STRETCH GROWTH

Teacher knowledge and observation determines how the teacher helps students stretch spelling growth. Students design spelling references for use during editing including personal spelling dictionaries or lists, word collections, and spelling logs (see pages 26-36). Students are taught spelling strategies and the teacher provides ongoing, authentic activities to stretch spelling skills using WTA&A mini-lessons (see Appendix B).

Spelling patterns or generalizations included in Appendix C may be needed at times for direct instruction. The teacher can plan and teach WTA&A mini-lessons with small, ad hoc groups when only some students need a special lesson. Planning for the mini-lessons need not be time consuming and will take no more of a teacher's time than grading spelling series workbooks and giving weekly spelling tests. No more than fifteen well-planned minutes per day should be used in addition to the work students do during the editing process.

Occasionally, the teacher may see the need for the study of a list of words by individuals, groups, or by the class as a whole. As an optional activity to assess student needs, the teacher can assess the class, small groups, or individuals using the Benchmark Spelling Lists. Results of the assessments can be used for planning and for reporting progress to parents. The writing process is the setting for learning to spell and spelling skill enhancement is placed within that process.

20

PLAN B

WRITE AND READ EVERYDAY

Students write and read everyday. Within editing, spelling is emphasized. Extensive reading provides the spelling models students need.

DIAGNOSE NEEDS

Spelling growth depends on continuous diagnosis and evaluation. Periodically, perhaps weekly, the teacher diagnoses needs and selects between five and ten words for class study. Words for the list can be drawn from several sources: words from students' writing, words from the U.S.D. 259 Benchmark Spelling Lists, words the class is encountering in reading or other subject matter areas, or words from the manual of the previous spelling adoption (Riverside *Spelling*). The teacher presents (perhaps on Monday) the master class list and students are given the opportunity to add five or ten words they would like to learn to spell to the master class list.

STRETCH GROWTH

Initially, words should be presented in a list, not in sentences or paragraphs. The teacher engages the class in a discussion of the words, their sources, meanings, patterns, and generalizations. The WTA&A model is used. A pre-test is given. Students check their own pre-tests. Research tells us that the self-corrected test is the most powerful technique a teacher can use to help students learn a list of words (Oregon Department of Education, 1987). Since it is much more important for students to explore words in their writing and reading than to have them write lists of words, writing process activities precede and follow the spelling activity each day.

Next, (perhaps on Tuesday) students study only the words they missed using a variety of spelling strategies and WTA&A teacher directed activities, and pair with another student to take a self-corrected test. WTA&A mini-lessons from the appendix can be used

21

to enhance the study. Writing process activities precede and follow the spelling activity.

Next, (perhaps on Wednesday) students pair and take self-corrected tests or the teacher gives a practice test. By reading the master list and expecting students to be responsible for the words each identified earlier for study, the teacher can avoid reading several lists. Again, students can check their own tests. The results of the practice test can be used for further strategy study that day or the next (perhaps Thursday). Writing process activities precede and follow the spelling activity.

Finally, the teacher can use the master list (perhaps on Friday) as a test list and can check each student's test. Re-teaching and re-testing for those in need follows. Writing process activities precede and follow the spelling activity.

PLAN C

Plan B and Plan C differ only in the respect that Plan C does not allow involvement of the students in selecting words for the master spelling list. Teacher judgment determines how much and how frequently student involvement in diagnosis and determination of study methods and strategies is needed.

SPELLING STRATEGIES AND RESOURCES

Spelling strategies are ways to recall word structures and letter combinations in words. To try to memorize every letter of every word in the English language is impossible for most of us and at the very least, inefficient. We learn to devise ways to remember words we need to spell. For example, many school people remember how to spell principal as opposed to principle by remembering, "The principal is a pal." Another common spelling strategy most of us have learned is, "I before e except after c, and when sounded like a as in neighbor or weigh." Still a third strategy is the learning style or method we use to study and recall words for a weekly spelling test.

CHUNKING

Chunking is the ability to perceive groups of letters as a whole. Encouraging students to use chunking to study and spell words helps form associations and generalizations by focusing on the visual characteristics of words. Chunks include
- words within words (**teach**er);
- common letter patterns, syllables, blends (ight, a/gain, bl, ai);
- base words, prefixes, suffixes (replay, play, played).

MORPHEMES

A morpheme is the smallest meaningful language unit. The word boys contains two morphemes - **boy** and **s**. Boy is a base word, and the **s** in boys is a unit which adds plurality. Morphemic knowledge includes the study of prefixes, suffixes and base words and the meaning and function of word parts. The understanding of these structures helps students see logic in spelling. An example of a morphemic study might include run, runner, runs, rerun, runny.

23

MNEMONICS

Mnemonic means helping the memory. Some students enjoy creating mnemonic devices but find the ones they create themselves most useful. Several mnemonic devices are mentioned in the STUDY-TRY-CHECK method. Others include

- Never end a fri<u>end</u>ship.
- People in <u>bus</u>iness sometimes take a bus.
- <u>A</u>ffect has an a for action.

PHONETICS AND SPELLING RULES

Phonetics is the study of the production and written representation of the sound-symbol relationships found in the English language. Phonics is a phonetic method of teaching reading. The sounds we hear in words are only one possible clue as to the spelling of the word. The recall of English words based on sound-symbol relationship knowledge is only one spelling strategy. Appendix C contains a chart of consonant and vowel spellings and a list of rules which are somewhat reliable. There are no spelling rules or generalizations which are 100% reliable. While these rules are considered by many as important to teach and learn, students also need to learn:

- some sounds in words contain no phonetic clues (knife).
- a letter or sequence of letters may represent different sounds (rough, through).
- a sound may be spelled with various letters or letter sequences (rain, eight, day).
- in some words, the sound will be different in different cultures (wash, idea).
- spelling depends on context (principal, principle, affect, effect).

LOGS

Have students make and continuously keep a log of words they want to learn to spell and to practice the words on their own. Forms for logs are included later in this section.

24

SPELLING STUDY WITH *STYLE*

Everyone has different ways of remembering spellings depending on their preferred learning style or styles. Spelling correctly depends primarily on visual memory, but the use of other learning styles for study can help visual memory. Have students determine their preferred styles by discussing how each best remembers. Then encourage them to use the knowledge when they study spelling words. The study, try, check model allows visual, auditory, kinesthetic, and tactile learners to use their preferred learning style to study a word list and involves five steps:

STUDY WITH *STYLE*

visual | Look at the word. Close your eyes and visualize (imagine) the word. Devise a visual memory clue (There is a pie in piece.)

auditory | Say the word to yourself. Listen to the sounds in the word. Say the letters to yourself. Devise an auditory memory clue (issss-land for island).

tactile | Write or trace over the word. Write the word in the palm of the hand. Notice the way the word feels as you write it. Devise a feeling memory clue to go with the way the word looks (imagine the letters in the word "burn" feeling hot). Imagine the letters in the word moving (imagine the letters in the word "fast" running).

TRY | Without looking, try spelling the word.

CHECK | Check the word immediately. If the word is correct, go on to the next word, if not, repeat the steps.

25

✏ SPELLING STUDY ✏

STUDY WITH
STYLE
(LOOK, SAY, WRITE)

TRY

CHECK

Wrong? Try again!

26

Words	Study with *Style*	Try and Check
- - - - - - - - - - - - - - -	- - - - - - - - - - - - - - -	- - - - - - - - - - - - -
- - - - - - - - - - - - - - -	- - - - - - - - - - - - - - -	- - - - - - - - - - - - -
- - - - - - - - - - - - - - -	- - - - - - - - - - - - - - -	- - - - - - - - - - - - -
- - - - - - - - - - - - - - -	- - - - - - - - - - - - - - -	- - - - - - - - - - - - -
- - - - - - - - - - - - - - -	- - - - - - - - - - - - - - -	- - - - - - - - - - - - -
- - - - - - - - - - - - - - -	- - - - - - - - - - - - - - -	- - - - - - - - - - - - -
- - - - - - - - - - - - - - -	- - - - - - - - - - - - - - -	- - - - - - - - - - - - -
- - - - - - - - - - - - - - -	- - - - - - - - - - - - - - -	- - - - - - - - - - - - -
- - - - - - - - - - - - - - -	- - - - - - - - - - - - - - -	- - - - - - - - - - - - -
- - - - - - - - - - - - - - -	- - - - - - - - - - - - - - -	- - - - - - - - - - - - -
- - - - - - - - - - - - - - -	- - - - - - - - - - - - - - -	- - - - - - - - - - - - -
- - - - - - - - - - - - - - -	- - - - - - - - - - - - - - -	- - - - - - - - - - - - -
- - - - - - - - - - - - - - -	- - - - - - - - - - - - - - -	- - - - - - - - - - - - -
- - - - - - - - - - - - - - -	- - - - - - - - - - - - - - -	- - - - - - - - - - - - -

27

Words	Study with *Style*	Try and Check

_____ words   **Word Collection**

- - - - - - - - - - - -	- - - - - - - - - - - - -	- - - - - - - - - - - -
- - - - - - - - - - - -	- - - - - - - - - - - - -	- - - - - - - - - - - -
- - - - - - - - - - - -	- - - - - - - - - - - - -	- - - - - - - - - - - -
- - - - - - - - - - - -	- - - - - - - - - - - - -	- - - - - - - - - - - -
- - - - - - - - - - - -	- - - - - - - - - - - - -	- - - - - - - - - - - -
- - - - - - - - - - - -	- - - - - - - - - - - - -	- - - - - - - - - - - -
- - - - - - - - - - - -	- - - - - - - - - - - - -	- - - - - - - - - - - -
- - - - - - - - - - - -	- - - - - - - - - - - - -	- - - - - - - - - - - -
- - - - - - - - - - - -	- - - - - - - - - - - - -	- - - - - - - - - - - -
- - - - - - - - - - - -	- - - - - - - - - - - - -	- - - - - - - - - - - -
- - - - - - - - - - - -	- - - - - - - - - - - - -	- - - - - - - - - - - -
- - - - - - - - - - - -	- - - - - - - - - - - - -	- - - - - - - - - - - -
- - - - - - - - - - - -	- - - - - - - - - - - - -	- - - - - - - - - - - -
- - - - - - - - - - - -	- - - - - - - - - - - - -	- - - - - - - - - - - -

29

_____ words   **Word Categories**

30

GIVE IT A TRY LOG

My Try	Word	Practice	Memory Clue

GIVE IT A TRY LOG

My Try	Word	Practice	Memory Clue

Spelling Dictionary

33

Spelling Dictionary

34

_____ SPELLING LOG

My Try	Correct Word	Memory Strategy

_____ **SPELLING LOG**

My Try	Correct Word	Memory Strategy

GRADE LEVEL AND SPECIAL STUDENT CONSIDERATIONS

EARLY PRIMARY

The success of formal spelling lessons is highly dependent upon whether students have developmentally reached the appropriate stage in writing. Children enter school exhibiting various stages of the development. The spelling program needs to be broad and varied in order to stretch the growth of all. Students can be assisted in their development by being provided extensive opportunities for talking, drawing, writing, and reading. Abundant manipulative materials are essential to the early primary program. Manipulatives include various types and sizes of writing tools (pencils, crayons, markers, sticks, magnetic letters, flannel letters, typewriters, computers) and various sizes and types of material on/in which to write (rough paper, smooth paper, chalkboards, magic slates, sandboxes, lined and unlined paper).

A variety of shared reading and writing experiences provides abundant opportunities to learn that writing conveys meaning and to look at words and word structures. Opportunities for shared reading include choral reading and any reading aloud where the students can see the print. Shared writing includes writing demonstrations and involvements with making big books, charts, poems, lists, signs, messages, captions, labels, wall stories, experience stories and sentences, rhymes, songs, and more. Much as we fill the child's world with spoken language as they learn to talk, we must fill the classroom with written language as they learn to write and spell.

Finally, early primary teachers can help most by encouraging invented spelling so students have abundant opportunities to discover spelling patterns as well as to learn for themselves the importance of spelling correctly as they share, edit, and publish. Encourage writing in visits prior to the first day of school. Most importantly, respond to student's written meaning and praise their attempts, regardless of their developmental stage.

37

PRIMARY

As students can begin to profit from more formal spelling instruction, it is still critical they attempt to spell every word they want to write and they develop a spelling conscience within the writing process. We must continue to provide a risk-free environment, abundant models, and extensive experiences for trial and error. Students should collect, combine, compile, classify, chant, sing, display, shout, whisper, manipulate, experiment, proofread, underline, circle, generalize, summarize, record, evaluate, analyze, and more to develop awareness of word patterns and structures.

INTERMEDIATE

Intermediate students profit most by observing, proofreading, and analyzing their own errors and by using a combination of strategies. Of particular importance as students become more and more sophisticated in their thinking skills is the study of morphemic and mnemonic strategies including the study of base words, roots, origins of words, and how the spelling of English words has changed over time.

STUDENTS WITH SPECIAL NEEDS

Teachers who identify students with special needs within the class should give special consideration to Plan A for their spelling program. Plan A has the best chance of being the most effective with these students.

EVALUATION, RECORD KEEPING, REPORTING PROGRESS

SPELLING EVALUATION

Evaluation must be based on the grade level and special needs considerations discussed in the previous section **AND** on a student's progress toward reaching the goals of the Wichita spelling program:

Independently attempt to spell any word as they draft.

Learn to use many spelling resources and strategies through the writing process.

Develop a spelling conscience or the sense of words spelled correctly and words spelled incorrectly.

Learn common letter groups and spelling patterns, spelling generalizations, and words most commonly used in writing.

> Within the writing process, spelling should become a consideration for evaluation only during the <u>editing</u> process. Teachers and students should work together until ideas are communicated to their satisfaction. Then spelling can become the focus especially if the writing is to be published or shared more formally.

Ideally, evaluation is tied to and used for diagnosis and for planning for teaching. Spelling evaluation should always be related to writing since spelling is for writing. The student's stage of development and progress in spelling must also be considered. The best and most complete form of evaluation is to compare current writing samples with previous samples. The chart on pages 8 and 9 or any part of the chart can be used to assess stage of development and progress.

Grading, based on improvement, benefits <u>all</u> students--especially students with special needs. Evaluation based on improvement allows <u>all</u> students to experience success at their own rate and level. The student writer's confidence and attitude improves. This, in turn, serves to boost the student writer's stage of language development providing further opportunities for growth and success.

For example, document the spelling strengths and weaknesses of one piece of writing but do not give it a "grade". After the student has completed the next piece of writing, compare the strengths and weaknesses of the spelling to the spelling in the first paper. Note progress and areas of need. Continue with this process throughout the year expecting spelling to improve at each step.

Effective evaluation must eventually become the student's responsibility. When you involve students in selecting words for study, in choosing methods for study, in the analysis of spelling within their writing, and in assessing progress, you help them learn responsibility for their own learning and progress. Teachers will vary in the amount of control they wish to have over their spelling program and its evaluation. You are urged to consider teaching responsibility as you teach spelling.

TESTS

Teacher constructed tests can be one useful part of evaluation within a spelling program. Appendix D contains the Benchmark Spelling Lists for K-2 and 3-5. Other word lists or standardized tests may be used.

RECORD KEEPING

Record keeping is less time consuming and more relevant when students are involved and the records relate to writing and not spelling in isolation. Goal setting or contracts which involve students in record keeping can also be useful. Checklists can be useful, but are frequently very time consuming.

40

PROGRESS REPORT TO PARENTS

The U.S.D. 259 *Report to Parents* is under revision for 1990-91. A supplement to this guide will be developed and distributed when the revision is complete.

SPELLING SELF EVALUATION

Name _____   Date_____

1. Prewrite
   a.
   b.
2. Draft
   a.
   b.
   c.
   d. I use several spelling strategies
      invented spelling
      spelling conscience
      chunking
      morphemes
3. Conference and revise
   a.
   b.
4. Edit
   a.
   b. I use several spelling resources
      spelling conscience
      study with style
      mnemonics
      dictionaries
      glossaries
      logs
      students
      other

41

APPENDIX A
LETTERS TO THE HOME

The Wichita Language Arts Program and Spelling

This year, our district is increasing the language arts program. The program is very different from what most students in other districts in our area experience. Last year, we adopted new reading texts which included instruction in all of the language arts areas: reading, writing, listening, and speaking. This year, we are adding to the rest of the language arts program, especially in writing.

In writing, we are giving students many more chances to write for real reasons every day. We want students to concentrate on getting ideas down and communicating meaning. The message is of great importance. The tools of writing (spelling, grammar, punctuation) help make the message clear.

We will still be teaching spelling and English (grammar and punctuation). These are the tools (skills) we need for writing. But, instead of teaching them apart from reading and writing with a separate spelling book and language/English book, we will be using the reading and writing students are doing every day to teach the tools. We will be using many different teacher resource materials to help with teaching the tools.

The papers your student brings home will probably look different to you at first. We want students, for example, to try to spell every word they want to when they write. We are stressing writing down a meaningful, clear, message. Some words may not be spelled in the way adults spell words. Please help us by having your student tell you about the meaning. Try not to say anything about the spelling or punctuation for now. You will be receiving more information soon about this new program.

42

Spelling Within the Writing Program

Our writing program helps students write in five steps. In the first step, **prewriting**, we use many ways to get ideas for writing. In the second step, **drafting**, we stress writing down a meaningful, clear, message. Third, we **conference and revise** to make our message even more clear. Fourth, we **edit and work on spelling**, punctuation, grammar, and usage again to make the message more clear. Last, we **postwrite**. In this step we share our writing more formally perhaps by publishing in some way and evaluate our skills for the next time we write.

Students can easily become discouraged with writing if we demand perfect spelling all the time. How writing is graded will depend on the objectives of the assignment, the topic, and the audience (who is going to read the writing). Not every piece of writing will be graded on perfection. Since the main emphasis in our writing program is communicating a meaningful, clear message, not every piece of writing will be edited (checked for spelling) and published.

Please help us by not demanding perfect writing and spelling all the time. When your student shares some writing with you, talk about the meaning or message. Also, help us provide your student with opportunities to explore writing. You can do this by encouraging writing at home with simple messages to one another, letters to relative, shopping lists, thank you notes, and so forth.

43

Spelling Is a Tool

We know that spelling correctly is a very important skill. Spelling is the art of forming words in the standard way society expects. Knowing how to spell words frees us to write what we want to write, whenever and wherever we want to write. In the world of work, spelling is valued and demanded.

Spelling is only one part of communicating meaning and can sometimes get in the way of putting ideas down when we're first drafting a meaningful message. When we demand perfect writing and spelling all the time from growing students, we can interfere with their growth. No one worries when a child's first drawing of a person is a circle on top of two sticks. Such an early drawing is not seen as a problem. Instead, the drawing is seen as a display of intelligence. Just so, children's misspellings should be seen as attempts to make sense of written English, a sign of intelligence. We must encourage them to explore and we must provide them with many models of correct writing.

For now, we are still stressing writing down a meaningful, clear, message. So, some words may not be spelled in the way adults spell words. Please help us by having your student tell you about the meaning. Try not to say anything about the spelling or punctuation for now. You will be receiving still more information soon about this new program.

Invented Spelling

Since the beginning of this school year, students have been writing every day. They have been writing messages, stories, reports, and more. We have been stressing getting a clear message on paper. We have expected them to try, without teacher help, to write any word they want to write. We have told students not to worry about spelling until they are ready to edit. We see no sense in most of the class waiting to write because they think they have to spell every word correctly during the drafting step. Thank you for helping us by not expecting perfect writing all of the time.

The kind of spelling students do when they try on their own to spell words is called invented spelling. All writers invent when they do not know. Invented spelling is the name for children's misspellings before they know as much as adults do about the way words are spelled. As they make judgments about how to spell words, they are learning rule systems. Like children learning to walk and draw, invented spelling does not produce habits to be overcome.

No one worries when a child's first drawing of a person is a circle on top of two sticks. Such an early drawing is not seen as a problem. Instead, the drawing is seen as a display of intelligence. Just so, children's misspellings should be seen as attempts to make sense of written English, a sign of intelligence, and a sign that children are getting better and better each day at spelling correctly.

As students practice writing, they practice and drill spelling at a pace and level of difficulty right for them. No teacher has the time to motivate, diagnose, and assign the materials for spelling that can match the work students do themselves as they write.

Analysis of spelling errors can give teachers and students pictures of spelling skills students are ready to learn. Students greater focus on their own work also guarantees more attention than they give to spelling worksheets or workbooks. As they explore spelling, students make written English spelling their own, forever.

45

We Are Teaching Spelling

We are still teaching spelling. We are teaching patterns, spelling rules and generalizations, and sometimes we have a class spelling list to work on. By analyzing the writing and spelling students are doing, and by encouraging them to analyze their own writing and spelling, we know what patterns, rules, words, and so forth students need to work on. This is better than having a workbook lesson which has skills and words some students already know and some words students are not ready for that week.

You can help by making the study of words a fun part of your life at home. Word or spelling games can stimulate student interest in words and how they are spelled. Play word games. If you don't know of any, your child probably does.

46

HOMEWORK ACTIVITIES

> Most activities in Appendix A have two parts. When there are two parts to activities, the first part is an example for you, the teacher. The second part is the activity on a form you can complete and send home. Some activities have just one part, the form.

Example:

Please help your child make a list of words which contain the letters_____. This may be done at home, at the store, or on a trip. To help you begin the list, some examples are given.

at home	at the store	on a trip
chair	peach	church
couch	pork chops	check
children	chives	chart

Spelling Homework

This homework is needed for class on _____.

Please help your child make a list of words which contain the letters_____. This may be done at home, at the store, or on a trip. To help you begin the list, some examples are given.

at home	at the store	on a trip
chair	peach	church
_____	_____	_____
_____	_____	_____
_____	_____	_____
_____	_____	_____

➡ Your child will be asked to add words to a class list.

Example:

Finding words within words is an easy and fun activity parents can help students do at home. Brothers, sisters, and cousins may want to join in. Please help your student find the little words in the word transportation.

transportation
ran
sport
or
at

Your child will be asked in class the number of words that were found. We will make a master list of the words found by all the students.

Spelling Homework

This homework is needed for class on _____.

Finding words within words is an easy and fun activity parents can help students do at home. Brothers, sisters, and cousins may want to join in. Please help your student find the little words in the word transportation.

_____   _____

Your child will be asked in class the number of words that were found. We will make a master list of the words found by all the students.

48

Example:

Please help your student find words with the letters **ch** in them in newspapers or magazines. Have your student cut out the words and paste them on the back of this note. This will help your student get needed visual practice with spelling words.

I will ask students to read the words they found. We will also count how many words they found.

Spelling Homework

This homework is needed for class on _____.

Please help your student find words with the letters **ch** in them in newspapers or magazines. Have your student cut out the words and paste them on the back of this note. This will help your student get needed visual practice with spelling words.

I will ask students to read the words they found. We will also count how many words they found.

Example:

This week's spelling words are listed below. Have your student draw pictures of <u>large fish</u> on another piece of paper. Then have them write one spelling word on each <u>fish</u>. As the spelling of each word is learned, let your child color the appropriate <u>fish</u>. When all the <u>fish</u> are colored, do something special. For example, allow your child to choose the main dish for Friday's dinner. Hanging the completed picture on the refrigerator can reinforce learning and give a feeling of accomplishment.

Spelling Homework

This homework is needed for class on _____.

This week's spelling words are listed below. Have your student draw pictures of _____ on another piece of paper. Then have them write one spelling word on each _____. As the spelling of each word is learned, let your child color the appropriate _____. When all the _____ are colored, do something special. For example, allow your child to choose the main dish for Friday's dinner. Hanging the completed picture on the refrigerator can to reinforce learning and give a feeling of accomplishment.

➱ Will your child know the spelling words for the test this week? Maybe not if you don't help.

50

Example:

Spelling Through the Seasons

Help your child make a simple seasonal shape such as a <u>fall tree,</u> <u>harvest moon, or pumpkin</u>. Post the shape on the refrigerator. Add words related to the season or the shape such as <u>autumn, leaf, and</u> <u>seed</u>. Help your child find these words in newspapers and magazines. Cut out the words and paste them on the shape.

I will be asking students to read the words on their shapes.

Spelling Homework

This homework is needed for class on _____.

Spelling Through the Seasons

Help your child make a simple seasonal shape such as a _____ _____. Post the shape on the refrigerator. Add words related to the season or the shape such as _____ _____. Help your child find these words in newspapers and magazines. Cut out the words and paste them on the shape.

⇨ I will be asking students to read the words on their shapes.

51

Example:

Rhyme of the Week

Post a piece of paper on the refrigerator. Use <u>an</u> as the word part for the week. Add beginning and ending letters such as <u>fan, ant, clan</u> to form as many words as possible. Practice spelling the words made.

We will use the words the children bring to school in our spelling list next week.

- -

Spelling Homework

This homework is needed for class on _____.

Rhyme of the Week

Post a piece of paper on the refrigerator. Use _____ as the word part for the week. Add beginning and ending letters such as _____to form as many words as possible. Practice spelling the words.

We will use the words the children bring to school in our spelling list next week.

52

Spelling Homework

This homework is needed for class on _____.

For homework tonight, help your child write and mail a letter to a friend or relative. The person chosen will enjoy hearing from your child and your child will get practice in writing and spelling. Please use the steps below which are the same steps we use to work on writing and spelling at school.

1. **Prewrite**: Talk about ideas for the letter.
2. **Draft**: Have your child draft the letter thinking only about meaning. Do not allow your child to think or worry about spelling, punctuation and so forth during this step. If you are asked about the spelling of any words, say, "Just try your best."
3. **Conference and revise**: Next, have your child read the letter to you. Talk again about the meaning and help your child make the meaning clear. Be sure to tell your child something you like about the letter.
4. **Edit**: Now help your child with spelling, punctuation, grammar, and so forth.
5. **Publish**: Mail the letter.

➪   When your child receives a reply, please send it to school for sharing.

Spelling Homework

This homework is needed for class on _____.

Ask your child to help with grocery shopping by spelling items you need them to find and put in the cart. For example, say, "We need g-r-e-e-n b-e-a-n-s. Get two cans, please."

➪   This week in spelling, we will be working on words found in grocery stores.

53

Spelling Homework

This homework is needed for class on _____.

Concentration is a fun and simple activity parents and children will enjoy. This takes no parent time or effort and provides purposeful spelling practice for the child! You may find this game less tedious than some as your own memory may be challenged. Your child's words for the week are listed somewhere on this paper.

Have your child cut out rectangles from heavy paper and write each spelling word for this week on two different cards. Mix the words up and place them face down. Turn over only two cards at a time. If the two words match **and** the player can spell the word without looking, the two cards belong to that player. The player with the most cards when all the cards are matched is the winner.

⇨ This week's spelling test will be given on _____.
Will your child spell all the words correctly?

Spelling Homework

This homework is needed for class on _____.

This week in spelling, we are learning about abbreviations. Please help your child cut out advertisements from the newspaper that have abbreviations. Paste the abbreviations on the back of this paper and help write the abbreviations in full.

⇨ I will ask students to write the abbreviations they found on the board for a partner to write out in full.

54

Spelling Homework

This homework is needed for class on _____.

This week in spelling, we are studying about the importance of spelling correctly. Please have your child write a letter asking you (the boss) for a job. Will words spelled correctly and incorrectly influence you as a boss? Decide how you (the boss) will talk to this job seeker.

⇨ Your child will be asked to tell what the "boss" said about spelling correctly.

Spelling Homework

This homework is needed for class on _____.

All Through the House

Select several items in one room of your house. Help your child make a label for each item. As your child learns to read and spell the names of the selected items, have him/her paste the label in a special spiral notebook. Each page of the notebook should be reserved for just one alphabet letter. When the room is label free, move to another room. Keep the notebook and practice reading and spelling the labels occasionally.

⇨ Your child will return the notebook later for future activities.

55

Name _____

I have a

GIGANTIC

memory!

I never forget my spelling homework.

Here's what you do:

1. Write your homework assignments on the lines.
2. Color in a book each time you turn in an assignment.

_____
_____
_____
_____
_____

Then have your teacher sign this award. Trade the award in for one homework assignment.

_____
teacher's signature

56

APPENDIX B
WTA&A MINI-LESSONS

The WTA&A model contains time effectiveness or lesson planning components:

FOCUS: The teacher provides a brief transition or preparation activity during the time that students are arriving or switching from the activity just finished to a new activity. Focus should occur at the beginning of a class and may occur at any time during a period when an instructional transition occurs or when the class has deviated from the intended topic. This transition or focus elicits attentive behavior and mental readiness for instruction. (Focus contains two parts: 1) get attention, 2) focus on content. Focus can include helping students transfer background knowledge to the current lesson.)

OBJECTIVE: The teacher states expectations for student achievement so that students will know what they will be able to do by the end of the lesson (not just a topic).

PURPOSE: The teacher identifies for students why it is important and/or useful to accomplish the objective(s) or content outlined at the beginning of a lesson. Purpose can include helping students transfer background knowledge to the current lesson. The more meaningful the task, the easier the learning.

INSTRUCTIONAL INPUT: The teacher provides appropriate instructional input when whatever the teacher does, gives, or says during a lesson is related to the lesson's objective(s) (activities match objective) and to the student behavior specified in the objective.

MODELING: The teacher provides visual, aural, tactile, oral, and/or olfactory representations so that learners have examples of what is being taught and the desired student behavior specified in the objective. (A definition is not a good example of a model.)

MONITORING: The teacher takes the time during instruction to make certain that students understand the material being presented. This can be done by questioning, observing, giving quizzes, etc. (signals, samples, choral responses, anything done to give the teacher an idea of who does and does not understands the material).

ADJUSTING: The teacher provides additional instructional input if it has been determined that students do not understand the material or have the skills necessary to accomplish the lesson's objectives (major additional instruction resulting from monitoring).

GUIDED PRACTICE*: While the teacher is available to provide help, students should be given opportunities to practice the behavior specified in the objectives after a lesson has been presented (available and/OR provides help during practice).

INDEPENDENT PRACTICE*: When students can perform the desired behavior, independent practice (related to objective), with no teacher guidance, is provided or assigned

*Practice Theory: how much - smallest part that maintains meaning, how long - short, motivated sessions, how often - massed for early, distributed for continued, how well - specific, immediate feedback

57

For the purposes of this guide only the components of objective, purpose, instructional input, modeling, monitoring, guided practice and independent practice will be specifically addressed. Focus activities will vary greatly depending on the context of the lesson. Adjusting is needed only if students do not understand or have the skills needed and again will vary greatly depending on the context of the lesson.

THE CASE OF THE MISSING LETTERS	
Objective	The learner will improve recall of correct word structure.
Purpose	"It is important to remember how words are spelled so we can use them when we write."
Model	On the board, write: L_st T_esday, we had birthd_y tre_ts.
Instructional Input	Have students act as detectives and find the missing letters in the sentence. Ask where they might have seen the words before today. Ask them to try to visualize the words and listen to the sounds as clues. Together complete the model sentence.
Monitor	Add one or more similar sentences. Use signaled responses (thumbs up or down) to check for agreement to sampled answers and monitor understanding.
Guided Practice	Add two more similar sentences including sentences students suggest. Circulate as students write the sentences on their own paper filling in the missing letters. Remind them of possible clues.
Independent Practice	Have students respond to sentences on their own.

SPOOK BOOK

Objective   The student will learn the spelling of the "oo" sounds.

Purpose   "When we are writing or reading it is important to know that the same letters can have different sounds in different words. This helps us be better spellers."

Model and   On the board write **spook.**
Instructional Input   Have children orally add words under spook with have the same oo sound. Next, write **book**. Repeat the activity with book.

Monitor and   Form small groups to further brainstorm words in each
Guided Practice   category. Suggest the groups look for patterns or letters that affect the sound. Share lists.

Independent Practice Have the same small groups produce "Spook Book" stories using words from their lists. This is a good Halloween activity as many words of the season (spook, boo, hoot, who-o-o) will come up in the brainstorming session. "Spook Book" stories may then be bound and put in the reading corner.

59

PENCIL TALKING #1	
Objective	The student will communicate using pictures and invented spelling.
Purpose	"We can 'talk' to each other using words and pictures, but no sounds."
Model and Instructional Input	Present four objects such as a ball, book, pencil, and hat. Folding newsprint in four sections. "Write" the names of the objects, one on each section, using pictures and invented spelling. To elicit invented spelling, ask students to suggest letters for the sounds they hear in the names of the objects.
Monitor and Guided Practice	Using four other objects, have students repeat the activity while you monitor and guide.
Independent Practice	Have students think of (but not tell or talk about) four different objects. Have them use pictures and invented spelling, but no talking, to tell about their objects on a four-fold piece of newsprint. Then have students "read" their papers.

PENCIL TALKING #2	
Objective	The student will create a story using pictures and invented spelling.
Purpose	"We can talk to each other with out talking out loud."
Model and Instructional Input	Demonstrate writing a story using pictures and invented spelling.
Monitor and Guided Practice	Divide the class into small groups. Help students with ideas for a story. Ask each group to work together to write a story using pictures and invented spelling. Circulate between groups. Next, have groups practice their stories and present them to the class. The stories can be put together in a book and shared with other classes. Be certain there is a title page.
Independent Practice	Have students individually write and share stories.

60

IN A FLASH	
Objective	The student will explore finding common spelling letter sequences in many words.
Purpose	The same letter sequences occur in many words. Seeing these sequences helps us learn to spell.
Model	Pick a letter sequence such as **ack**. Write a sentence on the board. such as, "A black jackass had a snack from a packet of crackers and began to quack."
Instructional Input	Have students read the sentence and identify the common letter sequence. Brainstorm IN A FLASH other words with the **ack** sequence. Say, "In a flash, we have found several words with the same letter sequence."
Monitor	As a group, write three sentences using the words that were brainstormed IN A FLASH.
Guided Practice	Circulate as students write their own sentences using as many words as possible containing the letter sequence.
Independent Practice	On the board write, "Sing a dingy song with a king and a thing that rings." Have students find the common sequence and IN A FLASH list more **ing** words.

NAMES #1

Objective	The students will recognize and duplicate their own printed names.
Purpose	"We need to learn to read our names so we can 'talk' to each other with writing."
Model	Write the students' names on sentence strips.
Instructional Input	Have the students use the model to refer to as they construct their names using magnetic or flannel letters.
Monitor	Have students name each letter, always working from left to right.
Guided Practice	Have several methods of "making" the names available: magnetic letters, felt letters, flash cards, primary typewriter. Have students use each method and say the letter names for you.
Independent Practice	Write four or five students' names on paper and place the lists at work stations. Have students go to the places where their names are located. Use the names on cards to signal who is to line up, sit down, and so forth. Begin using the written forms of their names as much as possible.

NAMES #2	
Objective	The students will write their names using correct spelling.
Purpose	"We need to learn to write our names so we can 'talk' to each other with writing."
Model	Provide students with their names written on sentence strips with orange or red marker.
Instructional Input	Have students trace their names on the strips using a variety of manipulatives (felt letters, magnetic letters, newspaper letters, flash cards, typewriter.)
Monitor and Guided Practice	Have students verbally say the letters contained in their names.
Independent Practice	Have students practice writing their names on the chalkboard or on paper until they perform independently

---

CONTRACTION ACTION

Objective The student will explore the spelling of contractions and will understand the function of the apostrophe in contractions.

Purpose "When using and spelling contractions, it is important to remember that two words that have been combined and also the special marking that must be in each contraction so others can understand what we mean."

Model and On the board write : **I will   I'll**

Instructional Input Ask students to look at the two lines and determine together what has happened. Pause and ponder. Facts elicited during discussion should include the following:

1) The second line is shorter (contracted).

2) The second line has a special mark (apostrophe).

3) The apostrophe takes the place of one or more letters in the first line.

4) Some of the letters are missing in second line.

5) The lines mean the same thing.

6) The second line is more like what we often say.

Monitor and Write additional examples on board. Have students come to

Guided Practice board and write the contraction beneath.

Independent Practice Have students write five groups of words which can be combined to make a contraction. Exchange papers and write the contractions. Have the original authors check for accuracy.

64

VOWEL + E

Objective   The student will improve spelling recall of vowel +e words and recognize exceptions.

Purpose   "We need to remember while reading and writing that a word with a **vowel + e** <u>usually</u> has a long vowel sound. This helps us spell words correctly so our readers understand our meaning."

Model   On the board write, "**lane, home, dive.**" Have students pronounce the words. Highlight the pattern of **vowel + e** with colored chalk. Have students add a few additional words from their spelling repertoire. Then add these words, "**come, give, live**." The discussion should include that the spelling of some words like "some" and "come" must simply be learned as exceptions, and others, like "live", from context clues.

Monitor and   Make vowel categories on the board using **a-o-i-u**. Have students
Guided Practice   pause, ponder, and participate by adding words to each category. Star (*) exceptions. Form small groups to enlarge lists. Share lists and star exceptions. Have students select ten to fifteen words for study for the week. After checking for accuracy, have students post their lists on their desks or place them in their writing folders. During the week, whenever students use words on their lists, have them use crayons or markers to highlight the words in their written work. As students gain mastery, have them turn in their lists.

Independent Practice Have students make contracts with you to use words from their lists and to spell them correctly in all written work for the week.

65

TRUCK WASH	
Objective	The student will spell consonant blends (initial and/or final) accurately.
Purpose	"We can expand our spelling knowledge and writing skills by using consonant blends with "chunks" (common phonograms) we already know."
Model and Instructional Input	Draw a truck shape on the board. Write tru__ __. on the shape. Elicit the blend for the blanks. Isolate the blend and demonstrate how two letters blend into one sound. Limit the number of blends used for this lesson. (Riverside has several good lessons to use as reference in Units 7-17.)
Monitor and Guided Practice	Have students suggest words that contain initial or final blends and write their correct suggestions on the board, highlighting the blend. Limit the list to ten or fifteen words. Pronounce and discuss all the words. Have students draw their own trucks and repeat the activity.
Independent Practice	Give each student a laminated truck. Have students write words with blends on their trucks. Check for accuracy. Pair students and direct them to take turns reading and spelling the words. If a word is spelled correctly, students may "wash" them from their trucks.

	ALPHABETICAL ORDER
Objective	The student will alphabetize the first letter of a word.
Purpose	"It is important to know alphabetical order so you can look up words you want to spell in a dictionary."
Model and Instructional Input	Put two letters on the board. Describe the thought process of putting the letters in alphabetical order. Sample student responses. Using three letters, repeat the activity.
Monitor and Guided Practice	"I'm going to put two letters on the board Say the alphabet silently to yourself and be ready to tell me which letter would come first in alphabetical order. Here are the letters (**b and f**). Everyone think. When I ask you to show me, put thumbs up if **b** comes first, thumbs down if **f** does. Ready, show me. Repeat the activity using student names.
Independent Practice	"I'm going to give each of you two letter cards. I want you to arrange them on your desk in alphabetical order. When you've finished, raise your hand and I'll come check your work. If you are correct, I'll give you a sheet of letters and words to alphabetize independently. If your incorrect, we'll try again." (Variation--use three letters or words to arrange in alphabetical order on desks.)

67

WALKING/TALKING	
Objective	The student will improve recall of the long vowel patterns in words.
Purpose	"We have studied one way long vowel sounds are made when we studied about **vowel + e**. Another way letters combine to make a long vowel sound is with two vowels together in the word. Knowing this helps us be better spellers."

Model	Put words that contain selected long vowel patterns (ai, ay, or oa) on the board. Have student volunteers pronounce words.
	
	Introduce the "rule"
	
	    "Sometimes, when two vowels go walking,
	     the first one does the talking."
	
	Add the exception: "The other thing you need to remember is that the first vowel <u>usually</u> says its own name. Beauty, leather, boot, and boil are exceptions.

Monitor and Guided Practice	Have students add to categories. If several have difficulty, move to cooperative groups. Have the groups use current reading material (Heath, Weekly Reader, etc.) to locate words that fit the categories. Have students make individual lists and post them on their desks. Have students set goals and repeat the highlighting activity.
Independent Practice	Have students use and highlight their words throughout week. Give a traditional spelling test by pronouncing from a master list. Have students be responsible for writing <u>only</u> words they have selected. This activity, writing self-selected words for tests, increases listening skills and word recall. It is difficult the first few times but produces good results and "individualizes" a traditional spelling test.

68

HIDDEN WORDS

Objective	The student will improve his/her spelling conscience.
Purpose	"It is important to develop a spelling conscience or a sense of whether or not words are spelled correctly so we can edit when we write."
Model	Place a word puzzle grid on the board with words which are familiar to the children.
Instructional Input	Have students act as detectives. Ask them to find words spelled correctly and words spelled incorrectly (vertically or horizontally). Make two lists, correct and incorrect, under the grid. After listing the word spelled incorrectly put the correct spelling in parenthesis.

s	w	h	a	t	b	m	f
v	b	c	r	u	l	i	i
o	t	h	e	r	o	x	n
j	m	u	t	h	e	r	d

correct   incorrect
what   ruli   (rule)
other   muther (mother)
are   bloe   (blue)

Monitor	Place another grid on the overhead or board. "I am going to say a word. After I say the word I will give you time to find it on the grid. When I ask you to show me, put your thumbs up if the word is spelled correctly; thumbs down if the word is spelled incorrectly. All right, let's begin. The word is <u>man</u>. Look at the grid carefully. Show me." (Students should show thumbs up). "The next word is <u>stay (stey)</u>. Look at the grid carefully. Show me." (Since stey is not spelled correctly, students should signal thumbs down). Continue with other words. Again make two columns under the grid.

s	l	e	e	p	u
h	m	a	n	a	n
u	s	e	o	l	t
t	o	s	t	e	y

Guided Practice	Give each student another small grid on paper at their seat. Ask them to raise their hands when they have found two words spelled correctly. Children should list them for teacher to see. Students with correct words may complete grid on their own.
Independent Practice	Have students create their own grids using their own spelling words then exchange papers with a friend. The friend should find words spelled correctly and incorrectly and list them under the grid.

69

PLURALS	
Objective	The student will spell plural words formed by adding **s** or **es** correctly.
Purpose	"When writing, it is important to know how to spell words that mean more than one so we can make our meaning clear to our readers."
Model	"The following words are all singular which means only one. I want to make them plural which means more than one." Change each word to plural by telling children what you are thinking as you work. Be sure to have the applicable spelling rules on the board or visible for all to see. Continue with more examples.
Monitor	1. Write these words on the board:

lunches   dress   beaches   losses
trunk   hearts   loss   boxes

Have student volunteers come to the board and circle the plural words and read the rule; or cross out a word that is not plural, state the rule, and make it plural. Remind students that the base word is the singular form of the word.

2. Write these words on the board:

passes   hands   sunglasses   tissue
bush   waxes   eggs   peaches

Have students circle the plural words, or cross out a word that is not plural and make it plural.

| **Guided Practice** | Write these words on the overhead: |

ghost   gases   pass
axes   watch   sales

Have children write the words in two columns. Ask them to make the words in the first column plural by adding **s** or **es**. Ask them to make the words in the second column singular. Students with correct answers may go on to independent practice. Students with incorrect answers will need additional practice.

| **Independent Practice** | Ask each student to write four sentences. Each sentence must contain a word that is plural. Trade papers with a neighbor. Students must find the plural words in each sentence, circle the base word, and underline the letter/letters that make the word plural. |

HOMOPHONES	
Objective	The student will spell six pairs of homophones correctly and be able to use them in written work.
Purpose	"It is important to learn to spell homophones and be able to use them in a sentence correctly so that you can use them when you write."
Instructional Input	"Homophones are words that sound the same when you say them, but they are not spelled in the same way and do not mean the same thing." Together, read the six pairs of homophones on the board. Discuss each pair as to meaning and spelling pattern."

two	by	their	ate	be	wood
to	buy	there	eight	bee	would

Model	On the board write sentences with missing homophones. Together discuss context clues and correct spelling for each missing homophone. Fill in the missing word in each sentence.

Ex: Hand the picture_____the clock.

Jess want to_____a radio.

Alice has_____dogs.

They went_____the pet store.

Monitor	"I have numbered the homophone pairs on the board. Listen to my sentence. Think about the homophone in the sentence. Think about its meaning and how it should be spelled. When I ask you to show me, hold up one finger if you would use the first homophone pair; hold up two fingers if you would use the second homophone pair."

1 two	1 by	1 their	1 ate	1 be	1 wood
2 to	2 buy	2 there	2 eight	2 bee	2 would

Example: I'll be eight on my birthday."

(Ask one child to identify the homophone in the sentence so everyone is focused on the correct word. Ask entire class to signal response to teacher.)

Guided Practice	Play the game Homophone Spell Down. Form two teams. Give Team A a card with a homophone. Have one player use the word in a sentence. Have a Team B player spell the word. Have another Team B player use the companion homophone in a sentence and a Team A player spell the homophone. If incorrect, the other team gets the turn. One point is awarded for each correct answer.
Independent Practice	Have students write sentences or a story using the homophones they have learned.

71

SPELLING THE LONG i SOUND

Objective — The student will spell long i words with the patterns i + e; or ending **y.**

Purpose — "It is important to understand the letter or letters that make the long i sound so you can use that knowledge when you write."

Instructional Input — Write the words **hide** and **my** on the chalkboard. Have a student pronounce each word. Ask what vowel sound is heard in each word. Make sure children hear the long i vowel sound. Point out to students that the same vowel sound is heard in both words, but the sound is spelled differently in each word. In the word **hide,** the long i sound is spelled with the pattern **i + e.** In the word **my,** the long i sound is spelled with the letter **y** at the end of the word.

Modeling — Write the following words on the board: **rice, bite, pray, cry, pry, rip, wipe, apply, advice, reply, bite, gripe, outside, invite.** Begin the modeling by reading the first three words, telling if the word does or does not have a long i sound, and if so, telling what pattern makes the sound. Continue with volunteers doing the other words.

Monitor — Tell students to raise their hands when they hear you say a word with the long i sound. As each word is identified, ask a student to write the word on the board. Ask another student to identify the letter/letters that make the long i sound.

Try these words: **dry, rice, cry, bite, why, nice, gripe**.

Guided Practice — Write the words **fly** and **ride** on the board. Ask students to list three words that use the same pattern to spell the long i sound under each of the words. Tell students to try to think of words that have not been used in this lesson. Ask students to think of words from their reading that follow these patterns. Examples of words might be outline, divide, identify, reply, describe, surprise, advice, survive, define. Students should raise hands for teacher to check. If correct, students may move to independent practice; if incorrect, adjust and try again.

Independent Practice — Ask students to underline the letter/letters in each of their words from the guided practice that make the long i sound and use each word in a sentence.

SPELLING CONSCIENCE	
Objective	The student will identify misspelled words from among a group of words.
Purpose	"Developing a spelling conscience and recognizing spelling errors is an important key to becoming a good writer. When you proofread and edit your work for spelling mistakes your writing will improve since you will catch problems before your reader either loses or confuses your meaning due to a spelling error."
Model	Write on the board: Wednesday, punkin, garbage, halo. (This may also be done with misspelled words in sentences.)
Instructional Input	Ask students to raise their hands when they locate the misspelled word. Encourage students to trust themselves when searching for the word that does not look correct. Their first guess is apt to be right. After identifying the incorrect word, you may want to have students give the correct spelling.
Monitor	Add more groups. Point to each word beginning with the first word listed. When students feel you are pointing out the misspelled word, they shut both eyes until the next word is called. Watch for open eyes on misspelled words. Again, discuss the intuitive first impression. Call attention to spelling patterns that are not common to the English language which is a strong indication of misspelled words.
Guided Practice	Provide more word groups to be written on paper. Circulate, giving extra assistance to struggling students.
Independent Practice	Have students locate misspelled words on their own. Or give points for finding misspelled words anywhere on the board at any time, then purposefully misspell words on the board occasionally.
Enrichment	Have students make up their own word groups. You may want to provide a word list from which to choose. They can exchange papers with a classmate and identify misspelled words.

73

SPELLING WITH MEANING	
Objective	The student will identify relationships between spelling and meaning.
Purpose	"If we can understand the meaning of two words that are alike, we can become better writers by using what we already know about some words to help us use and spell new words."
Model	Write microscope and microscopic on the board.
Instructional Input	Ask students to pronounce the two words. Discuss their related meanings. Call on students to use the two words in sentences. (I viewed the microscopic cells with my new microscope.) Identify similarities in spelling. microscope microscopic micro scope/ic
Monitor	Write gymnasium and gymnastics on the board. On lap boards or on paper, have students write spelling similarities found in the words. Have the students look at a classmate's answer. Have students raise their hand if they agree with a classmate's answer. Call on students to use each word in a sentence. Have students signal their agreement with raised hands.
Guided Practice	Provide more word pairs (entertainer, entertainment; temporary, temporarily etc.). On paper have students write word similarities and use words in sentences. Circulate, checking for accurate spelling similarities, and pointing out the meaning relationships.
Independent Practice	Provide more word pairs (photograph, photography; number, numeral, etc.) for students to respond to on their own.

74

APPENDIX C
RULES, GENERALIZATIONS, PATTERNS

SOMETIMES RELIABLE SPELLING RULES

RULE	EXAMPLES	EXCEPTIONS
1. Add **s** to make most nouns plural.	hat-hats	child-children
2. Add **es** to make most nouns ending with **s, ss, ch,** and **x** plural	pass-passes box-boxes	ox-oxen
3. To make some nouns that end with **y** plural, change the **y** to **i** and add **es**.	cry-cries sky-skies	Mary-Marys key-keys toy-toys
4. To make some nouns that end with **f** plural, change the **f** to **v** and add **es**.	calf-calves	gulf-gulfs
5. Some words that end in silent **e** drop the **e** when a vowel ending is added.	hope-hoping time-timer	dye-dyeing change-changeable gentle-gentling acre-acreage
6. Some words that end in silent **e** just add a consonant ending.	use-useful tire-tiresome	true-truly nine-ninth
7. Some short vowel words double the last letter when a vowel ending is added.	ship-shipping win-winning	end-ending
8. Some long vowel words contain that long vowel and one other vowel.	late soap dime	sigh go oh
9. **I** before **e** except after **c**, and when sounded like **a** as in neighbor or weigh.	receive pie	either weird their

75

COMMON SPELLING PATTERNS

VOWELS

Letter	Possible Spelling	Words
a	a, ai, au	hat, plaid, laugh
a	a_e, ay, ai, ay, ea, ei, ey	late, pay, bait, say, steak, veil, prey
e	e, a, ai, ay, ea, ie, eo	yet, many, said, says, read, friend, leopard
e	e, ea, e_e, ee, ei, eo, ey, y	she, eat, eve, see, seize, people, key, city
i	i, e, ee, ie, o, u	it, pretty, been, sieve, women, busy
i	i, y, ey, i-e, ie, igh, uy, y, ye	ice, my, eye, dime, pie, sigh, buy, try, lye
u	u, o, oe, oo, ou	cut, some, does, blood, young
o	o, ew, oa, oe, oh, oo, ou, ow	go, sew, soap, toe, oh, brooch, soul, grow
o, au, aw	o, a, au, aw, ou	hot, father, ball, fault, dawn, ought
oo	oo, u, ol, ou	look, full, wolf, could
oo	oo, o, ew, ui, ou, oe, ue	pool, who, drew, fruit, group, canoe, sue
oi, oy	oi, oy	boil, boy
ou	ou, ow, our	out, town, bough, hour
ar	are, air, ere, ear, eir, ur	care, fair, where, bear, their, bury
ar	ar, ear	far, heart
ur, ir, er	ur, ir, er, or, our	turn, bird, fern, worm, journal
any vowel	a, e, i, o, u	ago, lemon, pencil, above, butter

CONSONANTS

Letter	Possible Spelling	Words
b	b, bb	boy, bubble
c, k	c, k	cat, kettle
d	d, dd, ed	dog, ladder, called
f	f, ff	fun, off
g	g, gg	gum, giggle
h	h, wh	hot, who
j	j, g, dg	jet, gem, edge
l	l, ll	let, ball
m	m, mm, lm, mb	mom, hammer, palm, limb
n	n, nn, kn, pn, gn	not, banner, know, pneumonia, gnome
p	p, pp	put, happen
r	r, rr, wr	run, carry, write
s	s, ss, c, sc, ps	set, miss, cite, scissors, psalm
sh	sh, cean, ion	show, ocean, potion
sk, sch	sk, sch	skin, school
ch	ch, tch	chip, batch
t	t, tt, ed, ght, th	ten, butter, walked, caught, Thomas
th	th	think
th	th, the	this, bathe
v	v, f	vine, of
w	w	win
wh	wh	white
y	y	yet
z	z, zz, s, se	zip, puzzle, was, cause

APPENDIX D

WICHITA PUBLIC SCHOOLS
BENCHMARK SPELLING LISTS

K-2 Benchmark Spelling Words

A	B	C	D	E	F	G	H
a	back	call	day	each	fasten	gallon	had
about	backward	came	December	east	February	get	handle
African	bad	can	did	edit	fifth	getting	hard
after	bark	car	didn't	eight	find	gift	has
again	be	cheer	different	eighth	fire	girl	hasn't
all	beach	child	dinosaur	every	first	give	have
also	because	children	display		five	glove	having
always	been	chirp	do		fix	go	he
am	before	coast	doctor		float	good	head
American	belt	coin	dodge		fold	got	hear
an	best	cold	don't		follow	grandfather	help
and	better	come	down		for	grandmother	her
another	big	connect	doze		forty	great	here
any	bill	cook	Dr.		found	green	him
April	black	corner	draft		four	grey	hip
are	block	could	drag		fourth	grow	his
around	blocks	cousin	drive		Friday		home
as	blue	crib	dry		friend		hope
Asian	board	crisp			from		hospital
ask	boy	cup			fur		house
at	bring	curb					how
August	brother						husband
aunt	build						
	bulb						
	bump						
	but						
	by						

Continued			K-2 Benchmark Spelling Words				
I	**J**	**K**	**L**	**M**	**N**	**O**	**P**
I	January	keep	last	made	name	October	pan
if	joke	kick	late	make	never	of	palm
in	July	kind	Latino	man	new	off	park
Indian	June	know	leak	many	next	oil	part
into	just		least	map	night	old	pass
is			left	March	nine	on	passenger
it			lens	May	ninth	once	pave
			let	may	no	one	peel
			life	me	noon	only	people
			light	mean	north	or	pint
			lightning	meet	not	orange	pirate
			like	men	nothing	other	place
			line	Mexican	November	our	play
			little	Miss	now	out	please
			live	model	number	over	pleased
			log	Monday			pocket
			long	more			press
			look	most			prickly
			loud	Mr.			print
				Ms.			pull
				much			purple
				music			put
				must			
				my			

79

| Continued | | | | K-2 Benchmark Spelling Words | | | | |

Q	R	S	S	T	U	V	W	Y
quart	rag	safe	spout	tail	uncle	very	wage	year
	rail	said	stiff	take	under	violet	want	yellow
	rain	same	still	taste	up		was	yes
	rained	Saturday	stop	tell	us		waste	you
	raise	saw	stretch	ten	use		water	your
	ramp	say	sun	tenth			wave	
	ranch	scatter	Sunday	than			way	
	reach	school	sunny	that			we	
	red	scold		thaw			weary	
	right	seal		the			Wednesday	
	roast	second		their			weed	
	roof	see		them			well	
	room	seed		then			went	
		September		there			were	
		set		these			west	
		seven		they			what	
		seventh		thief			when	
		shape		thing			where	
		sharp		think			which	
		she		third			while	
		shock		this			white	
		shore		thought			who	
		short		thousand			why	
		should		three			wide	
		show		through			wife	
		sister		Thursday			wig	
		six		tight			will	
		sixth		time			wish	
		sleep		to			wished	
		slice		told			with	
		small		too			woke	
		smoke		took			woman	
		snack		torn			word	
		so		tow			work	
		some		track			world	
		something		trim			would	
		soon		try			write	
		sound		Tuesday			wrong	
		south		twig				
		Spanish		two				
		spent						
		split						

Benchmark Spelling Words 3-5

A	A	B	B	C	C	D	E
able	August	back	burnt	came	correct	damp	early
above	Australia	balance	burst	can't	country	dark	earth
across	autumn	bargain	bushel	candles	couple	data	east
add	away	base		cannot	cover	December	eastern
advisable		bathe		car	covered	decide	easy
African		beard		carefully	cried	decision	eat
after		became		carpet	cry	deep	edit
again		because		carry	cut	deliver	education
against		become		carrying		didn't	eight
ago		before		cent		different	eighteen
agree		began		certain		dignity	eighth
agreeable		begin		chance		discover	eighty
air		beginning		change		discuss	eleven
almost		behind		check		disease	end
along		being		cherry		disk	English
already		below		children		dislike	enough
also		better		china		disturb	environment
always		between		choir		divide	equation
am		big		circle		doctor	estimate
America		billion		city		does	Europe
American		birds		claims		dog	European
among		black		class		dollar	even
angle		blackboard		clear		don't	evening
animal		blanket		close		done	ever
animals		blaze		closet		door	every
another		blouse		cloudy		Dr.	example
answer		boat		coal		draft	explain
any		body		coin		draw	express
apart		book		college		drawn	eye
April		both		color		drive	eyes
area		bottom		column		drove	
argue		bought		common		during	
around		bowl		complain			
artic		box		complaint			
Asia		boy		complete			
Asian		branch		computer			
ask		bring		conference			
asked		brought		consonant			
Atlantic		building		contain			
		built		continue			
				cord			

81

Continued			Benchmark Spelling Words 3-5				
F	**F**	**G**	**H**	**I**	**J**	**K**	**L**
face	forty	game	half	I'll	January	Kansas	land
fact	found	games	hand	idea	jolly	keep	language
fade	four	gave	happened	important	July	kind	large
failed	fourteen	gentle	hard	inches	June	king	last
fall	fourth	gently	head	include	just	kitten	late
family	friends	ghost	hear	indeed		knee	lately
far	fright	girl	heard	independence		knew	later
farm	front	give	heat	Indian		knit	Latino
farther	frost	glow	heavy	Indians		knock	learn
fast	fruits	goats	help	inside		know	leave
fatal	full	good	here	inspire		known	left
father		got	hero	instrument			let
February		government	high	interesting			letter
feeds		grain	himself	island			letters
feel		grasp	hire	it's			life
feet		great	hold				light
few		green	hole				line
field		greet	home				list
fifteen		ground	horse				listen
fifth		group	hot				little
fifty		grow	hour				live
figure		guardian	hours				loan
fill		guilty	house				
filled			however				
finally			hundred				
first			hunger				
fish							
five							
flashlight							
flood							
fly							
follow							
following							
food							
fool							
force							
forehead							
forest							
forgotten							
form							
former							

Continued			Benchmark Spelling Words 3-5			
M	**M**	**N**	**O**	**P**	**Q**	**R**
machine	much	name	object	Pacific	quality	ran
magic	multiply	native	ocean	page	quest	ranch
man	music	near	October	pail	question	reached
March	must	need	off	paper	questions	read
mark	mystery	never	often	park	quickly	reading
marriage		new	oh	particular		real
marry		next	old	parties		really
material		nickname	oldest	partner		red
mathematics		night	omit	passed		refuse
matter		nine	once	pattern		regard
May		nineteen	one	peel		regardless
me		ninth	only	perform		region
mean		north	open	performance		regret
means		northern	opinion	person		remember
meant		note	orange	physical		repeat
measure		notice	orchestra	picture		respect
melt		noun	order	piece		rest
memory		November	Oriental	place		revise
men		number	our	plan		riddle
mercy		numeral	owl	plane		right
merry			own	planning		river
Mexican				plant		road
might				play		rock
mild				plow		room
mile				plural		round
miles				point		rule
million				power		run
minutes				praise		
miss				print		
money				prints		
morning				probably		
most				problem		
mostly				produce		
mother				products		
motion				public		
mountain				publish		
mountains				published		
move				put		
Mr.						
Mrs.						
Ms.						

83

Continued			Benchmark Spelling Words 3-5				
S	S	T	T	U	V	W	Y
same	social studies	table	trees	under	value	wagon	valley
sang	something	take	trial	understand	valued	wait	voice
saw	sometimes	talk	tried	united	vegetable	walk	year
say	song	tell	true	until	vegetation	walked	years
saying	soon	ten	try	upon	veil	want	yellow
school	sound	tenth	turn	us	vein	war	yet
science	sour	terrible	turned	usual	verb	warm	young
scientist	south	terribly	twelve	usually	very	Washington	
scout	southern	thing	twenty		violet	watch	
scream	space	things	twice		voice	waves	
sea	Spanish	think	two		vote	wax	
second	special	third			vowel	week	
seem	spell	thirteen				weekend	
seemed	square	those				well	
seen	stand	though				went	
selfish	stars	thought				west	
senior	start	thousand				western	
sentence	started	thousands				whale	
September	state	three				wheels	
set	states	through				where	
seven	stay	thrust				while	
seventeen	step	tide				white	
seventh	still	to				whole	
ship	stocking	today				why	
shipment	stood	together				Wichita	
shoes	stop	told				width	
shoot	story	too				wind	
short	street	took				without	
shortage	strong	top				woman	
should	study	Topeka				women	
show	studying	toward				wood	
shown	subtract	towel				wore	
side	such	town				work	
since	sure	toxic				world	
sing	surface	track				wound	
singular	sweater	trade				write	
six	swift	traded					
sixteen	swiftly	travel					
sixth	syllable	tree					
slice	syllables						
slowly							
small							

REFERENCES

Donoghue, Mildred. *The Child and the English Language Arts, 5th edition*. Dubuque, Iowa: William C. Brown, 1990.

Hudson, C. and M. O'Toole. *Spelling A Teachers' Guide, revised edition*. Melbourne, Australia: Globe Press, 1985.

Mazzio, F. "English Language Arts Concept Paper: Spelling." Salem, Oregon: Oregon Department of Education, May 1987.

Stetson, E. G. and F. Boutin. "Spelling Instruction: Diagnostic-Prescriptive Minus the Diagnostic." Unpublished paper, 1980. ERIC #205 980.

Watson, Dorothy. *Ideas and Insights*. Illinois: National Council of Teachers of English, 1987.

Wilde, S. "A Proposal for a New Spelling Curriculum." *The Elementary School Journal*, Vol. 9, # 3, 1990, pp 275-289.

9

IDEAS FOR SPECIAL PROJECTS IN LANGUAGE ARTS

by Carlota Cárdenas de Dwyer
English Teacher
Tom Clark High School, San Antonio, Texas

I don't think students should be asked to do projects unless they will learn something from the work!"
Mike Olson, grade 12

"Projects are fun! We get a chance to do something different and enjoy ourselves for a change."
Christina Ramirez, grade 2

"Projects should be graded fairly. Teachers shouldn't give everybody an A just because there was no real grading scale."
Grace Wang, grade 11

Ask students what they think about projects, and they'll be more than glad to tell you! Yet for every tale of woe and frustration, there are many more stories of excitement, involvement, energy, and pride. What is the role of such independent student activity in the English class? What goals—and assessments—should a teacher have in mind before launching a class on such a voyage of discovery, creation, and learning? How, specifically, do projects fit into curriculum programs of the twenty-first century?

Among the most frequently heard ideas in current discussions of school reform and restructuring is the suggestion that the out-dated factory metaphor for school be discarded for something more congruent with our modern age of communication and information. The notion of school as a creative "studio" has been offered by Ben Nelms (1992) and would seem to present a number of distinct advantages. Nelms enthusiastically remarks, "Say the word 'studio,' and images of light, space, creativity, works in progress, experimentation, and work come to mind" (13). While this artistic studio vision may have more to do with reader response to literature and other specifically writing-process expressions, there is no reason to limit creativity in English to writing portfolios. Imaginative projects might include any of the following:

- · a special edition of the *Rome News Gazette* covering the assassination of Julius Caesar
- · a set of watercolors designed to illustrate a collection of stories by Poe
- · an illustrated calendar noting a variety of diverse literary events gleaned form student research and accompanied by full documentation and bibliography

These varied creations represent the astounding multiplicity of alternatives available to a language arts teacher hoping to inject new energy and originality into a class. Because of the nearly limitless number of possible choices, teachers

should approach the structuring of a project assignment with care and deliberation. A few simple questions might be considered at the start:
· What is the *purpose* of the project?
· How will the project be assessed and ultimately graded?
· Will students be encouraged not only to utilize information on a topic, but also to incorporate original expression and critical thinking skills?
· Will students be encouraged to work collaboratively?

This discussion will serve to suggest an overall conceptualization of the fundamental elements of a class project as well as to list a series of viable and attractive possibilities that might be adapted to a classroom.

Before embarking on a detailed catalogue of specifics, examination of basic concepts might be most useful. First, one should appreciate that almost anything is possible in a project format. Shakespeare's Globe Theatre, Huck's raft, and Hester's scaffold might not need more than cardboard, paint, and staples, but the list of possibilities extends far beyond that. While details and materials may vary from one project to another, the goals of instruction and learning should be the same as for any class activity: to teach reading, writing, and the mental processes that underline these basic skills—discovery, perception, cognition, and imaginative manipulation, perhaps with an added dimension of creative invention.

A series of projects planned over an academic year should be a spiral of graduated complexity and sophistication, so that levels of growth and development might be experienced by the students. In addition, projects should provide opportunities for discovery and offer a supplemental mode of knowing and interaction. Content and skills learned in class should be enhanced, expanded, transferred, and applied inventively in a project. Finally, whatever differences might exist among specific project assignments, students should be challenged consistently to organize, clarify, and focus the relation of ideas; identify an effective rhetorical or presentational strategy; and select materials, language, and formats to achieve the highest standards of clarity, precision, and presuasive impact.

While most teachers would recognize that the essential characteristic of a project is that students (individually or collectively) create and produce a product beyond the conventional essay in response to a lesson, many might benefit from more detailed elaboration of how a worthwhile project is integrated into a lesson.

Anatomy of a Project

1. Students frequently work in groups or teams to develop and practice skills in communication, organization, and leadership or collaboration.
2. The project should be defined *but not limited by* the assignment presented by the teacher. Directions and specifications should establish goals, suggest methods, approaches, and material, plus clarify overall learning purposes.
3. Project possibilities should be invited a wide spectrum of responses either across product lines (creative writing or performance, illustrated graphics, skit or scenario) or within a specified form (magazine: cover, lead article, features, letters, advertisements, etc.).
4. Critiques and evaluation instruments should be incorporated into the original presentation if possible. Students, in any case, should have a clear idea of what they are supposed to do and how they will be graded. Distribution and weight of grades should be revealed at the start.
5. Some allowance should be made for students to venture into multidisciplinary approaches, especially art, music, and history.
6. The project process should be conceived in terms of multi-part stages with appropriate time and direction given for each aspect (e.g., a verbal component as opposed to the visual component; presenters vs. presentation; or research vs. record and report).
7. Special effort should be made for students to express or demonstrate their personal talents, backgrounds, interests, or views.
8. *Quality* of thought and effort must be stressed rather than obsessive expenditures of time, money, and mindless motion.
9. Anticipate realistic possibilities—does any classroom really need seventy or a hundred *Pequods?*
10. Make a special occasion of the due date. Bring a camera. Invite guests. Arrange for student work to be safely displayed in the library, front office, or lobby of the school.

Purpose

Language Skills

Perhaps one of the most important principles inherent in the project concept for teachers at all grade levels to consider most carefully and critically is that of *purpose*. Too often project assignments are product-driven, severely limiting what might otherwise be broad, expansive, and rich learning experiences. Because a chivalric shield or illustrated family tree (like Huck's raft and Hester's scaffold, mentioned earlier) are easily suggested by the text, some instructors are tempted to start and stop there. If expectations for learning and development are consistent in this segment of the curriculum, then more rigorous examination of purpose is required. Ideally, deliberation should ideally proceed from two distinct, yet complementary, points of departure.

First and most significantly, the numerous areas of potential learning should be considered. In this instance, *more is better.* Note the circular graph presented here (figure 1). When outlining directions, a teacher might review the various components of the project assignment to capture as many opportunities for learning as reasonably possible. For example, when students

are presenting and speaking, the listening skills of the rest of the class might be exercised through the use of a postpresentation quiz or evaluation. Or, at the start, class members might be given a partially completed outline of ideas that they should fill in during or after the project presentation.

In the same way, a project assignment that is substantially a crafted artifact designed for display and viewing, such as a picture or shield, might be augmented by the addition of an expository explanation or introduction expressed both orally and in writing. Conversely, a language project—expressive, persuasive, literary, or expository—might be complemented by a graphic or viewing component. In other words, minimal expansion and broadening of project activities might frequently result in increased learning and on enriched experience for an entire class.

Projects revolving around fairly specific ideas, such as a literary work in the uppper grades, might best be presented in a more general, thematic form at lower grade levels. Topics like voyages, the heroic experience, challenge, identity, or quests could legitimately encompass works from Dr. Suess and *Charlotte's Web* to series by C. S. Lewis and Lloyd Alexander.

FIGURE 1. AREAS OF POTENTIAL LEARNING

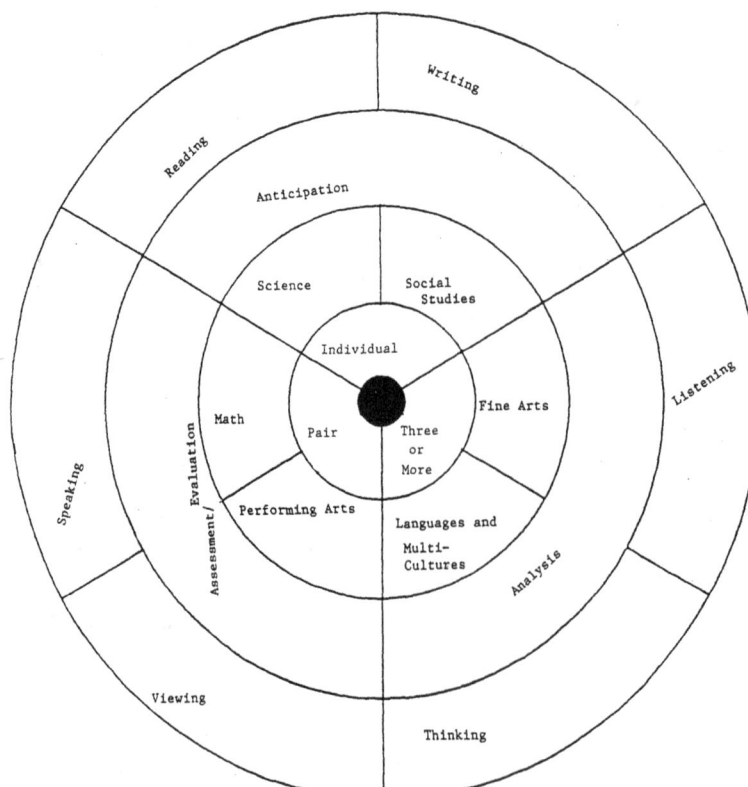

Thinking Skills

Thinking skills constitute a second dimension of potent cognitive potential that should function as the next point of departure. While critical thinking is too often conceived of as a rarefied and nebulous ideal, floating ethereally at the loftiest reaches of some abstract and elusive learning peak, the opposite is actually true. Once thinking skills are isolated into their own component parts, an orderly and manageable assortment of valuable, interrelated activities might be constructed at any grade level. Three general areas of thinking might be roughly sequenced into encompassing areas of before, during, and after. At the initial or preparatory stage, *anticipation* activities could assume the form of preliminary investigations or inventory of current knowledge, experience, or attitudes. Before a group begins library research, they could, for example, interview a family member or acquaintance. Before class members observed a project presentation, they might be invited to discuss their own views, prior experience, feelings, or opinions. Class members might be asked to complete a preproject inventory to express their expectations in the form of predictions, which are a key aspect of anticipation and frequently enhance interest and readiness.

Major thinking skills might be directed along central patterns of *organization*, such as illustration, comparison/contrast, classification, definition, process, and causality. While the essential elements of these thinking skills might be thought to be the most sophisticated, and, are perhaps most likely to be restricted to more mature students, again the opposite is true. Young learners, when given the opportunity, mechanism, and material, are capable of identifying, creating, and arranging categories at least as well as older students. The point to remember is that the specific character of the category created is not strategic; what *is* critical is the substantive quality of the decision-making process exercised. Therefore, any one of the following generic, analytic activities offers varied and rich rewards in a student's development of critical-thinking skills:

Example or Illustration
- Select individual and concrete examples of a general or abstract rule or principle.

Comparison/Contrast
- Identify similarities for comparison or differences for contrast from an array of elements.

Classification
- Group items into categories or classifications.

Definition
- Define or explain the meaning or multiple meanings of a word or term, considering both the standard, dictionary definition and how the word may have accumulated varied meanings in particular situations. Note the etymology, and consider the original meaning.

Progress
- Examine the chronological progression of elements involved, marking the pace or rate of the passage of time and events.

Causality
- Distinguish factors in a process that are specifically causal, distinguishing some by degrees of influence or responsibility.

Persuasion
- Persuade the audience or readers through argument, logic, or other cogent means.

While these seven areas are not exhaustive, they do represent some very practical and specific approaches to the otherwise untrammeled avenues of critical thinking.

This stage of the critical thinking process is unquestionably the most incisive, not because it relates most specifically to actual cognitive processes, but rather because it relates most essentially to the pivotal character of the lesson's content and effect. Whether at the kindergarten, elementary, middle school, or high school level, someone must make a decision about which of the various possible patterns of analysis would be most useful and appropriate to the material involved and to the learners. Although a fair amount of flexibility surely exists, a most significant—if not *the* most significant—principle applies here: Which of the available choices would be most fruitful? No facile, arbitrary choice should be made. This is the point where the product-driven project assignment fails most dramatically. Key questions at this point might be: What vital aspect of the material or work should be focused upon? What does the student learn that relates to, yet goes beyond, following mechanical directions? A simplistic and superficial purpose must be abandoned in favor of a more profound and critical one. The material or literary work itself should be carefully assessed by the instructor first, to identify crucial points of analysis.

For example, to exercise their thinking skills, younger students in the lower grades might simply gather individual examples of a broad concept. Or, conversely, they could create categories from randomly selected illustrations cut from magazines. They might also collect "found objects," devise a display, and explain an informing, pervasive principle or quality. More advanced students might be asked to gather examples of subtler, more refined categories. In either case, students should be directed toward what is most critical and appropriate to the content and its application to thinking activities of identifying categories and examples. Correctly noting time, its rate, pace, and relative measurement, might be important in the understanding of setting in some narratives. At more advanced levels of analysis, sophisticated skills might be required to identify the progress of events embedded in an associative network and, then, to recognize the logical sequence of causes and effects.

The works of Faulkner, such as "A Rose for Emily," or Robert Penn Warren's *All the King's Men* come to mind as graphic examples of the latter. In contrast to *The Sound and the Fury*, Faulkner's "A Rose for Emily" is relatively simple, involving just a handful of characters. Crucial to its most fundamental meaning is the reader's eventual "sorting out" of the narrator's somewhat disordered recounting of numerous details and episodes related to the life and times of Miss Emily Grierson. Only after conscientiously culling, sifting and re-ordering individual narrative items does the reader grasp the recurring principle of emotional trauma and subsequent reality denial apparent in the life of Emily Grierson, first as a result of her father's death and, later, as a result of the loss of Homer Baron, her "intended."

Similarly, in Penn Warren's *All the King's Men*, narrator Jack Burden's near-dizzying, backward-forward-backward perspective shifts begin with a rather misleading casualness that belies the final, powerful conclusion:

> The last time I saw Mason city I went up there in that big black Cadillac with the Boss and the gang, . . . and it was a long time ago—nearly three years, for it is now 1939, but it seems like forever. But the first time I went up there, it was a lot longer time ago back in 1922, and I went up there, in my Model-T . . . (51)

Right from the very start, Burden entices and then entangles the reader in a web of events that he relentlessly pursues until the eventual, devastating conclusion. With the reader in tow, Burden doggedly searches the past—his own as well as that of others—in pursuit of the now strangely contemporary question, "*What* was known and *when* was it known?" Gently but resolvedly extending the perimeters of past and present, Burden gradually accumulates a history of past events that "rewrites" his understanding of the present and the past with crushing impact.

In either case, students should be directed to use index cards to "track" individual events as they appear in the text. As additional details are elaborated, they can easily be added to the appropriate card. As a concluding activity, the numerous cards/events might be sequenced in proper chronological order. With some discussion and guidance from the instructor, patterns of causality might be affixed to chronological order.

The third and final dimension of critical thinking, *assessment* and *evaluation*, also requires careful and even somewhat cautious consideration. To venture beyond merely capricious and idiosyncratic expressions of praise and condemnation, precise criteria must be offered. While the process of examination and evaluation is an important one, its intrinsic value is ultimately determined by the validity and legitimacy of the standards themselves. Students at all levels should be stimulated to assess their own responses, encouraged to engage in such decision-making processes, and prompted to articulate their judgments reasonably and objectively. The mechanism for this vital process might be as simple as a checklist for rating their feelings as readers, viewers, or audience to a fully elaborated persuasive argument. Indeed, the crux of this point is that critical thinking is a flexible, multifaceted mode of perception and expression that can be infused into any array of lessons at any level.

Multidisciplinary Extensions/ Multicultural Connections

Many teachers are drawn to the creative appeal of the project assignment because they believe that students who are inventive and artistic rather then verbal and analytical will enjoy a welcome opportunity to engage in language arts in a new way. Indeed, students who hesitate and stumble in more conventional classroom activities often shine when enticed to pick up scissors and staples and paint, or to exchange textbook exposition for dramatic declamation. Some students are simply more successful at creating their own texts than they are at studying those of others. In any case, since a strong attraction of project assignments is their "differentness" or relative unorthodoxy, then expanding their reach to extend beyond the familiar perimeters of our content field, language arts, may be understood as another illustration of the "more is better" principle.

Instead of simply relying on the whims of random students, the instructor should carefully consider various options when planning the project assignment and strive to design some options in as many legitimate areas of cross-reference as possible. Differences in level, such as elementary vs. high school, should dictate the form or degree of specificity selected rather than the type or form of activity. In other words, differences in grade level would generate differences in degrees of precision or difficulty not in kind.

Many stories or narratives, whether a pre-schooler's brief text or a classic like *The Adventures of Huckleberry Finn* or *Moby Dick*, specify a particular setting, especially when a trip or voyage is involved. Students might be asked to engage in some social studies and find a map, draw a map, embellish an illustrated map, or even create a full-scale story-board-map based on the episodes of the text.

Literary sites themselves are prime targets for geographical study. Marcella Thum's *Exploring Literary America* (1979) profiles more than sixty authors whose homes or regional affiliation exerted substantial influence on their work, from Emily Dickinson and Harriet Beecher Stowe to Booker T. Washington and William Faulkner. This high-interest, readable reference not only provides useful information and background on Thum's chosen writers but also presents a sample format that could be adapted by young readers to explore their own local literary luminaries or preferred authors.

Other literary works are bound to the specifics of a precise historical epoch. Social, political, domestic, educational, or even culinary issues, or a specified time, might be studied and presented in project format.

Performing arts, fine arts, language, and ethnic cultures related to a course of study might be conceptualized as the suggested context of expression, as well as a source of supplemental enrichment. Students might be urged to create their own works of art, drawings, dance, song, etc., to express their feelings or to communicate related ideas and views. Turn a story into a song, turn a poem into a dance, or turn anything into a television commercial! Myths, legends, songs, and stories from traditional cultures endure in the memories and home cultures of many students, providing them with a range of connections and applications that are rarely given the opportunity to be shared. A class project collecting tales and lore might allow some students to construct a bridge between school and home that was not evident before.

While math and science may seem to be the most distant subjects from language arts at any level, their involvement in activities promises rich reward and might simply be more specialized. While relationships and applications may not abound, the few that exist may suggest connections that are strong in content and of powerful appeal. One somewhat obvious way of linking a reading activity to science, for example, would be to have students research the state of science, or medicine in particular, in some earlier historical era. Focus on a past historical era offers a simple but effective means for directing learners in diverse directions. The teacher might simply provide a "scavenger hunt" list of topics—people, events, terms, etc.—that would lead students into captivating and fascinating areas of knowledge and study.

Grouping—Individuals, Pairs, Groups, and Teams

One of the most remarkable conditions of the conventional classroom situation is that boys and girls sit for fairly extended periods of time in relative proximity to others they may know only superficially and are repeatedly cautioned against engaging in basic social conversation. Yet these same students are compelled to function as a cohesive unit—the class—and consistently obligated to perform in various patterns of synchronized conformity with otherwise virtual strangers. In most classes, students alternate between two extremes of personal responsibility congruent with their physical arrangement. On the one hand, they are mobilized and "collectified" in an amorphous conglomerate of diffused anonymity—"Class, open your books . . . " On the other hand, a miscellaneous individual may be singled out at any moment (usually when least expected!) and designated to perform alone—

"Mario, step up to the board" or "Read what you have just written to the class."

While the logistics of a regular classroom may discourage deviation from those two unhappy extremes, the project format offers welcome relief to the otherwise regimented and constricted classroom organization. Although the rise of collaborative learning theory in recent years has probably precipitated more change in interstudent activities in the last few years than had occurred in the century before, many more opportunities are available in theory than are being practiced. In out–of–class projects, pairing, partnering, and teaming in multiple guises should proliferate.

Assessment

Projects as Performance-Based Assessment

The dynamic, interactive, and open nature of projects literally projects them into the center of the most innovative arena of current professional discussion. Because projects challenge students to use their knowledge and skills, to think critically, and to transform the content of their learning through the use of their own imagination, at least one school system has adopted the project as a deciding assessment instrument (Rothman 1992). In this context, the project assignment (a research paper) is conceptualized as a demonstration assessment task or a performance based outcome for elementary students. People involved in the program at Littleton, Colorado, feel that such activities provide a "fuller picture of student assessment than do traditional tests."

Assessment—How, What, and Why

Whether the student project serves as a deciding performance-based assessment for a substantial course of study or as a simple, supplemental enrichment activity for a brief subunit of a few weeks' time, evaluation of the project and student effort should be as thorough, orderly, and educationally sound as the project design itself. Crucial issues center on two or three fundamental factors that the instructor must consider carefully.

Grading Scale. While pass/fail is not particularly desirable because of its neglect to consider and, hence, encourage high achievement, such a binary scale is the first example of a logical possibility. Because of the likely variety of performance from kindergarten to twelfth grade, a four- or five-segment rubric is recommended.

Four-Level Scale

A, B	Exceptional, above and beyond
C	Adequate, competent
D	Below expectations
F	Not acceptable

Five-Level Scale

A	Superior
B	Above Average, Exceptional
C	Satisfactory
D	Less than satisfactory
F	Not acceptable

In ideal situations, students who are to be graded will be given a complete grade sheet, along with a list of directions and expectations at the same time the project is first assigned. Students should have an opportunity to understand from the beginning how their efforts will be translated into grades (letter, number, or descriptive), thus alerting them to the casual relationship between time and effort (or lack thereof!) and final evaluation. In Littleton, for example, mere proficiency is distinguished from excellence; "A proficient letter is one in which the writer clearly states an opinion and uses facts to support it; uses the appropriate format and wording; and makes few grammatical errors." On the other hand, "an excellent letter is one in which the writer explains the writer's position and refutes an alternative position; uses interesting vocabulary and varied sentence structure; and makes essentially no errors." While specific profiles of critical assessment may vary from project to project, certain components remain consistent.

Criteria. What exactly is to be graded? Well, as has been more or less asserted earlier, the very components of the assignment should comprise the critical dimensions of assessment. Note the grading sheet for the *Moby Dick* novel project. The areas designated are exactly parallel to the goals noted on the original assignment sheet. *Standards or goals should dictate assessment criteria.*

Projects: Approaches and Suggestions

Twenty-Five Project Formats Based on a Single Literary Work

Writing

1. Revise the genre—rewrite a section of a novel into a dramatic scene or play; revise a

play into a poem, a poem into a short story, or a narrative into a children's book.

2. Write a television commercial in which a literary character endorses an appropriate product, such as Tom Sawyer endorsing white exterior paint.

3. Write a journal from the point of view of a designated literary character.

4. Devise correspondence between two literary characters.

5. Autobiographical essay from the perspective of a literary character.

6. Do a research report on the music, art, or an historical event of a specified time.

7. Write "formula" poems on a literary theme: acrostic, visual, limerick, or haiku.

8. Create a scene in any genre that might have occurred *before* the actual beginning of the literary work.

9. Create a scene implied but not included in the literary work.

10. Create a scene at some future time after the conclusion of the literary work.

Artistic/Inventive

11. Design a poster, T-shirt, or bumper sticker based on the work.

12. Design and illustrate a deck of cards, calendar, or book of days.

13. Illustrate a literary timeline.

14. Draw an illustrated literary map of the specified region.

15. Create a board game based on the work.

16. Build a theme mobile for classroom display.

17. Design illustrated literary theme paper products:

bookmarks, book covers, folders; note paper or stationery; buttons.

18. Design a vocabulary, crossword, or word-search.

19. Create a musical composition or song as "theme music" for the work.

20. Design a series of sketches, paintings, photographs, or illustrations to embellish the printed text.

Simulation Activities

21. Stage a debate on two opposing views of a central conflict or judgment of character in the literary work.

22. Conduct a trial in which a literary character is tried for an offense noted in the text, with students serving as attorneys, judge, and jury.

23. Create a product and stage an advertising campaign, including press releases, blurbs, magazine layouts, etc.

24. Create a museum exhibit of some cultural dimension of the literary work.

25. Stage an interview or talk-show appearance of the author or literary characters.

Student Portfolio/Curriculum Packet

As their culminating activity, students might do as many of the following as the instructor judges to be appropriate, beneficial, and practical.

1. Research the background of the work and its author, and write a report.

2. Write discussion questions, probable answers, quizzes, and a sample test.

3. Design varied writing assignments.

4. Suggest classroom strategies for small-group activities and reader-response writing activities.

5. Develop vocabulary lessons or activities (crossword puzzles, word-search, etc.)

6. Design critical-thinking activities.

7. Design artistic/creative projects for students.

8. Produce bulletin board and classroom decorations, such as posters.

Create a Classroom Literary Happening

1. Make decorations for the classroom.

2. Create promotional materials (posters, playbills, programs, etc.).

3. Demonstrate and display student writing–songs, stories, poems, and recitations.

4. Provide entertainment–performances, puppet shows, skits, all student created.

5. Provide background music.

6. Play games and hold contests designed by the student.

7. Wear literary costumes, have a parade, distribute awards.

8. Publish a special-edition newspaper for the day, covering events with related features.

9. Prepare and serve appropriate snacks (or banquet!).

10. Make a time capsule to commemorate the event for a future class.

Sample Group Assignment: *Moby Dick*

Underneath a comprehensive list of due dates for each step of the assignment process, the teacher explains group responsibilities and levels of research, as shown below.

Group Responsibilities

1. Quiz: Each group will prepare, administer, and correct a quiz on their chapters. A *typed* copy of the quiz must be given for duplication. Same due date for any other pages needing duplication!
2. Clarify, explain, and illuminate the chapters assigned. Highlight concepts. No tedious plot summaries, please.
3. Consider significant examples, confusions, and questions relating to:
    Plot: action, episode, structure
    Setting: time, place, atmosphere
    Characterization: major, minor, interaction, development, twists
    Theme: ideas, concepts, developments
    Literary devices: figurative language, symbols, ambiguity, irony
4. Selected vocabulary: choose items judiciously
5. Supplemental/enrichment research: Herman Melville, *Moby Dick*, the American romance novel, whaling, etc.

Levels of Research

1. General Reference: basic encyclopedias (*Britannica*)
2. Special Reference: literary encyclopedias (*American Writers*)
3. Books on American literature: Richard Chase, Alfred Kazin
4. Books on Herman Melville: as subject in card catalogue

Each group is responsible for presenting during the full fifty-minute class period, with no time wasted: no indecisiveness, no irrelevant chatter, no needless observations on the obvious.

Each member of the group will receive a major test grade for the group presentation. *As always, absence (excused, serious, tragic, fatal) is no excuse.*

Because of the schedule given above, groups will not be allowed to spill over into the next day's time. When it's all over, there is no more.

Examples of References for Information on *Moby Dick*:

· *American Writers*, vol. 3/R920.03/Ame
· *Critical Survey of Long Fiction*, Vol. 5 /R920.3/ Mag
· *DLB" Dictionary of Literary Biography*, Vol. 3, R920.03 Dictionary: ·· *Chelsea House Library of Literary Criticism: Major Authors*, Vol, 5/R820.9/Maj

Sample In-Class Assignment

For their set of chapters, each member of a group has a specific and independent assignment that is to be completed in the first thirty minutes of class, after which each person will explain his/her notes to the class on one of the following:

1. Ahab: descriptive passage(s) or his own words/quotes.
2. Moby Dick and other minor characters: key descriptive passages, quotes (humans), and important actions.
3. Encounters with other boats: name boat and key characters in episode; note highlights of actions, if any.
4. Identify passages in which Ishmael expresses some aspect of whaling or ship life (or whales!) as being symbolic (allegorical) of human life and experience.
5. Style: Identify passages with examples of any or all of the following: (*a*) allusion (*b*) metaphor (*c*) simile (*d*) personification (*e*) foreshadowing

Note: A minimum of three examples should be identified for each point.

Moby Dick Project Evaluation

The following is an example of what such an evaluation sheet might contain:

Group: _____ Date: _____ Period: _____
Chapters: _____ Students: _____
_____
_____

Assessment	*Points Earned*
Quiz (10)	_____
Vocabulary (10)	_____
Research/Scholarship (10)	_____
Elan (10)	_____
Plot (12)	_____
Setting (12)	_____
Characterization (12)	_____
Theme (12)	_____
Style (12)	_____
TOTAL	_____

Remarks:_____
_____

Representative Selection of Recommended National Contests

Grades: 9–12
Task: Design a time capsule to show people of the future what it was like to be young in the 1900s. Communicate choices through writing, art, video, song, or any other medium.
Prizes: $10,000 Grand Prize Scholarship
$1,000 First Grand Prize (3)
$500 Bond Second Prize (10)
Contact: Oxy 10 Scholarship Contest
c/o Mickey Ravenaugh
Scholastic, Inc.
730 Broadway
New York, NY 10003

Grades: 9–12
Task: Division One: Authorship–music, photography, video, computer program.
Division Two: Invention–devices, tools, mechanists, etc.–in areas of agriculture, environment, leisure (games, sports), new technology.
Contact: Ellen R. Cardwell
Foundation for a Creative America
U.S. Patent and Copyright Office
1255 23rd Street N.W., Suite 850
Washington, D.C. 20037

Title: Promising Writers Contest
Grade: 8
Task: One best writing sample and one 75-minute impromptu essay on a designated topic.
Eligibility: Student must be nominated by English teacher on appropriate forms and according to specified rules.
Contact: Promising Writers Contest
National Council of Teachers of English
1111 Kenyon Road
Urbana, IL 61801

Title: Junior Writing Achievement Contest
Grade: 11
Topic or Task: One best writing sample and one 75-minute impromptu essay on a designated topic.

Eligibility: Student must be nominated by English teacher on appropriate form and according to specified rules.
Contact: Junior Writing Achievement Contest
National Council of Teachers of English
1111 Kenyon Road
Urbana, IL 61801

Title: National PTA Reflections Program
Grades: Four Age Divisions:
Primary K–3
Intermediate 4–6
Junior High 7–9
Senior High 10–12
Task: Use creative talents to express self through original work in one of four categories: literature, music, photography, visual arts.
Eligibility: Student must attend a school where there is a PTA in good standing.
Contact: Program Division, Reflections
National PTA
700 North Rush Street
Chicago, IL 60611-2571

References

Nelms, Ben. 1992. "Editorial." *English Journal* (Jan.): 13.
Penn Warren, Robert. 1974. *All the King's Men.* New York: Harcourt Brace Jovanovich.
Rothman, Robert. 1992. "Testing Shifts from Memorization to Investigation in Littleton, Colorado." *Education Week* (Apr. 22): 1, 22-23.
Thum, Marcella. 1979. *Exploring Literary America.* New York: Atheneum.

10

CHILDREN'S TRADE BOOKS: A GUIDE TO RESOURCES

by Janice Kristo
Associate Professor of Education
University of Maine, Orono, Maine
and
Abigail Garthwait
Librarian, Asa Adams School, Orono, Maine

C URRICULUM development in today's English/language arts classrooms indicates a move from an exclusive use of textbooks to literature-based instruction. Teachers are integrating literature throughout the curriculum. For example, students are now exploring history through historical fiction and biography, and science through nonfiction and other genres. Planning for such an extensive use of trade books can be an overwhelming task. Fortunately, there are many resources available to teachers who wish to base some or all of their teaching on books other than textbooks.

This chapter includes a variety of helpful sources for the teacher who wants to incorporate more literature in the classroom. The purpose of this chapter is to provide a sampling of some of the more recent and most useful references; it is not an exhaustive list. Such sources as bibliographies and guides are specifically designated for appropriate grade-level use for all grades, from elementary school to high school.

Professional Resources

Books

Art and Design in Children's Picture Books: An Analysis of Caldecott Award-Winning Illustrators (Chicago: American Library Association, 1986), 229p. ISBN 0-8389-0446-7.
Art and Design examines in depth eleven Caldecott books. For example, "line" is discussed via *Make Way for Ducklings* and *Time of Wonder*. Includes glossary. Index: title/artist. **Related titles:** *Words about Pictures: The Narrative Art of Children's Picture Books,* by Perry Nodelman (New York: University of Georgia Press, 1988). *Notes on Books and Pictures,* by Maurice Sendak (New York: Farrar, Strauss & Giroux, 1989).

Beyond Words: Picture Books for Older Readers and Writers, ed. by Susan Benedict and Lenore Carlisle (Portsmouth, NH: Heinemann, 1992),142p. ISBN 0-435-08710-X
Beyond Words, comprised of fourteen chapters, focuses on the potential of using picture books from first grade to high school.

Children's Literature: A Guide to Criticism, by
Linnea Hendrickson (Boston: G. K. Hall,
1987), 664p. ISBN 0-8161-8670-7.
Citations for significant articles, books, and
dissertations relating to children's literature are
divided into two sections: "Authors and their
Works and Subjects," and "Themes and Genres."
Includes bibliography. Indexes: critic, author/title/
subject. **Related title:** *Art of the Children's Picture
Books: A Selective Reference Guide,* by Sylvia S.
Marantz and Kenneth A. Marantz (New York:
Garland, 1988).

*Children's Literature Awards and Winners: A
Directory of Prizes, Authors, and Illustrators,* 2d
ed., by Dolores Blythe Jones (New York: Neal-
Schuman, 1988), 671p. ISBN 0-8103-2741-4.
Part One lists awards given in the field of
children's literature. Annotations include agency,
address, purpose and history of the award,
frequency, selection criteria, categories, rules and
regulations, and the form of the award. Part Two
lists authors and illustrators. Includes selected
bibliography. Indexes: award, subject of award,
author/illustrator/translator, title. **Related title:**
*Winning Books for Children and Young Adults: An
Annual Guide,* by Betty Criscoe (Metuchen, NJ:
Scarecrow Press, 1990).

*Children's Literature in the Classroom: Weaving
Charlotte's Web,* ed. by Janet Hickman and
Bernice Cullinan (Norwood, MA: Christopher
Gordon, 1989), 274p. ISBN 0-926-842-00-5.
This volume, a tribute to children's literature
scholar Charlotte Huck, contains a section on
using literature in the classroom; chapters on picture books, fantasy, historical fiction, and poetry;
and ways to develop literature-based programs.

Children's Literature in the Elementary School, 4th
ed., by Charlotte Huck, Susan Hepler, and
Janet Hickman (Austin: Holt, Rinehart and
Winston, 1987), 753p. ISBN 0-03-041770-8.
Among its many chapters, *Children's Literature in
the Elementary School* discusses the importance of
using literature in the elementary school, responses to literature, the history of children's
literature, and major genres. **Related titles:**
*Thursday's Child: Trends and Patterns in Contem-
porary Children's Literature,* by Sheila A. Egoff
(Chicago: American Library Association, 1981).
*Jump over the Moon: Selected Professional Read-
ings,* ed. by Pamela Petrick Barron and Jennifer
Q. Burley (Austin: Holt, Rinehart, and Winston,

1984). *Children's Books of International Interest,*
ed. by Barbara Elleman (Chicago: American
Library Association, 1985). *Innocence and
Experience: Essays and Conversations on
Children's Literature,* ed. by Barbara Harrison and
Gregory Maguire (New York: Lothrop, Lee, and
Shepard, 1987). *Children and Literature,* 2d ed., by
John Warren Stewig (Boston: Houghton Mifflin,
1988). *Literature and the Child,* 2d ed., by Bernice
E. Cullinan (Orlando, FL: Harcourt Brace
Jovanovich, 1989). *A Critical Handbook of
Children's Literature,* 4th ed., by Rebecca Lukens
(Glenview, IL: Scott, Foresman, 1990). *Children's
Literature: Theory, Research, and Teaching,* by Kay
E. Vandergrift (Englewood, CO: Libraries
Unlimited, 1990). *Literature for the Young Child,*
2d ed., by Eileen M. Burke (Needham Heights,
MA: Allyn & Bacon, 1990). *Literature for Young
Children.* 3d ed., by Joan I. Glazer (Columbus,
OH: Merrill, 1991). *Through the Eyes of a Child,*
3d ed., by Donna Norton (Columbus, OH:
Merrill, 1991).

*Children's Literature—Resource for the Class-
room.,* ed. by Masha Kabakow Rudman
(Norwood, MA: Christopher Gordon, 1989),
258p. ISBN 0-926842-01-3.
This eleven-chapter text is divided into three
sections, "Context and Background for Using
Children's Literature in the Classroom"; "Perspectives on Evaluation and Selection in
Children's Literature"; and "Literature in and
beyond the Classrooms."

Children Tell Stories: A Teaching Guide, by Martha
Hamilton and Mitch Weiss (Katonah, NY:
Richard C. Owen, 1990), 225p. ISBN 0-913461-
20-2.
This text offers a bibiliography of stories to tell
and read aloud to students in grades 2–12.
Related titles: *The Storyteller's Sourcebook: A
Subject, Title, and Motif Index to Folklore Collec-
tions for Children,* ed. by Margaret Read
MacDonald (Detroit: Gale, 1982). *The Storyvine:
A Source Book of Unusual and Easy-to-Tell Stories
from around the World,* by Anne Pellowski (New
York: Collier Books, 1984). *Stories in the Class-
room,* by Bob Barton and David Booth (Ports-
mouth, NH: Heinemann, 1990). *Wise Women:
Folk and Fairy Tales from around the World,* by
Suzanne I. Barchers (Englewood, CO: Libraries
Unlimited, 1990). *Sit Tight, and I'll Swing You a
Tail: Using and Writing Stories with Young People,*
by Gregory Denman (Portsmouth, NH:

Heinemann, 1991). *Making Stories,* by Irene N. Watts (Portsmouth, NH: Heinemann, 1992).

The Child's Developing Sense of Theme: Responses to Literature, by Susan S. Lehr (New York: Teachers College Press, 1991), 216p. ISBN 0-8077-31056.
Lehr discusses the child's sense of theme from a variety of perspectives. Classroom profiles, response guides, and bibliography of children's literature are included.

Explore Poetry, by Donald H. Graves (Portsmouth, NH: Heinemann, 1992), 194p. ISBN 0-435-08489-5.
Reading, writing, and integrating poetry fill this final volume in *The Reading/Writing Teacher's Companion Series.* Other titles in the series include: *Experiment with Fiction; Investigate Nonfiction; Build a Literate Classroom; and Discover Your own Literacy.* **Related titles:** *When You've Made It Your Own... Teaching Poetry to Young People,* by Gregory Denman (Portsmouth, NH: Heinemann, 1988). *For the Good of the Earth and Sun,* by Georgia Heard (Portsmouth, NH: Heinemann, 1989). *Sunrises and Songs: Reading and Writing Poetry in an Elementary Classroom,* by Amy McClure, with Peggy Harrison and Sheryl Reed (Portsmouth, NH: Heinemann, 1990). *Listening to the Bells,* by Florence Grossman (Portsmouth, NH: Boynton/Cook, 1991).

Exploring Literature in the Classroom: Content and Methods, ed. by Karen D. Wood, with Anita Moss. (Norwood, MA: Christopher Gordon, 1992), 280p. ISBN 0-926842-11-0.
This ten-chapter text offers a philosophical understanding and strategies for implementing a literature-based curriculum.

Fairy Tales, Fables, Legends, and Myths: Using Folk Literature in Your Classroom. 2d ed., by Bette Bosma (New York: Teachers College Press, 1992), 200p. ISBN 0-8077-3134X.
This text offers teachers through the middle school level ways to involve students with folk literature. Includes a guide to recommended folk literature.

Focus on Literature: A Context for Literacy Learning, by Joy F. Moss (Katonah, NY: Richard C. Owen, 1990), 272p. ISBN 0-913461-17-2.
Designed for the elementary and middle school teacher, this text contains literature units such as

"Cinderella Tales: A Multicultural Experience and Wish Tales," and "The Literary Dialogue-Journal." **Related title:** *Novel Experiences: Literature Units for Book Discussion Groups in the Elementary Grades,* by Christine Jenkins and Sally Freeman (Englewood, CO: Teacher Ideas Press, 1991).

International Directory of Children's Literature, by MaryBeth Dunhouse (New York: Facts on File, 1986), 128p. ISBN 0-8160-1411-6.
This reference offers eight chapters on a wide selection of topics, such as children's literature publishers, magazines, organizations, fairs, seminars and conferences, major children's libraries and special collections, and statistics on children's books. Each chapter is arranged in alphabetical order by country. Entries are included for eighty-four countries.

Invitations: Changing as Teachers and Learners K–12, by Regie Routman (Portsmouth, NH: Heinemann, 1991), 502p. ISBN 0-435-08578-6.
This comprehensive resource offers seventeen chapters on organizing and managing literacy-oriented classrooms; an annotated bibliography of resources for teachers (including professional books, journal articles, theme journals, journals, newsletters, and literacy extension resources); recommended literature by grade level, K–12; supplemental lists; and ten appendices. **Related titles:** *This Way to Books,* by Caroline Feller Bauer (New York: H.W. Wilson, 1983). *Creating Connections: Books, Kits, and Games for Children: A Sourcebook,* by Betty P. Cleaver, Barbara Chatton, and Shirley Vittum Morrison (New York: Garland, 1986). *Stories, Songs and Poetry for Teaching Reading and Writing: Literacy through Literature,* by Robert A. McCracken and Marlene J. McCracken (New York: Teachers College Press, 1986). *Children's Literature in the Reading Program,* ed. by Bernice E. Cullinan (Newark, DE: International Reading Association, 1987). *Literature in the Classroom: Readers, Texts, and Contexts,* ed. by Ben Nelms (Urbana, IL: National Council of Teachers of English, 1988). *Literature-Based Reading Programs at Work,* ed. by Joelie Hancock and Susan Hill (Portsmouth, NH: Heinemann, 1988). *Using Literature in the Elementary Classroom,* ed. by John Warren Stewig and Sam Leaton Sebesta (Urbana, IL: National Council of Teachers of English, 1989). *An Integrated Language Perspective in the Elementary School: Theory into Action,* by Christine C. Pappas, Barbara Z. Kiefer, and Linda S. Levstik

(White Plains, NY: Longman, 1990). *Bringing It All Together: A Program for Literacy*, by Terry D. Johnson and Daphne R. Louis (Portsmouth, NH: Heinemann, 1990). *Grand Conversations: Literature Groups in Action*, by Ralph Peterson and Maryann Eeds (Richmond Hill, Ontario: Scholastic-TAB, 1990). *Responses to Literature, Grades K–8*, by James M. Macon, and Diane Bewell, Mary Ellen Vogt (Newark, DE: International Reading Association, 1990). *Talking about Books: Creating Literate Communities*, ed. by Kathy Gnagey Short and Kathryn Mitchell Pierce (Portsmouth, NH: Heinemann, 1990). *Workshop 2 by and for Teachers: Beyond the Basal*, ed. by Nancie Atwell (Portsmouth, NH: Heinemann, 1990). [See also Workshop 1; *Writing and Literature*; Workshop 3: *The Politics of Process*, ed. by Nancie Atwell, and Workshop 4: *The Teacher as Researcher*, ed. by Thomas Newkirk (Portsmouth, NH: Heinemann, 1992.)] *Other Worlds: The Endless Possibilities of Literature*, by Trevor H. Cairney (Portsmouth, NH: Heinemann, 1991). *Start with a Story*, by Linda Wasson-Ellam (Portsmouth, NH: Heinemann, 1991). *The Child as Critic: Teaching Literature in Elementary and Middle Schools*, by Glenna Davis Sloan (New York: Teachers College Press, 1991).

The Library/Classroom Connection, by Silvana Carletti, Suzanne Girard, and Kathlene Willing (Portsmouth, NH: Heinemann, 1991), 128p. ISBN 0-435-08711-8.
The Library/Classroom Connection discusses the expanded role of the librarian in whole-language programs and offers suggestions for teacher-librarian teams who want to explore curricular planning collaboratively.

Literature Activity Books: An Index, by Marybeth Green and Beverly Williams (Englewood, CO: Libraries Unlimited, 1992), 250p. ISBN 1-56308-011-7.
Over 1,000 quality children's titles may be accessed by an integrated author, title, subject arrangement. Entries give a brief description of contents, objectives, and interest levels. **Related title:** *Developing Learning Skills through Children's Literature: An Idea Book for K–5 Classrooms and Libraries*, by Mildred Knight Laughlin and Letty S. Watt (Phoenix, AZ: Oryx, 1986).

Literature for Today's Young Adults, 3d. ed., by Kenneth L. Donelson and Alleen Pace Nilsen (Glenview, IL: Scott, Foresman, 1989), 620p. ISBN 0-673-38400-4.

This text is devoted to the books that young adults read, with seven chapters focused on genres of young adult literature. Chapters dealing with evaluating books, mass media, and censorship are also included. **Related titles:** *Readers, Texts, Teachers*, ed. by Bill Corcoran and Emrys Evans (Portsmouth, NH: Boynton/Cook, 1987). *Response and Analysis: Teaching Literature in Junior and Senior High School*, by Robert E. Probst (Portsmouth, NH: Boynton/Cook, 1988).

Newbery and Caldecott Awards: A Guide to the Medal and Honor Books, by the Association for Library Service to Children (Chicago: American Library Association, n.d.), 137p. ISBN 0-8389-3398-X.
Entries are arranged in reverse chronological order. Each entry includes a paragraph commentary. There are chapters on awards and on media used in Caldecott picture books. Indexes: author/illustrator, title. **Related titles:** *For Reading Outloud! A Guide to Sharing Books With Children*, by Margaret Mary Kimmel and Elizabeth Segal (New York: Delacorte, 1983). *Prizewinning Books for Children: Themes and Stereotypes in U.S. Prizewinning Prose Fiction for Children*, by Jaqueline Shachter Weiss (New York: Lexington Books, 1983).

New Read Aloud Handbook, by Jim Trelease (New York: Penguin, 1989), 290p. ISBN 0-14-046881-1.
Several essays in the first half of this book address topics such as the importance of reading aloud and how to choose a book. The second section utilizes various headings: predictable books, short novels, and novels. Each of the 300 annotations includes grade level, plot summary, commentary, and related books. Includes bibliography. Index. **Related titles:** *For Reading Outloud! A Guide to Sharing Books with Children*, by Margaret Mary Kimmel and Elizabeth Segal (New York: Delcorte, 1983). *Books Kids Will Sit Still For: The Complete Read-Aloud Guide*, 2d ed., by Judy Freeman (New Providence, NJ: Bowker, 1990). *Hey! Listen to This—Stories to Read Aloud*, ed. by Jim Trelease (New York: Penguin, 1992).

The Oxford Companion to Children's Literature, by Humphrey Carpenter and Mari Prichard (New York: Oxford University Press, 1984), 587p. ISBN 0-19-211582-0.
This volume lists authors and descriptions of genres in alphabetical order. It includes summaries of the state of children's literature in all

languages, countries, and continents and provides readily-available information.

Read to Write: Using Children's Literature as a Springboard for Teaching Writing, by John Warren Stewig (Katonah, NY: Richard C. Owen, 1990, 296p. ISBN 0-913461-16-4.
This text discusses a three-part program for pre-K–8 students to help develop ability in writing fiction and poetry.

Touchstones: Reflections on the Best in Children's Literature, ed. by Perry Nodelman (Battle Creek, MI: Children's Literature Association, 1989), 309p. ISBN 0-318-1834-3.
This volume presents critical essays of fiction titles placed on the Children's Literature Association's Touchstones list. Also see vol. 2, *Fairy Tales, Fables, Myths, Legends, and Poetry.* 1987, and vol. 3, *Picture Books.* 1989.

Vital Connections: Children, Science, and Books, ed. by Wendy Saul and Sybille A. Jagusch (Portsmouth, NH: Heinemann, 1992), 176p. ISBN 0-435-08332-5.
Vital Connections describes the use of science trade books and the ways children become involved in these kinds of books. This text includes contributions from children's authors Seymour Simon, Jean Craighead George, and Patrica Lauber, as well as educators and science and literature specialists. **Related title:** *Science through Children's Literature*, by Carol M. Butzow and John W. Butzow (Englewood, CO: Teacher Ideas Press, 1989).

Whole Language Strategies for Secondary Students, by Carol Gilles, Mary Bixby, Paul Crowley, Shirley R. Crenshaw, Margaret Henrichs, Frances E. Reynolds, and Donelle Pyle (Katonah, NY: Richard C. Owen, 1988), 208p. ISBN 0-913461-84-9.
This text contains chapters on theory as well as strategies and activities for grades 5–12.

Journals
Teachers may wish to refer to the following journals for articles on using literature in the classroom and book reviews:

The ALAN Review. Assembly on Literature for Adolescents, National Council of Teachers of English.

Book Links. Booklist Publications, American Library Association.
Booklist. American Library Association. Includes the annual "Best Books for Young Adults."
The Bulletin of the Center for Children's Books. University of Illinois Press.
The Children's Literature Assembly Bulletin-Journal of the Children's Literature Assembly of National Council of Teachers of English. See also *The Best of the Bulletin*, ed. by Carolyn J. Bauer.
Children's Literature in Education: An International Quarterly. Agathon Press.
The English Journal. National Council of Teachers of English.
The Horn Book Magazine. Boston.
Interracial Books for Children Bulletin. Council on Interracial Books for Children.
Journal of Youth Services in Libraries. Joint publication of the Association for Library Service to Children and the Young Adult Services Division of the American Library Association.
Kirkus Reviews. Kirkus Service.
Language Arts. National Council of Teachers of English.
The Lion and The Unicorn. Johns Hopkins University Press, Journals Publishing Division.
The New Advocate: For Those Involved with Young People and Their Literature. Christopher Gordon.
New York Times Book Review (Fall and spring issues devoted primarily to children's books.)
Phaedrus: An International Annual of Children's Literature Research. Fairleigh Dickinson University.
The Reading Teacher and The Journal of Reading. International Reading Association. *The Reading Teacher* annually publishes two lists: "Teachers' Choices," "Children's Book Choices," and "The Journal of Reading" annually publishes "Young Adults Choices."
School Library Journal. R.R. Bowker Company.
Top of the News—Association for Library Services to Children and the Young Adult Services. Division of the American Library Association.
Voice of Youth Advocates (VOYA). Scarecrow Press.
Wilson Library Bulletin. H. W. Wilson Company.

Other Publications of Interest
American Library Association (ALA) offers annual lists of: "Best Books for Young Adults,"

"Quick Picks for Great Reading," and a pamphlet called "Becoming a Lifetime Reader."

The Children's Book Council (CBC) offers reprints of two lists: "Outstanding Science Trade Books for Children" (which appears annually in *Science and Children*) and "Notable Children's Trade Books in the Field of Social Studies" (which appears annually in *Social Education*).

International Reading Association/Children's Book Council Liaison Committee offers an annotated book list every two years that includes "Poetry and Verse," "Fiction for Young Readers," "Easy-to-Read Fiction for Older Readers," "Folklore," and "Non-Fiction."

Teachers Networking: The Whole-Language Newsletter. Richard C. Owen Publishers.

The WEB. The Ohio State University. Three issues offering reviews of books and ways they can be used in the classroom.

All Grades

American Indian Reference Books for Children and Young Adults, by Barbara J. Kuipers (Englewood, CO: Libraries Unlimited, 1991), 176p. ISBN 0-87287-745-0.
Over 200 selected nonfiction materials are arranged by Dewey Decimal number. The long annotations include subject area, reading level, strengths and weaknesses, and uses in the curriculum. Includes publisher information. Indexes: author/title, subject.

Basic Collection of Children's Books in Spanish, by Isabel Schon (Metuchen, NJ: Scarecrow, 1986), 230p. ISBN 0-8108-1904-X.
More than 500 selected titles are organized by Dewey decimal system. The text's brief annotations are basically descriptive. Appendices: list of dealers in books in Spanish. Indexes: author, title (Spanish only), subject.

Bibliography of Nonsexist Supplementary Books (K–12), developed by Karen Stone and the Northwest Regional Educational Laboratory Center for Sex Equity (Phoenix, AZ: Oryx, 1984), 108p. 0-89774-101-3.
This slim volume is arranged into twelve reading levels. Each entry gives a brief summary and the gender, ethnic group, or nationality of the major character, as well as qualitative information and

subject headings. Includes bibliography. Indexes: title, author, subject. **Related title:** *Guide to Nonsexist Children's Books*, by Judith Adell and Hilary Dole Klein, with an introduction by Alan Alda (Academy Chicago, 1976).

The Birthday Book, by Mary Hovas Munroe and Judith Rogers Banja (New York: Neal Schuman, 1991), 499p. ISBN 1-55570-051-9.
This book allows access to information on more than 7,200 American authors and illustrators. The main body is an alphabetical list that gives birth surname, pseudonym(s) birth date and birthplace, death date and citations for further information (thirty-four sources). Indexes: birth month, birth year, geographic. **Related titles:** *A State-by-State Guide to Children's and Young Adult Authors and Illustrators*, by David Loertscher (Englewood, CO: Libraries Unlimited, 1991). *Biographical Index to Children's and Young Adult Authors and Illustrators*, by David V. Loertscher (Englewood, CO: Libraries Unlimited, 1992).

Bookbrain, by E. A. Hass (Phoenix, AZ: Oryx, 1990). (For Apple II, Macintosh LC, and IBM.)
This interactive computer database helps students select books from thousands of titles. It allows for customizing any collection. Three separate programs are geared to different age levels. **Related programs:** *Bookwhiz*, the Educational Testing Service; *Fiction Finder*, Educational Support Services; and *Desk Top Library*, Scholastic.

Bookfinder 4: When Kids Need Books: Annotations of Books Published 1983–1986, by Sharon Spredemann Dreyer (Circle Pines: American Guidance, 1989). ISBN 0-913476-51-X.
This resource aids in finding books that address specific behavioral and developmental problems. Each entry includes a list of primary and secondary themes, several paragraphs of annotations, commentary, reading level, and other available formats. Volumes 1–3 are out of print, but *The Best of Bookfinder* (1992) replaces them. Includes list of publishers addresses. Indexes: subject, author, title. **Related titles:** *Children's Literature—An Issues Approach*, 2d ed., by Marsha Kabakow Rudman (White Plains, NY: Longman, 1984). *Single-Parent Family in Children's Books: An Annotated Bibliography*, 2d ed., by Catherine Townsend Horner (Metuchen, NJ: Scarecrow, 1988).

Books by African-American Authors and Illustrators for Children and Young Adults, by Helen E. Williams (Chicago: American Library Association, 1991), 270p. ISBN 0-8389-0570-6.
Over 1,260 briefly annotated entries are grouped into three scholastic levels. Includes awards and prizes, glossary and art terms, short bibliography. Index. **Related title:** *Black Authors and Illustrators of Children's Books: A Biographical Dictionary,* by Barbara Rollock (New York: Garland, 1988).

Books for the Gifted Child, vol. 2, by Paula Hauser and Gail A. Nelson (New Providence, NJ: Bowker, 1988), 244p. ISBN 0-8352-2467-8.
The 195 fiction and nonfiction titles listed in the text do not overlap with the first volume. Each entry includes the reading level, characters, style, and evaluative comments on the plot. Includes introductory chapters on gifted children. **Related titles:** *Picture Books for Gifted Programs,* by Nancy Palette (Metuchen, NJ: Scarecrow, 1981). *Educating the Gifted: A Sourcebook,* by M. Jean Greenlaw and Margaret E. McIntosh (Chicago: American Library Association, 1988).

Books to Help Children Cope with Separation and Loss: An Annotated Bibliography, vol. 3, by Joanne E. Bernstain and Masha Kabakow Rudman (New Providence, NJ: Bowker, 1989), 532p. ISBN 0-8352-2510-0.
The first section of this book consists of essays on why and how to use books with children who are coping with grief. The 606 entries are arranged in thematic categories, such as death, divorce, serious illness, etc. Includes bibliography for adult guides, directory of organizations. Indexes: author, title, subject, interest level, reading level.

Canadian Books for Young People, 4th ed., by Andre Gagnon and Ann Gagnon (Toronto: University of Toronto Press, 1988), 186p. ISBN 0-8020-6662-3.
This selected bibliography is arranged by genre (travel, history, social sciences, etc.). Books published in French are listed separately with brief annotations in French. Includes bibliography. Indexes: author, title, illustrator. **Related titles:** *Best of Children's Choices,* by Lenore Wilson and Jane Charlton (Citizens Committee on Children, 1988). *The New Republic of Childhood: A Critical Guide to Canadian Children's Literature in English,* by Shelia Egoff (New York: Oxford University, 1990). *Presenting Canscaip (Profiles of Canadian Children's Artists),* ed. by

Barbara Greenwood (Markham, Ontario: Pembroke, 1990). *Canadian Connections,* by Ron Jobe and Paula Hart (Markham, Ontario: Pembroke, 1991). *The Canscaip Companion,* ed. by Barbara Greenwood (Markham, Ontario: Pembroke, 1991).

Children's Book Review Index 1991 Annual (Detroit: Gale, 1991), 675p. ISBN 0-8103-7492-7.
Citations from over 500 periodicals allow easy access to reviewers' comments and opinions. Indexes: illustrators, titles. **Related titles:** *Children's Literature Review, Horn Book Index, Book Review Index,* and *Book Review Digest.*

Choosing Books for Children: A Commonsense Guide, by Betsy Hearne (New York: Delacorte, 1990), 150p. ISBN 0-385-3010-81.
The author provides suggestions for using a variety of literature and choosing books for children and young adults.

Collected Perspectives: Choosing and Using Books for the Classroom, by Hughes Moir, Melissa Cain, and Leslie Prosak-Beres (Norwood, MA: Christopher Gordon, 1990), 280p. ISBN 0-926842-03-X.
This resource provides reviews written by educators who have used books with children and young adults. Suggestions are offered for integrating books into the curriculum. Marginal notes are included throughout the text. Categories include picture storybooks; fiction for younger readers (ages 6-12); for older readers (ages 12 and up); poetry (all ages); and nonfiction (all ages). Indexes: author/title, subject area, entry number, publisher addresses, and toll-free numbers.

Dictionary of American Children's Fiction 1960-1984: Recent Books of Recognized Merit, by Alethea K. Helbig and Agnes Regan Perkins (Westport, CN: Greenwood, 1986), 914p. 0-313-25233-5.
Based on 489 books that have won awards, this resource lists 1,550 titles, authors, characters, and settings in dictionary format. Index. **Related titles:** *Dictionary of American Children's Fiction 1859-1959,* by Helbig and Perkins (Westport, CT: Greenwood, 1985); *Dictionary of British Children's Fiction: Books of Recognized Merit,* by Helbig and Perkins (Westport, CT: Greenwood, 1989); *Young Reader's Companion,* by Gorton Carruth and Eugene Ehrlich (New Providence, NJ: Bowker, 1992).

E Is for Environment: An Annotated Bibliography of Children's Books with Environmental Themes, by Patti Sinclair (New Providence, NJ: Bowker, 1992), 232p. ISBN 0-8352-3028-7.
Most of the 517 titles listed have been published during the last ten years in the fields of natural history, geology, meteorology, botany, and ecology (No field guides, natural history, or biology books have been included.) Both fiction and nonfiction books are arranged under broad topics. Annotations include interest level ratings and awards. Includes bibliography. Indexes: author, title, subject.

Eyeopeners! How to Choose and Use Children's Books about Real People, Places, and Things, by Beverly Kobrin (New York: Viking, 1988), 317p. ISBN 0-670-82073-3.
Kobrin discusses over 500 nonfiction titles and groups them by categories such as dinosaurs, holidays, and rocks. Each annotation includes recommended ages and teaching tips. A "Quick-Link Index" is also included for locating topics. **Related title:** *The Kobrin Letter,* a newsletter of reviews and recommendations of nonfiction titles for children.

Fantasy Literature for Children and Young Adults: An Annotated Bibliography, 3d ed., by Ruth Nadelman Lynn (New Providence, NJ: Bowker, 1989), 771p. ISBN 0-8352-2347-7.
Arranged by type of fantasy (time travel, animal, ghost, etc.), 3,300 recommended titles are listed. Each entry includes a one sentence synopsis, reading level, major awards, and citations from at least two reviewing sources. Neither the genres of science fiction or horror are included. Includes essays, "Outstanding Authors and Series." Indexes: author/illustrator, title, subject.

From Page to Screen, by Joyce Moss and George Wilson (Detroit: Gale, 1992), 450p. ISBN 0-8103-7893-0.
This directory lists media versions of hundreds of books. The 1,200 film, video and laser-disc versions are arranged alphabetically by title. Annotations include a brief synopsis, release date, viewing time, film technique, audience level, foreign language adaptations, review citations, prices, and rights. Indexes: film title, author, age level, subject, award, and sign-captioned availability.

Health, Illness and Disability: A Guide to Books for Children and Young Adults, by Pat Azarnoff

(New Providence, NJ: Bowker, 1983), 259p. ISBN 0-8352-1518-0.
Over 1,000 fiction and nonfiction titles are listed alphabetically by author. Each entry includes suggested the grade level, disability, and a brief summary. Also included is a directory of publishers. Indexes: title, subject, subject guide. **Related title:** *Understanding Abilities, Disabilities and Capabilities: A Guide to Children's Literature,* by Margaret F. Carlin (Englewood, CO: Libraries Unlimited, 1991).

Index to Collective Biographies for Young Readers, 4th ed., ed. by Karen Breen (New Providence, NJ: Bowker, 1988), 494p. 0-8352-2348-5.
Over 1,100 collective biographies for students ages 7–15 are indexed. The index is arranged by biographical subject, occupation or area of fame, and title of collective work.

Index to Fairy Tales, 1978–1986: Including Folklore, Legends and Myths in Collections, by Norma Olin Ireland, comp. by Joseph W. Sprug (Metuchen, NJ: Scarecrow, 1989), 575p. ISBN 0-8108-2194.
This fifth supplement to a monumental index lists 261 collection titles, using 2,700 subject headings. The index is arranged alphabetically by title and subject. No annotations are given. **Related titles:** *Guide to Folktales in the English Language,* by D. Ashliman (Westport, CN: Greenwood, 1987). *Folk Literature and Children: An Annotated Bibliography of Secondary Materials,* by George B. Shannon (Westport, CN: Greenwood, 1981).

Index to Poetry for Children and Young People 1976–1981, comp. by John E. Brewton, G. Meredith Blackburn II, and Lorraine A. Blackburn (New York: Wilson, 1984), 320p. ISBN 0-8242-0681-9.
This is a title, subject, author, and first line index. Over 100 poetry collections are included: 7,000 poems by 2,000 authors, classified under 2,000 subject headings. Collections are listed with suggested grade, number of poems, and how they are grouped. **Related title:** *Poetry Anthologies for Children and Young People,* by Marycile E. Olexer (Chicago: American Library Association, 1985).

Literature for Young People on War and Peace: An Annotated Bibliography, comp. by Harry Eiss (Westport, CN: Greenwood, 1989), 131p. ISBN 0742-6801.
This bibliography lists works for children dealing

with all aspects of war; the preface provides background on why children are interested in the topic. Including adult resources, there are 386 titles listed alphabetically by author. Annotations widely vary in length; approximate age range is given. Includes adult bibliography. **Related title:** *Nuclear Age Literature for Youth: The Quest for a Life-Affirming Ethic,* by Millicent Lenz (Chicago: American Library Association, 1990).

Magazines for Young People: A Children's Magazine Guide Companion Volume, 2d ed., by Bill Katz (New Providence, NJ: Bowker, 1991), 238p. ISBN 0-8352-3009-0 (formerly *Magazines for School Libraries: For Elementary, Junior High School and High School Libraries.*)
Ethnic and Canadian magazines and professional journals are reviewed; subject experts point out strengths and weaknesses of each periodical. Index: title, major subject. **Related titles:** *Magazines for Children,* ed. by Donald A. Stoll (Baltimore: Educational Press and International Reading Association, 1990). *Magazines for Children: A Guide for Parents, Teachers, and Librarians,* 2d ed., by Selma K. Richardson (Chicago: American Library Association, 1991).

Our Family, Our Friends, Our World: An Annotated Guide to Significant Multicultural Books for Children and Teenagers, by Lyn Miller-Lachmann (New Providence, NJ: Bowker, 1992), 710p. ISBN 0-8352-3025-2.
Approximately 1,000 books are arranged by country, ethnic group, and grade level. Each section was written by an expert in the field. Length of annotations vary from sixty to 300 words, depending on the complexity of the book. Includes essay, bibliography, directory of publishers. Indexes: author, title/series, subject. **Related titles:** *Literature for Children about Asians and Asian Americans: Analysis and Annotated Bibliography with Additional Readings for Adults,* by Esther C. Jenkins and Mary C. Austin (Westport, CN: Greenwood, 1987). *Multicultural Literature for Children and Young Adults: A Selected Listing of Books 1980-1990 by and about People of Color,* by Ginny Moore Kruse (Madison: Wisconsin Department of Public Instruction, 1991). *Teaching Multicultural Literature in Grades K–8,* ed. by Violet J. Harris (Norwood, MA: Christopher Gordon, 1992).

Plays for Children and Young Adults: An Evaluative Index and Guide, by Rashelle S. Karp and June

H. Schlessinger (New York: Garland, 1991), 580p. ISBN 0-8240-6112-8.
Evaluative information is given for over 3,500 plays, choral readings, skits, and reviews. Organized alphabetically by title, each entry gives audience level, evaluation, cast needs, playing time, setting, number of acts, royalty information, subject, type of play and summary. Indexes: author/title, cast (number of males and females), grade level, subject, playing time. **Related title:** *Index to Children's Plays in Collections 1975-1984* (Metuchen, NJ: Scarecrow, 1986).

Portraying the Disabled: A Guide to Juvenile Fiction, by Debra Robertson (New Providence, NJ: Bowker, 1991), 150p. ISBN 0-8352-3023-6 (Formerly *Notes from a Different Drummer* and *More Notes from a Different Drummer.*)
Portraying the Disabled: A Guide to Juvenile Non-Fiction, by Joan Brest Friedberg, June B. Mullins, and Adelaide Weir Sukiennik (New Providence, NJ: Bowker, 1991), 363p. ISBN 0-8352-3022-8 (Formerly *Accept Me As I Am: Best Books of Juvenile Non-fiction on Impairments and Disabilities.*)
These selective bibliographies list books about individuals with impairments and disabilities. About 350 nonfiction titles are arranged by the type of disability (e.g., physical problems, cognitive-behavior problems). More than 650 fiction titles promote acceptance and understanding of the disabled. Each entry lists reading level, specific disability, and about two paragraphs of annotation. Indexes: author, title, subject.

Primaryplots: A Book Talk Guide for Readers Ages 4-8, by Rebecca L. Thomas (New Providence, NJ: Bowker, 1989), 392p. ISBN 0-8352-2514-3.
Juniorplots 3: A Book Talk Guide for Use with Readers Ages 12-16, by John T. Gillespie and Corinne J. Naden (New Providence, NJ: Bowker, 1987), 352p. ISBN 0-8352-2367-1.
Seniorplots: A Book Talk Guide for Use with Readers Ages 15-18, by John T. Gillespie and Corinne J. Naden (New Providence, NJ: Bowker, 1989), 386p. ISBN 0-8352-251-5.
These guides introduce techniques for giving reading advice to groups. Each contain summaries, thematic information, page numbers for reading aloud, citations for further information, and other titles. **Related title:** *Booktalker,* by Joni Bodart (Englewood, CO: Libraries Unlimited, 1992).

Something about the Author: Facts and Pictures about Authors and Illustrators for Books for Young People, by Anne Commire (Detroit: Gale Research, 1990), 350p. ISBN 0-8103-0099-0.
This is a continuing volume that includes information on many authors. **Related titles:** *Illustrators of Children's Books 1967-1976,* by Lee Kingman and Grace Allen Hogarth (Boston: Horn Book, 1978). *Yesterday's Authors of Books for Children,* ed. by Anne Commire (Detroit: Gale, 1978). *American Writers for Children Since 1960: Poets, Illustrators, and NonFiction Authors,* ed. by Glenn E. Estes (Detroit: Gale, 1987). *Writers for Children: Critical Studies of Major Authors Since the Seventeenth Century,* ed. by Jane M. Bingham (New York: Scribner, 1988). *Authors and Artists for Young Adults,* vol. 1, ed. by Agnes Garrett and Helga P. McCue (Detroit: Gale, 1989). Semiannual. *Book People: A First Album* and *Book People: A Second Album,* by Sharron L. McElmeel (Englewood, CO: Libraries Unlimited, 1989). *Sixth Book of Junior Authors and Illustrators,* by Sally Holmes Holtze (New York: H.W. Wilson, 1989). *Twentieth-Century Children's Writers,* 3d ed., by Tracy Chevalier (Chicago: St. James Press, 1989). *Book People: A Multicultural Album,* by Sharron L. McElmeel (n.p.: 1992). *Something about the Author Autobiography Series,* by Joyce Nakamura (Detroit: Gale Research, 1992).

They Wrote for Children Too: An Annotated Bibliography of Children's Literature by Famous Writers for Adults, comp. by Marilyn Fain Apseloff (Westport, CT: Greenwood, 1989), 202p. ISBN 0742-6801.
The main body is divided into three centuries. The notes for 511 numbered entries (60 authors) run about one-fourth to one-half page and include subject headings. Science fiction or abridged versions rewritten for children are not included. Indexes: author/translator/reteller, illustrator, title, subject. **Related title:** *Bookbait: Detailed Notes on Adult Books Popular with Young People,* 4th ed., comp. by Elinor Walker (Chicago: American Library Association, 1988).

Using Picture Storybooks to Teach Literary Devices: Recommended Books for Children and Young Adults, by Susan Hall (Phoenix, AZ: Oryx, 1990), 168p. ISBN 0-89774-582-5.
Over 270 simple but selected picture books illustrate thirty literary devices (e.g., inference, foreshadowing). Entries contain a brief summary, a description of how the primary literary device is used, and any secondary devices. Includes essays, bibliography. Index.

World History for Children and Young Adults: An Annotated Bibliographic Index, by Vandelia VanMeter (Englewood, CO: Libraries Unlimited, 1992), 266p. ISBN 0-87287-732-9.
Hundreds of fiction and nonfiction titles are arranged by time period; they are further subdivided by subject and indexed by grade level. Versions for Apple, Macinstosh, and IBM computers allow this bibliography to be printed and tailored to the user's library. **Related title:** *Reference Guide to Historical Fiction for Children and Young Adults,* by Lynda G. Adamson (Westport, CT: Greenwood, 1987).

Elementary Level

Adventuring with Books: A Booklist for Pre-K–Grade 6, 9th ed., ed. by Mary Jett-Simpson (Urbana, IL: National Council of Teachers of English, 1989), 550p. ISBN 0-8141-0078-3.
This booklist contains annotations for almost 1,800 children's books published between 1984 and 1988. The organization of this resource is designed to help teachers develop units. Each entry includes bibliographic information; interest age-range; annotation; ways the book connects with other areas of the curriculum; and book awards, if applicable.

A to Zoo: Subject Access to Children's Picture Books, 3d ed., by Carolyn W. Lima and John A. Lima (New Providence, NJ: Bowker, 1989), 939p. ISBN 0-8352-2599-2.
A to Zoo categorizes nearly 12,000 fiction and informational titles (preschool to second grade) under 700 subject headings. No summaries or evaluations are given. Includes "Genesis of the English-Language Picture Book," bibliography. Indexes: title, illustrator. **Related title:** *Wordless/Almost Wordless Picture Books: A Guide,* by Virginia H. Richey and Katharyn E. Puckett (Englewood, CO: Libraries Unlimited, 1992).

Alphabet Books as a Key to Language Patterns: An Annotated Action Bibliography, by Patricia Roberts (Hamden, CT: Shoe String Press, Library Professional Publications, 1987), 263p. ISBN 0-208-02151-5.

Approximately 500 titles are listed here. Each main entry is arranged by the language pattern featured in the book (e.g., word associations, names and occupations, alliteration). The annotations give a brief summary and often include response activity. Includes bibliography. Index: author/title.

Best Books for Children: Preschool through Grade 6, 4th ed., by John T. Gillespie and Corinne J. Naden (New Providence, NJ: Bowker, 1990), 1002p. ISBN 0-8352-2668-9.
Each of the more than 12,000 fiction and informational books have been recommended by at least two sources. Nonfiction titles are organized first by detailed subject headings, fiction by genre and author. Each entry contains a brief annotation; grade range; sequels; Dewey decimal number; and review citations. Appendices: "For Advanced Students," bibliography. Indexes: author, title, subject/grade.

Best in Children's Books: Guide to Children's Literature, 1985-1990, ed. by Zena Sutherland, Betsy Hearne, and Roger Sutton (Chicago: University of Chicago Press, 1991), 547p. ISBN 0-226-78064.
Over 1,110 information and fiction titles are listed alphabetically by author. Each numbered annotation was gleaned from the *Bulletin of the Center for Children's Books*, as well as from other review sources. Three other volumes in this series cover recommended books published since 1966. Indexes: title, developmental values, curricular use, reading level, subject, type of literature. **Related title:** *Picture Books for Children*, by Patricia J. Cianciolo (Chicago: American Library Association, 1990).

Beyond Picture Books: A Guide to First Readers, by Barbara Barstow and Judith Riggle (New Providence, NJ: Bowker, 1989), 336p. ISBN 0-8352-2515-1.
Over 1,600 titles qualify as first readers (e.g., containing large print, short sentences, limited number of words per page, with plenty of illustrations). These first- or second-grade reading level books are listed alphabetically by author. Each entry includes a brief summary, subject, series, and reading level. Includes outstanding first readers (200 titles). Indexes: subject, title, illustrator, readability, series.

Children's Literature from A to Z: A Guide for

Parents and Teachers, by Jon C. Stott (New York: McGraw-Hill, 1984), 318p. ISBN 0-07-061791-0.
Children's Literature from A to Z is a selective guide that includes short essays on major authors and illustrators; brief notes on a sampling of other authors and illustrators; essays on several popular folktales and heroic figures; and essays on major kinds of children's literature and Newbery and Caldecott winners. Includes "Tips for Parents and Teachers."

Counting Books Are More than Numbers: An Annotated Action Bibliography, by Patricia L. Roberts (Hamden, CT: Shoe String Press, Library Professional Publications, 1990), 270p. ISBN 0-208-02216-3.
Roberts believes that counting books aid in the development of basic problem-solving abilities. The 350 titles are arranged within four broad categories (e.g., collections of related items). Annotations range from 50–300 words and include suggested grade and interest levels, suggestions for use, and a mathematical feature. Includes essays; bibliography; "Selected Counting Books." Indexes: title, artist/author.

Kids' Favorite Books: Children's Choices 1989–1991 (Newark, DE: The Children's Book Council and International Reading Association, 1992), 96p. ISBN 0-87207-370-X.
This resource contains 300 titles selected by children and organized by categories, such as books for all ages, those for beginning independent readers, young readers, middle grade students, and those for older readers. Each entry includes bibliographic information and an annotation. Indexes: authors, illustrators, titles.

Literature-Based Social Studies: Children's Books and Activities to Enrich the K–5 Curriculum, by Mildred Knight and Patricia Payne Kardaleff (Phoenix, AZ: Oryx Press, 1991), 148p. ISBN 0-89774-605-8.
This resource discusses the use of children's literature in the social studies program and units that include trade book suggestions for each grade level. **Related titles:** *Peoples of the American West: Historical Perspectives through Children's Literature*, by Mary Hurlbut Cordier and María A. Pérez-Stable (Metuchen, NJ: The Scarecrow Press, 1989). *American History for Children and Young Adults: An Annotated Bibliographic Index*, by Vandelia VanMeter (Englewood, CO: Librar-

ies Unlimited, 1990). *Adventures with Social Studies (through Literature)* by Sharron L. McElmeel (Englewood, CO: Libraries Unlimited, 1991). *Social Studies through Children's Literature: An Integrated Approach,* by Anthony D. Fredericks (Englewood, CO: Teacher Ideas Press, 1991).

More Exciting, Funny, Scary, Short, Different and Sad Books Kids Like about Animals, Science, Sports, Families, Songs and Other Things, ed. by Frances Laverne Carroll and Mary Meacham (Chicago: American Library Association, 1992), 180p. ISBN 0-8389-05854.

This book could be used either by adults who work with children or by students as a personal reading guide. The 100 topic headings are of proven interest to children and include such loose groupings as: "I want a book about . . . islands . . . or a sad story. . . ." Short annotations are written in a popular style. Index: author/title. **Related title:** *Literature of Delight: A Critical Guide to Humorous Books for Children,* by Kimberly Olson Fakih (New Providence, NJ: Bowker, 1992).

The Oxford Dictionary of Nursery Rhymes, ed. by Iona Opie and Peter Opie (Clarendon Press, 1966), 467p. No ISBN.

This volume contains nursery rhymes, nonsense jingles, humorous songs, character rhymes, lullabies, riddles, and more, all arranged in alphabetical order. Indexes: first line; figures associated with the invention, diffusion, or illustration of nursery rhymes.

Read Any Good Math Lately? Children's Books for Mathematical Learning, K–6, by David J. Whitin and Sandra Wilde (Portsmouth, NH: Heinemann, 1992), 220p. ISBN 0-435-08334-1.

Read Any Good Math Lately? is a resource of children's books addressing mathematical concepts. **Related titles:** *Books You Can Count On: Linking Mathematics and Literature,* by Rachel Griffiths and Margaret Clyne (Portsmouth, NH: Heinemann, 1991). *Raps and Rhymes in Maths,* by Ann and Johnny Baker (Portsmouth, NH: Heinemann, 1991).

Science and Technology in Fact and Fiction: A Guide to Children's Books, by DayAnn M. Kennedy, Stella S. Spangler, Mary Ann Vanderwerf (New Providence, NJ: Bowker, 1990), 319p. ISBN 0-8352-2708-1.

This resource is divided into two major areas: science and technology. These are further

subdivided into fiction and nonfiction, and the titles are arranged alphabetically by author. Entries are usually a half page, with age and grade level, summary, and authoritative evaluation. Includes bibliography. Indexes: author, title, illustrator, subject, reading level.

Middle Level

Adolescent Female Portraits in the American Novel (see under *High School Level,* below).

Adventuring with Books: A Booklist for Pre–K– Grade 6 (see under *Elementary Level,* above).

Beacham's Guide to Literature for Young Adults, 6 vol., ed. by Kirk H. Beetz and Suzanne Niemeyer (Washington DC: Beacham, 1989), ISBN 0-933833-11-3.

This series examines in depth about 450 titles and includes information about the author, overview, setting, themes and characters, literary qualities, and a social sensitivity. Includes topics for discussion, ideas for reports, titles of adaptations, bibliography. Approximately five to nine pages are devoted to each alphabetically arranged book. Includes glossary, Newbery winners, thematic grouping (vol. 3–6). Index: vol. 3–6. **Related title:** *Masterplots II: Juvenile and Young Adult Fiction,* 4 vol., by Frank N. Magill (Englewood Cliffs, NJ: Salem, 1991).

Best Books for Junior High Readers, by John T. Gillespie (New Providence, NJ: Bowker, 1991), 567p. ISBN 0-8352-3020-1.

All of the 6,848 fiction and informational titles have been recommended by at least two sources. The books are organized under detailed subject headings for nonfiction, and genre for fiction, with entries arranged alphabetically by author. Each entry gives a brief annotation, grade range, sequels, if any, Dewey decimal number, and review citations. Includes for advanced students, bibliography. Indexes: author, title, subject, grade.

Best in Children's Books (see under *Elementary Level,* above).

Comics to Classics—A Parent's Guide to Books for Teens and Preteens, by Arthea J. S. Reed (Newark, DE: International Reading Association, 1988), 121p. ISBN 0-87207-798-5.

Comics to Classics includes a discussion of teens

and preteens; books for teens and preteens; sharing books; locating books; and an appendix. The characters in the book selections are between the ages of ten and twenty. The annotated bibliography lists books appropriate for readers from ages ten through eighteen and are divided into fiction and nonfiction titles. Information on whether males or females will prefer the books and are appropriate for low-level readers is included. Those books that are partcularly good for sharing aloud are also suggested. Includes Book Publishers.

Fiction Sequels for Readers 10 to 16: An Annotated Bibliography of Books in Succession, by Vicki Anderson (Jefferson, NC: McFarland, 1990). 150p. ISBN 0-89950-519-8.
More than 1,500 titles by 350 authors are listed alphabetically. Brief summaries and sequence in the series are provided. **Related titles:** *Sequences: An Annotated Guide to Children's Fiction in Series,* by Susan Roman (Chicago: American Library Association, 1985); *Mirrors of American Culture Children's Series in the Twentieth Century,* by Paul Deane (Metuchen, NJ: Scarecrow, 1991). *Happily Ever After: A Guide to Reading Interests in Romance Fiction* (see *High School,* below).

Happily Ever After: A Guide to Reading Interests (see under *High School,* below).

High Interest–Easy Reading: A Booklist for Junior and Senior High School Students, 6th ed., by William G. McBride (Urbana, IL: National Council of Teachers of English, 1990), 132p. ISBN 0-8141-2097-0.
This source presents an annotated bibliography of books for reluctant readers in junior high and high school. The books are arranged in categories, and indexed by author, title, and subject. Twenty-four categories of books are included from adventure to travel. This source is renewed on a regular basis. The entries are written for students. No grade level, reading level, or sophistication level is indicated; however, notes are included for those books containing mature subject matter. Includes directory of publishers. Indexes: author, title, and subject. **Related titles:** *Easy Reading: Book Series and Periodicals for Less Able Readers,* 2d ed., by Randall J. Ryder, Bonnie B. Graves, and Michael F. Graves (Newark, DE: International Reading Association, 1989). *The Best: High/Low Books for Reluctant Readers,* by Marianne Laino Pilla (Englewood, CO: Libraries Unlimited, 1990).

High/Low Handbook: Encouraging Literacy in the 1990s, 3d ed., ed. by Ellen V. Libretto (New Providence, NJ: Bowker, 1990), 264p. ISBN 0-8352-2804-5.
A distinction is made between the disabled teenage reader (scoring at a fourth grade reading level or below) and the reluctant reader (scoring above fourth grade but lacking motivation). This edition lists 412 books, arranged alphabetically by author. Critical annotations and reading and interest levels are given. Includes essays, list of publishers, bibliography. Indexes: title, subject.

Nonfiction for Young Adults: From Delight to Wisdom. Betty Carter and Richard F. Abrahamson (Phoenix, AZ: Oryx, 1990), 233p. ISBN 0-89774-555-8.
Nonfiction is examined from many angles: popularity, uses, and evaluation techniques. This neglected genre takes its place squarely in the forefront of teenage reading interests. Includes interviews with six authors, bibliographies. Index.

Teaching Multicultural Literature in Grades K–8 (see under *Elementary Level,* above).

Young Adult Reader's Advisor (New Providence, NJ: Bowker, 1992), 1312p. ISBN 0-8352-3068-6.
Modeled on the adult version from the same publisher, this two-volume set could be used for browsing or research. The main arrangement is by broad discipline areas, divided into sections and subsections so that the reader is led from the general to the specific. Over 850 noteworthy people are profiled, with general reading lists and books included. Includes list of publishers. Indexes: profiles in both volumes, author, title. **Related title:** *Olderr's Young Adult Fiction Index for 1990,* by Steven Olderr and Candace Smith (Chicago: St. James Press, 1990).

Your Reading: A Booklist for Junior High and Middle School School Students, 7th ed., by James E. Davis and Hazel K. Davis (Urbana, IL: National Council of Teachers of English, 1988), 494p. ISBN 0-8141-5939-7.
Nearly 2,000 books recommended for junior high and middle school students are arranged categori-cally. **Related titles:** *Books for the Junior High Years,* ed. by James E. Davis and Hazel K. Davis (Urbana, IL: National Council of Teachers of English, 1989). *Kliatt Young Adult Paperback Book Guide* (journal).

High School Level

Adolescent Female Portraits in the American Novel 1961–1981, by Jane S. Bakerman and Mary Jean DeMarr (New York: Garland, 1983), 254p. ISBN 0-8240-9136-1.
This bibliography focuses on 580 novels whose significant female characters are striving to establish their identity within the adult world. Entries are listed alphabetically by the 477 authors. A checklist also categorizes books under fourteen group images such as friends, heroes, rebellious daughters, and victims. Suggested grade levels are not given. Adult novels are included. Short annotations describe the plot, theme, and significance of the adolescent female. Indexes: title, subject.

America as Story: Historical Fiction for Secondary Schools, by Elizabeth F. Howard (Chicago: American Library Association, 1988), 126p. ISBN 0-8389-0492.
America as Story lists 154 titles under seven broad chronological, topical categories. A short summary introducing the plot precedes a commentary on historical place and accuracy. Ideas for reports and activities are aimed towards middle-level and high school readers. Index: author/title.

Beacham's Guide to Literature for Young Adults (see under *Middle Level,* above).

Best Books for Senior High Readers, by John T. Gillespie (New Providence, NJ: Bowker, 1991), 931p. ISBN 0-8352-3021-X.
This newest addition to the *Best Books* series lists over 10,800 books. Short annotations indicate if the book is for advanced readers (intellectually challenging), or for mature readers (using explicit adult situations). Indexes: author, title, subject, grade.

Books for You: A Booklist for Senior High Students, ed. by Richard F. Abrahamson and Betty Carter (Urbana, IL: National Council of Teachers of English, 1988), 507p. ISBN 0-8141-0364-2.
Nearly 1,200 books appropriate for teenage readers are grouped in forty-eight alphabetically arranged categories. **Related titles:** *Book Bait: Detailed Notes on Adult Books Popular with Young People,* 4th ed., ed. by Eleanor Walker (Chicago: American Library Association, 1988). *Books for the Teen Age* (New York: New York Public Library).

Careers in Fact and Fiction: A Selective List of Books for Career Backgrounds, by June Klein Bienstock, and Ruth Bienstock Anolik (Chicago: American Library Association, 1985), 178p. ISBN 0-8389-0424-6.
Divided by main career types (e.g., business and industry, education, law). this bibliography is geared toward students who wish to develop their values and interests in occupations. Includes appendix for teaching a unit on careers. Index: author, title.

Feminist Resources for Schools and Colleges: A Guide to Curricular Materials, 3d ed., ed. by Anne Chapman (New York: The Feminist Press at the City University of New York, 1986), 190p. ISBN 0-935312-35-8.
This resource is divided into two sections: print and audiovisual materials. Each of the 445 entries are grouped under subject areas that encompass major disciplines. Annotations of one quarter to half-page include both descriptive and evaluative comments. Includes directory of publishers and distributors. Indexes: author/title, subject.

Happily Ever After: A Guide to Reading Interests in Romance, by Kristin Ramsdell (Englewood, CO: Libraries Unlimited, 1987), 203p. ISBN 0-87287-479-6.
Useful for the reading advisor attempting to elevate standards of this popular genre, this bibliography includes works by Jane Austin, Joan Aiken, and other famous authors. Also included are definitions, historical perspective, descriptions, and annotations grouped by subgenres.

High Interest—Easy Reading—A Booklist for Junior and Senior High School Students (see under *Middle Level,* above).

High/Low Handbook (see above under *Middle Level*).

Nonfiction for Young Adults: From Delight to Wisdom (see under *Middle Level,* above).

Science and Technology in Fact and Fiction: A Guide to Young Adult Books, by DayAnn M. Kennedy, Stella S. Spangler, and Mary Ann Vanderwerf (New Providence, NJ: Bowker 1990), 363p. ISBN 0-8352-2710-3.
Science and technology form the two major sections of this resource; each part is divided into fiction or nonfiction, and the titles are arranged

alphabetically by author. Entries are usually a half page and contain age and grade levels, a summary, authoritative evaluation. Indexes: author, title, illustrator, subject, readability.

Supernatural Fiction for Teens: More than 1300 Good Paperbacks to Read for Wonderment, Fear and Fun, 2d ed., by Cosette Kies (Englewood, CO: Libraries Unlimited, 1992), 200p. ISBN 0-87287-940-2.
This bibliography includes subgenres such as parapsychology, psychic phenomena, tales and legends, occult, and traditional and modern horror. Each entry describes the book and includes series and/or sequel information and other works by the same author. **Related title:** *Genreflecting: A Guide to Reading Interests in Genre Fiction,* by Betty Rosenberg and Diana Tixler Herald (Englewood, CO: Libraries Unlimited, 1991).

Whole Language Strategies for Secondary Students (see under *Professional Resources,* above).

Young Adult Reader's Advisor (see under *Middle Level,* above).

CURRICULUM MATERIAL PRODUCERS

THIS chapter provides information on publishers and producers of English/language arts curriculum materials, textbooks, supplementary materials, software, and other items. For some of the larger publishers, we have provided a listing of English/ language arts series and book titles. For other companies, we provide a description of products. Much of the information in this chapter is based on the publishers' catalogues; for more details, you should contact the publishers and producers directly. The addresses and phone numbers given are for the offices that will supply catalogues and other promotion material; note that these phone numbers are not for the editorial offices.

Academic Therapy Publications
20 Commercial Boulevard
Novato, CA 94949-6191
1-800-422-7249

Grades pre-K–12. Tests, supplementary curriculum materials, parent/teacher resources, remediation programs

Active Learning Corporation
P.O. Box 254
New Paltz, NY 12561
914-255-0844

The Active Reader for Writers
High school. Textbook, reading model booklets, answer key

Essays/Letters/Reports
High school. Student handbook

Writing Guides, 2E
Junior high/high school (remedial). Student

edition, student management forms, instructor's manual

Writing Paragraphs
Grade 6/junior high (remedial). Softcover text

Addison-Wesley Publishing Company
Jacob Way
Reading, MA 01867
1-800-447-2226

Happily Ever After (series)
Pre-K–grade 1. Complete literature-based early reading program. Big books classics package, teacher's guide, supplementary materials including English and Spanish audio cassette packages

Now Presenting: Classic Tales for Readers Theatre (series)
Elementary grades. Teacher's resource book, poster set

Story Chest (series)
Grades 1–3. Folktale storybooks, teacher's guides, audio cassettes

Superkids (series)
Grade K–1. Multilevel reading program. Student reader, teacher's resource kit, supplementary materials including audio cassettes

Teaching Language, Literature, and Culture (series)
Grades K–2. Multicultural early childhood program. Books, program binder, audio cassettes, posters

Ten Best Ideas for Reading Teachers

Advantage Learning Systems, Inc.
210 Market Avenue
P.O. Box 95
Port Edwards, WI 54469-0095
800-338-4204

The Accelerated Reader
Grades 3–12. Software for Apple/IBM, Core book list, teacher's manual, supplementary materials

Agency for Instructional Technology (AIT)
Box A
Bloomington, IN 47402-0120
800-457-4509

Grades K–12. Video cassette series, interactive videodisc/instructional software (Apple/Macintosh), teacher's guides. For communication skills, literature, library skills

AGS
Publishers' Building
Circle Pines, MN 55014-1796
1-800-328-2560

Grades K-12. Diagnostic tests, supplementary programs including software for language, speech and auditory development, reading

The American Association of School Administrators
1801 North Moore Street
Arlington, VA 22209-9988
703-875-0730

Guidelines for the teaching of reading and writing

American Education Publishing
3790 East Fifth Avenue
Columbus, OH 43219
800-542-7833

Distributes materials from Creative Education, The Child's World, Listening Library, and Milliken. Books, cassettes, posters

American Language Academy
Suite 550
1401 Rockville Pike, MD 20852
1-800-346-3469

Skills levels: beginning through advanced, ESL and EFL students. Software for Apple/IBM, teacher's handbooks, interactive sound/graphic programs. For grammar, reading, vocabulary

American School Publishers
SRA School Group
P.O. Box 5380
Chicago, IL 60680-5380
1-800-843-8855

Grades 1–12. Supplementary programs in whole language, reading, content area reading, test preparation, composition, grammar, writing (see also under SRA School group)

American Teaching Aids
4424 West 78th Street
Bloomington, MN 55435
800-526-9907

Grades pre-K-6. Resource books, badges, borders, calendars/accessories, charts, "Drill-It" workbooks, game pieces, incentive charts, interactive posters, stickers, teacher resources

Amsco School Publications, Inc.
315 Hudson Street
New York, NY 10013-1085
212-675-7000

Grammar

Drill for Skill

English Alive
Workbook

English Language Arts
Textbook, workbook

English Made Easier

English, Plain and Simple

Essentials of English
Textbook, workbook

Laugh Your Way through Grammar: Blue, Yellow, Green
Textbook, teacher's manual, test book

Composition

Achieving Competence in Reading and Writing

Amsco Writing English Series
Includes "Composition: Prewriting, Response, Revision," "Paragraph Power," "Sense of Sentences," "Writing English: Foundations"

Building Power in Reading and Writing

Building Power in Writing

A Common-Sense Approach to Composition

Fifteen Steps to Better Writing
Workbook, teacher's manual, tests

Paragraph Play

Sentence Play

Thirteen Steps to Better Writing

Vocabulary and Composition through Pleasurable Reading

Writing about Amusing Things

Writing about Curious Things

Writing about Fascinating Things

Writing about People

Writing Creatively

Writing Logically

Writing Practically

Reading and Literature

Action Stories of Yesterday and Today

Aiming High: Stirring Tales and Poems

All about the Dictionary

Americans of Dreams and Deeds
Reading skills workbook

Amsco Literature Program
Novels, reader's guides, teacher's editions

Amsco Literature Series

Building Power in Reading

Building Power in Reading and Writing

High Marks: Stories that Make Good Reading

Introducing the Short Story

More Powerful Reading

Myths and Folklore

The Newspaper and You
Reading skills workbook

Poems: American Themes

The Reader as Detective

Reading and Growing

Reading around the World
Textbook, workbook, teacher's manual, unit tests

Reading Comprehension...Lessons and Tests

Reading Skills

Reading Today

RSVP: With Etymology
Workbook

Short Stories

Skillbook in Reading

Springboards (A College Reader)

Stories from Four Corners

Stories Here and Now

Stories that Live

Stories to Teach and Delight

Tales from World Epics

Vocabulary

Adventures with Words

Instant Word Power

101 Ways to Learn Vocabulary

The Joy of Vocabulary

Reading, Spelling, Vocabulary, Pronunciation (RSVP)

Three Dimensions of Vocabulary Growth

Vocabulary for the College-Bound Student

Vocabulary for Enjoyment

Vocabulary for the High School Student

Vocabulary through Pleasurable Reading

Vocabulary and Composition through Pleasurable Reading

Wide World of Games

Word Games

Word Play

Barnell-Loft
SRA School Group
P.O. Box 5380
Chicago, IL 60680-5380
1-800-843-8855

Grades pre-K–8. Supplementary programs for comprehension, phonics, specific skills, multiple skills, reading, spelling (see also under SRA School Group)

Beacon Films
(Altschul Group Corporation)
930 Pitner Avenue
Evanston, IL 60202
800-323-5448

Videocassettes and films for language arts/ English, including "The Kids of DeGrassi Street Series," "The Ray Bradbury Series," "Storybook International Series," "The Beacon Short Story Collection," "Shakespeare from Page to Stage"

Bantam Doubleday Dell, Education and Library Division
666 Fifth Avenue
New York, NY 10103
800-223-6834

Grades 7-12. Bantam Classics editions including "The Bantam Shakespeare"

Barron's Educational Series, Inc.
P.O. Box 8040, 250 Wireless Boulevard
Hauppauge, NY 11788
800-645-3476

Children's books for all ages. Study guides for English/language arts and literature

BGR Publishing
4520 North 12th Street
Phoenix, AZ 85014
800-892-BOOK

Grades pre-K-6. Books and materials with emphasis on whole language and multiculturalism

BLS Tutorsystems
Woodmill Corporate Center
5153 West Woodmill Drive
Wilmington, DE 19808
1-800-545-7766

Grades 3–12. Software for Apple/IBM, student manuals, teacher's guides, supplementary materials. In career English, reading, grammar, spelling

Book-Lab
P.O. Box 7316
500 74th Street
North Bergen, NJ 07047
1-800-654-4081

Instructional materials for language-delayed learners. Readers, spelling workbooks, and teacher's guides

Branden
17 Station Street, Box 843
Brookline Village, MA 02147
617-734-2045

Classics, fiction, general nonfiction, microcomputer software, women's studies, and biographies

Brown Roa Publishing Media
P.O. Box 539
Dubuque, IA 52001
1-800-338-5578

Grades 7–12. English curriculum units, lesson plans, student handouts, tests. Series include literature, world literature, mythology, advanced-placement English, poetry, writing, creative

writing, basic and advanced composition, research, speech, thinking, reading and writing,
junior high language arts, fiction-nonfiction,
drama, short story, Shakespeare

Charlesbridge Publishing
85 Main Street
Watertown, MA 02172
800-225-3214
617-926-0329

Alphabet Books (series)
Grades K–6

Charlesbridge Reading Skills Units (series)
Grades 3–8. Student workbooks

Dictionary Skills
Grades 3–8. Student books, answer guides

Insights: Comprehension (series)
Grades K–8. Reading-comprehension program.
Student workbooks and teacher's resources

Insights: Reading as Thinking (series)
Grades K–8. Reading strategies program. Student
workbooks

Lessons in Library Skills
Grades 3–8. Student books, answer guide

Networks (series)
Grades K–3. Whole-language reading program.
Teacher's planning guides, anthologies, big books,
small books, activity books, action packs, puppets

Sparks for Learning
Special needs. Grades K–8. Teacher's resource
book

Strategies for Independent Reading (series)
Grades 4–6. Student books, teacher's manuals

Strategies for Language Expansion (series)
Grades 1–3. Teacher's manual, blackline masters

Time and Space Adventure Series
Remedial. Grades 5–8. Student books, teacher's
guides

Understanding Language
Grades 3–8. Student books, teacher's manual,
teacher's resource book

Writing and Thinking (series)
Grades 1–6. Student books, teacher's manuals,
Spanish blackline masters, transparencies

Writing and Thinking: Secondary (series)
Grades 7–12. Process writing program. Student
books and teacher's manuals

Young Discovery Library (series)
Grades 3–6

Chelsea Curriculum Publications
School Division, Dept. CUR
P.O. Box 5186
Yeadon, PA 19050-0686

Grades 4–12. Biographical and mythological
literature collections with teacher's guides,
literary criticism collections

Chariot Software Group
3659 India Street, Suite 100C
San Diego, CA 92103
800-800-4540

Grades K-12. Macintosh educational software for
english/language arts, including English grammar
computer, grammar tutorials, linkword, pronunciation tutors, reading maze, "Sounds of English,"
"Spell It Plus"

Clark Publishing, Inc.
P.O. Box 4875
Topeka, KS 66604
913-271-8668

Junior high/high school. Softcover texts include
"38 Basic Speech Experiences," "Mastering
Competitive Debate," "Basic Drama Projects,"
"Writing and Editing School News"

Communicad, The Communications Academy
Box 541
Wilton, CT 06897
800-762-7464

Grades 4-12. Multimedia vocabulary and study-
skills program

Communication Skill Builders
3830 E. Bellevue
P.O. Box 42050
Tucson, AZ 85733
800-866-4446

Grades K–12. Culturally and linguistically diverse materials for speech and language therapy. curriculum guides, teacher's manuals, assessment forms, activity books and kits, audio and video cassettes, computer software

Compu-Teach
78 Olive Street
New Haven, CT 06511
800-448-3224

Grades pre-K–6. Software for IBM/Macintosh/Apple. In reading, story composition, writing

CONDUIT
The University of Iowa
Oakdale Campus
Iowa City, IA 52242
1-800-365-9774

Writer's Helper
Software for Windows /Macintosh/Apple/IBM-DOS. Prewriting and revising software includes teacher's manual, student edition, instructional video cassette

SEEN: Tutorials for Critical Reading
Software for Apple/IBM. Includes teacher's manual

Continental Press
520 East Bainbridge Street
Elizabethtown, PA 17022
800-233-0759

Grades K–12. Activity units, manipulative sets, skills series, literature-based reading, software, teacher's resource books, phonics programs, Spanish resources

Cottonwood Press
305 W. Magnolia, Suite 398
Fort Collins, CO 80521
303-493-1286

Grades 5–12. Activity books, resource books, books, posters

Creative Publications
5040 West 11th Street
Oak Lawn, IL 60453
800-624-0822

Teacher's resource books. Grades pre-K–6. Series titles include: "Themeworks," "Language Through Literature," "Early Childhood Language," "Language Arts and Problem-Solving," "Storytelling and Writing"

Creative Teaching Press
P.O. Box 6017
Cypress, CA 0630-0017
1-800-444-4CTP

Grades K–8. Resource guides, activity books, overhead transparencies, big book kits, shape book kits

Critical Thinking Press & Software
Midwest Publications
P.O. Box 448
Pacific Grove, CA 93950
800-458-4849

Grades K–12. Remedial—average—gifted—at risk. Activity books, resource books, software, tests

Curriculum Associates, Inc.
5 Esquire Road
North Billerica, MA 01862-2589
800-225-0248
508-667-8000

Grades 2–adult ed. Handbooks, workbooks, teacher's guides, software in spelling, writing, language development, reading

Dandy Lion Publications
3563 Sueldo
San Luis Obispo, CA 93401
1-800-776-8032

Literature, reading, poetry, and language workbooks, guides, and activity books

Davidson & Associates, Inc.
P.O. Box 2961
Torrance, CA 90509
800-545-7677

Pre-K–adult. Software for Apple/Macintosh/IBM/Tandy/Commodore, interactive (audio) programs, teacher materials. In grammar, spelling, journalism, reading

Delmar Publishers, Inc.
2 Computer Drive West
P.O. Box 15015
Albany, NY 12212-5015
800-347-7707

Early Childhood. "Growing Up with Literature, "Early Childhood Experiences in Language Arts: Emerging Literacy"

Didax, Inc.
One Centennial Drive
Peabody, MA 01960
1-800-458-0024

Preschool, elementary, special needs. Speech and language educational activities, reading-readiness materials, clearview materials, literature topical sets/whole language, ladybird books, games

Diskovery Educational Systems
1860 Old Okeechobee Road, Suite 105
West Palm Beach, FL 33409
800-331-5489

Grades pre-K–12. Software for Apple/IBM/Macintosh/CD-ROM

DLM
P.O. Box 4000
One DLM Park
Allen, TX 75002
800-527-4747

Grades K–12. Alternative instructional materials for early childhood, reading, writing, grammar, spelling, language development, speech, remedial/basic skills

Econo-Clad Books
P.O. Box 1777
Topeka, KS 66601
1-800-255-3502

Grades pre-K–12. Literature-based and whole-language teaching materials. Literature collections, teacher's guides, teacher's resource packages, video cassettes

ECS Learning Systems, Inc.
P.O. Box 791437
San Antonio, TX 78279-1437
1-800-68-TEACH

Grades pre-K–12. Whole language learning materials, language arts/English supplementary materials, writing programs, reading resources, novels units, teacher's resources, software

EDL
P.O. Box 210726
Columbia, SC 29221
1-800-227-1606

Reading levels 1–13 (remedial). Vocabulary, reading comprehension, fluency, and writing programs. Student books, teacher's guides and supplementary materials including audio and video cassettes, and software

Educational Activities, Inc.
P.O. Box 392
Freeport, NY 11520
1-800-645-3739

Grades K–adult. Software for Apple/Macintosh/MS-DOS, voice- interactive programs, support materials. In English, basics, vocabulary, spelling, writing

Entry Publishing, Inc.
P.O. Box 20277
New York, NY 10025
1-800-736-1405

Reading-disabled grades 5–adult. Teacher's guides, workbooks, novels, software, audio and video cassettes, bilingual materials

Everbind Books
Marco Book Company
P.O. Box 331
Bayonne, NJ 07002-0331
800-842-4234

Junior high/high school. Collections of drama, prose and poetry, young adult literature, biography and autobiography, ethnic studies, myths and legends, teacher's guides, reference materials

Facts On File, Inc.
460 Park Avenue South
New York, NY 10016-7382
800-322-8755

Reference materials in language arts and literature, including bibliographies and dictionaries

Fearon/Janus/Quercus
500 Harbor Boulevard
Belmont, CA 94002
800-877-4283

Special education/remedial programs. Language arts/reading softcover texts, curriculum guides, study guides, novels, audio cassettes, workbooks, magazines

Focus Media, Inc.
839 Stewart Avenue
P.O. Box 865
Garden City, NY 11530
800-645-8989

Grades pre-K–12. Software for Apple/MS-DOS/ Macintosh/Commodore, support materials. In reading, writing, vocabulary, spelling

Franklin Learning Resources
122 Burrs Road
Mt. Holly, NJ 08060
800-525-9673

Hand-held electronic learning products. Spelling, dictionary companion, language master, wordmaster and encyclopedia series. Also Franklin curriculum series and secondary whole-language writing-language arts program

Gamco Industries, Inc.
P.O. Box 1862N1
Big Spring, TX 79721-1911
800-351-1404

Grades K–12. Software for Apple/MS-DOS/ Macintosh, support materials. In phonics, spelling, vocabulary, reading comprehension, writing, grammar

Glencoe/Macmillan/McGraw-Hill
P.O. Box 543
Blacklick, OH 43004-0543
1-800-334-7344

English

The Art of Writing: A Modern Rhetoric
Softcover text, instructor's manual

Business Communications
Textbook, teacher's guide, activities book

The CORT Thinking Program
Textbook, student workcards, teacher's notes

Effective Speech
Textbook, teacher's edition, teacher's resource binder, audio and video cassettes

English Skills Series
Student editions, teacher's Editions. Includes "Sentence Mechanics," "Usage," "Editing and Proofreading," "Writing about Literature"

Glencoe English (series)
Grades 7–8. Textbooks, teacher's editions, teacher's resource book, supplementary materials

Glencoe English (series)
Grades 9–12. Textbooks, teacher's editions, teacher's resource book, supplementary materials including software

Introduction to Literature-Based Composition
Textbook, teacher's manual

The Laidlaw English Series
Grades 9–12. "Composition and Grammar," textbooks, teacher's editions, supplementary materials

Literature-Based Composition
Student's edition, teacher's manual

Macmillan English: Thinking and Writing Processes (series)
Grades 9–12. Textbooks, teacher's editions, teacher's resource book, supplementary materials including software

McGraw-Hill Handbook of English
Grades 9–12. Textbook, teacher's manual and key

PWR: Macmillan Literature Composition Software
Grades 7–12. Software, user manual, teaching notes

PWR: Macmillan English Composition Software
Grades 9–12. Software, user manual, teaching notes

Word Clues
Student Edition, teacher's manual with tests

Drama

Reading Drama: An Anthology of Plays
Textbook, teacher's guide

The Stage and the School
Textbook, teacher's manual, scenes and monologues

Literature

The American Tradition in Literature
Textbook

The Contemporary Shakespeare Series
Texts, teacher's guides. Includes "Hamlet," "Romeo and Juliet," "Julius Caesar," "Macbeth"

Literature Reading: Fiction, Poetry, Drama, and the Essay
Textbook, instructor's manual

Macmillan Literary Heritage (series)
Grades 7–12. Textbooks, teacher's editions. Includes "Literature to Remember," "Literature to Enjoy," "Currents in Literature," "Designs in Literature," "The American Experience," "The English Tradition"

Macmillan Literature Series, Signature Edition, 1991
Grades 6–12. Textbooks, teacher's editions, teacher's classroom resources, supplementary materials including audio and video cassette, and software. Includes "Discovering Literature," "Introducing Literature," "Enjoying Literature," "Understanding Literature," "Appreciating Literature," "World Literature," "American Literature," "English Literature with World Masterpieces"

McGraw-Hill Literature Series, New Treasury Edition
Grades 7–12. Textbooks, teacher's classroom resources, supplementary materials. Includes "Focus," "Perception," "Insights," "Encounters," "American Literature," "English Literature," "British and Western Literature"

Reading Fiction: An Anthology of Short Stories
Student edition, teacher's guide

Reading Poetry: An Anthology of Poems
Student edition, teacher's guide

Scribner Literature Series, Signature Edition, 1989
Grades 7–12. Textbooks, teacher's editions, teacher's classroom resources, supplementary materials including audio and video cassettes, and software. Includes "Introducing Literature," "Enjoying Literature," "Understanding Literature," "Appreciating Literature," "American Literature," "English Literature with World Masterpieces"

The Supernatural in Fiction
Textbook

Globe Book Company
Simon and Schuster
4350 Equity Drive
P.O. Box 2649
Columbus, Ohio 43216
1-800-848-9500

The African-American Literature Collection
Softcover texts, activity sheets

Be a Better Reader (series)
Grades 4–12. Softcover texts, teacher's editions, teacher's guides

Communication Skills Resources
Reading Levels 4–6. Softcover texts, teacher's manuals. Includes "Grammar and Composition for Everyday English," "Reading Road to Writing," "Newspaper Workshop," "Unlocking Test Taking"

Experiencing Poetry
Softcover text, teacher's manual

Foundations for Learning: Language (series)
Softcover texts, teacher's manuals, literature guides, supplementary readings, assessment kit

Globe Anthology Series
Reading levels 5–9. Texts, student workbooks, teacher's manuals with tests

Globe African American Biographies
Softcover text, teacher's manual

Globe Biographies (series)
Softcover texts, teacher's manuals. Includes "Globe Hispanic Biographies," "Globe World Biographies," "Globe American Biographies"

Globe Literature (series)
Grades 7–12. Textbooks, teacher's editions, teacher's resource books, supplementary materials including workbooks for limited English-proficient students

The Globe Reader's Collection (series)
Reading Levels 3–8. Softcover texts, teacher's manuals

Globe Reading Comprehension Program (series)
Reading levels 4–7. Softcover texts, teacher's editions

Globe Writing Program
Grades 6–12. Softcover texts, teacher's editions

Globe's Adapted Classics (series)
Reading levels 3–8. 17 Softcover texts, teacher's manuals

Life Skills Resources
Softcover texts, teacher's manuals. Includes "Forms in Your Future," and "Writing for Life"

Reading Improvement Resources
Reading Levels 3–7. Softcover texts, teacher's manuals. Includes "A Better Reading Workshop," "The Real Stories Series," "Open-Ended Plays and Open-Ended Stories"

The Shakespeare Classics (series)
Softcover texts, teacher's manuals

Spell It Out
Reading Levels 4–7. Softcover text, teacher's manual

The World of Vocabulary (series)
Reading Levels 2–8. Softcover texts, teacher's manuals

Graphic Learning
61 Mattatuck Heights Road
Waterbury, CT 06705
1-800-874-0029

Grades K–12. Integrated language arts/social studies programs. Student desk maps, activity pages, teacher's guides, workbooks, supplementary materials. Integrates geography, history, economics, politics, sociocultural concepts, map and globe skills, language/study skills, thinking skills

Hammond Education Catalog
515 Valley Street
Maplewood, New Jersey 07040
1-800-526-4935

Grades K–12. Reading skills series. Classroom packs, softcover texts, teacher's answer key

Harlan Davidson, Inc.
3110 North Arlington Heights Road
Arlington Heights, IL 60004-1592
312-253-9720

The Crofts Classics series contains classic works in English, American, and world literature; Goldentree bibliographies in language and literature

Harcourt Brace Jovanovich, Inc.
School Department
6277 Sea Harbor Drive
Orlando, FL 32821-9989
1-800-CALL-HBJ

Early Childhood

Bill Martin Big Books
Big books, audio cassettes, teacher's guides

Bright Start
Pre-K. Themepacks include lap book and class library books, read-at-home books (available in Spanish), supplementary materials; teacherpacks; teacher's resource video; parent partners program

The HBJ Kindergarten Literature Collection (series)
Grade K. Lap book, class library books, audio cassette

Handwriting

HBJ Handwriting (series)
Student editions, teacher's editions, teacher's resource materials, supplementary materials

Reading/Language

Basic Drills in English Skills I–IV
Grades 3–6. Workbooks, answer keys

Focus on Writing (series)
Grades 3–8. Workbooks

HBJ Language (series)
Grades K–8. Textbooks, teacher's editions, teacher's resource banks, supplementary materials include home activities (Spanish), audio cassettes, software

Imagination (series)
Grades K–6. Textbooks, teacher's editions, teacher's resource banks, supplementary materials including audio cassettes, software, video workshop

Impressions (series)
K–6. Readers, student anthologies, teacher resource books, supplementary materials including audio cassettes

Reading/Literature

Discoveries in Reading (series)
Middle school/junior high (remedial). Textbooks, teacher's editions, supplementary materials including audio cassettes

HBJ Lectura (series)
Grades K–5. Spanish reading program. Textbooks, teacher's editions, supplementary materials

HBJ Reading Program (series)
Grades K–8. Textbooks, teacher's editions, teacher's resource banks, supplementary materials including audio and video cassettes, software

HRW Reading: Reading Today and Tomorrow (series)

Grades K–8. Textbooks, teacher's editions, teacher's resource materials, supplementary materials including audio cassettes, software

Spelling

HBJ Spelling (series)
Levels 1–8. Student editions (consumable), teacher's editions, teacher's resource books, supplementary materials include audio cassettes, software

D. C. Heath and Company
School Division
125 Spring Street
Lexington, MA 02173
1-800-235-3565

Better Spelling: Fourteen Steps to Spelling Improvement
High school (advanced placement). Softcover text

Building Vocabulary for College
High school (advanced placement). Softcover text, teacher's guide

Correct Writing
High school (advanced placement). Softcover text, teacher's edition

The Essay Connection
High school (advanced placement). Softcover text, instructor's guide

Explore-a-Story (series)
Grades K–5. Storybooks, software, activity books

The Heath Anthology of American Literature
High school. Softcover texts, instructor's guide

Heath English (series)
Grades 9–12. Textbooks, teacher's editions, teacher's resource packages, workbooks, transparencies

Heath Grammar and Composition with a Process Approach to Writing
Grades 6–8. Student editions, teacher's editions, teacher's resource binders, supplementary materials

The Heath Guide to Writing a Research Paper
High school (advanced placement). Student edition

Heath Introduction to Drama
High school (advanced placement). Softcover text

Heath Introduction to Fiction
High school (advanced placement). Softcover text

The Heath Introduction to Literature
High school (advanced placement). Softcover text, instructor's guide

Heath Introduction to Poetry
High school (advanced placement). Softcover text

The Heath Reader
High school (advanced placement). Softcover text, instructor's guide

Heath Reading (series)
Grades K–8. Textbooks, teacher's edition packages, teacher's resource materials, supplementary materials including audio cassettes, video cassettes, literature collections, software, Spanish resources

The Humanities: Cultural Roots and Continuities
Advanced. Softcover texts, instructor's guide, test item file

Language Enrichment Program: A Companion to Heath Reading (series)
Levels R–6. Student studytext, teacher's edition

Paragraphs and Themes
High school (advanced placement). Softcover text, instructor's guide

The Reading Edge: Thirteen Ways to Build Reading Comprehension
High school (advanced placement). Softcover text, instructor's guide

Working Words in Spelling (series)
Grades 6–8. Student editions, teacher's editions, software, activity booklets

Heinemann Boynton/Cook
361 Hanover Street
Portsmouth, NH 03801-3959
1-800-541-2086

Teacher's resource books for reading, writing, literature, whole language, poetry, drama

Hoffman Educational Systems
1863 Business Center Drive
Duarte, CA 91010
1-800-472-2625

Laser Learning Barcode Application
Videodiscs, user's guides, laserdisc player, barcode reader. Videodisc reading program, process writing program

Holt, Rinehart, and Winston
6277 Sea Harbor Drive
Orlando, FL 32821-9989
800-225-5425

Literature

Adventures in Literature (series)
Grades 7–12. Textbook, teacher's resource package, supplementary materials including test-generator software

African-American Literature
High school. Textbook, teacher's manual, tests

Eight Classic American Novels
High school (advanced placement). Text

Elements of Literature (series)
Grades 7–12. Textbooks, teacher's edition, supplementary materials including audio cassettes, test generator software, video series

Emerging Voices: A Cross-Cultural Reader
High school (advanced placement). Text, instructor's manual

HBJ Shakespeare Series
High school. Student edition, teacher's guide, posters

Heritage of American Literature
High school (advanced placement). Softcover texts, instructor's manuals

Impact: Fifty Short Short Stories
High school. Student edition, teacher's manual

Introduction to Literature
Grade 6. Textbook, teacher's edition, teacher's resource binder, supplementary materials including audio cassettes, test generator software

Journeys: A Reading and Literature Program (series)
High school. Textbook, teacher's manual, tests

Literature: Reading, Reacting, Writing
High school (advanced placement). Text, instructor's manual

Literature: Structure, Sound and Sense
High school (advanced placement). Text, instructor's manual

Literature: Uses of the Imagination
High school. Textbooks, teacher's manuals.
Includes "Man the Myth-Maker," "A World
Enclosed: Tragedy"

Mexican American Literature
High school. Textbook, teacher's manual

Perspectives in Literature (series)
High school. Textbooks, teacher's manuals. Books
on drama, nonfiction, poetry, short stories

Shakespeare in Performance: Hamlet
High school. Student edition, teacher's manual

Short Essays
High school (advanced placement). Softcover
text, instructor's manual

Short Stories: Characters in Conflict
High school. Student edition, teacher's manual

Sound and Sense: An Introduction to Poetry
High school (advanced placement). Text

Story and Structure
High school (advanced placement). Text,
instructor's manual

Strategies in Reading (series)
High school. Textbook, teacher's edition

To Read Literature
High school (advanced placement). Softcover
text, instructor's manual

To Read a Poem
High school (advanced placement). Softcover
text, instructor's manual

World Literature
High school. Textbook, teacher's edition,
teacher's resource binder, supplementary materials including audiovisual resources, test generator
software

The World of Fiction
High school (advanced placement). Softcover
text, companion handbook

Composition

Composition: Models and Exercises
Grades 7–12. Student edition, teacher's manual

Elements of Writing (series)
Grades 6–12. Student editions, teacher's editions,
teacher's resouce bank, supplementary materials
including test generator software

English Workshop
Grades 6–12. Student edition, mastery tests,
teacher's answer key

From Sight to Insight: Stages in the Writing Process
High school (advanced placement). Text,
instructor's manual

Harbrace College Handbook
High school (advanced placement). Text,
instructor's manual, supplementary materials
including test generator software

The Holt Handbook
High school (advanced placement). Text, research
sourcebook, supplementary materials including
software

Practical Writer
High school (advanced placement). Softcover text

Practical Writer with Readings
High school (advanced placement). Softcover text

*Steps to Writing Well: A Concise Guide to Compo-
sition*
High school (advanced placement). Softcover
text, instructor's manual

*Visions across the Americas: Multicultural Prose
Models*
High school (advanced placement). Softcover
text, instructor's manual

Vocabulary Workshop
Grades 6–12. Student edition, test booklet,
teacher's answer key

*We Are America: A Cross-Cultural Reader and
Guide*
High school (advanced placement). Softcover
text, instructor's manual

Writing Research Papers across the Curriculum
High school (advanced placement). Softcover
text, instructor's manual

Warriner's High School Handbook
Student edition, teacher's manual

Language Arts Supplementary Programs

Acting Is Believing: A Basic Method
High school (advanced placement). Text

English 2200, 2600, and 3200
High school. Student edition, teacher's manual

HRW Handy Guides
High school (advanced placement). Includes
"Writing the Research Report," "Developing
Your Vocabulary," "Improving Spelling Skills"

Learning How to Learn
High school. Student edition, teacher's manual

Looking Out/Looking In
High school (advanced placement). Text, instructor's manual, supplementary materials including test bank software, video cassettes

Reporting for the Print Media
High school (advanced placement). Text, instructor's manual

The Speaker's Handbook
High school (advanced placement). Text, instructor's manual

Speech for Effective Communication
Textbook, teacher's resource package, supplementary materials including audio and video cassettes

Understanding Human Communication
High school (advanced placement). Softcover text, instructor's manual, supplementary materials with test bank software, video cassettes

Vocabulary for College
High school. Student edition, teacher's manual, tests

Vocabulary Workshop
Grades 6–12. Student edition, test booklet, teacher's answer key

Houghton Mifflin
Department J
One Beacon Street
Boston, MA 02108-9971
1-800-323-5663

English

Computer Software
Grades K–8. Including "FirstWriter," "The Grolier Writer," "Language Activities Courseware: Grammar and Study Skills," "Microcourse Language Arts," "Computer Activities for the Writing Process"

Houghton Mifflin English Levels K–8 (series)
Grades K–8. Textbooks, teacher's editions, teacher's resources, student workbooks, supplementary materials including audio cassettes, limited English proficiency activity masters

Troubleshooter I and II (series)
Grades 7–8. Student workbooks, teacher's editions. Topics include spelling, puncutation, vocabulary, reading

Reading/Literature

Houghton Mifflin Reading (series)
Grades K–8. Student readers, teacher's guides, teacher's resource file, supplementary materials

Houghton Mifflin Reading/Language Arts Program (series)
Grades K–8. Literary readers, teacher's guides, supplementary materials

Houghton Mifflin Reading: The Literature Experience (series)
Grades K–8. Student anthologies, theme books, read along books, teacher's editions, teacher's resource materials, supplementary materials including audio cassettes

Houghton Mifflin Transition
Grades K–8. Limited English-proficient student program. Student readers, workbooks, teacher's guides

New Directions in Reading (series)
Grades 4–12. High interst/low level reading program. Student readers, teacher's guides, teacher's resource book, supplementary materials

Programa de lectura en español de Houghton Mifflin
Grades K–6. Literature-based reading program in Spanish. Spanish trade books, teacher's guides, student workbooks, supplementary materials

Reading Resources
Grades K–8. Literature collections, book and audio cassette programs, children's books and story plans, trade-author video cassettes, reading software

Vocabulary

Houghton Mifflin Spelling and Vocabulary (series)
Grades 1–8. Student books, teacher's editions, teacher's resource books, supplementary materials

Houghton Mifflin Vocabulary for Achievement (series)
Grades 6–8. Student editions, teacher's editions, teacher's resource masters

Humanities Software, Inc.
408 Columbia Street, Suite 222
P.O. Box 950
Hood River, OR 97031
1-800-245-6737

Grades K–12. Software for IBM/Tandy/Apple/
Macintosh, support materials. In writing, reading,
whole language

Hunter & Joyce Publishing Company
Federal Hill No. 1
R.D. 2, Box 54
Delhi, NY 13753
800-462-7483

The Hunter Writing System: Sentence Sense (series)
Grades 7 and above. Textbooks, skills practice
books, teacher's guides, supplementary materials

IBM Direct
PC Software Department 829
One Culver Road
Dayton, NJ 08810
1-800-222-7257

Pre-K–adult. Software for IBM, Support materials, multimedia materials including CD-ROM,
videodisks, video cassettes. In reading comprehension, writing, spelling, grammar, vocabulary.
Spanish program

I/CT—Instructional/Communications Technology, Inc.
10 Stepar Place
Huntington Station, NY 11746
516-549-3000

Grades K–adult. Software for Apple/MS-DOS
and support materials, filmstrips, books, activity
books, audio cassettes. For oral language development, visual efficiency, perceptual accuracy
and efficiency, word recognition, decoding and
spelling, vocabulary development, reading,
comprehension skills, expressive skills, computer
awareness

Intellimation
Library for the Macintosh
Department 2SCK
P.O. Box 219
Santa Barbara, CA 93116-9954
1-800-346-8355

Grades K–12. Software for Macintosh, multimedia programs. In writing, grammar, spelling,
literature

Interact
Box 997-H92
Lakeside, CA 92040
1-800-359-0961

Grades K–12. Simulation programs. Student
guides, teacher's guides, supplementary materials
including software. Topics include american
literature, world literature, humanities, reading
and editing skills, genealogy, poetry, media
studies/mythology, public speaking, writing

International Society for Technology in Education
1787 Agate Street
Eugene, OR 97403-1923
503-346-4414

Journals, books, courseware, teacher's guides to
meet the needs of educators integrating computer
technology in the classroom

IRI/Skylight Publishing, Inc.
200 East Wood Street, Suite 274
Palatine, IL 60067
800-348-4474

Grades K–12. Teacher's resource books, handbooks, video cassettes

Jamestown Publishers
P.O. Box 9168
Providence, RI 02940
1-800-USA-READ

Grades K–12. Anthologies, big books (English
and Spanish), readers, skills series, literature
programs, comprehension programs, classic
author kits, reading the content fields kits

Jostens Learning Corporation

7878 North 16th Street
Suite 100
Phoenix, AZ 85020-4402
1-800-422-4339

Pre-K–12. Software for Apple/IBM/Tandy. In language development (available in Spanish), reading, writing

Judy/Instructo

4424 West 78th Street
Bloomington, MN 55435
800-832-5228

Grades pre-K-2. Educational materials for English/language arts, including desk tapes, sorting boxes, picture cards, puzzles, alphabet wall charts

K-12 MicroMedia Publishing

6 Arrow Road
Ramsey, NJ 07446
201-825-8888

Grades 2–12. Software for Apple/Macintosh/IBM/Tandy. For writing, literature

Kendall/Hunt Publishing Company

2460 Kerper Boulevard
P.O. Box 539
Dubuque, IA 52004-0539
1-800-258-5622

Active Composing and Thinking II
Grade 7. Student book, writer's notebook, teacher's guide

Active Composing and Thinking III
Grade 8. Student book, writer's notebook, teacher's guide

Content Reading Including Study Systems (CRISS)
Softcover text. Includes two-day teacher in-service

Kendall/Hunt Spelling: Improving Spelling Performance (series)
Grades 1–6, Softcover texts, teacher's guides

Kendall/Hunt Spelling: Learning to Spell
Special-needs students, grades 3–adult. Softcover texts

Kendall/Hunt Spelling: Spelling the Written Word (series)
Grades 7–10. Softcover texts, administrator guides

Pegasus: Integrating Themes in Literature and Language (series)
Grades (K–6). Student anthologies, books, writer's resource books, teacher's implementation guides, teacher's resource books, supplementary materials including audio cassettes

Project Write! (series)
Student materials packages, teacher tool kits

Thomas S. Klise Company

Old Chelsea Station
P.O. Box 1877
New York, NY 10113-0950
1-880-937-0092

Grades 6–12. Audio and video cassettes, film-strips, records, posters, teacher's guides. In English, world and American literature, language and writing, grammar, fiction, poetry, drama, mythology and fantasy

Knowledge Unlimited, Inc.

Box 52
Madison, WI 53701-0052
1-800-356-2303

Teacher's guides, filmstrips, audio cassettes for poetry, journalism, composition; posters; video cassettes of literature classics

H.P. Kopplemann, Inc.

Paperback Book Service
P.O. Box 145
Hartford, CT 06141-0145
1-800-243-7724

Grades K–12. Multi-cultural, literature-based and whole-language materials, software, video cassettes, reading collections, teacher's guides, filmstrips, literature tests

Krell Software

Flowerfield Building #7
Saint James, NY 11780-1502

Software for standardized-test preparation

Lakeshore Learning Materials

2695 E. Dominguez Street
P.O. Box 6261
Carson, CA 90749
800-421-5354

Lakeshore Lifeskills (series)
Junior high/high school. Skill-building materials for reading, writing, grammar, spelling. Textbooks, workbooks, activity books, teacher's guides, software

Laureate Learning Systems, Inc.

110 East Spring Street
Winooski, VT 05404-1837
1-800-562-6801

Talking software for special needs, compatible with Apple/IBM/Tandy. For language development, concept development and processing, reading and advanced cognitive skills

Learning Links, Inc.

2300 Marcus Avenue
New Hyde Park, NY 11042
516-437-9071

Grades K–12. Literature-based study guides, individual books, whole-language sets, reading books for social studies and science, thematic units, read alouds, Spanish language books for young readers

LEGO Dacta

555 Taylor Road
Enfield, CT 06082
P.O. Box 1600
1-800-527-8339

Grades pre-K–2. Manipulatives, curriculum support materials. Scope and sequence includes cognitive development; transportation; animals

and the environment; homes, family, and neighborhoods; problem solving and whole language; themes and project work
Grades 3–12. Technic sets for simple machines through technic control sets for robotics, physics, and artifical intelligence

Longman Publishing Group

10 Bank Street
White Plains, NY 10606
1-800-447-2226

Grades 4–12. Student texts, teacher's guides, workbooks in grammar, writing, vocabulary, reading, poetry, mythology, drama, literature

Loyola University Press

3441 North Ashland Avenue
Chicago, IL 60657
1-800-621-1008

Exercises in English (series)
Grades 3–8. Grammar workbooks, teacher's editions

Voyages in English (series)
Grades 1–8. Text-workbooks, teacher's guides, test booklets

Writing Step-by-Step
Grades 3–8. Text-workbooks, teacher's edition

Macmillan/McGraw-Hill

School Division
220 East Danieldale Road
De Soto, Texas 75115-9990
1-800-442-9685

Reading

Connections (series)
Grades K–8. Thematic-literature units, teacher's editions, student workbooks, supplementary materials including in-service videotapes, software

Early Childhood Programs
Complete reading and language programs with supplementary materials. Includes "Big Books," "Once upon a Time," "Beginning to Read, Write and Listen," "Superstart"

McGraw-Hill Reading (series)
Grades K–8. Textbooks, teacher's editions, teacher's resource centers, student workbooks, supplementary materials

Reading Express (series)
Grades K–8. Textbooks, teacher's editions, teacher's resource centers, supplementary materials including software

Supplementary Materials
Grades K–8. Classroom libraries, literature collections, teacher's guides

Spanish Reading

Campanitas de Oro (series)
Grades R–6. Complete Spanish basal reading program. Textbooks, teacher's editions, teacher's resource packages, supplementary materials

Por el Mundo del Cuentro y la Aventura (series)
grades r–6. Spanish basal-reading series. Textbooks, teacher's guides, workbooks

Language Arts

Language Arts Today (series)
Grades K–8. Integrated language arts program. Textbooks, teacher's editions, teacher's resource packages, supplementary materials, software

McGraw-Hill English (series)
Grades K–8. Textbooks, teacher's editions, teacher's resource packages, supplementary materials including software

McGraw-Hill Spelling (series)
Grades 1–8. Softcover texts, teacher's editions, teacher's resource packages, supplementary materials including software

Merrill Spelling
Grades K–8. Textbooks, teacher's editions, teacher's resource package, supplementary materials including software

Palmer Method Handwriting (series)
Grades K–8. Softcover texts, teacher's editions, teacher's resource package

The MASTER Teacher
Leadership Lane
P.O. Box 1207
Manhattan, KS 66502
1-800-669-9633

Grades pre-K–5. Video cassette series, software

McDonald Publishing Company
10667 Midwest Industrial Bouevard
St. Louis, MO 63132
1-800-722-8080

Grades 4–9. Teaching poster sets, activity sheets, teacher's guides, reproducible and duplicating books for reading, writing, spelling, vocabulary

McDougal, Littell & Company
P.O. Box 8000
St. Charles, IL 60174
1-800-225-3809

Composition/Grammar

Basic Skills in English (series)
Grade 7–12. Textbooks, teacher's editions, teacher's resource binders, supplementary materials

Building English Skills (series)
Grades 9–12. Textbooks, teacher's editions, teacher's resource binders, supplementary materials

Grammar and Usage
Grades 9–12. Textbook, teacher's edition, vocabulary development workbook

McDougal, Littell English (series)
Grades 9–12. Textbooks, teacher's editions, teacher's resource files, software

Thinking and Writing (series)
Grades 9–12. Textbooks, teacher's editions, vocabulary development workbook

Writing: Process to Product
Grades 9–12. Softcover text, special workshops booklet, teacher's manual

English and Literature

Contemporary Short Stories

Grades 9–12. Textbooks, teacher's guides

Literature and Language (series)
Grades 9–12. Textbooks, teacher's editions, teacher's resource file, student workbooks, supplementary materials including software

Multicultural Perspectives

Grades 9–12. Textbooks, teacher's guides

Responding to Literature (series)
Grades 9–12. Textbooks, teacher's guides

Study Guides for Novels (series)
Grades 7–12. Study guide packs

The Writer's Craft (series)
Grades 9–12. Textbooks, teacher's editions, teacher's resource file, supplementary materials including software

Literature

McDougal, Littell Literature (series)
Grades 7–12. Textbooks, teacher's editions, teacher's resource files, study guides for novels

Reading Literature (series)
Grades 9–12. Textbooks, teacher's manuals, teacher's resource binders, student workbooks, supplementary materials

Middle School Materials

Language Handbook for Student Writers (series)
Grades 6–8. Softcover texts, teacher's editions

McDougal, Littell English (series)
Grades 6–8. Textbooks, teacher's editions, teacher's resource files, student workbooks, supplementary materials including software

McDougal, Littell Handwriting (series)
Grades 6–8. Textbooks, teacher's editions, teacher's resource binder, supplementary materials

McDougal, Littell Spelling (series)
Grades 6–8. Textbooks, teacher's editions, teacher's resource binders, supplementary materials including software

Vistas in Reading Literature (series)
Grades 5–8. Textbooks, teacher's editions, teacher's resource binders, student workbooks, supplementary materials

The Young Writer's Handbook
Grades 5–8. Softcover edition

Vocabulary

Daily Analogies (series)
Grades 1–8. Teacher's manuals or overhead transparency packages with answer keys

Daily Analogies and Antonyms
Grades 9–12. Teacher's manual

Vocabulary Development Workbooks (series)
Grades 6–12. Student Workbooks, teacher's editions

Wordskills (series)

Grades 6–12. Textbooks, teacher's editions, tests (blackline)

MECC
6160 Summit Drive North
Minneapolis, MN 55430-4003
800-685-MECC

Grades Pre-K–adult. Software for Macintosh/Apple/MS-DOS, multimedia materials. In reading, spelling, grammar, composition

Merrill
SRA School Group
P.O. Box 5380
Chicago, IL 60680-5380
800-621-0476

Grades K–12. supplementary programs in reading, phonics, grammar, composition, vocabulary. (See also under SRA School Group for supplementary programs; see under Glencoe/Macmillan/McGraw-Hill for grades 6–12 texts; see under Macmillan McGraw-Hill for grades K–8 texts)

Micrograms Publishing
1404 North Main Street
Rockford, IL 61103
1-800-338-4726

Grades K–6. Software for Apple. In reading, punctuation, capitalization, grammar, spelling

The Millbrook Press, Inc.
2 Old New Milford Road-Box 335
Brookfield, CT 06804
800-462-4703

Grades K-2, 4, and 8. Reading materials, including biographies and autobiographies

Milliken Publishing Company
1100 Research Boulevard
P.O. Box 21579
St. Louis, MO 63132-0579
1-800-643-0008

Pre-K–8. Books, posters, teacher's resource guides, duplicating masters, blackline reproducibles, workbooks, filmstrips, video cassettes, whole-language resource guides

Modern Curriculum Press
13900 Prospect Road
Cleveland, OH 44136
1-800-321-3106

Whole Language

Concept Science (series)
Grades K–3. Available in Spanish. Student books, big books, teacher's guides. Special teacher's guides for ESL/LEP students. Set themes include "Matter," "Energy," "The Universe," "Animals," "Plants," "Our Earth"

The Content Connection
Grades K–6. Read-a-loud books, student editions, audio cassettes. Trade books grouped by theme

Folklore: A Multi-Cultural Treasury
Grades 1–8. Student anthologies, teacher's guides, activity cards

Folklore: On Stage
Grades 1–8. Dramatic adaptations of folk tales. Student scripts, director's handbook

Language Works: Developing Language
Grades pre-K–1. Available in Spanish. Integrated program. Student books, teacher's reference book

Language Works: Exploring Our World
Grades K–4. Integration of science and social studies. Student books, teacher's reference book

Language Works: Folktales
Grades K–3. Integrated program. Student books, teacher's book

Language Works: Stories and Rhymes
Grades K–4. Integrated program. Student books, teacher's reference book

Literary Life Lines (series)
Grades 4–8. Student books, teacher's idea books. Author sets include Irene Hunt, Eleanor Heady, Milton Meltzer, Carol Ann Bales, Countee Cullen, Sydney Taylor, Arna Bontemps

MCP Literature (series)
Grades 1–6. Student anthologies, teacher's guides, workbooks

Poetry Works
Grades pre-K–3. Posters, teacher's idea book, audio cassette

Poetry Works! Second Stanza
Grades 3–6. Posters, teacher's idea book, audio cassette

Swinging Out Language Development Program
Grade pre-K–1. Big books, books, mini-books, teacher's sourcebooks, supplementary materials

Reading Friends (series)
Grades K–3. Language acquisition. Story packs, organizer binders, puppet friends

What Do You Think? (series)
Grades K–2. Skills integration. Big books, student books, teacher's idea books, supplementary materials

The Writing Program (series)
Grades 1–9. Softcover texts, teacher's guides, writing folders

Writing Skills (series)
Grades 2–6. Softcover texts. Includes "Writing Sentences, Paragraphs and Composition," "Mastering Writing Skills for Editing and Test-Taking," "Mastering Capitalization," "Mastering Punctuation," "Mastering Usage"

Yes, I Can! (series)
Grades pre-K–2. Available in Spanish. Language acquisition. Big books, student books, teacher's guides

Young Explorers (series)
Grades K–4. Student books, big books, teaching companions, supplementary materials. Series themes include social studies, mathematics, science

Phonics

Discovery Phonics: An Integrated Approach to Decoding Stategies (series)
Grades K–2. Big books, small books, audio cassettes, teacher's resources

Literature First: Phonics with a Purpose (series)
Grades K–3. Softcover texts, teacher's guides, posters

MCP Phonics Program (series)
Grades 1–6. Student workbooks, teacher's edition, supplementary materials

MCP Phonics Riddles
Grades 1–3. Big books, student books, workbooks, teacher's guides

MCP Spelling Program (series)
Grades 1–8. Student editions, teacher's edition

Mortimer Moose Turns the Alphabet Loose (series)
Grades pre-K–6. Student books, teacher's handbook, supplementary materials including audio cassettes, puppets

Phonics Practice Readers (series)
Grades 1–3. Student readers, teacher's guides, skillmasters

Phonics Workbook Series
Grades K–4. Student workbooks, teacher's guides. Series titles include "Phonics First, " "Phonics Is Fun," "Phonics Plus," "Phonics Works," "Schoolhouse Phonics," "Starting off with Phonics"

Reading/Thinking Skills

Classroom Reading
Grades 1–3. Books, teacher's guides. Series include "Beginning-to-Read Library," "Just Beginning-To-Read Collection," "Sharing and Caring Collection," "The Fantasy Collection," "The Science and Technology Collection," "The Social Awareness Collection," "The Dragons and Dinosaurs Collection," "Star Series Readers," "The High Action Treasure Chest," "The Books of Myths," "MCP Endangered Species Readers"

Workbooks
Grades 1–8. Student workbooks, teacher's guides. Series include "Keystones for Reading," "Vocabulary Works," "Reading in the Content Areas," "Stepping into Reading: A Guide to Critical Thinking," "Thinking about Reading," "High Action Reading," "Comprehension Plus," "My Kindergraph," "Skill-By-Skill Workbooks," "Skill Stations"

Modern Educational Resource Guide
5000 Park Street North
St. Petersburg, FL 33709
800-243-6877

K-12. Free loan programs, free teaching materials, media for the classroom, videos for inservice training, computer and network-based programs, interactive learning systems, and filmstrips

National Council of Teachers of English
1111 Kenyon Road
Urbana, IL 61801
217-328-3870

Grades K–college. Booklists, guidebooks, teacher's resource books, staff development materials, audio cassettes, video cassettes

National Resource Center for Middle Grades Education
University of South Florida
College of Education-EDU-118
Tampa, Florida 33620-5650
813-974-2530

Curriculum guides, resource books, reproducible interdisciplinary units, activity books. For reading, writing, thinking skills, self-concept, study skills

National Textbook Company
4255 West Touhy Avenue
Lincolnwood, IL 60646-1975
1-800-323-4900

Literature/Writing

An Anthology for Young Writers
High school (advanced placement). Textbook, teacher's guide

The Art of Composition
High school (advanced placement). Textbook, teacher's guide

Creative Writing: Forms and Techniques
High school. Textbook, teacher's manual

The Detective Story
High school. Softcover text, teacher's guide

Handbook for Proofreading
High school. Handbook

How to Write Term Papers and Reports
Softcover Text

Literature by Doing: Responding to Poetry, Essays, Drama and Short Stories
High school. Textbook, teacher's manual

Lively Writing: The Process of Creative Communication
Junior high/high school. Textbook, teacher's manual

Look, Think and Write
High school. Softcover text, teacher's guide

Mythology and You
Softcover text, teacher's guide

Poetry by Doing
High school. Textbook, teacher's manual

Publishing the Literary Magazine
High school. Softcover text, teacher's manual

The Short Story and You: An Introduction to Understanding and Appreciation
Junior high/high school. Textbook, teacher's guide

Snap, Crackle and Write
Junior high/high school. Textbook

Sports in Literature
Junior high/high school. Textbook, teacher's manual

Welcome to Ancient Rome/Welcome to Ancient Greece
High school. Softcover texts

World Literature: An Anthology of Great Short Stories, Drama, and Poetry
High school. Textbook, teacher's manual

World Mythology
High school. Textbook, teacher's manual

Write to the Point
High school. Textbook, teacher's manual

The Writer's Handbook: A Guide to the Essentials of Good Writing
High school. Handbook

Writing by Doing: Learning to Write Effectively
Textbook, teacher's manual

Writing in Action
High school (advanced placement). Textbook, teacher's guide

You and Science Fiction
High school. Softcover text, teacher's guide

Media Communication/Theatre

The Book of Cuttings for Acting abd Directing
High school. Softcover text, teacher's guide

The Book of Scenes for Acting Practice
High school. Softcover text, teacher's guide

The Dynamics of Acting
High school. Textbook, teacher's guide

Fundamentals of Copy and Layout
High school. Softcover text

Getting Started in Journalism
Junior high/senior high. Softcover text, teacher's guide

Getting Started in Mass media
High school. Softcover text, teacher's manual

A Guide to TV Production
High school. Textbook, teacher's resource book

An Introduction to Modern One-Act Plays
High school. Softcover text, teacher's guide

An Introduction to Theatre and Drama
High school. Softcover text

Journalism Today!
High school. Textbook, teacher's manual, workbook

The Mass Media Workbook
High school. Student workbook, teacher's guide

Photography in Focus
High school. Textbook, teacher's manual

Play Production Today!
High school. Textbook, teacher's guide

Resources for Theatre Arts
Softcover texts on stagecraft, acting, directing

Understanding Mass Media
High school. Textbook, teacher's manual

Understanding the Film: An Introduction to Film Appreciation
High school. Softcover text, teacher's manual

Skills Reinforcement

Softcover Texts for Reading, Vocabulary, Study Skills, Life Skills, Basic English Skills

Speech Communication/Debate

Activities for Effective Communication
High school. Workbooks, teacher's guide, audio cassettes

Advanced Debate
High school. Textbook

Basic Debate
Junior high/high school. Textbook, teacher's guide

The Basics of Speech
Junior high/high school. Textbook, workbook, teacher's guide, teacher's resource book

Business Communication Today!
High school. Textbook, teacher's resource book

Contemporary Speech
Textbook, teacher's guide

Creative Speaking
High school. Textbook, individual booklets

Dynamics of Speech
High school. Textbook, teacher's resource book

Getting Started in Debate
Junior high/high school. Textbook, teacher's manual

Getting Started in Public Speaking
Junior high/high school. Textbook, teacher's guide

Handbook for Business Writing
High school. Handbook

Literature Alive!
Textbook, teacher's guide

Moving from Policy to Value Debate (A CEDA Handbook)
High school. Softcover texts

Person to Person
High school. Textbook, workbook, teacher's resource book including Audio Cassettes

Public Speaking Today!
High school. Textbook, teacher's resource book

Resources for Debate Teams
Resource handbooks, special events resources, flow chart pads, award certificates

Self-Awarenss: Communicating with Yourself and Others
Junior high/high school. Textbook, teacher's guide

Speaking by Doing
Junior high/high school. Textbook, teacher's resource book

Strategic Debate
High school. Textbook, teacher's guide

Successful Business Series
High school. Softcover texts

New Dimensions in Education
61 Mattatuck Heights Road
Waterbury, CT 06705
800-227-9120

Grades pre-K–3. Language immersion and reading readiness programs. Student readers, teacher's editions, supplementary materials including audio and video cassettes

New Readers Press
Department 72
P.O. Box 888
Syracuse, NY 13210
800-448-8878

Challenger (series)
High school (remedial). Integrated program of reading, writing, and reasoning skills. Work-texts, teacher's guides, supplementary materials

Newsweek Education Program
The Newsweek Building
P.O. Box 414
Livingston, NJ 07039
800-526-2595

Newsweek education program for English. Includes cross-curriculum guide and free teacher's resources

Novel Units
P.O. Box 1461, Dept. C
Palatine, IL 60078
708-253-8200

Grades K-12. Support materials for the study of literature. Also integrated whole- language approach, including literature units, vocabulary, and writing materials

Open Court Publishing Company
315 Fifth Street
Peru, IL 61354
1-800-435-6850

The Headway Program (series)
Grades K–6. Readers, teacher's editions, workbooks, supplementary materials

Magazines
Grades K–6. Includes "Ladybug Classroom Library," "Cricket Classroom Library"

Open Court Reading and Writing (series)
Grades K–6. Student workbooks, teacher's guides, teacher's resource books, supplementary materials

Special Purpose Programs and Materials
Includes "Gifted and Talented Language Arts: The RISE Program," "Reading Comprehension: Catching On," "Remedial Reading: Breaking the Code," "Skills Recovery Program: The Reading Connection"

Supplemental Reading Kits
Grades K–6. Books grouped by grade and interest level

Orange Cherry/ Talking Schoolhouse Software

P.O. Box 390, Dept. S
Pound Ridge, NY 10576-0390
1-800-672-6002

Grades pre-K–8. Software for Apple/Macintosh/ IBM/Tandy, support materials, multimedia programs. For phonics, reading, vocabulary, grammar, spelling

Peguis Publishers

520 Hargrave Street
Winnipeg Manitoba
Canada R3A OX8
1-800-667-9673

Grades K–7. McCracken, whole language, and native literature programs; teacher's resource books, readers, classroom literature

Peal Software, Inc.

P.O. Box 8188
Calabasas, CA 91372
800-541-1318

Grade pre-K. Software for early acquisition of language

The Peoples Publishing Group, Inc.

P.O. Box 70
365 W. Passaic Street
Rochelle Park, NJ 07662
1-800-822-1080

Students-at-risk. Series in practical writing, survival reading, contemporary fiction

Perfection Learning

1000 North Second Avenue
Logan, IA 51546-1099
1-800-831-4190

Grades pre-K–12. Classic, contemporary, and multicultural literature, workbooks, posters, teacher's guides, tests, video cassettes, software

Phoenix Learning Resources

468 Park Avenue South
New York, NY 10016
1-800-221-1274

Grades K–12. Programmed reading series, whole-language series, language skills text-workbooks, teacher's guides

Players Press, Inc.

P.O. Box 1132
Studio City, CA 91614
818-784-8918

Play anthologies, activity books, teacher's guides. For drama, clowning and mime, costume reference, make-up, technical theatre, writing

Prentice Hall

School Division of Simon & Schuster
Englewood Cliffs, NJ 07632-9940
1-800-848-9500

Elective/Advanced Placement

Key to a Powerful Vocabulary, Levels I and II
Grades 9–10. Softcover texts, instructor's manuals

Prentice Hall Handbook for Writers
Grades 11–12. Textbook, student workbook, diagnostic tests, exercise bank

The Prentice Hall Reader
Grades 10–12. Textbook, teacher's resource guide

Programmed College Vocabulary 3600
Grades 10–12. Softcover text, instructor's manual

Public Speaking: An Audience-Centered Approach
Grades 10–12. Textbook, instructor's resource manual, test item file

Simon and Schuster Handbook for Writers
Grades 10–12. Textbook, student workbook, diagnostic tests

Writing Clear Essays
Grades 10–12. Softcover text, teacher's manual

Writing Skills for Technical Students
Grades 10–12. Softcover text, teacher manuals with tests

Grammar/Composition

Developing Writing Skills
Grades 9–12. Textbook, teacher's guide

Models for Clear Writing
Grades 10–12. Softcover text, teacher's manual

Prentice Hall Grammar and Composition (series)
Grades 6–12. Textbooks, teacher's editions, teacher's resource book, supplementary materials including test bank software

Steps in Composition
Grades 9–12. Softcover text, teacher's edition, teacher's resource book

Thinking and Writing about Literature
Grades 10–12. Textbook, teacher's guide

Writing Clear Paragraphs
Grades 9–12. Softcover text, teacher's manual

Writing Model Transparencies (series)
Grades 6–12. Transparencies, teacher's guide

Writing the 500-Word Theme
Grades 9–12. Textbook, teacher's guide, workbook, supplementary materials

Writing Themes about Literature
Grades 10–12. Softcover text

Journalism

Journalism
Grades 9–12. Textbook, teacher's resource book

Press Time
Grades 9–12. Textbook, teacher's guide, practice books

Literature

Fiction: An Introduction to Reading and Writing
Grades 10–12. Softcover text

Literature: An Introduction to Reading and Writing

Grades 10–12. Textbook, teacher's manual

Literature Classroom Resources
Transparencies, computer test bank, study guides, great works library, video classics, audio cassettes, cross-curriculum ancillaries

Myths and Their Meaning
Grades 7–12. Textbook, teacher's guide

Prentice Hall Literature (series)
Grades 6–12. Textbooks, teacher's editions, teaching portfolio, supplementary materials including test bank software and audio cassettes

Speech

Communication: An Introduction to Speech
Grades 7–9. Textbook, teacher's resource book

Speech: Exploring Communication
Grades 9–12. Textbook, teacher's resource book

Queue, Inc.
338 Commerce Drive
Fairfield, CT 06430
800-232-2224

Grades K–12. Software for Apple/IBM/Macintosh, support materials, multimedia materials. In creative writing, reading comprehension, writing skills, life skills, grammar, vocabulary, spelling

The Right Combination
Cornerstone Division
6025 Sandy Springs Circle
Atlanta, GA 30328
1-800-458-3219

Workbooks, blackline masters, teacher's guides for standardized test preparation

Sadlier-Oxford
11 Park Place
New York, NY 10007
1-800-221-5175

Building an Enriched Vocabulary
Grades 11–12. Textbook, teacher's edition, testing program

Composition Workshop (series)
Grades 6–11. Softcover texts, teacher's guides

Spelling Skill (series)
Grades 1–8. Softcover texts, teacher's editions, spelling masters

Vocabulary Workshop Series
Grades 6–12. Softcover texts, teacher's guides, supplementary materials

Scholastic, Inc.
2931 East McCarty Street
P.O. Box 7502
Jefferson City, MO 65102-9968
800-325-6149

Elementary Language Arts/Reading

Basal Breaks: Applying Reading Strategies (series)
Grades 1–6. Grade units including paperback titles, teacher's guides

Big Books Collections
Grades K–3. Predictables, classic and contemporary favorites, content area, and emergent reader collections with supplementary materials

Book Center: A Whole-Language Program from Scholastic (series)
Grades 2–6. Literature units, student resource cards, teacher's resource book, supplementary materials including audio cassettes

Bookshelf (series)
Grades K–2. Whole-language libraries, teacher's resource books, audio packages

Bridges: Moving from the Basal into Literature (series)
Grades 1–6. Whole-class books, small group books, buddy books, read alouds books, teacher's guides, supplementary materials including readalong cassettes

Doing Research and Writing Reports (series)
Grades 4–6. Student workbooks, teacher's editions

Innovations: Experiencing Literature in the Classroom
Grades K–9. Teaching guides for paperback literature

The International Stewed Rhubarb Show
Grade 4–6. Actor's script and supplementary materials

Language Arts Phonics (series)
Grades 1–3. Student workbooks, teacher's editions, software

Perform! (series)
Grades 1–6. Whole-class books, theatre workshop playbooks, teaching guide, supplementary materials including audio cassettes

Phonics (series)
Grades 1–3. Student workbooks, teacher's editions

Reading Comprehension Series
Grades 3–6. Student workbooks, teacher's editions, includes "Reading for Information," "Critical Reading," "Read and Think"

Reading Explorers (series)
Grades 4–6. Interactive reading program. Software, activity sheets, lesson plans, supplementary materials

Resource Materials
Filmstrips, magazines, activity packages, literature collections

Scholastic Banners: Teaching with Themes (series)
Grades K–2. Big books, little books, read-a-loud books, audio cassettes, song charts, teaching theme folders

Scholastic Bookline (series)
Grades K–6. Science and social studies libraries with supplementary materials

Scholastic Listening Skills (series)
Grades 1–6. Short story audio cassettes, worksheets, teaching guide

Scholastic primeros libros de lectura
Grades K–2. Spanish beginning reading collection. Big books, books, audiocassettes, activity cards, teaching guides

Scholastic SuperPrint (series)
Grades K–12. Classroom publishing software, graphics activity packs, teacher's editions

Special Reading Collections
Grades K–9. Series include "Literature Links," "Reluctant Reader Collections," "Read By Reading Collection," "Celebrated Books," "Pleasure Reading," "Sprint Libraries," "Text Extenders," "Multi-Cultural Paperbacks"

Sprint Reading Skills Program (series)
Grades 4–6. Developmental reading program. Skills books, story books, play books, teaching guides, supplementary materials

Vocabulary Skills (series)
Grades 1–6. Student workbooks, teacher's editions

Writer's Workshop
Grades 1–6. Student workbooks, teacher's editions

Secondary Language Arts/Reading

Action 2000 (series)
Grades 7–12. Reading program for hard-to-reach students. Student anthologies, teacher's resource binders. Includes "Jobs in Your Future," "Friends and Families," "Making Decisions"

How to Read Literature (series)
Grades 7–12. Student workbooks, teacher's editions

Improve Your Grades (series)
Grades 6–12. Student work-texts, teacher's editions

Project Achievement: Reading
Grades 5–12 . Developmental reading program. Softcover texts, teacher's resource manuals, supplementary materials

Scholastic Literature Anthologies (series)
Grades 7–12. Softcover anthologies, teacher's resource manuals with print masters

Scholastic Literature Units (series)
Grades 7–12. Scholastic literature anthologies, teacher's resource books, classroom libraries units

Scholastic Literature Units for Cooperative Learning (series)
Grades 7–12. Literature anthologies, paperbacks, teachers resource books

Scholastic Scope Literature (series)
Grades 6–12. Textbooks, teacher's editions, teacher's resource packages, literature libraries

Scope Activity Kit (series)
Grades 7–12. Student booklets, masters, teaching guides

Scope English: Writing and Language (series)
Grades 6–8. Textbooks, teacher's editions, teacher's resource binders, supplementary materials

Scope English: Writing and Language Skills (series)
Grades 9–12. Textbooks, teacher's editions, teacher's resource binders, supplementary materials

Scope Plays (series)
Grades 7–12. Anthologies of plays, teacher's guides

Scope Skills Books (series)
Grades 7–12. Student workbooks, teacher's guides

Scope Visuals (series)
Grades 7–12. Transparencies, teaching guides. Includes "Reading Comprehension Skills," "Writing Skills," "Word Skills," "Close Reading Skills," Reference Skills," "Language Skills," "Career and Consumer Skills"

Springboard Publisher
Grades 7–12. Software, teacher's edition

Success with Literature : A Computer-Based Approach to Writing about Literature (series)
Grades 7–12. Student booklets, software, teaching guides

Success with Writing
Grades 7–12. Software/text approach to the complete writing process. Program/student activity disks, activity book, teaching guide

The Triple Action Unit (series)
Grades 7–12. Unit books, teacher's guide, supplementary materials

ScottForesman
1900 East Lake Avenue
Glenview, IL 60025
1-800-554-4411

Language Arts

Assignments in Exposition
High school (advanced placement, honors). Softcover text

College Reading and Study Skills
High school (advanced placement, honors). Softcover text

How to Design and Deliver a Speech
High school (advanced placement, honors). Text, instructor's manual

Inside High School Journalism
Textbook, teacher's manual

Intercultural Journeys through Reading and Writing
High school (advanced placement, honors). Softcover text

Language: Structure and Use (series)
Grades 9–12. Textbooks, teacher's editions, workbooks, test booklets, language handbook

The Little, Brown Handbook
High school (advanced placement, honors).
Textbook, instructor's manual

The Little English Handbook
High school (advanced placement, honors).
Softcover text

Modern Mass Media Communication in Society
High school (advanced placement, honors).
Softcover text, instructor's manual, test bank

Patterns of Exposition
High school (advanced placement, honors).
Softcover text

The Practical Stylist
High school (advanced placement, honors).
Softcover text, instructor's manual

The Practical Stylist with Reading
High school (advanced placement, honors).
Softcover text

Principles and Types of Speech Communication
High school (advanced placement, honors).
Textbook

Robert's Rules of Order
Cloth/Leather/Paperbound

Scott Foresman D'Nealian® Handwriting Program (series)
Grades K–8. Textbooks, teacher's editions, supplementary materials

The Scott Foresman Handbook with Writing Guide
High school (advanced placement, honors).
Textbook

Scott Foresman Language (series)
Grades K–8. Textbooks, teacher's editions, teacher's resource files, student workbooks, supplementary materials including software

Scott Foresman Spelling (series)
Grades 1–8. Textbooks, teacher's editions, teacher's resource books, supplementary materials including software

Short Takes: Model Essays for Composition
High school (advanced placement, honors).
Softcover text

Speech: Principles and Practice
Grades 7–12. Textbook, teacher's resource book

Strategies of Rhetoric with Handbook
High school (advanced placement, honors).
Softcover text

Theater: Preparation and Performance
Grades 9–12. Textbook, teacher's planbook, teacher's resource book

Types of Drama
High school (advanced placement, honors).
Softcover text

The Write Connection
Grades 7–8. Software package, teacher's guide, blackline masters

The Writer's Options: Combining to Composing
High school (advanced placement, honors).
Softcover text, instructor's manual

A Writer's Reader
High school (advanced placement, honors).
Softcover text

Writing Research Papers
High school (advanced placement, honors).
Softcover text, instructor's manual

Writing Well
High school (advanced placement, honors).
Softcover text, instructor's manual

Literature and Reading

America Reads, Classic Edition (series)
Grades 6–12. Textbook, teacher's editions, teacher's resource files, supplementary materials including audio cassettes, software, literature guides. Includes "Beginnings in Literature," "Discoveries in Literature," "Explorations in Literature," "Patterns in Literature," "Traditions in Literature," "United States in Literature," "England in Literature," "Classics in World Literature"

American Short Stories
High school (advanced placement, honors).
Softcover text

Collections—An Anthology Series
Grades preprimer–6. Textbooks, teacher's editions, literature journal, software

Focus: Reading for Success (series)
Grades K–8 (less able readers). Textbook, teacher's editions, student workbooks, teacher's resource materials, supplementary materials

The Gateway Literature Series
Grades 7–12. Textbooks, teacher's guidebooks, workbooks, assessment materials. Includes "Pursuits," "Outposts," "Reflections," "Travels," "Album USA," "Landmarks"

The Harper Anthology of Fiction
High school (advanced placement, honors).
Softcover text, instructor's manual

An Introduction to Literature: Fiction, Poetry, Drama
High school (advanced placement, honors).
Softcover text, instructor's manual

An Introduction to Poetry
High school (advanced placement, honors).
Softcover text, instructor's manual

Literature: An Introduction to Fiction, Poetry, and Drama
High school (advance placement). Textbook, instructor's manual

Literature and Interpretive Techniques
High school (advanced placement, honors).
Softcover text, instructor's manual

The Literature of England
High school (advanced placement, honors).
Textbook

Of Time and Place: Comparative World Literature in Translation
Grades 11–12. Textbook

Reflections on a Gift of Watermelon Pickle
Grades 7–10. Paperback poetry collection

Scott Foresman Reading (series)
Grades K–8. Big books, readiness books, preprimer books, textbooks, teacher's editions, teacher's resource files, student workbooks, supplementary materials including video cassettes

Scott, Foresman Reading Workshop
Grades 7–8. Software package, teacher's guides

Seven Contemporary Novels
High school (advanced placement, honors).
Softcover text

Supplementary Materials
Scott Foresman/HarperCollins literature libraries, reading software programs

Dale Seymour Publications
P.O. Box 10888
Palo Alto, CA 94303-0879
800-USA-1100

Grades K–8. Teacher's source books, big books, story books and novels, activity books, self-study guides, reading kits, word games, software, teacher's resources

Silver Burdett and Ginn
4350 Equity Drive
P.O. Box 2649
Columbus, OH 43216
1-800-848-9500

World of Reading (series)
Grades K–8. Textbooks, teacher's editions, teacher's resource kits, early literacy program, supplementary materials including trade book collections, assessment materials, software, reader's journals and workbooks, and interactive teaching kits of audio and video cassettes, posters, activity guides, theme cards

World of Language (series)
Grades K–8. Textbooks, teacher's editions, teacher's resource file, software, primary literature program, writing and spelling activity books, classroom libraries, assessment materials, multimedia resources including audio and video cassettes

Skills Bank Corporation
15 Governor's Court
Baltimore, MD 21207-2791
1-800-222-3681

Software for MS-DOS/Apple/Macintosh/Tandy.
In reading, language, writing

Tom Snyder Productions
90 Sherman Street
Cambridge, MA 02140
1-800-342-0236

Grades K–12. Software for Apple/Macintosh/IBM/Tandy/MS-DOS, support materials, multimedia materials. For grammar, writing

Soft-Kat
20630 Nordhoff Street
Chatsworth, CA 91311
800-641-1057

Grades K-12. Software for language arts—reading, spelling, writing, grammar, and vocabulary

South-Western Publishing Co.

5101 Madison Road
Cincinnati, OH 45227
1-800-543-7972

Applied Penmanship
Text-workbook, teacher's manual

Audioactive, Inc.—A Communication Simulation
High school. Text-workbook, teacher's manual

Basic Letter and Memo Writing
High school. Text-workbook, tests, software

The Business of Oral Communication
Study guides, audio and video cassettes

Communication that Works!
Softcover text, teacher's manual

The Computer-Writing Book
High school. Text-workbook, software

Easy Rules Series
High school. Software programs with text-workbooks. Topics include the comma, spelling, capitalization and number expression, word choice, punctuation

Effective Communication for Today
High school. Textbook, workbook, tests, software

English for the Disenchanted
High school. Textbook

English Skill Builder Reference Manual
High school. Reference manual, software

English the Easy Way
Text-workbook, test package, teacher's edition

Food for Thought: Reading and Thinking Critically
Reading levels 4–14. Text-workbooks, test package, teacher's manual

Language Works
Text-workbook, teacher's manual

A Manual of Style for Business Letters, Memos, and Reports
Manual

The Perfect Score: Computer Preparation for the SAT
User's manual, software

Pro-Grammar/Pro-Sentence
High school. Text-workbook, software

Punctuation: A Simplified Approach
Text-workbook, teacher's manual

Reading in Focus: Learning to Get the Message (series)
Reading levels 4–10. Text-workbooks, placement tests, instructor's manual

Word Studies
Text-workbook, tests, teacher's edition

Words, Words, Words
High school. Text-workbook, test, teacher's manual

Working with Words
High school. Text-workbook, audio cassette, teacher's manual

Write Now! A Process-Writing Program
Grades 6–9. Text-workbook, teacher's manual

Writing with Appleworks
High school. Text-workbook, teacher's manual, software

SRA School Group

American School Publishers
Barnell Loft-Merrill-SRA
P.O. Box 5380
Chicago, IL 60680-5380
800-843-8855

Grades K–12. Supplementary programs in reading, literature, life skills, comprehension, handwriting, composition-grammar, process writing, spelling, vocabulary

Steck-Vaughn Company

P.O. Box 26015
Austin, TX 78755
1-800-531-5015

Reading

Developing Reading Strategies
Grades 6–12, Reading levels 2.5–6. Student workbooks, teacher's editions, classroom libraries

First-Time Phonics
Reading levels K–1. Student workbooks, picture cards, classroom library, teacher's editions

Mastering Basic Reading Skills
Grade levels 3–10, reading levels 2–7. Text-workbooks, teacher's editions

Novel Collections for Special-Needs Students
Includes "Short Classics," "Great Unsolved

Mysteries," "The Great Series," "Steck-Vaughan Spotlight," "Superstars in Action"

On Stage: A Reader's Theater Collection
Grades 4–10, reading levels 2–6. Readers, teacher's guides

Phonics and Sight Word Programs
Grades K–6. Student editions, teacher's guides. Includes "Building Sight Vocabulary," "Power-Word Programs," "Sounds, Words, and Meanings"

Phonics Readers (series)
Reading levels K–2. Readers, teacher's guides

Reading Comprehension Series
Grades 1–6. Student workbooks, teacher's editions, classroom library

Reading Links
Grades 1–2. Phonics/literature kit includes big books, lap books, student story books, teacher's resource box

Steck-Vaughn Comprehension Skills (series)
Grades 6–12, reading levels 2–6. Text-workbooks, teacher's guides, classroom libraries

Steck-Vaughan Critical Thinking (series)
Grades 1–6. Student workbooks, teacher's editions

Steck-Vaughan Phonics
Grades 1–4. Student workbooks, teacher's editions, picture cards

Spelling/Language

Language Exercises (series)
Grades 1–8. Student workbooks, teacher's guides, skills books, review books

Steck-Vaughan Handwriting (series)
Grades 1–6. Student workbooks, teacher's edition, alphabet cards

Steck-Vaughan Spelling (series)
Grades 1–8. Textbooks, teacher's editions, activity and comprehension masters, software

Target: Spelling (series)
Grades 2–10, reading levels 1–6. Softcover texts, teacher's editions

Vocabulary Connections: A Content Area Approach (series)
Grades 3–8. Softcover text-workbooks, classroom library

Writing for Competency
Grades 7–10, reading level 7. Softcover text

Whole Language

Classroom Libraries
Whole-language collections for primary, middle and junior high students; high-interest, low-level readers for middle school and secondary students; thinking, reading, comprehension, vocabulary skills sets; hot topic sets

The Highgate Collection (series)
Grades 2–4, reading levels 2–4. Book collections for thematic or topical study, teacher's guides

My World (series)
Grades 1–3. Big books, softcover nonfiction books, teacher's guides, Spanish editions. Science and social studies themes

New Way: Learning with Literature (series)
Grade levels pre-K–3, reading levels 0–3. Big books, student books, teacher's guides, audio cassettes

Real rea pre-K–4, reading levels 0–2. Fiction and non-fiction series, teacher's guides

Steck-Vaughan Writing Dictionary
Grades 1–2. Softcover workbook-dictionary

Steppingstone Stories (series)
Grades K–2. Student books, big books, teacher's guide

Who's Behind the Door? (series)
Grades 1–2. Student books, lap books, teacher's guides

Sundance
P.O. Box 1326
Newton Road
Littleton, MA 01460
1-800-343-8204

Grades pre-K–6. Early childhood materials, literature programs, developmental writing guides, thematic learning units, cross-curriculum units, classroom libraries, audio and video cassettes

SVE—Society for Visual Education, Inc.
Department JT
1345 Diversey Parkway
Chicago, IL 60614-1299
1-800-829-1900

Grades pre-K–9. Audio and video cassettes, filmstrips, software, videodiscs. For children's literature, reading, writing, whole language skills

Swan Books
P.O. Box 2498
Fair Oaks, CA 95628
916-961-8778

Grades 5-12. Presents Shakespeare's plays to suit the grade level and/or special needs of students. "Shakespeare for Young People," "Shakespeare on Stage"

Teacher Support Software
1035 Northwest 57th Street
Gainesville, Florida 32605-4486
800-228-2871

Grades pre-K–adult. Software for Apple/MS-DOS, support materials. For whole language, reading, writing, vocabulary

Teacher Ideas Press
Libraries Unlimited, Inc.
P.O. Box 3988
Englewood, CO 80155-3988
1-800-237-6124

Teacher's resource books, activity books for literature, reading, storytelling, research skills, writing, gifted and talented students

United Learning, Inc.
6633 W. Howard Street
Niles, IL 60648-3305
800-424-0362

Grades K–12. Video cassettes, filmstrips, slides. In reading, literature, presentation skills

Videodiscovery, Inc.
1700 Westlake Avenue North, Suite 600
Seattle, WA 98109-3012
1-800-548-3472

Videodiscs, software for Macintosh/Apple/MS-DOS. For reading, writing, mythology, film

Wadsworth School Group
10 Davis Drive
Belmont, CA 94002-3098
1-800-831-6996

College textbooks appropriate for use by college-bound, honors, or advanced placement students in reading/study skills, grammar and composition, critical thinking/writing, journalism, business english/communication, speech/forensics/communication, theatre, mass communication, telecommunication/film studies

J. Weston Walch, Publisher
321 Valley Street
P.O. Box 658
Portland, ME 04104-0658
1-800-341-6094

Materials for meeting literacy needs, whole language approaches, skills programs in reading and writing, story collections. Photocopy masters, activity cards, audio cassettes, student books, teacher's guides

Watten/Poe Teaching Resource Center
P.O. Box 1509
14023 Catalina Street
San Leandro, CA 94577
1-800-833-3389

Integrated curriculum materials, teacher's resource books, nursery rhyme strips, easels, pocket charts and stands, theme kits, big books, book/audio cassette packages, chalkboards, markboards

Weaver Instructional Systems
6161 28th Street, Southeast
Grand Rapids, MI 49506
616-942-2891

Reading Efficiency System
Software for Apple/Franklin/Radio Shack/Acorn/ IBM/Atari/Commodore

English Grammar Instructional System
Grades 6 and above. Software for Apple/Franklin/ Radio Shack/Acorn/IBM/Atari/Commodore

Weekly Reader Corporation
3000 Cindel Drive
P.O. Box 8037
Delran, NJ 08075

Weekly Reader Skills Books (series)
Grades pre-K–6. Reading, writing, speech, vocabulary, and library skills workbooks, supplementary materials

WICAT
The Learning Improvement Company
1875 South State Street
Orem, UT 84058
800-759-4228

Grades K–12. Software programs for capitalization, punctuation, grammar, usage and parts of speech, writing, whole-language writing activity

William K. Bradford Publishing Company
310 School Street
Acton, MA 01720
800-421-2009

Grades K-12. Software programs for reading and language arts

WINGS for Learning/Sunburst
1600 Green Hills Road
P.O. Box 660002
Scotts Valley, CA 95067-0002
800-321-7511

Grades K–college. Software for Apple/Macintosh/IBM/Tandy, multimedia materials. For reading, sequencing/categorization, handwriting, spelling, literature, writing

The Wright Group
19201 120th Avenue, NE
Bothell, WA 98011-9512
800-523-2371

Grades K-6. Learning resources, with whole-language approach. For reading and writing

Write Source
Educational Publishing House
Box J
Burlington, WI 53105

Language arts handbooks, teacher's guides, activity books, workbooks, posters, literature collections

Zaner-Bloser
2200 West Fifth Avenue
P.O. Box 16764
Columbus, OH 43216-6764
1-800-421-3018

Breakthroughs: Language Development Supplements (series)
Teacher's folder with teaching notes, worksheets, and reproducible picture glossary

Day-by-Day Kindergarten Program
Cross-curriculum resource program. Teacher's resource book, student activity book, teacher's guide, supplementary materials

Developing Reading Power
Grades 1–8. Comprehension skills assessment program

Let's Read and Think (series)
Grades 1–3. Student text-workbooks, teacher's editions

Literacy Plus (series)
Grades K–8. Integrated language arts program. Teacher's guides, teacher's reference book, student reference book, student word books, trade book collections, supplementary materials including inservice video cassettes

Spelling Connections (series)
Grades 1–8. Textbooks, teacher's editions, teacher's resource binder, supplementary materials including in-service video cassettes, software

Supplementary Materials
Critical-thinking programs, guided practice books, independent readers, duplicating masters

Zaner-Bloser Handwriting: A Way to Self-Expression
Grades K–8. Student workbooks, teacher's edition's, teacher's resource binders, supplementary materials including in-service video cassettes

Zaner-Bloser Vocabulary Building (series)
Grades 1–9. Softcover texts, teacher's editions

Zephyr Press
3316 North Chapel Avenue
P.O. Box 13448-E
Tucson, AZ 85732-3448
1-800-350-0851

Grades K–12. Whole-language source books,
activity books

■

STATEWIDE TEXTBOOK ADOPTION

THERE are twenty-two states that have statewide adoption of textbooks and other instructional materials: Alabama, Arizona, Arkansas, California, Florida, Georgia, Idaho, Indiana, Kentucky, Louisiana, Mississippi, Nevada, New Mexico, North Carolina, Oklahoma, Oregon, South Carolina, Tennessee, Texas, Utah, Virginia, and West Virginia.

The policies and procedures for textbook adoption are similar in all twenty-two states, with some minor variations.

Textbook Advisory Committee

In general, the state board of education is responsible for developing guidelines and criteria for the review and selection of textbooks and for appointing members to a textbook advisory committee. However, in a few states, the appointment of committee members is the responsibility of the governor or of the Commissioner of Education.

The textbook advisory committee is usually composed of educators, lay citizens, and parents, and can have from nine to twenty-seven appointees, depending upon the state. Membership is weighted, however, toward individuals who are educators: elementary and secondary teachers in the subject areas in which textbooks are to be adopted, instructors of teacher education and curriculum from local universities and colleges, school administrators, and school board members. Lay citizens, in order to sit on the committee, should be interested in and conversant with educational issues. An effort is made to select

appointees who reflect the diversity of their state's population, and therefore decisions about appointments are often made with the purpose of having a wide representation of ethnic backgrounds and geographical residence within the state.

Adoption Process

The textbook and instructional materials adoption process takes approximately twelve months.

Once the textbook advisory committee is formed, the members conduct an organizational meeting to formulate policy on such issues as adoption subjects and categories; standards for textbook evaluation, allocation of time for publisher presentations, and location of regional sites for such; sampling directions for publishers; and publisher contact. The committee may appoint subcommittees--made up of curriculum and/or subject specialists--to assist them in developing criteria for evaluating instructional materials.

After these procedural matters are agreed upon, the committee issues an official textbook call or "invitation to submit" to the textbook publishers. This document provides the publisher with adoption information and subject area criteria, which can either be the curriculum framework or essential skills list. Those publishers interested in having their materials considered for adoption submit their intention to bid, which shows the prices at which the publishers will agree to sell their material during the adoption period. Publishers usually bid current wholesale prices or lowest existing contract prices at which textbooks or other instructional materials are being sold elsewhere in the country.

If their bid has been accepted by the committee, the publishers submit sample copies of their textbooks for examination. The committee then hears presentations by the publishers. This meeting allows the publisher to present the texts submitted for adoption and to answer any questions the committee may have on the material. After publisher presentations, the textbooks are displayed in designated areas throughout the state for general public viewing. The committee then holds public hearings (usually two) which provide citizens with the opportunity to give an opinion on the textbooks offered for adoption. After much discussion and evaluation, the committee makes a recommendations for textbook adoption to the state board of education.

When the board of education approves the committee's recommendations, it negotiates the contract with the chosen publishers and disseminates the list of instructional materials to the school districts. The school districts will then make their textbook selections from this list. A few states also allow their school districts to use materials for the classroom that are not on the adoption list.

Textbook and Instructional Materials

There are two categories of instructional materials: basal and supplementary. Basal, or basic, materials address the goals, objectives, and content identified for a particular subject. Supplementary materials, used in conjunction with the basic text, enhance the teaching of the subject.

Instructional materials may include all or some of the following: hardcover books, softcover books, kits, workbooks, dictionaries, maps and atlases, electronic/computer programs, films, filmstrips, and other audiovisual materials.

The textbook adoption period generally runs from four to six years (California, the exception, has an eight-year contract period for K-8 only). The grade levels for adoption are usually K-12, with the following subject areas: English/language arts, social studies, foreign languages, English as a second language (ESL), science, mathematics, fine arts, applied arts.

Textbooks and instructional materials are ultimately judged by how well they reflect the state curriculum framework and/or essential skills objectives. Materials are rated on the following criteria: organization, accuracy, and currency of subject content; correlation with grade level requirements for the subject; adaptability for students with different abilities, backgrounds, and experiences; types of teacher aids provided; author's background and training; physical features; and cost.

In addition, some states have social content requirements that textbooks have to meet. For instance, textbooks should be objective in content and impartial in interpretation of the subject, and should not include "offensive" language or illustrations. American values (e.g., democracy, the work ethic, free enterprise), culture, traditions, and government should be presented in a positive manner. Respect for the individual's rights, and for the cultural and racial diversity of American society, can also be addressed in the text. Finally, some states declare that textbooks should not condone civil disorder, lawlessness, or "deviance."

Kraus thanks the personnel we contacted at the state departments of education, for their help in providing the states' textbook adoption lists.

List of Textbooks

Following is a compilation of the textbooks and instructional materials approved by the twenty-two states that have statewide textbook adoption. This listing is based on the relevant publications submitted to Kraus by the textbook division of the respective departments of educations.

The list is alphabetized by state; under each state, the materials are organized by subject (e.g., English, handwriting, reading, literature, etc.). Note that the categories are those used by each state, and therefore they are not always consistent from state to state. In some cases, supplemental material is also noted. For each textbook (and supplemental publication), the title, grade level, publisher, and copyright date are provided, as well as the termination year of the textbook's adoption period.

Alabama

English

Glencoe English: Grades 9–12
Glencoe, 1985 (Termination Date: 1994)

Macmillan English, Thinking and Writing: Grades 9–12
Glencoe, 1988 (Termination Date: 1994)

The Stage and the School: Grades 9–12
Glencoe, 1982 (Termination Date: 1994)

The Write Steps: Grades 3–6
Hammond, 1983 (Termination Date: 1994)

Language for Daily Use: Grades 1–8
Harcourt, 1986 (Termination Date: 1994)

Heath Language Arts: Grades K–8
Heath, 1988 (Termination Date: 1994)

English Composition and Grammar: Grades 6–12
Holt, 1988 (Termination Date: 1994)

English: Writing and Skills, First–Sixth Course: Grades 7–12
Holt, 1988 (Termination Date: 1994)

Houghton Mifflin English, Levels K–8: Grades K–8
Houghton, 1988 (Termination Date: 1994)

Macmillan English: Grades K–8
Macmillan, 1987 (Termination Date: 1994)

Macmillan English, Thinking and Writing Processes: Grades 6–8
Macmillan, 1987 (Termination Date: 1994)

Laidlaw English: Grades K–8
Macmillan, 1987 (Termination Date: 1994)

McDougal, Littell English: Grades K–8
McDougal, 1987 (Termination Date: 1994)

Building English Skills: Grades 9–12
McDougal, 1988 (Termination Date: 1994)

Prentice Hall Grammar and Composition: Grades 6–12
Prentice, 1987 (Termination Date: 1994)

Press Time: Grades 9–12
Prentice, 1985 (Termination Date: 1994)

Language: Skills and Use: Grades K–8
Scott, 1986 (Termination Date: 1994)

Silver Burdett and Ginn English: Grades 1–8
Silver Burdett and Ginn, 1988 (Termination Date: 1994)

Basic Skills in English: Grades 7–12
McDougal, 1985 (Termination Date: 1994)

Supplemental Materials, English

Amsco Writing English Series: Grades 8–12
Amsco, 1982 (Termination Date: 1994)

English Language Arts: Grades 8–12
Amsco, 1982 (Termination Date: 1994)

English for the College Boards: Grades 10–12
Amsco, 1987 (Termination Date: 1994)

Thirteen Steps to Better Writing: Grades 9–12
Amsco, 1987 (Termination Date: 1994)

Guide to Writing Term Papers: Grades 9–12
Amsco, 1971 (Termination Date: 1994)

Writing the Research Paper: Grades 10–12
Amsco, 1978 (Termination Date: 1994)

Word Play: Grades 7–12
Amsco, 1984 (Termination Date: 1994)

Word Game: Grades 6–12
Amsco, 1987 (Termination Date: 1994)

Vocabulary for Enjoyment, Books One and Two: Grades 6–12
Amsco, 1986, 1987 (Termination Date: 1994)

Vocabulary for the High School Student: Grades 9–12
Amsco, 1983 (Termination Date: 1994)

Vocabulary for the College Bound Student: Grades 11–12
Amsco, 1983 (Termination Date: 1994)

The Joy of Vocabulary, Grades 11–12
Amsco, 1986 (Termination Date: 1994)

Writing about Amusing Things: Grades 6–12
Amsco, 1982 (Termination Date: 1994)

Writing about Curious Things: Grades 7–12
Amsco, 1981 (Termination Date: 1994)

Writing about Fascinating Things: Grades 8–12
Amsco, 1980 (Termination Date: 1994)

Literature-Based Composition: Grades 9–12
Glencoe, 1988 (Termination Date: 1994)

Laidlaw English, Composition and Grammar:
Grades 9–12
Glencoe, 1985 (Termination Date: 1994)

Lively Writing: Grades 9–12
National, 1985 (Termination Date: 1994)

Supplemental Materials-Advanced, English
Compositions: Models and Exercises: Grades 7–12
Holt, 1986 (Termination Date: 1994)

Art of Composition: Grades 9–12
National, 1984 (Termination Date: 1994)

Proficiency in Written English: Grades 7–12
Hammond, 1986 (Termination Date: 1994)

KoKo's Clubhouse (kit) *for Laidlaw English:*
Grades K–1
Macmillan, n.d. (Termination Date: 1994)

Handwriting
HBJ Handwriting, Readiness-Book 6: Grades 1–6
Harcourt, 1987 (Termination Date: 1994)

Palmer Method, Manuscript: Transition to Cursive:
Grades K–8
Macmillan, 1987 (Termination Date: 1994)

Bowmar/Noble Handwriting, Book A-I: Grades 1–8
Macmillan, 1987 (Termination Date: 1994)

McDougal, Littell Handwriting: Grades K–8
McDougal, 1987 (Termination Date: 1994)

Scott, Foresman D'Nealian Handwriting: Grades
K–8
Scott, 1987 (Termination Date: 1994)

*Zaner-Bloser Handwriting: Basic Skills and
Applications, Readiness-Book 8:* Grades K–8
Zaner, 1987 (Termination Date: 1994)

Supplementary Materials, Handwriting
Steck-Vaughn Handwriting, Book 1–6: Grades 1–6
Steck, 1988 (Termination Date: 1994)

Supplementary Materials for HBJ Handwriting:
Grades 1–6
Harcourt, n.d. (Termination Date: 1994)

*Supplementary Materials for Scott, Foresman
D'Nealian Handwriting:* Grades 1–8
Scott, n.d. (Termination Date: 1994)

*Supplementary Materials for Steck-Vaughn Hand-
writing:* Grades 1–6
Steck, n.d. (Termination Date: 1994)

Literature
Macmillan Literature Series: Grades 7–12
Glencoe, 1989 (Termination Date: 1995)

McGraw-Hill Literature Series: Grades 7–12
Glencoe, 1989 (Termination Date: 1995

Adventures in Literature: Grades 7–12
Holt, 1989 (Termination Date: 1995)

Adventures in Reading: Grade 9
Holt, 1989 (Termination Date: 1995)

Elements of Literature, First-Sixth Course: Grades
7–12
Holt, 1989 (Termination Date: 1995)

McDougal, Littell Literature: Grades 7–12
McDougal, 1989 (Termination Date: 1995)

Prentice Hall Literature: Grades 7–10
Prentice, 1989 (Termination Date: 1995)

Prentice Hall Literature: Grades 11–12
Prentice, 1989 (Termination Date: 1995)

America Reads: Grades 6–12
Scott, 1989 (Termination Date: 1995)

Scope English Anthologies, Level Z–6: Grades 6–12
Scholastic, 1988 (Termination Date: 1995)

Supplementary Material, Literature
Short Stories: Grades 8–12
Amsco, 1988 (Termination Date: 1995)

Amsco Literature Program: Grades 9–12
Amsco, 1971–74 (Termination Date: 1995)

On Stage: Grades 6–12
Amsco, 1986 (Termination Date: 1995)

The Reader as Detective, Books II and III: Grades 7–12
Amsco, 1986–87 (Termination Date: 1995)

Beyond Basics: Grades 4–12
Jamestown, 1986 (Termination Date: 1995)

Best Short Stories, Middle and Advanced Levels: Grades 6–10, 9–12
Jamestown, 1980, 1983 (Termination Date: 1993)

Best Selling Chapters, Middle and Advanced Levels: Grades 9–12
Jamestown, 1982, 1979 (Termination Date: 1995)

MCP Literature Anthology, Levels C-F: Grades 3–6
MCP, 1987 (Termination Date: 1995)

The Short Story and You: Grades 9–12
National, 1987 (Termination Date: 1995)

Myths and Their Meanings; Grades 9–12
Prentice, 1984 (Termination Date: 1995)

Collections: An Anthology Series: Grades 1–6
Scott, 1989 (Termination Date: 1995)

Reading

Kites: Grades R-1
Harcourt, 1989 (Termination Date: 1995)

HBJ Beginning Readers' Library: Grades R-1
Harcourt, 1989 (Termination Date: 1995)

HBJ Reading Program: Grades K–8
Harcourt, 1989 (Termination Date: 1995)

Imagination: An Odyssey through Literature: Grades K–6
Harcourt, 1989 (Termination Date: 1995)

HRW Reading: Reading Today and Tomorrow: Grades K–8
Harcourt, 1989 (Termination Date: 1995)

Heath Reading: Grades K–8
Heath, 1989 (Termination Date: 1995)

Houghton Mifflin Reading: Grades K–8
Houghton, 1989 (Termination Date: 1995)

Houghton Mifflin Reading Program: Grades K–8
Houghton, 1983 (Termination Date: 1995)

Macmillan Reading Program: Connections: Grades K–8
Macmillan, 1988, 1989 (Termination Date: 1995)

McGraw-Hill Reading: Grades K–8
Macmillan, 1989 (Termination Date: 1995)

Open Court Reading and Writing Student-Reader Anthologies: Grades K–6
Open Court, 1989 (Termination Date: 1995)

Scott-Foresman Reading: Grades K–8
Scott, 1989 (Termination Date: 1995)

Silver, Burdett and Ginn World of Reading: Grades K–8
Silver, Burdett and Ginn, 1989 (Termination Date: 1995)

Scribner Reading Series: Grades K–8
Macmillan, 1989 (Termination Date: 1995)

Journeys: A Reading and Literature Program: Grades 7–12
Holt, 1986 (Termination Date: 1995)

Houghton Mifflin Reading, Levels 1–10: Grades 6–8
Houghton, 1986 (Termination Date: 1995)

Reading Express: Grades 1–8
Macmillan, 1986 (Termination Date: 1995)

Focus: Reading for Success: Grades: K–8
Scott, 1988 (Termination Date: 1995)

Supplementary Materials, Reading

Random House Phonics, Books 1-3: Grades 1-3
Random House, 1988 (Termination Date: 1995)

Alpha Time Complete Program: Grades K–1
Dimensions, 1988 (Termination Date: 1995)

Read-To-Me Library: Grades K–2
Dimensions, 1981 (Termination Date: 1995)

Alpha One Complete Program: Grades 1-2
Dimensions, 1988 (Termination Date: 1995)

Complete Alpha Phonics Program: Grades 1-2
Dimensions, 1988 (Termination Date: 1995)

Alpha Time Plus Complete Program: Grades 1-2
Dimensions, 1988 (Termination Date: 1995)

*Special A Complete Program with Large Huggables;
Special A Complete Program with Small Huggables*:
Grades K–1
Dimensions, 1988 (Termination Date: 1995)

Alpha Time Complete Pre-Reading Program:
Grades K–1
Dimensions, 1988 (Termination Date: 1995)

Star Books Complete Program: Grades K–1
Dimensions, 1980 (Termination Date: 1995)

Comprehension Skills Laboratories: Grades 1–6
Dimensions, 1976 (Termination Date: 1995)

Reading Vocabulary Laboratories: Grades 2–8
Dimensions, 1978 (Termination Date: 1995)

Rebus Reading: Beginning Sentence Building:
Grades 1-4
DLM, 1982 (Termination Date: 1995)

Sound Foundations, Programs I-IV: Grades 2-4
DLM, 1973–81 (Termination Date: 1995)

Bill Martin's Treasure Chest: Grades K–5
DLM, 1987 (Termination Date: 1995)

Read Aloud Predictables for Beginners: Grades K–1
DLM, 1987 (Termination Date: 1995)

Sight Word Lab: Grades 1-2
DLM, 1982 (Termination Date: 1995)

Predictable Storybooks, I-III: Grades K–3
DLM, 1987 (Termination Date: 1995)

Bobber Books: Grades K–2
DLM, 1988 (Termination Date: 1995)

Teddy Bear Bear Books: Grades K–2
DLM, 1988 (Termination Date: 1995)

Bridges to Understanding: Grades K–1
DLM, 1988 (Termination Date: 1995)

Reading Skills Series: Grades 1–6
Hammond, 1982–86 (Termination Date: 1995)

Reading Skills in the Content Areas: Grades 4–8
Hammond, 1980, 1986 (Termination Date: 1995)

Learning to Study: Grades 2–8
Jamestown, 1983 (Termination Date: 1995)

Starting Off with Phonics, Books 1–6: Grades K–1
MCP, 1986 (Termination Date: 1995)

MCP Phonics, Levels A-B: Grades 1-2
MCP, 1988 (Termination Date: 1995)

Phonics First, Levels A-B: Grades 1-2
MCP, 1988 (Termination Date: 1995)

Swinging Out, Mini Books: Grades K–1
MCP, 1986 (Termination Date: 1995)

Going Places: Grades K–6
SRA, 1988 (Termination Date: 1995)

Merrill Focus on Reading, Books I-III: Grades 7–9
SRA, 1989 (Termination Date: 1995)

Sight Word Skills 1-4: Grades 1-3
Mid-America, 1984, 1986 (Termination Date: 1995)

Reading by Doing: Grades 9–12
National, 1988 (Termination Date: 1995)

Talespinners II: Grades 8–12
Fearon, 1988 (Termination Date: 1995)

Pacemaker True Adventures Set: Grades 8–12
Fearon, 1970–73 (Termination Date: 1995)

Bestsellers IV Set: Grades 8–12
Fearon, 1988 (Termination Date: 1995)

High Stakes Set: Grades 8–12
Fearon, 1987 (Termination Date: 1995)

Five-Minute Thrillers Set: Grades 8–12
Fearon, 1988 (Termination Date: 1995)

Fastback Mystery Series Set: Grades 8–12
Fearon, 1984 (Termination Date: 1995)

Fastback Romance Series Set: Grades 8–12
Fearon, 1984 (Termination Date: 1995)

Fastback Spy Series Set: Grades 8–12
Fearon, 1985 (Termination Date: 1995)

Fastback Sport Series Set: Grades 8–12
Fearon, 1984 (Termination Date: 1995)

Fastback Crime and Detection Series Set: Grades
8–12
Fearon, 1986 (Termination Date: 1995)

Fastback Science Series Set: Grades 8–12
Fearon, 1987 (Termination Date: 1995)

Double Fastback Romance Series Set: Grades 8–12
Fearon, 1987 (Termination Date: 1995)

Double Fastback Mystery Series Set: Grades 8–12
Fearon, 1987 (Termination Date: 1995)

Double Fastback Spy Series Set: Grades 8–12
Fearon, 1988 (Termination Date: 1995)

Flashback Series Set: Grades 8–12
Fearon, 1987 (Termination Date: 1995)

Flashback War Series Set: Grades 8–12
Fearon, 1987 (Termination Date: 1995)

Flashback Sport Series Set: Grades 8–12
Fearon, 1987 (Termination Date: 1995)

Merrill Linguistic Reading: Grades K–3
SRA, 1986 (Termination Date: 1995)

Spelling

Spelling is Important: Grades 9–12
Hammond, 1986 (Termination Date: 1994)

HBJ Spelling: Grades 1–8
Harcourt Brace Jovanovich, 1988 (Termination
Date: 1994)

Houghton Mifflin Spelling: Grades 1–8
Houghton Mifflin, 1988 (Termination Date: 1994)

Riverside Spelling: Grades K–8
Houghton Mifflin, 1988 (Termination Date: 1994)

Series S: Macmillan Spelling: Grades 1–8
Macmillan, 1987 (Termination Date: 1994)

Laidlaw Spelling: Grades 1–8
Macmillan, 1987 (Termination Date: 1994)

Basic Goals in Spelling: Grades 1–8
Macmillan, 1988 (Termination Date: 1994)

Spelling for Word Mastery: Grades 1–8
Macmillan, 1987 (Termination Date: 1994)

McDougal, Littell Spelling: Grades 1–8
McDougal, Littell, 1988 (Termination Date: 1994)

Scott, Foresman Spelling: Grades 1–8
Scott, Foresman, 1988 (Termination Date: 1994)

Spelling Connections: Words into Language:
Grades 1–8
Zaner-Bloser, 1988 (Termination Date: 1994)

A Presciptive Spelling Program: Grades 2–8
Barnell, 1980 (Termination Date: 1994)

Supplementary Materials, Spelling
Spelling Word Lists for HBJ Spelling: Grades 1–8
Harcourt Brace Jovanovich, n.d. (Termination
Date: 1994)

Readiness Kit for Laidlaw Spelling: Grades K–1
Macmillan (Termination Date: 1994)

Bonus Pack for Scott, Foresman Spelling: Grades 1–8
Scott, Foresman (Termination Date: 1994)

Arizona

Language Arts
Holt Impressions: Grades 1-3
Holt, Rinehart and Winston, 1984–86 (Termina-
tion Date: 1993)

McDougal, Littell English: Grades K–6
McDougal, Littell, 1987, 1989 (Termination Date:
1993)

Language for Daily Use: Grades K–8
Harcourt Brace Jovanovich, 1986 (Termination
Date: 1993)

Houghton Mifflin English: Grades K–8
Houghton Mifflin, 1986 (Termination Date: 1993)

Macmillan English: Grades K–8
Macmillan, 1987 (Termination Date: 1993)

Language: Skills and Use: Grades K–8
Scott, Foresman, 1984–86 (Termination Date: 1993)

Silver Burdett English: Grades K–8
Silver, Burdett, and Ginn, 1985–87 (Termination Date: 1993)

Heath Grammar and Composition: Grades 6–8
D.C. Heath, 1987 (Termination Date: 1993)

Houghton Mifflin English: Grammar and Composition: Grades 7–9
Houghton Mifflin, 1986 (Termination Date: 1993)

Building English Skills: Grades 7–9
McDougal, Littell, 1984–88 (Termination Date: 1993)

Language Arts—Special Needs
Learning to Spell: Grades 7–9
Kendall/Hunt, 1986 (Termination Date: 1993)

Basic Skills in English: Grades 7–9
McDougal, Littell, 1989 (Termination Date: 1993)

Basic Skills in English: Grade 9
Media Materials, 1985 (Termination Date: 1993)

Writing Composition
Writing and Thinking: A Process Approach: Grades 1–6
Mastery Education, 1985 (Termination Date: 1993)

Writing Guides: Grade 6
Active Learning Corporation, 1986 (Termination Date: 1993)

Language Arts—Accelerated Basal
Warriner's English Grammar and Composition, Liberty Edition: Grades 7–9
Harcourt Brace Jovanovich, 1986 (Termination Date: 1993)

Language Arts—Supplemental
Skills Sharpeners: Grades 6–12
Addison-Wesley, 1984, 1991 (Termination Date: 1993)

Write 1: Grades 7–12
Addison-Wesley, 1985 (Termination Date: 1993)

America: The Early Years, Book 1: Grades 5–12
Addison-Wesley, 1987 (Termination Date: 1993)

High Hat Early Reading Program: Grades K–1
American Guidance Service, 1986 (Termination Date: 1993)

Early Writing Program: Grades K–6
American Guidance Service, 1985 (Termination Date: 1993)

Listening to the World: Grades K–2
American Guidance Service, 1980 (Termination Date: 1993)

Peabody Language Development Kits: Grades K–2
American Guidance Service, 1981 (Termination Date: 1993)

Ideas for Fun: Grades K–8
Ballard and Tighe, 1985 (Termination Date: 1993)

Writing: The Business Letter: Grades 8–9
Competency, 1980 (Termination Date: 1993)

Writing: The Report: Grades 8–9
Competency, 1980 (Termination Date: 1993)

Writing: The Composition: Grades 8–9
Competency, 1980 (Termination Date: 1993)

Writing: Personal Expression: Grades 4-5
Competency, 1986 (Termination Date: 1993)

Writing: Personal Narrative: Grades 4-5
Competency, 1986 (Termination Date: 1993)

Language Skills: Grades 2–6
Curriculum Associates, 1983–84, 1986 (Termination Date: 1993)

Paragraphs: A Writing Strategy: Grade 6
David M. Bishop Management Services, 1985 (Termination Date: 1993)

Passport to Reading: Grades 6–12
EMC, 1982 (Termination Date: 1993)

Writing Makes Sense: Grades 6–12
Fearon Education, 1987 (Termination Date: 1993)

Capitalization and Punctuation Make Sense: Grades 6–12
Fearon Education, 1987 (Termination Date: 1993)

Basics of Writing: Grades 6–12
Globe Book, 1985–86 (Termination Date: 1993)

Grammar and Composition for Everyday English:
Grades 6–12
Globe Book, 1987 (Termination Date: 1993)

Kendall/Hunt Study Skills Program: Grades 6–8
Kendall/Hunt, 1985 (Termination Date: 1993)

Odyssey: A Curriculum for Thinking: Grades 4–8
Mastery Education, 1986 (Termination Date: 1993)

MCP Writing Mastery Books: Grades 3–6
Modern Curriculum, 1983 (Termination Date: 1993)

Writing Sentences, Paragraphs, and Compositions:
Grades 2–6
Modern Curriculum, 1984, 1986 (Termination
Date: 1993)

Developing Reading Comprehension Skills: Grades
1–8
Oceana Educational Communications, 1977–80,
1983, 1986 (Termination Date: 1993)

Building Reading Competencies: Grades 1–6
Oceana Educational Communications, 1981
(Termination Date: 1993)

Figurative Language: Grades 1–6
Oceana Educational Communications, 1982
(Termination Date: 1993)

Rhyming: Grades 1–6
Oceana Educational Communications, 1982
(Termination Date: 1993)

Breaking the Code: Grades 4–12
Open Court, 1975, 1979 (Termination Date: 1993)

Catching On: Grades 1–6
Open Court, 1987 (Termination Date: 1993)

The Reading Connection: Grades 7–12
Open Court, 1982–86 (Termination Date: 1993)

Individual Corrective English: Grades 2–6
Random House, 1983 (Termination Date: 1993)

Language Roundup: Grades 1–6
Random House, 1986 (Termination Date: 1993)

Plain English: Grades 7–8
Random House, 1987 (Termination Date: 1993)

Practicing Capitalization and Punctuation: Grades
2–8
Random House, 1984 (Termination Date: 1993)

Practicing Grammar: Grades 2–8
Random House, 1984 (Termination Date: 1993)

Practicing Standard Usage: Grades 2–8
Random House, 1984 (Termination Date: 1993)

Practicing Vocabulary in Context: Grades 2–8
Random House, 1984 (Termination Date: 1993)

Spotlight on Writing: Grades 1–8
Random House, 1983 (Termination Date: 1993)

English that We Need: Grades K–8
Richards, 1986 (Termination Date: 1993)

Learning to Communicate: Grades K–8
Richards, 1986 (Termination Date: 1993)

More English that We Need: Grades K–8
Richards, 1984 (Termination Date: 1993)

Using the Telephone: Grades K–8
Richards, 1983 (Termination Date: 1993)

Reading/Writing and Speaking: Grades K–8
Richards, 1986 (Termination Date: 1993)

Reading for Mathematics: Grades K–8
Richards, 1984 (Termination Date: 1993)

Understanding English: Grades K–8
Richards, 1982 (Termination Date: 1993)

Reading for Survival: Grades K–8
Richards, 1985 (Termination Date: 1993)

Vocabulary Workshop: Grades 6–8
Sadlier-Oxford, 1982, 1984 (Termination Date:
1993)

Buho: Grades K–1
Santillana, 1985 (Termination Date: 1993)

Aguila: Grades K–1
Santillana, 1985 (Termination Date: 1993)

Canguro: Grades K–1
Santillana, 1985 (Termination Date: 1993)

Writer's Workshop: Grades 1–6
Scholastic, 1986 (Termination Date: 1993)

Distar Language I and II: Grades K–3
Science Research, 1977, 1987 (Termination Date: 1993)

Corrective Spelling through Morphographs: Grades 4–12
Science Research, 1977 (Termination Date: 1993)

Spelling Mastery: Grades 1–6
Science Research, 1980–81 (Termination Date: 1993)

Tap the Deck, An Early Composition Book: Grades 9–12
Stack the Deck, 1985 (Termination Date: 1993)

Open the Deck, An Introductory Composition Book: Grades 9–12
Stack the Deck, 1982 (Termination Date: 1993)

Cut the Deck, A Basic Composition Book: Grades 9–12
Stack the Deck, 1985 (Termination Date: 1993)

Stack the Deck, An Intermediate Composition Book: Grades 9–12
Stack the Deck, 1980 (Termination Date: 1993)

Pass the Deck, A Developmental Composition Book: Grades 9–12
Stack the Deck, 1983 (Termination Date: 1993)

Zaner-Bloser Vocabulary Building: Process, Principles, and Application: Grades 1–8
Zaner-Bloser, 1986 (Termination Date: 1993)

Spelling

Improving Spelling Performance: Grades 1–6
Kendall/Hunt, 1986 (Termination Date: 1993)

Working Words in Spelling: Grades 1–8
D. C. Heath, 1985 (Termination Date: 1993)

Macmillan Spelling: Grades 1–8
Macmillan, 1987 (Termination Date: 1993)

Building Spelling Skills: Grades 1–8
McDougal, Littell, 1985 (Termination Date: 1993)

Spelling: Words and Skills: Grades 1–8
Scott, Foresman, 1986 (Termination Date: 1993)

Zaner-Bloser Spelling: Basic Skills and Applications: Grades 1–8
Zaner-Bloser, 1983–84 (Termination Date: 1993)

Spelling and the Written Word: Grades 7–9
Kendall/Hunt, 1986 (Termination Date: 1993)

Bilingual Spelling

Ortografia Santillana: Grades K–2
Santillana, 1986 (Termination Date: 1993)

Handwriting

Italic Handwriting, Getty/Dubay 2d Edition: Grades K–6
Continuing Education, 1986 (Termination Date: 1993)

Bowmar/Noble Handwriting: Grades K–8
McGraw-Hill, 1987 (Termination Date: 1993)

Palmer Method Handwriting, Centennial Edition: Grades K–6
Macmillan, 1987 (Termination Date: 1993)

Scott, Foresman D'Nealian Handwriting Program: Grades K–8
Scott, Foresman, 1987 (Termination Date: 1993)

Zaner-Bloser Handwriting: Basic Skills and Application: Grades 1–8
Zaner-Bloser, 1987 (Termination Date: 1993)

Dictionaries

HBJ School Dictionary: Grades 3–8
Harcourt Brace Jovanovich, 1985 (Termination Date: 1993)

Holt School Dictionary of American English: Grades 3–8
Holt, Rinehart and Winston, 1981 (Termination Date: 1993)

My Picture Dictionaries: Grades K–2
Silver, Burdett, and Ginn, 1985 (Termination Date: 1993)

Webster's Dictionaries: Grades 3–8
Silver, Burdett, and Ginn, 1982 (Termination Date: 1993)

Webster's School Thesaurus: Grades 6–8
Silver, Burdett, and Ginn, 1978 (Termination Date: 1993)

Student's Dictionary: Grades 7–8
Houghton Mifflin, 1981 (Termination Date: 1993)

The American Heritage Dictionary: High School Edition: Grades 7–8
Houghton Mifflin, 1982 (Termination Date: 1993)

Student's Dictionary: Grades K–8
National Textbook, 1984 (Termination Date: 1993)

Building Dictionary Skills in English: Grades K–8
National Textbook, 1984 (Termination Date: 1993)

Macmillan Dictionaries: Grades K–8
Macmillan, 1987 (Termination Date: 1993)

Webster's New World Dictionary: Grades 3–8
Modern Curriculum, 1983 (Termination Date: 1993)

Webster's New World Dictionary: Grades 7–8
Prentice Hall, 1983 (Termination Date: 1993)

Random House School Dictionary: Grades 3–8
Random House, 1984 (Termination Date: 1993)

Webster's II Riverside Beginning Dictionary: Grades 3–8
Riverside, 1984 (Termination Date: 1993)

Scott, Foresman Dictionary Program: Grades K–8
Scott, Foresman, 1983 (Termination Date: 1993)

Scott, Foresman Pictionary/Picture Dictionary Program: Grades K–2
Scott, Foresman, 1982–83 (Termination Date: 1993)

In Other Words Thesauri Program: Grades 3–8
Scott, Foresman, 1982–83 (Termination Date: 1993)

Everyday American English Dictionary: Grades K–8
Voluntad, 1984 (Termination Date: 1993)

Dictionaries—Supplemental
Addison-Wesley Picture Dictionary: Grades K–2
Addison-Wesley, 1984 (Termination Date: 1993)

Addison-Wesley Picture Dictionary Skills Book: Grades K–2
Addison-Wesley, 1986 (Termination Date: 1993)

Reading
Heath American Readers: Grades K–8
D.C. Heath, 1986 (Termination Date: 1992)

HBJ Bookmark Reading Program, Eagle Edition: Grades K–8
Harcourt Brace Jovanovich, 1983 (Termination Date: 1992)

Macmillan Reading Express: Grades K–6
Macmillan, 1986 (Termination Date: 1992)

The Headway Reading Program: Grades K–6
Open Court, 1985 (Termination Date: 1992)

Gateway Literature: Grades 7–8
Scott, Foresman, 1984 (Termination Date: 1992)

Macmillan Literature: Grades 7–8
Glencoe, 1985 (Termination Date: 1992)

McDougal, Littell Literature: Grades 7–8
McDougal, Littell, 1982 (Termination Date: 1992)

McGraw-Hill Literature, Treasury Edition: Grades 7–8
McGraw-Hill, 1985 (Termination Date: 1992)

Ginn Literature: Grades 7–8
Prentice Hall, 1986 (Termination Date: 1992)

Adventures in Literature, Heritage Edition: Grades 7–8
Harcourt Brace Jovanovich, 1985 (Termination Date: 1992)

Economy Reading: Grades K–8
McGraw-Hill, 1986 (Termination Date: 1992)

Ginn Reading Program: Grades K–8
Silver, Burdett, and Ginn, 1985 (Termination Date: 1992)

Magic Circle Libraries: Grades K–4
Silver, Burdett, and Ginn, 1985 (Termination Date: 1992)

Ready Steps Language Survey: Grades K–8
Houghton Mifflin, 1986 (Termination Date: 1992)

Houghton Mifflin Reading: Grades K–8
Houghton Mifflin, 1986 (Termination Date: 1992)

Riverside Reading Program: Grades K–8
Houghton Mifflin, 1989 (Termination Date: 1992)

Scott, Foresman Reading: Grades K–8
Scott, Foresman, 1985 (Termination Date: 1992)

Spanish Reading Keys: Grades 1–6
McGraw-Hill, 1980–85 (Termination Date: 1992)

Macmillan Mil Marvillas: Grades K–6
Macmillan, 1986 (Termination Date: 1992)

Merrill Linguistic Reading Program: Grades K–6
Merrill, 1986 (Termination Date: 1992)

Beginning to Read, Write and Listen: Grades K–1
Macmillan, 1988 (Termination Date: 1992)

Keytext: Grades 1–8
McGraw-Hill, 1984 (Termination Date: 1992)

Reading for Success: Grades K–8
Scott, Foresman, 1985 (Termination Date: 1992)

The Reader's Anthology: Grades 7–8
Globe Book, 1986 (Termination Date: 1992)

Journeys: A Reading and Literature Program:
Grades 7–8
Harcourt Brace Jovanovich, 1982–84 (Termination Date: 1992)

New Directions in Reading: Grades 7–8
Houghton Mifflin, 1986 (Termination Date: 1992)

Scope English Anthologies: Grades 7–8
Scholastic, 1986 (Termination Date: 1992)

Reading—Supplemental
Aiming High: Grades 7–8
Amsco, 1983 (Termination Date: 1992)

The Reader as Detective: Grades 7–8
Amsco, 1983 (Termination Date: 1992)

High Marks: Grades 7–8
Amsco, 1981 (Termination Date: 1992)

Cloze Connections: Grades 1–9
Barnell Loft, 1990 (Termination Date: 1992)

Developing Key Concepts in Comprehension:
Grades 1–10
Barnell Loft, 1984 (Termination Date: 1992)

Specific Skills: Grades K–8
Barnell Loft, 1990 (Termination Date: 1992)

Barnell Loft 500: Grades 1–6
Barnell Loft, 1986 (Termination Date: 1992)

Multiple Skills: Grades K–9
Barnell Loft, 1990 (Termination Date: 1992)

Rookie Readers: Grades K–2
Children's Press, 1982–92 (Termination Date: 1992)

Clues for Better Reading: Grades 1-5
Curriculum Associates, 1987, 1991 (Termination Date: 1992)

Phonetic Keys to Reading for Keys to Independence in Reading: Grades K–3
McGraw-Hill, 1983 (Termination Date: 1992)

Economy Supplementary Reading, Spanish Edition:
Grades K–5
McGraw-Hill, 1986 (Termination Date: 1992)

Economy Supplementary Reading, English Edition:
Grades K–6
McGraw-Hill, 1986 (Termination Date: 1992)

Creatures Wild and Free: Grades K–6
EMC, 1981 (Termination Date: 1992)

Animals around Us: Grades K–6
EMC, 1982 (Termination Date: 1992)

Passport to Reading: Grades 2-5
EMC, 1982 (Termination Date: 1992)

Easy to Read Classics: Grades 3–6
EMC, 1967–68, 1980 (Termination Date: 1992)

Ginn Word Enrichment Program: Grades K–3
Silver, Burdett, and Ginn, 1985 (Termination
Date: 1992)

A Better Reading Workshop: Grades 6–12
Globe Book, 1984 (Termination Date: 1992)

Spell It Out: Grades 5–8
Globe Book, 1985–86 (Termination Date: 1992)

Real Stories: Grades 6–12
Globe Book, 1985 (Termination Date: 1992)

The World of Vocabulary: Grades 6–12
Globe Book, 1984 (Termination Date: 1992)

Odyssey: An HBJ Literature Program: Grades K–8
Harcourt Brace Jovanovich, 1986 (Termination
Date: 1992)

Chicago Mastery Learning Reading: Grades K–8
Mastery Education, 1982–83 (Termination Date:
1992)

Merrill Reading Skilltext: Grades K–6
Merrill, 1983 (Termination Date: 1992)

Reading Reinforcement Skilltext: Grades 1–8
Merrill, 1982 (Termination Date: 1992)

Phonics Is Fun: Grades 1-3
Modern Curriculum, 1985 (Termination Date: 1992)

Primary Phonetic Readers: Grades 1-3
Modern Curriculum, 1981–82 (Termination Date:
1992)

Primary Sight-Word Readers: Grades K–1
Modern Curriculum, 1981–83 (Termination Date:
1992)

Star Series Readers: Grades K–2
Modern Curriculum, 1988 (Termination Date: 1992)

Getting the Main Idea: Grades 2–6
Modern Curriculum, 1983 (Termination Date: 1992)

Increasing Comprehension: Grades 2–6
Modern Curriculum, 1983 (Termination Date: 1992)

Building Word Power: Grades 2–6
Modern Curriculum, 1983 (Termination Date: 1992)

Following Directions: Grades 2-4
Modern Curriculum, 1983 (Termination Date: 1992)

Working with Facts and Details: Grades 3–6
Modern Curriculum, 1983 (Termination Date: 1992)

Organizing Information: Grades 3–6
Modern Curriculum, 1983 (Termination Date: 1992)

Using References: Grades 3–6
Modern Curriculum, 1983–86 (Termination Date:
1992)

HM Study Skills Program, Levels I-III: Grades 5–12
National Association of Secondary School
Principals, 1980, 1982, 1986 (Termination Date:
1992)

Developing Comprehension: Grades 1-4
Random House, 1983 (Termination Date: 1992)

Structural Reading: Grades K–3
Random House, 1984 (Termination Date: 1992)

Practicing Comprehension: Grades 2–8
Random House, 1984 (Termination Date: 1992)

Triple Takes: Grades 1–8
Random House, 1984 (Termination Date: 1992)

Spotlight on Reading: Grades 2–8
Random House, 1984 (Termination Date: 1992)

Skill Builders: Grades 1–6
Random House, 1986 (Termination Date: 1992)

Reading Mastery Program: Direct Instruction:
Grades 1–6
Science Research, 1982–84 (Termination Date:
1992)

Corrective Reading: Grades 3–12
Science Research, 1978 (Termination Date: 1992)

SRA Lunchbox Library: Grades K–2
Science Research, 1990 (Termination Date: 1992)

Reading Laboratory: Grades 1–8
Science Research, 1989–90 (Termination Date:
1992)

Skills for Reading: Grades 7–12
Scott, Foresman, 1984 (Termination Date: 1992)

America Reads: Grades 6–8
Scott, Foresman, 1985–87 (Termination Date: 1992)

Lippincott Basic Reading: Grades K–6
Macmillan, 1981 (Termination Date: 1992)

The Wonder Story Books: Grades K–6
Macmillan, 1976 (Termination Date: 1992)

SUPER Books: Grades K–6
Macmillan, 1974–78 (Termination Date: 1992)

Codebook: Grades K–2
Macmillan, 1975 (Termination Date: 1992)

Mastering Basic Reading Skills: Grade 8
Steck-Vaughn, 1985 (Termination Date: 1992)

Reading Comprehension: Grade 8
Steck-Vaughn, 1989 (Termination Date: 1992)

Competency Reading: Grades 5–10
Steck-Vaughn, 1984 (Termination Date: 1992)

Building Sight Vocabulary: Grades K–3
Steck-Vaughn, 1985 (Termination Date: 1992)

Power Words: Grades 2–6
Steck-Vaughn, 1985 (Termination Date: 1992)

Arkansas

Language Arts—Elementary
HBJ Language: Grades 1–6
Harcourt Brace Jovanovich, 1990 (Termination Date: 1998)

Houghton Mifflin English: Grades 1–6
Houghton Mifflin, 1990 (Termination Date: 1998)

Language Arts Today: Grades 1–6
Macmillan/McGraw-Hill, 1991 (Termination Date: 1998)

World of Language: Grades 1–6
Silver, Burdett and Ginn, 1990 (Termination Date: 1998)

Supplementary Language Arts—Elementary
English Basics, I and II: Grades 4–6
Educational Activities, 1988 (Termination Date: 1998)

Punctuation: Grades 4–6
Educational Activities, 1988 (Termination Date: 1998)

Quotation Marks: Grades 4–6
Educational Activities, 1988 (Termination Date: 1998)

Capitalization: Grades 4–6
Educational Activities, 1988 (Termination Date: 1998)

Library and Media Skills: Grades 2–6
Educational Activities, 1988 (Termination Date: 1998)

E.A. Core Vocabulary Worksheet: Grades 1–6
Educational Activities, 1988 (Termination Date: 1998)

Developing Basic Writing Skills: Grades 3-5
Educational Activities, 1986 (Termination Date: 1998)

WordFind: Grades 1–6
Educational Activities, 1984 (Termination Date: 1998)

Gentle Art of Punctuation: Grades 5–6
Educational Activities, 1985 (Termination Date: 1998)

Creative Punctuation: Grades 5–6
Educational Activities, 1985 (Termination Date: 1998)

Capital Letters...and How to Use Them: Grades 5–6
Educational Activities, 1985 (Termination Date: 1998)

Imagination: An Odyssey through Language: Grades 1–6
Harcourt, Brace, 1989 (Termination Date: 1998)

The Writing Program: Grades 1–6
Modern Curriculum, 1989 (Termination Date: 1998)

Writing Folders: Grades 1-5
Modern Curriculum, 1989 (Termination Date: 1998)

Vocabulary Booster: Grades 4–6
Phoenix Learning Resources, 1989 (Termination Date: 1998)

Prentice Hall Grammar and Composition Series: Grade 6
Prentice Hall, 1990 (Termination Date: 1998)

Journalism

Getting Started in Journalism: Grades 7–12
National Textbook, 1989 (Termination Date: 1998)

Journalism Today!: Grades 7–12
National Textbook, 1986 (Termination Date: 1998)

Understanding Mass Media: Grades 7–12
National Textbook, 1991 (Termination Date: 1998)

Inside High School Journalism: Grades 9–12
Scott, Foresman, 1986 (Termination Date: 1998)

Press Time: Grades 9–12
Prentice Hall, 1985 (Termination Date: 1998)

Language, Grammar, and Composition, High School

HBJ Language Series: Grades 7–8
Harcourt Brace Jovanovich, 1990 (Termination Date: 1998)

Heath Grammar and Composition: Grades 6–12
D. C. Heath, 1990 (Termination Date: 1998)

English Composition and Grammar: Grades 7–12
Holt, Rinehart and Winston, 1988 (Termination Date: 1998)

English Workshop: Grades 7–12
Holt, Rinehart and Winston, 1986 (Termination Date: 1998)

Vocabulary Workshop: Grades 7–12
Holt, Rinehart and Winston, 1988 (Termination Date: 1998)

Composition: Models and Exercises: Grades 7–12
Holt, Rinehart and Winston, 1986 (Termination Date: 1998)

Vocabulary for College Vanguard Edition with Analogies: Grades 9–12
Holt, Rinehart and Winston, 1989 (Termination Date: 1998)

Houghton Mifflin English: Grades 7–12
Houghton Mifflin, 1990 (Termination Date: 1998)

Writer's Notebook: Grades 9–12
Houghton Mifflin, 1990 (Termination Date: 1998)

The Pocket Writer: Grades 9–12
Houghton Mifflin, 1990 (Termination Date: 1998)

Writer's Portfolio: Grades 9–12
Houghton Mifflin, 1992 (Termination Date: 1998)

Writing Process Videotape: Grades 9–12
Houghton Mifflin, 1992 (Termination Date: 1998)

McDougal Littell English Series: Grades 7–8
McDougal, Littell, 1990 (Termination Date: 1998)

The Writer's Craft Series: Grades 9–12
McDougal, Littell, 1991 (Termination Date: 1998)

Language Arts Today: Grades 7–8
Macmillan/McGraw-Hill, 1991 (Termination Date: 1998)

Literature Alive!: Grades 7–12
National Textbook, 1976 (Termination Date: 1998)

Write to the Point!: Grades 7–12
National Textbook, 1991 (Termination Date: 1998)

Lively Writing: Grades 7–12
National Textbook, 1985 (Termination Date: 1998)

Creative Writing: Grades 7–12
National Textbook, 1990 (Termination Date: 1998)

The Art of Composition: Grades 7–12
National Textbook, 1984 (Termination Date: 1998)

Prentice Hall Grammar and Composition Series: Grades 7–12
Prentice Hall, 1990 (Termination Date: 1998)

World of Language: Grades 7–8
Silver, Burdett and Ginn, 1990 (Termination Date: 1998)

Speech and Drama

Effective Speech: Grades 9–12
Glencoe/Macmillan McGraw-Hill, 1988 (Termination Date: 1998)

Speech Cassettes: Grades 9–12
Glencoe/Macmillan McGraw-Hill, 1988 (Termination Date: 1998)

Video Media: Grades 9–12
Glencoe/Macmillan McGraw-Hill, 1988 (Termination Date: 1998)

The Stage and the School: Grades 9–12
Glencoe/Macmillan McGraw-Hill, 1988 (Termination Date: 1998)

Scenes and Monologues: Grades 9–12
Glencoe/Macmillan McGraw-Hill, 1989 (Termination Date: 1998)

Speech for Effective Communication: Grades 9–12
Holt, Rinehart and Winston, 1988 (Termination Date: 1998)

Basic Debate: Grades 11–12
National Textbook, 1989 (Termination Date: 1998)

Speech: Exploring Communication: Grades 9–12
Prentice Hall, 1988 (Termination Date: 1998)

Communication: An Introduction to Speech: Grades 9–12
Prentice Hall, 1988 (Termination Date: 1998)

Theater: Preparation and Performance: Grades 9–12
Scott, Foresman, 1989 (Termination Date: 1998)

**Supplemental Language, Grammar
and Composition, High School**
Vocabulary for the High School: Grades 9–12
Amsco, 1983 (Termination Date: 1998)

Vocabulary for the College Bound: Grades 10–12
Amsco, 1983 (Termination Date: 1998)

Classroom News International: Grades 7–12
Educational Activities, 1990 (Termination Date: 1998)

Newspaper Literacy: Grades 7–12
Educational Activities, 1990 (Termination Date: 1998)

Descriptive Language Arts Development: Grades 7–12
Educational Activities, 1986 (Termination Date: 1998)

Writing Process Workshop: Grades 7–12
Educational Activities, 1990 (Termination Date: 1998)

Developing Basic Writing Skills: Grades 7–12
Educational Activities, 1986 (Termination Date: 1998)

Writing Competency Program: Grades 7–12
Educational Activities, 1986 (Termination Date: 1998)

CAW: Computer Assisted Writing: Grades 7–12
Educational Activities, 1986 (Termination Date: 1998)

Analyzing and Writing about Literature: Grades 7–12
Educational Activities, 1986 (Termination Date: 1998)

Writing Competency Practice: Grades 7–12
Educational Activities, 1991 (Termination Date: 1998)

English 2200 Nova Edition with Writing Applications: Grades 9–12
Holt, Rinehart and Winston, 1989 (Termination Date: 1998)

English 2600 Nova Edition with Writing Applications: Grades 9–12
Holt, Rinehart and Winston, 1989 (Termination Date: 1998)

English 3200 Nova Edition with Writing Applications: Grades 9–12
Holt, Rinehart and Winston, 1989 (Termination Date: 1998)

The Writing Program: Grades 7–9
Modern Curriculum, 1989 (Termination Date: 1998)

Speaking by Doing: Grades 7–12
National Textbook, 1990 (Termination Date: 1998)

Person to Person: Grades 7–12
National Textbook, 1990 (Termination Date: 1998)

The Basics of Speech: Grades 7–12
National Textbook, 1988 (Termination Date: 1998)

Dynamics of Speech: Grades 7–12
National Textbook, 1988 (Termination Date: 1998)

Public Speaking Today!: Grades 7–12
National Textbook, 1989 (Termination Date: 1998)

Vocabulary by Doing: Grades 7–12
National Textbook, 1990 (Termination Date: 1998)

Writing by Doing: Grades 7–12
National Textbook, 1990 (Termination Date: 1998)

The Dynamics of Acting: Grades 7–12
National Textbook, 1989 (Termination Date: 1998)

The Book of Scenes for Acting Practice: Grades 7–12
National Textbook, 1989 (Termination Date: 1998)

The Book of Cuttings for Acting and Directing:
Grades 7–12
National Textbook, 1989 (Termination Date: 1998)

Webster's New World High School: Grades 9–12
Prentice Hall, 1988 (Termination Date: 1998)

Stanford Vocabulary: Grade 7
Phoenix Learning Resources, 1988 (Termination
Date: 1998)

Guidebook to Better English: Grade 7
Phoenix Learning Resources, 1989 (Termination
Date: 1998)

Arkansas Basic Skillpack: Language Arts: Grade 8
Rainbow Educational Concepts, 1991 (Termination Date: 1998)

Supplemental, Journalism
The Communicator's Handbook: Grades 10–12
Maupin House, 1990 (Termination Date: 1998)

Photography: Grades 10–12
Scott, Foresman, 1989 (Termination Date: 1998)

Modern Mass Media: Communications in Society:
Grades 10–12
Scott, Foresman, 1990 (Termination Date: 1998)

Literature
Basic English Revisited: Grades 7–12
Econo-Clad, 1989 (Termination Date: 1998)

Eight Plus One: Grades 9–12
Econo-Clad, 1980 (Termination Date: 1998)

*Barron's Book Notes: Glass Menagerie/Streetcar
Named Desire:* Grades 9–12
Econo-Clad, 1984 (Termination Date: 1998)

*Barron's Book Notes (Glass Menagerie/Streetcar
Named Desire/Old Man and the Sea/My Antonia)*
Grades 7–12
Econo-Clad, 1954, 1984 (Termination Date: 1998)

Summer of My German Soldier: Grades 7–12
Econo-Clad, 1973 (Termination Date: 1998)

Wrinkle in Time: Grades 4–8
Econo-Clad, 1962 (Termination Date: 1998)

Westmark: Grades 4–8
Econo-Clad, 1984 (Termination Date: 1998)

Myths and Their Meanings: Grades 9–12
Allyn and Bacon, 1984 (Termination Date: 1998)

*New Voices in Literature, Language and Composi-
tion*: Grades 9–12
Allyn and Bacon, 1984 (Termination Date: 1998)

The Amsco Literature Series: Grades 7–12
Amsco, 1970–75 (Termination Date: 1998)

Afro-American Literature: Grades 11–12
Gamco Industries, 1978 (Termination Date: 1998)

The Devil in American Literature: Grades 11–12
Gamco Industries, 1976 (Termination Date: 1998)

The Globe Anthologies of Literature: Grades 7–12
Globe, 1986 (Termination Date: 1998)

*Journeys: A Reading and Literature Program, Re-
vised Edition with Writing Supplement:* Grades 7–12
Harcourt Brace Jovanovich, 1986 (Termination
Date: 1998)

Strategies in Reading: Grades 7–12
Harcourt Brace Jovanovich, 1984 (Termination
Date: 1998)

Impact: Fifty Short Stories: Grades 7–12
Harcourt Brace Jovanovich, 1986 (Termination
Date: 1998)

Reading/Writing Workshop, Heritage Edition:
Grades 7–10
Harcourt Brace Jovanovich, 1982 (Termination
Date: 1998)

Perspectives in Literature: Grades 7–12
Harcourt Brace Jovanovich, 1983 (Termination Date: 1998)

Adventures in Literature, Heritage Edition Revised: Grades 7–12
Harcourt Brace Jovanovich, 1970, 1979 1985, (Termination Date: 1998)

Reading Literature: Grades 7–12
McDougal, Littell, 1986 (Termination Date: 1998)

McDougal, Littell Literature: Grades 7–12
McDougal, Littell, 1987 (Termination Date: 1998)

McGraw-Hill Literature Series, Treasury Edition: Grades 7–12
McGraw-Hill, 1985 (Termination Date: 1998)

Ginn Literature Series: Grades 7–12
Prentice Hall, 1986 (Termination Date: 1998)

Scope English Anthology: Grades 7–12
Scholastic, 1983–84 (Termination Date: 1998)

America Reads: Grades 7–12
Scott, Foresman, 1987 (Termination Date: 1998)

The Gateway Literature Series: Grades 9–12
Scott, Foresman, 1984 (Termination Date: 1998)

Macmillan Literature Series: Grades 7–12
Scribner, 1985, 1984 (Termination Date: 1998)

Reading
HBJ Reading Program: Grades 1–6
Harcourt Brace Jovanovich, 1989 (Termination Date: 1994)

Heath Reading: Grades 1–6
D.C. Heath, 1989 (Termination Date: 1994)

HRW Reading: Reading Today and Tomorrow: Grades 1–6
Holt, Rinehart and Winston, 1989 (Termination Date: 1994)

Houghton Mifflin Reading: Grades 1–6
Houghton Mifflin, 1989 (Termination Date: 1994)

Macmillan Reading Program: Connections: Grades 1–6
Macmillan, 1989 (Termination Date: 1994)

Scott Foresman Reading: Grades 1–6
Scott, Foresman, 1989 (Termination Date: 1994)

World of Reading: Grades 1–6
Silver, Burdett and Ginn, 1989 (Termination Date: 1994)

Dictionaries
My Picture Dictionary: Grades 1-2
Ginn, 1985 (Termination Date: 1994)

My Second Picture Dictionary: Grades 1-2
Ginn, 1985 (Termination Date: 1994)

Webster's Elementary Dictionary: Grades 3–6
Ginn, 1986 (Termination Date: 1994)

HBJ School Dictionary: Grades 4–8
Harcourt Brace Jovanovich, 1985 (Termination Date: 1994)

Houghton Mifflin Primary Dictionary: Grades 1-2
(Termination Date: 1994)

HBJ School Dictionary: Grades 4–8
Harcourt Brace Jovanovich, 1985 (Termination Date: 1994)

Houghton Mifflin Primary Dictionary: Grades 1-2
Houghton Mifflin, 1986 (Termination Date: 1994)

Houghton Mifflin Intermediate Dictionary: Grades 3–6
Houghton Mifflin, 1986 (Termination Date: 1994)

Vocabulary Building and Dictionary Skills Workbook: Grades 1–6
Houghton Mifflin, 1986 (Termination Date: 1994)

Macmillan Dictionary Series: Grades 1–8
Macmillan, 1981, 1983, 1987 (Termination Date: 1994)

Webster's New World Dictionary, Basic School Edition: Grades 3–6
Modern Curriculum, 1983 (Termination Date: 1994)

My Dictionary: Grade 1
Scott, Foresman, 1987 (Termination Date: 1994)

My First Picture Dictionary: Grade 1
Scott, Foresman, 1987 (Termination Date: 1994)

My Second Picture Dictionary: Grade 2
Scott, Foresman, 1987 (Termination Date: 1994)

*In Other Words (Beginning and Junior Thesaurus
Exercise Book):* Grades 3-4
Scott, Foresman, 1987 (Termination Date: 1994)

Scott, Foresman Beginning Dictionary: Grades 3-5
Scott, Foresman, 1983 (Termination Date: 1994)

Scott, Foresman Intermediate Dictionary: Grades 5-8
Scott, Foresman, 1983 (Termination Date: 1994)

Webster's Intermediate Dictionary: Grades 7-9
Ginn, 1986 (Termination Date: 1994)

Webster's School Thesaurus: Grades 7-9
Ginn, 1978 (Termination Date: 1994)

Webster's High School Dictionary: Grades 7-12
Globe, 1982 (Termination Date: 1994)

Webster's Ninth Collegiate Dictionary: Grades 7-12
Globe, 1985 (Termination Date: 1994)

Houghton Mifflin Student Dictionary: Grades 7-9
Houghton Mifflin, 1986 (Termination Date: 1994)

*Vocabulary Building and Dictionary Skills Work-
book:* Grades 7-9
Houghton Mifflin, 1986 (Termination Date: 1994)

*The American Heritage Dictionary of the English
Language, High School Edition:* Grades 9-12
Houghton Mifflin, 1982 (Termination Date: 1994)

Houghton Mifflin College Dictionary: Grades 9-12
Houghton Mifflin, 1986 (Termination Date: 1994)

The American Heritage Dictionary: Grades 10-12
Houghton Mifflin, 1982 (Termination Date: 1994)

Roget's II, The New Thesaurus: Grades 9-12
Houghton Mifflin, 1980 (Termination Date: 1994)

The Concise American Heritage Dictionary: Grades
9-12
Houghton Mifflin, 1980 (Termination Date: 1994)

The Word Desk Set: Grades 7-12
Houghton Mifflin, 1983 (Termination Date: 1994)

Macmillan Dictionary: Grades 7-12
Macmillan, 1987 (Termination Date: 1994)

Webster's New World Dictionary: Grades 7-12
Prentice Hall, 1983 (Termination Date: 1994)

*Webster's New World Dictionary, Revised School
Printing:* Grades 7-12
Prentice Hall, 1985 (Termination Date: 1994)

Random House College Dictionary: Grades 7-12
Random House, 1983 (Termination Date: 1994)

Robert's Rules of Order: Grade 12
Scott, Foresman, 1981 (Termination Date: 1994)

Scott, Foresman Advanced Dictionary: Grades 7-12
Scott, Foresman, 1983 (Termination Date: 1994)

Handwriting

Bowmar/Noble Handwriting Series: Grades 1-7
Economy, 1987 (Termination Date: 1994)

HBJ Handwriting: Grades 1-6
Harcourt Brace Jovanovich, 1987 (Termination
Date: 1994)

McDougal, Littell Handwriting: Grades 1-8
McDougal, Littell, 1987 (Termination Date: 1994)

Palmer Method Handwriting, Centennial Edition:
Grades 1-6
A.N. Palmer, 1987 (Termination Date: 1994)

D'Nealian Handwriting: Grades 1-6
Scott, Foresman, 1987 (Termination Date: 1994)

Zaner-Bloser Handwriting: Grades 1-8
Zaner-Bloser, 1987 (Termination Date: 1994)

Spelling

HBJ Spelling: Grades 1-8
Harcourt Brace Jovanovich, 1983 (Termination
Date: 1994)

Houghton Mifflin Spelling: Grades 1-8
Houghton Mifflin, 1985 (Termination Date: 1994)

Building Spelling Skills: Grades 1-8
McDougal, Littell, 1985 (Termination Date: 1994)

Series S: Macmillan Spelling: Grades 1-8
Macmillan, 1987 (Termination Date: 1994)

Spelling for Word Mastery: Grades 1–8
Merrill, 1984 (Termination Date: 1994)

Spelling: Words and Skills: Grades 1–8
Scott, Foresman, 1986 (Termination Date: 1994)

Silver Burdett Spelling: Grades 1–8
Silver Burdett and Ginn, 1986 (Termination Date: 1994)

Steck-Vaughn Spelling Series: Grades 1–8
Steck-Vaughn, 1984 (Termination Date: 1994)

Basic Skills and Application: Grades 1–8
Zaner-Bloser, 1984 (Termination Date: 1994)

California

Elements of Literature: Grades 7–8
Holt, Rinehart and Winston, 1988, 1989 (Termination Date: 1996)

English: Writing and Skills: Grades 7–8
Holt, Rinehart and Winston, 1988 (Termination Date: 1996)

Houghton Mifflin English: Grades K–8
Houghton Mifflin, 1988 (Termination Date: 1996)

McDougal, Littell English Series: Grades K–8
McDougal, Littell, 1987-1989 (Termination Date: 1996)

McGraw-Hill English: Grades K–8
McGraw-Hill, 1989 (Termination Date: 1996)

Scott, Foresman Language: Grades K–8
Scott, Foresman, 1989 (Termination Date: 1996)

Scott Foresman Computer Management System: Grades K–8
Scott, Foresman, 1987 (Termination Date: 1996)

Scott, Foresman Language Objectives Disks: Grades K–8
Scott, Foresman, 1989 (Termination Date: 1996)

The Write Connection: Grades 1–8
Scott, Foresman, 1988 (Termination Date: 1996)

Silver, Burdett and Ginn: Grades K–3
Silver, Burdett and Ginn, 1989 (Termination Date: 1996)

Florida

Dictionaries
Scribner Dictionary Series: Grades 3–8
Glencoe, 1986 (Termination Date: 1993)

The American Heritage Dictionary of the English Language, High School Edition: Grades 11–12
Glencoe, 1982 (Termination Date: 1994)

HBJ School Dictionary: Grades 4–6
Harcourt Brace Jovanovich, 1985 (Termination Date: 1993)

Houghton Mifflin Dictionary Series: Grades K–8
Houghton Mifflin, 1986 (Termination Date: 1993)

Houghton Mifflin College Dictionary: Grades 9–12
Glencoe, 1986 (Termination Date: 1994)

Scribner Dictionary: Grades 8–12
Glencoe, 1986 (Termination Date: 1994)

Macmillan Dictionary Series: Grades K–12
Macmillan, 1983, 1987 (Termination Date: 1993/94)

The Random House School Dictionary: Grades 5–8
McGraw-Hill Educational Resources (Random House), 1984 (Termination Date: 1993)

Webster's New World Dictionary, Basic School Edition: Grades 3–6
Modern Curriculum, 1983 (Termination Date: 1993)

Webster's New World Dictionary: Grades 7–10
Prentice Hall, 1989 (Termination Date: 1994)

Scott, Foresman Dictionary Series: Grades K–8
Scott, Foresman, 1983, 1987 (Termination Date: 1993)

Scott, Foresman Advanced Dictionary: Grades 6–12
Scott, Foresman, 1988 (Termination Date: 1994)

Ginn Dictionary Series: Grades K–8
Silver, Burdett and Ginn, 1985, 1986 (Termination Date: 1993)

Handwriting
HBJ Handwriting: Grades K–6
Harcourt Brace Jovanovich, 1987 (Termination Date: 1993)

Bowmar/Noble Handwriting Series: Grades K–8
Macmillan/McGraw-Hill, 1987 (Termination
Date: 1993)

McDougal, Littell Handwriting: Grades K–8
McDougal, Littell, 1987 (Termination Date: 1993)

Scott, Foresman D'Nealian Handwriting Program:
Grades K–8
Scott, Foresman, 1987 (Termination Date: 1993)

*Zaner-Bloser Handwriting: Basic Skills and
Applications:* Grades K–8
Zaner-Bloser, 1987 (Termination Date: 1993)

Composition
Language for Daily Use, Voyager Edition: Grades
K–8
Harcourt Brace Jovanovich, 1986 (Termination
Date: 1993)

Your English: Grades K–8
Holt (Coronado), 1984 (Termination Date: 1993)

Houghton Mifflin English: Grades K–8
Houghton Mifflin, 1986 (Termination Date: 1993)

Laidlaw English: Grades K–8
Macmillan/McGraw-Hill, 1987 (Termination
Date: 1993)

Macmillan English: Grades K–8
Macmillan/McGraw-Hill, 1987 (Termination
Date: 1993)

Silver, Burdett English: Grades K–8
Silver, Burdett and Ginn, 1987 (Termination
Date: 1993)

Glencoe English: Grades 9–12
Glencoe, 1985 (Termination Date: 1994)

Houghton Mifflin English: Grades 6–8
Glencoe, 1988 (Termination Date: 1994)

*Houghton Mifflin English Grammar and Composi-
tion:* Grades 9–12
Glencoe, 1986 (Termination Date: 1994)

*Macmillan English: Thinking and Writing Pro-
cesses:* Grades 9–12
Glencoe, 1988 (Termination Date: 1994)

English Composition and Grammar: Grades 6–12
Harcourt Brace Jovanovich, 1988 (Termination
Date: 1994)

Heath Grammar and Composition: Grades 6–12
D.C. Heath, 1988 (Termination Date: 1994)

Heath Language Arts: Grades 6–8
D.C. Heath, 1988 (Termination Date: 1994)

English: Writing and Skills: Grades 7–12
Holt, Rinehart and Winston, 1988 (Termination
Date: 1994)

*Macmillan English: Thinking and Writing Pro-
cesses:* Grades 6–8
Macmillan, 1987 (Termination Date: 1994)

Basic Skills in English Series: Grade 7–12
McDougal, Littell, 1985 (Termination Date: 1994)

The McDougal, Littell English Program: Grades 7–12
McDougal, Littell, 1988 (Termination Date: 1994)

Prentice Hall Grammar and Composition Series:
Grades 6–12
Prentice Hall, 1987 (Termination Date: 1994)

Scope English: Writing and Language Skills:
Grades 6–12
Scholastic, 1987 (Termination Date: 1994)

Thirteen Steps to Better Writing: Grade 9
Amsco, 1987 (Termination Date: 1994)

Literature-Based Composition: Grades 9–12
Glencoe, 1988 (Termination Date: 1994)

The Art of Composition: Grades 11–12
National Textbook, 1984 (Termination Date: 1994)

Lively Writing: Grades 9–12
National Textbook, 1985 (Termination Date: 1994)

Writing by Doing: Grades 9–12
National Textbook, 1990 (Termination Date: 1994)

Developing Writing Skills: Grades 9–10
Prentice Hall, 1988 (Termination Date: 1994)

Thinking and Writing about Literature: Grades 11–12
Prentice Hall, 1984 (Termination Date: 1994)

Literature

Jamestown Heritage Readers: Grades K–6
Jamestown, 1991 (Termination Date: 1997)

Adventures in Literature Series: Grades 6–12
Holt, Rinehart and Winston, 1989 (Termination
Date: 1997)

Elements of Literature Series: Grades 7–12
Holt, Rinehart and Winston, 1989 (Termination
Date: 1997)

Prentice Hall Literature Series: Grades 6–12
Prentice Hall, 1991 (Termination Date: 1997)

Scholastic Scope Literature Series: Grades 6–12
Scholastic, 1991 (Termination Date: 1997)

America Reads Series: Grades 6–12
Scott, Foresman, 1991 (Termination Date: 1997)

World Literature

Prentice Hall Literature: World Masterpieces:
Grades 9–12
Prentice Hall, 1991 (Termination Date: 1997)

Classics in World Literature: Grades 9–12
Scott, Foresman, 1991 (Termination Date: 1997)

Speech

Speaking by Doing: Grades 6–12
National Textbook, 1986 (Termination Date:1993)

Speech: Exploring Communication: Grades 9–12
Prentice Hall, 1984 (Termination Date: 1993)

Speech: Principles and Practice: Grades 6–12
Scott, Foresman, 1987 (Termination Date: 1993)

Stagecraft

Play Production Today: Grades 9–12
National Textbook, 1983 (Termination Date: 1993)

Theatre History and Literature

Introduction to Theatre and Drama: Grades 9–12
National Textbook, 1975 (Termination Date: 1993)

Reading, Basal Programs

Imagination: An Odyssey through Literature:
Grades 1–6
Harcourt Brace Jovanovich, 1989/90 (Termination
Date: 1996)

Heath Reading: Grades K–8
D.C. Heath, 1989 (Termination Date: 1996)

Houghton Mifflin Reading/Language Arts: Grades
K–8
Houghton Mifflin, 1989 (Termination Date: 1996)

McGraw-Hill Reading/Integrated Language Arts:
Grades K–8
McGraw-Hill, 1989 (Termination Date: 1996)

World of Reading: Grades K–8
Silver, Burdett and Ginn, 1989 (Termination
Date: 1996)

HBJ Reading: Grades K–8
Harcourt Brace Jovanovich, 1989 (Termination
Date: 1996)

Houghton Mifflin Reading: Grades K–8
Houghton Mifflin, 1989 (Termination Date: 1996)

Connections: Grades K–8
McGraw-Hill, 1989 (Termination Date: 1996)

Open Court Reading and Writing: Grades K–6
Open Court, 1989 (Termination Date: 1996)

Scott, Foresman Reading: Grades K–8
Scott, Foresman, 1989 (Termination Date: 1996)

Reading Specific Skills, Grades K–5 6–8, 9–12

Random House Phonics: Grades 1-3
American School, 1988 (Termination Date: 1996)

Scoring High in Reading: Grades 1-5
American School, 1985 (Termination Date: 1996)

Experiences for Literacy: Grades K–2
DLM Teaching Resources, 1989 (Termination
Date: 1996)

Impressions: Grades K–3
Holt, Rinehart, 1984–88 (Termination Date: 1996)

Reading Express: Grades K–5
Macmillan/McGraw-Hill, 1986–90 (Termination Date: 1996)

Language Works: Grades K–4
Modern Curriculum, 1987–89 (Termination Date: 1996)

MCP Literature: Grades 1–6
Modern Curriculum, 1988 (Termination Date: 1996)

MCP Phonics Program: Grades 1–6
Modern Curriculum, 1986, 1988 (Termination Date: 1996)

Swinging Out: Grade K
Modern Curriculum, 1986 (Termination Date: 1996)

Bridges: Grades K–5
Scholastic, 1987 (Termination Date: 1996)

Focus: Reading for Success: Grades K–5
Scott, Foresman, 1988 (Termination Date: 1996)

Steck-Vaughn Literature Library: Grade 5
Steck-Vaughn, 1996 (Termination Date: 1996)

Vocabulary Connections: Grades 3-5
Steck-Vaughn, 1989 (Termination Date: 1996)

Sunshine Reading Program: Grades K–1
Wright Group, 1986–88 (Termination Date: 1996)

Scoring High in Reading: Grade 6
American School, 1985 (Termination Date: 1996)

Strategies for Effective Writing: Grades 6–8
DLM Teaching Resources, 1988 (Termination Date: 1996)

Be a Better Reader: Grades 6–8
Globe, 1989 (Termination Date: 1996)

Critical Reading Skills Series: Grades 6–8
Jamestown, 1982–87 (Termination Date: 1996)

Learning to Study: Grades 6–8
Jamestown, 1996 (Termination Date: 1996)

Reading the Newspaper: Grades 6–8
Jamestown, 1987 (Termination Date: 1996)

Reading Express: Grades 6–8
McGraw Hill, 1986–90 (Termination Date: 1996)

McDougal Littell Wordskills Series: Grades 7–8
McDougal, Littell, 1986 (Termination Date: 1996)

Vistas in Reading Literature Series: Grades 6–8
McDougal, Littell, 1989 (Termination Date: 1996)

The Writing Program: Grades 6–8
Modern Curriculum, 1989 (Termination Date: 1996)

Reading about Science: Grades 6–8
Phoenix Learning Resources, 1990 (Termination Date: 1996)

Bridges: Grade 6
Scholastic, 1987 (Termination Date: 1996)

Focus: Reading for Success: Grades 6–8
Scott, Foresman, 1988 (Termination Date: 1996)

The Reader as Detective Series: Grades 9–12
Amsco, 1996 (Termination Date: 1996)

Be a Better Reader Series: Grades 9–12
Globe Book, 1989 (Termination Date: 1996)

Beyond Basics: Grades 9–12
Jamestown, 1986 (Termination Date: 1996)

Jamestown Classics: Grades 9–12
Jamestown, 1976, 1980, 1982 (Termination Date: 1996)

Reading the Newspapers: Grades 9–12
Jamestown, 1989 (Termination Date: 1996)

Six-Way Paragraphs: Grades 9–12
Jamestown, 1983 (Termination Date: 1996)

Skimming and Scanning: Grades 9–12
Jamestown, 1989 (Termination Date: 1996)

Vocabulary Drills: Grades 9–12
Jamestown, 1986 (Termination Date: 1996)

McDougal Littell Wordskills Series: Grades 9–12
McDougal, Littell, 1986 (Termination Date: 1996)

Reading in the Content Area: Grades 9–12
Media Materials, 1989 (Termination Date: 1996)

Reading by Doing: Grades 9–12
National Textbook, 1988 (Termination Date: 1996)

The Reading Connection: A Skills Recovery Program: Grades 9–12
Open Court, 1982, 1984 (Termination Date: 1996)

Project Achievement Reading: Grades 9–12
Scholastic, 1987 (Termination Date: 1996)

Focus on Reading: A Merrill Skilltext Series: Grades 9–12
Science Research Associates (Merrill), 1989 (Termination Date: 1996)

Spelling
Houghton Mifflin Spelling: Grades 1–8
Houghton Mifflin, 1985 (Termination Date: 1993)

Laidlaw Spelling: Grades 1–8
Macmillan/McGraw-Hill, 1987 (Termination Date: 1993)

Series S: Macmillan Spelling: Grades 1–8
Macmillan/McGraw-Hill, 1987 (Termination Date: 1993)

Spelling for Word Mastery: Grades 1–8
Macmillan/McGraw-Hill, 1987 (Termination Date: 1993)

Spelling: Words and Skills: Grades 1–8
Scott, Foresman, 1986 (Termination Date: 1993)

Silver Burdett Spelling: Grades 1–8
Silver, Burdett and Ginn, 1986 (Termination Date: 1993)

Zaner-Bloser Spelling: Basic Skills and Applications: Grades 1–8
Zaner-Bloser, 1984 (Termination Date: 1993)

Debate
Basic Debate: Grades 9–12
National Textbook, 1986 (Termination Date: 1993)

Strategic Debate: Grades 9–12
National Textbook, 1993 (Termination Date: 1993)

Drama
The Stage and the School: Grades 9–12
Glencoe/ (McGraw-Hill/School Division), 1982 (Termination Date: 1993)

Theatre: Preparation and Performance: Grades 9–12
Scott, Foresman, 1987 (Termination Date: 1993)

Humanities
The Humanities: Cultural Roots and Continuities: Grades 9–12
D.C. Heath, 1985 (Termination Date: 1993)

Journalism Today: Grades 9–12
National Textbook, 1986 (Termination Date: 1993)

Press Time: Grades 9–12
Prentice Hall, 1985 (Termination Date: 1993)

Inside High School Journalism: Grades 6–12
Scott, Foresman, 1986 (Termination Date: 1993)

Georgia

Communications/Applied Language Arts
Effective Speech: Grades 9–12
Glencoe/McGraw-Hill, 1988 (Termination Date: 1994)

Speech for Effective Communication: Grades 9–12
Harcourt, Brace, 1988 (Termination Date: 1994)

English for the World of Work: Grades 7–12
Media Materials, 1984 (Termination Date: 1994)

Life Skills English: Grades 7–12
Media Materials, 1984 (Termination Date: 1994)

The Basics of Speech: Grades 7–9
National Textbook, 1988 (Termination Date: 1994)

Public Speaking Today!: Grades 9–12
National Textbook, 1988 (Termination Date: 1994)

Person to Person: Grades 9–12
National Textbook, 1990 (Termination Date: 1994)

Dynamics of Speech: Grades 9–12
National Textbook, 1988 (Termination Date: 1994)

Communication: An Introduction to Speech: Grades 7–8
Prentice Hall, 1988 (Termination Date: 1994)

Speech: Exploring Communication: Grades 9–12
Prentice Hall, 1988 (Termination Date: 1994)

Speech: Principles and Practices: Grades 6–9
Scott, Foresman, 1987 (Termination Date: 1994)

Dictionaries

Webster's Elementary Dictionary: Grades 3–6
Encyclopaedia Britannica, 1986 (Termination Date: 1994)

Webster's Intermediate Dictionary: Grades 5–8
Encyclopaedia Britannica, 1986 (Termination Date: 1994)

Webster's School Dictionary: Grades 7–12
Encyclopaedia Britannica, 1986 (Termination Date: 1994)

Webster's Ninth New Collegiate Dictionary: Grades 9–12
Encyclopaedia Britannica, 1987 (Termination Date: 1994)

Webster's School Thesaurus: Grades 7–12
Encyclopaedia Britannica, 1989 (Termination Date: 1994)

Webster's Collegiate Thesaurus: Grades 9–12
Encyclopaedia Britannica, 1988 (Termination Date: 1994)

Scribner Dictionary: Grades 8–12
Glencoe/McGraw-Hill, 1986 (Termination Date: 1994)

Macmillan Dictionary: Grades 9–12
Glencoe/McGraw-Hill, 1987 (Termination Date: 1994)

Scribner Intermediate Dictionary: Grades 6–8
Glencoe/McGraw-Hill, 1986 (Termination Date: 1994)

The Lincoln Reading Dictionary: Grades 1-3
Harcourt Brace Jovanovich, 1990 (Termination Date: 1994)

The Lincoln Writing Dictionary: Grades 3–8
Harcourt Brace Jovanovich, 1989 (Termination Date: 1994)

HBJ School Dictionary, 3rd Edition: Grades 4–8
Harcourt Brace Jovanovich, 1990 (Termination Date: 1994)

Houghton Mifflin Picture Dictionary: Grades K–1
Houghton Mifflin, 1989 (Termination Date: 1994)

Houghton Mifflin Primary Dictionary: Grades 1-2
Houghton Mifflin, 1990 (Termination Date: 1994)

Houghton Mifflin Intermediate Dictionary: Grades 3–6
Houghton Mifflin, 1989 (Termination Date: 1994)

Houghton Mifflin Student Dictionary: Grades 6–9
Houghton Mifflin, 1989 (Termination Date: 1994)

Houghton Mifflin College Dictionary: Grades 9–12
Houghton Mifflin, 1986 (Termination Date: 1994)

American Heritage Dictionary of the English Language: Grades 11–12
Houghton Mifflin, 1982 (Termination Date: 1994)

Macmillan Picture Dictionary: Grades K–1
Macmillan/McGraw-Hill, 1983 (Termination Date: 1994)

Macmillan First Dictionary: Grades 1-2
Macmillan/McGraw-Hill, 1987 (Termination Date: 1994)

Macmillan School Dictionary, 1 and 2: Grades 3–7
Macmillan/McGraw-Hill, 1990 (Termination Date: 1994)

A Big Book of Words: Grades K–3
Macmillan/McGraw-Hill, 1988 (Termination Date: 1994)

Webster's New World Dictionary: Grades 3–8
Modern Curriculum, 1989 (Termination Date: 1994)

Webster's New World Dictionary: Grades 9–12
Prentice Hall, 1988 (Termination Date: 1994)

Pictionary/Picture Dictionary Program: Grades K–1
Scott, Foresman, 1990 (Termination Date: 1994)

Scott, Foresman Thorndike-Barnhart Dictionaries: Grades 3–12
Scott, Foresman, 1988 (Termination Date: 1994)

Thesauri Program: Grades 3–12
Scott, Foresman, 1987 (Termination Date: 1994)

Webster's Elementary Dictionary: Grades 3–6
Silver Burdett and Ginn, 1986 (Termination
Date: 1994)

Webster's Intermediate Dictionary: Grades 6–8
Silver Burdett and Ginn, 1986 (Termination
Date: 1994)

Handwriting
Ready! Set! Keyboard!: Grades 3–6
Harcourt Brace Jovanovich, 1988 (Termination
Date: 1994)

HBJ Handwriting: Grades K–8
Harcourt Brace Jovanovich, 1987 (Termination
Date: 1994)

McDougal, Littell Handwriting: Grades K–8
McDougal, Littell, 1990 (Termination Date: 1994)

*Scott, Foresman D'Nealian Handwriting Program,
2nd Edition:* Grades K–8
Scott, Foresman, 1991 (Termination Date: 1994)

Handwriting: Basic Skills and Application: Grades
1–8
Zaner-Bloser, 1989 (Termination Date: 1994)

Language and/or Composition
Practicing the Writing Process: Grades 7–9
EDI, 1986, 1988 (Termination Date: 1994)

HBJ Language: Grades K–8
Harcourt Brace Jovanovich, 1990 (Termination
Date: 1994)

*English Composition and Grammar, Benchmark
Edition:* Grades 6–12
Harcourt Brace Jovanovich, 1988 (Termination
Date: 1994)

English Workshop, Liberty/Benchmark Edition:
Grades 6–12
Harcourt Brace Jovanovich, 1986, 1988 (Termina-
tion Date: 1994)

*Composition: Models and Exercises, Liberty/
Benchmark Edition:* Grades 7–12
Harcourt Brace Jovanovich, 1986, 1989 (Termina-
tion Date: 1994)

Heath Grammar and Composition: Grades 6–12
D.C. Heath, 1988 (Termination Date: 1994)

Houghton Mifflin English: Grades K–12
Houghton Mifflin, 1990 (Termination Date: 1994)

Project Write, 2nd Edition: Grades 6–8
Kendall Hunt, 1988 (Termination Date: 1994)

Active Composing and Thinking: Grades 7–8
Kendall Hunt, 1988 (Termination Date: 1994)

Language Arts Today: Grades K–8
Macmillan/McGraw-Hill, 1990 (Termination
Date: 1994)

McGraw-Hill English: Grades K–8
Macmillan/McGraw-Hill, 1989 (Termination
Date: 1994)

Basic Skills in English: Grades 7–12
McDougal, Littell, 1989 (Termination Date: 1994)

McDougal, Littell English: Grades 6–12
McDougal, Littell, 1990 (Termination Date: 1994)

The Writing Program: Grades 1–9
Modern Curriculum, 1989 (Termination Date: 1994)

Lively Writing: Grades 9–12
National Textbook, 1985 (Termination Date: 1994)

Writing by Doing: Grades 9–12
National Textbook, 1990 (Termination Date: 1994)

Prentice Hall Grammar and Composition: Grades
6–12
Prentice Hall, 1990 (Termination Date: 1994)

Project Achievement: Writing: Grades 6–12
Scholastic, 1989 (Termination Date: 1994)

Scope English Writing and Language: Grades 6–12
Scholastic, 1989 (Termination Date: 1994)

Scott, Foresman Language: Grades K–8
Scott, Foresman, 1989 (Termination Date: 1994)

World of Language: Grades K–8
Silver, Burdett and Ginn, 1990 (Termination
Date: 1994)

Literature
AMSCO Literature Series: Grades 9–12
AMSCO, 1989, 1988 (Termination Date: 1994)

Scribner Literature Series: Grades 6–12
Glencoe/McGraw-Hill, 1986, 1989, 1991 (Termination Date: 1994)

Globe Literature: Grades 7–12
Globe, 1990 (Termination Date: 1994)

Imagination: An Odyssey through Language:
Grades K–6
Harcourt Brace Jovanovich, 1989 (Termination Date: 1994)

Impact: Fifty Short Stories: Grades 7–12
Harcourt Brace Jovanovich, 1986 (Termination Date: 1994)

Adventures in Literature: Grades 6–12
Harcourt Brace Jovanovich, 1986, 1989, 1991 (Termination Date: 1994)

Elements of Literature: Grades 6–12
Holt, Rinehart and Winston, 1989, 1991 (Termination Date: 1994)

African-American Literature: Grades 9–12
Holt, Rinehart and Winston, 1991 (Termination Date: 1994)

Houghton Mifflin Reading/Language Arts Program:
Grades K–8
Houghton Mifflin, 1989 (Termination Date: 1994)

McDougal, Littell Literature: Grades 7–12
McDougal, Littell, 1989 (Termination Date: 1994)

The Short Story and You: Grades 9–12
National Textbook, 1987 (Termination Date: 1994)

Prentice Hall Literature: Grades 6–12
Prentice Hall, 1991, 1989 (Termination Date: 1994)

Scope English Anthologies: Grades 6–12
Scholastic, 1988 (Termination Date: 1994)

Collections: An Anthology Series: Grades 1–6
Scott, Foresman, 1989 (Termination Date: 1994)

America Reads: Grades 6–12
Scott, Foresman, 1989 (Termination Date: 1994)

Spelling

HBJ Spelling: Grades 1–8
Harcourt Brace Jovanovich, 1988 (Termination Date: 1994)

Houghton Mifflin Spelling and Vocabulary: Grades 1–8
Houghton Mifflin, 1990 (Termination Date: 1994)

Riverside Spelling: Grades K–8
Houghton Mifflin, 1988 (Termination Date: 1994)

McGraw-Hill Spelling: Grades 1–8
McGraw-Hill, 1990 (Termination Date: 1994)

Merrill Spelling: Grades 1–8
McGraw-Hill, 1990 (Termination Date: 1994)

McDougal, Littell Spelling: Grades 1–8
McDougal, Littell, 1990 (Termination Date: 1994)

Scott, Foresman Spelling: Grades 1–8
Scott, Foresman, 1988 (Termination Date: 1994)

Steck-Vaughn Spelling: Grades 1–8
Steck-Vaughn, 1990 (Termination Date: 1994)

Spelling Connections: Words into Language:
Grades 1–8
Zaner-Bloser, 1988 (Termination Date: 1994)

Reading

Early Bird: Grade K
Delmar, 1990 (Termination Date: 1995)

Experiences for Literacy: Grade K
DLM, 1989, 1990 (Termination Date: 1995)

Reading Bridge: Grades 6–12
Dormac, 1989, 1990 (Termination Date: 1995)

Discoveries in Reading: Grades 6–8
Harcourt, Brace, 1990 (Termination Date: 1995)

HBJ Reading: Grades K–8
Harcourt, Brace, 1990 (Termination Date: 1995)

Heath Reading: Grades K–8
D.C. Heath, 1991 (Termination Date: 1995)

Houghton Mifflin Reading: The Literature Experience: Grades K–8
Houghton Mifflin, 1991 (Termination Date: 1995)

Connections: Grades 1–8
Macmillan/McGraw-Hill, 1991 (Termination Date: 1995)

Reading Literature: Grades 9–12
McDougal, Littell, 1990 (Termination Date: 1995)

Vistas in Reading Literature: Grades 5–8
McDougal, Littell, 1990, 1989 (Termination Date: 1995)

Language Immersion Experience: Grade K
New Dimensions in Education, 1981, 1989, 1990 (Termination Date: 1995)

Open Court Reading and Writing: Grades K–6
Open Court, 1989 (Termination Date: 1995)

Bridges: Grades 1–6
Scholastic, 1987, 1990 (Termination Date: 1995)

Focus: Reading for Success: Grades K–8
Scott, Foresman, 1988 (Termination Date: 1995)

Scott Foresman Reading: Grades K–8
Scott, Foresman, 1987–89 (Termination Date: 1995)

World of Reading: Grades K–8
Silver, Burdett and Ginn, 1991 (Termination Date: 1995)

Idaho

Basic Integrated Language Arts

Impressions: Grades K–6
Harcourt Brace Jovanovich, 1989, 1990 (Termination Date: 1995)

Imagination: An Odyssey through Language: Grades K–8
Harcourt Brace Jovanovich, 1989 (Termination Date: 1995)

Heath Reading: Grades K–8
D. C. Heath, 1991 (Termination Date: 1995)

Houghton Mifflin Reading/Language Arts: Houghton Mifflin Literary Readers: Grades K–8
Houghton Mifflin, 1989 (Termination Date: 1995)

Introduction to Literature: Grade 6
Holt, Rinehart and Winston/Harcourt Brace Jovanovich, 1991 (Termination Date: 1995)

Vistas in Reading Literature Series: Grades 5–8
McDougal, Littell, 1990 (Termination Date: 1995)

Strategies Series: Grades 4–6
McDougal, Littell, 1991 (Termination Date: 1995)

Prentice Hall Literature Series: Grades 6–12
Prentice Hall, 1989-1991 (Termination Date: 1995)

Scholastic Scope Literature: Grades 6–12
Scholastic, 1991 (Termination Date: 1995)

America Reads: Grades 6–12
Scott, Foresman, 1991 (Termination Date: 1995)

Collections: Grades 1–6
Scott, Foresman, 1989 (Termination Date: 1995)

Story Box Series: Grade K
Wright Group, 1990 (Termination Date: 1995)

The Sunshine Box Series, Levels 1–11: Grades 1-5
Wright Group, 1990 (Termination Date: 1995)

Reading

HBJ Reading: Grades K–8
Harcourt Brace Jovanovich, 1989 (Termination Date: 1995)

Houghton Mifflin Reading: Grades K–8
Houghton Mifflin, 1991 (Termination Date: 1995)

Connections: Grades K–8
Macmillan/McGraw-Hill, 1991 (Termination Date: 1995)

Reading Express: Grades K–8
Macmillan/McGraw-Hill, 1990 (Termination Date: 1995)

Scribner Reading Series: Grades K–8
Macmillan/McGraw-Hill, 1989 (Termination Date: 1995)

Open Court Reading and Writing: Grades K–6
Open Court, 1989 (Termination Date: 1995)

World of Reading: Grades K–8
Silver, Burdett and Ginn, 1991 (Termination Date: 1995)

Focus: Reading for Success: Grades K–8
Scott, Foresman, 1989 (Termination Date: 1995)

Scott, Foresman Reading: Grades K–8
Scott, Foresman, 1989 (Termination Date: 1995)

Supplemental

Be a Better Reader: Grades 4–12
Globe, 1989 (Termination Date: 1995)

Lincoln Reading Dictionary: Grades K–3
Harcourt Brace Jovanovich, 1990 (Termination
Date: 1995)

Bill Martin Big Books: Grades K–2
Harcourt Brace Jovanovich, 1970 (Termination
Date: 1995)

Treasury of Lap Books: Grades K–1
Harcourt Brace Jovanovich, 1989 (Termination
Date: 1995)

Beginning to Read, Write and Listen: Grades K–1
Macmillan/McGraw-Hill, 1988 (Termination
Date: 1995)

Once upon a Time: Grade K
Macmillan/McGraw-Hill, 1989 (Termination
Date: 1995)

McDougal, Littell Magic Bean Series: Grades K–4
McDougal, Littell, 1989 (Termination Date: 1995)

Eureka Treasure Chest Series: Grades K–2
McDougal, Littell, 1991 (Termination Date: 1995)

My First Thesaurus: Grades 1-4
McDougal, Littell, 1990 (Termination Date: 1995)

Young Writer's Thesaurus: Grades 4–8
McDougal, Littell, 1990 (Termination Date: 1995)

Book Centers: Grades 2–6
Scholastic, 1988, 1990 (Termination Date: 1995)

Bridges: Grades 1–6
Scholastic, 1988, 1990 (Termination Date: 1995)

Big Books: Grades K–3
Scholastic, (Termination Date: 1995)

Perform!: Grades 1–6
Scholastic, 1990 (Termination Date: 1995)

Project Achievement: Reading: Grades 5–12
Scholastic, 1987 (Termination Date: 1995)

Sprint Libraries Gold Medal Collection: Grades 3–6
Scholastic, 1989 (Termination Date: 1995)

Action 2000: Grades 7–12
Scholastic, 1989 (Termination Date: 1995)

Highgate Collection: Grades 1-4
Steck-Vaughn, 1990 (Termination Date: 1995)

*Complete Literature Library: Folk Tales from
around the World:* Grades 4–10
Steck-Vaughn, 1990 (Termination Date: 1995)

*Complete Literature Library: Moments in American
History:* Grades 4–10
Steck-Vaughn, 1989 (Termination Date: 1995)

**Composition/Grammar Usage
Elementary/Junior High Basic**

Early Foundations Program Kit: Grade Pre-K
Coronado, 1986 (Termination Date: 1996)

Your English Readiness Program: Grade K
Coronado, 1985 (Termination Date: 1996)

Your English: Grades 1–8
Coronado, 1984–85, 86 (Termination Date: 1991)

English Workshop, Liberty Edition: Grades 6–12
Harcourt Brace Jovanovich, 1988 (Termination
Date: 1996)

Language for Daily Use, Voyager Edition: Grades
K–8
Harcourt Brace Jovanovich, 1986 (Termination
Date: 1996)

Vocabulary Workshop, Liberty/Benchmark Edition:
Grades 6–12
Harcourt Brace Jovanovich, 1988 (Termination
Date: 1996)

*Composition: Models and Exercises, Liberty/
Benchmark Edition:* Grades 7–12
Harcourt Brace Jovanovich, 1986 (Termination
Date: 1996)

*English 2200 with Writing Applications, Nova
Edition:* Grades 7–12
Harcourt Brace Jovanovich, 1989 (Termination
Date: 1996)

*English 2600 with Writing Applications, Nova
Edition:* Grades 7–12
Harcourt Brace Jovanovich, 1989 (Termination
Date: 1996)

English 3200 with Writing Applications, Nova Edition: Grades 7–12
Harcourt Brace Jovanovich, 1989 (Termination Date: 1996)

Heath Language Arts: Grades K–8
D. C. Heath, 1988 (Termination Date: 1996)

Houghton Mifflin English, Omega Edition: Grades K–8
Houghton Mifflin, 1988 (Termination Date: 1996)

Laidlaw English: Grades K–8
Laidlaw Brothers, 1987 (Termination Date: 1996)

Macmillan English: Grades K–8
Macmillan/McGraw-Hill, 1987 (Termination Date: 1996)

Macmillan English: Thinking and Writing Process: Grades 6–8
Macmillan/McGraw-Hill, 1987 (Termination Date: 1996)

Macmillan English: Grades 9–12
Macmillan/McGraw-Hill, 1988 (Termination Date: 1996)

McGraw-Hill English: Grades K–8
McGraw-Hill, 1989 (Termination Date: 1996)

McDougal, Littell English Series: Grades 7–8
McDougal, Littell, 1987 (Termination Date: 1996)

McDougal, Littell English Series: Grades K–6
McDougal, Littell, 1987 (Termination Date: 1996)

Silver Burdett English: Grades K–8
Silver, Burdett and Ginn, 1986 (Termination Date: 1996)

Scott Foresman Language: Grades K–8
Scott, Foresman, 1989 (Termination Date: 1996)

Zaner-Bloser Vocabulary Building: Process, Principles, and Application: Grades 1–8
Zaner-Bloser, 1986 (Termination Date: 1996)

Supplemental

Action Sequence Stories Program-ACT I: Grades K–12
Ballard & Tighe, 1988 (Termination Date: 1996)

Evaluating within the Writing Process: Grades K–8
Coronado, 1988 (Termination Date: 1996)

Your English Computer Program Kit: Grades 3–8
Coronado, 1984 (Termination Date: 1996)

Warriners English Grammar and Composition, Liberty Edition (Introductory Course) Grade 6
Harcourt Brace Jovanovich, 1986 (Termination Date: 1996)

Houghton Mifflin Vocabulary for Achievement: Grades 6–12
Houghton Mifflin, 1988 (Termination Date: 1996)

Practicing Grammar, Levels 2–8: Grades 2–8
Random House, 1984 (Termination Date: 1996)

Practicing Standard Usage: Grades 2–8
Random House, 1984 (Termination Date: 1996)

Practicing Capitalization and Punctuation: Grades 2–8
Random House, 1984 (Termination Date: 1996)

Spotlight on Writing: Grades 1–8
Random House, 1984 (Termination Date: 1996)

Individual Corrective English: Grades 2–6
Random House, 1983 (Termination Date: 1996)

Language Roundup: Grades 1–6
Random House (Termination Date: 1996)

Silver Burdett English Micro Manager: Grades 1–8
Silver, Burdett and Ginn, 1987 (Termination Date: 1996)

Language Arts Phonics: Grades 1-3
Scholastic, 1986 (Termination Date: 1996)

Writer's Workshop: Grades 1–6
Scholastic, 1986 (Termination Date: 1996)

Comprehension Test Strategies: Grades 4–6
Scholastic, 1986 (Termination Date: 1996)

The Three "I's": Grades 2-3
Scholastic, 1983 (Termination Date: 1996)

Distar Language Series I, II, III: Grades 1-3
Science Research, 1973, 1977, 1987 (Termination Date: 1996)

Spelling

Spelling for Word Mastery. Grades K–8
Merrill, 1987 (Termination Date: 1996)

Working Words in Spelling. Grades 1–8
Curriculum Associates, 1985 (Termination Date: 1996)

HBJ Spelling. Grades 1–8
Harcourt Brace Jovanovich, 1983 (Termination Date: 1996)

HBJ Spelling. Grades 1–8
Harcourt Brace Jovanovich, 1988 (Termination Date: 1996)

Houghton Mifflin Spelling. Grades 1–8
Houghton Mifflin, 1988 (Termination Date: 1996)

Laidlaw Spelling. Grades 1–8
Laidlaw Brothers, 1987 (Termination Date: 1996)

Macmillan Spelling. Grades 1–8
Macmillan, 1986 (Termination Date: 1996)

Basic Goals in Spelling. Grades 1–8
Mark Hart, William Brown, 1984 (Termination Date: 1996)

Building Spelling Skills Series. Grades 1–8
McDougal, Littell, 1985 (Termination Date: 1996)

Wordskill Series. Grades 6–12
McDougal, Littell, 1982, 1985, 1986 (Termination Date: 1996)

The Riverside Spelling Program. Grades K–8
Riverside, 1988 (Termination Date: 1996)

Silver Burdett Spelling. Grades 1–8
Silver, Burdett and Ginn, 1986 (Termination Date: 1996)

Silver Burdett Spelling, Complete Courseware. K–6
Silver, Burdett and Ginn, 1985 (Termination Date: 1996)

Scott Foresman Spelling. Grades 1–8
Scott, Foresman, 1988 (Termination Date: 1996)

Spelling: Words and Skills. Grades 1–8
Scott, Foresman, 1986 (Termination Date: 1992)

Steck-Vaughn Spelling. Grades 1–8
Steck-Vaughn, 1984 (Termination Date: 1992)

Elementary/Junior High Handwriting—Basic

HBJ Handwriting. Grades K–8
Harcourt Brace Jovanovich, 1987, 1989 (Termination Date: 1996)

Palmer Method Handwriting. Grades K–8
Macmillan, 1987 (Termination Date: 1996)

Bowmar/Noble Handwriting. Grades K–8
McGraw-Hill, 1987 (Termination Date: 1996)

McDougal, Littell Handwriting Series. Grades K–8
McDougal, Littell, 1990 (Termination Date: 1996)

Italic Handwriting Series. Grades K–8
Portland State University, 1986 (Termination Date: 1996)

Scott Foresman D'Nealian Handwriting Program. Grades K–8
Scott, Foresman, 1987 (Termination Date: 1999)

Zaner Bloser Handwriting: Basic Skills and Application. Grades K–8
Zaner-Bloser, 1989 (Termination Date: 1996)

Elementary Handwriting—Supplemental

My Alphabet Workbook. Grade K
Peterson Directed Handwriting, 1986 (Termination Date: 1996)

We Write to Read. Grades K–8
Peterson Directed Handwriting, 1986 (Termination Date: 1996)

The Write Way. Grades K–8
Peterson Directed Handwriting, 1987 (Termination Date: 1996)

Transfer of Learning. Grades 6–8
Peterson Directed Handwriting, 1989 (Termination Date: 1996)

Cursive Writing Program. Grades 3-4
Science Research, 1980 (Termination Date: 1996)

Steck Vaughn Handwriting. Grades 1–6
Steck Vaughn Handwriting, 1988 (Termination Date: 1996)

Zaner Bloser Handwriting: A Way to Self Expression: Grades K–8
Zaner-Bloser, 1991 (Termination Date: 1996)

**Elementary/Junior High—
Supplemental Dictionaries**
HBJ School Dictionary: Grades 3–8
Harcourt Brace Jovanovich, 1985 (Termination Date: 1996)

Houghton Mifflin Primary Dictionary, HM Ed.: Grades 1-2
Houghton Mifflin, 1986 (Termination Date: 1996)

Houghton Mifflin Intermediate Dictionary, HM Ed.: Grades 3–6
Houghton Mifflin, 1986 (Termination Date: 1996)

Houghton Mifflin Student Dictionary, HM Ed.: Grades 6–9
Houghton Mifflin, 1986 (Termination Date: 1996)

Picture Dictionary: Grades K–1
Macmillan, 1982 (Termination Date: 1996)

Macmillan Beginning Dictionary: Grades 1-2
Macmillan, 1981–87 (Termination Date: 1996)

Macmillan School Dictionary: Grades 3-5
Macmillan, 1981–87 (Termination Date: 1996)

Macmillan Dictionary: Grades 8–12
Macmillan, 1981–87 (Termination Date: 1996)

Scribner Beginning Dictionary: Grades 3-5
Scribner, 1986 (Termination Date: 1996)

Scribner Intermediate Dictionary: Grades 5–7
Scribner, 1986 (Termination Date: 1996)

My Pictionary: Grades K–1
Scott, Foresman, 1987 (Termination Date: 1996)

My First Picture Dictionary: Grade 1
Scott, Foresman, 1987 (Termination Date: 1996)

My Second Picture Dictionary: Grade 2
Scott, Foresman, 1987 (Termination Date: 1996)

Scott Foresman Thesauri Program: Grades 3–8
Scott, Foresman, 1987 (Termination Date: 1996)

Scott Foresman Beginning Dictionary: Grades 3-5
Scott, Foresman, 1988 (Termination Date: 1996)

Scott Foresman Intermediate Dictionary: Grades 5–8
Scott, Foresman, 1988 (Termination Date: 1996)

In Other Words: A Beginning Thesaurus: Grades 3-4
Scott, Foresman, 1987 (Termination Date: 1996)

In Other Words: A Junior Thesaurus: Grades 5–8
Scott, Foresman, 1987 (Termination Date: 1996)

**Secondary—Basic Integrated
English Language Arts**
Macmillan Literature Series: Grades 7–12
Glencoe/Macmillan/McGraw-Hill, 1991 (Termination Date: 1995)

Globe Literature: Grades 7–12
Globe, 1990 (Termination Date: 1995)

Adventures in Literature: Grades 7–12
Holt, Rinehart and Winston/Harcourt Brace Jovanovich, 1989 (Termination Date: 1995)

Elements of Literature: Grades 7–12
Holt, Rinehart and Winston/Harcourt Brace Jovanovich, 1989 (Termination Date: 1995)

Themes in World Literature: Grades 10–12
Houghton Mifflin, 1989 (Termination Date: 1995)

McDougal Littell Literature Series: Grades 7–10
McDougal, Littell, 1989 (Termination Date: 1995)

Reading Literature Series: Grades 9–12
McDougal, Littell, 1990 (Termination Date: 1995)

Prentice Hall Literature Series: Grades 6–12
Prentice Hall, 1989, 1991 (Termination Date: 1995)

Scholastic Scope Literature: Grades 6–12
Scholastic, 1991 (Termination Date: 1995)

America Reads: Grades 6–12
Scott, Foresman, 1991 (Termination Date: 1995)

Supplemental
Be a Better Reader: Grades 4–12
Globe, 1989 (Termination Date: 1995)

Reading by Doing: Grades 9–12
National Textbook, 1988 (Termination Date: 1995)

Time: We the People: Grades 9–12
National Textbook, 1990 (Termination Date: 1995)

Project Achievement: Reading: Grades 5–12
Scholastic, 1987 (Termination Date: 1995)

Action 2000: Grades 7–12
Scholastic, 1990 (Termination Date: 1995)

Complete Literature Library: Folk Tales from around the World: Grades 4–10
Steck-Vaughn, 1990 (Termination Date: 1995)

Complete Literature Library: Moments in American History: Grades 4–10
Steck-Vaughn, 1989 (Termination Date: 1995)

Grammar and Composition
Secondary—Basic
Developing Writing Skills: Grades 9–12
Allyn & Bacon/Prentice Hall, 1988 (Termination Date: 1995)

English Writing and Skills (Advanced): Grades 7–12
Coronado, 1985–86 (Termination Date: 1996)

Glencoe/English: Grades 7–12
Glencoe, 1984–85 (Termination Date: 1996)

Literature-Based Composition: Grades 6–8
Glencoe/Macmillan/McGraw-Hill, 1987 (Termination Date: 1996)

English Workshop, Liberty/Benchmark Edition:
Grades 7–12
Harcourt Brace Jovanovich, 1988 (Termination Date: 1996)

Vocabulary Workshop, Liberty/Benchmark Edition:
Grades 6–12
Harcourt Brace Jovanovich, 1988 (Termination Date: 1996)

Composition: Models and Exercises, Liberty/ Benchmark Ed.: Grades 7–12
Harcourt Brace Jovanovich, 1986 (Termination Date: 1996)

English 2200 with Writing Applications, Nova Ed.:
Grades 7–12

Harcourt Brace Jovanovich, 1989 (Termination Date: 1996)

English 2600 with Writing Applications, Nova Ed.:
Grades 7–12
Harcourt Brace Jovanovich, 1989 (Termination Date: 1996)

English 3200 with Writing Applications, Nova Ed.:
Grades 7–12
Harcourt Brace Jovanovich, 1989 (Termination Date: 1996)

Warriner's English Composition and Grammar, Liberty Ed.: Grades 6–12
Harcourt Brace Jovanovich, 1988 (Termination Date: 1996)

Heath Grammar and Composition: Grades 6–12
D.C Heath, 1986–87 (Termination Date: 1996)

Houghton Mifflin English Grammar and Composition: Grades 7–12
Holt, Rinehart and Winston/Harcourt Brace Jovanovich, 1986–87 (Termination Date: 1996)

From Sight to Insight: Grades 9–12
Laidlaw Brothers, 1988 (Termination Date: 1996)

Building English Skills: Grades 9–12
McDougal, Littell, 1989 (Termination Date: 1996)

Basic Skills in English Series: Grades 7–12
McDougal, Littell, 1985 (Termination Date: 1996)

McDougal, Littell English Series: Grades 9–12
McDougal, Littell, 1989 (Termination Date: 1996)

Prentice Hall Grammar and Composition: Grades 6–12
Prentice Hall, 1987 (Termination Date: 1996)

Macmillan English: Grades 9–12
Scribner Educational, 1986 (Termination Date: 1996)

Secondary-Supplemental
Writing Guides: Grades 7–8
Active Learning Corporation, 1986 (Termination Date: 1996)

Writing: Process to Product: Grades 9–12
Addison-Wesley, 1987 (Termination Date: 1996)

Basic Grammar and Writing Workbook: Grades 7–8
Basic English Revisited, 1986 (Termination Date: 1996)

Study Skills and Writing Process Workbook: Grades 9–10
Basic English Revisited, 1985 (Termination Date: 1996)

Practical Writing Skills Workbook: Grades 11–12
Basic English Revisited, 1984 (Termination Date: 1996)

The Revising Process: Grades 7–12
Basic English Revisited, 1986 (Termination Date: 1996)

The Mechanics of Writing: Grades 7–12
Basic English Revisited, 1984 (Termination Date: 1996)

Basic English Revisited, A Student Handbook: Grades 7–12
Basic English Revisited, 1985 (Termination Date: 1996)

Evaluating within the Writing Process: Grades 7–12
Coronado, 1985 (Termination Date: 1996)

Basic Drills in English Skills: Grades 7–12
Harcourt Brace Jovanovich, 1984 (Termination Date: 1996)

Houghton Mifflin Vocabulary for Achievement: Grades 7–12
Houghton Mifflin, 1988 (Termination Date: 1996)

The Art of Composition: Grades 9–12
National Textbook, 1984 (Termination Date: 1996)

Lively Writing: Grades 6–8
National Textbook, 1985 (Termination Date: 1996)

Writing by Doing: Grades 9–12
National Textbook, 1983 (Termination Date: 1996)

Composition Notebooks: Grades 6–8
Random House, (Termination Date: 1996)

Macmillan English: Grades 9–12
Scribner, 1988 (Termination Date: 1996)

Vocabulary Workshop: Grades 6–12
Sadler/Oxford, 1984 (Termination Date: 1996)

Building an Enriched Vocabulary: Grades 11–12
Sadler/Oxford, 1983 (Termination Date: 1996)

SRA Writing for Independence: Grades 9–12
Science Research, 1985 (Termination Date: 1996)

Pro-Grammar/Pro-Sentence: Grades 9–12
South-Western, 1986 (Termination Date: 1996)

Appleworks—Integrated Applications for the Microcomputer: Grades 9–12
South-Western, 1987 (Termination Date: 1996)

Spelling
Secondary—Basic
Wordskills Series: Grades 6–12
McDougal, Littell, 1982, 1985, 1986 (Termination Date: 1996)

Secondary—Supplemental
Corrective Spelling through Morphographs: Grades 4–12
Science Research, 1979 (Termination Date: 1996)

Secondary Journalism—Basic
Journalism: Grades 8–12
Allyn & Bacon/Prentice Hall, 1984 (Termination Date: 1996)

Journalism Today!: Grades 6–8
National Textbook, 1986–87 (Termination Date: 1996)

Press Time: Grades 7–12
Prentice Hall, 1985 (Termination Date: 1996)

Inside High School Journalism: Grades 9–12
Scott, Foresman, 1986 (Termination Date: 1996)

Secondary Journalism—Supplemental
Writing and Editing School News: Grades 6–8
Clark Publishing, 1983 (Termination Date: 1996)

Newspaper Workshop: Grades 7–12
Globe, 1985 (Termination Date: 1996)

Getting Stared in Journalism: Grades 9–12
National Textbook, 1989 (Termination Date: 1996)

Secondary Dictionaries--Supplemental

Houghton Mifflin Student Dictionary: Grades 6–9
Houghton Mifflin, 1986 (Termination Date: 1996)

Houghton Mifflin College Dictionary (Advanced Level), American Heritage Dictionary of the English Language: Grades 9–12
Houghton Mifflin, 1982 (Termination Date: 1996)

Macmillan School Dictionary: Grades 8-12
Macmillan (Termination Date: 1996)

Macmillan Dictionary: Grades 7–9
Macmillan, 1981–87 (Termination Date: 1996)

Websters High School Dictionary: Grades 7–12
Merriam Webster, 1982 (Termination Date: n.d.)

Websters Ninth New Collegiate Dictionary: Grades 7–12
Merriam Webster, 1985 (Termination Date: n.d.)

Scribner Intermediate Dictionary: Grades 5–7
Scribner, 1986 (Termination Date: 1996)

Scribner Dictionary: Grades 8–12
Scribner, 1985 (Termination Date: 1996)

Scott Foresman Thesauri Program: Grades 3–8
Scott, Foresman, 1987 (Termination Date: 1996)

Scott Foresman Intermediate Dictionary: Grades 5–8
Scott, Foresman, 1988 (Termination Date: 1996)

Scott Foresman Advanced Dictionary: Grades 7–12
Scott, Foresman, 1988 (Termination Date: 1996)

Speech
Secondary—Basic

Communicating Message and Meaning. Grades 9–12
Allyn & Bacon/Prentice Hall, 1984 (Termination Date: 1996)

Communication: An Introduction to Speech: Grades 9–12
Allyn & Bacon/Prentice Hall, 1988 (Termination Date: 1996)

Effective Speech: Grades 6–8
Glencoe/Macmillan/McGraw-Hill, 1988 (Termination Date: 1996)

Speech for Effective Communication: Grades 9–12
Harcourt Brace Jovanovich, 1988 (Termination Date: 1996)

The Basics of Speech: Grades 9–12
National Textbook, 1988 (Termination Date: 1996)

Person to Person: Grades 7–9
National Textbook, 1984 (Termination Date: 1996)

Contemporary Speech: Grades 10–12
National Textbook, 1982 (Termination Date: 1996)

Dynamics of Speech: Grades 9–12
National Textbook, 1988 (Termination Date: 1996)

Public Speaking Today!: Grades 9–12
National Textbook, 1989 (Termination Date: 1996)

Basic Debate: Grades 9–12
National Textbook, 1989 (Termination Date: 1996)

Strategic Debate: Grades 9–12
National Textbook, 1985 (Termination Date: 1996)

Getting Started in Debate: Grades 9–12
National Textbook, 1987 (Termination Date: 1996)

Speech: Exploring Communication: Grades 7–12
Prentice Hall, 1988 (Termination Date: 1996)

Secondary—Supplemental

38 Basic Speech Experience: Grades 6–8
Clark, 1987 (Termination Date: 1996)

Mastering Competitive Debate: Grades 6–8
Clark, 1987 (Termination Date: 1996)

More than Talking: Grades 6–8
Clark, 1983 (Termination Date: 1996)

Speech: Principles and Practice: Grades 8–12
Scott, Foresman, 1987 (Termination Date: 1996)

Drama
Secondary—Basic

Theater: Preparation and Performance: Grades 10–12
Scott, Foresman, 1989 (Termination Date: 1996)

Secondary—Supplemental

Basic Drama Projects: Grades 6–8
Clark, 1987 (Termination Date: 1996)

Creative Communication: Grades 6–8
Clark, 1985 (Termination Date: 1996)

Readers Theater Fundamentals: Grades 6–8
Clark, 1987 (Termination Date: 1996)

The Dynamics of Acting: Grades 9–12
National Textbook, 1989 (Termination Date: 1996)

Television Production Today: Grades 9–12
National Textbook, 1987 (Termination Date: 1996)

Play Production Today: Grades 9–12
National Textbook, 1989 (Termination Date: 1996)

Preparation and Performance: Grades 10–12
Scott, Foresman, 1987 (Termination Date: 1996)

Indiana

English

HBJ Language: Grades 1–8
Harcourt Brace Jovanovich, 1990 (Termination Date: 1996)

Houghton Mifflin English: Grades 1–12
Houghton Mifflin, 1990 (Termination Date: 1996)

Language Arts Today: Grades 1–8
Macmillan, 1990 (Termination Date: 1996)

McGraw-Hill English: Grades 1–8
McGraw-Hill, 1990 (Termination Date: 1996)

Series E: Macmillan English: Grades 3–6
Macmillan, 1984 (Termination Date: 1996)

Building English Skills: Grades 7–11
McDougal, Littell, 1984 (Termination Date: 1996)

Scott, Foresman Language: Grades K–8
Scott, Foresman, 1989 (Termination Date: 1996)

Scott, Foresman Language, D'Nealian: Grades 1-2
Scott, Foresman, 1989 (Termination Date: 1996)

World of Language: Grade 1
Silver, Burdett and Ginn, 1990 (Termination Date: 1996)

Heath Grammar and Composition: Grades 6–12
D. C. Heath, 1988 (Termination Date: 1996)

English Composition and Grammar, Benchmark Edition: Grades 6–12
Harcourt Brace Jovanovich, 1988 (Termination Date: 1996)

Warriner's English Grammar and Composition: Grade 11
Harcourt, Brace, 1982 (Termination Date: 1996)

Harper and Row English (Nonconsumable): Grades 7–8
Harper and Row, 1983 (Termination Date: 1996)

Basic Language: Messages and Meanings: Grades 9–10
Harper and Row, 1982 (Termination Date: 1996)

Holt English: Grades 7–8
Holt, Rinehart, and Winston, 1984 (Termination Date: 1996)

Grammar and Composition: Grades 9–10
Hougton Mifflin, 1984 (Termination Date: 1996)

McDougal, Littell English: Grades 6–12
McDougal, Littell, 1990 (Termination Date: 1996)

Basic Skills in English: Grades 7–12
McDougal, Littell, 1989, 1981 (Termination Date: 1996)

Prentice Hall Grammar and Composition: Grades 6–12
Prentice Hall, 1990 (Termination Date: 1996)

Scope English Writing and Language Skills: Grades 6–12
Scholastic, 1990 (Termination Date: 1996)

Spelling

HBJ Spelling: Grades 1–8
Harcourt Brace Jovanovich, 1983, 1988 (Termination Date: 1996)

Working Words in Spelling: Grades 1–8
D. C. Heath, 1990 (Termination Date: 1996)

Houghton Mifflin Spelling: Grades 1–8
Houghton Mifflin, 1984 (Termination Date: 1996)

Houghton Mifflin Spelling and Vocabulary: Grades 1–8
Houghton Mifflin, 1990 (Termination Date: 1996)

McDougal, Littell Spelling: Grades 1–8
McDougal, Littell, 1990 (Termination Date: 1996)

McGraw-Hill Spelling: Grades 1–8
McGraw-Hill, 1990 (Termination Date: 1996)

Merrill Spelling: Grades 1–8
Merrill, 1990 (Termination Date: 1996)

The Riverside Spelling Program: Grades 1–8
Riverside, 1984 (Termination Date: 1996)

Scott Foresman Spelling: Grades 1–8
Scott, Foresman, 1988 (Termination Date: 1996)

Scott Foresman Spelling D'Nealian: Grades 1-3
Scott, Foresman, 1988 (Termination Date: 1996)

Silver Burdett Spelling: Grades 1–8
Silver Burdett and Ginn, 1983 (Termination
Date: 1996)

Steck-Vaughn Spelling: Grades 1–8
Steck-Vaughn, 1990 (Termination Date: 1996)

Spelling Connections: Words into Language:
Grades 1–8
Zaner-Bloser, 1988 (Termination Date: 1996)

Literature
Scribner Literature Series: Grades 7–12
Glencoe/McGraw-Hill, 1989 (Termination Date:
1996)

Globe Literature: Grades 7–12
Globe, 1990 (Termination Date: 1996)

Adventures in Literature: Grades 7–12
Harcourt Brace Jovanovich, 1989 (Termination
Date: 1996)

Adventures for Readers, Heritage Edition: Grades
9–10
Harcourt Brace Jovanovich, 1989 (Termination
Date: 1996)

Journeys: A Reading and Literature Program:
Grades 8–11
Harcourt Brace Jovanovich, 1982 (Termination
Date: 1996)

Elements of Literature: Grades 7–12
Holt, Rinehart and Winston, 1989 (Termination
Date: 1996)

Houghton Mifflin Literary Readers: Grades 7–8
Houghton Mifflin, 1989 (Termination Date: 1996)

Houghton Mifflin Literature Bookshelf: Grades 7–8
Houghton Mifflin, 1989 (Termination Date: 1996)

Themes in World Literature: Grade 12
Houghton Mifflin, 1989 (Termination Date: 1996)

McDougal, Littell Literature: Grades 7–12
McDougal, Littell, 1989 (Termination Date: 1996)

Vistas in Reading Literature: Grades 7–8
McDougal, Littell, 1989 (Termination Date: 1996)

Reading Literature: Grades 9–12
McDougal, Littell, 1989 (Termination Date: 1996)

Prentice Hall Literature: Grades 7–12
Prentice Hall, 1989 (Termination Date: 1996)

Scope English Anthology: Grades 7–12
Scholastic, 1988 (Termination Date: 1996)

America Reads: Grades 7–12
Scott, Foresman, 1989 (Termination Date: 1996)

America Reads, Medallion Edition: Grades 7–12
Scott, Foresman, 1982 (Termination Date: 1996)

American Literature
American Literature: Grades 9–12
Glencoe/McGraw-Hill, 1989 (Termination Date:
1996)

Globe Literature: Grades 9–12
Globe, 1990 (Termination Date: 1996)

The American Anthology: Grades 9–12
Globe, 1983 (Termination Date: 1996)

Adventures in American Literature: Grades 9–12
Harcourt, Brace 1989 (Termination Date: 1996)

*Adventures in American Literature, Heritage
Edition*: Grades 9–12
Harcourt, Brace 1980 (Termination Date: 1996)

Elements of Literature: Grades 9–12
Holt, Rinehart and Winston, 1989 (Termination
Date: 1996)

McDougal, Littell Literature: Grades 9–12
McDougal, Littell, 1984 (Termination Date: 1996)

Prentice Hall: The American Experience: Grades 9–12
Prentice Hall, 1989 (Termination Date: 1996)

Scope English Anthology: Grades 9–12
Scholastic, 1988 (Termination Date: 1996)

The United States in Literature: Grades 9–12
Scott, Foresman, 1989, 1982 (Termination Date: 1996)

English Literature
English Literature with World Masterpieces: Grades 9–12
Glencoe/McGraw-Hill, 1989 (Termination Date: 1996)

Globe Literature: Grades 9–12
Globe, 1990 (Termination Date: 1996)

Adventures in English Literature: Grades 9–12
Harcourt Brace Jovanovich, 1989 (Termination Date: 1996)

Adventures in English Literature, Heritage Edition: Grades 9–12
Harcourt Brace Jovanovich, 1980 (Termination Date: 1996)

Elements of Literature: Grades 9–12
Holt, Rinehart and Winston, 1989 (Termination Date: 1996)

Prentice Hall: The English Tradition: Grades 9–12
Prentice Hall, 1989 (Termination Date: 1996)

England in Literature (Macbeth, Hamlet Editions): Grades 9–12
Scott, Foresman, 1982, 1986 (Termination Date: 1996)

World Literature
Globe Literature: Grades 7–12
Globe, 1990 (Termination Date: 1996)

Adventures in World Literature: Grades 7–12
Harcourt Brace, 1970 (Termination Date: 1996)

Themes in World Literature: Grades 7–12
Houghton Mifflin, 1989 (Termination Date: 1996)

Literature: An Introduction to Reading and Writing: Grades 7–12
Prentice Hall, 1989 (Termination Date: 1996)

Scope English Anthology: Grades 7–12
Scholastic, 1988 (Termination Date: 1996)

Classics in World Literature: Grades 7–12
Scott, Foresman, 1989 (Termination Date: 1996)

Grammar
English Workshop, Liberty/Benchmark: Grades 9–12
Harcourt Brace Jovanovich, 1986 (Termination Date: 1996)

Advanced Grammar and Composition
Warriner's English Grammar and Composition: Grades 9–12
Harcourt Brace Jovanovich, 1982 (Termination Date: 1996)

Basic Language: Messages and Meanings: Grades 9–12
Harper and Row, 1982 (Termination Date: 1996)

Basic Language: Grades 9–12
Harper and Row, 1983 (Termination Date: 1996)

Grammar and Composition: Grades 9–12
Houghton Mifflin, 1984 (Termination Date: 1996)

Building English Skills: Grades 9–12
McDougal, Littell, 1981 (Termination Date: 1996)

Basic Skills in English: Grades 9–12
McDougal, Littell, 1981 (Termination Date: 1996)

Dramatics
The Stage and the School: Grades 9–12
Glencoe/McGraw-Hill, 1989 (Termination Date: 1996)

Play Production Today: Grades 9–12
National Textbook, 1989 (Termination Date: 1996)

The Dynamics of Acting: Grades 9–12
National Textbook, 1989 (Termination Date: 1996)

Theater:Preparation and Performance: Grades 9–12
Scott, Foresman, 1989 (Termination Date: 1996)

Speech

Effective Speech: Grades 9–12
Glencoe/McGraw-Hill, 1989 (Termination Date: 1996)

Speech for Effective Communication: Grades 9–12
Harcourt Brace Jovanovich, 1988 (Termination Date: 1996)

The Basics of Speech: Grades 9–12
National Textbook, 1988 (Termination Date: 1996)

Dynamics of Speech: Grades 9–12
National Textbook, 1988 (Termination Date: 1996)

Public Speaking Today: Grades 9–12
National Textbook, 1989 (Termination Date: 1996)

Person to Person: Grades 9–12
National Textbook, 1990 (Termination Date: 1996)

Communication: An Introduction to Speech:
Grades 9–12
Prentice Hall, 1988 (Termination Date: 1996)

Speech Exploring Communications: Grades 9–12
Prentice Hall, 1988 (Termination Date: 1996)

Speech Principles and Practice: Grades 9–12
Scott, Foresman,, 1987 (Termination Date: 1996)

Mass Media

Understanding Mass Media: Grades 9–12
National Textbook, 1986 (Termination Date: 1996)

Writing for the Media: Film, Television, Video:
Grades 9–12
Prentice Hall, 1988 (Termination Date: 1996)

Composition

Literature-Based Composition: Grades 9–12
Glencoe/McGraw-Hill, 1988 (Termination Date: 1996)

Composition: Models and Exercises: Grades 9–12
Harcourt Brace Jovanovich, 1989 (Termination Date: 1996)

Lively Writing: Grades 9–12
National Textbook, 1985 (Termination Date: 1996)

Writing by Doing: Grades 9–12
National Textbook, 1990 (Termination Date: 1996)

The Writing Clinic: Grades 9–12
Prentice Hall, 1988 (Termination Date: 1996)

Handwriting

HBJ Handwriting: Grades 1–6
Harcourt Brace Jovanovich, 1987 (Termination Date: 1995)

Palmer Handwriting: Grades 1–6
Macmillan, 1987 (Termination Date: 1995)

McDougal, Littell Handwriting: Grades 1–6
McDougal, Littell, 1987 (Termination Date: 1995)

Bowmar/Noble Handwriting: Grades 1–6
McGraw-Hill, 1987 (Termination Date: 1995)

D'Nealian Handwriting: Grades 1–6
Scott, Foresman, 1987 (Termination Date: 1995)

Steck-Vaughn Handwriting: Grades 1–6
Steck-Vaughn, 1988 (Termination Date: 1995)

Zaner-Bloser Handwriting: Grades 1–6
Zaner-Bloser, 1989 (Termination Date: 1995)

Creative Growth with Handwriting: Grades 1–6
Zaner-Bloser, 1979 (Termination Date: 1995)

Reading

HBJ Reading Program: Grades 1–8
Harcourt Brace Jovanovich, 1989 (Termination Date: 1995)

Heath Reading: Grades 1–8
D.C. Heath, 1989 (Termination Date: 1995)

Reading: Today and Tomorrow: Grades 1–8
Holt, Rinehart and Winston, 1989 (Termination Date: 1995)

Houghton Mifflin Reading: Grades 1–8
Houghton Mifflin, 1989 (Termination Date: 1995)

Macmillan Reading Program: Connections: Grades 1–8
Macmillan, 1989 (Termination Date: 1995)

McGraw-Hill Reading: Grades 1–8
McGraw-Hill, 1989 (Termination Date: 1995)

Open Court Reading and Writing: Grades 1–6
Open Court, 1989 (Termination Date: 1995)

The Riverside Reading Program: Grades 1–8
Riverside, 1989 (Termination Date: 1995)

World of Reading: Grades 1–8
Silver, Burdett and Ginn, 1989 (Termination Date: 1995)

Scott Foresman Reading: Grades 1–8
Scott, Foresman, 1989 (Termination Date: 1995)

Scribner Literature Series: Grades 7–8
Glencoe, 1989 (Termination Date: 1995)

Kentucky

Language
HBJ Language for Daily Use: Grades K–8
Harcourt Brace Jovanovich, 1986 (Termination Date: 1994)

Heath Language Arts: Grades K–8
D. C. Heath, 1988 (Termination Date: 1994)

Houghton Mifflin English, Omega: Grades K–8
Houghton Mifflin, 1988 (Termination Date: 1994)

Laidlaw English: Grades K–8
Laidlaw, 1987 (Termination Date: 1994)

Language: Skills and Use: Grades K–8
Scott, Foresman, 1986 (Termination Date: 1994)

Silver Burdett and Ginn English: Grades 1–8
Silver Burdett and Ginn, 1988 (Termination Date: 1994)

McDougal, Littell English: Grades K–8
McDougal, Littell, 1988 (Termination Date: 1994)

English Composition
HBJ English Composition/Grammar: Grades 6–8
Harcourt Brace Jovanovich, 1988 (Termination Date: 1994)

Holt English: Writing Skills: Grades 7–8
Holt, Rinehart and Winston, 1988 (Termination Date: 1994)

Macmillan English: Thinking/Writing Processes: Grades 6–8
Macmillan, 1988 (Termination Date: 1994)

Prentice Hall Grammar/Composition: Grades 6–8
Prentice Hall, 1987 (Termination Date: 1994)

Basic Skills in English: Grades 7–8
McDougal, Littell, 1985 (Termination Date: 1994)

Scope English: Writing/Language Skills: Grades 6–8
Scholastic, 1987 (Termination Date: 1994)

Spelling
HBJ Spelling: Grades 1–8
Harcourt Brace Jovanovich, 1988 (Termination Date: 1994)

Working Words/Spelling: Grades 1–8
D.C. Heath, 1988 (Termination Date: 1994)

Houghton Mifflin Spelling: Grades 1–8
Houghton Mifflin, 1988 (Termination Date: 1994)

Laidlaw Spelling: Grades 1–8
Laidlaw, 1987 (Termination Date: 1994)

Spelling for Word Mastery: Grades 1–8
Charles E. Merrill, 1987 (Termination Date: 1994)

Foresman Spelling: Grades 1–8
Scott, Foresman, 1988 (Termination Date: 1994)

Basic Goals/ Spelling: Grades 1–8
Webster Division, McGraw-Hill, 1988 (Termination Date: 1994)

Spelling Connections: Grades 1–8
Zaner-Bloser, 1988 (Termination Date: 1994)

McDougal Spelling: Grades 1–8
McDougal, Littell, 1988 (Termination Date: 1994)

Riverside Spelling: Grades K–8
Riverside, 1988 (Termination Date: 1994)

Handwriting

HBJ Handwriting: Grades K–6
Harcourt Brace Jovanovich, 1987 (Termination Date: 1994)

Palmer Method: Grades K–8
A. N. Palmer, 1987 (Termination Date: 1994)

D'Nealian Handwriting: Grades K–8
Scott, Foresman, 1987 (Termination Date: 1994)

Steck-Vaughn Handwriting: Grades 1–6
Steck Vaughn, 1988 (Termination Date: 1994)

Bowmar Noble Handwriting: Grades 1–8
Webster Division McGraw-Hill, 1987 (Termination Date: 1994)

Basic Skills and Application: Grades K–8
Zaner-Bloser, 1987 (Termination Date: 1994)

McDougal Handwriting: Grades K–8
McDougal, Littell, 1987 (Termination Date: 1994)

Reading

Journeys Reading/Literature Program: Grades 9–12
Harcourt Brace Jovanovich, 1986 (Termination Date: 1994)

Reading Drills: Grades 9–12
Jamestown, 1975 (Termination Date: 1994)

Skimming and Scanning: Grades 9–12
Jamestown, 1978 (Termination Date: 1994)

Vocabulary Drills: Grades 9–12
Jamestown, 1986 (Termination Date: 1994)

Dictionary Drills: Grades 9–12
Jamestown, 1982 (Termination Date: 1994)

Graphical Comprehension: Grades 9–12
Jamestown, 1981 (Termination Date: 1994)

Six/Way Paragraphs: Grades 9–12
Jamestown, 1983 (Termination Date: 1994)

Gateway Literature: Grades 9–12
Scott, Foresman, 1984 (Termination Date: 1994)

Oral Communications

Communication: An Introduction to Speech: Grades 9–12
Allyn and Bacon, 1988 (Termination Date: 1994)

Effective Speech: Grades 9–12
Glencoe, 1988 (Termination Date: 1994)

HBJ Speech for Effective Communication: Grades 9–12
Harcourt Brace Jovanovich, 1988 (Termination Date: 1994)

Speech: Exploring Communication: Grades 9–12
Prentice Hall, 1988 (Termination Date: 1994)

Speech: Principles and Practice: Grades 9–12
Scott, Foresman, 1987 (Termination Date: 1994)

The Basics of Speech: Grades 9–12
National Textbook, 1988 (Termination Date: 1994)

Dynamics of Speech: Grades 9–12
National Textbook, 1988 (Termination Date: 1994)

Person to Person: Grades 9–12
National Textbook, 1984 (Termination Date: 1994)

Dramatics

Theater: Preparation Performance: Grades 9–12
Scott, Foresman, 1987 (Termination Date: 1994)

The Stage and the School: Grades 9–12
Webster Division McGraw-Hill, 1982 (Termination Date: 1994)

Journalism

Journalism: Grades 9–12
Allyn & Bacon, 1986 (Termination Date: 1994)

Mass Media and the School Newspaper: Grades 9–12
Wadsworth, 1985 (Termination Date: 1994)

English

Glencoe/English: Grades 9–12
Glencoe, 1985 (Termination Date: 1994)

HBJ English Composition/Grammar: Grades 9–12
Harcourt Brace Jovanovich, 1988 (Termination Date: 1994)

Holt English: Writing Skills: Grades 9–12
Holt, Rinehart and Winston, 1988 (Termination Date: 1994)

Laidlaw English Series: Grades 9–12
Laidlaw, 1985 (Termination Date: 1994)

Prentice Hall Grammar and Composition: Grades 9–12
Prentice Hall, 1987 (Termination Date: 1994)

Building English Skills: Grades 9–12
McDougal, Littell, 1988 (Termination Date: 1994)

Scope English: Writing and Language Skills:
Grades 9–12
Scholastic, 1987 (Termination Date: 1994)

Macmillan English: Grades 9–12
Scribner/Macmillan, 1988 (Termination Date: 1994)

Composition
Developing Writing Skills: Grades 9–12
Allyn & Bacon, 1988 (Termination Date: 1994)

Composition Notebook: Grades 9–12
Random House, 1986 (Termination Date: 1994)

Scholastic Composition: Grades 9–12
Scholastic, 1985 (Termination Date: 1994)

Lively Writing: Grades 9–12
National Textbook, 1985 (Termination Date: 1994)

Advanced Placement Language and Composition
Thinking and Writing about Literature: Grade 12
Prentice Hall, 1984 (Termination Date: 1994)

Functional English
Foundations for Learning Language: Grades 9–12
Scribner, 1986 (Termination Date: 1994)

Basic Skills in English: Grades 9–12
McDougal, Littell, 1985 (Termination Date: 1994)

Reading Program
The Economy Company Reading Program: Grades K–8
The Economy, 1986 (Termination Date: 1992)

Ginn Reading Program: Grades K–8
Ginn, 1985 (Termination Date: 1992)

Bookmark Reading Program, Eagle Edition:
Grades K–8
Harcourt Brace Jovanovich, 1983 (Termination Date: 1992)

Heath American Readers: Grades K–8
D. C. Heath, 1986 (Termination Date: 1992)

Holt Basic Reading: Grades K–8
Holt, Rinehart and Winston, 1986 (Termination Date: 1992)

Houghton Mifflin Reading: Grades K–8
Houghton Mifflin, 1986 (Termination Date: 1992)

Macmillan Reading Program: Grades K–7
Macmillan, 1986 (Termination Date: 1992)

Scott Foresman Reading: Grades K–8
Scott, Foresman, 1985 (Termination Date: 1992)

Reading Literature: Grades 7–8
McDougal, Littell, 1985 (Termination Date: 1992)

The Riverside Reading Program: Grades K–8
Riverside, 1986 (Termination Date: 1992)

Functional Level Reading
The Economy Company Reading: Grades RR–8
The Economy, 1984 (Termination Date: 1992)

Journeys Reading: Grades 7–8
Harcourt Brace Jovanovich, 1982 (Termination Date: 1992)

New Directions in Reading: Grades 4–8
Houghton Mifflin, 1986 (Termination Date: 1992)

Reading Express: Grades PP–6
Macmillan, 1986 (Termination Date: 1992)

Merrill Linguistic Reading Program: Grades PP-3
Charles E. Merrill, 1986 (Termination Date: 1992)

FOCUS: Reading for Success: Grades K–8
Scott, Foresman, 1985 (Termination Date: 1992)

Literature

Ginn Literature: Grades 7–12
Ginn, 1986 (Termination Date: 1992)

Odyssey: Grades 1–6
Harcourt Brace Jovanovich, 1986 (Termination Date: 1992)

Adventures in Literature, Heritage Edition: Grades 7–12
Harcourt Brace Jovanovich, 1985 (Termination Date: 1992)

Laidlaw Literature: Grades 1–6
Laidlaw, 1984 (Termination Date: 1992)

America Reads: Grades 6–12
Scott, Foresman, 1985 (Termination Date: 1992)

Scribner Literature Program: Grades K–7
Scribner, 1976 (Termination Date: 1992)

Macmillan Literature: Grades 7–12
Scribner, 1984, 1985 (Termination Date: 1992)

Treasury Edition: Grades 7–12
Webster Division McGraw Hill, 1985 (Termination Date: 1992)

McDougal, Littell Literature: Grades 7–12
McDougal, Littell, 1982–85 (Termination Date: 1992)

Myths and Their Meaning: Grade 9
Allyn & Bacon, 1984 (Termination Date: 1992)

The Reader's Anthology: Grade 9
Globe, 1986 (Termination Date: 1992)

The American Anthology: Grade 10
Globe, 1983 (Termination Date: 1992)

The World Anthology: Grade 11
Globe, 1983 (Termination Date: 1992)

Best-Selling Chapters, Middle Level: Grade 9
Jamestown, 1982 (Termination Date: 1992)

Literary Tales: Grade 10
Jamestown, 1980 (Termination Date: 1992)

Best Short Stories, Middle Level: Grade 10
Jamestown, 1983 (Termination Date: n.d.)

Best-Selling Chapters, Advanced Level: Grade 11
Jamestown, 1979 (Termination Date: 1992)

Best Short Stories, Advanced Level: Grade 12
Jamestown, 1983 (Termination Date: n.d.)

Louisiana

Language and Composition

Language for Daily Use, Voyager Edition: Grades K–8
Harcourt Brace Jovanovich, 1986 (Termination Date: 1992)

Warriner's English Grammar and Composition, Liberty Edition: Grades 6–12
Harcourt Brace Jovanovich, 1986 (Termination Date: 1992)

Houghton Mifflin English: Grades K–8
Houghton Mifflin, 1986 (Termination Date: 1992)

Laidlaw English: Grades K–8
Macmillan, 1987 (Termination Date: 1992)

McDougal, Littell English Series: Grades K–8
McDougal, Littell, 1987 (Termination Date: 1992)

Macmillan English: Grades K–12
Macmillan, 1987, 1985 (Termination Date: 1992)

Prentice Hall Grammar and Composition: Grades 6–12
Prentice Hall, 1987 (Termination Date: 1992)

Language: Skills and Use: Grades K–8
Scott, Foresman, 1986 (Termination Date: 1992)

Silver Burdett English: Grades K–8
Silver, Burdett, 1986 (Termination Date: 1992)

Glencoe/English: Grades 9–12
Glencoe, 1985 (Termination Date: 1992)

Heath Grammar and Composition: Grades 6–12
D. C. Heath, 1986,87 (Termination Date: 1992)

Houghton Mifflin English Grammar and Composition: Grades 9–12
Houghton Mifflin, 1986 (Termination Date: 1992)

Laidlaw English Series: Grades 9–12
Macmillan, 1985 (Termination Date: 1992)

Literature

Odyssey, An HBJ Literature Program: Grades 1–6
Harcourt Brace Jovanovich, 1986 (Termination
Date: 1992)

Macmillan Reading Express: Grades K–6
Macmillan, 1986 (Termination Date: 1992)

Wonder Story Books: Grades K–6
Scribner, 1976 (Termination Date: 1992)

Adventures in Literature, Heritage Edition: Grades
7–12
Harcourt Brace Jovanovich, 1985 (Termination
Date: 1992)

Journeys, A Reading and Literature Program:
Grades 7–12
Harcourt Brace Jovanovich, 1986 (Termination
Date: 1992)

McDougal Littell Literature Series: Grades 7–12
McDougal, Littell, 1987 (Termination Date: 1992)

Macmillan Literature Series: Grades 7–12
Scribner, 1984–85 (Termination Date: 1992)

America Reads Literature Series: Grades 7–12
Scott, Foresman, 1987 (Termination Date: 1992)

McGraw-Hill Literature Series, Treasury Edition:
Grades 7–12
Webster, 1985 (Termination Date: 1992)

Speech

Communicating Message and Meaning: Grades 9–12
Allyn & Bacon, 1982 (Termination Date: 1992)

Contemporary Speech: Grades 9–12
National Textbook, 1982 (Termination Date: 1992)

Speech: Exploring Communication: Grades 9–12
Prentice Hall, 1984 (Termination Date: 1992)

The Stage and the School: Grades 9–12
Webster, 1982 (Termination Date: 1992)

Journalism

Journalism: Grades 9–12
Silver Burdett and Ginn, 1984 (Termination
Date: 1992)

Scholastic Journalism: Grades 9–12
Iowa State University, n.d. (Termination Date:
1992)

Journalism: Print and Broadcast: Grades 9–12
Glencoe, 1983 (Termination Date: 1992)

Journalism Today!: Grades 9–12
National Textbook, 1984 (Termination Date: 1992)

Press Time: Grades 9–12
Prentice Hall, 1985 (Termination Date: 1992)

Inside High School Journalism: Grades 9–12
Scott, Foresman, 1986 (Termination Date: 1992)

Spelling

HBJ Spelling: Grades 1–8
Harcourt Brace Jovanovich, 1983 (Termination
Date: 1992)

Houghton Mifflin Spelling: Grades 1–8
Houghton Mifflin, 1985 (Termination Date: 1992)

Laidlaw Spelling: Grades 1–8
Macmillan, 1987 (Termination Date: 1992)

Macmillan Spelling: Grades 1–8
Macmillan, 1987 (Termination Date: 1992)

Building Spelling Skills Series: Grades 1–8
McDougal, Littell, 1985 (Termination Date: 1992)

Spelling: Words and Skills: Grades 1–8
Scott, Foresman, 1986 (Termination Date: 1992)

Silver Burdett Spelling: Grades 1–8
Silver Burdett and Ginn, 1986 (Termination
Date: 1992)

Basic Goals in Spelling: Grades 1–8
Webster, 1984 (Termination Date: 1992)

Zaner-Bloser Spelling: Basic Skills and Application:
Grades 1–8
Zaner-Bloser, 1984 (Termination Date: 1992)

Reading, Basal

HBJ Reading Program: Grades K–8
Harcourt Brace Jovanovich, 1987 (Termination
Date: 1992)

Houghton Mifflin Reading: Grades K–8
Houghton Mifflin, 1986 (Termination Date: 1992)

Economy Reading Series: Grades K–8
McGraw-Hill, 1988 (Termination Date: 1992)

Connections: Grades K–8
Macmillan, 1987 (Termination Date: 1992)

The Riverside Reading Program: Grades K–8
Riverside, 1989 (Termination Date: 1992)

Scott Foresman Reading: An American Tradition:
Grades K–8
Scott, Foresman, 1987 (Termination Date: 1992)

Scribner Reading Series: Grades K–8
Scribner-Laidlaw, 1989 (Termination Date: 1992)

Ginn Reading Program: Grades K–8
Silver Burdett and Ginn, 1987 (Termination
Date: 1992)

Handwriting
D'Nealian Handwriting: Grades K–8
Scott, Foresman, 1991 (Termination Date: 1998)

McDougal Littell Handwriting: Grades K–8
McDougal, Littell, 1990 (Termination Date: 1998)

HBJ Handwriting: Grades K–8
Harcourt Brace Jovanovich, 1987, 1989 (Termination Date: 1998)

Zaner-Bloser Handwriting: A Way to Self-Expression: Grades K–12
Zaner-Bloser, 1991 (Termination Date: 1998)

Mississippi

Reading (Grade Level and Extended)
HBJ Reading: Grades 1–8
Harcourt Brace Jovanovich, 1989 (Termination Date: 1997)

Heath Reading: Grades 1–8
D. C. Heath, 1991 (Termination Date: 1997)

Houghton Mifflin Reading: The Literature Experience: Grades 1–8
Houghton Mifflin, 1991 (Termination Date: 1997)

Connections: Grades K–8
Macmillan/McGraw-Hill, 1991 (Termination Date: 1997)

Vistas in Reading Literature: Grades 5–8
McDougal, Littell, 1990 (Termination Date: 1997)

Open Court Reading and Writing: Grades K–6
Open Court, 1989 (Termination Date: 1997)

Scott, Foresman Reading: Grades K–8
Scott, Foresman, 1989 (Termination Date: 1997)

World of Reading: Grades K–8
Silver, Burdett and Ginn, 1991 (Termination Date: 1997)

Reading (Below Grade Level)
Reading Express: Grades K–8
Macmillan/McGraw-Hill, 1990 (Termination Date: 1997)

Strategies: Grades 4–6
McDougal, Littell, 1991 (Termination Date: 1997)

FOCUS: Reading for Success: Grades K–8
Scott, Foresman, 1988 (Termination Date: 1997)

Reading (Supplemental)
Bill Martin Big Books (HBJ): Grade 1
Harcourt Brace Jovanovich, 1970 (Termination Date: 1997)

Steck-Vaughn Phonics Program: Grades 1-4
Steck-Vaughn, 1990 (Termination Date: 1997)

Aesop's Fables: Grades 1-4
Trillium Press, 1988 (Termination Date: 1997)

Reading (Low Vocabulary High Interest)
Discoveries in Reading: Grades 6–12
Harcourt Brace Jovanovich, 1990–91 (Termination Date: 1997)

New Directions in Reading: Grades 4–12
Houghton Mifflin, 1986 (Termination Date: 1997)

New Practice Readers: Grades 4–6
Phoenix Learning Resources, 1988 (Termination Date: 1997)

Reading for Concepts: Grades 3–6
Phoenix Learning Resources, 1988 (Termination Date: 1997)

Reading about Science: Grades 4–6
Phoenix Learning Resources, 1990 (Termination Date: 1997)

Great Series: Grades 6–12
Steck-Vaughn, 1990 (Termination Date: 1997)

Superstars in Action: Grades 5–12
Steck-Vaughn, 1990 (Termination Date: 1997)

English (Grade Level and Extended)
HBJ Language: Grades 1–8
Harcourt Brace Jovanovich, 1990 (Termination Date: 1998)

Houghton Mifflin English: Grades 1–12
Houghton Mifflin, 1990 (Termination Date: 1998)

Language Arts Today: Grades 1–6
Macmillan/McGraw-Hill, 1991 (Termination Date: 1998)

McDougal, Littell English: Grades 6–12
McDougal, Littell, 1990 (Termination Date: 1998)

Prentice Hall Grammar and Composition: Grades 6–12
Prentice Hall, 1990 (Termination Date: 1998)

Scott, Foresman Language: Grades 1–8
Scott, Foresman, 1989 (Termination Date: 1998)

World of Language: Grades 1–6
Silver Burdett and Ginn, 1990 (Termination Date: 1998)

Philosophy for Young Thinkers: Grades 1–6
Trillium, 1989 (Termination Date: 1998)

Macmillan English: Thinking and Writing Processes: Grades 9–12
Glencoe/McGraw-Hill, 1988 (Termination Date: 1998)

Heath Grammar and Composition: Grades 7–12
D. C. Heath, 1988–90 (Termination Date: 1998)

English Composition and Grammar: Grades 7–12
Holt, Rinehart and Winston/HBJ, 1988 (Termination Date: 1998)

English (Below Grade Level)
Basic Skills in English: Grades 7–12
McDougal, Littell, 1989 (Termination Date: 1998)

Study Skills and Strategies: Grades 7–12
Media Materials, 1987 (Termination Date: 1998)

Guidebook to Better English: Grades 7–12
Phoenix Learning Resources, 1989 (Termination Date: 1998)

Written Communication
Globe Writing Program: Grades 7–12
Globe, 1989 (Termination Date: 1998)

Project Write: Grades 7–12
Kendall/Hunt, 1988 (Termination Date: 1998)

Webster's New World School Writer's Handbook: Grades 9–12
Prentice Hall, 1988 (Termination Date: 1998)

Composition
Lively Writing: Grades 7–12
National Textbook, 1985 (Termination Date: 1998)

The Paragraph System for Successful Writing: Grades 7–12
Trillium, 1990 (Termination Date: 1998)

Vocabulary
World of Vocabulary: Grades 7–12
Globe, 1991 (Termination Date: 1998)

Wordskills: Grades 9–12
McDougal, Littell, 1991 (Termination Date: 1998)

Vocabulary by Doing: Grades 7–12
National Textbook, 1990 (Termination Date: 1998)

Stanford Vocabulary: Grades 7–12
Phoenix Learning Resources, 1988 (Termination Date: 1998)

The Word within the Word: Grades 7–12
Trillium, 1990 (Termination Date: 1998)

Journalism
Journalism Today: Grades 7–12
National Textbook, 1986 (Termination Date: 1998)

Press Time: Grades 9–12
Prentice Hall, 1985 (Termination Date: 1998)

Inside High School Journalism: Grades 9–12
Scott, Foresman, 1986 (Termination Date: 1998)

Oral Communication
The Basics of Speech: Grades 7–12
National Textbook, 1988 (Termination Date: 1998)

Person to Person: Grades 7–12
National Textbook, 1990 (Termination Date: 1998)

Dynamics of Speech: Grades 7–12
National Textbook, 1988 (Termination Date: 1998)

Communication: An Introduction to Speech:
Grades 7–9
Prentice Hall, 1988 (Termination Date: 1998)

Speech: Exploring Communication: Grades 9–12
Prentice Hall, 1988 (Termination Date: 1998)

Debate
Basic Debate: Grades 7–12
National Textbook, 1989 (Termination Date: 1998)

Strategic Debate: Grades 7–12
National Textbook, 1989 (Termination Date: 1998)

Public Speaking
Speech for Effective Communication: Grades 9–12
Holt, Rinehart and Winston/HBJ, 1988 (Termination Date: 1998)

Public Speaking Today!: Grades 7–12
National Textbook, 1989 (Termination Date: 1998)

Speech: Principles and Practice: Grades 8–12
Scott, Foresman, 1987 (Termination Date: 1998)

Creative Writing
Active Composing and Thinking: Grades 88
Kendall/Hunt, 1988 (Termination Date: 1998)

Creative Writing: Grades 7–12
National Textbook, 1990 (Termination Date: 1998)

Drama
The Stage and the School: Grades 9–12
Glencoe/McGraw-Hill, 1989 (Termination Date: 1998)

Play Production Today!: Grades 7–12
National Textbook, 1989 (Termination Date: 1998)

The Dynamics of Acting: Grades 7–12
National Textbook, 1989 (Termination Date: 1998)

Theater: Preparation and Performance: Grades 9–12
Scott, Foresman, 1989 (Termination Date: 1998)

Other Interrelated English/Literature
Reading Drama: An Anthology of Plays: Grade 12
Glencoe/McGraw-Hill, 1990 (Termination Date: 1998)

Reading Fiction: Anthology of Short Stories: Grade 12
Glencoe/McGraw-Hill, 1988 (Termination Date: 1998)

Reading Poetry: An Anthology of Poems: Grade 12
Glencoe/McGraw-Hill, 1989 (Termination Date: 1998)

Satire and Irony: Grades 7–9
Trillium, 1985 (Termination Date: 1998)

Message and Meaning: Grades 7–9
Trillium, 1984 (Termination Date: 1998)

Cartoons for Thinking: Grades 10–12
Trillium, 1988 (Termination Date: 1998)

Read to Study: Grades 7–12
Trillium, 1987 (Termination Date: 1998)

Elementary Literature
Just One More Program: Grades K–1
Childrens Press, 1990 (Termination Date: 1997)

DLM Literature Collection: Grades 1-2
DLM, 1986–90 (Termination Date: 1997)

Nystrom Three Packs: Grades 1-3
Nystrom Division of Herff Jones, 1990 (Termination Date: 1997)

Prentice Hall Literature: Grade 6
Prentice Hall, 1991 (Termination Date: 1997)

Collections: Grades K–6
Scott, Foresman, 1989 (Termination Date: 1997)

Sunshine Fiction: Grades 1-4
Wright Group, 1986–88 (Termination Date: 1997)

Sunshine Fact and Fantasy: Grades 1-2
Wright Group, 1988–89 (Termination Date: 1997)

Literature (Grade Level and Extended)
Macmillan Literature: Grades 7–12
Glencoe/McGraw-Hill, 1991 (Termination Date: 1997)

Adventures in Literature, HBJ: Grades 7–12
Holt, Rinehart and Winston, 1989 (Termination Date: 1997)

Elements of Literature: Grades 7–12
Holt, Rinehart and Winston, 1989 (Termination Date: 1997)

Prentice Hall Literature: Grades 7–12
Prentice Hall, 1991 (Termination Date: 1997)

America Reads: Grades 7–12
Scott, Foresman, 1991 (Termination Date: 1997)

Literature (Below Grade Level)
Journey's (HBJ): Grades 7–12
Holt, Rinehart and Winston, 1986 (Termination Date: 1997)

Reading Literature: Grades 9–12
McDougal, Littell, 1990 (Termination Date: 1997)

Short Stories
The Short Story and You: Grades 7–12
National Textbook, 1987 (Termination Date: 1997)

Mississippi Writers
Mississippi Writers: An Anthology: Grades 7–12
University Press of Mississippi, 1991 (Termination Date: 1997)

Spelling
HBJ Spelling: Grades 1–8
Harcourt Brace Jovanovich, 1988 (Termination Date: 1998)

Working Words in Spelling: Grades 1–8
D. C. Heath, 1990 (Termination Date: 1998)

Houghton Mifflin Spelling and Vocabulary: Grades 1–8
Houghton Mifflin, 1990 (Termination Date: 1998)

McDougal, Littell Spelling: Grades 1–8
McDougal, Littell, 1990 (Termination Date: 1998)

Scott, Foresman Spelling: Grades 1–8
Scott, Foresman, 1988 (Termination Date: 1998)

Language Connections: Grades 2–6
Wright Group, 1988 (Termination Date: 1998)

Spelling Connections: Words into Language: Grades 1–8
Zaner-Bloser, 1991 (Termination Date: 1998)

Handwriting
HBJ Handwriting: Grades 1–6
Harcourt Brace Jovanovich, 1989 (Termination Date: 1998)

McDougal, Littell Handwriting: Grades 1–8
McDougal, Littell, 1990 (Termination Date: 1998)

Scott, Foresman D'Nealian Handwriting Program: Grades 1–8
Scott, Foresman, 1991 (Termination Date: 1998)

Zaner-Bloser Handwriting: A Way to Self-Expression: Grades 1–8
Zaner-Bloser, 1991 (Termination Date: 1998)

Dictionaries
Scribner Dictionary Program: Grades 6–12
Glencoe/McGraw-Hill, 1986 (Termination Date: 1998)

The Lincoln Reading Dictionary: Grades 1-3
Harcourt Brace Jovanovich, 1990 (Termination Date: 1998)

HBJ School Dictionary: Grades 3–8
Harcourt Brace Jovanovich, 1990 (Termination Date: 1998)

The Lincoln Writing Dictionary: Grades 3–8
Harcourt Brace Jovanovich, 1989 (Termination Date: 1998)

Houghton Mifflin Dictionary Program: Grades K–12
Houghton Mifflin, 1989 (Termination Date: 1998)

Macmillan Dictionary Series: Grades 1–8
Macmillan/McGraw-Hill, 1990–91 (Termination
Date: 1998)

McDougal, Littell Dictionary Series: Grades 1–12
McDougal, Littell, 1990 (Termination Date: 1998)

Prentice Hall Dictionary Program: Grades 7–12
Prentice Hall, 1983–88 (Termination Date: 1998)

Scott, Foresman Dictionary Program: Grades 1–12
Scott, Foresman, 1988–90 (Termination Date: 1998)

Silver, Burdett and Ginn Dictionary Program:
Grades 1–8
Silver, Burdett and Ginn, 1985–90 (Termination
Date: 1998)

Nevada

Reading

Scribner Literature Series: Grades 7–8
Glencoe, 1989 (Termination Date: 1994)

HBJ Reading Program: Grades K–8
Harcourt Brace Jovanovich, 1989 (Termination
Date: 1994)

Imagination: An Odyssey through Language:
Grades 1–6
Harcourt Brace Jovanovich, 1989 (Termination
Date: 1993)

Discoveries in Reading: Grades 6–8
Harcourt Brace Jovanovich, 1990 (Termination
Date: 1994)

Impressions: Grades K–6
Harcourt Brace Jovanovich, 1990 (Termination
Date: 1994)

Heath Reading Program: Grades K–6
D. C. Heath, 1989 (Termination Date: 1994)

Houghton Mifflin Literary Reader: Grades K–6
Houghton Mifflin, 1989 (Termination Date: 1994)

Houghton Mifflin Reading: Grades K–8
Houghton Mifflin, 1989 (Termination Date: 1993)

Scott Foresman Reading: Grades K–8
Scott, Foresman, 1989 (Termination Date: 1994)

World of Reading: Grades 7–8
Silver, Burdett and Ginn, 1989 (Termination
Date: 1994)

McGraw-Hill Reading Series: Grades K–8
McGraw-Hill, 1989 (Termination Date: 1993)

Scott Foresman Reading: An American Tradition:
Grades K–8
Scott, Foresman, 1989 (Termination Date: 1993)

World of Reading: Grades K–6
Silver, Burdett and Ginn, 1989 (Termination
Date: 1993)

Macmillan Connections: Grades 1–6
Macmillan, 1987 (Termination Date: 1993)

Spelling

Working Words in Spelling: Grades 1–6
D.C. Heath, 1988 (Termination Date: 1993)

HBJ Spelling: Grades 1–6
Harcourt Brace Jovanovich, 1988 (Termination
Date: 1993)

Houghton Mifflin Spelling: Grades 2–6
Houghton Mifflin, 1988 (Termination Date: 1993)

Laidlaw Spelling: Grades K–8
Macmillan, 1989 (Termination Date: 1993)

Series S: Macmillan Spelling: Grades 6–8
Macmillan, 1987 (Termination Date: 1993)

McDougal Littell Spelling: Grades 6–8
McDougal, Littell, 1988 (Termination Date: 1993)

Spelling for Word Mastery: Grades 6–8
Merrill, 1987 (Termination Date: 1993)

Scott Foresman Spelling: Grades 1–8
Scott, Foresman, 1988 (Termination Date: 1993)

Spelling Connections: Words into Language:
Grades K–8
Zaner-Bloser, 1988 (Termination Date: 1993)

Spelling Connections: Grades K–8
Zaner-Bloser, 1991 (Termination Date: 1993)

Merrill Spelling. Grades 5–8
Merrill, 1990 (Termination Date: 1996)

Handwriting
D'Nealian Handwriting. Grades 1–8
Scott, Foresman, 1987 (Termination Date: 1993)

Speech
Effective Speech. Grades 7–8
Glencoe, 1988 (Termination Date: 1993)

Communications: An Introduction in Speech:
Grades 7–8
Prentice Hall, 1988 (Termination Date: 1993)

Literature
Adventures in Literature: Grades 11–12
Harcourt Brace Jovanovich, 1989 (Termination
Date: 1993)

Elements of Literature Series: Grades
Holt, Rinehart and Winston, 1989 (Termination
Date: 1993)

Themes in World Literature: Grades
Houghton Mifflin, 1989 (Termination Date: 1993)

McDougal Littell Literature: Grades 9–12
McDougal, Littell, 1989 (Termination Date: 1993)

Reading Literature: Grades 9–12
McDougal, Littell, 1989 (Termination Date: 1993)

Prentice Hall Literature: Grades 9–12
Prentice Hall, 1989 (Termination Date: 1993)

Scope English Anthologies: Grades 9–12
Scholastic, 1988 (Termination Date: 1993)

America Reads: Grades 9–12
Scott, Foresman, 1989 (Termination Date: 1993)

Scribner Literature Series: Grades 9–12
Glencoe, 1989 (Termination Date: 1993)

Globe Literature: Grades 10–12
Globe, 1990 (Termination Date: 1996)

Responding to Literature: Grades 9–12
McDougal, Littell, 1992 (Termination Date: 1996)

World Mythology. Grades 9–12
National Textbook, 1986 (Termination Date: 1996)

Composition and Grammar
*Heath Grammar and Composition with a Process
Approach to Writing.* Grades 6–12
D.C. Heath, 1988 (Termination Date: 1992)

Heath English: Grades 9–12
D.C. Heath, 1992 (Termination Date: n.d.)

Paragraphs and Themes: Grades 9–12
D.C. Heath, 1983 (Termination Date: n.d.)

The Heath Reader. Grades 9–12
D.C. Heath, 1987 (Termination Date: n.d.)

The Essay Connection: Grades 9–12
D.C. Heath, 1988 (Termination Date: n.d.)

The Lexington Reader. Grades 9–12
D.C. Heath, 1987 (Termination Date: n.d.)

Literature Based Composition: Grades 9–12
Glencoe, 1988 (Termination Date: n.d.)

Macmillan English: Thinking and Writing Processes: Grades 9–12
Macmillan, 1988 (Termination Date: n.d.)

Composition: Models and Exercises: Grades 9–12
Harcourt Brace Jovanovich, 1986 (Termination
Date: n.d.)

English Composition and Grammar. Grades 9–12
Harcourt Brace Jovanovich, 1988 (Termination
Date: n.d.)

Advanced Composition—Models for Writing.
Grades 9–12
Harcourt Brace Jovanovich, 1986 (Termination
Date: n.d.)

English Workshop. Grades 9–12
Harcourt Brace Jovanovich, 1986 (Termination
Date: n.d.)

English Writing and Skills, Coronado Ediition:
Grades 9–12
Holt, Rinehart and Winston, 1988 (Termination
Date: n.d.)

Houghton Mifflin English: Grades K–12
Houghton Mifflin, 1990 (Termination Date: 1993)

Grammar and Composition: Grades 9–12
Houghton Mifflin, 1986 (Termination Date: n.d.)

Writing with a Purpose: Grades 9–12
Houghton Mifflin, 1988 (Termination Date: n.d.)

Macmillan English: Grades 1–6
Macmillan, 1987 (Termination Date: 1996)

McDougal Littell English: Grades K–8
McDougal, Littell, 1989 (Termination Date: 1993)

Basic Skills in English: Grades 9–12
McDougal, Littell, 1985 (Termination Date: n.d.)

Building English Skills: Grades 9–12
McDougal, Littell, 1988 (Termination Date: n.d.)

The Writer's Craft: Grades 9–12
McDougal, Littell, 1992 (Termination Date: n.d.)

Literature and Language: Grades 9–12
McDougal, Littell, 1992 (Termination Date: n.d.)

Grammar and Composition: Grades 9–12
Prentice Hall, 1990, 1984 (Termination Date: n.d.)

Writing Themes about Literature: Grades 9–12
Prentice Hall, 1986 (Termination Date: n.d.)

Scope English: Writing and Language Skills:
Grades 9–12
Scholastic, 1987 (Termination Date: n.d.)

Cut the Deck: Grades 9–12
Stack the Deck, 1985 (Termination Date: n.d.)

Fan the Deck: Grades 9–12
Stack the Deck, 1980 (Termination Date: n.d.)

Pass the Deck: Grades 9–12
Stack the Deck, 1983 (Termination Date: n.d.)

Stack the Deck: Grades 9–12
Stack the Deck, 1988 (Termination Date: n.d.)

McGraw-Hill English: Grades K–8
McGraw-Hill, 1989 (Termination Date: n.d.)

Scott Foresman Language: Grades K–8
Scott, Foresman, 1989 (Termination Date: n.d.)

Silver Burdett and Ginn English: Grades K–8
Silver, Burdett and Ginn, 1989 (Termination Date: n.d.)

HBJ Language: Grades 6–8
Harcourt, Brace, 1990 (Termination Date: 1995)

Language Arts Today: Grades 6–8
Macmillan, 1990 (Termination Date: 1995)

Laidlaw English Series: Composition and Grammar: Grades 9–12
Laidlaw (Glencoe), 1985 (Termination Date: n.d.)

New Mexico

Reading Anthology
The Literature Bridge: Grades 4–12
Berrent, 1989 (Termination Date: 1997)

Coleccion Antologia Comunicativa: Grades 1–9
D.D.L. 1990 (Termination Date: 1997)

Touchstones Project: Grades 6–12
C.Z.M., 1985–91 (Termination Date: 1997)

Literature by Doing: Grades 9–12
National Textbook, 1990 (Termination Date: 1997)

Globe Literature: Grades 7–12
Globe, 1990 (Termination Date: 1997)

Introduction to Literature: Grade 6
Holt, Rinehart and Winston, 1991 (Termination Date: 1997)

Reading Literature: Grades 9–12
McDougal, Littell, 1990 (Termination Date: 1997)

Spotlight on Literature: Grades 7–12
American School, 1988 (Termination Date: 1997)

Achievement Program in Literature: Grades 1–8
American School, 1986 (Termination Date: 1997)

Bilingual
Isabel y Su Cama Nueva: Grades K–1
D.D.L., 1989 (Termination Date: 1997)

Coleccion Punto Infantil: Grades 6–8
D.D.L., 1987 (Termination Date: 1997)

Don Quijote de la Mancha: Grades 9–12
D.D.L., 1987 (Termination Date: 1997)

A Toda Maquina: Grades K–12
D.D.L., 1989–90 (Termination Date: 1997)

Illustrated Children's Dictionary: Grades K–2
D.D.L., 1989 (Termination Date: 1997)

Nuevo Auriga Series: El Lazarillo de Tormes:
Grades 7–12
D.D.L., 1988–89 (Termination Date: 1997)

Castell 3 Diccionario Enciclopedia: Grades 9–12
D.D.L., 1989 (Termination Date: 1997)

Historia de America: Grades 9–12
D.D.L., 1984 (Termination Date: 1997)

Reference Library: Grades K–12
D.D.L., 1988–90 (Termination Date: 1997)

Hombres Famosos: Grades 7–12
D.D.L., 1990–91 (Termination Date: 1997)

Torre de Papel: Grades 6–12
D.D.L., 1987 (Termination Date: 1997)

Coleccion Ardilla: Grades K–1
D.D.L., 1989 (Termination Date: 1997)

The Flying Horse: Grades 4–12
D.D.L., 1988 (Termination Date: 1997)

La Espiral Magica: Grades K–5
D.D.L., 1990 (Termination Date: 1997)

Agatha Christie's Complete Works: Grades 9–12
D.D.L., 1988 (Termination Date: 1997)

Coleccion Punto Juvenil: Grades 9–12
D.D.L., 1987–88 (Termination Date: 1997)

Coleccion Tu Gran Libro de Cuentos: Grades K–2
D.D.L., 1987 (Termination Date: 1997)

Coleccion Palabras: Grades K–1
D.D.L., 1987 (Termination Date: 1997)

Richard Scarry: Grades K–1
D.D.L., 1988 (Termination Date: 1997)

Coleccion Julio Verne: Grades 7–12
D.D.L., 1989 (Termination Date: 1997)

Coleccion Coediciones Latino Americanas: Grades
7–12
D.D.L., 1984–85 (Termination Date: 1997)

Coleccion Abra Palabra: Grades K–12
D.D.L., 1987–89 (Termination Date: 1997)

*Touchstones Project: Touchstones en Espanol, Vol.
1:* Grades 6–12
C.Z.M., 1990 (Termination Date: 1997)

Diccionario Enciclopedico: Grades 3–12
Encyclopedia Britannica, 1989 (Termination
Date: 1997)

Children's Classic Tales—Spanish: Grades K–6
Encyclopedia Britannica, 1989 (Termination
Date: 1997)

Rhythms to Reading: Grades K–2
Hawthorne, 1989 (Termination Date: 1997)

Chiquilines Gigantes: Grades K–4
Flame, 1988 (Termination Date: 1997)

Endangered Species: Grades 1-3
Modern Curriculum, 1986 (Termination Date:
1997)

Language Works: Spanish Developing Language:
Grades K–1
Modern Curriculum, 1990 (Termination Date: 1997)

Dedalin: Grades K–3
Modern Curriculum, 1990 (Termination Date: 1997)

Concept Science en Espanol: Grades 1-4
Modern Curriculum, 1990–91 (Termination Date:
1997)

Campanitas de Oro: Grades K–6
Macmillan, 1987 (Termination Date: 1997)

Bravo! Bravo!: Grades 1–6
Santillana, 1989 (Termination Date: 1997)

German Today: Grades 9–12
Houghton Mifflin, 1989 (Termination Date: 1997)

Kaleidoskop: Grades 9–12
Houghton Mifflin, 1987 (Termination Date: 1997)

Focus: Leer Para Triumfar: Grades K–5
Scott, Foresman, 1986 (Termination Date: 1997)

Nopalitos: Grade K–1
Scott, Foresman, 1987 (Termination Date: 1997)

Scott, Foresman Spanish Reading: Grades K–5
Scott, Foresman, 1987–90 (Termination Date: 1997)

La Constitucion: Grades 2-4
Childrens Press, 1989 (Termination Date: 1997)

La Carta de Derechos: Grades 2-4
Childrens Press, 1989 (Termination Date: 1997)

Todos mis juguentes: Grades K–2
Childrens Press, 1989 (Termination Date: 1997)

Puedo ser maestra: Grades K–2
Childrens Press, 1989 (Termination Date: 1997)

Lucio el sucio: Grades K–2
Childrens Press, 1989 (Termination Date: 1997)

Quien es quien?: Grades K–2
Childrens Press, 1989 (Termination Date: 1997)

Arriba y abajo: Grades K–2
Childrens Press, 1989 (Termination Date: 1997)

Los tres osos: Grades K–2
Childrens Press, 1989 (Termination Date: 1997)

Sal y entra: Grades K–2
Childrens Press, 1989 (Termination Date: 1997)

El principe rana: Grades K–2
Childrens Press, 1989 (Termination Date: 1997)

Manzano! Manzano!: Grades K–2
Childrens Press, 1989 (Termination Date: 1997)

Pequeno Coala busca casa: Grades K–2
Childrens Press, 1989 (Termination Date: 1997)

Raintree Hispanic Stories: Grades 3-4
Raintree, 1990 (Termination Date: 1997)

Our Hispanic Heritage: Grades 3-4
Raintree, 1990 (Termination Date: 1997)

Children's Book Press: Grades 3-4
Raintree, 1990 (Termination Date: 1997)

Spanish Sunshine: Grades K–1
Wright, 1990 (Termination Date: 1997)

Literature/Other

Readalong Skill Motivators: Grades K–3
Spoken Arts, 1988–89 (Termination Date: 1997)

Story Stations: Grades 1-5
Econo-Clad, 1990 (Termination Date: 1997)

React: Grades 9–12
Sundance, 1989–90 (Termination Date: 1997)

Insight: Grades 6–12
Sundance, 1987–89 (Termination Date: 1997)

Ananlit: Grades 7–12
Sundance, 1984–88 (Termination Date: 1997)

The Write Way: Grades 7–12
Sundance, 1984–90 (Termination Date: 1997)

Persona: Grades 6–12
Sundance, 1987–89 (Termination Date: 1997)

Literature Plus: Grades 1–6
Merrill, 1990 (Termination Date: 1997)

Prentice Hall Literature World Masterpieces: Grade 12
Prentice Hall, 1991 (Termination Date: 1997)

Prentice Hall Literature, Copper: Grade 6
Prentice Hall, 1991 (Termination Date: 1997)

Webster's New World High School Writers' Handbook: Grades 9–12
Prentice Hall, 1988 (Termination Date: 1997)

Scott, Foresman Classroom Libraries: Grades k–8
Scott, Foresman, 1989 (Termination Date: 1997)

The Education of Little Tree: Grades 4–12
University of New Mexico Press, 1986 (Termination Date: 1997)

The Wright Collections: Grades K–2
Wright, 1989 (Termination Date: 1997)

The Windmill Series: Grades K–1
Wright, n.d., (Termination Date: 1997)

Buddy Books: Grades K–3
Wright, 1987–88 (Termination Date: 1997)

Fables from Aesop: Grades K–2
Wright, 1986–87 (Termination Date: 1997)

Giggling Gerties: Grades K–3
Wright, 1989 (Termination Date: 1997)

Once upon a Time: Grades K–2
Wright, 1986–88 (Termination Date: 1997)

Tales from Hans Andersen: Grades K–2
Wright, 198689 (Termination Date: 1997)

Tales from Long Ago: Grades K–3
Wright, 1986–88 (Termination Date: 1997)

The Wright Way Home: Grades K–1
Wright, n.d., (Termination Date: 1997)

Classic Big Books Series: Grades K–1
Wright, 1986 (Termination Date: 1997)

The Rainbow Series: Grade 1
Wright, 1986 (Termination Date: 1997)

Rhyme Readers: Grades K–1
Wright, 1987 (Termination Date: 1997)

Balloons: Grades K–2
Wright, 1987 (Termination Date: 1997)

Don't Do That: Grades K–2
Wright, 1987 (Termination Date: 1997)

Joe's Gang!: Grades K–2
Wright, 1988 (Termination Date: 1997)

Starpol Action Series: Grades 2–8
Wright, 1987 (Termination Date: 1997)

Start with Rhymes: Grades K–1
Wright, n.d., (Termination Date: 1997)

Traditional Tales from around the World: Grades 5–8
Wright, 1986–88 (Termination Date: 1997)

Story Starters: Grades K–1
Wright, 1984–85 (Termination Date: 1997)

Let's Celebrate: Grades 1-4
Wright, 1987 (Termination Date: 1997)

Wesley and the Dinosaurs: Grades K–3
Wright, 1987 (Termination Date: 1997)

Story Poems: Grades 1-4
Wright, 1987 (Termination Date: 1997)

The Giant Series: Grades 1-4
Wright, 1988 (Termination Date: 1997)

Joanna Troughton Folk Tales: Grades 1-4
Wright, 1988 (Termination Date: 1997)

Celebration Series: Grades 1-4
Wright, 1986 (Termination Date: 1997)

Junior Great Books: Grades K–1, 3–10
Great Books, 1984–90 (Termination Date: 1997)

Introduction to Great Books: Grades 10–12
Great Books, 1990 (Termination Date: 1997)

Reading Alternative
Informational Book Sets: Grades 3–6
Rigby, 1987–89 (Termination Date: 1997)

Traditional Collections and Plays: Grades 3–6
Rigby, 1989 (Termination Date: 1997)

Literacy 2,000 Stories for Shared Reading: Grades K–4
Rigby, 1988–89 (Termination Date: 1997)

Informazing Titles: Content Area Reading—Science: Grades K–6
Rigby, 1988 (Termination Date: 1997)

Read-Along/Contemporary Stories: Grades K–2
Rigby, 1988 (Termination Date: 1997)

Poetry and Rhymes for Shared Reading: Grade K
Rigby, 1989 (Termination Date: 1997)

Wild, Weird and Wonderful: Grades 3–6
Berrent, 1991 (Termination Date: 1997)

Barnaby Brown Books: Grades 3-5
Berrent, 1991 (Termination Date: 1997)

Comprehension through CLOZE: Grades 1–10
Berrent, 1992 (Termination Date: 1997)

Understanding What You Read: Grades 3–8
Berrent, 1988 (Termination Date: 1997)

Exploring Social Studies through CLOZE: Grades 2–8
Berrent, 1992 (Termination Date: 1997)

CLOZE in on Social Studies: Grades 2–6
Berrent, 1990 (Termination Date: 1997)

Discovering Science through CLOZE: Grades 2–8
Berrent, 1991 (Termination Date: 1997)

Reading Success with CLOZE: Grades 2–12
Berrent, 1990 (Termination Date: 1997)

Early Birds: Grade K
Charlesbridge, 1990–91 (Termination Date: 1997)

Dolch Read and Comprehend: Grades 1-3
DLM, 1990 (Termination Date: 1997)

Sounds of Language: Grades K–2
DLM, 1990 (Termination Date: 1997)

Experiences for Literacy: Grades K–2
DLM, 1990 (Termination Date: 1997)

Bill Martin Junior Library: Grades K–3
DLM, 1989–90 (Termination Date: 1997)

Bill Martin's Sounds of Language: Grades K–4
DLM, 1990 (Termination Date: 1997)

Early Childhood Activity Books: Grades K–2
DLM, 1989 (Termination Date: 1997)

Read with Me Poetry: Grades K–2
DLM, 1990 (Termination Date: 1997)

Once upon a Time: An Encyclopedia for Successfully Using Literature: Grades K–2
DLM, 1990 (Termination Date: 1997)

Long Ago and Far Away: An Encyclopedia for Successfully Using Literature: Grades 3–6
DLM, 1990 (Termination Date: 1997)

Predictable Storybooks: Social Studies: Grades K–2
DLM, 1990 (Termination Date: 1997)

ABC Read Books: Grades K–2
DLM, 1990 (Termination Date: 1997)

Poetry to Share: Grades K–2
DLM, 1990 (Termination Date: 1997)

Numbers in Rhyme: Grades K–2
DLM, 1990 (Termination Date: 1997)

DLM's Legacy Collection of Children's Literature: Grades K–4
DLM, 1990 (Termination Date: 1997)

McCracken's Survival Handbook: Grades 3–6
DLM, 1990 (Termination Date: 1997)

Journeys: Grades 1–6
Ginn Canada, 1988–90 (Termination Date: 1997)

Ready to Read: Grades K–2
Richard C. Owen, 1982–86 (Termination Date: 1997)

Phoenix Everyreaders: Grades 4–12
Phoenix Learning Resources, 1988–89 (Termination Date: 1997)

Vocabulary Booster: Grades 4–6
Phoenix, 1989 (Termination Date: 1997)

MCP Phonics Program: Grades 1–6
Modern Curriculum, 1991 (Termination Date: 1997)

Big Books: Predictables: Grades 1-3
Scholastic, 1988 (Termination Date: 1997)

Favorite Books: Grades K–6
Scholastic, 1986 (Termination Date: 1997)

Predictable Theme Libraries: Grades 1-2
Scholastic, 1988 (Termination Date: 1997)

Predictable Book Collections: Grades K–2
Scholastic, 1989 (Termination Date: 1997)

Whole Language Theme Units: Grades K–4
Scholastic, n.d., (Termination Date: 1997)

Bookcenter Unit: Grades 2–6
Scholastic, n.d., (Termination Date: 1997)

Basal Breaks: Grades 1–6
Scholastic, n.d., (Termination Date: 1997)

Bridges II Unit: Grades 1–6
Scholastic, 1990 (Termination Date: 1997)

Perform!: Grades 1–6
Scholastic, 1990 (Termination Date: 1997)

Innovations: Literature Guides: Grades K–6
Scholastic, n.d., (Termination Date: 1997)

Discoveries in Reading: Grades 6–8
Holt, Rinehart and Winston, 1990–91 (Termination Date: 1997)

Reading Express: Grades K–8
Macmillan, 1990 (Termination Date: 1997)

HM Reading/Language Arts Program: Literary Reader: Grades K–8
Houghton Mifflin, 1989 (Termination Date: 1997)

Focus: Reading for Success: Grades K–8
Scott, Foresman, 1988 (Termination Date: 1997)

Reading Comprehension Series: Grades 1–6
Steck-Vaughn, 1989 (Termination Date: 1997)

New Way Series: Grades K–3
Steck-Vaughn, 1989 (Termination Date: 1997)

Vocabulary Connections: Grades 3–8
Steck-Vaughn, 1989 (Termination Date: 1997)

Folk Tales from around the World: Grades 4–6
Steck-Vaughn, 1990 (Termination Date: 1997)

Great Series: Grades 6–7
Steck-Vaughn, 1990 (Termination Date: 1997)

My World Series: Grades 1-3
Steck-Vaughn, 1990 (Termination Date: 1997)

Reading Bridge: Grades 4–12
Dormac, 1989 (Termination Date: 1997)

Midnight Reading Series: Grades 7–12
EDL, 1990 (Termination Date: 1997)

An American Family: Colony of Fear: Grades 7–12
Fearon, 1989–91 (Termination Date: 1997)

Quercus Caught Reading: Grades 7–12
Fearon, 1989–91 (Termination Date: 1997)

Quercus Content Reading: Grades 7–12
Fearon, 1989–91 (Termination Date: 1997)

Novels Set: Grades 7–12
Fearon, 1988–91 (Termination Date: 1997)

American Biographies: Grades 7–12
Fearon, 1987–91 (Termination Date: 1997)

Just One More: Grades K–2
Childrens Press, 1983–88 (Termination Date: 1997)

American Indian Stories: Grades 4-5
Raintree, 1990 (Termination Date: 1997)

Real Readers: Grade 1
Raintree, 1989 (Termination Date: 1997)

Ready-Set-Read: Grades K–3
Raintree, 1990 (Termination Date: 1997)

Raintree Science Adventures: Grade 3
Raintree, 1990 (Termination Date: 1997)

Publish-A-Book: Grades 2-4
Raintree, 1990 (Termination Date: 1997)

Networks: Grades 1-3
Charlesbridge, 1991 (Termination Date: 1997)

World of Reading: Grades K–8
Silver, Burdett and Ginn, 1989–90 (Termination Date: 1997)

Heath Reading: Grades K–8
D. C. Heath, 1991 (Termination Date: 1997)

Impressions: Grades K–6
Holt, Rinehart and Winston, 1989–90 (Termination Date: 1997)

Connections: Grades K–8
Macmillan, 1991 (Termination Date: 1997)

Basic Reading Series: Grades K–2
Science Research, 1985 (Termination Date: 1997)

Programa de Lectura en Espanol: Grades 1–6
Houghton Mifflin, 1987 (Termination Date: 1997)

The Literature Experience: Grades K–8
Houghton Mifflin, 1991 (Termination Date: 1997)

Scott, Foresman Reading: Grades K–8
Scott, Foresman, 1989 (Termination Date: 1997)

Vistas in Reading: Grades 5–8
McDougal, Littell, 1989 (Termination Date: 1997)

Open Court Reading and Writing: Grades K–6
Open Court, 1989 (Termination Date: 1997)

Reading—Other

Story Strategies: Grades 1–8
Econo-Clad, 1958–82 (Termination Date: 1997)

Bank Street Ready to Read: Grades K–3
Econo-Clad, 1989–90 (Termination Date: 1997)

Children's Classic Tales—English: Grades K–6
Encyclopedia Britannica, 1989 (Termination Date: 1997)

Creative Short Story Library: Grade 5
Encyclopedia Britannica, 1982–90 (Termination Date: 1997)

We the People: Grade 3
Encyclopedia Britannica, 1987 (Termination Date: 1997)

The NFL Today: Grade 4
Encyclopedia Britannica, 1986 (Termination Date: 1997)

Safety First: Grade 2
Encyclopedia Britannica, 1986 (Termination Date: 1997)

The Entertainers: Grade 4
Encyclopedia Britannica, 1979–86 (Termination Date: 1997)

Thunder the Dinosaur: Grade 2
Encyclopedia Britannica, 1987 (Termination Date: 1997)

Mr. Books: Grade 2
Encyclopedia Britannica, 1971–78 (Termination Date: 1997)

Turning Points: Grade 4
Encyclopedia Britannica, 1981 (Termination Date: 1997)

Amazing Fact Books: Grade 4
Encyclopedia Britannica, 1987 (Termination Date: 1997)

Baseball: The American Game: Grade 4
Encyclopedia Britannica, 1987 (Termination Date: 1997)

Limited Editions: Grade 5
Encyclopedia Britannica, 1978–89 (Termination Date: 1997)

NBA Today: Grade 4
Encyclopedia Britannica, 1989 (Termination Date: 1997)

Living Philosophies: Grade 6
Encyclopedia Britannica, 1985 (Termination Date: 1997)

The Value of Self-Esteem: Grade 5
Encyclopedia Britannica, 1986 (Termination Date: 1997)

Skills for Living: Grade 4
Encyclopedia Britannica, 1984 (Termination Date: 1997)

Rose Blanche: Grade 2
Encyclopedia Britannica, 1985 (Termination Date: 1997)

Fairy Tales: Grade 6
Encyclopedia Britannica, 1983–84 (Termination Date: 1997)

Zoobooks: Grade 3
Encyclopedia Britannica, 1988 (Termination Date: 1997)

Sun Signs: Grade 3
Encyclopedia Britannica, 1990 (Termination Date: 1997)

Great Moments in Sports: Grade 4
Encyclopedia Britannica, 1990 (Termination Date: 1997)

The NHL Today: Grade 4
Encyclopedia Britannica, 1990 (Termination Date: 1997)

Pinocchio: Grade 4
Encyclopedia Britannica, 1988 (Termination Date: 1997)

Mozart: Grade 4
Encyclopedia Britannica, 1989 (Termination Date: 1997)

Riverside Big Books: Grades K–3
Houghton Mifflin, 1989 (Termination Date: 1997)

Wit!: Grades 9–12
Sundance, 1989–91 (Termination Date: 1997)

ACT: Grades 2–6
Sundance, 1989–91 (Termination Date: 1997)

LIFT: Grades 4–8
Sundance, 1987–90 (Termination Date: 1997)

Kinderbooks: Grades K–2
Sundance, 1987–91 (Termination Date: 1997)

Four Star Library I, II, II, IV: Grades K–2
Sundance, 1989–91 (Termination Date: 1997)

LEAP: Grades 2–6
Sundance, 1987–91 (Termination Date: 1997)

Wild about Series: Grades 1–6
Sundance, 1989–91 (Termination Date: 1997)

Alert Reader Program: Grades 2–12
Sundance, 1987–90 (Termination Date: 1997)

Kinderpress: Grades K–2
Sundance, 1990 (Termination Date: 1997)

Kindercooks: Grades K–2
Sundance, 1990 (Termination Date: 1997)

Wordless Books: Grades K–1
Sundance, 1986 (Termination Date: 1997)

Poetry in Motion: Grades 4–6
Sundance, 1984 (Termination Date: 1997)

Connect: Grades 3–6
Sundance, 1990 (Termination Date: 1997)

America's Story Book, I–IV: Grades 4–8
Sundance, 1989–90 (Termination Date: 1997)

Intermediate Persona, Books I, II: Grades 4–6
Sundance, 1989 (Termination Date: 1997)

Reading for Concepts: Grades 2–12
Phoenix, 1988 (Termination Date: 1997)

New Practice Readers: Grades 2–12
Phoenix, 1988 (Termination Date: 1997)

Endangered Species: Grades 1–3
Modern Curriculum, 1986 (Termination Date: 1997)

Concept Science: Grades 1–3
Modern Curriculum, 1991 (Termination Date: 1997)

Our Earth Collection: Grades 1–3
Modern Curriculum, 1990 (Termination Date: 1997)

Quest for America Treasure Chest: Grades 5–9
Modern Curriculum, 1989 (Termination Date: 1997)

Globe Hispanic Biographies: Grades 7–12
Globe, 1989 (Termination Date: 1997)

Globe African American Biographies: Grades 7–12
Globe, 1989 (Termination Date: 1997)

Bill Martin Big Books: Grade 1
Holt, Rinehart and Winston, 1970 (Termination Date: 1997)

HBJ Libraries: Grades K–6
Holt, Rinehart and Winston, 1989 (Termination Date: 1997)

The K Literature Collection: Grade K
Holt, Rinehart and Winston, 1990 (Termination Date: 1997)

Bright Start Themepacks: Grade K
Holt, Rinehart and Winston, 1990 (Termination Date: 1997)

Houghton Mifflin Reading: Minibooks: Grade 1
Houghton Mifflin, 1989 (Termination Date: 1997)

Literature en Espagnol de HM: Grades K–6
Houghton Mifflin, 1990 (Termination Date: 1997)

Happily Ever After Program: Grades K–1
Addison-Wesley, 1991 (Termination Date: 1997)

Man in the Black Coat: Grades 6–12
Dormac, 1990 (Termination Date: 1997)

The Black Mexican Necklace: Grades 6–12
Dormac, 1990 (Termination Date: 1997)

Achievement Program in Comprehension: Grades 1–8
American School, 1986 (Termination Date: 1997)

Scoring High in Reading: Grades 2–8
American School, 1985 (Termination Date: 1997)

Spotlight on . . . Series: Grades 3–8
American School, 1989 (Termination Date: 1997)

New York Times Reader: Grades 6–8
American School, 1989 (Termination Date: 1997)

Phonics Readers for Writers: Grade 1
American School, 1990 (Termination Date: 1997)

Fearon's U.S. Geography: Grades 7–12
Fearon, 1990 (Termination Date: 1997)

Fearon's World History: Grades 7–12
Fearon, 1990 (Termination Date: 1997)

Fearon's United States History: Grades 7–12
Fearon, 1990 (Termination Date: 1997)

Fearon's American Government: Grades 7–12
Fearon, 1990 (Termination Date: 1997)

Fearon's General Science: Grades 7–12
Fearon, 1990 (Termination Date: 1997)

Fearon's Biology: Grades 7–12
Fearon, 1990 (Termination Date: 1997)

Fearon's Health: Grades 7–12
Fearon, 1990 (Termination Date: 1997)

Nystrom Theme Packs: Grades K–3
Nystrom, 1990 (Termination Date: 1997)

Composition/Journalism
Macmillan English: Grades 9–12
Glencoe, 1988 (Termination Date: 1995)

Literature-Based Composition: Grades 7–12
Glencoe, 1987 (Termination Date: 1995)

Understanding Mass Media: Grades 7–12
National Textbook, 1986 (Termination Date: 1995)

The Art of Composition: Grades 7–12
National Textbook, 1984 (Termination Date: 1995)

Journalism Today!: Grades 7–12
National Textbook, 1986 (Termination Date: 1995)

Lively Writing: Grades 7–12
National Textbook, 1985 (Termination Date: 1995)

Look, Think and Write: Grades 7–12
National Textbook, 1985 (Termination Date: 1995)

An Anthology for Young Writers: Grades 7–12
National Textbook, 1975 (Termination Date: 1995)

Writing in Action: Grades 7–12
National Textbook, 1984 (Termination Date: 1995)

Globe Writing Program: Grades 6–12
Globe, 1989 (Termination Date: 1995)

Newspaper Workshop: Grades 7–12
Globe, 1985 (Termination Date: 1995)

The Basics of Writing: Grades 7–12
Globe, 1986 (Termination Date: 1995)

Heath Language Arts: Grades K–8
D. C. Heath, 1988 (Termination Date: 1995)

Heath Grammar and Composition: Grades 6–12
D. C. Heath, 1988 (Termination Date: 1995)

English Composition and Grammar: Grades 6–12
Holt, Rinehart and Winston, 1988 (Termination Date: 1995)

English 2200: Nova Edition: Grades 7–12
Holt, Rinehart and Winston, 1989 (Termination Date: 1995)

English 2600, Nova Edition: Grades 7–12
Holt, Rinehart and Winston, 1989 (Termination Date: 1995)

English 3200: Grades 7–12
Holt, Rinehart and Winston, 1989 (Termination Date: 1995)

English Workshop: Grades 6–12
Holt, Rinehart and Winston, 1986 (Termination Date: 1995)

Language for Daily Use: Grades K–8
Holt, Rinehart and Winston, 1986 (Termination Date: 1995)

Vocabulary Workshop: Grades 6–12
Holt, Rinehart and Winston, 1988 (Termination Date: 1995)

The Lincoln Writing Dictionary: Grades 3–8
Holt, Rinehart and Winston, 1989 (Termination Date: 1995)

Business Communication for the Information Age:
Grades 9–12
Holt, Rinehart and Winston, 1988 (Termination
Date: 1995)

Composition: Models & Exercises: Grades 7–12
Holt, Rinehart and Winston, 1986 (Termination
Date: 1995)

Prentice Hall Grammar and Composition: Grades
6–12
Prentice Hall, 1987 (Termination Date: 1995)

Press Time: Grades 9–12
Prentice Hall, 1985 (Termination Date: 1995)

Thinking and Writing about Literature: Grades 10–12
Prentice Hall, 1984 (Termination Date: 1995)

Developing Writing Skills: Grades 9–12
Prentice Hall, 1988 (Termination Date: 1995)

Journalism: Grades 9–12
Prentice Hall, 1984 (Termination Date: 1995)

Writing and Thinking: Grades 1–6
Mastery Education, 1985 (Termination Date: 1995)

Houghton Mifflin English: Grades K–8
Houghton Mifflin, 1988 (Termination Date: 1995)

Inside High School Journalism: Grades 9–12
Scott, Foresman, 1986 (Termination Date: 1995)

Writing Practically: Grades 9–12
Amsco, 1976 (Termination Date: 1995)

Writing Creatively: Grades 10–12
Amsco, 1977 (Termination Date: 1995)

Writing Logically: Grades 11–12
Amsco, 1978 (Termination Date: 1995)

Wordplay: Grades 7–12
Amsco, 1984 (Termination Date: 1995)

Sentence Play: Grades 5–10
Amsco, 1984 (Termination Date: 1995)

Paragraph Play: Grades 5–10
Amsco, 1977 (Termination Date: 1995)

Word Game: Grades 6–10
Amsco, 1988 (Termination Date: 1995)

Fifteen Steps to Better Writing: Grades 10–12
Amsco, 1988 (Termination Date: 1995)

McGraw-Hill English: Grades K–8
McGraw-Hill, 1989 (Termination Date: 1995)

Active Composing and Thinking: Grades 7–8
Kendall/Hunt, 1988 (Termination Date: 1995)

Write and Read: Grades 7–12
EDL, 1981 (Termination Date: 1995)

The Write Track: Grades K–12
ERA/CCR, 1984–87 (Termination Date: 1995)

Every Page Perfect, Vol. 1: Grades 7–12
Compupress, 1987 (Termination Date: 1995)

Grammar/Handbooks
Language Skills: Grades 1-5
Curriculum Associates, 1984–88 (Termination
Date: 1995)

Silver Burdett and Ginn English: Grades K–8
Silver, Burdett and Ginn, 1989 (Termination
Date: 1995)

Grammar for Use: Grades 7–12
National Textbook, 1986 (Termination Date: 1995)

Essentials of English Grammar: Grades 7–12
National Textbook, 1987 (Termination Date: 1995)

Grammar Step-by-Step: Grades 7–12
National Textbook, 1985 (Termination Date: 1995)

Grammar and Composition for Everyday English:
Grades 7–12
Globe, 1987 (Termination Date: 1995)

Grammar and Composition for Today: Grades 7–12
Globe, 1983 (Termination Date: 1995)

Language Workshop: Guide to Better English:
Grades 7–12
Globe, 1984 (Termination Date: 1995)

English: Writing and Skills: Grades 6–12
Holt, Rinehart and Winston, 1988 (Termination
Date: 1995)

Macmillan English: Grades K–8
Macmillan, 1987 (Termination Date: 1995)

Macmillan English: Thinking and Writing Processes: Grades 6–8
Macmillan, 1987 (Termination Date: 1995)

Prentice Hall Handbook for Writers: Grades 10–12
Prentice Hall, 1988 (Termination Date: 1995)

Houghton Mifflin English: Grammar and Composition: Grades 7–12
Houghton Mifflin, 1986 (Termination Date: 1995)

Scott, Foresman Language: Grades K–8
Scott, Foresman, 1989 (Termination Date: 1995)

McDougal, Littell English: Grades K–12
McDougal, Littell, 1989 (Termination Date: 1995)

Basic Skills in English: Grades 7–12
McDougal, Littell, 1989 (Termination Date: 1995)

Literature

First Fairy Tales: Grades K–1
Ladybird, 1988 (Termination Date: 1995)

Well-Loved Tales: Grades 1-5
Ladybird, 1987 (Termination Date: 1995)

Children's Classics: Grades 4–7
Ladybird, 1986 (Termination Date: 1995)

Walker Plays for Reading: Grades 3–8
Curriculum Associates, 1978 (Termination Date: 1995)

Plays for Oral Reading: Grades 1-4
Curriculum Associates, 1979 (Termination Date: 1995)

Unified Language Series: Grades 1-5
Curriculum Associates, 1987 (Termination Date: 1995)

Scribner Literature Series: Grades 7–12
Glencoe, 1989 (Termination Date: 1995)

World Mythology: Grades 7–12
National Textbook, 1986 (Termination Date: 1995)

The Short Story and You: Grades 7–12
National Textbook, 1987 (Termination Date: 1995)

You and Science Fiction: Grades 7–12
National Textbook, 1976 (Termination Date: 1995)

Mythology and You: Grades 7–12
National Textbook, 1984 (Termination Date: 1995)

The Detective Story: Grades 7–12
National Textbook, 1975 (Termination Date: 1995)

Big Books: Content Area Titles: Grades 1-3
Scholastic, 1988 (Termination Date: 1995)

Big Books: Classics and Contemporary Favorites: Grades K–3
Scholastic, 1988 (Termination Date: 1995)

Big Books: Predictables: Grades 1-3
Scholastic, 1988 (Termination Date: 1995)

Bookshelf: Grades K–2
Scholastic, 1988 (Termination Date: 1995)

Globe's Adapted Classics: Grades 7–12
Globe, 1978–88 (Termination Date: 1995)

The Globe Reader's Collection: Grades 7–12
Globe, 1980 (Termination Date: 1995)

Legends for Everyone: Grades 7–12
Globe, 1978 (Termination Date: 1995)

Imagination: Grades K–6
Holt, Rinehart and Winston, 1989–90 (Termination Date: 1995)

Odyssey: Grades 1–8
Holt, Rinehart and Winston, 1982–85 (Termination Date: 1995)

Adventures in Literature: Grades 7–12
Holt, Rinehart and Winston, 1989–90 (Termination Date: 1995)

Journeys: Grades 7–12
Holt, Rinehart and Winston, 1986 (Termination Date: 1995)

Literature: Man the Myth-Maker: Grades 9–12
Holt, Rinehart and Winston, 1981 (Termination Date: 1995)

Adventures in Modern Literature: Grades 12
Holt, Rinehart and Winston, 1970 (Termination Date: 1995)

Adventures in World Literature: Grades 12
Holt, Rinehart and Winston, 1970 (Termination Date: 1995)

Perspectives in Literature: Grades 9–12
Holt, Rinehart and Winston, 1983 (Termination Date: 1995)

Impact: Fifty Short Stories: Grades 7–10
Holt, Rinehart and Winston, 1986 (Termination Date: 1995)

Short Stories: Characters in Conflict: Grades 9–12
Holt, Rinehart and Winston, 1981 (Termination Date: 1995)

Elements of Literature: Grades 7–12
Holt, Rinehart and Winston, 1989 (Termination Date: 1995)

Macmillan Classroom Library: Grades K–8
Macmillan, 1987 (Termination Date: 1995)

Wonder Story Books: Grades K–6
Macmillan, 1987 (Termination Date: 1995)

Prentice Hall Literature: Grades 7–12
Prentice Hall, 1989 (Termination Date: 1995)

Myths and Their Meanings: Grades 7–12
Prentice Hall, 1985 (Termination Date: 1995)

Aesop's Fables: My Book about Reading-Writing-Thinking, Vol. I-IV: Grades 2-4
Trillium, 1988 (Termination Date: 1995)

Houghton Mifflin Literature, Bookshelf: Grades K–8
Houghton Mifflin, 1989 (Termination Date: 1995)

America Reads: Grades 6–12
Scott, Foresman, 1989 (Termination Date: 1995)

Collections: An Anthology Series: Grades 1–6
Scott, Foresman, 1989 (Termination Date: 1995)

McDougal, Littell Literature: Grades 7–12
McDougal, Littell, 1989 (Termination Date: 1995)

Amsco Literature Program: Grades 7–12
Amsco, 1970–93 (Termination Date: 1995)

Short Stories: Grades 9–12
Amsco, 1988 (Termination Date: 1995)

McGraw-Hill Literature Series: Grades 7–12
McGraw-Hill, 1989 (Termination Date: 1995)

Literary Reflections: Grades 9–12
McGraw-Hill, 1982 (Termination Date: 1995)

Introduction to Literature: Grades 9–12
McGraw-Hill, 1985 (Termination Date: 1995)

McGraw-Hill Reader: Grades 9–12
McGraw-Hill, 1989 (Termination Date: 1995)

The Earth Did Not Devour Him: Grades 9–12
Arte Publico, 1987 (Termination Date: 1995)

The House on Mango Street: Grades 5–12
Arte Publico, 1988 (Termination Date: 1995)

Jamestown Literature Series: Grades 6–12
Jamestown, 1979–83 (Termination Date: 1995)

Phonetic Readers for Short Vowels: Grades K–2
Sizzy Books, 1988 (Termination Date: 1995)

Story Box: Grades K–3
Wright, 1980–84 (Termination Date: 1995)

The Kick-A-Lot Shoes Big Book: Grade 1
Wright, 1981 (Termination Date: 1995)

Hungry Monster: Grade 1
Wright, 1981 (Termination Date: 1995)

The You and Me Series: Grades K–2
Wright, 1985 (Termination Date: 1995)

Sunshine Series: Grades K–6
Wright, 1986–88 (Termination Date: 1995)

Tail Tigerswallow and The Great Tobacco War: Grades 8–12
Amador, 1988 (Termination Date: 1995)

Speech/Drama
Opposing Viewpoints—Civil Liberties: Grades 8–12
Greenhaven, 1988 (Termination Date: 1995)

Effective Speech: Grades 7–12
Glencoe, 1988 (Termination Date: 1995)

Creative Speaking: Grades 7–12
National Textbook, 1981 (Termination Date: 1995)

Play Production Today!: Grades 7–12
National Textbook, 1989 (Termination Date: 1995)

Introduction to Theatre and Drama: Grades 7–12
National Textbook, 1975 (Termination Date: 1995)

Book of Scenes for Acting Practice: Grades 7–12
National Textbook, 1985 (Termination Date: 1995)

The Dynamics of Acting: Grades 7–12
National Textbook, 1989 (Termination Date: 1995)

Literature Alive: Grades 7–12
National Textbook, 1976 (Termination Date: 1995)

Basic Debate: Grades 7–12
National Textbook, 1989 (Termination Date: 1995)

Strategic Debate: Grades 7–12
National Textbook, 1989 (Termination Date: 1995)

The Basics of Speech: Grades 7–12
National Textbook, 1988 (Termination Date: 1995)

Person to Person: Grades 7–12
National Textbook, 1984 (Termination Date: 1995)

Public Speaking Today!: Grades 7–12
National Textbook, 1989 (Termination Date: 1995)

Dynamics of Speech: Grades 7–12
National Textbook, 1988 (Termination Date: 1995)

Speaking by Doing: Grades 7–12
National Textbook, 1986 (Termination Date: 1995)

Television Production Today!: Grades 7–12
National Textbook, 1987 (Termination Date: 1995)

Getting Started in Public Speaking: Grades 7–12
National Textbook, 1985 (Termination Date: 1995)

Getting Started in Debate: Grades 7–12
National Textbook, 1987 (Termination Date: 1995)

Understanding the Film: Grades 7–12
National Textbook, 1986 (Termination Date: 1995)

Speech for Effective Communication: Grades 9–12
Holt, Rinehart and Winston, 1988 (Termination Date: 1995)

Vocabulary for College: Grades 9–12
Holt, Rinehart and Winston, 1989 (Termination Date: 1995)

Speech: Exploring Communication: Grades 9–12
Prentice Hall, 1988 (Termination Date: 1995)

Communication: An Intro to Speech: Grades 7–9
Prentice Hall, 1988 (Termination Date: 1995)

Speech: Principles and Practice: Grades 8–12
Scott, Foresman, 1987 (Termination Date: 1995)

Theater: Preparation and Performance: Grades 10–12
Scott, Foresman, 1989 (Termination Date: 1995)

The Stage and the School: Grades 9–12
McGraw-Hill, 1989 (Termination Date: 1995)

Spelling/Handwriting

Spellex Word Finder: Grades 3–9
Curriculum Associates, 1988 (Termination Date: 1995)

Handwriting: I Grades 3–8
Curriculum Associates, 1988 (Termination Date: 1995)

Spelling to Be Somebody: Grades 7–12
Curriculum Associates, 1987 (Termination Date: 1995)

Quick-Word Handbook: Grades 1–6
Curriculum Associates, 1987 (Termination Date: 1995)

Spell It Out: Grades 7–12
Globe, 1985–86 (Termination Date: 1995)

Working Words in Spelling: Grades 1–8
D. C. Heath, 1988 (Termination Date: 1995)

Wordfinder: Grades 1–8
D. C. Heath, 1988 (Termination Date: 1995)

HBJ Handwriting: Grades K–6
Holt, Rinehart and Winston, 1987 (Termination Date: 1995)

HBJ Spelling: Grades 1–8
Holt, Rinehart and Winston, 1988 (Termination Date: 1995)

Laidlaw Spelling: Grades K–8
Macmillan, 1987 (Termination Date: 1995)

Palmer Method Handwriting: Grades K–8
Macmillan, 1987 (Termination Date: 1995)

Merrill Spelling for Word Mastery: Grades K–8
Macmillan, 1990 (Termination Date: 1995)

Cursive Writing Program: Grades 3-4
Science Research, 1985 (Termination Date: 1995)

Spelling Mastery: Grades 2–6
Science Research, 1985 (Termination Date: 1995)

Houghton Mifflin Spelling: Grades 1–8
Houghton Mifflin, 1988 (Termination Date: 1995)

Riverside Spelling: Grades K–8
Houghton Mifflin, 1988 (Termination Date: 1995)

Spelling Is Special: Grades 1-4
Scott, Foresman, 1984 (Termination Date: 1995)

D'Nealian Handwriting Readiness: Grades 1-2
Scott, Foresman, 1987 (Termination Date: 1995)

D'Nealian Handwriting: Grades K–8
Scott, Foresman, 1987 (Termination Date: 1995)

Scott, Foresman Spelling: Grades 1–8
Scott, Foresman, 1988 (Termination Date: 1995)

Spelling Connections: Grades 1–8
Zaner-Bloser, 1988 (Termination Date: 1995)

Handwriting: Basic Skills and Application: Grades
1–8
Zaner-Bloser, 1989 (Termination Date: 1995)

McDougal, Little Spelling: Grades 1–8
McDougal, Littell, 1988 (Termination Date: 1995)

McDougal, Littell Handwriting: Grades K–8
McDougal, Littell, 1988 (Termination Date: 1995)

Bowmar/Nobel Handwriting Series: Grades 1–8
McGraw-Hill, 1987 (Termination Date: 1995)

Spelling the Written Word: Grades 7–10
Kendall/Hunt, 1984–85 (Termination Date: 1995)

Study Skills
Skills for School Success: Grades 3–6
Curriculum Associates, 1988 (Termination Date:
1995)

Study Skills and Strategies: Grades 9–12
Media Materials, 1987 (Termination Date: 1995)

Listening by Doing: Grades 7–12
National Textbook, 1985 (Termination Date: 1995)

Reading for Study Skills: Grades 4–7
Hammond, 1986 (Termination Date: 1995)

Insights: Reading as Thinking: Grades 3–8
Mastery Education, 1987 (Termination Date: 1995)

Critical Thinking: Grades 1–6
Steck-Vaughn, 1987 (Termination Date: 1995)

Learning to Study: Grades 2–8
Jamestown, 1983 (Termination Date: 1995)

Beyond Basics: Grades 4–12
Jamestown, 1986 (Termination Date: 1995)

Scoring High in Language: Grades 2–8
American School, 1987 (Termination Date: 1995)

Skills on Studying, Help Is on the Way for . . . :
Grades 4–6
Childrens Press, 1984 (Termination Date: 1995)

Vocabulary
How to Develop a College-Level Vocabulary:
Grades 9–12
Media Materials, 1985 (Termination Date: 1995)

A Basic and Root Vocabulary Builder: Grades 7–12
Media Materials, 1984 (Termination Date: 1995)

How To Build an "Educated" Vocabulary: Grades
11–12
Media Materials, 1986 (Termination Date: 1995)

Integrated Vocabulary Development: Grades 7, 9–10
Educational Design, 1987 (Termination Date: 1995)

Vocabulary for Competency: Grades 8, 11–12
Educational Design, 1986–87 (Termination Date:
1995)

The World of Vocabulary: Grades 7–12
Globe, 1979–87 (Termination Date: 1995)

Keys to a Powerful Vocabulary: Grades 9–12
Prentice Hall, 1983–88 (Termination Date: 1995)

Houghton Mifflin Vocabulary for Achievement:
Grades 6–12
Houghton Mifflin, 1988 (Termination Date: 1995)

Wordskills: Grades 7–12
McDougal, Littell, 1986 (Termination Date: 1995)

Building Word Skills: Grade 6
McDougal, Littell, 1982 (Termination Date: 1995)

The Joy of Vocabulary: Grades 11–12
Amsco, 1984 (Termination Date: 1995)

Vocabulary for Enjoyment: Grades 6–8
Amsco, 1986–88 (Termination Date: 1995)

English for the College Boards: Grades 11–12
Amsco, 1987 (Termination Date: 1995)

Vocabulary Drills: Grades 6–12
Jamestown, 1986 (Termination Date: 1995)

Vocabulary Workshop: Grades 6–12
Sadlier-Oxford, 1988 (Termination Date: 1995)

The Write Track: Grades 3–12
ERA/CCR, 1986 (Termination Date: 1995)

Rookie Readers: Grades K–1
Childrens Press, 1985 (Termination Date: 1995)

Great Unsolved Mysteries: Grade 5
Raintree, 1986 (Termination Date: 1995)

Quest, Adventure, Survival: Grade 5
Raintree, 1986 (Termination Date: 1995)

Raintree Short Classics: Grade 4
Raintree, 1986 (Termination Date: 1995)

Science Fiction Shorts: Grade 5
Raintree, 1986 (Termination Date: 1995)

Raintree Stories Clippers: Grades 2-4
Raintree, 1986 (Termination Date: 1995)

Raintree Stories American: Grades 2-4
Raintree, 1986 (Termination Date: 1995)

Raintree Stories International: Grades 2-4
Raintree, 1986 (Termination Date: 1995)

Reading Rainbow Group: Grades 1-4
Raintree, 1986 (Termination Date: 1995)

Dictionaries
Mi Primer Libro: Grades K–2
D.D.L., 1990 (Termination Date: 1998)

1000 Preguntas, 1000 Respuestas: Grades 4–9
D.D.L., 1990 (Termination Date: 1998)

Mi Diccionario Gigante: Grades 1-3
D.D.L., 1990 (Termination Date: 1998)

Diccionario de Simbolos: Grades 9–12
D.D.L., 1988 (Termination Date: 1998)

Diccionario de la Mitologia Mundial: Grades 9–12
D.D.L., 1984 (Termination Date: 1998)

Diccionario Enciclopedico Castell: Grades 9–12
D.D.L., 1985–90 (Termination Date: 1998)

Webster's Elementary Dictionary: Grades 1–6
Encyclopaedia Britannica, 1986 (Termination
Date: 1998)

Webster's Intermediate Dictionary: Grades 6–8
Encyclopaedia Britannica, 1986 (Termination
Date: 1998)

Webster's New Geographical Dictionary: Grades 8-12
Encyclopaedia Britannica, 1988 (Termination
Date: 1998)

Webster's New Ideal Dictionary: Grades 8–12
Encyclopaedia Britannica, 1989 (Termination
Date: 1998)

Webster's New Biographical Dictionary: Grades 8-12
Encyclopaedia Britannica, 1988 (Termination
Date: 1998)

Webster's Dictionary of English Usage: Grades 10–12
Encyclopaedia Britannica, 1989 (Termination
Date: 1998)

Webster's Word Histories: Grades 10–12
Encyclopaedia Britannica, 1989 (Termination
Date: 1998)

Webster's 3rd International Dictionary: Grades 10–12
Encyclopaedia Britannica, 1986 (Termination
Date: 1998)

12,000 Words: Grades 10–12
Encyclopaedia Britannica, 1987 (Termination
Date: 1998)

Webster's 9th New Collegiate Dictionary: Grades
10–12
Encyclopaedia Britannica, 1987 (Termination
Date: 1998)

Webster's School Dictionary: Grades 9–12
Encyclopaedia Britannica, 1986 (Termination
Date: 1998)

Scribner Intermediate Dictionary: Grades 7–9
Glencoe/McGraw-Hill, 1986 (Termination Date:
1998)

Scribner Dictionary: Grades 9–12
Glencoe/McGraw-Hill, 1986 (Termination Date:
1998)

Random Hosue Webster's College Dictionary:
Grades 9–12
Glencoe/McGraw-Hill, 1992 (Termination Date:
1998)

Schoolhouse Dictionary: Grades 2-4
Modern Curriculum, 1986 (Termination Date:1998)

Webster New World Dictionary Explorer/Language:
Grades 2-4
Modern Curriculum, 1991 (Termination Date: 1998)

Webster New World Dictionary Basic School:
Grades 3–8
Modern Curriculum, 1989 (Termination Date: 1998)

Webster's New World Dictionary, School Edition:
Grades 5–8
Silver, Burdett and Ginn, 1990 (Termination
Date: 1998)

*Webster's New World Dictionary for Young Readers
and Writers:* Grades 3-5
Silver, Burdett and Ginn, 1991 (Termination
Date: 1998)

Lincoln Reading Dictionary: Grades 1-2
Harcourt Brace Jovanovich, 1990 (Termination
Date: 1998)

HBJ School Dictionary: Grades 3–8
Harcourt Brace Jovanovich, 1990 (Termination
Date: 1998)

Macmillan/McGraw-Hill Picture Word Book:
Grades K–1
Macmillan/McGraw-Hill, 1991 (Termination
Date: 1998)

Macmillan/McGraw-Hill Primary Dictionary:
Grades 1-2
Macmillan/McGraw-Hill, 1991 (Termination
Date: 1998)

Macmillan/McGraw-Hll School Dictionary: Grades
3 –8
Macmillan/McGraw-Hill, 1990 (Termination
Date: 1998)

Webster's New World Dictionary: Grades 7–12
Prentice Hall, 1988 (Termination Date: 1998)

The American Heritage Dictionary: Grades 11–12
Houghton Mifflin, 1982 (Termination Date: 1998)

The Concise American Heritage Dictionary: Grades
9–12
Houghton Mifflin, 1987 (Termination Date: 1998)

Houghton Mifflin Student Dictionary: Grades 6–9
Houghton Mifflin, 1989 (Termination Date: 1998)

Houghton Mifflin Intermediate Dictionary: Grades
3–6
Houghton Mifflin, 1989 (Termination Date: 1998)

Houghton Mifflin Primary Dictionary: Grades 1-2
Houghton Mifflin, 1989 (Termination Date: 1998)

Houghton Mifflin College Dictionary: Grades 9–12
Houghton Mifflin, 1986 (Termination Date: 1998)

Houghton Mifflin Picture Dictionary: Grades K–1
Houghton Mifflin, 1989 (Termination Date: 1998)

The Dictionary of Cultural Legacy: Grades 9–12
Houghton Mifflin, 1988 (Termination Date: 1998)

Word Desk Set: Grades 7–12
Houghton Mifflin, 1990 (Termination Date: 1998)

Scott, Foresman-Barnhart Dictionary: Grades 3–12
Scott, Foresman, 1988 (Termination Date: 1998)

My Pictionary. Grades K–1
Scott, Foresman, 1990 (Termination Date: 1998)

My First Picture Dictionary: Grade 1
Scott, Foresman, 1990 (Termination Date: 1998)

My Second Picture Dictionary: Grade 2
Scott, Foresman, 1990 (Termination Date: 1998)

HarperCollins Bilingual Spanish Dictionary.
Grades 7–12
Scott, Foresman, 1990 (Termination Date: 1998)

HarperCollins Bilingual French Dictionary. Grades
7–12
Scott, Foresman, 1990 (Termination Date: 1998)

American Heritage Picture Dictionary. Grades K–1
Perma-Bound/Hertzberg New Method, 1986
(Termination Date: 1998)

American Heritage Student's Dictionary. Grades 7–
10
Perma-Bound/Hertzberg New Method, 1986
(Termination Date: 1998)

American Heritage Larousse Spanish Dictionary.
Grades 7–12
Perma-Bound/Hertzberg New Method, 1987
(Termination Date: 1998)

Diccionario de Sinonimos y Antonimos. Grades 7–12
Perma-Bound/Hertzberg New Method, 1988
(Termination Date: 1998)

Macmillan First Dictionary. Grades K–3
Perma-Bound/Hertzberg New Method, 1990
(Termination Date: 1998)

*American Heritage Dictionary of the English
Language:* Grades 7–12
Perma-Bound/Hertzberg New Method, 1983
(Termination Date: 1998)

University of Chicago Spanish/English Dictionary.
Grades 9–12
Perma-Bound/Hertzberg New Method, 1977
(Termination Date: 1998)

Random House Basic Dictionary: Spanish-English:
Grades 8–12
Perma-Bound/Hertzberg New Method, 1981
(Termination Date: 1998)

French Dictionary. Grades 7–12
Amsco, 1988 (Termination Date: 1998)

Spanish Dictionary. Grades 7–12
Amsco, 1987 (Termination Date: 1998)

A First Dictionary. Grades 2-4
Childrens Press, 1990 (Termination Date: 1998)

Encyclopedias

La Naturaleza en 101 Preguntas. Grades 2-5
D.D.L., 1990 (Termination Date: 1998)

Como Nacemos, Crecemos, Funciona Nuestro:
Grades 3-5
D.D.L., 1990 (Termination Date: 1998)

Nueva Acta 2000. Grades 9–12
D.D.L., 1985 (Termination Date: 1998)

Mega Junior. Grades 5–9
D.D.L., 1989 (Termination Date: 1998)

Mega Benjamin. Grades 2–6
D.D.L., 1989 (Termination Date: 1998)

Mega Chiquitin. Grades 1-3
D.D.L., 1989 (Termination Date: 1998)

Gran Enciclopedia Rialp. Grades 9–12
D.D.L., 1989 (Termination Date: 1998)

Dime Enciclopedia: Grades 4–7
D.D.L., 1983 (Termination Date: 1998)

Enciclopedia Tematica: Grades 9–12
D.D.L., 1986 (Termination Date: 1998)

Enciclopedia Larousse Juvenil: Grades 6–12
D.D.L., 1990 (Termination Date: 1998)

Enciclopedia de los Museos: Grades 9–12
D.D.L., 1986 (Termination Date: 1998)

Consultor Juvenil: Grades 6–12
D.D.L., 1984 (Termination Date: 1998)

Historia Universal: Grades 7–12
D.D.L., 1990 (Termination Date: 1998)

Enciclopedia de Saber. Grades 9–12
D.D.L., 1989 (Termination Date: 1998)

Enciclopedia Por Que: Grades 5–9
D.D.L., 1988 (Termination Date: 1998)

El Mundo de Hoy: Grades 7–12
D.D.L., 1990 (Termination Date: 1998)

Combi Visual: Grades 7–12
D.D.L., 1990 (Termination Date: 1998)

Children's Britannica: Grades 3–8
Encyclopaedia Britannica, 1991 (Termination Date: 1998)

Comptom's Encyclopedia: Grades 6–9
Encyclopaedia Britannica, 1991 (Termination Date: 1998)

Encyclopaedia Britannica: Grades 9–12
Encyclopaedia Britannica, 1991 (Termination Date: 1998)

Compton's Multi-Media Encyclopedia: Grades 4–12
Encyclopaedia Britannica, 1991 (Termination Date: 1998)

Encyclopedia Americana: Grades 7–12
Grolier, 1992 (Termination Date: 1998)

New Book of Knowledge: Grades 2–8
Grolier, 1992 (Termination Date: 1998)

Academic American Encyclopedia: Grades 6–12
Grolier, 1992 (Termination Date: 1998)

Thesauruses
Webster's New Dictionary of Synonyms: Grades 8–12
Encyclopaedia Britannica, 1984 (Termination Date: 1998)

Webster's School Thesaurus: Grades 9–11
Encyclopaedia Britannica, 1989 (Termination Date: 1998)

Webster's Collegiate Thesaurus: Grades 10–12
Encyclopaedia Britannica, 1988 (Termination Date: 1998)

A First Thesaurus: Grades 2-5
Modern Curriculum, 1986 (Termination Date: 1998)

Webster's New World Thesaurus: Grades 6–8
Silver, Burdett and Ginn, 1990 (Termination Date: 1998)

Roget's II: The New Thesaurus: Grades 9–12
Houghton Mifflin, 1988 (Termination Date: 1998)

In Other Words: Grades 3–8
Scott, Foresman, 1987 (Termination Date: 1998)

Clear and Simple Thesaurus Dictionary: Grades 4–9
Perma-Bound/Hertzberg New Method, 1971
(Termination Date: 1998)

A First Thesaurus: Grades 2-4
Childrens Press, 1985 (Termination Date: 1998)

North Carolina

Handwriting
HBJ Handwriting: Grades 1-5
Harcourt Brace Jovanovich, 1987 (Termination Date: 1996)

McDougal, Littell Handwriting: Grades 1-5
McDougal, Littell, 1990 (Termination Date: 1996)

Scott Foresman D'Nealian Handwriting: Grades 1-5
Scott, Foresman, 1991 (Termination Date: 1996)

Zaner-Bloser Handwriting: Grades 1-5
Zaner-Bloser, 1991 (Termination Date: 1996)

Reading and Literature
DLM Literature Collection: Grades 1-2
DLM, 1990 (Termination Date: 1996)

Houghton Mifflin Readers: Grades 1–6
Houghton Mifflin (Termination Date: 1996)

Scholastic Reading: Grades 1–6
Scholastic, 1987, 1990 (Termination Date: 1996)

Ginn Readers: Grades 1–6
Ginn, 1989 (Termination Date: 1996)

Heath Reading: Grades 1–6
D.C. Heath, 1991 (Termination Date: 1996)

Houghton Mifflin Reading: Grades 1–6
Houghton Mifflin, 1991 (Termination Date: 1996)

Macmillan/McGraw Hill Reading: Grades 1–6
Macmillan, 1991 (Termination Date: 1996)

Open Court Reading and Writing: Grades 1–6
Open Court, 1989 (Termination Date: 1996)

Scott, Foresman Reading: Grades 1–6
Scott, Foresman, 1989 (Termination Date: 1996)

Silver, Burdett and Ginn Reading: Grades 1–6
Silver, Burdett and Ginn, 1991 (Termination Date: 1996)

The Wright Group Reading: Grades 1-3
Wright, 1990 (Termination Date: 1996)

Macmillan/McGraw Hill Reading Express: Grades 1–8
Macmillan, 1991 (Termination Date: 1996)

Discovering Literature: Grade 6–8
Glencoe, 1991 (Termination Date: 1996)

HBJ Discoveries in Reading: Grades 6–8
Harcourt Brace Jovanovich, 1990 (Termination Date: 1996)

Introduction to Literature: Grades 6–7
Holt, Rinehart and Winston, 1991 (Termination Date: 1996)

Globe Literature: Grades 7–8
Globe, 1990 (Termination Date: 1996)

Adventures for Readers: Grades 7–8
Holt, Rinehart and Winston, 1989 (Termination Date: 1996)

Elements of Literature: Grades 7–8
Holt, 1989 (Termination Date: 1996)

Vistas in Reading Literature: Grades 6–8
McDougal, Littell, 1989 (Termination Date: 1996)

McDougal, Littell Literature: Grades 7–8
McDougal, Littell, 1989 (Termination Date: 1996)

Prentice Hall Literature: Grades 6–8
Prentice Hall, 1991 (Termination Date: 1996)

America Reads: Grades 6
Scott, Foresman, 1991 (Termination Date: 1996)

Discoveries in Literature Reading Series: Grade 7
Scott, Foresman, 1991 (Termination Date: 1996)

Language

HBJ Language: Grades 1–8
Harcourt Brace Jovanovich, 1990 (Termination Date: 1995)

Houghton Mifflin English: Grades 1–8
Houghton Mifflin, 1990 (Termination Date: 1995)

Language Arts Today: Grades 1–8
Macmillan, 1990 (Termination Date: 1995)

World of Language: Grades 1–8
Silver, Burdett and Ginn, 1990 (Termination Date: 1995)

McDougal, Littell English: Grades 6–8
McDougal, Littell, 1990 (Termination Date: 1995)

McGraw-Hill English: Grades 6–8
McGraw-Hill, 1990 (Termination Date: 1995)

Scope English Writing and Language: Grades 6–8
Scholastic, 1990 (Termination Date: 1995)

Basic Skills in English: Grades 7–8
McDougal, Littell, 1989 (Termination Date: 1995)

Spelling

Houghton Mifflin Spelling: Grades 2–8
Houghton Mifflin, 1988 (Termination Date: 1992)

Macmillan Spelling: Grades 2–8
Macmillan, 1983 (Termination Date: 1992)

The Riverside Spelling Program: Grades 2–8
Riverside, 1984 (Termination Date: 1992)

Spelling: Words and Skills: Grades 2–8
Scott, Foresman, 1984 (Termination Date: 1992)

Steck-Vaughn Spelling: Grades 2–8
Steck-Vaughn, 1984 (Termination Date: 1992)

Language and Composition

Basic Skills in English: Grades 9–12
McDougal, Littell, 1989 (Termination Date: 1994)

Scope English Writing and Language Skills: Grades 9–12
Scholastic, 1987 (Termination Date: 1994)

English Composition and Grammar. Grades 9–12
Harcourt, 1988 (Termination Date: 1994)

English: Writing and Skills: Grades 9–12
Holt, Rinehart and Winston, 1988 (Termination Date: 1994)

McDougal, Littell English: Grades 9–12
McDougal, Littell, 1989 (Termination Date: 1994)

Writing

Lively Writing: Grades 9–12
National, 1985 (Termination Date: 1994)

Writing Guides: Grades 9–12
Active, 1986 (Termination Date: 1994)

Composition: Models and Exercises: Grades 9–10
Harcourt, 1987 (Termination Date: 1994)

Advanced Composition: Grades 9–12
Harcourt, 1987 (Termination Date: 1994)

Developing Writing Skills: Grades 9–12
Prentice, 1988 (Termination Date: 1994)

Practicing the Writing Process: Grades 9–12
Educational Design, 1989 (Termination Date: 1994)

Writing: Process to Product: Grades 9–12
Addison-Wesley, 1987 (Termination Date: 1994)

Literature

Macmillan Literature Series: Grades 9–12
Glencoe, 1991 (Termination Date: 1996)

Globe Literature: Grades 9–12
Globe, 1990 (Termination Date: 1996)

Adventures in Literature: Grades 9, 11–12
Holt, Rinehart and Winston (Termination Date: n.d.)

Elements of Literature: Grades 9, 11–12
Holt, Rinehart and Winston, 1989 (Termination Date: 1996)

McDougal, Littell Literature: Grades 9, 11–12
McDougal, Littell, 1989 (Termination Date: 1996)

Prentice Hall Literature: Grades 9–12
Prentice Hall, 1991 (Termination Date: 1996)

America Reads: Grade 10
Scott, Foresman, 1987 (Termination Date: 1994)

America Reads: Grades 9–12
Scott, Foresman, 1991 (Termination Date: 1996)

Speech

Effective Speech: Grades 9–12
Glencoe, 1988 (Termination Date: 1996)

Speech for Effective Communication: Grades 9–12
Holt, Rinehart and Winston, 1988 (Termination Date: 1996)

Communication: An Introduction to Speech:
Grades 9–12
Prentice Hall, 1988 (Termination Date: 1996)

Speech: Exploring Communication: Grades 9–12
Prentice Hall, 1988 (Termination Date: 1996)

Oklahoma

Dictionaries

Macmillan Picture Dictionary: Grades 1-3
Macmillan, 1983 (Termination Date: 1993)

Macmillan First Dictionary: Grades 1-3
Macmillan, 1987 (Termination Date: 1993)

Houghton Mifflin Picture Dictionary: Grade 1
Houghton Mifflin, 1986 (Termination Date: 1993)

Houghton Mifflin Dictionaries: Grades 1–12
Houghton Mifflin, 1986 (Termination Date: 1993)

Scribner Dictionaries: Grades 1–6
Scribner Educational, 1986 (Termination Date: 1993)

A Big Book of Words: Grades 1-3
McGraw-Hill, 1988 (Termination Date: 19993)

Pictionary/Picture Dictionaries: Grades 1-3
Scott, Foresman, 1987 (Termination Date: 1993)

Scott, Foresman Thorndike-Barnhart Dictionaries: Grades 1–8
Scott, Foresman, 1988 (Termination Date: 1993)

My Picture Dictionaries: Grades 1-3
Silver, Burdett, and Ginn, 1985 (Termination Date: 1993)

Macmillan School Dictionaries: Grades 4–8
Macmillan, 1990 (Termination Date: 1993)

HBJ School Dictionary: Grades 4–6
Harcourt Brace Jovanovich, 1985 (Termination Date: 1993)

Webster's New World Dictionary: Basic School Edition: Grades 4–6
Modern Curriculum, 1989 (Termination Date: 1993)

Webster's II Riverside Beginning Dictionary: Grades 4–6
Riverside, 1984 (Termination Date: 1993)

In Other Words (thesaurus series): Grades 4–6
Scott, Foresman, 1987 (Termination Date: 1993)

Webster's Dictionaries: Grades 4–8
Silver, Burdett, and Ginn, 1986 (Termination Date: 1993)

Random House School Dictionary: Grades 4–6
Random House, 1984 (Termination Date: 1993)

Webster's New World Dictionary: Grades 7–8
Prentice Hall, 1983 (Termination Date: 1993)

Webster's School Thesaurus: Grades 7–8
Silver, Burdett, and Ginn, 1978 (Termination Date: 1993)

Webster's High School Dictionary: Grades 7–8
Globe Book, 1986 (Termination Date: 1993)

Macmillan Dictionary: Grades 9–12
Macmillan, 1987 (Termination Date: 1993)

Dictionary of Essential English: Grades 9–12
Media Materials, 1987 (Termination Date: 1993)

The American Heritage Dictionaries: Grades 9–12
Houghton Mifflin, 1982 (Termination Date: 1993)

Roget's II, The New Thesaurus: Grades 9–12
Houghton Mifflin, 1988 (Termination Date: 1993)

The Concise American Heritage Dictionary: Grades 9–12
Houghton Mifflin, 1987 (Termination Date: 1993)

Scribner Dictionary: Grades 9–12
Scribner, 1986 (Termination Date: 1993)

Word Clues, The Vocabulary Builder: Grades 9–12
Scribner, 1984 (Termination Date: 1993)

Webster's New World Dictionary: Grades 9–12
Prentice Hall, 1988 (Termination Date: 1993)

Webster's New World Dictionary: Grades 9–12
Globe Book, 1982 (Termination Date: 1993)

Grammar and Language
Alpha One Complete Program: Grade K
Arista, 1981 (Termination Date: 1993)

Alpha Time Plus: Grade K
Arista, 1972–81 (Termination Date: 1993)

Macmillan English: Grades K–8
Macmillan, 1987 (Termination Date: 1993)

Heath Language Arts: Grades K–8
D.C. Heath, 1988 (Termination Date: 1993)

Houghton Mifflin English: Grades K–8
Houghton Mifflin, 1988 (Termination Date: 1993)

McDougal, Littell English: Grades K–6
McDougal, Littell, 1987 (Termination Date: 1993)

Laidlaw English: Grades K–8
Scribner, 1987 (Termination Date: 1993)

Language for Daily Use: Grades K–8
Harcourt Brace Jovanovich, 1986 (Termination Date: 1993)

Language: Skills and Use: Grades K–8
Scott, Foresman, 1986 (Termination Date: 1993)

Language: Skills and Use, D'Nealian: Grades K–2
Scott, Foresman, 1986 (Termination Date: 1993)

McGraw-Hill Superstart Program: Grade K
McGraw-Hill, 1982–88 (Termination Date: 1993)

Scott, Foresman Language Pre-Readiness: Grade 1
Scott, Foresman, 1989 (Termination Date: 1993)

Scott, Foresman Language Pre-Readiness, D'Nealian: Grade 1
Scott, Foresman, 1989 (Termination Date: 1993)

Scott, Foresman Language: Grades 1–6
Scott, Foresman, 1989 (Termination Date: 1993)

Scott, Foresman Language, D'Nealian: Grades 1-2
Scott, Foresman, 1989 (Termination Date: 1993)

Silver, Burdett and Ginn English: Grades K–8
Silver, Burdett, and Ginn, 1988 (Termination Date: 1993)

Wordless Picture Books: Silver, Burdett and Ginn English: Grades K–2
Silver, Burdett, and Ginn, 1988 (Termination Date: 1993)

Thinking and Writing Processes: Grades 6–8
Macmillan, 1987 (Termination Date: 1993)

English Writing and Skills: Grades 7–12
Holt, Rinehart and Winston, 1988 (Termination Date: 1993)

Heath Grammar and Composition: Grades 7–12
D.C. Heath, 1988 (Termination Date: 1993)

English Composition and Grammar: Grades 7–12
Harcourt Brace Jovanovich, 1988 (Termination Date: 1993)

English Workshop, Liberty Edition: Grades 7–12
Harcourt Brace Jovanovich, 1986 (Termination Date: 1993)

Grammar and Composition I-IV
Basic Skills in English: Grades 11–12
McDougal, Littell, 1985 (Termination Date: 1993)

Houghton Mifflin English Grammar and Composition: Grades 9–12
Houghton Mifflin, 1986 (Termination Date: 1993)

Building English Skills: Grades 9–12
McDougal, Littell, 1988 (Termination Date: 1993)

Macmillan English: Thinking and Writing Processes: Grades 9–12
Scribner, 1988 (Termination Date: 1993)

Glencoe/English: Grades 9–12
Glencoe, 1985 (Termination Date: 1993)

Prentice Hall Grammar and Composition: Grades 9–12
Prentice Hall, 1987 (Termination Date: 1993)

Advanced Composition
Writing Logically: Grades 9–12
Amsco School, 1978 (Termination Date: 1993)

The Laidlaw English Series: Grades 9–12
Scribner, 1985 (Termination Date: 1993)

Composition: Models and Exercises: Grades 9–12
Harcourt Brace Jovanovich, 1986 (Termination Date: 1993)

Advanced Composition: A Book of Models for Writing: Grades 9–12
Harcourt Brace Jovanovich, 1986 (Termination Date: 1993)

Thinking and Writing about Literature: Grades 9–12
Prentice Hall, 1984 (Termination Date: 1993)

Simon and Schuster Handbook for Writers: Grades 9–12
Prentice Hall, 1987 (Termination Date: 1993)

Strategies of Rhetoric: Grades 9–12
Scott, Foresman, 1987 (Termination Date: 1993)

Writing Research Papers: Grades 9–12
Scott, Foresman, n.d. (Termination Date: 1993)

Creative Writing
Writing Creatively: Grades 9–12
Amsco School, 1977 (Termination Date: 1993)

Literature-Based Composition: Grades 9–12
Glencoe, 1988 (Termination Date: 1993)

Developing Writing Skills: Grades 9–12
Allyn & Bacon, 1988 (Termination Date: 1993)

Lively Writing: Grades 9–12
National Textbook, 1985 (Termination Date: 1993)

Debate-Dramatics (I-III)
The Dynamics of Acting: Grades 9–12
National Textbook, 1989 (Termination Date: 1996)

The Stage and the School: Grades 9–12
Glencoe/McGraw-Hill, 1989 (Termination Date: 1996)

Theater: Preparation and Performance: Grades 9–12
Scott, Foresman, 1989 (Termination Date: 1996)

Play Production Today!: Grades 9–12
National Textbook, 1989 (Termination Date: 1996)

Basic Debate: Grades 9–12
National Textbook, 1989 (Termination Date: 1996)

An Introduction to Theater and Drama: Grades 9–12
National Textbook, 1975 (Termination Date: 1996)

Strategic Debate: Grades 9–12
National Textbook, 1989 (Termination Date: 1996)

Advanced Debate: Grades 9–12
National Textbook, 1987 (Termination Date: 1996)

Journalism
Press Time: Grades 9–12
Prentice Hall, 1985 (Termination Date: 1993)

Journalism: Grades 9–12
Allyn & Bacon, 1984 (Termination Date: 1993)

Inside High School Journalism: Grades 9–12
Scott, Foresman, 1986 (Termination Date: 1993)

Literature
The Writing Program: Grades 1–8
Modern Curriculum, 1989 (Termination Date: 1996)

Literature First: Grades 1-3
Modern Curriculum, 1989 (Termination Date: 1996)

MCP Literature: Grades 1–6
Modern Curriculum, 1988 (Termination Date: 1996)

Prentice Hall Literature Series: Grades 6–12
Prentice Hall, 1991 (Termination Date: 1996)

Macmillan Literature Series: Grades 6–12
Glencoe/McGraw-Hill, 1991 (Termination Date: 1996)

America Reads: Grades 6–12
Scott, Foresman, 1991 (Termination Date: 1996)

Introduction to Literature: Grade 6
Holt, Rinehart and Winston/Harcourt Brace Jovanovich, 1991 (Termination Date: 1996)

Adventures in Literature: Grades 7–12
Holt, Rinehart and Winston/Harcourt Brace Jovanovich, 1989 (Termination Date: 1996)

Elements of Literature: Grades 7–12
Holt, Rinehart and Winston/Harcourt Brace Jovanovich, 1989 (Termination Date: 1996)

Literature by Doing: Grades 9–12
National Textbook, 1990 (Termination Date: 1996)

The Short Story and You: Grades 9–12
National Textbook, 1989 (Termination Date: 1996)

Reading Literature Series: Grades 9–12
McDougal, Littell, 1990 (Termination Date: 1996)

American Literature
Prentice Hall Literature Series: Grades 9–12
Prentice Hall, 1991 (Termination Date: 1996)

Explore: A Course in Literature: Grades 9–12
Media Materials, 1991 (Termination Date: 1996)

Reading Literature Series: Grades 9–12
McDougal, Littell, 1990 (Termination Date: 1996)

Macmillan Literature Series: Grades 9–12
Glencoe/McGraw-Hill, 1991 (Termination Date: 1996)

America Reads: Grades 9–12
Scott, Foresman, 1991 (Termination Date: 1996)

Adventures in Literature: Grades 9–12
Holt, Rinehart and Winston/Harcourt Brace Jovanovich, 1989 (Termination Date: 1996)

Elements of Literature: Grades 9–12
Holt, Rinehart and Winston/Harcourt Brace Jovanovich, 1989 (Termination Date: 1996)

Globe Literature: Grades 9–12
Globe Book, 1990 (Termination Date: 1996)

English Literature
Prentice Hall Literature Series: Grades 9–12
Prentice Hall, 1991 (Termination Date: 1996)

Reading Literature Series: Grades 9–12
McDougal, Littell, 1990 (Termination Date: 1996)

Macmillan Literature Series: Grades 9–12
Glencoe/McGraw-Hill, 1991 (Termination Date: 1996)

America Reads: Grades 9–12
Scott, Foresman, 1991 (Termination Date: 1996)

Adventures in Literature: Grades 9–12
Holt, Rinehart and Winston/Harcourt Brace
Jovanovich, 1989 (Termination Date: 1996)

Elements of Literature: Grades 9–12
Holt, Rinehart and Winston/Harcourt Brace
Jovanovich, 1989 (Termination Date: 1996)

Globe Literature: Grades 9–12
Globe Book, 1990 (Termination Date: 1996)

World Literature
Prentice Hall Literature Series: Grades 9–12
Prentice Hall, 1991 (Termination Date: 1996)

Macmillan Literature Series: Grades 9–12
Glencoe/McGraw-Hill, 1991 (Termination Date: 1996)

America Reads: Grades 9–12
Scott, Foresman, 1991 (Termination Date: 1996)

Responding to Literature: Grades 9–12
McDougal, Littell, 1992 (Termination Date: 1996)

Handwriting
Palmer Method, Manuscript: Grades K–2
A. N. Palmer, 1987 (Termination Date: 1993)

Palmer Method, Transition: Grades 2-3
A. N. Palmer, 1987 (Termination Date: 1993)

Palmer Method, Cursive: Grades 4–8
A. N. Palmer, 1987 (Termination Date: 1993)

*Zaner-Bloser Handwriting: Basic Skills and
Application, Readiness:* Grades K–8
Zaner-Bloser, 1987 (Termination Date: 1993)

Zaner-Bloser Handwriting: A Way to Self-Expression: Grades K–8
Zaner-Bloser, 1991 (Termination Date: 1993)

McDougal, Littell Handwriting: Grades K–7
McDougal, Littell, 1987 (Termination Date: 1993)

HBJ Handwriting: Grades K–6
Harcourt Brace Jovanovich, 1987 (Termination
Date: 1993)

Bowmar/Noble Handwriting: Grades K–7
McGraw-Hill, 1987 (Termination Date: 1993)

D'Nealian Handwriting: Grades K–7
Scott, Foresman, 1987 (Termination Date: 1993)

Steck-Vaughn Handwriting: Grades 1–6
Steck-Vaughn, 1988 (Termination Date: 1993)

Reading
Bill Martin Big Books: Grade K
Harcourt Brace Jovanovich, 1970 (Termination
Date: 1996)

Getting Started: Grade K
Macmillan, 1991 (Termination Date: 1996)

Language Immersion/Alpha: Grade K
New Dimensions in Education, 1990 (Termination Date: 1996)

All about Color: Grade K
New Dimensions in Education, 1989 (Termination Date: 1996)

Story Box Series: Grade K
Wright Group, 1990 (Termination Date: 1996)

Macmillan Reading Program: Grades K–8
Macmillan, 1986–91 (Termination Date: 1996)

Heath Reading: Grades K–8
D. C. Heath, 1991 (Termination Date: 1996)

World of Reading: Grades K–8
Silver, Burdett and Ginn, 1991 (Termination
Date: 1996)

Open Court Reading and Writing: Grades K–6
Open Court, 1989 (Termination Date: 1996)

Scott, Foresman Reading: Grades K–8
Scott, Foresman, 1989 (Termination Date: 1996)

Houghton Mifflin Reading: The Literature Experience: Grades K–8
Houghton Mifflin, 1991 (Termination Date: 1996)

DLM Alternative Reading Collection: Grades K–4
DLM, 1980–91 (Termination Date: 1996)

M.O.R.E., Units I-III: Grades 1–6
Perma-Bound, n.d., (Termination Date: 1996)

The Sunshine Series: Grades 1-3
Wright Group, 1986–89 (Termination Date: 1996)

Basic Learning Systems/Reading Plus: Grades K–3
Jostens Learning, 1990 (Termination Date: 1996)

Basic Learning Systems/Reading Plus: Grades 4–8
Jostens Learning, 1990 (Termination Date: 1996)

Basic Learning Systems/Reading Plus: Grades K–8
Jostens Learning, 1990 (Termination Date: 1996)

Dolch Classic Stories: Grade 3
DLM, 1962 (Termination Date: 1996)

Dolch Class Pleasure Readers: Grade 4
DLM, 1962 (Termination Date: 1996)

Vistas in Reading Literature: Grades 5–8
McDougal, Littell, 1990 (Termination Date: 1996)

Discoveries in Reading: Grades 7–8
Harcourt Brace Jovanovich, 1990 (Termination Date: 1996)

Globe Literature: Grades 7–8
Globe Book, 1990 (Termination Date: 1996)

Myths and Folklore: Grades 9–12
Amsco, 1989 (Termination Date: 1996)

Amsco Literature Program: Grades 9–12
Amsco, 1970–89 (Termination Date: 1996)

Globe Literature: Grades 9–12
Globe Book, 1990 (Termination Date: 1996)

Living Literature Series: Grades 9–12
Perma-Bound, 1927–90 (Termination Date: 1996)

Remedial Reading

Collamore Phonics: Grades 1–6
D. C. Heath, 1987 (Termination Date: 1993)

The Chall-Popp Reading Books: Grades 1–6
Continental Press, 1986 (Termination Date: 1993)

Houghton Mifflin Reading, Levels 1-5: Grades 1-3
Houghton Mifflin, 1987 (Termination Date: 1993)

MCP Phonics: Grades 1–6
Modern Curriculum, 1991 (Termination Date: 1993)

Phonetic Keys to Independence in Reading: Grades 1-3
McGraw-Hill, 1983 (Termination Date: 1993)

Focus: Reading for Success: Grades 1–8
Scott, Foresman, 1988 (Termination Date: 1993)

Riverside Phonics: Grades 1–6
Riverside, 1988 (Termination Date: 1993)

Ginn Reading Text Workbook Series: Grades 1–6
Silver, Burdett, and Ginn, 1985–87 (Termination Date: 1993)

Barnell Loft Reading Program: Grades 1–12
Barnell Loft, 1977–90 (Termination Date: 1993)

Developing Key Concepts in Comprehension: Grades 1–12
Barnell Loft, 1984–85 (Termination Date: 1993)

Developing a Basic Sight Vocabulary: Grade 1
Barnell Loft, 1983 (Termination Date: 1993)

Phonics to Meaning: Grades 1-2
Barnell Loft, 1990 (Termination Date: 1993)

Steck-Vaughn Phonics: Grades 1-4
Steck-Vaughn, 1989 (Termination Date: 1993)

Let's Think Together: Grades 2-3
Barnell Loft, 1987 (Termination Date: 1993)

A Word Recognition Program: Grades 3-4
Barnell Loft, 1982 (Termination Date: 1993)

Project Achievement: Reading: Grades 7–8
Scholastic, 1987 (Termination Date: 1993)

The Reading Scene I-III: Grades 7–8
Continental Press, 1987 (Termination Date: 1993)

New Directions in Reading: Grades 7–8
Houghton Mifflin, 1986 (Termination Date: 1993)

RALLY! Levels A-C: Grades 7–8
Harcourt Brace Jovanovich, 1979–80 (Termination Date: 1993)

Globe's Adapted Classics: Grades 7–12
Globe Book, 1978–86 (Termination Date: 1993)

New Practice Readers: Grades 7–8
Phoenix Learning, 1988 (Termination Date: 1993)

Reading for Concepts: Grades 7–8
Phoenix Learning, 1988 (Termination Date: 1993)

Steck-Vaughn Comprehension Skills: Grades 7–8
Steck-Vaughn, 1987–88 (Termination Date: 1993)

Aiming High: Grades 9–12
Amsco, 1983 (Termination Date: 1993)

High Marks: Grades 9–12
Amsco, 1981 (Termination Date: 1993)

On Stage: Grades 9–12
Amsco, 1986 (Termination Date: 1993)

The Reader as Detective: Grades 9–12
Amsco, 1985–86 (Termination Date: 1993)

Be a Better Reader: Grades 9–12
Prentice Hall, 1989 (Termination Date: 1993)

Words Are Important: Grades 9–12
Hammond, 1985 (Termination Date: 1993)

Reading for Independence Series: Grades 9–12
Science Research, 1985 (Termination Date: 1993)

Reading Laboratory Kit: Grades 9–12
Science Research, 1988 (Termination Date: 1993)

Reading Road to Writing: Grades 9–12
Globe Book, 1984 (Termination Date: 1993)

Reading for Today: Grades 9–12
Steck-Vaughn, 1987 (Termination Date: 1993)

Communication for Today: Grades 9–12
Steck-Vaughn, 1987 (Termination Date: 1993)

Spelling

Working Words in Spelling: Grades 1–8
D. C. Heath, 1990 (Termination Date: 1996)

HBJ Spelling: Grades 1–8
Harcourt Brace Jovanovich, 1988 (Termination Date: 1996)

Language: Grades 1–6
Zaner-Bloser, 1991 (Termination Date: 1996)

McDougall, Littell Spelling: Grades 1–8
McDougal, Littell, 199- (Termination Date: 1996)

Scott, Foresman Spelling: Grades 1–8
Scott, Foresman, 1988 (Termination Date: 1996)

Houghton Mifflin Spelling and Vocabulary: Grades 1–8
Houghton Mifflin, 1990 (Termination Date: 1996)

Language Connections: Grades 2–6
Wright Group, 1988 (Termination Date: 1996)

Spelling Connections: Words into Language: Grades 7–8
Zaner-Bloser, 1991 (Termination Date: 1996)

Spell It Out: Grades 7–8
Globe Book, 1991 (Termination Date: 1996)

Speech

Speech for Effective Communication: Grades 9–12
Harcourt Brace Jovanovich, 1988 (Termination Date: 1993)

Effective Speech: Grades 9–12
Glencoe, 1988 (Termination Date: 1993)

Speech: Exploring Communication: Grades 9–12
Prentice Hall, 1988 (Termination Date: 1993)

Communication: An Introduction to Speech: Grades 9–12
Allyn & Bacon, 1988 (Termination Date: 1993)

Speech: Principles and Practice: Grades 9–12
Scott, Foresman, 1987 (Termination Date: 1993)

The Basics of Speech: Grades 9–12
National Textbook, 1988 (Termination Date: 1993)

Oregon

Handwriting
The Italic Handwriting Series: 1986 Grades K–8
Continuing Ed, PSU, 1986 (Termination Date: 1993)

HBJ Handwriting: Grades K–6
Harcourt Brace Jovanovich, 1987 (Termination Date: 1993)

Spelling
HBJ Spelling: Grades 1–8
Harcourt Brace Jovanovich, 1988 (Termination Date: 1993)

Working Words in Spelling: Grades 1–8
D. C. Heath, 1985 (Termination Date: 1993)

Houghton Mifflin Spelling: Grades 1–8
Houghton Mifflin, 1985 (Termination Date: 1993)

Laidlaw Spelling: Grades K–8
Laidlaw, 1987 (Termination Date: 1993)

Building Spelling Skills: Grades 1–8
McDougal, Littell, 1985 (Termination Date: 1993)

Spelling for Word Mastery: Grades K–8
Merrill, 1987 (Termination Date: 1993)

Spelling Mastery: Grades 2–6
Science Research (Termination Date: 1993)

Scott, Foresman Spelling: Grades K–8
Scott, Foresman, 1988 (Termination Date: 1993)

Spelling Connections: Words into Language:
Grades 1–8
Zaner-Bloser, 1988 (Termination Date: 1993)

Language and Composition
Language for Daily Use, Voyager Edition: Grades K–8
Harcourt Brace Jovanovich, 1986 (Termination Date: 1993)

Heath Language Arts: Grades K–8
D. C Heath, 1988 (Termination Date: 1993)

Impressions Series: K–3
Holt, Rinehart and Winston/Harcourt Brace Jovanovich, 1984 (Termination Date: 1993)

Houghton Mifflin English: Grades K–8, Houghton Mifflin, 1986, 1988 (Termination Date: 1993)

McDougal, Littell English Series: Grades K–6
McDougal, Littell, 1987 (Termination Date: 1993)

McDougal, Littell English Series: Grades 7–8
McDougal, Littell, 1988 (Termination Date: 1993)

Macmillan English: Grades K–8
Macmillan, 1987 (Termination Date: 1993)

Macmillan English: Thinking and Writing Processes: Grades 6–8
Macmillan, 1987 (Termination Date: 1993)

Silver Burdett English: Grades K–8
Silver, Burdett, 1988 (Termination Date: 1993)

Language and Composition
English: Writing and Skills: Grades 7–12
Coronado, 1985 (Termination Date: 1993)

Glencoe/English Series: Grades 7–12
Glencoe/Macmillan/McGraw-Hill, 1984–85 (Termination Date: 1993)

English Grammar and Composition, Liberty Edition: Grades 7–12
Harcourt Brace Jovanovich, 1986 (Termination Date: 1993)

English Composition and Grammar: Benchmark Edition: Grades 7–12
Harcourt Brace Jovanovich, 1988 (Termination Date: 1993)

Heath Grammar and Composition: Grades 6–12
D. C. Heath, 1986–87 (Termination Date: 1993)

The Laidlaw English Series: Grades 9–12
Laidlaw Brothers, 1985 (Termination Date: 1993)

Macmillan English: Grades 7–8
Macmillan, 1987 (Termination Date: 1993)

Macmillan English: Thinking and Writing Processes: Grades 7–8
Macmillan, 1987 (Termination Date: 1993)

Macmillan English: Thinking and Writing Processes: Grades 9–12
Macmillan, 1988 (Termination Date: 1993)

Foundations: Language: Grades 9–12
Scribner, 1986 (Termination Date: 1993)

Silver Burdett English: Grades 7–8
Silver, Burdett, 1987 (Termination Date: 1993)

Oral Communication

Communication: An Introduction to Speech: Grades 7–12
Allyn & Bacon/Prentice Hall, 1988 (Termination Date: 1993)

Glencoe/English Series: Grades 7–12
Glencoe/Macmillan/McGraw-Hill, 1984–85 (Termination Date: 1993)

Speech for Effective Communication: Grades 7–12
Harcourt Brace Jovanovich, 1988 (Termination Date: 1993)

Person to Person: Grades 9–12
National Textbook, 1984 (Termination Date: 1993)

Speaking by Doing: Grades 9–12
National Textbook, 1986 (Termination Date: 1993)

Speech: Exploring Communication: Grades 9–12
Prentice Hall, 1988 (Termination Date: 1993)

Reading

Economy Reading Series: Grades K–8
Economy, 1986 (Termination Date: 1993)

HBJ Reading, 1st Ed: Grades K–8
Harcourt Brace Jovanovich, 1987 (Termination Date: 1993)

Impressions Series: Grades K–3
Holt, Rinehart and Winston/Harcourt Brace Jovanovich, 1984 (Termination Date: 1993)

Houghton Mifflin Reading: Grades K–8
Houghton Mifflin, 1986 (Termination Date: 1993)

Connections: Grades K–8
Macmillan, 1987 (Termination Date: 1993)

Reading Literature Series: Grades 7–8
McDougal, Littell, 1988 (Termination Date: 1993)

The Headway Reading Program: K–6
Open Court, 1985 (Termination Date: 1993)

Reading Mastery Series: Grades 1–6
Science Research, 1982–83, 1988 (Termination Date: 1993)

Scott, Foresman Reading: An American Tradition: Grades K–8
Scott, Foresman, 1987 (Termination Date: 1993)

Scribner Reading Series: Grades K–8
Scribner, 1987 (Termination Date: 1993)

Ginn Reading Program: Grades K–8
Silver, Burdett and Ginn, 1987 (Termination Date: 1993)

Reading—Low Level

Reading Express: Grades 1–6
Macmillan, 1986 (Termination Date: 1993)

Focus: Reading for Success: Grades K–8
Scott, Foresman, 1985 (Termination Date: 1993)

Literature

Adventures in Literature: Grades 7–12
Harcourt Brace Jovanovich, 1985 (Termination Date: 1993)

The McDougal, Littell Literature Series: Grades 7–12
McDougal, Littell, 1987 (Termination Date: 1993)

Reading Literature Series: Grades 9–12 (low level)
McDougal, Littell, 1985–86 (Termination Date: 1993)

McGraw-Hill Literature Series: Grades 7–12
McGraw-Hill, 1985 (Termination Date: 1993)

America Reads: Grades 7–12
Scott, Foresman, 1987 (Termination Date: 1993)

Macmillan Literature Series: Grades 7–12
Macmillan, 1984–85, 1987 (Termination Date: 1993)

South Carolina

Composition and Grammar
Houghton Mifflin English: Grades 3–8
Houghton Mifflin, 1990 (Termination Date: 1994)

Language Arts Today: Grades 3–8
Macmillan/McGraw-Hill, 1990 (Termination Date: 1994)

McDougal, Littell English: Grades 6–8
McDougal, Littell, 1990 (Termination Date: 1994)

Scope English Writing and Language: Grades 6–8
Scholastic, 1990 (Termination Date: 1994)

World of Language: Grades 3–8
Silver, Burdett, and Ginn, 1990 (Termination Date: 1994)

English Composition and Grammar: Grades 9–12
Harcourt Brace Jovanovich, 1988 (Termination Date: 1993)

English: Writing and Skills: Grades 9–12
Holt, Rinehart and Winston, 1988 (Termination Date: 1993)

Basic Skills in English: Grades 9–12
McDougal, Littell, 1989 (Termination Date: 1993)

McDougal, Littell English: Grades 9–12
McDougal, Littell, 1989 (Termination Date: 1993)

Scope English: Writing and Language Skills: Grades 9–12
Scholastic, 1987 (Termination Date: 1993)

Macmillan English: Thinking and Writing Processes: Grades 9–12
Scribner-Laidlaw Educational, 1988 (Termination Date: 1993)

Composition and Grammar—Supplementary
Practicing the Writing Process: Grades 9–12
Educational Design, 1988 (Termination Date: n.d.)

Life Skills Writing: Grades 9–12
Educational Design, 1985 (Termination Date: n.d.)

Writing for the World of Work: Grades 9–12
Educational Design, 1987 (Termination Date: n.d)

The Writer's Tool Box: Grades 9–12
Educational Design, 1988 (Termination Date: n.d.)

Developing Comprehension Skills: Grades 9–12
Glencoe, 1989 (Termination Date: n.d.)

Writing for Competency: Grade 9
Steck-Vaughn, 1988 (Termination Date: n.d.)

Advanced Composition
Advanced Composition: A Book of Models for Writing: Grade 12
Harcourt Brace Jovanovich, 1986 (Termination Date: 1993)

Developing Writing Skills: Grade 12
Prentice Hall, 1988 (Termination Date: 1993)

Thinking and Writing about Literature: Grade 12
Prentice Hall, 1984 (Termination Date: 1993)

Literature: An Introduction to Reading and Writing: Grade 12
Prentice Hall, 1986 (Termination Date: 1993)

Developmental Reading
Globe Classroom Libraries: The Black Experience: Grades 9–12
Globe, 1989 (Termination Date: 1994)

Globe Classroom Libraries: The Teen Years: Grades 9–12
Globe, 1989 (Termination Date: 1994)

Globe Classroom Libraries: Survivors: Grades 9–12
Globe, 1989 (Termination Date: 1994)

Globe Classroom Libraries: Science Fiction: Grades 9–12
Globe, 1989 (Termination Date: 1994)

Journalism
Journalism Today!: Grades 11–12
National Textbook, 1986 (Termination Date: 1994)

Press Time: Grades 11–12
Prentice Hall, 1985 (Termination Date: 1994)

Inside High School Journalism: Grades 11–12
Scott, Foresman, 1986 (Termination Date: 1994)

Literature

Adventures in Literature, Heritage Edition: Grades 7–12
Harcourt Brace Jovanovich, 1985 (Termination Date: 1991)

McDougall, Littell Literature: Grades 7–12
McDougal, Littell, 1987 (Termination Date: 1991)

Reading Literature: Grades 7–12
McDougal, Littell, 1985 (Termination Date: 1991)

Scope English Anthologies: Grades 7–12
Scholastic, 1983–84 (Termination Date: 1991)

Macmillan Literature: Grades 7–12
Scribner, 1984–85 (Termination Date: 1991)

Myths and Their Meaning: Grades 7–12
Allyn & Bacon, 1984 (Termination Date: 1991)

Reading

HBJ Reading Program: Grades 1–8
Harcourt Brace Jovanovich, 1989 (Termination Date: 1993)

HRW Reading: Reading Today and Tomorrow:
Grades 1–8
Holt, Rinehart and Winston, 1989 (Termination Date: 1993)

Connections: Grades 1–8
Macmillan, 1989 (Termination Date: 1993)

Scott, Foresman Reading: An American Tradition:
Grades 1–8
Scott, Foresman, 1989 (Termination Date: 1993)

World of Reading: Grades 1–8
Silver Burdett and Ginn, 1989 (Termination Date: 1993)

Basic Reading

New Directions in Reading: Grades 5–8
Houghton Mifflin, 1986 (Termination Date: 1993)

Reading Express: Grades 1–8
Macmillan, 1986–88 (Termination Date: 1993)

Quest: A Scholastic Reading Improvement Series:
Grades 4–8
Scholastic, 1987–88 (Termination Date: 1993)

Focus: Reading for Success: Grades 1–8
Scott, Foresman, 1988 (Termination Date: 1993)

Reading—Special Education (Basal)

Language Clues: Grades 1–10
EDL, 1980–86 (Termination Date: 1993)

Reading Strategies: Grades 1–10
EDL, 1980–85 (Termination Date: 1993)

Thinking Strategies: Grades 7–10
EDL, 1985 (Termination Date: 1993)

Raising Your Test Scores: Grades 7–12
Educational Design, 1986–88 (Termination Date: 1993)

New Practice Readers: Grades 2–12
Phoenix Learning Resources, 1988 (Termination Date: 1993)

Reading for Concepts: Grades 2–12
Phoenix Learning Resources, 1988 (Termination Date: 1993)

Reading about Science: Grades 2–12
Phoenix Learning Resources, 1988 (Termination Date: 1993)

Learning Skills Series: Language Arts: Grades 6–12
Phoenix Learning Resources, 1989 (Termination Date: 1993)

Janus Book Life Skills Reading Books: Grades 9–12
Janus, 1976–88 (Termination Date: 1993)

Merrill Linguistic Reading: Grades 1–8
Merrill, 1986 (Termination Date: 1993)

Reading Mastery: Grades 1–6
Science Research, 1988 (Termination Date: 1993)

Corrective Reading: Grades 3–12
Science Research, 1978–88 (Termination Date: 1993)

Mastering Basic Reading Skills: Grades 3–10
Steck-Vaughn, 1985 (Termination Date: 1993)

Reading Comprehension Skills: Grades 1–6
Steck-Vaughn, 1989 (Termination Date: 1993)

Building Sight Vocabulary: Grades K–3
Steck-Vaughn, 1985 (Termination Date: 1993)

Power Words Program: Grades 2–6
Steck-Vaughn, 1985 (Termination Date: 1993)

Remedial Reading and Composition
Globe Reading Comprehension Program: Grades 9–10
Globe, 1989 (Termination Date: 1994)

Journeys: A Reading and Literature Program:
Grades 9–10
Harcourt Brace Jovanovich, 1986 (Termination Date: 1994)

Reading for Better Comprehension: Grades 9–10
Media Materials, 1988 (Termination Date: 1994)

Developing Grammar and Composition Skills:
Grades 9–10
Media Materials, 1989 (Termination Date: 1994)

Focus on Reading: Grades 9–10
Merrill, 1989 (Termination Date: 1994)

Speech
Effective Speech: Grades 11–12
Glencoe, 1988 (Termination Date: 1992)

Speech for Effective Communication: Grades 11–12
Harcourt Brace Jovanovich, 1988 (Termination Date: 1992)

Dynamics of Speech: Grades 11–12
National Textbook, 1988 (Termination Date: 1992)

Speech: Exploring Communication: Grades 11–12
Prentice Hall, 1988 (Termination Date: 1992)

Speech: Principles and Practice: Grades 11–12
Scott, Foresman, 1987 (Termination Date: 1992)

Spelling
Houghton Mifflin Spelling and Vocabulary: Grades 2–8
Houghton Mifflin, 1990 (Termination Date: 1995)

McDougal, Littell Spelling: Grades 2–8
McDougal, Littell, 1990 (Termination Date: 1995)

Merrill Spelling: Grades 2–8
Macmillan/McGraw-Hill, 1990 (Termination Date: 1995)

Scott, Foresman Spelling: Grades 2–8
Scott, Foresman, 1988 (Termination Date: 1995)

Spelling Connections: Words into Language:
Grades 2–8
Zaner-Bloser, 1991 (Termination Date: 1995)

Vocabulary
Vocabulary for the High School Student: Grades 9–10
Amsco, 1983 (Termination Date: 1990)

Vocabulary for the College-Bound Student: Grades 10–11
Amsco, 1983 (Termination Date: 1990)

The Joy of Vocabulary: Grades 11–12
Amsco, 1984 (Termination Date: 1990)

Three Dimensions of Vocabulary Growth: Grade 12
Amsco, 1971 (Termination Date: 1990)

Vocabulary for Competency: Grades 9–12
Educational Design, 1985 (Termination Date: 1990)

McDougal, Littell Wordskills: Grades 9–12
McDougal, Littell, 1985–86 (Termination Date: 1990)

Vocabulary Workshop: Grades 9–12
Sadlier-Oxford, 1982–84 (Termination Date: 1990)

Building an Enriched Vocabulary: Grades 11–12
Sadlier-Oxford, 1983 (Termination Date: 1990)

Words, Words, Words: Grades 9–12
South-Western, 1986 (Termination Date: 1990)

Vocabulary—Supplementary
Vocabulary for the World of Work: Grades 9–12
Educational Design, 1985 (Termination Date: 1990)

Handwriting
HBJ Handwriting: Grades 1–8
Harcourt Brace Jovanovich, 1987 (Termination Date: 1995)

McDougal, Littell Handwriting: Grades 1–8
McDougal, Littell, 1990 (Termination Date: 1995)

Scott, Foresman D'Nealian Handwriting: Grades 1–8
Scott, Foresman, 1991 (Termination Date: 1995)

Zaner-Bloser Handwriting: A Way to Self-Expression: Grades 1–8
Zaner-Bloser, 1991 (Termination Date: 1995)

Tennessee

Grammar and Composition
HBJ Language: Grades: R–8
Harcourt Brace Jovanovich, 1990 (Termination Date: 1998)

English Composition and Grammar: Grades 6–12
Harcourt Brace Jovanovich, 1988 (Termination Date: 1998)

Heath Grammar and Composition: Grades 6–8
D. C. Heath, 1990 (Termination Date: 1998)

D. C. Heath English Program: Grades 9–12
D. C. Heath, 1992 (Termination Date: 1998)

Houghton Mifflin English: Grades 1–8, 9–12
Houghton Mifflin, 1992 (Termination Date: 1998)

Language Arts Today: Grades 1–8
McDougall, Littell, 1991 (Termination Date: 1998)

McDougall, Littell English Series: Grades 6–8
McDougall, Littell, 1990 (Termination Date: 1998)

Basic Skills in English: Grades 7–12
McDougall, Littell, 1989 (Termination Date: 1998)

The Writer's Craft Series: Grades 9–12
McDougall, Littell, 1992 (Termination Date: 1998)

McDougall, Littell Literature and Language Series: Grades 9–12
McDougall, Littell, 1992 (Termination Date: 1998)

The Writer's Handbook: Grades 9–12
National Textbook, 1990 (Termination Date: 1998)

Write to the Point: Grades 9–12
National Textbook, 1991 (Termination Date: 1998)

Creative Writing: Grades 9–12
National Textbook, 1990 (Termination Date: 1998)

Essentials of English Grammar: Grades 9–12
National Textbook, 1987 (Termination Date: 1998)

Write by Doing: Grades 9–12
National Textbook, 1990 (Termination Date: 1998)

Prentice Hall Grammar and Composition: Grades 6–12
Prentice Hall, 1990 (Termination Date: 1998)

World of Language: Grades 1–8
Silver Burdett and Ginn, 1990 (Termination Date: 1998)

The Computer Writing Book: Grades 9–12
South-Western, 1992 (Termination Date: 1998)

Language Arts: Grades 9–12
South-Western, 1992 (Termination Date: 1998)

Literacy Plus: Grades 9–12
Zaner-Bloser, 1991 (Termination Date: 1998)

English Handbooks
Warriner's High School Handbook: Grades 9–12
Holt, Rinehart and Winston, 1992 (Termination Date: 1998)

Harbrace College Handbook: Grades 9–12
Holt, Rinehart and Winston, 1990 (Termination Date: 1998)

Elements of English Grammar Rules Explained Simply: Grades 9–12
Mancorp, 1990 (Termination Date: 1998)

Webster's New World High School Writer's Handbook: Grades 9–12
Prentice Hall, 1988 (Termination Date: 1998)

Literature
Reading Literature: Grade 7
Silver Burdett and Ginn, 1986 (Termination Date: 1992)

Exploring Literature: Grade 8
Ginn (Silver Burdett/Ginn), 1986 (Termination Date: 1992)

Understanding Literature: Grade 9
Ginn, 1986 (Termination Date: 1992)

Types of Literature: Grade 10
Ginn, 1986 (Termination Date: 1992)

American Literature: Grade 11
Ginn, 1986 (Termination Date: 1992)

English Literature: Grade 12
Ginn, 1986 (Termination Date: 1992)

New Voices, 1-4: Grades 9–12
Ginn (Prentice-Hall) (Termination Date: 1992)

Adventures in Literature Series: Grades 7–12
Harcourt Brace Jovanovich, 1985 (Termination Date: 1992)

Journeys: A Reading and Literature Program:
Grades 7–12
Harcourt Brace Jovanovich, 1986 (Termination Date: 1992)

Myths and Their Meaning: Grades 9–12
Prentice-Hall, 1984 (Termination Date: 1992)

McDougal, Littell Literature: Grades 7–12
McDougal, Littell, 1985 (Termination Date: 1992)

Reading Literature Series: Grades 7–12
McDougal, Littell, 1987 (Termination Date: 1992)

Focus: Grade 7
McGraw-Hill/Webster Division (Glencoe), 1986
(Termination Date: 1992)

Perception: Grade 8
McGraw-Hill/Webster Division (Glencoe), 1986
(Termination Date: 1992)

Insights: Grade 9
McGraw-Hill/Webster Division (Glencoe), 1986
(Termination Date: 1992)

Encounters: Grade 10
McGraw-Hill/Webster Division (Glencoe), 1986
(Termination Date: 1992)

American Literature: Grade 11
McGraw-Hill/Webster Division (Glencoe), 1986
(Termination Date: 1992)

English Literature: Grade 12
McGraw-Hill/Webster Division (Glencoe), 1986
(Termination Date: 1992)

Reading Express Series: Grades 1–6
Macmillan, (Termination Date: 1992)

Scope English Anthologies: Grades 7–12
Scolastic, 1983, 1984 (Termination Date: 1992)

Beginnings in Literature: Grade 6
Scott, Foresman, 1985 (Termination Date: 1992)

Discoveries in Literature: Grade 7
Scott, Foresman, 1985 (Termination Date: 1992)

Exploration in Literature: Grade 8
Scott, Foresman, 1985 (Termination Date: 1992)

Patterns in Literature: Grade 9
Scott, Foresman, 1985 (Termination Date: 1992)

Traditions in Literature: Grade 10
Scott, Foresman, 1985 (Termination Date: 1992)

The United States in Literature: Grade 11
Scott, Foresman, 1985 (Termination Date: 1992)

England in Literature: Grade 12
Scott, Foresman, 1985 (Termination Date: 1992)

Pursuits: Grade 7
Scott, Foresman, 1984 (Termination Date: 1992)

Outposts: Grade 8
Scott, Foresman, 1984 (Termination Date: 1992)

Reflections: Grade 9
Scott, Foresman, 1984 (Termination Date: 1992)

Travels: Grade 10
Scott, Foresman, 1984 (Termination Date: 1992)

Album, U.S.A.: Grade 11
Scott, Foresman, 1984 (Termination Date: 1992)

Landmarks: Grade 12
Scott, Foresman, 1984 (Termination Date: 1992)

Supplementary
Language Handbook: Grades 9–12
Scott, Foresman, 1981 (Termination Date: 1992)

Spelling
Keys to Spelling Mastery Series: Grades 1–8
The Economy Company (Macmillan Publishing),
1984 (Termination Date: 1992)

Follet Spelling Series, Books 1–8: Grades 1–8
Ginn, 1984 (Termination Date: 1992)

HBJ Spelling: Grades 1–8
Harcourt Brace Jovanovich, 1983 (Termination
Date: 1992)

Houghton Mifflin Spelling: Grades 1–8
Houghton Mifflin, 1985 (Termination Date: 1992)

Building Spelling Skills: Grades 1–8
McDougal, Littell, 1985 (Termination Date: 1992)

Macmillan Spelling: Grades 1–8
Macmillan, 1987 (Termination Date: 1992)

Spelling for Word Mastery: Grades 1–8
Merrill, 1984 (Termination Date: 1992)

The MCP Spelling Workout Program: Grades 1–6
Modern Curriculum, 1990 (Termination Date: 1992)

Spelling: Words and Skills: Grades 1–8
Scott, Foresman, 1986 (Termination Date: 1992)

Silver Burdett Spelling: Grades 1–8
Silver Burdett, 1986 (Termination Date: 1992)

Steck-Vaughn Spelling: Grades 1–8
Steck-Vaughn, 1984 (Termination Date: 1992)

Zaner-Bloser Spelling: Basic Skills and Applications: Grades 1–8
Zaner-Bloser, 1984 (Termination Date: 1992)

Handwriting
McDougal, Littell Handwriting Series: Grades 1–8
McDougal, Littell, 1990 (Termination Date: 1998)

Scott, Foresman D'Nealian Handwriting: Grades 1–8
Scott, Foresman, 1991 (Termination Date: 1998)

Zaner-Bloser Handwriting: A Way to Self Expression: Grades 1–8
Zaner-Bloser, 1991 (Termination Date: 1998)

Dictionaries
Webster's New Ideal Dictionary #49: Grades 9–12
Encyclopedia Britannica Educational, 1989
(Termination Date: 1998)

Webster's School Thesaurus #78: Grades 9–11
Encyclopedia Britannica Educational, 1989
(Termination Date: 1998)

Webster's Collegiate Thesaurus #69: Grades 10–11
Encyclopedia Britannica Educational, 1988
(Termination Date: 1998)

Webster's Elementary Dictionary #75: Grades 1–6
Encyclopedia Britannica Educational, 1986
(Termination Date: 1998)

Webster's Intermediate Dictionary #79: Grades 6–8
Encyclopedia Britannica Educational, 1986
(Termination Date: 1998)

Webster's School Dictionary #80: Grades 9–12
Encyclopedia Britannica Educational, 1986
(Termination Date: 1998)

Webster's Ninth Collegiate Dictionary #8: Grades 9–12
Encyclopedia Britannica Educational, 1991
(Termination Date: 1998)

Random House Webster's College Dictionary, Plain Edged Version: Grades 10–12
Glencoe, 1991 (Termination Date: 1998)

Random House Webster's College Dictionary, Thumb Index Version: Grades 10–12
Glencoe, 1991 (Termination Date: 1998)

Scribner Intermediate Dictionary: Grades 5–7
Glencoe, 1986 (Termination Date: 1998)

Scribner Dictionary: Grades 8–12
Glencoe, 1986 (Termination Date: 1998)

Webster's New World Dictionary for Young Readers and Writers: Grades 3-5
Silver Burdett and Ginn, 1991 (Termination Date: 1998)

Webster's New World Dictionary, School Edition: Grades 5–8
Silver Burdett and Ginn, 1982 (Termination Date: 1998)

HBJ School Dictionary: Grades 4–8
Harcourt Brace Jovanovich, 1985, 1990 (Termination Date: 1998)

The Lincoln Writing Dictionary: Grades 3–8
Harcourt Brace Jovanovich, 1989 (Termination Date: 1998)

Houghton Mifflin Picture Dictionary: Grades K–1
Houghton Mifflin, 1989 (Termination Date: 1998)

Houghton Mifflin Primary Dictionary: Grades 1-2
Houghton Mifflin, 1989 (Termination Date: 1998)

Houghton Mifflin Intermediate Dictionary: Grades 3–6
Houghton Mifflin, 1989 (Termination Date: 1998)

Houghton Mifflin Student Dictionary: Grades 6–9
Houghton Mifflin, 1989 (Termination Date: 1998)

Houghton Mifflin College Dictionary: Grades 9–12
Houghton Mifflin, 1988 (Termination Date: 1998)

The American Heritage Dictionary of the English Language, High School Edition: Grades 11–12
Houghton Mifflin, 1982 (Termination Date: 1998)

Picture Word Book: Grades K–1
Macmillan, 1991 (Termination Date: 1998)

Primary Dictionary: Grades 1-2
Macmillan, 1991 (Termination Date: 1998)

Macmillan School Dictionary, 1 and 2: Grades 3–8
Macmillan, 1991 (Termination Date: 1998)

Webster's Dictionary for Young Explorers of Language: Grades 2-4
Modern Curriculum, 1992 (Termination Date: 1998)

Webster's New World Dictionary: Basic School Education: Grades 3–8
Modern Curriculum, 1990 (Termination Date: 1998)

Webster's New World Dictionary: Third College Edition: Grades 7–10
Prentice Hall, 1988 (Termination Date: 1998)

My Pictionary: Grade 1
Scott, Foresman, 1990 (Termination Date: 1998)

My First Picture Dictionary: Grade 1
Scott, Foresman, 1990 (Termination Date: 1998)

My Second Picture Dictionary: Grade 2
Scott, Foresman, 1990 (Termination Date: 1998)

Scott, Foresman Beginning, Intermediate and Advanced Dictionaries: Grades 3–12
Scott, Foresman, 1988 (Termination Date: 1998)

Reading

HBJ Reading: Grades 1–8
Harcourt Brace Jovanovich, 1989 (Termination Date: 1995)

Heath Reading Program: Grades 1–8
D. C. Heath, 1989 (Termination Date: 1995)

Reading: Today and Tomorrow: Grades 1–8
Holt, Rinehart and Winston, 1989 (Termination Date: 1995)

Houghton Mifflin Reading: Grades 1–8
Houghton Mifflin, 1989 (Termination Date: 1995)

Connections: Grades 1–8
Macmillan, 1989 (Termination Date: 1995)

Vistas in Reading Literature: Grades 6–8
McDougal, Littell, 1989 (Termination Date: 1995)

McGraw-Hill Reading: Grades 1–8
McGraw-Hill, 1989 (Termination Date: 1995)

Scott Foresman Reading: An American Tradition: Grades 1–8
Scott, Foresman, 1989 (Termination Date: 1995)

Scribner Reading Series: Grades 1–8
Scribner-Laidlaw, 1989 (Termination Date: 1995)

World of Reading: Grades 1–8
Silver Burdett and Ginn, 1989 (Termination Date: 1995)

Imagination: An Odyssey through Language: Grades 1–8
Harcourt Brace Jovanovich, 1989 (Termination Date: 1995)

New Directions in Reading (Houghton Mifflin)
Houghton Mifflin, 1986 (Termination Date: 1995)

Reading Express: Grades 7–8
Macmillan, 1988 (Termination Date: 1995)

Merrill Linguistic Reading Program: Grades 1-3
Merrill, 1986 (Termination Date: 1995)

Open Court Reading and Writing: Grades 1–6
Open Court, 1989 (Termination Date: 1995)

Collections: An Anthology Series: Grades 1–6
Scott, Foresman, 1989 (Termination Date: 1995)

Focus: Reading for Success: Grades 1–8
Scott, Foresman, 1988 (Termination Date: 1995)

Texas

Pre-kindergarten Teacher's Resource Packet
Brigance Prescriptive Readiness: Strategies and Practice 1E
Curriculum, 1985 (Termination Date: 1992)

Early Foundations 1E
Coronado, 1986 (Termination Date: 1992)

Beginning Foundations 1E
DLM, 1986 (Termination Date: 1992)

Supplementary Pre-Kindergarten Learning Systems English and Spanish
Milestones, Materials and Manipulatives 1E (also in Spanish edition)
DLM, 1988 (Termination Date: 1994)

Crosscuts 1E (also in Spanish edition)
Nelson-Remington, 1988 (Termination Date: 1994)

Kindergarten Learning Systems English and Spanish
Springboards to Learning Sunrise Edition: Grade K (also in Spanish edition)
DLM, 1988 (Termination Date: 1994)

McGraw-Hill Superstart: Grade K (also in Spanish edition)
McGraw-Hill, 1988 (Termination Date: 1994)

Sunshine Days: Grade K (also in Spanish edition)
Scott, Foresman, 1988 (Termination Date: 1994)

Basal Readers—Readiness (including Spanish editions)
Connections: I Think I Can: Grade 1
Macmillan/McGraw-Hill, 1987 (Termination Date: 1993)

Come Along: Grade 1
Scott, Foresman, 1987 (Termination Date: 1993)

HBJ Pinwheels: Grade 1
Harcourt Brace Jovanovich, 1987 (Termination Date: 1993)

Getting Ready: Grade 1
Houghton Mifflin, 1986 (Termination Date: 1993)

Let's Begin (Scribner): Grade 1
Macmillan/McGraw-Hill, 1987 (Termination Date: 1993)

Campanitas De Oro: Grade 1
Macmillan/McGraw-Hill, 1987 (Termination Date: 1993)

Scott, Foresman Spanish Reading: Grade 1
Scott, Foresman, 1987 (Termination Date: 1993)

HBJ Lectura: Grade 1
Harcourt Brace Jovanovich, 1987 (Termination Date: 1993)

Programa De Lectura En Espanol De Houghton Mifflin: Grade 1
Houghton Mifflin, 1987 (Termination Date: 1993)

Economy Spanish Reading Series: Grade 1
Macmillan/McGraw-Hill, 1987 (Termination Date: 1993)

Basal Readers—Pre-primer (including Spanish editions)
Connections: Grade 1
Macmillan/McGraw-Hill, 1987 (Termination Date: 1993)

Scott Foresman Reading: Grade 1 (also in Spanish edition)
Scott, Foresman, 1987 (Termination Date: 1993)

HBJ Reading Program Series: Grade 1 (also in Spanish edition)
Harcourt Brace Jovanovich, 1987 (Termination Date: 1993)

Houghton Mifflin Reading: Grade 1
Houghton, Mifflin, 1986 (Termination Date: 1993)

Scribner Reading Series: Grade 1
Macmillan/McGraw-Hill, 1987 (Termination Date: 1993)

Campanitas De Oro: Grade 1
Macmillan/McGraw-Hill, 1987 (Termination
Date: 1993)

Economy Spanish Reading Series: Grade 1
Macmillan/McGraw-Hill, 1987 (Termination
Date: 1993)

**Supplementary Readers—Pre-primer
(including Spanish editions)**
Reading Express: Grade 1
Macmillan/McGraw-Hill, 1986 (Termination
Date: 1992)

Economy Supplementary Reading Series: Grade 1
(also in Spanish edition)
Macmillan/McGraw-Hill, 1986 (Termination
Date: 1992)

Focus: Reading for Success: Grade 1 (also in
Spanish edition)
Scott, Foresman, 1985 (Termination Date: 1992)

Odyssey: An HBJ Literature Program: Grade 1
Harcourt Brace Jovanovich, 1986 (Termination
Date: 1992)

*Mil Maravillas: Mama, Papa, Y Yo/Yo Solita!/Con
Mis Amigos:* Grade 1
Macmillan/McGraw-Hill, 1986 (Termination
Date: 1992)

Hagamos Caminos Partimos, Pre-Primer: Grade 1
Addison-Wesley, 1986 (Termination Date: 1992)

**Basal Readers—Primers
(including Spanish editions)**
Connections: Grade 1
Macmillan/McGraw-Hill, 1987 (Termination
Date: 1993)

Campanitas De Oro: Grade 1
Macmillan/McGraw-Hill, 1987 (Termination
Date: 1993)

Scott, Foresman Reading: Grade 1
Scott, Foresman, 1987 (Termination Date: 1993)

Scott Foresman Spanish Reading: Grade 1
Scott, Foresman, 1987 (Termination Date: 1993)

HBJ Reading Program: Grade 1
Harcourt Brace Jovanovich, 1987 (Termination
Date: 1993)

HBJ Lectura: Grade 1
Harcourt Brace Jovanovich, 1987 (Termination
Date: 1993)

Houghton Mifflin Reading: Grade 1
Houghton Mifflin, 1986 (Termination Date: 1993)

*Programa de Lectura en Espanol de Houghton
Mifflin:* Grade 1
Houghton Mifflin, 1986 (Termination Date: 1993)

Scribner Reading Series: Grade 1
Macmillan/McGraw-Hill, 1987 (Termination
Date: 1993)

Economy Spanish Reading Series: Grade 1
Macmillan/McGraw-Hill, 1987 (Termination
Date: 1993)

Supplementary Readers
Reading Express: Grades 1–8
Macmillan/McGraw-Hill, 1986, 1988 (Termina-
tion Date: 1992)

Mil Maravillas: Grades 1-5
Macmillan/McGraw-Hill, 1986 (Termination
Date: 1992)

Economy Supplementary Reading Series: Grades
1–6 (also in Spanish edition)
Macmillan/McGraw-Hill, 1986 (Termination
Date: 1992)

Focus: Reading for Success: Grade 1–8 (also in
Spanish edition)
Scott, Foresman 1985 (Termination Date: 1992)

Odyssey: An HBJ Literature Program: Grades 1–8
Harcourt Brace Jovanovich, 1986 (Termination
Date: 1992)

Hagamos Caminos Corremos: Grades 1-3
Addison-Wesley, 1986 (Termination Date: 1992)

Basal Readers (including Spanish editions)
Connections: Grades 1–8
Macmillan/McGraw-Hill, 1987 (Termination
Date: 1993)

Campanitas De Oro: Grades 1-5
Macmillan/McGraw-Hill, 1987 (Termination
Date: 1993)

Scott Foresman Reading: Grades 1–8
Scott, Foresman, 1987 (Termination Date: 1993)

Scott Foresman Spanish Reading: Grades 1-5
Scott, Foresman, 1987 (Termination Date: 1993)

HBJ Reading Program: Grades 1–8
Harcourt Brace Jovanovich, 1987 (Termination Date: 1993)

HBJ Lectura: Grades 1-5
Harcourt Brace Jovanovich, 1987 (Termination Date: 1993)

Houghton Mifflin Reading: Grades 1–8
Houghton Mifflin, 1986 (Termination Date: 1993)

Program de Lectura en Espanol de Houghton Mifflin: Grades 1-5
Houghton Mifflin, 1987 (Termination Date: 1993)

Scribner Reading Series: Grades 1–8
Macmillan/McGraw-Hill, 1987 (Termination Date: 1993)

Economy Spanish Reading Series: Grades 1-5
Macmillan/McGraw-Hill, 1987 (Termination Date: 1993)

Reading Improvement

Journeys: A Reading and Literature Program with Writing Supplement: Grades 7–8
Harcourt Brace Jovanovich, 1986 (Termination Date: 1994)

New Directions in Reading: Grades 7–8
Houghton Mifflin, 1986 (Termination Date: 1994)

Reading Express: Grades 7–8
Macmillan/McGraw-Hill, 1988 (Termination Date: 1994)

Scope English Anthology: Grades 7–8
Scholastic, 1988 (Termination Date: 1994)

Quest: Grades 7–8
Scholastic, 1985 (Termination Date: 1994)

Focus: Reading for Success: Grades 7–8
Scott, Foresman, 1988 (Termination Date: 1994)

Handwriting

Zaner-Bloser Handwriting: Grades 1–6
Zaner-Bloser, 1987 (Termination Date: 1993)

Palmer Method Handwriting: Grades 1–6
Macmillan/McGraw-Hill, 1987 (Termination Date: 1993)

McDougal, Littell Handwriting: Grades 1–6
McDougal, Littell, 1987 (Termination Date: 1993)

Scott Foresman D'Nealian Handwriting: Grades 1–6
Scott, Foresman, 1987 (Termination Date: 1993)

HBJ Handwriting: Grades 1–6
Harcourt Brace Jovanovich, 1987 (Termination Date: 1993)

Spelling

HBJ Spelling: Grades 1–6
Harcourt Brace Jovanovich, 1988 (Termination Date: 1994)

Houghton Mifflin Spelling: Grades 1–6
Houghton Mifflin, 1988 (Termination Date: 1994)

Spelling for Word Mastery (Merrill): Grades 1–6
Macmillan/McGraw-Hill, 1987 (Termination Date: 1994)

Riverside Spelling: Grades 1–6
Riverside, 1988 (Termination Date: 1994)

Scott, Foresman Spelling: Grades 1–6
Scott, Foresman, 1988 (Termination Date: 1994)

Laidlaw Spelling (Scribner): Grades 1–6
Macmillan/McGraw-Hill, 1987 (Termination Date: 1994)

Spelling Connections Words into Language: Grades 1–6
Zaner-Bloser, 1988 (Termination Date: 1994)

Series S: Macmillan Spelling: Grades 6–8
Macmillan/McGraw-Hill, 1987 (Termination Date: 1994)

Composition and Language

HBJ Language: Grades 1–8
Harcourt Brace Jovanovich, 1990 (Termination Date: 1996)

Houghton Mifflin English: Grades 1–8
Hougton Mifflin, 1990 (Termination Date: 1996)

Macmillan Language Arts Today: Grades 1–8
Macmillan/McGraw Hill, 1990 (Termination Date: 1996)

McGraw-Hill English: Grades 1–8
Macmillan/McGraw Hill, 1990 (Termination Date: 1996)

World of Language: Grades 1–8
Silver, Burdett and Ginn, 1990 (Termination Date: 1996)

English Composition and Grammar: Grades 6–8
Harcourt Brace Jovanovich, 1988 (Termination Date: 1996)

Heath Grammar and Composition: Grades 6–8
D. C. Heath, 1990 (Termination Date: 1996)

Scholastic Scope English Writing and Language: Grades 6–8
Scholastic, 1990 (Termination Date: 1996)

Literature
Pegasus Edition Adventures for Readers: Grades 7–12
Harcourt Brace Jovanovich, 1989 (Termination Date: 1995)

Elements of Literature: Grades 7–12
Holt, Rinehart, 1989 (Termination Date: 1995)

McDougal, Littell Literature: Grades 7–12
McDougal, Littell, 1988 (Termination Date: 1995)

Reading Literature: Grades 7–8
McDougal, Littell, 1988 (Termination Date: 1995)

Prentice Hall Literature: Grades 7–12
Prentice Hall, 1989 (Termination Date: 1995)

America Reads: Grades 7–8
Scott, Foresman, 1989 (Termination Date: 1995)

Patterns in Literature, Etc: Grades 9–12
Scott, Foresman, 1989 (Termination Date: 1995)

Scribner Literature Series: Grades 7–12
Glencoe/McGraw-Hill, 1989 (Termination Date: 1995)

England in Literature Series: Grades 9–12
Scott, Foresman, 1989 (Termination Date: 1995)

Correlated Language Arts (High School)
McDougal, Littell Correlated Language Arts Program: Grades 9–12
McDougal, Littell, 1985 (Termination Date: 1992)

Scope English Anthology: Grades 9–12
Scholastic, 1983 (Termination Date: 1992)

Journeys: A Reading and Literature Program: Grades 9–12
Harcourt Brace Jovanovich, 1986 (Termination Date: 1992)

English Language and Composition (High School)
Glencoe English: Grades 9–12
Glencoe/McGraw-Hill, 1985 (Termination Date: 1992)

English: Writing and Skills: Grades 9–12
Coronado, 1985 (Termination Date: 1992)

Macmillan English: Grades 9–12
Glencoe/McGraw-Hill, 1986 (Termination Date: 1992)

McDougall, Littell Building English Skills: Grades 9–12
McDougall, Littell, 1985 (Termination Date: 1992)

Introduction to Speech Communication
Effective Speech: Grades 9–12
Glencoe/McGraw-Hill, 1988 (Termination Date: 1994)

Speech for Effective Communication: Grades 9–12
Harcourt Brace Jovanovich, 1988 (Termination Date: 1994)

Dynamics of Speech: Grades 9–12
National Textbook, 1988 (Termination Date: 1994)

Speech: Exploring Communication: Grades 9–12
Prentice Hall, 1988 (Termination Date: 1994)

Debate
Strategic Debate: Grades 9–12
National Textbook, 1989 (Termination Date: 1995)

Public Speaking
Public Speaking Today!: Grades 9–12
National Textbook, 1989 (Termination Date: 1995)

Journalism
Journalism: Grades 9–12
Prentice Hall, 1984 (Termination Date: 1992)

Mass Media and the School Newspaper. Grades 9–12
Wadsworth, 1985 (Termination Date: 1992)

Inside High School Journalism: Grades 9–12
Scott, Foresman, 1986 (Termination Date: 1992)

Journalism Today. Grades 9–12
Scott, Foresman, 1986 (Termination Date: 1992)

Press Time: Grades 9–12
Prentice Hall, 1985 (Termination Date: 1992

Utah

Note: Utah did not provide list.

Virginia

Dictionaries
Random House School Dictionary. Grades 4–7
American School, 1984 (Termination Date: 1993)

Fearon New School Dictionary. Grades 9–12
Fearon/Janus/Quercus, 1987 (Termination Date:
1993)

Scribner Beginning Dictionary. Grades 3-5
Glencoe/Macmillan/McGraw-Hill, 1986 (Termination Date: 1993)

Scribner Intermediate Dictionary. Grades 5–7
Glencoe/Macmillan/McGraw-Hill, 1986 (Termination Date: 1993)

Scribner Dictionary: Grades 9–12
Glencoe/Macmillan/McGraw-Hill, 1986 (Termination Date: 1993)

Webster's High School Dictionary: Grades 9–12
Globe, 1986 (Termination Date: 1993)

Webster's Ninth New Collegiate Dictionary: Grades
9–12
Globe, 1985 (Termination Date: 1993)

HBJ School Dictionary, 2d Ed.: Grades 4–7
Harcourt Brace Jovanovich, 1985 (Termination
Date: 1993)

Houghton Mifflin Intermediate Dictionary. Grades
3–6
Houghton Mifflin, 1986 (Termination Date: 1993)

Houghton Mifflin Student Dictionary: Grades 9-12
Houghton Mifflin, 1986 (Termination Date: 1993)

Houghton Mifflin College Dictionary: Grades 9–12
Houghton Mifflin, 1986 (Termination Date: 1993)

*The American Heritage Dictionary of English
Language*
Houghton Mifflin, 1982 (Termination Date: 1993)

Macmillan School Dictionary 1: Grades 2-5
Macmillan, 1990 (Termination Date: 1993)

Macmillan School Dictionary 2: Grades 4–7
Macmillan, 1990 (Termination Date: 1993)

Macmillan Dictionary: Grades 9–12
Macmillan, 1987 (Termination Date: 1993)

Webster's New World Dictionary. Grades 4–7
Modern Curriculum, 1989 (Termination Date: 1993)

Webster's New World Dictionary: Grades 9–12
Prentice Hall, 1983 (Termination Date: 1993)

Wester's New World Dictionary: Grades 9–12
Prentice Hall, 1985 (Termination Date: 1993)

Random House College Dictionary: Grades 9–12
Random House, 1983 (Termination Date: 1993)

Scott, Foresman Beginning Dictionary. Grades 4-5
Scott, Foresman, 1988 (Termination Date: 1993)

Scott, Foresman Intermediate Dictionary. Grades 5–7
Scott, Foresman, 1988 (Termination Date: 1993)

Scott, Foresman Advanced Dictionary: Grades 9–12
Scott, Foresman, 1988 (Termination Date: 1993)

Webster's Elementary Dictionary: Grades 4–6
Silver, Burdett and Ginn, 1986 (Termination Date: 1993)

Webster's Intermediate Dictionary: Grades 6–7
Silver Burdett, 1986 (Termination Date: 1993)

Language Arts—Handwriting
HBJ Handwriting: Grades 1–6
Harcourt Brace Jovanovich, 1987 (Termination Date: 1993)

McDougal, Littell Handwriting: Grades 1–7
McDougal, Littell, 1987 (Termination Date: 1993)

D'Nealian Handwriting: Grades 1–7
Scott, Foresman, 1987 (Termination Date: 1993)

Zaner-Bloser Handwriting: Grades 1–7
Zaner-Bloser, 1989 (Termination Date: 1993)

Journalism
Journalism Today!: Grades 9–12
National Textbook, 1986 (Termination Date: 1993)

Press Time: Grades 9–12
Prentice Hall, 1985 (Termination Date: 1993)

Language, Grammar, and Composition
Glencoe/English: Grades 7–8
Glencoe/Macmillan/McGraw-Hill, 1984 (Termination Date: 1993)

Macmillan English: Thinking and Writing Processes
Glencoe/Macmillan/McGraw-Hill, 1988 (Termination Date: 1993)

HBJ Language: Grades 3-5
Harcourt Brace Jovanovich, 1990 (Termination Date: 1993)

Language for Daily Use, Phoenix Ed.: Grades 6–8
Harcourt Brace Jovanovich, 1983 (Termination Date: 1993)

Your English: Grades 6–8
Holt, Rinehart and Winston/Harcourt Brace Jovanovich, 1984 (Termination Date: 1993)

English: Writing and Skills: Grades 7–8
Holt, Rinehart and Winston/Harcourt Brace Jovanovich, 1985 (Termination Date: 1993)

English: Composition and Grammar: Grades 9–12
Holt, Rinehart and Winston/Harcourt Brace Jovanovich, 1988 (Termination Date: 1993)

Houghton Mifflin English: Grades 6–8
Houghton Mifflin, 1983 (Termination Date: 1993)

Grammar and Composition: Grades 7–8
Houghton Mifflin, 1984 (Termination Date: 1993)

Houghton Mifflin English: Grades 9–12
Houghton Mifflin, 1990 (Termination Date: 1993)

Expressways: Grades 6–8
Macmillan/McGraw-Hill, 1984 (Termination Date: 1993)

Macmillan English, Series E: Grades 6–8
Macmillan/McGraw-Hill, 1984 (Termination Date: 1993)

McDougal Littell English: Grades 9–12
McDougal, Littell, 1989 (Termination Date: 1993)

Basic Skills in English: Grades 7–8
McDougal, Littell, 1985 (Termination Date: 1993)

Building English Skills: Grades 6–8
McDougal, Littell, 1984 (Termination Date: 1993)

The Writing Process: Grades 7–8
Prentice Hall, 1982 (Termination Date: 1993)

Scholastic Composition: Grades 7–8
Scholastic, 1985 (Termination Date: 1993)

Silver, Burdett English: Grades 6–8
Silver, Burdett, 1985 (Termination Date: 1993)

World of Language: Grades 3-5
Silver, Burdett, 1990 (Termination Date: 1993)

Literature
Macmillan Literature Series: Grades 7–12
Macmillan, 1987 (Termination Date: 1993)

McGraw Literature Series: Grades 7–12
McGraw-Hill, 1985 (Termination Date: 1993)

Adventures for Readers: Grades 7–9
Harcourt Brace Jovanovich, 1985 (Termination Date: 1993)

Adventures in Appreciation: Grade 10
Harcourt Brace Jovanovich, 1985 (Termination Date: 1993)

Adventures in American Literature: Grade 11
Harcourt Brace Jovanovich, 1985 (Termination Date: 1993)

Adventures in English Literature: Grade 12
Harcourt Brace Jovanovich, 1985 (Termination Date: 1993)

Literature Series: Grades 7–12
McDougal, Littell, 1982–85 (Termination Date: 1993)

Ginn Literature Series: Grades 7–12
Prentice Hall, 1984 (Termination Date: 1993)

Scope English Anthology: Grades 7–12
Scholastic, 1983 (Termination Date: 1993)

America Reads Series: Grades 6–12
Scott, Foresman, 1985 (Termination Date: 1993)

Reading

Heath Reading: Grades 1–8
D. C. Heath, 1989 (Termination Date: 1993)

Journeys: Grades 1–6
Ginn Publishing Canada, 1984–88 (Termination Date: 1993)

HBJ Reading Program: Laureate Edition: Grades K–8
Harcourt Brace Jovanovich, 1989 (Termination Date: 1993)

Reading Today and Tomorrow: Grades 1–8
Holt, Rinehart and Winston/Harcourt Brace Jovanovich, 1989 (Termination Date: 1993)

Vistas in Reading Literature: Grades 6–8
McDougal, Littell, 1989 (Termination Date: 1993)

McGraw-Hill Reading: Grades K–8
Macmillan/McGraw-Hill, 1989 (Termination Date: 1993)

World of Reading: Grades K–8
Silver, Burdett, 1989 (Termination Date: 1993)

Reading—Alternatives

Globe Anthology Series: Grades 6–8
Globe, 1992 (Termination Date: 1993)

New Directions in Reading: Grades 5–8
Houghton Mifflin, 1986 (Termination Date: 1993)

Reading Express: Grades 1–8
Macmillan/McGraw-Hill, 1986/88 (Termination Date: 1993)

Merrill Linguistic Reading Program: Grades 1-3
Merrill, 1986 (Termination Date: 1993)

Quest: Grades 4–8
Scholastic, 1986–88 (Termination Date: 1993)

Focus: Reading for Success: Grades K–8
Scott, Foresman, 1988 (Termination Date: 1993)

Speech

Effective Speech: Grades 9–12
McGraw-Hill, 1988 (Termination Date: 1993)

Speech for Effective Communication: Grades 9–12
Holt, Rinehart and Winston/Harcourt Brace Jovanovich, 1988 (Termination Date: 1993)

Person to Person: Grades 9–12
National Textbook, 1990 (Termination Date: 1993)

The Basics of Speech: Grades 9–12
National Textbook, 1988 (Termination Date: 1993)

Dynamics of Speech: Grades 9–12
National Textbook, 1988 (Termination Date: 1993)

Communication: An Introduction to Speech: Grades 7–9
Prentice Hall, 1988 (Termination Date: 1993)

Speech: Exploring Communication: Grades 9–12
Prentice Hall, 1988 (Termination Date: 1993)

Spelling

HBJ Spelling: Grades 2–7
Harcourt Brace Jovanovich, 1988 (Termination Date: 1993)

McDougal, Littell Spelling: Grades 2–7
McDougal, Littell, 1988 (Termination Date: 1993)

Scott, Foresman Spelling: Grades 2–7
Scott, Foresman, 1988 (Termination Date: 1993)

Spelling Connection: Words into Language: Grades
2–7
Zaner-Bloser, 1988 (Termination Date: 1993)

Theater
The Stage and the School: Grades 9–12
Glencoe/Macmillan/McGraw-Hill, 1988 (Termination Date: 1993)

Theater:Preparation and Performance: Grades 9–12
Scott, Foresman, 1989 (Termination Date: 1993)

West Virginia

Correlated Language Arts
Heath Reading: Grades K–8
D. C. Heath, 1989 (Termination Date: 1994)

Imagination: An Odyssey through Language:
Grades K–6
Harcourt Brace Jovanovich, 1989 (Termination
Date: 1994)

Connections: Grades K–8
Macmillan, n.d. (Termination Date: 1994)

McGraw-Hill Integrated Language Arts: Grades K–8
McGraw-Hill, 1989 (Termination Date: 1994)

Scott, Foresman Reading: An American Tradition:
Grades K–8
Scott, Foresman, 1989 (Termination Date: 1994)

Focus: Reading for Success: Grades K–8
Scott, Foresman, 1988 (Termination Date: 1994)

Scott Foresman Spelling: Grades 1–8
Scott, Foresman, 1988 (Termination Date: 1994)

Scott, Foresman Language: Grades K–8
Scott, Foresman, 1989 (Termination Date: 1994)

Open Court Reading and Writing: Grades K–6
Open Court, 1989 (Termination Date: 1994)

Reading
Heath Reading: Grades K–8
D. C. Heath, 1989 (Termination Date: 1995)

HBJ Reading: Grades K–8
Harcourt Brace Jovanovich, 1989 (Termination
Date: 1995)

Reading: Today and Tomorrow: Grades K–8
Holt, Rinehart and Winston/Harcourt Brace
Jovanovich, 1989 (Termination Date: 1995)

Houghton Mifflin Reading: 1989 Grades K–8
Houghton Mifflin, 1989 (Termination Date: 1995)

Connections: Grades K–8
Macmillan, 1988 (Termination Date: 1995)

McGraw-Hill Reading: Grades K–8
McGraw-Hill, 1989 (Termination Date: 1995)

The Riverside Reading Program: Grades K–8
Riverside, 1989 (Termination Date: 1995)

Scott, Foresman Reading: An American Tradition:
Grades K–8
Scott, Foresman, 1989 (Termination Date: 1995)

Scribner Reading Series: Grades K–8
Scribner Laidlaw, 1989 (Termination Date: 1995)

World of Reading: Grades K–8
Silver, Burdett, 1989 (Termination Date: 1995)

New Directions in Reading: Grades 4–8 (Low
Ability)
Houghton Mifflin, 1986 (Termination Date: 1995)

Reading Express: Grades K–8
Macmillan, 1986 (Termination Date: 1995)

Focus: Reading for Success: Grades K–8
Scott, Foresman, 1989 (Termination Date: 1995)

Open Court Reading: Grades K–8
Open Court, 1989 (Termination Date: 1995)

Spelling
Working Words in Spelling: Grades 1–8
D. C. Heath, 1988 (Termination Date: 1995)

HBJ Spelling, Signature: Grades 1–8
Harcourt Brace Jovanovich, 1988 (Termination Date: 1995)

Laidlaw Spelling: Grades 1–8
Macmillan, 1987 (Termination Date: 1995)

Spelling for Word Mastery: Grades 1–8
Merrill, 1987 (Termination Date: 1995)

McDougal, Littell Spelling Series: Grades 1–8
McDougal, Littell, 1988 (Termination Date: 1995)

Basic Goals in Spelling: Grades 1–8
McGraw-Hill, 1988 (Termination Date: 1995)

Scott, Foresman Spelling: Grades 1–8
Scott, Foresman, 1988 (Termination Date: 1995)

Spelling Connections: Words into Language:
Grades 1–8
Zaner-Bloser, 1988 (Termination Date: 1995)

Literature
Scribner Literature Series: Grades 7–12
Glencoe/Macmillan/McGraw-Hill, 1989 (Termination Date: 1995)

Adventures in Literature: Grades 7–12
Harcourt Brace Jovanovich, 1989 (Termination Date: 1995)

Journeys: A Literature Program: Grades 7–12
Harcourt Brace Jovanovich, 1986 (Termination Date: 1995)

Elements in Literature: Grades 7–12
Holt, Rinehart and Winston/Harcourt Brace Jovanovich, 1989 (Termination Date: 1995)

McDougal, Littell Literature Series: Grades 7–12
McDougal, Littell, 1989 (Termination Date: 1995)

Reading Literature Series: Grades 7–12
McDougal, Littell, 1988 (Termination Date: 1995)

The McGraw-Hill Literature Series by Carlsen:
Grades 7–12
McGraw-Hill, 1989 (Termination Date: 1995)

Prentice Hall Literature Series: Grades 7–12
Prentice Hall, 1989 (Termination Date: 1995)

America Reads: Classic Edition: Grades 6–10
Scott, Foresman, 1989 (Termination Date: 1995)

Globe Anthology Series: Grades 7–12 (Low Ability)
Globe, 1986, 1987, 1989 (Termination Date: 1995)

Reading Literature Series: Grades 7–12 (Low Ability)
McDougal, Littell, 1989 (Termination Date: 1995)

English
Heath Grammar and Composition: Grades 6–8
D.C Heath, 1988 (Termination Date: 1996)

HBJ Language: Grades K–8
Harcourt Brace Jovanovich, 1990 (Termination Date: 1996)

Houghton Mifflin English: Grades K–8
Houghton Mifflin, 1990 (Termination Date: 1996)

McDougal, Littell English Series: Grades 6–8
McDougal, Littell, 1990 (Termination Date: 1996)

McGraw-Hill English: Grades K–8
McGraw-Hill, 1989 (Termination Date: 1996)

Prentice Hall Grammar and Composition Series:
Grade 6
Prentice Hall, 1990 (Termination Date: 1996)

Scott, Foresman Language: Grades K–8
Scott, Foresman, 1989 (Termination Date: 1996)

World of Language: Grades K–8
Silver Burdett, 1990 (Termination Date: 1996)

Basic Skills in English Series: Grades 7–8 (Low Ability)
McDougal, Littell, 1989 (Termination Date: 1996)

Language Arts Today: Grades K–8
Macmillan/McGraw-Hill, 1990 (Termination Date: 1996)

Composition/Grammar
Heath Grammar and Composition: Grades 6–12
D. C. Heath, 1988 (Termination Date: 1996)

Macmillan English: Thinking and Writing Processes: Grades 9–12
Glencoe/Macmillan/McGraw-Hill, 1988 (Termination Date: 1996)

English Composition and Grammar: Benchmark Edition: Grades 6–12
Harcourt Brace Jovanovich, 1988 (Termination Date: 1996)

Houghton Mifflin English: Grades 9–12
Houghton Mifflin, 1990 (Termination Date: 1996)

Prentice Hall Grammar and Composition Series: Grades 6–12
Prentice Hall, 1990 (Termination Date: 1996)

Basic Skills in English Series: Grades 9–12 (Low Ability)
McDougal, Littell, 1989 (Termination Date: 1996)

Scope English Writing and Language: Grades 7–12
Scholastic, 1987/90 (Termination Date: 1996)

Oral Composition
Effective Speech: Grades 9–12
Glencoe/Macmillan/McGraw-Hill, 1988 (Termination Date: 1996)

Speech for Effective Communication: Grades 9–12
Harcourt Brace Jovanovich, 1988 (Termination Date: 1996)

Communication: An Introduction to Speech: Grades 7–8
Prentice Hall, 1988 (Termination Date: 1996)

The Basics of Speech, The Dynamics of Speech, Public Speaking Today!, Person to Person: Grades 7–12
National Textbook, 1990 (Termination Date: 1996)

An Introduction to Speech: Grades 7–12
Prentice Hall, 1988 (Termination Date: 1996)

Handwriting
HBJ Handwriting: Grades K–8
Harcourt Brace Jovanovich, 1989 (Termination Date: 1996)

McDougal, Littell Handwriting Series: Grades K–8
McDougal, Littell, 1990 (Termination Date: 1996)

Scott, Foresman D'Nealian Handwriting Program: Grades K–8
Scott, Foresman, 1987 (Termination Date: 1996)

Zaner-Bloser Handwriting: Basic Skills and Application: Grades K–8
Zaner-Bloser, 1989 (Termination Date: 1996)

Combined Subjects in Kindergarten
Alpha Time Complete Program: Grade K
Arista, 1981 (Termination Date: 1994)

Springboards to Learning, Sunrise Edition: Grade K
DLM Teaching Resources, 1987 (Termination Date: 1994)

Superstart (Big Books): Grade K
McGraw-Hill, 1988 (Termination Date: 1994)

Sunshine Days—Learning System: Grade K
Scott, Foresman, 1988 (Termination Date: 1994)

Beginning to Read, Write and Listen: Grade K
Scribner, 1978 (Termination Date: 1994)

Correlated Language Arts (partial listing 7–12)
Journeys: Grades 7–12
Harcourt Brace Jovanovich, 1986 (Termination Date: 1994)

Correlated Language Arts: Grades 7–12
McDougal, Littell, 1988 (Termination Date: 1994)

INDEX TO REVIEWS OF
EDUCATIONAL MATERIALS

T HIS index cites reviews of recently published materials for use in English/language arts classes, including curriculum guides, lesson plans, project books, software programs, videos, and filmstrips. The citations cover reviews from the past two years (up to March 1992), and they reflect a search of educational journals, magazines, and newsletters that would include reviews of social studies materials. The journals chosen are those that are available in teacher college libraries, in other college and university collections, and in many public libraries. They also include the major publications sent to members of the appropriate educational organizations. The review for each item can be found under the following listings:

- the title of the item
- the author(s)
- the publisher or producer/distributor
- school level (elementary, middle school, or high school)
- subject (a broad subject arrangement is used)

Activities

All Sides of the Issue: Activities for Cooperative Jigsaw Groups, by Elizabeth Coelho, Lise Winer, and Judy Winn-Bell (Old Tappan, NJ: Prentice Hall, 1989). Reviewed in: *Journal of Reading* 34, no. 2 (Oct. 1990): 156

Listening: The Basic Connection, by M. Micallef (Carthage, IL: Good Apple, 1984). Reviewed in: *Reading Teacher* 43, no. 9 (May 1990): 675–76

Spelling Puzzles and Tests, software (n.p.: Educational Computing Corp., n.d.). Reviewed in: *School Library Journal* 37, no. 3 (Mar. 1991): 142

Write On!, software (Hood River, OR: Humanities Software, 1989). Reviewed in: *Journal of Reading* 34, no. 4 (Dec./Jan. 1990–91): 314

Writing Exercises for High School Students, by Barbara Vulaggio (Bloomington, IN: ERIC Clearinghouse on Reading and Communication Skills, 1989). Reviewed in: *Journal of Reading* 34, no. 7 (Apr. 1991): 577–78

Aims Media

European Folk Tales, video (Chatsworth, CA: Aims Media, 1990). Reviewed in: *School Library Journal* 37, no. 10 (Oct. 1991): 73

Akin, Berdell J.
Comprehension Checkups Grades 1–5: Strategies for Success, by Berdell J. Akin and Patricia R. Conley (Englewood, CO: Libraries Unlimited, 1990). Reviewed in: *Curriculum Review* 31, no. 3 (Nov. 1991): 28

All Sides of the Issue: Activities for Cooperative Jigsaw Groups
by Elizabeth Coelho, Lise Winer, and Judy Winn-Bell (Old Tappan, NJ: Prentice Hall, 1989). Reviewed in: *Journal of Reading* 34, no. 2 (Oct. 1990): 156

American School
Following the Drinking Gourd, video (Chicago: American School, n.d.). Reviewed in: *School Library Journal* 37, no. 2 (Feb. 1991): 53

The Little Snowgirl, video (Chicago: American School, n.d.). Reviewed in: *School Library Journal* 37, no. 10 (Oct. 1991): 80

The Secret Life of the Underwear Champ, video (Chicago: American School, 1989). Reviewed in: *School Library Journal* 37, no. 1 (Jan. 1991): 60–61

Barnard, Tom
Write Ahead, by Tom Barnard (New York: Macmillan, 1989). Reviewed in: *Child Language Teaching and Therapy* 6, no. 1 (Feb. 1990): 104–5

Baskwill, Jane
The Whole Language Source Book, by Jane Baskwill and Paulette Whitman (Ontario, Canada: Scholastic, 1986). Reviewed in: *Language Arts* 68, no. 2 (Feb. 1991): 150

Bissinger, Kristen
Leap into Learning, by Kristen Bissinger and Nancy Renfro (Austin: Nancy Renfro Studios, 1990). Reviewed in: *Curriculum Review* 31, no. 7 (Mar. 1992): 26

Bolton, F.
Bookshelf Stage 1, by F. Bolton, R. Green, J. Pollock, B. Scarff, and D. Snowball (New York: Scholastic, 1986). Reviewed in: *Reading Teacher* 43, no. 8 (Apr. 1990): 592

Books Alive! Using Literature in the Classroom
by Susan Hill (Portsmouth, NH: Heinemann, 1986). Reviewed in: *Language Arts* 68, no. 2 (Feb. 1991): 149

Bookshelf Stage 1
by F. Bolton, R. Green, J. Pollock, B. Scarff, and D. Snowball (New York: Scholastic, 1986). Reviewed in: *Reading Teacher* 43, no. 8 (Apr. 1990): 592

Building Elementary Reading Skills through Whole Language and Literature
by Donald C. Cushenbery (Springfield, IL: Charles C. Thomas, 1989). Reviewed in: *Curriculum Review* 30, no. 3 (Nov. 1990): 27

Charles C. Thomas (publishers)
Building Elementary Reading Skills through Whole Language and Literature, by Donald C. Cushenbery (Springfield, IL: Charles C. Thomas, 1989). Reviewed in: *Curriculum Review* 30, no. 3 (Nov. 1990): 27

Comprehensive Reading Strategies for All Secondary Students, by Donald C. Cushenbery (Springfield, IL: Charles C. Thomas, 1988). Reviewed in: *Journal of Reading* 33, no. 6 (Mar. 1990): 477

Child's Play (publishers)
The Princess and the Dragon/Scaredy Cats, video (New York: Child's Play, 1990). Reviewed in: *School Library Journal* 37, no. 6 (June 1991): 60–61

Chip Taylor Communications
The Storyteller Series: Serena of the River, video (Derry, NH: Chip Taylor Communications, 1991). Reviewed in: *School Library Journal* 37, no. 12 (Dec. 1991): 64

Coelho, Elizabeth
All Sides of the Issue: Activities for Cooperative Jigsaw Groups, by Elizabeth Coelho, Lise Winer, and Judy Winn-Bell (Old Tappan, NJ: Prentice Hall, 1989). Reviewed in: *Journal of Reading* 34, no. 2 (Oct. 1990): 156

College Board Publications
The Student's Guide to Good Writing, by Marianne Dalton and Rick Dalton (New York: College Board Publications, 1990). Reviewed in: *Journal of Reading* 34, no. 1 (Sept. 1990): 76

Comley, Nancy R.
Text Book: An Introduction to Literary Language, by Nancy R. Comley, Robert Scholes, and Gregory L. Ulmer (New York: St. Martin's, 1988). Reviewed in: *English Journal* 79, no. 5 (Sept. 1990): 98

Composition. *See* Writing skills

Comprehension (*see also* Reading)
Comprehension Checkups Grades 1–5: Strategies for Success, by Berdell J. Akin and Patricia R. Conley (Englewood, CO: Libraries Unlimited, 1990). Reviewed in: *Curriculum Review* 31, no. 3 (Nov. 1991): 28

Team Series: Reading Comprehension, software (Torrance, CA: Davidson and Associates, 1990). Reviewed in: *Journal of Reading* 34, no. 5 (Feb. 1991): 410</rv

Understanding Unreliable Narrators: Reading between the Lines in the Literature Classroom, by Michael W. Smith (Urbana, IL: National Council of Teachers of English, 1991). Reviewed in: *Curriculum Review* 31, no. 2 (Oct. 1991): 28–29

Comprehension Checkups Grades 1–5: Strategies for Success
by Berdell J. Akin and Patricia R. Conley (Englewood, CO: Libraries Unlimited, 1990). Reviewed in: *Curriculum Review* 31, no. 3 (Nov. 1991): 28

Comprehensive Reading Strategies for All Secondary Students
by Donald C. Cushenbery (Springfield, IL: Charles C. Thomas, 1988). Reviewed in: *Journal of Reading* 33, no. 6 (Mar. 1990): 477

Computers. *See* Technology

CONDUIT (publishers)
SEEN: Tutorials for Critical Reading, software (Iowa City: CONDUIT, 1989). Reviewed in: *Journal of Reading* 33, no. 6 (Mar. 1990): 476

Conley, Patricia R.
Comprehension Checkups Grades 1–5: Strategies for Success, by Berdell J. Akin and Patricia R. Conley (Englewood, CO: Libraries Unlimited, 1990). Reviewed in: *Curriculum Review* 31, no. 3 (Nov. 1991): 28

Continental Press
Teaching Reading Skills, by B. C. Holmes (Elizabethtown, PA: Continental Press, 1988). Reviewed in: *Reading Teacher* 43, no. 7 (Mar. 1990): 503

Coronet/MTI
The Early Romantic Age, video (Deerfield, IL: Coronet/MTI, 1990). Reviewed in: *School Library Journal* 37, no. 6 (Jun. 1991)

Crisman, Ruth
Hot Off the Press, by Ruth Crisman (Minneapolis: Lerner, 1991). *Curriculum Review* 31, no. 1 (Sept. 1991): 28

Critical thinking
Understanding Unreliable Narrators: Reading between the Lines in the Literature Classroom, by Michael W. Smith (Urbana, IL: National Council of Teachers of English, 1991). Reviewed in: *Curriculum Review* 31, no. 2 (Oct. 1991): 28–29

Cushenbery, Donald C.
Building Elementary Reading Skills through Whole Language and Literature, by Donald C. Cushenbery (Springfield, IL: Charles C. Thomas, 1989). Reviewed in: *Curriculum Review* 30, no. 3 (Nov. 1990): 27

Comprehensive Reading Strategies for All Secondary Students, by Donald C. Cushenbery (Springfield, IL: Charles C. Thomas, 1988). Reviewed in: *Journal of Reading* 33, no. 6 (Mar. 1990): 477

Dalton, Marianne and Rick
The Student's Guide to Good Writing, by Marianne Dalton and Rick Dalton (New York: College Board Publications, 1990). Reviewed in: *Journal of Reading* 34, no. 1 (Sept. 1990): 76

Daniels, Harvey
Teaching Writing in the Junior and Senior High Schools, by Harvey Daniels and Steven Zemelman (Portsmouth, NH: Heinemann, 1988). Reviewed in: *Reading Research and Instruction* 30, no. 1 (Fall 1990): 72

Danny and the Dinosaur
video (Weston, CT: Weston Woods, 1990). Reviewed in: *School Library Journal* 37, no. 2 (Feb. 1991): 52

Davidson, Josephine
Teaching and Dramatizing Greek Myths, by Josephine Davidson (Englewood, CO: Libraries Unlimited, 1989). Reviewed in: *Curriculum Review* 30, no. 3 (Nov. 1990): 28

Davidson and Associates
Headline Harry and the Great Paper Race, software (Torrance, CA: Davidson and Associates, 1991). Reviewed in: *Media and Methods* 28, no. 2 (Nov./Dec. 1991): 56

Team Series: Reading Comprehension, software (Torrance, CA: Davidson and Associates, 1990). Reviewed in: *Journal of Reading* 34, no. 5 (Feb. 1991): 410

Team Series: Vocabulary, software (Torrance, CA: Davidson and Associates, 1990). Reviewed in: *School Library Journal* 37, no. 5 (May 1991): 55

Dougill, P.
The Primary Language Book, by P. Dougill and R. Knott (Buckingham, England: Open Univ. Press, 1988; distr. by Taylor & Francis, New York). Reviewed in: *Child Language Teaching and Therapy* 6, no. 1 (Feb. 1990): 103

Drama
Teaching and Dramatizing Greek Myths, by Josephine Davidson (Englewood, CO: Libraries Unlimited, 1989). Reviewed in: *Curriculum Review* 30, no. 3 (Nov. 1990): 28

The Early Romantic Age
video (Deerfield, IL: Coronet/MTI, 1990). Reviewed in: *School Library Journal* 37, no. 6 (Jun. 1991)

Educational Computing Corp.
Grammar Monsters, software (n.p.: Educational Computing, 1991). Reviewed in: *School Library Journal* 37, no. 7 (July 1991): 33

Spelling Puzzles and Tests, software (n.p.: Educational Computing Corp., n.d.). Reviewed in: *School Library Journal* 37, no. 3 (Mar. 1991): 142

Educational Design (publishers)
Good Sentences, by Steve Wiesinger (New York: Educational Design, 1990). Reviewed in: *Curriculum Review* 30, no. 9 (May 1991): 26

Educators Publishing Service
Keeping A Head in School: A Student's Book about Learning Abilities and Learning Disorders, by Dr. Melvin D. Levine (Cambridge, MA: Educators Publishing Service, 1990). Reviewed in: *Journal of Reading* 34, no. 4 (Dec./Jan. 1990–91): 317

Elementary materials
Bookshelf Stage 1, by F. Bolton, R. Green, J. Pollock, B. Scarff, and D. Snowball (New York: Scholastic, 1986). Reviewed in: *Reading Teacher* 43, no. 8 (Apr. 1990): 592

Building Elementary Reading Skills through Whole Language and Literature, by Donald C. Cushenbery (Springfield, IL: Charles C. Thomas, 1989). Reviewed in: *Curriculum Review* 30, no. 3 (Nov. 1990): 27

Comprehension Checkups Grades 1–5: Strategies for Success, by Berdell J. Akin and Patricia R. Conley (Englewood, CO: Libraries Unlimited, 1990). Reviewed in: *Curriculum Review* 31, no. 3 (Nov. 1991): 28

Danny and the Dinosaur, video (Weston, CT: Weston Woods, 1990). Reviewed in: *School Library Journal* 37, no. 2 (Feb. 1991): 52

European Folk Tales, video (Chatsworth, CA: Aims Media, 1990). Reviewed in: *School Library Journal* 37, no. 10 (Oct. 1991): 73

Following the Drinking Gourd, video (n.p.: American School, n.d.). Reviewed in: *School Library Journal* 37, no. 2 (Feb. 1991): 53

The Fool and the Flying Ship, video (Universal City, CA: Uni, 1991). Reviewed in: *School Library Journal* 37, no. 12 (Dec. 1991): 63

Grammar Monsters, software (n.p.: Educational Computing, 1991). Reviewed in: *School Library Journal* 37, no. 7 (July 1991): 33

The Happy Lion, video (Weston, CT: Weston Woods, 1991). Reviewed in: *School Library Journal* 37, no. 1 (Jan. 1991): 56–57

Hot Off the Press, by Ruth Crisman (Minneapolis: Lerner, 1991). *Curriculum Review* 31, no. 1 (Sept. 1991): 28

Elementary materials *(cont'd)*
Journal Keeping with Young People, by Kathleen Phillips and Barbara Steiner (Englewood, CO: Libraries Unlimited, 1991). Reviewed in: *Curriculum Review* 31, no. 3 (Nov. 1991): 28

Leap into Learning, by Kristen Bissinger and Nancy Renfro (Austin: Nancy Renfro Studios, 1990). Reviewed in: *Curriculum Review* 31, no. 7 (Mar. 1992): 26

Learning through Literature, by Carol Sue Kruise (Englewood, CO: Libraries Unlimited, 1990). Reviewed in: *Curriculum Guide* 30, no. 8 (Apr. 1991): 29–30

Listening: The Basic Connection, by M. Micallef (Carthage, IL: Good Apple, 1984). Reviewed in: *Reading Teacher* 43, no. 9 (May 1990): 675–76

The Little Snowgirl, video (n.p.: American School, n.d.). Reviewed in: *School Library Journal* 37, no. 10 (Oct. 1991): 80

Madeline and the Bad Hat, video (Weston, CT: Weston Woods, 1991). Reviewed in: *School Library Journal* 37, no. 3 (Mar. 1991): 150

Max's Library: Beginning to Write, video (Chicago: SVE, 1991). Reviewed in: *School Library Journal* 37, no. 9 (Sept. 1991): 212

Reading Beyond the Basal Plus, by D. Roettager (Logan, IA: Perfect Form, 1989). Reviewed in: *Reading Teacher* 43, no. 8 (Apr. 1990): 593

Reading Skills Registrar, by K. Smith (Laguna Niguel, CA: The Monkey Sisters, 1983). Reviewed in: *Reading Teacher* 43, no. 7 (Mar. 1990): 503

S-P-E-L-L: The Reading/Writing Connection Grade 4, software (Pleasantville, NY: Sunburst Communications, 1990). Reviewed in: *School Library Journal* 37, no. 9 (Sept. 1991): 204

Spelling Strategies You Can Teach, by Mary Tarasoff (Victoria, Canada: M. V. Egan, 1990). Reviewed in: *Curriculum Review* 30, no. 3 (Nov. 1990): 27

Spelling Puzzles and Tests, software (n.p.: Educational Computing Corp., n.d.). Re-viewed in: *School Library Journal* 37, no. 3 (Mar. 1991): 142

Stepping Into Reading, by V. Herold (Cleveland: Modern Curriculum Press, 1988). Reviewed in: *Reading Teacher* 43, no. 7 (Mar. 1990): 503

Stories and More, software (Boca Raton, FL: IBM, n.d.). *Technology and Learning* 12, no. 4 (Jan. 1992): 17–18

Story Tailor, software (Hood River, OR: Humanities Software, 1989). Reviewed in: *Reading Horizons* 30, no. 3 (Apr. 1990): 258

Super Solvers Spellbound, software (Fremont, CA: The Learning Company, 1991). Reviewed in: *Technology and Learning* 12, no. 6 (Mar. 1992): 11–14

Teaching Reading Skills, by B. C. Holmes (Elizabethtown, PA: Continental Press, 1988). Reviewed in: *Reading Teacher* 43, no. 7 (Mar. 1990): 503

The Whole Language Source Book, by Jane Baskwill and Paulette Whitman (Ontario, Canada: Scholastic, 1986). Reviewed in: *Language Arts* 68, no. 2 (Feb. 1991): 150

The Wind in the Willows, video (Princeton: Films for the Humanities, 1991). Reviewed in: *School Library Journal* 37, no. 9 (Sept. 1991): 126

Wordtis, software (Alameda, CA: Spectrum HoloByte, 1991). Reviewed in: *Technology and Learning* 12, no. 6 (Mar. 92): 6

World of Reading, software (Fairfield: Queue, 1989). Reviewed in: *Curriculum Review* 30, no. 4 (Dec. 1990): 28

The Writing-Center School Edition, software (Fremont, CA: The Learning Company, 1991). Reviewed in: *Technology and Learning* 12, no. 3 (Nov./Dec. 1991): 9

The English Classroom in the Computer Age: Thirty Lesson Plans
ed. by William Wresch (Urbana, IL: National Council of Teachers of English, 1991). Re-viewed in: *Curriculum Review* 31, no. 4 (Nov. 1991): 28–9

ERIC Clearinghouse on Reading and Communication Skills
Writing Exercises for High School Students, by Barbara Vulaggio (Bloomington, IN: ERIC Clearinghouse on Reading and Communication Skills, 1989). Reviewed in: *Journal of Reading* 34, no. 7 (Apr. 1991): 577–78

European Folk Tales
video (Chatsworth, CA: Aims Media, 1990). Reviewed in: *School Library Journal* 37, no. 10 (Oct. 1991): 73

Fearon Teacher Aids
Writers Triangle: A Literature-based Writing Program, by Carla Heymsfeld and Joan Lewis (Belmont, CA: Fearon Teacher Aids, 1989). Reviewed in: *Journal of Reading* 34, no. 3 (Nov. 1990): 232

Films for the Humanities
The Wind in the Willows, video (Princeton: Films for the Humanities, 1991). Reviewed in: *School Library Journal* 37, no. 9 (Sept. 1991): 126

Films/videos
Danny and the Dinosaur, video (Weston, CT: Weston Woods, 1990). Reviewed in: *School Library Journal* 37, no. 2 (Feb. 1991): 52

The Early Romantic Age, video (Deerfield, IL: Coronet/MTI, 1990). Reviewed in: *School Library Journal* 37, no. 6 (Jun. 1991)

European Folk Tales, video (Chatsworth, CA: Aims Media, 1990). Reviewed in: *School Library Journal* 37, no. 10 (Oct. 1991): 73

Following the Drinking Gourd, video (Chicago: American School, n.d.). Reviewed in: *School Library Journal* 37, no. 2 (Feb. 1991): 53

The Fool and the Flying Ship, video (Universal City, CA: Uni, 1991). Reviewed in: *School Library Journal* 37, no. 12 (Dec. 1991): 63

The Happy Lion, video (Weston, CT: Weston Woods, 1991). Reviewed in: *School Library Journal* 37, no. 1 (Jan. 1991): 56–57

The Little Snowgirl, video (Chicago: American School, n.d.). Reviewed in: *School Library Journal* 37, no. 10 (Oct. 1991): 80

Madeline and the Bad Hat, video (Weston, CT: Weston Woods, 1991). Reviewed in: *School Library Journal* 37, no. 3 (Mar. 1991): 150

Max's Library: Beginning to Write, video (Chicago: SVE, 1991). Reviewed in: *School Library Journal* 37, no. 9 (Sept. 1991): 212

The Princess and the Dragon/Scaredy Cats, video (New York: Child's Play, 1990). Reviewed in: *School Library Journal* 37, no. 6 (Jun. 1991): 60–61

The Secret Life of the Underwear Champ, video (Chicago: American School, 1989). Reviewed in: *School Library Journal* 37, no. 1 (Jan. 1991): 60–61

The Storyteller Series: Serena of the River, video (Derry, NH: Chip Taylor Communications, 1991). Reviewed in: *School Library Journal* 37, no. 12 (Dec. 1991): 64

The Wind in the Willows, video (Princeton: Films for the Humanities, 1991). Reviewed in: *School Library Journal* 37, no. 9 (Sept. 1991): 126

Following the Drinking Gourd
video (Chicago: American School, n.d.). Reviewed in: *School Library Journal* 37, no. 2 (Feb. 1991): 53

Folklore
European Folk Tales, video (Chatsworth, CA: Aims Media, 1990). Reviewed in: *School Library Journal* 37, no. 10 (Oct. 1991): 73

Student Worlds, Student Words: Teaching Writing through Folklore, by Elizabeth Radin Simons (Portsmouth, NH: Heinemann, 1990). Reviewed in: *The Reading Teacher* 45, no. 4 (Dec. 1991): 327

The Fool and the Flying Ship
video (Universal City, CA: Uni, 1991). Reviewed in: *School Library Journal* 37, no. 12 (Dec. 1991): 63

Good Apple
Listening: The Basic Connection, by M. Micallef (Carthage, IL: Good Apple, 1984). Reviewed in: *Reading Teacher* 43, no. 9 (May 1990): 675–76

Good Sentences
by Steve Wiesinger (New York: Educational Design, 1990). Reviewed in: *Curriculum Review* 30, no. 9 (May 1991): 26

Grammar (*see also* Writing skills)
Good Sentences, by Steve Wiesinger (New York: Educational Design, 1990). Reviewed in: *Curriculum Review* 30, no. 9 (May 1991): 26

Grammar Monsters, software (n.p.: Educational Computing, 1991). Reviewed in: *School Library Journal* 37, no. 7 (July 1991): 33

Green, R.
Bookshelf Stage 1, by F. Bolton, R. Green, J. Pollock, B. Scarff, and D. Snowball (New York: Scholastic, 1986). Reviewed in: *Reading Teacher* 43, no. 8 (Apr. 1990): 592

Haggard, M. R.
Thinking about Reading, by M. R. Haggard and R. B. Ruddell (Cleveland: Modern Curriculum Press, 1987). Reviewed in: *Reading Teacher* 43, no. 7 (Mar. 1990): 503

The Happy Lion
video (Weston, CT: Weston Woods, 1991). Reviewed in: *School Library Journal* 37, no. 1 (Jan. 1991): 56–57

Headline Harry and the Great Paper Race
software (Torrance, CA: Davidson and Associates, 1991). Reviewed in: *Media and Methods* 28, no. 2 (Nov./Dec. 1991): 56

Heinemann
Books Alive! Using Literature in the Classroom, by Susan Hill (Portsmouth, NH: Heinemann, 1986). Reviewed in: *Language Arts* 68, no. 2 (Feb. 1991): 149

Student Worlds, Student Words: Teaching Writing through Folklore, by Elizabeth Radin Simons (Portsmouth, NH: Heinemann, 1990). Reviewed in: *The Reading Teacher* 45, no. 4 (Dec. 1991): 327

Teaching Writing in the Junior and Senior High Schools, by Harvey Daniels and Steven Zemelman (Portsmouth, NH: Heinemann, 1988). Reviewed in: *Reading Research and Instruction* 30, no. 1 (Fall 1990): 72

Herold, V.
Stepping Into Reading, by V. Herold (Cleveland: Modern Curriculum Press, 1988). Reviewed in: *Reading Teacher* 43, no. 7 (Mar. 1990): 503

Heymsfeld, Carla
Writers Triangle: A Literature-based Writing Program, by Carla Heymsfeld and Joan Lewis (Belmont, CA: Fearon Teacher Aids, 1989). Reviewed in: *Journal of Reading* 34, no. 3 (Nov. 1990): 232

High school materials
All Sides of the Issue: Activities for Cooperative Jigsaw Groups, by Elizabeth Coelho, Lise Winer, and Judy Winn-Bell (Old Tappan, NJ: Prentice Hall, 1989). Reviewed in: *Journal of Reading* 34, no. 2 (Oct. 1990): 156

Books Alive! Using Literature in the Classroom, by Susan Hill (Portsmouth, NH: Heinemann, 1986). Reviewed in: *Language Arts* 68, no. 2 (Feb. 1991): 149

Comprehensive Reading Strategies for All Secondary Students, by Donald C. Cushenbery (Springfield, IL: Charles C. Thomas, 1988). Reviewed in: *Journal of Reading* 33, no. 6 (Mar. 1990): 477

The Early Romantic Age, video (Deerfield, IL: Coronet/MTI, 1990). Reviewed in: *School Library Journal* 37, no. 6 (Jun. 1991)

The English Classroom in the Computer Age: Thirty Lesson Plans, ed. by William Wresch (Urbana, IL: National Council of Teachers of English, 1991). Reviewed in: *Curriculum Review* 31, no. 4 (Nov. 1991): 28–9

Headline Harry and the Great Paper Race, software (Torrance, CA: Davidson and Associates, 1991). Reviewed in: *Media and Methods* 28, no. 2 (Nov./Dec. 1991): 56

Keeping A Head in School: A Student's Book about Learning Abilities and Learning Disorders, by Dr. Melvin D. Levine (Cambridge, MA: Educators Publishing Service, 1990). Reviewed in: *Journal of Reading* 34, no. 4 (Dec./Jan. 1990–91): 317

High school materials *(cont'd)*

Novels of Initiation: A Guidebook for Teaching Literature to Adolescents, by David Peck (New York: Teachers College Press, 1989). Reviewed in: *Adolescents* 25, no. 100 (Winter 1990): 999

One of a Kind: Creativity with Words, software (Pleasantville, NY: Sunburst Communications, 1989). Reviewed in: *Journal of Reading* 34, no. 2 (Oct. 1990): 154

Opening the Door to Classroom Research, ed. by Mary W. Olson (Newark, DE: International Reading Association, 1990). Reviewed in: *Journal of Reading* 34, no. 1 (Sept. 1990): 80

Personal Press, software (San Diego: Silicon Beach Software, 1992). Reviewed in: *Technology & Learning* 12, no. 1 (Sept. 1991): 9–10

Reader's Quest, software (Hood River, OR: Humanities Software, 1990). Reviewed in: *Journal of Reading* 33, no. 7 (Apr. 1990): 569–70

SEEN: Tutorials for Critical Reading, software (Iowa City: CONDUIT, 1989). Reviewed in: *Journal of Reading* 33, no. 6 (Mar. 1990): 476

Spelling Puzzles and Tests, software (n.p.: Educational Computing Corp., n.d.). Reviewed in: *School Library Journal* 37, no. 3 (Mar. 1991): 142

Student Worlds, Student Words: Teaching Writing through Folklore, by Elizabeth Radin Simons (Portsmouth, NH: Heinemann, 1990). Reviewed in: *The Reading Teacher* 45, no. 4 (Dec. 1991): 327

The Student's Guide to Good Writing, by Marianne Dalton and Rick Dalton (New York: College Board Publications, 1990). Reviewed in: *Journal of Reading* 34, no. 1 (Sept. 1990): 76

Teaching Writing in the Junior and Senior High Schools, by Harvey Daniels and Steven Zemelman (Portsmouth, NH: Heinemann, 1988). Reviewed in: *Reading Research and Instruction* 30, no. 1 (Fall 1990): 72

Team Series: Reading Comprehension, software (Torrance, CA: Davidson and Associates,

1990). Reviewed in: *Journal of Reading* 34, no. 5 (Feb. 1991): 410

Team Series: Vocabulary, software (Torrance, CA: Davidson and Associates, 1990). Reviewed in: *School Library Journal* 37, no. 5 (May 1991): 55

Text Book: An Introduction to Literary Language, by Nancy R. Comley, Robert Scholes, and Gregory L. Ulmer (New York: St. Martin's, 1988). Reviewed in: *English Journal* 79, no. 5 (Sept. 1990): 98

Understanding Unreliable Narrators: Reading between the Lines in the Literature Classroom, by Michael W. Smith (Urbana, IL: National Council of Teachers of English, 1991). Reviewed in: *Curriculum Review* 31, no. 2 (Oct. 1991): 28–29

Word Weaving: A Creative Approach to Reading and Writing Poetry, by David M. Johnson (Urbana, IL: National Council of Teachers of English, 1990). Reviewed in: *Curriculum Review* 30, no. 6 (Feb. 1991): 27–8

Write On!, software (Hood River, OR: Humanities Software, 1989). Reviewed in: *Journal of Reading* 34, no. 4 (Dec./Jan. 1990–91): 314

Write Source 2000, by Dave Kemper, Verne Meyer, and Patrick Sebranek (Burlington, WI: Write Source Educational, 1990). Reviewed in: *Curriculum Review* 31, no. 1 (Sept. 1991): 28

Writing Exercises for High School Students, by Barbara Vulaggio (Bloomington, IN: ERIC Clearinghouse on Reading and Communication Skills, 1989). Reviewed in: *Journal of Reading* 34, no. 7 (Apr. 1991): 577–78

The Writing-Center School Edition, software (Fremont, CA: The Learning Company, 1991). Reviewed in: *Technology and Learning* 12, no. 3 (Nov./Dec. 1991): 9

Hill, Susan

Books Alive! Using Literature in the Classroom, by Susan Hill (Portsmouth, NH: Heinemann, 1986). Reviewed in: *Language Arts* 68, no. 2 (Feb. 1991): 149

Holmes, B. C.
   Teaching Reading Skills, by B. C. Holmes
   (Elizabethtown, PA: Continental Press, 1988).
   Reviewed in: *Reading Teacher* 43, no. 7 (Mar.
   1990): 503

Hot Off the Press
   by Ruth Crisman (Minneapolis: Lerner, 1991).
   Curriculum Review 31, no. 1 (Sept. 1991): 28

Humanities Software
   Reader's Quest, software (Hood River, OR:
   Humanities Software, 1990). Reviewed in:
   Journal of Reading 33, no. 7 (Apr. 1990): 569–
   70

   Story Tailor, software (Hood River, OR:
   Humanities Software, 1989). Reviewed in:
   Reading Horizons 30, no. 3 (Apr. 1990): 258

   Write On!, software (Hood River, OR: Humanities Software, 1989). Reviewed in: *Journal
   of Reading* 34, no. 4 (Dec./Jan. 1990–91): 314

IBM
   Stories and More, software (Boca Raton, FL:
   IBM, n.d.). *Technology and Learning* 12, no. 4
   (Jan. 1992): 17–18

International Reading Association
   Opening the Door to Classroom Research, ed. by
   Mary W. Olson (Newark, DE: International
   Reading Association, 1990). Reviewed in:
   Journal of Reading 34, no. 1 (Sept. 1990): 80

Johnson, David M.
   *Word Weaving: A Creative Approach to Reading
   and Writing Poetry,* by David M. Johnson
   (Urbana, IL: National Council of Teachers of
   English, 1990). Reviewed in: *Curriculum
   Review* 30, no. 6 (Feb. 1991): 27–8

Journal Keeping with Young People
   by Kathleen Phillips and Barbara Steiner
   (Englewood, CO: Libraries Unlimited, 1991).
   Reviewed in: *Curriculum Review* 31, no. 3
   (Nov. 1991): 28

Journalism
   Headline Harry and the Great Paper Race,
   software (Torrance, CA: Davidson and Associates, 1991). Reviewed in: *Media and Methods*
   28, no. 2 (Nov./Dec. 1991): 56

Hot Off the Press, by Ruth Crisman (Minneapolis: Lerner, 1991). *Curriculum Review* 31, no. 1
(Sept. 1991): 28

*Keeping A Head in School: A Student's Book about
Learning Abilities and Learning Disorders*
   by Dr. Melvin D. Levine (Cambridge, MA:
   Educators Publishing Service, 1990). Reviewed
   in: *Journal of Reading* 34, no. 4 (Dec./Jan.
   1990–91): 317

Kemper, Dave
   Write Source 2000, by Dave Kemper, Verne
   Meyer, and Patrick Sebranek (Burlington, WI:
   Write Source Educational, 1990). Reviewed
   in: *Curriculum Review* 31, no. 1 (Sept. 1991): 28

Knott, R.
   The Primary Language Book, by P. Dougill and
   R. Knott (Buckingham, England: Open Univ.
   Press, 1988; distr. by Taylor & Francis, New
   York). Reviewed in: *Child Language Teaching
   and Therapy* 6, no. 1 (Feb. 1990): 103

Kruise, Carol Sue
   Learning through Literature, by Carol Sue
   Kruise (Englewood, CO: Libraries Unlimited,
   1990). Reviewed in: *Curriculum Guide* 30, no.
   8 (Apr. 1991): 29–30

Leap into Learning
   by Kristen Bissinger and Nancy Renfro (Austin: Nancy Renfro Studios, 1990). Reviewed
   in: *Curriculum Review* 31, no. 7 (Mar. 1992): 26

The Learning Company
   Super Solvers Spellbound, software (Fremont,
   CA: The Learning Company, 1991). Reviewed
   in: *Technology and Learning* 12, no. 6 (Mar.
   1992): 11–14

   The Writing-Center School Edition, software
   (Fremont, CA: The Learning Company, 1991).
   Reviewed in: *Technology and Learning* 12, no. 3
   (Nov./Dec. 1991): 9

Learning skills
   *Keeping A Head in School: A Student's Book
   about Learning Abilities and Learning Disorders,*
   by Dr. Melvin D. Levine (Cambridge, MA:
   Educators Publishing Service, 1990). Reviewed
   in: *Journal of Reading* 34, no. 4 (Dec./Jan.
   1990–91): 317

Learning skills *(cont'd)*
   Leap into Learning, by Kristen Bissinger and
   Nancy Renfro (Austin: Nancy Renfro Studios,
   1990). Reviewed in: *Curriculum Review* 31, no.
   7 (Mar. 1992): 26

Learning through Literature
   by Carol Sue Kruise (Englewood, CO: Libraries Unlimited, 1990). Reviewed in: *Curriculum
   Guide* 30, no. 8 (Apr. 1991): 29–30

Lerner (publishers)
   Hot Off the Press, by Ruth Crisman (Minneapo-
   lis: Lerner, 1991). *Curriculum Review* 31, no. 1
   (Sept. 1991): 28

Lesson plans (*see also* Activities)
   *The English Classroom in the Computer Age:
   Thirty Lesson Plans,* ed. by William Wresch
   (Urbana, IL: National Council of Teachers of
   English, 1991). Reviewed in: *Curriculum
   Review* 31, no. 4 (Nov. 1991): 28–9

Levine, Melvin D.
   *Keeping A Head in School: A Student's Book
   about Learning Abilities and Learning Disorders,*
   by Dr. Melvin D. Levine (Cambridge, MA:
   Educators Publishing Service, 1990). Reviewed
   in: *Journal of Reading* 34, no. 4 (Dec./Jan.
   1990–91): 317

Lewis, Joan
   *Writers Triangle: A Literature-based Writing
   Program,* by Carla Heymsfeld and Joan Lewis
   (Belmont, CA: Fearon Teacher Aids, 1989).
   Reviewed in: *Journal of Reading* 34, no. 3 (Nov.
   1990): 232

Libraries Unlimited
   *Comprehension Checkups Grades 1–5: Strategies
   for Success,* by Berdell J. Akin and Patricia R.
   Conley (Englewood, CO: Libraries Unlimited,
   1990). Reviewed in: *Curriculum Review* 31, no.
   3 (Nov. 1991): 28

   Journal Keeping with Young People, by Kathleen
   Phillips and Barbara Steiner (Englewood, CO:
   Libraries Unlimited, 1991). Reviewed in:
   Curriculum Review 31, no. 3 (Nov. 1991): 28

   Learning through Literature, by Carol Sue
   Kruise (Englewood, CO: Libraries Unlimited,
   1990). Reviewed in: *Curriculum Guide* 30, no.
   8 (Apr. 1991): 29–30

Teaching and Dramatizing Greek Myths, by
   Josephine Davidson (Englewood, CO: Librar-
   ies Unlimited, 1989). Reviewed in: *Curriculum
   Review* 30, no. 3 (Nov. 1990): 28

Listening: The Basic Connection
   by M. Micallef (Carthage, IL: Good Apple,
   1984). Reviewed in: *Reading Teacher* 43, no. 9
   (May 1990): 675–76

Literature
   Books Alive! Using Literature in the Classroom,
   by Susan Hill (Portsmouth, NH: Heinemann,
   1986). Reviewed in: *Language Arts* 68, no. 2
   (Feb. 1991): 149

   Bookshelf Stage 1, by F. Bolton, R. Green, J.
   Pollock, B. Scarff, and D. Snowball (New York:
   Scholastic, 1986). Reviewed in: *Reading
   Teacher* 43, no. 8 (Apr. 1990): 592

   *Building Elementary Reading Skills through
   Whole Language and Literature,* by Donald C.
   Cushenbery (Springfield, IL: Charles C.
   Thomas, 1989). Reviewed in: *Curriculum
   Review* 30, no. 3 (Nov. 1990): 27

   The Early Romantic Age, video (Deerfield, IL:
   Coronet/MTI, 1990). Reviewed in: *School
   Library Journal* 37, no. 6 (Jun. 1991)

   European Folk Tales, video (Chatsworth, CA:
   Aims Media, 1990). Reviewed in: *School
   Library Journal* 37, no. 10 (Oct. 1991): 73

   Following the Drinking Gourd, video (n.p.:
   American School, n.d.). Reviewed in: *School
   Library Journal* 37, no. 2 (Feb. 1991): 53

   Learning through Literature, by Carol Sue
   Kruise (Englewood, CO: Libraries Unlimited,
   1990). Reviewed in: *Curriculum Guide* 30, no.
   8 (Apr. 1991): 29–30

   *Novels of Initiation: A Guidebook for Teaching
   Literature to Adolescents,* by David Peck (New
   York: Teachers College Press, 1989). Reviewed in: *Adolescents* 25, no. 100 (Winter
   1990): 999

   Success with Literature, software (New York:
   Scholastic Software, 1989). Reviewed in:
   Journal of Reading 34, no. 3 (Nov. 1990): 231

Literature *(cont'd)*

Teaching and Dramatizing Greek Myths, by Josephine Davidson (Englewood, CO: Libraries Unlimited, 1989). Reviewed in: *Curriculum Review* 30, no. 3 (Nov. 1990): 28

Text Book: An Introduction to Literary Language, by Nancy R. Comley, Robert Scholes, and Gregory L. Ulmer (New York: St. Martin's, 1988). Reviewed in: *English Journal* 79, no. 5 (Sept. 1990): 98

Understanding Unreliable Narrators: Reading between the Lines in the Literature Classroom, by Michael W. Smith (Urbana, IL: National Council of Teachers of English, 1991). Reviewed in: *Curriculum Review* 31, no. 2 (Oct. 1991): 28–29

Watership Down, software, by Bev Nelson and Sue Warren (Pleasantville, NY: Sunburst Communications, n.d.). Reviewed in: *Journal of Reading* 34, no. 7 (Apr. 1991): 576

The Whole Language Source Book, by Jane Baskwill and Paulette Whitman (Ontario, Canada: Scholastic, 1986). Reviewed in: *Language Arts* 68, no. 2 (Feb. 1991): 150

The Wind in the Willows, video (Princeton: Films for the Humanities, 1991). Reviewed in: *School Library Journal* 37, no. 9 (Sept. 1991): 126

Word Weaving: A Creative Approach to Reading and Writing Poetry, by David M. Johnson (Urbana, IL: National Council of Teachers of English, 1990). Reviewed in: *Curriculum Review* 30, no. 6 (Feb. 1991): 27–8

Writers Triangle: A Literature-based Writing Program, by Carla Heymsfeld and Joan Lewis (Belmont, CA: Fearon Teacher Aids, 1989). Reviewed in: *Journal of Reading* 34, no. 3 (Nov. 1990): 232

The Little Snowgirl
video (Chicago: American School, n.d.). Reviewed in: *School Library Journal* 37, no. 10 (Oct. 1991): 80

M. V. Egan (publishers)
Spelling Strategies You Can Teach, by Mary Tarasoff (Victoria, Canada: M. V. Egan, 1990).

Reviewed in: *Curriculum Review* 30, no. 3 (Nov. 1990): 27

Macmillan
Write Ahead, by Tom Barnard (New York: Macmillan, 1989). Reviewed in: *Child Language Teaching and Therapy* 6, no. 1 (Feb. 1990): 104–5

Madeline and the Bad Hat
video (Weston, CT: Weston Woods, 1991). Reviewed in: *School Library Journal* 37, no. 3 (Mar. 1991): 150

Max's Library: Beginning to Write
video (Chicago: SVE, 1991). Reviewed in: *School Library Journal* 37, no. 9 (Sept. 1991): 212

Meyer, Verne
Write Source 2000, by Dave Kemper, Verne Meyer, and Patrick Lewis (Burlington, WI: Write Source Educational, 1990). Reviewed in: *Curriculum Review* 31, no. 1 (Sept. 1991): 28

Micallef, M.
Listening: The Basic Connection, by M. Micallef (Carthage, IL: Good Apple, 1984). Reviewed in: *Reading Teacher* 43, no. 9 (May 1990): 675–76

Middle school materials
European Folk Tales, video (Chatsworth, CA: Aims Media, 1990). Reviewed in: *School Library Journal* 37, no. 10 (Oct. 1991): 73

Following the Drinking Gourd, video (n.p.: American School, n.d.). Reviewed in: *School Library Journal* 37, no. 2 (Feb. 1991): 53

Good Sentences, by Steve Wiesinger (New York: Educational Design, 1990). Reviewed in: *Curriculum Review* 30, no. 9 (May 1991): 26

One of a Kind: Creativity with Words, software (Pleasantville, NY: Sunburst Communications, 1989). Reviewed in: *Journal of Reading* 34, no. 2 (Oct. 1990): 154

Personal Press, software (San Diego: Silicon Beach Software, 1992). Reviewed in: *Technology & Learning* 12, no. 1 (Sept. 1991): 9–10

Middle school materials *(cont'd)*
Reader's Quest, software (Hood River, OR: Humanities Software, 1990). Reviewed in: *Journal of Reading* 33, no. 7 (Apr. 1990): 569–70

The Secret Life of the Underwear Champ, video (n.p.: American School, 1989). Reviewed in: *School Library Journal* 37, no. 1 (Jan. 1991): 60–61

The Storyteller Series: Serena of the River, video (Derry, NH: Chip Taylor Communications, 1991). Reviewed in: *School Library Journal* 37, no. 12 (Dec. 1991): 64

Student Worlds, Student Words: Teaching Writing through Folklore, by Elizabeth Radin Simons (Portsmouth, NH: Heinemann, 1990). Reviewed in: *The Reading Teacher* 45, no. 4 (Dec. 1991): 327

Success with Literature, software (New York: Scholastic Software, 1989). Reviewed in: *Journal of Reading* 34, no. 3 (Nov. 1990): 231

Teaching Writing in the Junior and Senior High Schools, by Harvey Daniels and Steven Zemelman (Portsmouth, NH: Heinemann, 1988). Reviewed in: *Reading Research and Instruction* 30, no. 1 (Fall 1990): 72

Teaching and Dramatizing Greek Myths, by Josephine Davidson (Englewood, CO: Libraries Unlimited, 1989). Reviewed in: *Curriculum Review* 30, no. 3 (Nov. 1990): 28

Team Series: Vocabulary, software (Torrance, CA: Davidson and Associates, 1990). Reviewed in: *School Library Journal* 37, no. 5 (May 1991): 55

Watership Down, software, by Bev Nelson and Sue Warren (Pleasantville, NY: Sunburst Communications, n.d.). Reviewed in: *Journal of Reading* 34, no. 7 (Apr. 1991): 576

Write Source 2000, by Dave Kemper, Verne Meyer, and Patrick Sebranek (Burlington, WI: Write Source Educational, 1990). Reviewed in: *Curriculum Review* 31, no. 1 (Sept. 1991): 28

Write Ahead, by Tom Barnard (New York: Macmillan, 1989). Reviewed in: *Child Language Teaching and Therapy* 6, no. 1 (Feb. 1990): 104–5

Writers Triangle: A Literature-based Writing Program, by Carla Heymsfeld and Joan Lewis (Belmont, CA: Fearon Teacher Aids, 1989). Reviewed in: *Journal of Reading* 34, no. 3 (Nov. 1990): 232

Modern Curriculum Press
Stepping Into Reading, by V. Herold (Cleveland: Modern Curriculum Press, 1988). Reviewed in: *Reading Teacher* 43, no. 7 (Mar. 1990): 503

Thinking about Reading, by M. R. Haggard and R. B. Ruddell (Cleveland: Modern Curriculum Press, 1987). Reviewed in: *Reading Teacher* 43, no. 7 (Mar. 1990): 503

The Monkey Sisters (publishers)
Reading Skills Registrar, by K. Smith (Laguna Niguel, CA: The Monkey Sisters, 1983). Reviewed in: *Reading Teacher* 43, no. 7 (Mar. 1990): 503

Mythology
Teaching and Dramatizing Greek Myths, by Josephine Davidson (Englewood, CO: Libraries Unlimited, 1989). Reviewed in: *Curriculum Review* 30, no. 3 (Nov. 1990): 28

Nancy Renfro Studios
Leap into Learning, by Kristen Bissinger and Nancy Renfro (Austin: Nancy Renfro Studios, 1990). Reviewed in: *Curriculum Review* 31, no. 7 (Mar. 1992): 26

National Council of Teachers of English
The English Classroom in the Computer Age: Thirty Lesson Plans, ed. by William Wresch (Urbana, IL: National Council of Teachers of English, 1991). Reviewed in: *Curriculum Review* 31, no. 4 (Nov. 1991): 28–9

Understanding Unreliable Narrators: Reading between the Lines in the Literature Classroom, by Michael W. Smith (Urbana, IL: National Council of Teachers of English, 1991). Reviewed in: *Curriculum Review* 31, no. 2 (Oct. 1991): 28–29

National Council of Teachers of English *(cont'd)*
Word Weaving: A Creative Approach to Reading and Writing Poetry, by David M. Johnson (Urbana, IL: National Council of Teachers of English, 1990). Reviewed in: *Curriculum Review* 30, no. 6 (Feb. 1991): 27–8

Nelson, Bev
Watership Down, software, by Bev Nelson and Sue Warren (Pleasantville, NY: Sunburst Communications, n.d.). Reviewed in: *Journal of Reading* 34, no. 7 (Apr. 1991): 576

Novels of Initiation: A Guidebook for Teaching Literature to Adolescents
by David Peck (New York: Teachers College Press, 1989). Reviewed in: *Adolescents* 25, no. 100 (Winter 1990): 999

Olson, Mary W., ed.
Opening the Door to Classroom Research, ed. by Mary W. Olson (Newark, DE: International Reading Association, 1990). Reviewed in: *Journal of Reading* 34, no. 1 (Sept. 1990): 80

One of a Kind: Creativity with Words
software (Pleasantville, NY: Sunburst Communications, 1989). Reviewed in: *Journal of Reading* 34, no. 2 (Oct. 1990): 154

Open University Press
The Primary Language Book, by P. Dougill and R. Knott (Buckingham, England: Open University Press, 1988; distr. by Taylor & Francis, New York). Reviewed in: *Child Language Teaching and Therapy* 6, no. 1 (Feb. 1990): 103

Opening the Door to Classroom Research
ed. by Mary W. Olson (Newark, DE: International Reading Association, 1990). Reviewed in: *Journal of Reading* 34, no. 1 (Sept. 1990): 80

Peck, David
Novels of Initiation: A Guidebook for Teaching Literature to Adolescents, by David Peck (New York: Teachers College Press, 1989). Reviewed in: *Adolescents* 25, no. 100 (Winter 1990): 999

Perfect Form
Reading Beyond the Basal Plus, by D. Roettager (Logan, IA: Perfect Form, 1989). Reviewed in: *Reading Teacher* 43, no. 8 (Apr. 1990): 593

Personal Press
software (San Diego: Silicon Beach Software, 1992). Reviewed in: *Technology & Learning* 12, no. 1 (Sept. 1991): 9–10

Phillips, Kathleen
Journal Keeping with Young People, by Kathleen Phillips and Barbara Steiner (Englewood, CO: Libraries Unlimited, 1991). Reviewed in: *Curriculum Review* 31, no. 3 (Nov. 1991): 28

Poetry
Word Weaving: A Creative Approach to Reading and Writing Poetry, by David M. Johnson (Urbana, IL: National Council of Teachers of English, 1990). Reviewed in: *Curriculum Review* 30, no. 6 (Feb. 1991): 27–8

Pollock, J.
Bookshelf Stage 1, by F. Bolton, R. Green, J. Pollock, B. Scarff, and D. Snowball (New York: Scholastic, 1986). Reviewed in: *Reading Teacher* 43, no. 8 (Apr. 1990): 592

Prentice Hall
All Sides of the Issue: Activities for Cooperative Jigsaw Groups, by Elizabeth Coelho, Lise Winer, and Judy Winn-Bell (Old Tappan, NJ: Prentice Hall, 1989). Reviewed in: *Journal of Reading* 34, no. 2 (Oct. 1990): 156

The Primary Language Book
by P. Dougill and R. Knott (Buckingham, England: Open Univ. Press, 1988; distr. by Taylor & Francis, New York). Reviewed in: *Child Language Teaching and Therapy* 6, no. 1 (Feb. 1990): 103

The Princess and the Dragon/Scaredy Cats
video (New York: Child's Play, 1990). Reviewed in: *School Library Journal* 37, no. 6 (Jun. 1991): 60–61

Queue
World of Reading, software (Fairfield: Queue, 1989). Reviewed in: *Curriculum Review* 30, no. 4 (Dec. 1990): 28

Reader's Quest
software (Hood River, OR: Humanities Software, 1990). Reviewed in: *Journal of Reading* 33, no. 7 (Apr. 1990): 569–70

Reading

All Sides of the Issue: Activities for Cooperative Jigsaw Groups, by Elizabeth Coelho, Lise Winer, and Judy Winn-Bell (Old Tappan, NJ: Prentice Hall, 1989). Reviewed in: *Journal of Reading* 34, no. 2 (Oct. 1990): 156

Books Alive! Using Literature in the Classroom, by Susan Hill (Portsmouth, NH: Heinemann, 1986). Reviewed in: *Language Arts* 68, no. 2 (Feb. 1991): 149

Bookshelf Stage 1, by F. Bolton, R. Green, J. Pollock, B. Scarff, and D. Snowball (New York: Scholastic, 1986). Reviewed in: *Reading Teacher* 43, no. 8 (Apr. 1990): 592

Building Elementary Reading Skills through Whole Language and Literature, by Donald C. Cushenbery (Springfield, IL: Charles C. Thomas, 1989). Reviewed in: *Curriculum Review* 30, no. 3 (Nov. 1990): 27

Comprehension Checkups Grades 1–5: Strategies for Success, by Berdell J. Akin and Patricia R. Conley (Englewood, CO: Libraries Unlimited, 1990). Reviewed in: *Curriculum Review* 31, no. 3 (Nov. 1991): 28

Comprehensive Reading Strategies for All Secondary Students, by Donald C. Cushenbery (Springfield, IL: Charles C. Thomas, 1988). Reviewed in: *Journal of Reading* 33, no. 6 (Mar. 1990): 477

Danny and the Dinosaur, video (Weston, CT: Weston Woods, 1990). Reviewed in: *School Library Journal* 37, no. 2 (Feb. 1991): 52

Following the Drinking Gourd, video (n.p.: American School, n.d.). Reviewed in: *School Library Journal* 37, no. 2 (Feb. 1991): 53

The Fool and the Flying Ship, video (Universal City, CA: Uni, 1991). Reviewed in: *School Library Journal* 37, no. 12 (Dec. 1991): 63

The Happy Lion, video (Weston, CT: Weston Woods, 1991). Reviewed in: *School Library Journal* 37, no. 1 (Jan. 1991): 56–57

Learning through Literature, by Carol Sue Kruise (Englewood, CO: Libraries Unlimited,

1990). Reviewed in: *Curriculum Guide* 30, no. 8 (Apr. 1991): 29–30

The Little Snowgirl, video (n.p.: American School, n.d.). Reviewed in: *School Library Journal* 37, no. 10 (Oct. 1991): 80

Madeline and the Bad Hat, video (Weston, CT: Weston Woods, 1991). Reviewed in: *School Library Journal* 37, no. 3 (Mar. 1991): 150

Max's Library: Beginning to Write, video (Chicago: SVE, 1991). Reviewed in: *School Library Journal* 37, no. 9 (Sept. 1991): 212

Novels of Initiation: A Guidebook for Teaching Literature to Adolescents, by David Peck (New York: Teachers College Press, 1989). Reviewed in: *Adolescents* 25, no. 100 (Winter 1990): 999

One of a Kind: Creativity with Words, software (Pleasantville, NY: Sunburst Communications, 1989). Reviewed in: *Journal of Reading* 34, no. 2 (Oct. 1990): 154

Opening the Door to Classroom Research, ed. by Mary W. Olson (Newark, DE: International Reading Association, 1990). Reviewed in: *Journal of Reading* 34, no. 1 (Sept. 1990): 80

The Primary Language Book, by P. Dougill and R. Knott (Buckingham, England: Open Univ. Press, 1988; distr. by Taylor & Francis, New York). Reviewed in: *Child Language Teaching and Therapy* 6, no. 1 (Feb. 1990): 103

The Princess and the Dragon/Scaredy Cats, video (New York: Child's Play, 1990). Reviewed in: *School Library Journal* 37, no. 6 (Jun. 1991): 60–61

Reader's Quest, software (Hood River, OR: Humanities Software, 1990). Reviewed in: *Journal of Reading* 33, no. 7 (Apr. 1990): 569–70

Reading Beyond the Basal Plus, by D. Roettager (Logan, IA: Perfect Form, 1989). Reviewed in: *Reading Teacher* 43, no. 8 (Apr. 1990): 593

Reading Skills Registrar, by K. Smith (Laguna Niguel, CA: The Monkey Sisters, 1983). Reviewed in: *Reading Teacher* 43, no. 7 (Mar. 1990): 503

Romantic literature
The Early Romantic Age, video (Deerfield, IL: Coronet/MTI, 1990). Reviewed in: *School Library Journal* 37, no. 6 (Jun. 1991)

Ruddell, R. B.
Thinking about Reading, by M. R. Haggard and R. B. Ruddell (Cleveland: Modern Curriculum Press, 1987). Reviewed in: *Reading Teacher* 43, no. 7 (Mar. 1990): 503

S-P-E-L-L: The Reading/Writing Connection Grade 4
software (Pleasantville, NY: Sunburst Communications, 1990). Reviewed in: *School Library Journal* 37, no. 9 (Sept. 1991): 204

St. Martin's Press
Text Book: An Introduction to Literary Language, by Nancy R. Comley, Robert Scholes, and Gregory L. Ulmer (New York: St. Martin's, 1988). Reviewed in: *English Journal* 79, no. 5 (Sept. 1990): 98

Scholastic
Bookshelf Stage 1, by F. Bolton, R. Green, J. Pollock, B. Scarff, and D. Snowball (New York: Scholastic, 1986). Reviewed in: *Reading Teacher* 43, no. 8 (Apr. 1990): 592

Success with Literature, software (New York: Scholastic Software, 1989). Reviewed in: *Journal of Reading* 34, no. 3 (Nov. 1990): 231

The Whole Language Source Book, by Jane Baskwill and Paulette Whitman (Ontario, Canada: Scholastic, 1986). Reviewed in: *Language Arts* 68, no. 2 (Feb. 1991): 150

Scholes, Robert
Text Book: An Introduction to Literary Language, by Nancy R. Comley, Robert Scholes, and Gregory L. Ulmer (New York: St. Martin's, 1988). Reviewed in: *English Journal* 79, no. 5 (Sept. 1990): 98

Scott Foresman
The Whole Language Companion, Grades 4–8, by David Clark Yager (Glenview, IL: Scott Foresman, 1991). Reviewed in: *Curriculum Review* 30, no. 7 (Mar. 1991): 27–8

Sebranek, Patrick
Write Source 2000, by Dave Kemper, Verne Meyer, and Patrick Sebranek (Burlington, WI: Write Source Educational, 1990). Reviewed in: *Curriculum Review* 31, no. 1 (Sept. 1991): 28

The Secret Life of the Underwear Champ
video (Chicago: American School, 1989). Reviewed in: *School Library Journal* 37, no. 1 (Jan. 1991): 60–61

SEEN: Tutorials for Critical Reading
software (Iowa City: CONDUIT, 1989). Reviewed in: *Journal of Reading* 33, no. 6 (Mar. 1990): 476

Silicon Beach Software
Personal Press, software (San Diego: Silicon Beach Software, 1992). Reviewed in: *Technology & Learning* 12, no. 1 (Sept. 1991): 9–10

Simons, Elizabeth Radin
Student Worlds, Student Words: Teaching Writing through Folklore, by Elizabeth Radin Simons (Portsmouth, NH: Heinemann, 1990). Reviewed in: *The Reading Teacher* 45, no. 4 (Dec. 1991): 327

Smith, K.
Reading Skills Registrar, by K. Smith (Laguna Niguel, CA: The Monkey Sisters, 1983). Reviewed in: *Reading Teacher* 43, no. 7 (Mar. 1990): 503

Smith, Michael W.
Understanding Unreliable Narrators: Reading between the Lines in the Literature Classroom, by Michael W. Smith (Urbana, IL: National Council of Teachers of English, 1991). Reviewed in: *Curriculum Review* 31, no. 2 (Oct. 1991): 28–29

Software packages
Grammar Monsters, software (n.p.: Educational Computing, 1991). Reviewed in: *School Library Journal* 37, no. 7 (July 1991): 33

Headline Harry and the Great Paper Race, software (Torrance, CA: Davidson and Associates, 1991). Reviewed in: *Media and Methods* 28, no. 2 (Nov./Dec. 1991): 56

Spelling Strategies You Can Teach
by Mary Tarasoff (Victoria, Canada: M. V. Egan, 1990). Reviewed in: *Curriculum Review* 30, no. 3 (Nov. 1990): 27

Spelling Puzzles and Tests
software (n.p.: Educational Computing Corp., n.d.). Reviewed in: *School Library Journal* 37, no. 3 (Mar. 1991): 142

Steiner, Barbara
Journal Keeping with Young People, by Kathleen Phillips and Barbara Steiner (Englewood, CO: Libraries Unlimited, 1991). Reviewed in: *Curriculum Review* 31, no. 3 (Nov. 1991): 28

Stepping Into Reading
by V. Herold (Cleveland: Modern Curriculum Press, 1988). Reviewed in: *Reading Teacher* 43, no. 7 (Mar. 1990): 503

Stories and More
software (Boca Raton, FL: IBM, n.d.). *Technology and Learning* 12, no. 4 (Jan. 1992): 17–18

Story Tailor
software (Hood River, OR: Humanities Software, 1989). Reviewed in: *Reading Horizons* 30, no. 3 (Apr. 1990): 258

The Storyteller Series: Serena of the River
video (Derry, NH: Chip Taylor Communications, 1991). Reviewed in: *School Library Journal* 37, no. 12 (Dec. 1991): 64

Student Worlds Student Words: Teaching Writing through Folklore
by Elizabeth Radin Simons (Portsmouth, NH: Heinemann, 1990). Reviewed in: *The Reading Teacher* 45, no. 4 (Dec. 1991): 327

The Student's Guide to Good Writing
by Marianne Dalton and Rick Dalton (New York: College Board Publications, 1990). Reviewed in: *Journal of Reading* 34, no. 1 (Sept. 1990): 76

Success with Literature
software (New York: Scholastic Software, 1989). Reviewed in: *Journal of Reading* 34, no. 3 (Nov. 1990): 231

Sunburst Communications
One of a Kind: Creativity with Words, software (Pleasantville, NY: Sunburst Communications, 1989). Reviewed in: *Journal of Reading* 34, no. 2 (Oct. 1990): 154

S-P-E-L-L: The Reading/Writing Connection Grade 4, software (Pleasantville, NY: Sunburst Communications, 1990). Reviewed in: *School Library Journal* 37, no. 9 (Sept. 1991): 204

Watership Down, software, by Bev Nelson and Sue Warren (Pleasantville, NY: Sunburst Communications, n.d.). Reviewed in: *Journal of Reading* 34, no. 7 (Apr. 1991): 576

Super Solvers Spellbound
software (Fremont, CA: The Learning Company, 1991). Reviewed in: *Technology and Learning* 12, no. 6 (Mar. 1992): 11–14

SVE (publishers)
Max's Library: Beginning to Write, video (Chicago: SVE, 1991). Reviewed in: *School Library Journal* 37, no. 9 (Sept. 1991): 212

Tarasoff, Mary
Spelling Strategies You Can Teach, by Mary Tarasoff (Victoria, Canada: M. V. Egan, 1990). Reviewed in: *Curriculum Review* 30, no. 3 (Nov. 1990): 27

Teachers College Press
Novels of Initiation: A Guidebook for Teaching Literature to Adolescents, by David Peck (New York: Teachers College Press, 1989). Reviewed in: *Adolescents* 25, no. 100 (Winter 1990): 999

Teaching Writing in the Junior and Senior High Schools
by Harvey Daniels and Steven Zemelman (Portsmouth, NH: Heinemann, 1988). Reviewed in: *Reading Research and Instruction* 30, no. 1 (Fall 1990): 72

Teaching Reading Skills
by B. C. Holmes (Elizabethtown, PA: Continental Press, 1988). Reviewed in: *Reading Teacher* 43, no. 7 (Mar. 1990): 503

KRAUS CURRICULUM DEVELOPMENT LIBRARY CUSTOMERS

T HE following list shows the current subscribers to the Kraus Curriculum Development Library (KCDL), Kraus's annual program of curriculum guides on microfiche. Customers marked with an asterisk (*) do not currently have standing orders to KCDL, but do have recent editions of the program. This information is provided for readers who want to use KCDL for models of curriculum in particular subject areas or grade levels.

Alabama

Auburn University
Ralph Brown Draughton Library/Serials
Mell Street
Auburn University, AL 36849

Jacksonville State University
Houston Cole Library/Serials
Jacksonville, AL 36265

University of Alabama at Birmingham
Mervyn H. Sterne Library
University Station
Birmingham, AL 35294

*University of Alabama at Tuscaloosa
University Libraries
204 Capstone Drive
Tuscaloosa, AL 35487-0266

Alaska

*University of Alaska—Anchorage
Library
3211 Providence Drive
Anchorage, AK 99508

Arizona

Arizona State University, Phoenix
Fletcher Library/Journals
West Campus
4701 West Thunderbird Road
Phoenix, AZ 85069-7100

Arizona State University, Tempe
Library/Serials
Tempe, AZ 85287-0106

Northern Arizona University
University Library
Flagstaff, AZ 86011

University of Arizona
Library/Serials
Tucson, AZ 85721

Arkansas

Arkansas State University
Dean B. Ellis Library
State University, AR 72467

Southern Arkansas University
The Curriculum Center
SAU Box 1389
Magnolia, AR 71753

University of Central Arkansas
The Center for Teaching & Human Development
Box H, Room 104
Conway, AR 72032

California

California Polytechnic State University
Library/Serials
San Luis Obispo, CA 93407

California State Polytechnic University
Library/Serials
3801 West Temple Avenue
Pomona, CA 91768

California State University at Chico
Meriam Library
Chico, CA 95929-0295

*California State University, Dominguez Hills
Library
800 East Victoria Street
Carson, CA 90747

California State University at Fresno
Henry Madden Library/Curriculum Department
Fresno, CA 93740

California State University at Fresno
College of the Sequoia Center
5241 North Maple, Mail Stop 106
Fresno, CA 93740

California State University at Fullerton
Library Serials BIC
Fullerton, CA 92634

California State University at Long Beach
Library/Serials Department
1250 Bellflower Boulevard
Long Beach, CA 90840

*California State University at Sacramento
Library
2000 Jed Smith Drive
Sacramento, CA 95819

California State University, Stanislaus
Library
801 West Monte Vista Avenue
Turlock, CA 95380

*La Sierra University
Library
Riverside, CA 92515

Los Angeles County Education Center
Professional Reference Center
9300 East Imperial Highway
Downey, CA 90242

National University
Library
4007 Camino del Rio South
San Diego, CA 92108

San Diego County Office of Education
Research and Reference Center
6401 Linda Vista Road
San Diego, CA 92111-7399

San Diego State University
Library/Serials
San Diego, CA 92182-0511

*San Francisco State University
J. Paul Leonard Library
1630 Holloway Avenue
San Francisco, CA 94132

San Jose State University
Clark Library, Media Department
San Jose, CA 95192-0028

*Stanford University
Cubberly Library
School of Education
Stanford, CA 94305

*University of California at Santa Cruz
Library
Santa Cruz, CA 95064

Colorado

Adams State College
Library
Alamosa, CO 81102

University of Northern Colorado
Michener Library
Greeley, CO 80639

Connecticut

*Central Connecticut State University
Burritt Library
1615 Stanley Street
New Britain, CT 06050

District of Columbia

The American University
Library
Washington, DC 20016-8046

*United States Department of Education/OERI
Room 101
555 New Jersey Avenue, N.W., C.P.
Washington, DC 20202-5731

*University of the District of Columbia
Learning Resource Center
11100 Harvard Street, N.W.
Washington, DC 20009

Florida

*Florida Atlantic University
Library/Serials
Boca Raton, FL 33431-0992

Florida International University
Library/Serials
Bay Vista Campus
North Miami, FL 33181

Florida International University
Library/Serials
University Park
Miami, FL 33199

Marion County School Board
Professional Library
406 S.E. Alvarez Avenue
Ocala, FL 32671-2285

*University of Central Florida
Library
Orlando, FL 32816-0666

University of Florida
Smathers Library/Serials
Gainesville, FL 32611-2047

*University of North Florida
Library
4567 St. John's Bluff Road South
Jacksonville, FL 32216

*University of South Florida
Library/University Media Center
4202 Fowler Avenue
Tampa, FL 33620

University of West Florida
John C. Pace Library/Serials
11000 University Parkway
Pensacola, FL 32514

Georgia

*Albany State College
Margaret Rood Hazard Library
Albany, GA 31705

Atlanta University Center in Georgia
Robert W. Woodruff Library
111 James P. Brawley Drive
Atlanta, GA 30314

*Columbus College
Library
Algonquin Drive
Columbus, GA 31993

Kennesaw College
TRAC
3455 Frey Drive
Kennesaw, GA 30144

University of Georgia
Main Library
Athens, GA 30602

Guam

*University of Guam
Curriculum Resources Center
College of Education
UOG Station
Mangilao, GU 96923

Idaho

*Boise State University
Curriculum Resource Center
1910 University Drive
Boise, ID 83725

Illinois

Community Consolidated School District 15
Educational Service Center
505 South Quentin Road
Palatine, IL 60067

Illinois State University
Milner Library/Periodicals
Normal, IL 61761

Loyola University
Instructional Materials Library
Lewis Towers Library
820 North Michigan Avenue
Chicago, Illinois 60611

National–Louis University
Library/Technical Services
2840 North Sheridan Road
Evanston, IL 60201

Northeastern Illinois University
Library/Serials
5500 North St. Louis Avenue
Chicago, IL 60625

*Northern Illinois University
Founders Memorial Library
DeKalb, IL 60115

Southern Illinois University
Lovejoy Library/Periodicals
Edwardsville, IL 62026

*University of Illinois at Chicago
Library/Serials
Box 8198
Chicago, IL 60680

University of Illinois at Urbana–Champaign
246 Library
1408 West Gregory Drive
Urbana, IL 61801

Indiana

Indiana State University
Cunningham Memorial Library
Terre Haute, IN 47809

Indiana University
Library/Serials
Bloomington, IN 47405-1801

Kentucky

Cumberland College
Instructional Media Library
Williamsburg, KY 40769

*Jefferson County Public Schools
The Greens Professional Development Academy
4425 Preston Highway
Louisville, KY 40213

Maine

University of Maine
Raymond H. Fogler Library/Serials
Orono, ME 04469

Maryland

*Bowie State University
Library
Jericho Park Road
Bowie, MD 20715

Western Maryland College
Hoover Library
2 College Hill
Westminster, MD 21157

Massachusetts

*Barnstable Public Schools
230 South Street
Hyannis, MA 02601

Boston College
Educational Resource Center
Campion Hall G13
Chestnut Hill, MA 02167

Framingham State College
Curriculum Library
Henry Whittemore Library
Box 2000
Framingham, MA 01701

Harvard University
School of Education
Monroe C. Gutman Library
6 Appian Way
Cambridge, MA 02138

*Lesley College
Library
30 Mellen Street
Cambridge, MA 02138

*Salem State College
Professional Studies Resource Center
Library
Lafayette Street
Salem, MA 01970

Tufts University
Wessell Library
Medford, MA 02155-5816

*University of Lowell
O'Leary Library
Wilder Street
Lowell, MA 01854

*Worcester State College
Learning Resource Center
486 Chandler Street
Worcester, MA 01602

Michigan

*Grand Valley State University
Library
Allendale, MI 49401

*Wayne County Regional Educational Servic
  Agency
Technical Services
5454 Venoy
Wayne, MI 48184

Wayne State University
Purdy Library
Detroit, MI 48202

*Western Michigan University
Dwight B. Waldo Library
Kalamazoo, MI 49008

Minnesota

Mankato State University
Memorial Library
Educational Resource Center
Mankato, MN 56002-8400

Moorhead State University
Library
Moorhead, MN 56563

University of Minnesota
170 Wilson Library/Serials
309 19th Avenue South
Minneapolis, MN 55455

Winona State University
Maxwell Library/Curriculum Laboratory
Sanborn and Johnson Streets
Winona, MN 55987

Mississippi

Mississippi State University
Mitchell Memorial Library
Mississippi State, MS 39762

University of Southern Mississippi
Cook Memorial Library/Serials
Box 5053
Hattiesburg, MS 39406-5053

Missouri

Central Missouri State University
Ward Edwards Library
Warrensburg, MO 64093-5020

Missouri Southern State College
George A. Spiva Library
3950 Newman Road
Joplin, MO 64801-1595

Northeast Missouri State University
Pickler Library/Serials
Kirksville, MO 63501

Southwest Baptist University
ESTEP Library
Bolivar, MO 65613-2496

Southwest Missouri State University
#175 Library
Springfield, MO 65804-0095

*University of Missouri at Kansas City
Instructional Materials Center
School of Education
5100 Rockhill Road
Kansas City, MO 64110-2499

University of Missouri at St. Louis
Library
St. Louis, MO 63121

Webster University
Library
470 East Lockwood Avenue
St. Louis, MO 63119-3194

Nebraska

Chadron State College
Library
10th and Main Streets
Chadron, NE 69337

University of Nebraska
University Libraries
Lincoln, NE 68588

University of Nebraska at Kearney
Calvin T. Ryan Library/Serials
Kearney, NE 68849-0700

*University of Nebraska at Omaha
Education Technology Center/Instructional
   Material
Kayser Hall, Room 522
Omaha, NE 68182-0169

Nevada

*University of Nevada, Las Vegas
Materials Center—101 Education
Las Vegas, NV 89154

*University of Nevada, Reno
Library (322)
Reno, NV 89557-0044

New Hampshire

Plymouth State College
Herbert H. Lamson Library
Plymouth, NH 03264

New Jersey

Caldwell College
Library
9 Ryerson Avenue
Caldwell, NJ 07006

Georgian Court College
Farley Memorial Library
Lakewood, NJ 08701

Jersey City State College
Forrest A. Irwin Library
2039 Kennedy Boulevard
Jersey City, NJ 07305

*Kean College of New Jersey
Library
Union, NJ 07083

Paterson Board of Education
Media Center
823 East 28th Street
Paterson, NJ 07513

*Rutgers University
Alexander Library/Serials
New Brunswick, NJ 08903

St. Peter's College
George F. Johnson Library
Kennedy Boulevard
Jersey City, NJ 07306

Trenton State College
West Library
Pennington Road CN4700
Trenton, NJ 08650-4700

William Paterson College
Library
300 Pompton Road
Wayne, NJ 07470

New Mexico

University of New Mexico
General Library/Serials
Albuquerque, NM 87131

New York

*BOCES–REPIC
Carle Place Center Concourse
234 Glen Cove Road
Carle Place, NY 11514

*Canisius College
Curriculum Materials Center
Library
2001 Main Street
Buffalo, NY 14208

Fordham University
Duane Library
Bronx, NY 10458

Hofstra University
Library
1000 Hempstead Turnpike
Hempstead, NY 11550

*Hunter College
Library
695 Park Avenue
New York, NY 10021

*Lehman College
Library/Serials
Bedford Park Boulevard West
Bronx, NY 10468

*New York University
Bobst Library
70 Washington Square South
New York, NY 10012

*Niagara University
Library/Serials
Niagara, NY 14109

Queens College
Benjamin Rosenthal Library
Flushing, NY 11367

St. John's University
Library
Grand Central and Utopia Parkways
Jamaica, NY 11439

State University of New York at Albany
University Library/Serials
1400 Washington Avenue
Albany, NY 12222

State University of New York, College at Buffalo
E. H. Butler Library
1300 Elmwood Avenue
Buffalo, NY 14222

State University of New York, College at
    Cortland
Teaching Materials Center
Cortland, NY 13045

State University of New York, College at
    Oneonta
James M. Milne Library
Oneonta, NY 13820

Teachers College of Columbia University
Millbank Memorial Library/Serials
525 West 120th Street
New York, NY 10027

North Carolina

*Appalachian State University
Instructional Materials Center
Belk Library
Boone, NC 28608

Charlotte–Mecklenburg Schools
Curriculum Resource Center
Staff Development Center
428 West Boulevard
Charlotte, NC 28203

*East Carolina University
Joyner Library
Greenville, NC 27858-4353

North Carolina A&T State University
F. D. Bluford Library
Greeensboro, NC 27411

North Carolina State University
D. H. Hill Library
Box 7111
Raleigh, NC 27695-7111

University of North Carolina at Chapel Hill
Davis Library/Serials
Campus Box 3938
Chapel Hill, NC 27599-3938

University of North Carolina at Charlotte
Atkins Library
UNCC Station
Charlotte, NC 28223

University of North Carolina at Wilmington
William M. Randall Library
601 South College Road
Wilmington, NC 28403-3297

Ohio

Bowling Green State University
Curriculum Center
Jerome Library
Bowling Green, OH 43403-0177

Miami University
Library
Oxford, OH 45056

*Ohio State University
2009 Millikin Road
Columbus, OH 43210

University of Akron
Bierce Library/Serials
Akron, OH 44325

*University of Rio Grande
Davis Library
Rio Grande, OH 45674

*Wright State University
Educational Resource Center
Dayton, OH 45435

Oklahoma

Southwestern Oklahoma State University
Al Harris Library
809 North Custer Street
Weatherford, OK 73096

*University of Tulsa
McFarlin Library
600 South College
Tulsa, OK 74104

Oregon

Oregon State University
Kerr Library/Serials
Corvallis, OR 97331-4503

Portland State University
Library/Serials
Portland, OR 97207

University of Oregon
Knight Library/Serials
Eugene, OR 97403

Pennsylvania

*Bucks County Intermediate Unit #22
705 Shady Retreat Road
Doylestown, PA 18901

*Cheyney University
Library
Cheyney, PA 19319

East Stroudsburg University of Pennsylvania
Library
East Stroudsburg, PA 18301

Holy Family College
Grant and Frankford Avenues
Philadelphia, PA 19114

*Indiana University of Pennsylvania
Media Resource Department
Stapleton Library
Indiana, PA 15705

Kutztown University
Curriculum Materials Center
Rohrbach Library
Kutztown, PA 19530

La Salle College
Instructional Materials Center
The Connelly Library
Olney Avenue at 20th Street
Philadelphia, PA 19141

Lock Haven University of Pennsylvania
Library
Lock Haven, PA 17745

*Millersville University
Ganser Library
Millersville, PA 17551-0302

*Pennsylvania State University
Pattee Library/Serials
University Park, PA 16802

*Shippensburg University of Pennsylvania
Ezra Lehman Library
Shippensburg, PA 17257-2299

*Slippery Rock University
Bailey Library
Instructional Materials Center
Slippery Rock, PA 16057

University of Pittsburgh
Hillman Library/Serials
Pittsburgh, PA 15260

West Chester University
Francis H. Green Library
West Chester, PA 19383

Rhode Island

Rhode Island College
Curriculum Resources Center
600 Mt. Pleasant Avenue
Providence, RI 02908

South Dakota

Northern State University
Williams Library
Aberdeen, SD 57401

University of South Dakota
I. D. Weeks Library
414 East Clark
Vermillion, SD 57069

Tennessee

Tennessee Technological University
Library
Cookeville, TN 38505

Trevecca Nazarene College
Curriculum Library
Mackey Library
333 Murfreesboro Road
Nashville, TN 37210-2877

*University of Tennessee at Chattanooga
Library/Serials
Chattanooga, TN 37403

*University of Tennessee at Martin
Instructional Improvement
Gooch Hall—Room 217
Martin, TN 38238

*Vanderbilt University
Curriculum Laboratory
Peabody Library
Peabody Campus, Magnolia Circle
Nashville, TN 37203-5601

Texas

Baylor University
School of Education
Waco, TX 76798-7314

East Texas State University
Curriculum Library
Commerce, TX 75429

*East Texas State University
Library
Texarkana, TX 75501

*Houston Baptist University
Moody Library
7502 Fondren Road
Houston, TX 77074

*Incarnate Word College
Library
4301 Broadway
San Antonio, TX 78209

*Sam Houston State University
Library
Huntsville, TX 77341

*Southern Methodist University
Fondren Library
Dallas, TX 75275-0135

Stephen F. Austin State University
Library/Serials
Box 13055 SFA Station
Nacogdoches, TX 75962

Texas A&M University
Library/Serials
College Station, TX 77843-5000

*Texas Tech University
Library
Lubbock, TX 79409

Texas Woman's University
Library
Box 23715 TWU Station
Denton, TX 76204

University of Houston—University Park
University of Houston Library
Central Serial
4800 Calhoun
Houston, TX 77004

University of North Texas
Library
Denton, TX 76203

University of Texas at Austin
General Libraries/Serials
Austin, TX 78713-7330

University of Texas at El Paso
Library
El Paso, TX 79968-0582

Utah

Utah State University
Educational Resources Center
College of Education
Logan, UT 84322-2845

Vermont

University of Vermont
Guy W. Bailey Library/Serials
Burlington, VT 05405

Virginia

Longwood College
Dabney Lancaster Library
Farmville, VA 23909-1897

*Regent University
Library
Virginia Beach, VA 23464-9877

University of Virginia
Alderman Library
Serials/Periodicals
Charlottesville, VA 22901

*Virginia Beach Public Schools
Instruction and Curriculum
School Administration Building
2512 George Mason Drive
Virginia Beach, VA 23456

Washington

Central Washington University
Library/Serials
Ellensburg, WA 98926

University of Puget Sound
Collins Library
Tacoma, WA 98416

University of Washington
Library/Serials
Seattle, WA 98195

Washington State University
Library
Pullman, WA 99164-5610

Western Washington University
Wilson Library
Bellingham, WA 98225

Wisconsin

University of Wisconsin—Eau Claire
Instructional Media Center
Eau Claire, WI 54702-4004

University of Wisconsin—Madison
Instructional Materials Center
225 North Mills
Madison, Wisconsin 53706

University of Wisconsin—Oshkosh
F. R. Polk Library
Oshkosh, WI 54901

University of Wisconsin—Platteville
Library
One University Plaza
Platteville, WI 53818-3099

University of Wisconsin—Whitewater
Learning Resources
Whitewater, WI 53190

Wyoming

*University of Wyoming
Coe Library
15th and Lewis
Laramie, WY 82071

AUSTRALIA

Griffith University
Library
Mount Gravatt Campus
Nathan, Queensland 4111

CANADA

The Ontario Institute for Studies in Education
Library
252 Bloor Street West
Toronto, Ontario M5S 1V6

*University of New Brunswick
Harriet Irving Library/Serials
Fredericton, New Brunswick E3B 5H5

University of Regina
Library/Serials
Regina, Saskatchewan S4S 0A2

University of Saskatchewan
Library
Saskatoon, Saskatchewan S7N 0W0

University of Windsor
Leddy Library/Serials
Windsor, Ontario N9B 3P4

*Vancouver School Board
Teachers' Professional Library
123 East 6th Avenue
Vancouver, British Columbia V5T 1J6

HONG KONG

*The Chinese University of Hong Kong
University Library
Shatin, N.T.

THE NETHERLANDS

National Institute for Curriculum Development
(Stichting voor de Leerplanontwikkeling)
7500 CA Enschede

INDEX

D

E

S

www.ingramcontent.com/pod-product-compliance
Lightning Source LLC
Chambersburg PA
CBHW062017090426
42811CB00005B/885